The War of 1812 in the Chesapeake

Johns Hopkins Books on the War of 1812

DONALD R. HICKEY, *Series Editor*

THE WAR OF 1812

IN THE CHESAPEAKE

A Reference Guide to Historic Sites in Maryland, Virginia, and the District of Columbia

Ralph E. Eshelman, Scott S. Sheads, and Donald R. Hickey

THE JOHNS HOPKINS UNIVERSITY PRESS · BALTIMORE

© 2010 The Johns Hopkins University Press
All rights reserved. Published 2010
Printed in the United States of America on acid-free paper

9 8 7 6 5 4 3 2 1

The Johns Hopkins University Press
2715 North Charles Street
Baltimore, Maryland 21218-4363
www.press.jhu.edu

Library of Congress Cataloging-in-Publication Data
Eshelman, Ralph E.
  The War of 1812 in the Chesapeake : a reference guide to historic
sites in Maryland, Virginia, and the District of Columbia / Ralph E.
Eshelman, Scott S. Sheads, Donald R. Hickey.
      p. cm.
  "With appendixes of battles, skirmishes, raids, and grave sites of War
of 1812 veterans."
  Includes bibliographical references and index.
  ISBN-13: 978-0-8018-9235-6 (hardcover : alk. paper)
  ISBN-10: 0-8018-9235-X (hardcover : alk. paper)
  1. United States—History—War of 1812. 2. Chesapeake Bay Region
(Md. and Va.)—History, Military—19th century. 3. Chesapeake Bay
Region (Md. and Va.)—History, Local. 4. Historic sites—Chesapeake
Bay Region (Md. and Va.)—Guidebooks. 5. Historic sites—Maryland—
Guidebooks. 6. Historic sites—Virginia —Guidebooks. 7. Historic
sites—Washington (D.C.)—Guidebooks. 8. United States—History—
War of 1812—Registers. 9. Soldiers—Chesapeake Bay Region (Md.
and Va.)—Registers. 10. Cemeteries—Chesapeake Bay Region (Md.
and Va.)—Guidebooks. I. Sheads, Scott S., 1952– II. Hickey, Donald R.,
1944– III. Title.
  E355.1.C485E84 2009
  973.5'23—dc22   2008042175

A catalog record for this book is available from the British Library.

*Special discounts are available for bulk purchases of this book. For
more information, please contact Special Sales at 410-516-6936 or
specialsales@press.jhu.edu.*

The Johns Hopkins University Press uses environmentally friendly
book materials, including recycled text paper that is composed of at
least 30 percent post-consumer waste, whenever possible. All of our
book papers are acid-free, and our jackets and covers are printed on
paper with recycled content.

CONTENTS

INTRODUCTION

This guide to War of 1812 sites in Maryland, Virginia, and the District of Columbia is an annotated inventory, not a conventional narrative or analytical history, although much new information of historical importance is presented here. The guide brings together the known sites related to the War of 1812 in the Chesapeake region. It includes sites where battles, raids, and skirmishes took place or where forts, earthworks, or batteries were established. It also includes buildings and sites where buildings once stood in which important events took place; monuments, memorials, and statues; museums that have pertinent collections and displays; and other resources, such as the homes and gravesites of individuals associated with the War of 1812. Selected sites from West Virginia (then part of Virginia), North Carolina, Delaware, and Pennsylvania are also included when they have a connection to the Chesapeake campaigns.

Today, the War of 1812 is not well remembered and is often misunderstood. Hence, on some plaques, monuments, and roadside markers the information provided is misleading or even wrong. Whenever we mention these sources, we try to set the record straight. We have corrected these when necessary. Whenever possible, we have used the words of the participants in the war to impart information. We have relied heavily on such primary sources as diaries, journals, newspapers, contemporary accounts, and other documents from the period. For the more significant entries, such as battlefield and raid sites, we have tried to include information from British as well as American sources.

This project grew out of a serendipitous meeting of a small group of War of 1812 enthusiasts in 1979. That year, the Calvert Marine Museum, located at the mouth of the Patuxent River in Solomons, Maryland, and then headed by Ralph Eshelman, and Nautical Research Associates, Inc., a nonprofit group of underwater archeologists headed by Donald Shomette, established a partnership to seek out the remains of the U.S. Chesapeake Flotilla, which had been scuttled in the Patuxent River during the War of 1812. This collaboration prompted representatives from various other sites in Maryland to launch the Maryland War of 1812 Initiative, whose purpose was to promote public awareness of, and interest in, the war. Not long thereafter, the Maryland Historical Trust and the Maryland Office of Tourism Development secured two grants from the American Battlefield Protection Program of the National Park Service in part to develop a list of War of 1812 sites in Maryland. Although investigators working under this grant expected to find 100 to 150 sites, they actually located 338, including at least one in each of Maryland's twenty-three counties and many in the City of Baltimore.

The Maryland inventory provided impetus for locating and identifying other 1812 sites in the region. The result of that expanded search is this guide. Our final inventory includes 804 sites (including burial grounds): 623 in Maryland, 124 in Virginia (including present-day West Virginia), 53 in the District of Columbia, and 5 in North Carolina, Delaware, and Pennsylvania. The following cities have 5 or more sites (not including burial grounds) within their jurisdictions: Alexandria (5); Annapolis (20, including 14 at the U.S. Naval Academy); Baltimore (80, including 8 at Fort McHenry and 9 in Fells Point); Bladensburg (13); Elkton (5); Hampton (8); Havre de Grace (10); Norfolk (8); St. Michaels (12); and Washington, D.C. (47, including 5 at the Washington Navy Yard).

More than 70 percent of the sites we identified in the Chesapeake region are located in Maryland (see appendix D) because Maryland was the site of more battles, skirmishes, and raids (103) than any other state in the Union. Maryland also suffered more damage and destruction than any other state.[1] The scars left by the British on the Maryland landscape and in the minds of the victims of these depredations did not heal quickly, nor were they soon forgotten after the war was over.

This guide is a condensed version of a more comprehensive inventory. This version includes the important sites but omits some background information mostly unrelated to the War of 1812, homes of less important veterans, folktales, gravestone epitaphs, and text on plaques and historic markers. A copy of the full version is available at the National Park Service Research Library, Fort McHenry National Monument and Historic Shrine, Baltimore.

In preparing this inventory, we soon realized how many War of 1812 sites had been lost because of neglect, ignorance, erosion, or modern development. In general, sites connected to the War of 1812 have not fared as well as those related to the American Revolution or the Civil War. This is hardly surprising given the relative significance of these wars. The War of 1812 may be important, but it hardly compares, in either scope or consequences, with the Revolution or the Civil War, nor has it generated anything like the same public interest over the years.

Still, a few remarkable and unexpected resources have survived. On Maryland's Eastern Shore, for example, the battlefield of Caulks Field as well as two earthworks, Fort Stokes and Fort Point, are in private hands and remain in nearly pristine condition.

The Battle of Caulks Field, fought in the early morning hours of August 31, 1814, was of little strategic importance, although it did mark one of the few times that Maryland militia withstood a larger and veteran British force. This engagement also raised the morale and confidence of the American forces who later defended Baltimore. Caulks Field battlefield can be viewed from a monument erected in 1902 along a county road. Looking north in the spring or summer, one can usually see corn growing much as it grew in these fields in 1814. A line of trees along the field edges is nearly identical to a timber line that appears in a British sketch of the battlefield made the day after the engagement. There is no better preserved battlefield from the War of 1812 in the Mid-Atlantic states. In fact, Caulks Field may be the best preserved battlefield from this era in eastern North America.

Most of the trees around Fort Stokes, the earthwork that protected Easton from a water attack, were leveled for townhouses, but the site of the fort itself remains open space. This fort has suffered some shoreline erosion, although approximately 90 percent of the structure survives in remarkably good condition. The developers plan to add interpretative signage at the fort site; we hope that they will also take measures to stem the threat of continued shoreline erosion. Fort Point, an earthwork that protected Centreville from a

water attack, is not accessible and can be viewed only by water. These earthworks, including a surviving dry moat, have also suffered from shoreline erosion but are now protected by riprap (a stone barrier) put there by the property owners. Fort Point is the best preserved earthwork fortification in Maryland and possibly in the Mid-Atlantic region.

By contrast, two of the main battlefields in Maryland have been almost entirely lost, and the most important fort in the region no longer looks like it did during the War of 1812. The land around Bladensburg (where an American defeat opened the door to the British occupation of Washington in 1814) and North Point (where the American defenders slowed the British advance on Baltimore that same year) have been heavily developed, and Fort McHenry looks largely like it did during the Civil War. Fortunately, a campaign to purchase the last large undeveloped nine-acre parcel of land at North Point Battlefield has succeeded, and a pedestrian bridge has been built across the Anacostia River, affording a good view of the very spot where the British army stormed across the waterway to meet the American defenders at Bladensburg. Moreover, at Fort McHenry, the National Park Service has re-created a hundred-foot section of the three hundred-foot-long water battery that existed during the War of 1812. A new visitor center, which is scheduled to be completed in 2010, will help commemorate the bicentennial of this post's important role in the War of 1812.

In Virginia, efforts at historic preservation also have met with mixed results. The Battle of Craney Island, fought in 1813, was a major American success, while the capture and burning of Hampton only four days later was a major failure. Craney Island has no historic integrity, as it has been surrounded by landfill and sustained other alterations made by the U.S. Army and U.S. Navy. Burned by the Confederates in 1861, Hampton retains little from the War of 1812. The extensive earthworks of forts Boykin and Powhatan date largely from the Civil War era, not the War of 1812. Yet, Fort Norfolk, the last surviving harbor fort of nineteen that were authorized by George Washington in 1794, is little altered, although public access is limited to only a few days a year.

The future of many surviving War of 1812 sites, especially those in private hands, is unclear. But the more we know about these sites and the better we publicize their historical significance, the more likely we are to preserve them. Fortunately, some War of 1812 sites have already been preserved, either by their private owners, by public entities, or by civic-minded volunteers, and public interest in preserving more sites seems to be growing. It is our hope that this guide, in conjunction with the coming bicentennial commemorating of the War of 1812, will promote additional preservation initiatives for the remaining vestiges of this largely forgotten conflict. If the guide contributes to that end, we will consider it a success.

Methodology

To prepare this guide, the single most valuable step was to physically visit and explore each site, especially raid, skirmish, and battlefield sites. Topography, relationship of roads, contemporary structures, water, and land, all help one to better visualize and understand the site. The senior author visited every pertinent site that was accessible. We also visited most of the archives and libraries in Maryland, Virginia, and the District of Columbia. We used the resources of many local and county libraries and historical societies, particularly their vertical files, which contain numerous fugitive newspaper articles, rare pamphlets, and unpublished manuscript material shedding light on the sites and on the events that took place at them during the war. Contemporary newspaper accounts offer a particularly rich vein of information on battles, skirmishes, raids, riots, and other events of local interest. Our visits to the Maryland Law Library, the Maryland State Archives, the Library of Virginia, the National Archives, the Library of Congress, and the Fort McHenry Research Library were especially fruitful. We also profited from conversations with local authors and experts as well as with the land owners who controlled sites that were part of our inventory.

We examined the site files of the Maryland Historical Trust for information on specific standing structures, many of which are listed on the National Register of Historic Places. To locate graves, we looked at county cemetery records as well as the web pages of the Maryland Tombstone Transcription Project. Also useful was Edward F. Wright's "Maryland Militia, War of 1812" series, recently made available on compact disk; and the Maryland roster of some 12,000 War of 1812 veterans compiled by Louis Henry Dielman in 1913 and published in William M. Marine's *British Invasion of Maryland 1812–1814*. We spent a great deal of time visiting cemeteries in Maryland, and this produced numerous pertinent gravesites that otherwise would have been missed.

Scholars interested in Virginia's military history are fortunate because many of the relevant records are available online from the Library of Virginia in Richmond. Under the Virginia Historical Inventory are 169 entries related to the War of 1812, ranging from a survey of Craney Island to a spike from Com. Oliver Hazard Perry's flagship *Niagara*.

Many homes of War of 1812 veterans are included in this resource. Within the online military records and inventory are the names of some forty thousand Virginia militia. The Society of the War of 1812 in Virginia has a project under way to locate as many War of 1812 veteran graves as possible. As of January 2007, more than 2,300 graves had been identified. Maryland is far behind Virginia in developing this kind of information and making it readily available to the public. Therefore, veteran graves in Maryland are included in this inventory, while only the more significant or previously undocumented graves in Virginia are included. A. Douglas Rawlinson has developed a comprehensive list of Maryland veteran graves from the war and has graciously consented to the reproduction of this information in appendix B.

It will come as no surprise to those who have studied history that we found discrepancies in some of the sources that we consulted. We came across three different dates, for example, for the British raid on Queenstown, Maryland, in 1813: August 2, August 7, and August 13. In other cases, the sources agreed but their claims rested on very thin evidence, such as oral tradition or a document written decades after the event. The story, for example, that the residents of St. Michaels, Maryland, tricked the British into aiming their artillery fire too high by hanging lanterns in trees and second-story windows did not surface until the 1880s and did not gain currency until the early twentieth century during the battle's centennial observation. In all such cases, we have tried to use the most reliable contemporary sources to resolve discrepancies and get at the truth. When we could not find a definitive answer, we base our conclusion on the most logical result supported by the documents of the period.

We have chosen not to compare costs during the War of 1812 with costs today by converting the original figures into current dollars using a consumer price index table. Such a comparison greatly understates the cost of things in 1812–15. People have so much more wealth today that many can now afford what few could buy 200 years ago. For example, although prices increased about 14-fold between 1812 and 2005, a much larger proportion of the population could afford a $148 rifle in 2005 than could afford a $10 rifle in 1812. If the comparison is based on prevailing unskilled wages, that same $10 rifle would cost $1,709 in 2005. Similarly, as a per capita share of the gross domestic product, $10 in 1812 is equivalent to $4,154 in 2005.[2]

How to Use This Guide

The sites in our inventory are arranged alphabetically within each state. Most appear in chapters 3-5, which cover Maryland, Virginia (including West Virginia), and the District of Columbia. Chapter 5 also includes sites in North Carolina, Delaware, and Pennsylvania that are connected to the Chesapeake campaigns. There is another small list in appendix A of sites whose precise location we could not establish. The sites within each chapter are listed alphabetically. When we found multiple sites at a larger site—such as in Baltimore, Fort McHenry, or the U.S. Naval Academy—we listed the individual sites alphabetically under the heading of the larger site. We did this to reduce the need for flipping through the guide to locate all the sites at a given location.

Each entry is listed by its most current name followed by any alternative names that were ever in use. The location of the site is given next, with directions on how to get there if the location is unlikely to be readily known. We also indicate when a site has been designated as a National Historic Landmark (NHL) or is on the National Register of Historic Places (NRHP). Sites that are located on private property are so indicated. An asterisk (*) indicates that additional information about persons and places can be found by going to the index. Finally, sites of special interest that are open to the public are marked with a star (★). This basic information is followed by a short history of the site focusing on its role in the War of 1812. We use current spellings of place names as they appear on U.S. topographic maps. Thus the apostrophe has been dropped from names like Poole's Island, and the apostrophe and *s* has been dropped from names like St. Leonard's Creek.

We have supplied the rank that all military personnel held at the time of the event that occurred at the site. Thus, George Armistead, the celebrated commander of Fort McHenry when it came under bombardment in 1814, is listed as a major for that site but as a captain or lieutenant colonel for other sites.

Any contemporary quotation that we use to explain a site is reproduced (even with misspelled words, mis-punctuation, or lack of punctuation) exactly as it appears in the document to retain the original voices of the authors. Any changes made to the text and any additional information supplied have been given in square brackets. When forced to guess at missing words or at undecipherable words, we so indicate with a question mark within square brackets.

While there is no consistency in the usage of naval ship names, and while U.S.S. and H.M.S. are customarily used today to preface American and English ships, during the War of 1812 such usage was rarely used. American ships were often identified by U.S. followed by the specific kind of vessel such as sloop, schooner, or frigate and then the name of the ship. British ships were often identified by H.M. typically followed by the generic term *ship* and then the name of the vessel. We have chosen to indicate the specific type of vessel for both American and British ships to provide this information to the reader.

In reproducing the illustrations and maps that appear in this work, we have usually included the original key that identified the location of military units and other objects of interest. When necessary, however, we have corrected the key or added information. In some cases, we have also added or enlarged letters or numbers to pinpoint locations.

A Cautionary Note

Some of the sites in this guide are located in high-congestion areas, such as Bladensburg, Annapolis, Baltimore, Norfolk, or Washington, D.C., while others are located on narrow, winding, or hilly rural roads. Those wishing to visit these sites, whether on foot or by car, should exercise caution. Many sites are located on private property. Some cannot be seen from public roads; others can be seen from public roads but no parking is available. Please respect private property and only pass by such sites. *Do not trespass.* Finally, remember that it is against the law to relic-hunt on public property or on any lands submerged below the high water mark. It is also against the law to relic-hunt or trespass on private property without the permission of the owner. Please take nothing but photographs and leave with nothing but good memories.

ABBREVIATIONS

Adj. Gen.	Adjutant General	Mas. Com.	Master Commandant
Adm.	Admiral	NHD	National Historic District
Brig. Gen.	Brigadier General	NHL	National Historic Landmark
Capt.	Captain	NHS	National Historic Site
Col.	Colonel	NRHP	National Register of Historic Places
Com.	Commodore	NSDAR	National Society Daughters American Revolution
Cpl.	Corporal	NSUSD 1812	National Society United States Daughters of 1812
DAR	Daughters of the American Revolution	Pvt.	Private
D.C.	District of Columbia	Q.M.	Quarter Master
Gen.	General	Rev.	Reverend
HABS	Historic American Buildings Survey	RM	Royal Marines
H.M.	His or Her Majesty's	RN	Royal Navy
H.M.S.	His or Her Majesty's Ship	Sgt.	Sergeant
Hon.	Honorable	Surg.	Surgeon
Lieut.	Lieutenant	U.S.	United States
Lt.	Lieutenant	U.S.S.	United States Ship
Maj.	Major	&c. =	etc.

The War of 1812 in the Chesapeake

The War of 1812: An Overview

While it is not the purpose of this guide to present a full history of the War of 1812, this chapter provides some general background on the conflict to place the war in the Chesapeake and the sites that we have inventoried in their larger wartime context. For additional information about the War of 1812, readers are urged to consult the works cited in the bibliographical essay at the end of this guide.

What Was the War of 1812?

The War of 1812 was an armed conflict between the United States and Great Britain that officially began with the declaration of war on June 18, 1812, and ended on February 16, 1815, with the ratification of the Treaty of Ghent. Because the United States sought to win the war by conquering Canada, the principal theaters of operation were located on the Canadian-American border, but the Chesapeake Bay, the Gulf Coast, and the high seas were also important theaters.

Compared to other American wars—the Revolution, the Civil War, and the two world wars—the War of 1812 was not a major conflict, although at the time many Americans considered it an essential struggle to vindicate the new nation's independence. In fact, Republicans at the time claimed that it was a "second war of independence," and historians have echoed that cry ever since. British subjects in Canada and their Indian allies, however, also believed—and probably more justly—that their own independence was at stake in the war.

The War of 1812 was not simply an Anglo-American conflict waged mainly on the Canadian-American border. There were also two Indian wars, one in the Old Northwest and another in the Old Southwest, which blended into the larger conflict. The Indian war in the Northwest began with the Battle of Tippecanoe on November 7, 1811, in present-day Indiana, and once the War of 1812 began the British eagerly cultivated America's Indian foes in this region to off-

set the manpower and logistical advantages that the young republic enjoyed. The Indian war in the Southwest—the Creek War—began in present-day Alabama with the Battle of Burnt Corn on July 27, 1813. The British were slower to cultivate the southern Indians, and their efforts were less successful than in the Northwest.

The War of 1812 may be seen as the last of the North American colonial wars fought to determine who would dominate the continent. In the first series of colonial wars (1689–1763), the British had prevailed over the French and had emerged as the dominant power in North America. In the final series (1775–1815), Americans contested British control, first by successfully establishing their independence in the American Revolution and then by challenging British control over Canada in the War of 1812. In each of these wars, Indians, acutely aware that their own fate hung in the balance, played a significant role.

What Caused the War of 1812?

The War of 1812 was a direct overgrowth of the French Revolutionary and Napoleonic Wars (1793–1815), a group of wars that constituted the final stage in a long series of Anglo-French wars sometimes called the Second Hundred Years War (1689–1815). In this phase of the Second Hundred Years War, France and Great Britain were contending for domination in Europe and the wider world. France controlled the Continent of Europe, while Britain was Mistress of the Seas. Both nations targeted neutral trade and in other ways encroached on American rights in the hope of putting pressure on the enemy. As a result, the central problem that American policy makers faced in this era was this: How could a second-rate power like the United States best preserve its maritime rights and promote its commercial interests in the midst of a world war?

The United States had already been drawn into this

phase of the Second Hundred Years War in the 1790s. French depredations on American trade in the mid-1790s had prompted the United States to initiate the Quasi-War (1798–1801), an undeclared naval war that targeted armed French ships—warships and privateers—on the high seas. The U.S. Navy had made a good showing in this limited war, cruising successfully against French privateers and warships in the Caribbean and significantly reducing the threat to American trade in those waters. The war ended in 1801 when both sides ratified the Convention of 1800. Although the navy had done conspicuous service and probably had paid for itself several times over, this lesson was lost on Jeffersonian Republicans when they assumed power in 1801. Ever frugal and suspicious of any military establishment in peacetime, they reduced the army and navy and thus left the new nation ill-equipped to deal with the dangerous world it confronted.

Great Britain and France agreed to the Peace of Amiens in 1801, but this was little more than an armed truce that settled nothing. By 1803, the two nations were again at war, and again neutral rights came under attack as each belligerent sought to maximize its pressure on the other. Most Americans considered Great Britain the greater menace. As undisputed Mistress of the Seas, she not only threatened American trade but encroached on other American rights at sea and in American waters. The two leading issues that led to the War of 1812 were the Orders-in-Council, a series of executive orders issued by the British government between 1807 and 1809 that restricted American trade with the Continent, and impressment, the Royal Navy's practice of stopping American merchantmen on the high seas to reclaim seamen that were considered British subjects. More than four hundred American ships and cargoes were seized by the British from 1807 to 1812, and by accident, negligence, or design, some six thousand American citizens were impressed into the British navy between 1803 and 1812.

At first President Thomas Jefferson and his successor, James Madison, sought to avoid war by employing economic sanctions in the hope of forcing Britain (and to a lesser degree, France) to show greater respect for American maritime rights. Congress adopted a partial non-importation law in 1806 that prohibited a select list of British imports. This law did not actually go into effect until late 1807, when it was joined by a more controversial and more comprehensive non-exportation law known as the Embargo, which prohibited American ships and goods from leaving port. When these measures failed to win any concessions from the European belligerents, they were repealed in 1809 in favor of a non-intercourse act that reopened trade with the rest of the world while prohibiting all trade with Britain and France and their colonies. When this measure was repealed in 1810, a period of open trade followed, but it lasted only until 1811, when Congress enacted the last prewar trade restriction, a non-importation act that barred all British ships and goods from American ports.

The restrictive system, as these measures were called, was designed to spare the United States from the horrors of war by using trade as an instrument of foreign policy. But the restrictions boomeranged on the new nation, undermining prosperity and sharply reducing government revenue without winning any concessions from Britain or France. By the end of 1811, a growing number of Republicans were talking about going to war against one or both of the nation's European antagonists. Since a "triangular war" against both great powers was impractical, Republicans opted to target Great Britain, whose encroachments on American rights seemed both greater and more threatening to the fledgling republic's hard-won independence.

When the Twelfth, or War, Congress convened in November 1811, President James Madison called for war preparations. A small coterie of War Hawks headed by Kentuckian Henry Clay, who was elected Speaker of the U.S. House of Representatives, was eager to declare war on Great Britain to uphold national honor and open European markets if concessions on the maritime issues were not forthcoming. By April 1812, Clay and his allies had shepherded a program of war preparations through Congress, and Republicans now marked time, waiting to see if the U.S. sloop *Hornet,* which was expected to return from Europe shortly, brought any news of British concessions. When the ship arrived empty-handed, President Madison on June 1 sent a secret message to Congress recommending, indirectly but unmistakably, a declaration of war.

Congress complied with the president's request, but the vote on the declaration of war, 79–49 in the House and 19–13 in the Senate, was far from unanimous. In fact, it was the closest vote on any formal declaration of war in American history. All the Federalists voted against the war bill, and so, too, did many Republicans. This vote suggests that perhaps as many as 35 to 40 percent of the American people questioned the wisdom of the war.

Republican leaders hoped that the decision for war would unify the country, forcing everyone, Republican and Federalist alike, to rally to the flag. Although most Republican dissidents now fell into line, Federalists did not. They considered the war unnecessary and unwise and insisted that it would boomerang on the United States without winning any concessions from Great Britain. Try as they might, Republicans could do little to change their minds. Far from winning over the Federalists, Republican actions shortly after the declaration of war had the opposite effect. The decision by the Republican-dominated Congress to retain trade restrictions against Great Britain (even though these had always been defended as an alternative to war) and to embrace a selective tax policy (which favored Republican districts) coupled with a series of vicious pro-war riots in Baltimore (which made the war look like a pretext for suppressing free speech) drove Federalists deeper into opposition. Thus, throughout the conflict, there was a strong Federalist antiwar movement that significantly hampered the American war effort.

What Were the Principal Campaigns of the War of 1812?

The United States went to war in the hope of forcing Britain to give up certain maritime practices, but since it was impractical to challenge Britain's immense power on the high seas, the young republic targeted Britain's North American colonies in what is today Canada. The plan was to invade and occupy Canada with a view to holding it for ransom on the maritime issues. Thus, even though the war was fought to uphold "Free Trade and Sailors' Rights," it was waged mainly on the Canadian-American border.

In the summer of 1812, the United States launched a three-pronged invasion of Canada. The results were disastrous. One American army under Brig. Gen. William Hull was supposed to invade across the Detroit River at the western end of Lake Erie but surrendered to an Anglo-Indian force under Maj. Gen. Isaac Brock and the great Indian leader Tecumseh. A second army under the command of Stephen Van Rensselaer (a major general in the New York militia) invaded across the Niagara River at the eastern end of Lake Erie, but it, too, surrendered when the New York militia refused to cross the border to reinforce it. A third army under the command of Maj. Gen. Henry Dearborn was supposed to follow the traditional invasion route along Lake Champlain and the Richelieu River into Canada, but it retreated after little more than light skirmishing. By the time the campaigning season closed in late 1812, the United States had little to show for its efforts.

The United States launched another three-pronged invasion of Canada in 1813, and this time it enjoyed greater success, but only in the West. After Mas. Com. Oliver H. Perry

had won control of Lake Erie by defeating the British squadron on those waters, Maj. Gen. William Henry Harrison crossed the Detroit River into Canada and defeated an Anglo-Indian force at the Battle of the Thames about fifty miles east of Detroit. Britain's great Indian ally, Tecumseh, was killed in the battle. The successful campaign left the United States in control of much of the Old Northwest and induced many Indian tribes to make peace, but this region was too remote from the centers of power and population farther east to bring the republic any closer to its goal of conquering Canada. Farther east, after initial success on the Niagara frontier, American forces withdrew from the British side of the river but burned the town of Niagara, or Newark (now Niagara-on-the-Lake), before leaving. The British retaliated by crossing the Niagara River, capturing Fort Niagara, and torching the nearby American settlements. Meanwhile, on the Saint Lawrence River, a large American force under the leadership of Maj. Gen. James Wilkinson was defeated by a small British force in the Battle of Crysler's Farm, while farther east on the Chateauguay River another sizeable American force under the command of Maj. Gen. Wade Hampton was checked by a mostly French Canadian force in the Battle of Chateauguay.

In the spring of 1814, the war in Europe ended when the allies entered Paris and Napoleon abdicated and was forced into exile. Freed from the European war, the British shifted military and naval assets to the New World and seized the initiative in the American war. Forced on the defensive, the United States managed just one more offensive. An American army under Maj. Gen. Jacob Jennings Brown crossed the Niagara River in the summer of 1814 and did well in heavy fighting on the Canadian side but ultimately withdrew without making any significant gains. Meanwhile, a British army under Sir George Prevost invaded upper New York as far as Plattsburgh but withdrew after Mas. Com. Thomas Macdonough threatened British supply lines by defeating a Royal Navy squadron on Lake Champlain. The fighting came to an end on the Canadian-American frontier without either side being able to claim a significant advantage.

On the high seas, the U.S. Navy prevented the British navy from blockading its coast for six months by cruising in squadrons. This allowed hundreds of American merchantmen loaded with cargoes to get safely into port. The U.S. Navy also won a series of single-ship duels that were strategically unimportant but produced joy and boasting in the United States and anger and consternation in Great Britain. The British subsequently gave as good as they got in the naval war, and in the end the naval victories at sea were about equal.

The British used their naval power not simply to even the score on the high seas but also to put pressure on the United States in other ways. After the British proclaimed a blockade of the Chesapeake Bay and Delaware River in December 1812, the Royal Navy arrived in force the following February to enforce it. Although some American warships and privateers could still occasionally slip out to sea, the impact of the British blockade on the American economy and U.S. government revenue was devastating.

The British also targeted Americans living on the Atlantic and the Gulf coasts. In 1813–14, the British conducted extensive predatory raids in the Chesapeake and occasionally farther south. In the summer of 1814, they burned the public buildings in Washington but were rebuffed when they threatened Baltimore. That summer they also occupied a hundred miles of the Maine coast, and shortly thereafter they targeted Mobile and New Orleans on the Gulf Coast. Although Mobile ultimately fell to the Royal Navy, by then the British had been checked by Maj. Gen. Andrew Jackson's spectacular victory at New Orleans, which proved to be the last major engagement of the war. The fighting on the Gulf and Atlantic coasts, like that on the Canadian-American border, ended without either side being able to claim clear and unmistakable victory.

How Did the War of 1812 End?

The United States sent out peace feelers within a week of the declaration of war, hoping that news of the decision for war would itself elicit concessions from the British. Although the British had repealed the Orders-in-Council about the same time that the United States went to war, they were unwilling to make any concessions on impressment, so hostilities continued.

Two years later, in August 1814, delegations from the two nations met in the European city of Ghent (in modern-day Belgium) to try again to reach a settlement that would end the war. By this time, the United States had dropped its demands on impressment, but the end of the war in Europe had put the British in the driver's seat in the American war, and they now sought to capitalize on their position by demanding concessions to protect their Canadian provinces and Indian allies from future aggression. The British called upon the United States to make territorial concessions in northern Minnesota and Maine, to agree to the establishment of an Indian barrier state in the Old Northwest, to unilaterally demilitarize the Great Lakes, and to surrender fishing privileges in Canadian waters.

When the American delegates resisted these demands, the negotiations threatened to break up. To prevent this, the British gradually retreated from their terms, and on December 24, 1814, the two sides signed the Treaty of Ghent, also known as the Peace of Christmas Eve, which provided for ending the war and returning to the *status quo ante bellum,* that is, the state that had existed before the war. This meant that each side returned any enemy territory that it held and that neither side gained any concessions.

The signing of the Treaty of Ghent did not actually end the war. Fearing that the United States might insist on changes before ratifying the agreement (as it had on three earlier occasions when American agents had signed treaties with Great Britain in 1794, 1803, and 1806), the British insisted that hostilities be suspended only after both nations had ratified the treaty. Since London was near, the British ratified the Treaty of Ghent on December 27, 1814, but the agreement did not reach Washington until February 14, 1815. The U.S. Senate unanimously approved it on the 16th, and when President Madison signed off on the agreement later that day, the ratification process was complete, thus ending the war. Both sides immediately sent orders to all military and naval commanders to cease operations. It took time for the news to reach distant theaters, and the last hostile action took place in the Indian Ocean on June 30, 1815, when the U.S. sloop *Peacock* fired on the East India cruiser *Nautilus,* killing and wounding fifteen members of its crew.

What Won the War of 1812?

More than a half century ago, Canadian historian Charles P. Stacey suggested that everyone was happy with the outcome of the War of 1812. Americans were happy because they remembered it as a naval war in which they had humiliated the Mistress of the Seas. Canadians were happy because they remembered it as defensive war in which they had saved their homeland from conquest. And the British were happiest of all because they had forgotten all about the conflict.

Stacey, of course, was speaking partly in jest, but there is considerable merit in his assessment. Although it is hard to imagine a war in which all sides win, it is not difficult to imagine one in which all sides claim victory. Much depends on one's point of view as well as how selective the memory is.

From the American perspective, the unexpected naval victories on the high seas as well as on Lake Erie and Lake Champlain, coupled with the successful defense of Baltimore and the spectacularly one-sided victory at New Orleans, all suggested that the young republic could hold its head high and claim to have bested Great Britain. In fact, in the years that followed, most Americans ignored the causes of the war and the many defeats suffered on land and at sea. Instead, they focused on the last year of the war and remembered how they had beaten back British threats at Plattsburgh, Baltimore, and New Orleans. They had preserved their country and vindicated their independence by defeating the army that had conquered Napoleon and the navy that was Mistress of the Seas.

To Canadians, the War of 1812 looked very different. To them the conflict was little more than a war of territorial aggression launched by their American neighbors to the south. As Canadians saw it, they had waged a successful war to ward off an American attempt to conquer Canada. Victory had preserved their unique identify as well as their connection to the British Empire and thus laid the foundation for the emergence later on of an independent Canadian Confederation. This war came closer than any other Canadians have fought to being a war of independence, and it is still remembered as a defining moment in Canadian history.

What about the British? Stacey was right that the War of 1812 was all but forgotten in Britain, lost in the larger and more important contest with Napoleonic France. But those who did remember the war could certainly take pride in Great Britain's showing. After several strategically unimportant defeats on the high seas, Great Britain had confirmed its naval preeminence by defeating American warships, capturing American privateers, blockading the American coast, burning the public buildings in the U.S. capital, and occupying, at least for short periods of time, large chunks of American territory. In the end, Great Britain remained Mistress of the Seas and held on to her North American possessions even though she waged most of this war with the bulk of her military and naval resources tied up in the Napoleonic Wars.

The only real losers in the War of 1812, and Stacey did not mention them, were the Indians. In the Old Northwest, the United States defeated the Indians in the Battle of the Thames in 1813, and in the Old Southwest in the Battle of Horseshoe Bend in 1814. Although the last tribes in the Northwest did not come to terms with the United States until 1817, and remnants of the Creeks fought in the Seminole wars for decades, the fate of North American Indians had been sealed. The Treaty of Ghent was supposed to restore all the rights, privileges, and territories that the Indians held in 1811, but this provision was a dead letter. Americans were determined to ignore the provision, and the British refused to make an issue of it. British leaders had lost all interest in cultivating the Indians, which left the tribes in North America without any bargaining power, and those in American territory particularly vulnerable. The Indians were therefore the biggest losers in the War of 1812.

What Was the Legacy of the War of 1812?

The War of 1812 may have been a small war by any objective standard, but it loomed large in the minds of the participants, and in a host of ways it shaped the future of people living in North America. It tested both the United States and Great Britain, and in the process further undermined their relationship until common interests finally brought the two English-speaking nations together in the late nineteenth century. For people in Canada, the war meant preserving their identity and accustomed way of life, while for Indians it meant just the opposite. For everyone involved, the War of 1812 cast a long shadow across the nineteenth century.

People in the United States remembered the conflict as a second war of independence, and although the new nation's independence was never really at stake, the war certainly had a visible impact on American development. It fostered nationalism and patriotism, boosted territorial expansionism, and stimulated pride in the republic's armed services, particularly the navy. The war shaped a generation of presidents—James Monroe and John Quincy Adams, Andrew Jackson and Martin Van Buren, William Henry Harrison and Zachary Taylor—and a host of lesser leaders who held federal, state, and local offices. Any candidate seeking public office who had played a role in this war was at a decided advantage at election time, and if, perchance, he had been at any one of the celebrated American victories—at the Thames or New Orleans, or on the Niagara frontier, Plattsburgh, or Baltimore—his chances were even better.

The U.S. Army and U.S. Navy were also shaped by the war. The modern army was arguably born in the fighting on the Niagara frontier in 1814 in the battles at Chippawa, Lundy's Lane, and Fort Erie; and until the Civil War, army leadership was dominated by 1812 veterans like Andrew Jackson, Winfield Scott, and Jacob Brown. The navy certainly burnished its reputation in its duels on the high seas and its victories on the northern lakes, and navy leadership in the years that followed was dominated by 1812 veterans like Stephen Decatur, William Bainbridge, and Charles Stewart. Without the War of 1812, the U.S. Army and U.S. Navy probably would have had a very different look in the years after 1815.

As the war receded into history, many symbols and sayings survived to remind Americans of the contest. Among these were the U.S. frigate *Constitution,* also known as "Old Ironsides," which survived long enough to be recommissioned as a ship in the U.S. Navy and is now on display at the Charlestown Navy Yard in Boston; the Fort McHenry flag, which became one of the most prized treasures in collections of the Smithsonian Institution; "The Star-Spangled Banner," which was heard over and over before finally becoming the nation's official anthem in 1931; and Uncle Sam, who made his first appearance during the war although he did not assume his modern form until cartoonist Thomas Nast portrayed him later in the nineteenth century. Generations of Americans also have been stirred by the words of Capt. James Lawrence's of the U.S. frigate *Chesapeake*—"Don't give up the ship"—or by those of Mas. Com. Oliver H. Perry of Lake Erie fame—"We have met the enemy and they are ours."

People in Canada also remembered the war as a watershed event. It gave them national heroes like Sir Isaac Brock, Laura Secord, and the Indian leaders Tecumseh and John Norton. It brought a diverse population of British, French, and native people together and helped forge an identity for the future nation. At the same time, it also reinforced Canada's ties to Great Britain, ensuring that even independent Canada would be part of the British Commonwealth of Nations.

For Indians on both sides of the border, the outcome was much sadder. In the United States, Indians were forced to accede to the American will, deprived of their lands and, effectively, too, of their way of life. In Canada, the process was slower and more benevolent, but the outcome for Indians was much the same, for there, too, the First Nations (as they are now called) saw their lands shrink and their traditional way of life deteriorate. The demographic clock, already ticking against Indians on both sides of the border, pointed to a dismal future. For this unfortunate race, the War of 1812 was even more of a watershed than it was for the United States or Canada.

The last surviving veteran of the war was Hiram Cronk, who died on May 13, 1905, at the age 105. The last surviving widow was Caroline King, who died June 28, 1936. Her age is unknown. And the last surviving dependent who was entitled to a pension was Esther A. H. Morgan, who died on March 12, 1946, at the age of eighty-nine. These Americans were simply the last of a large number of citizens whose lives were shaped by the War of 1812.

CHAPTER 2

Warfare in the Chesapeake

As early as November 1812, Adm. Sir John Borlase Warren, who was the Royal Navy's commander on the American Station, suggested that the British conduct predatory raids on the Atlantic and Gulf coasts to draw American forces away from Canada. On December 26, 1812, the Admiralty ordered the Royal Navy to blockade the Chesapeake Bay. On February 4, 1813, a British squadron arrived at the mouth of the Bay and effectively blockaded the U.S. frigate *Constellation* at Norfolk, Virginia. On February 5 6, the Royal Navy in the Chesapeake issued a pair of proclamations establishing a blockade. Rear Adm. Sir George Cockburn arrived on the scene on March 3, and over the next eighteen months he was the driving force behind a series of predatory raids that may not have eased the pressure on Canada but certainly had a dramatic impact on people living in Maryland, Virginia, and Washington, D.C. Coupled with the British blockade, these raids brought the war home to Americans living in the Chesapeake region.

The Chesapeake sustained more enemy raids, and thus more property damage and other losses, than any other theater of operations in the war, and the bulk of these raids took place in Maryland (see endnote 1, introduction). British raiding parties in the Chesapeake had a free hand because there were few regulars available here to resist them, and the militia was usually slow to respond and quick to flee. British commanders normally kept a tight rein on their troops to minimize looting, and they paid in cash for the food and other supplies that they needed. They burned only what they considered legitimate targets, such as buildings used for military purposes, and they took only property that they considered legitimate prize, such as public assets and maritime goods. But their interpretation of the law was often loose. When they met with resistance, they felt justified in burning everything, and when they came across vacant homes they sometimes burned them on the grounds that their owners must be away serving with the militia.

To Americans living in the Chesapeake, Cockburn's raids seemed to be little more than robbery and arson. Exposed towns were left in ruins, the countryside was devastated, and many people were left destitute. The nation's leading magazine, *Niles' Weekly Register,* which was published in Baltimore, called Cockburn a "Great *Bandit*" and "THE LEADER OF A HOST OF BARBARIANS" and branded his troops "water-*Winnebagoes,*" a reference to the militant Indians in the Old Northwest.[1] The scars that the raids left on the landscape and its people did not soon heal.

What Were the Principal Engagements in the Chesapeake?

Although desultory raids were the norm in the Chesapeake, there also were some conventional battles as well as some raids that deserve special notice.

The Battle of Craney Island, Virginia (June 22, 1813)

Craney Island served as the first line of defense for Norfolk and Portsmouth as well as for the Gosport Navy Yard and the U.S. frigate *Constellation,* which was anchored there. Despite its importance, Craney Island was defended by only eight hundred men and its fortifications were incomplete when the British launched a two-pronged attack on it in 1813. One British force, 2,400 strong, landed on the mainland two and a half miles to the west, but with the tide in the troops could not ford the water to get to Craney Island. A second British force approached by water in some fifty barges, with a British artillery and Congreve rocket battery providing covering fire. This assault force, 1,500 men in all, included several Independent Companies of Foreigners made up of French deserters and prisoners of war who had joined the British army.

With American artillery guns raining fire down on them, the British boats cleared the deep water but then ran into thick mud, which made an amphibious landing nearly im-

Chesapeake Bay Region

possible and thus forced a retreat. As the British withdrew, a detachment of Americans waded out and seized a grounded barge and took prisoners. British accounts claim that one boat with thirty Independent Foreigners had capsized and that its occupants were massacred. The British reported three killed, sixteen wounded, and sixty-two missing. There were no reported American casualties. Thus ended the only attempt in the war to threaten the navy yard and the U.S. frigate *Constellation* at Norfolk. Shortly after the battle, the Independent Companies of Foreigners took their revenge on Hampton, Virginia.

The British Raid on Hampton, Virginia (June 25, 1813)

Three days after their rebuff at Craney Island, the British attacked Hampton, sweeping aside the defending militia and then taking control of the city. The occupation force included the Independent Companies of Foreigners. Habitually unruly and smarting because their French officers were stealing their pay, the French soldiers responded to the atrocities they thought had been committed at Craney Island by going on a rampage of murder, rape, robbery, and arson. Lt. Col. Charles James Napier, who later gained fame in India, was now a junior officer whose command included the French units. "Every horror was committed with impunity," he said, "and not a man was punished."[2] After this incident, the Independent Foreigners were exiled to Halifax, Nova Scotia, where they continued to cause trouble until they were finally shipped back to Europe and their units disbanded. The rampage at Hampton was long remembered in the United States. Like Fort Mims and the River Raisin (both of which were sites of Indian massacres in the West), Hampton became a byword among Americans for enemy atrocities during this war.

The Battles of St. Leonard Creek, Maryland (June 8–10 and June 26, 1814)

In an effort to protect people and property in the Chesapeake from the Royal Navy, Capt. Joshua Barney on July 4, 1813, presented a plan to the Navy Department to construct a flying squadron of shallow-draft gunboats and barges capable of shadowing and pursuing British landing parties in shoal waters, out of range of the larger and deeper draft British warships. The plan was adopted, and Barney was appointed commodore of the "Chesapeake Flotilla," which ultimately included 18 vessels and some 500 men. Barney took his squadron from Baltimore down the Chesapeake Bay on May 24, 1814, to engage the British at their naval base on Tangier Island, Virginia. Encountering a superior

British force on June 1 near the mouth of the Potomac River, he retreated to the safety of the Patuxent River after a brief skirmish.

After moving upriver into St. Leonard Creek, Barney was attacked by the British on June 8, 9, and 10. Wave after wave of British gunboats, schooners, and barges attempted to destroy the American flotilla. In this series of engagements, known as the First Battle of St. Leonard Creek, Barney repulsed each attack. Casualties on both sides were light.

Next, in an attempt to draw Barney from his lair, the British began a campaign of destruction along the Patuxent. In response, the Americans launched a poorly coordinated predawn attack on June 26. Shore batteries (manned by U.S. Marines and flotillamen and supported by U.S. regulars and militia) pounded the British at the mouth of the creek, followed shortly thereafter by a waterborne flotilla attack. This engagement, known as the Second Battle of St. Leonard Creek, ended in a draw, and again casualties on each side were light. The engagement, however, did enable Barney to slip out of the creek and move his flotilla up the Patuxent River.

Determined to destroy the flotilla, British boats moved up the Patuxent in August 1814. Just above where Maryland Route 4 now crosses the Patuxent, the British discovered the flotilla on August 22, only to watch it blown up by the Americans to keep it out of enemy hands. Leaving only a small detachment of men to destroy the flotilla, Barney and his men already had left for Washington to take part in the defense of the capital city.

The Burning of Washington, D.C. (August 24–25, 1814)

On August 19–20, the British fleet in the Chesapeake landed some four thousand men under the command of Maj. Gen. Robert Ross at Benedict, Maryland, for an assault on Washington. Accompanying Ross was Rear Adm. Sir George Cockburn. Marching overland via Upper Marlboro, the British decided not to take the most direct route to Washington because the waters of the Anacostia River there were unfordable and the bridges across the river could easily be destroyed by the Americans. Instead, they headed for Bladensburg, where the water was shallow enough to ford if the bridge there was out of commission.

In charge of the approaches at Bladensburg was the hapless American commander, Brig. Gen. William H. Winder, the nephew of Maryland's Federalist governor, Levin Winder. General Winder's force, about 7,000 strong, included some 1,400 regulars, marines, and flotillamen but consisted mostly of raw militiamen from Maryland, Virginia, and

Inaccurate British depiction of the destruction of the U.S. Chesapeake Flotilla (Patuxent River) and Washington City (Anacostia River or Eastern Branch). Composite illustration depicting the events surrounding the capture of Washington. Although the artist shows the British destroying the American flotilla, in fact the Americans blew it up. Key: A. Maj. Gen. Robert Ross and the British army at Battle of Bladensburg. B. Cannons taken from the Americans at Battle of Bladensburg. C. The City of Washington. D. U.S. Chesapeake Flotilla. E. Washington Naval Yard and Greenleaf Point Federal Arsenal (arsenal is actually west of this position). F. Rope walk (should be farther inland). G. Anacostia River. H. 1,500-foot-long Eastern Branch Bridge, Virginia side destroyed by Americans and Maryland side destroyed by British. I. War Office. L. Senate Wing of Capitol (there was no dome as suggested here). M. Treasury (actual location is farther west). (1814 wood engraving by G. Thompson; Library of Congress, Prints and Photographs Division)

the District of Columbia. Winder also had twenty-six cannon, but most were light 6 pounders. Forming his troops on the high ground behind the river, Winder made no attempt to destroy the bridge despite having ample time to do so.

British soldiers stormed across the bridge under heavy American fire. Although repulsed at first, they soon got across the river and forced the first American line, which consisted of militia, to give way. This, in turn, panicked the second line, which also consisted of militia. Soon the road to Washington was filled with fleeing militia, a scene that

was remembered in song and verse as "The Bladensburg Races." Only the third line, anchored by the flotillamen under Barney's command and U.S. Marines under Capt. Samuel Miller, stood their ground. Firing their 12 and 18 pounder guns until they were outflanked, the Americans were finally overwhelmed. Both Barney and Miller were wounded in the engagement. Although captured, Barney was immediately released on parole by their British counterparts, who were impressed with his courage and professionalism under fire. Although the British had won the battle, they had taken heavy casualties: 64 killed and 185 wounded. American losses, by contrast, were much lighter: 26 killed and 51 wounded.

By this time, government officials and most of the inhabitants had fled Washington. Although the road to the capital city was now open, the British rested for two hours at Bladensburg before marching in. During their twenty-six-hour occupation of Washington, they burned most of the public buildings, including the Capitol, the building housing the War and Treasury departments, and a federal arsenal. The White House was also burned, although not before British officers sampled food and wine that had been laid out for an afternoon meal. The superintendent of patents, Dr. William Thornton, persuaded the British to spare the Patent Office on the grounds that it housed scientific apparatus that was private property. Congress used this building for its chambers when it later reconvened in the city.

The British were generally respectful of private property, although most accounts reported that they destroyed the office facade and burned the presses and the records of the *Daily National Intelligencer* as well as three rope walks that did government work on contract. Acting on standing orders, Capt. Thomas Tingey, commandant of the Washington Naval Yard, burned it as well as two ships under construction there. The fires in Washington were so intense that the glow in the sky could be seen thirty-five to forty miles away in Leesburg, Virginia, and Baltimore, Maryland. This was undoubtedly the low point for the United States during the war, but it was followed less than three weeks later by one of the high points at Fort McHenry.

The Surrender of Alexandria, Virginia (August 29, 1814)

While the main British force was marching to Washington, a squadron of Royal Navy ships under the command of Capt. James Gordon was laboriously working its way up the shallow Potomac River. The squadron met no resistance from Fort Washington, which was evacuated and then blown up by its commander, Capt. Samuel Dyson, who was subsequently cashiered from the army for not making a stand. When Gordon reached the prosperous city of Alexandria, the city fathers quickly agreed to his terms of surrender. All public property, all naval stores, and all goods intended for export were turned over to the British. The ransom was considerable. Gordon loaded his warships and some twenty-one prize ships with commodities and sailed down the Potomac for the Chesapeake Bay. His booty included 16,000 barrels of flour, 1,000 hogshead of tobacco, 150 bales of cotton, and sugar and wine worth nearly $5,000. Although he

was attacked by shore batteries and fire ships during his withdrawal and was forced to unload and then reload ships that ran aground, he got his squadron and prize goods back to the main British fleet intact. British naval officers applauded his feat, one calling it "as brilliant an achievement . . . as grace the annals of our naval history."[3] Many Americans, by contrast, found the craven surrender of Alexandria disgraceful.

The Battle of Caulks Field, Maryland (August 31, 1814)

Charged with conducting a diversion on the upper Eastern Shore to prevent militia there from interfering with the main British operation against Baltimore, Capt. Sir Peter Parker, scion of a prominent naval family, launched a night attack on the American camp at Caulks Field. Parker's force of 260 sailors and marines was opposed by some 200 American militiamen under the command of Lt. Col. Philip Reed, a Revolutionary War veteran and U.S. senator. The British sustained heavy fire from the militia, and Parker was mortally wounded. Although the Americans were out of ammunition and giving way, the British abandoned the attack and carried the dying Parker back to his ship. The British lost fourteen killed and twenty-seven wounded compared to only three wounded for the Americans. This rare militia victory against a British force boosted American morale and deprived the Royal Navy of one of its bright young stars.

The Battle for Baltimore, Maryland (September 12–14, 1814)

After its impressive victory at Washington, the main British force targeted Baltimore. With more than forty thousand people, Baltimore was the third largest city in the nation. It was fiercely Republican, a hotbed of Anglophobia, and a leading port for privateers that preyed upon British commerce. With the American forces dispersed, the British probably could have taken the city by marching overland from Washington, but having no cavalry for reconnoitering, they chose instead to retreat to the safety of their ships and approach Baltimore by water. This gave Americans extra time to strengthen the city's defenses.

Maj. Gen. Samuel Smith, Baltimore's leading Republican and ranking militia officer, turned the city into a beehive of activity, preparing its defenses. Militia from Maryland, Delaware, Pennsylvania, and Virginia poured into the city, and ultimately Smith had no less than 15,000 men to defend the earthworks on Baltimore's eastern flank. Another 4,000 Pennsylvania militia stood ready near the Maryland state line. Although mostly militia, Smith's force included 600 U.S. infantry, 125 U.S. light dragoons, 60 U.S. artillerymen,

500 U.S. flotillamen, 170 U.S. marines, and 700 U.S. sailors. The British naval force that threatened the city was formidable. It consisted of 50 warships, including 10 ships-of-the-line, 20 frigates, 5 bomb-vessels, and a rocket-vessel. The British fleet also included 6 troop transports and numerous armed schooners and barges. The British army making the assault was commanded by Maj. Gen. Robert Ross and consisted of 4,200 men, including a detachment of 600 sailors, but Ross only had 2 field howitzers and no cavalry.

The British landed at North Point to approach Baltimore from the east. At Godly Wood (site of the Battle of North Point), Brig. Gen. John Sticker, commanding a force of 3,200 men of the 3rd Brigade of the Maryland militia, faced the advancing British army. In an early skirmish Ross was mortally wounded. A capable officer who had distinguished himself in the Peninsular War, Ross was popular with his men, and his loss cast a pall over the entire operation. In the ensuing Battle of North Point, the British sustained losses of 46 killed, 295 wounded, and 50 missing. The Americans, by contrast, lost only 24 killed, 139 wounded, and 50 captured. Instead of pursuing them, the British, now under the command of Col. Arthur Brooke, chose to camp for the night. The next day Brooke reconnoitered the American defenses on Hampstead Hill and estimated that the British faced 15,000 men and 120 guns. Brooke's own army had been reduced to about 3,600 men. Brooke attempted a flanking movement to the north, but American scouts detected it, and American troops were quickly rushed in to protect the exposed flank.

Brooke then encamped about mile below the American defenses. Here he waited for the Royal Navy to pummel Fort McHenry into submission and then bring its heavy guns close enough to bear on the American line. But despite twenty-five hours of bombardment (from 6:00 a.m. on September 13 to 7:00 a.m. the following day), Fort McHenry held. Although over 1,500 shots were fired, only 400 fell within the works, and these did comparatively little damage. Fort McHenry sustained just 4 killed and 24 wounded. A British attempt to flank the fort at night with barges also failed. Unable to prevail over Fort McHenry, Royal Navy officials ordered the attacking force to withdraw and notified Brooke that they could not provide support for his land attack. In response, Brooke gave up his assault and ordered his forces to withdraw to North Point and then re-embark aboard their troop ships. Baltimore was thus saved from British occupation and perhaps destruction.

What Was the Genesis of "The Star-Spangled Banner"?

When the British withdrew through Upper Marlboro, some stragglers began plundering the small nearby farms. Robert Bowie, a former governor of Maryland, enlisted several men, including his cousin, Dr. William Beanes, to seize the stragglers, at least one of whom was clearly a deserter. The captives were confined at nearby Queen Anne's Town. One of the prisoners managed to escape and take word of the captures to his comrades. When Major General Ross learned of the captures, he ordered a contingent of mounted horsemen to seek their release and to arrest Beanes, whom he held responsible for the captures. When the British search party was told that the prisoners had been taken "into the interior," they seized several Americans (including Beanes), holding them as hostages and threatening to torch Upper Marlboro if the prisoners were not returned. With little choice, the townsmen released their captives, and the British, in turn, released all their American hostages except Doctor Beanes, who was taken some thirty-five miles away to the British flagship, H.M. ship-of-the-line *Tonnant,* where he was confined.

A friend of Beanes, Richard E. West, hurried to Georgetown to urge his brother-in-law, Francis Scott Key, a prominent attorney in the District of Columbia, to seek Beanes's release. Key consulted with President James Madison, who sent the young attorney to Brig. Gen. John Mason, the U.S. commissary for prisoners. Mason gave Key a letter addressed to the British asking for Beanes's release on the grounds that he was a civilian noncombatant. Mason then sent Key to Baltimore to meet John S. Skinner, the U.S. agent for the exchange of prisoners, who was to join Key on his mission. The two men set sail in a cartel, or truce, ship, the Baltimore-Norfolk packet-sloop *President.* They made their way down the Patapsco River into the Chesapeake Bay, where on September 7, 1814, they met the British fleet at the mouth of Potomac River and boarded *Tonnant.*

Vice Adm. Sir Alexander Cochrane graciously invited the American visitors to dinner. To buttress their case for Beanes's release, Skinner presented letters from wounded British soldiers left behind after the Battle of Bladensburg giving testimony to the kind treatment that they had received from their American captors, including Doctor Beanes. Major General Ross, who probably had already decided to release Beanes, was moved by these letters and informed Skinner and Key that the doctor could return with them, but only after a planned attack on Baltimore was over

Circa 1815 view of the bombardment of Fort McHenry. Key: A. Fort McHenry with garrison flag (center). B. Lazaretto Gun Battery and gun-barges positioned across channel. C. Fort Babcock with American flag. Note sunken ships between forts McHenry and Babcock. D. North Point. E. Troop ships behind the bombarding warships. (Aquatint by John Bower, *A View of the Bombardment of Fort McHenry, Near Baltimore by the British Fleet, Taken from the Observatory, Under the Command of Admirals Cochrane & Cockburn, on the Morning of the 13th of Sepr. 1814*; courtesy Maryland Historical Society)

lest the Americans share any intelligence that they might have picked up during their visit.

Because the *Tonnant* was crowded, the two American visitors and Beanes moved to their truce ship for the night. Key spent that night—September 13–14—pacing the deck as he watched the bombardment of Fort McHenry. The next morning, he saw that the British assault squadron had called off its attack and was heading back down the Patapsco River toward the Chesapeake Bay. The successful defense of Fort McHenry so moved him that he composed a poem commemorating the occasion. The three Americans soon returned to Baltimore, and Key spent the night at the Indian Queen Tavern perfecting his work. "The bombs bursting in air" in the poem refers to the British 190-pound mortar shells, many of which exploded over the fort. The "rockets' red glare" refers to the Congreve rockets (similar to modern sky rockets) that were fired at the fort.

Joseph H. Nicholson took Key's composition to the newspaper office of the Baltimore *American,* which published it in a handbill on September 17 under the title of the "Defence of Fort M'Henry." The handbill did not mention Key but explained how the work had come to be written and suggested that it be sung to the British drinking song, "Anacreon in Heaven," written in 1780. The Baltimore *Patriot* published the poem on September 20, and within a month it showed up in newspapers all along the eastern seaboard. The song, which was soon re-titled "The Star-Spangled Banner," was an instant hit and remained popular throughout the nineteenth century, although it was not until March 3, 1931, that Congress proclaimed it the national anthem.

What Did Privateers Contribute to the War of 1812?

Once the British blockade closed the Chesapeake, American warships could not leave port, but swift-sailing privateers, many of which were Baltimore clippers, could sometimes still slip out to sea. These privately owned vessels sailed with a government commission that authorized them to carry guns and cruise against the enemy's commerce, although the prizes they took were subject to the usual import taxes. In the course of the war, the U.S. government issued about 1,100 privateering commissions. Baltimore was the home port for more than 15 percent of all American privateers, including several of the most famous and successful. In 1812, the *Rossie,* Joshua Barney commanding, reportedly took 18 British merchantmen valued at $1,500,000. Two years later, under the command of Thomas Boyle, the *Chasseur*— known locally as "the Pride of Baltimore"—sailed into a British port and posted an announcement establishing a mock blockade of the British Isles. Although privateers usually sought to avoid combat with warships, in February 1815 the *Chasseur* defeated the H.M. schooner *St. Lawrence* off the coast of Cuba.

Privateers could not win the war, but they could annoy British commerce and drive up insurance rates. Because of the damage done by American privateers to British trade early in the war, London officials ordered all merchant vessels to sail in armed convoys. This order did not apply to vessels involved in the coasting trade, and even ocean-going merchantmen often broke away from their convoys when they neared their destination, both to make better time and to get their goods to market first. American privateers found lucrative cruising waters in the West Indies, in the Gulf of Saint Lawrence, and around the British Isles. In fact, American depredations in the Irish Sea forced up insurance rates to unprecedented levels, prompting angry British merchants to bombard the Royal government with petitions demanding protection. American privateering cannot be credited with shortening the war, but it may have made the British government more amenable to peace. Privateers from the Baltimore did more than their fair share of damage to enemy trade, prompting the British to label the port a "nest of pirates."

What Role Did Maryland Play in the War of 1812?

Although much of southern Maryland and the Eastern Shore supported the antiwar Federalist Party, the state nonetheless contributed to the war effort in a host of ways. With 380,518 people in 1810, Maryland's population was 5.3 percent of the nation's total. Maryland subscriptions to the government war loans exceeded those of the northeastern states and even those of Virginia, which had a much larger population in 1810. Baltimore merchants in 1813 subscribed for more than $3 million in government war loans. Baltimore raised an additional $600,000 for its own defense. Early in the war Maryland manufactured twice the amount of gunpowder than the better known du Pont mill in Delaware.

Maryland militia units were frequently called out and by and large did not distinguish themselves, although they successfully defeated British attacks at Elkton (twice), St. Michaels (twice), and Caulks Field. They also fought well at North Point and played a crucial role in preparing the defenses of Baltimore. The U.S. Chesapeake Flotilla was manned by Marylanders, including African American freemen. This unit fought bravely in all the battles that it engaged in, including the Battle of Bladensburg. The British lost two of their most popular officers on Maryland soil, Maj. Gen. Robert Ross and Capt. Peter Parker.

Maryland had a rich tradition of public service, and many prominent residents played a significant role in the war effort.

Comm. Joshua Barney (1759–1818). Born in Baltimore County, Barney went to sea at the age of thirteen. After a distinguished naval and privateering career in the American Revolution, Barney served his country again at sea during the War of 1812, commanding the successful privateer *Rossie* early in the conflict. Later he became commodore of the U.S. Chesapeake Flotilla, a squadron of gunboats and barges that he persuaded the federal government to build to protect the region from the Royal Navy. This squadron took part in several battles, including two at St. Leonard Creek, before the flotilla was blown up to prevent it from falling into British hands. Barney also played a conspicuous part in the Battle of Bladensburg. Wounded in that battle, he was paroled by the British and sat out the remainder of the war. Three years after the war, he decided to move to Kentucky but died while en route at Pittsburgh when the leg wound he had sustained at Bladensburg flared up.

Brig. Gen. Leonard Covington (1768–1813). Born in Aquasco, Maryland, Covington served as a junior officer in the U.S.

Army in the early 1790s, distinguishing himself at the Battle of Fallen Timbers in 1794. Resigning in 1795, he rejoined the army in 1808 as a lieutenant colonel of the Light Dragoons. Sent to New Orleans, he took part in the occupation of West Florida in 1810 and remained in the South during the first year of the War of 1812. Dispatched to the northern frontier and appointed a brigadier general in 1813, he was mortally wounded in the Battle of Crysler's Farm on November 11. He died three days later at French Mills, New York, and was buried there, although his remains were moved to Sackets Harbor in 1820. Fort Covington in Baltimore harbor, built in the spring of 1814, was named in his honor.

Samuel Hambleton (1777–1851). Born in Talbot County, Maryland, Hambleton joined the navy in 1806 as a purser. Assigned to Mas. Com. Oliver H. Perry's command on Lake Erie during the War of 1812, Hambleton designed the banner that Perry flew during the Battle of Lake Erie that echoed Capt. James Lawrence's words, "Don't Give Up the Ship." Hambleton was severely wounded during the battle while serving as an acting lieutenant on Perry's flagship. Commended by Perry for his courage during the battle, Hambleton survived his wounds and spent most of his time after the war at Perry's Cabin, the estate in Talbot County that he named after his commanding officer.

Alexander Contee Hanson (1786–1819). Born into a distinguished Maryland family, Hanson founded the Baltimore *Federal Republican and Commercial Gazette* in 1808 and built it into one of the leading Federalist newspapers in the South by publishing unrestrained attacks on domestic and foreign policies of the Republican administration in Washington. Shortly after the declaration of war in June 1812, a mob in Baltimore destroyed the *Federal Republican* office. When Hanson resumed publication the following month from a new office, a mob again destroyed his office and then broke into the county jail, where Hanson and a number of friends had been placed for protective custody. Hanson and his fellow Federalists sustained severe injuries at the hands of the mob. Unbowed, Hanson resumed publication yet again and his paper remained a powerful antiwar voice for the rest of the war. Catapulted into the limelight, Hanson was elected to the U.S. House and then U.S. Senate, serving from 1813 until his death in 1819. Apparently never fully recovering from the internal injuries that he sustained in the mob violence of 1812, he died at the age of thirty-three at his estate, Belmont, near Elkridge, Maryland.

Lt. Col. Jacob H. Hindman (1789–1827). A native of Centreville, Queen Anne County, Hindman was one of three brothers who served in the U.S. Army during the War of 1812. Joining the army in 1808, Hindman by 1812 had become a captain in the 2nd U.S. Artillery. Promoted to major in 1813, he saw extensive service on the Niagara frontier in 1814 and was rewarded with a brevet promotion to lieutenant colonel. He received another brevet promotion, this time to colonel, shortly after the war. He is buried in Old St. Paul's Cemetery in Baltimore.

Pvt. John Pendleton Kennedy (1795–1870). Born in Baltimore to a prosperous mercantile family, Kennedy was a member of the Baltimore United Volunteers, 5th Maryland Regiment. In 1814, he fought in the battles of Bladensburg and North Point. After the war, he took up the practice of law and then launched a career as a writer. An active Whig, he was a member of the U.S. House of Representatives (1838–45) and served as secretary of the navy (1852–53). Buried in Green Mount Cemetery in Baltimore, he is best remembered today for his novels and political and satirical writings.

Lt. Col. George Edward Mitchell (1781–1832). Born in Elkton, Cecil County, to a physician who served in the Revolutionary War, Mitchell was trained as a physician, but in 1812 he accepted a commission as a major in the 3rd Regiment of the U.S. Artillery. Promoted to lieutenant colonel in 1813, he was wounded in the American occupation of York (now Toronto), Canada, in April. After serving as the commanding officer of Fort Niagara, he was ordered in 1814 to Oswego, New York, where he oversaw the defense of Fort Ontario. When the British attacked, he was forced to retreat but was judged to have mounted an effective defense. Brevetted a colonel, he commanded a force on the Niagara front during the closing months of the war. He remained in the service after the war, retiring in 1821 to the family estate, Fair Hill, which he had inherited from his father. Later he served several terms in Congress.

Capt. Joseph Hopper Nicholson (1770–1817). Born in Chestertown on Maryland's Eastern Shore, Nicholson was a prominent member of the U.S. House of Representatives before accepting a Maryland state judicial appointment in 1806, a position he held until his death. During the War of 1812 he commanded a company of artillery known as the Baltimore Fencibles that he had raised at his own expense. In 1814, his company served in the Battle of Bladensburg and in the defense of Fort McHenry. When Nicholson learned that his brother-in-law, Francis Scott Key, had penned a poem that later became "The Star-Spangled Banner," he secured its publication.

Hezekiah Niles (1777–1839). A native of Chester, Pennsylvania, Niles learned the printing trade in Philadelphia and then launched several publishing ventures in Wilmington, Delaware. In 1805, he moved to Baltimore, where he became editor of the Baltimore *Evening Post*. When this paper was sold in 1811, Niles established the *Weekly Register* (later *Niles' Weekly Register*), which he published until 1836. The magazine quickly became one of the most widely circulated and influential periodicals in the United States, reaching almost ten thousand subscribers by the end of the War of 1812. Niles promoted Republican and later Whig policies in his journal, but what set it apart from other newspapers and magazines was the wide compendium of statistics, government papers, and other contemporary documents that Niles published. *Niles' Weekly Register* remains today one of the best sources of information on the United States during the War of 1812.

Mary Pickersgill (1776–1857). Born into a flag-making family in Philadelphia, Pickersgill learned the trade as a young girl. Her family moved to Baltimore after the Revolution, but she moved back to Philadelphia after she married in 1795. In 1807, after the death of her husband, she returned to Baltimore, where she and her daughter opened a flag-making business. Pickersgill made flags and standards for all the military services as well as for merchantmen. In 1813, she filled an order for Maj. George Armistead for a 30 by 42 foot garrison flag and a 17 by 25 foot storm flag for Fort McHenry. The garrison flag was run up the flag staff the morning after the failed British bombardment of the fort and inspired Francis Scott Key to write "The Star-Spangled Banner." From 1828 to 1851, Pickersgill served as president of the Impartial Female Humane Society that opened the Aged Widows' Home in 1850. Today, the Impartial Female Humane Society is known as the Pickersgill Retirement Community, relocated to Towson, Maryland. The garrison flag that Pickersgill made survives today at the National Museum of American History as one of our most revered symbols from the War of 1812.

Maj. William Pinkney (1764–1822). Born in Annapolis, Maryland, Pinkney was an accomplished Baltimore lawyer and onetime Federalist who was sent to London in 1806 to join resident minister James Monroe in negotiating a new British treaty. Known as the Monroe–Pinkney Treaty, this agreement was rejected by President Thomas Jefferson because it made no provision for ending impressment. Pinkney remained in London as Monroe's replacement and was the last U.S. minister to Great Britain before the War of 1812. Returning home in 1811, he served as President James Madison's attorney general from 1811 to 1814. In this capacity, he drafted the bill declaring war and gave the govern-

ment legal advice on various war-related matters. Pinkney commanded a battalion of volunteer militia at the Battle of Bladensburg in 1814 and was severely wounded in the arm. Although he served in the U.S. House and Senate after the war, his greatest postwar contribution came in several major cases that he argued before the U.S. Supreme Court.

Brig. Gen. Philip Reed (1760–1829). A native of Chestertown and veteran of the American Revolution, Reed served in the U.S. Senate from 1806 to 1813. In 1807, he was commissioned lieutenant colonel of the 21st Maryland Regiment, and in 1814, he headed the militia force that rebuffed the British at Caulks Field. In the spring of 1815, he was commissioned a brigadier general in the state militia for his services during the war. In the postwar era, he spent his last years as a member of Congress.

Com. John Rodgers (1771–1838). A native of Havre de Grace, Rodgers distinguished himself in the Quasi-War (1798–1801) and the Tripolitan War (1801–5). In 1811, he was in command of the U.S. frigate *President* when it fired on the H.M. sloop-of-war *Little Belt,* an action that many Americans considered just retaliation for the *Chesapeake–Leopard* affair in 1807. By 1812, Rodgers was the senior naval officer on active duty. In command of a squadron of ships headed by the *President* at the beginning of the war, he sought to chase down the H.M. frigate *Belvidera*. On June 23, with the *Belvidera* as his target, he sited the naval gun that fired the first shot of the war. Rodgers was wounded when the gun later blew up, and the British ship got away. In 1814, when the British threatened Baltimore, Rodgers played a significant role in preparing the defenses of the city, and he headed the force charged with defending Hampstead Hill, arguably the most important part of the American line. After the war he served for many years as head of the newly created U.S. Board of Navy Commissioners.

Maj. Gen. Samuel Smith (1752–1839). Born in Carlisle, Pennsylvania, but raised mostly in Baltimore, Smith served in the American Revolution. A wealthy land speculator and former Federalist, he headed the Republican Party in Baltimore in the age of Jefferson. A member of the U.S. Senate from 1803 to 1815, he was part of a group of Republican dissidents known as the "Invisibles," who frequently clashed with the Jefferson and Madison administrations and especially with their longtime secretary of the treasury, Albert Gallatin. Smith supported the War of 1812, but he continued to be a maverick, opposing certain administration legislative initiatives to support the war effort. As the ranking militia officer in Baltimore, he took charge of the defenses of the city in 1814 and did such a good job that the British ultimately withdrew without making their planned assault. Smith remained an important force in Congress for many years after the War of 1812 and closed out his public life as mayor of Baltimore.

1st Lt. John Stansbury (1788–1814). Born in Baltimore County, Stansbury was the son of Brig. Gen. Tobias E. Stansbury. Commissioned a 2nd lieutenant in the U.S. Navy in 1809, the younger Stansbury served under Com. Stephen Decatur aboard the U.S. frigate *President* when it defeated and captured the H.M. frigate *Macedonian* near the Madeira islands in October 1812. Promoted to 1st lieutenant, Stansbury was ordered to Lt. Stephen Cassin's U.S. brig *Ticonderoga* on Lake Champlain. He was killed in the Battle of Lake Champlain on September 11, 1814, when struck by a cannon ball.

Brig. Gen. Tobias E. Stansbury (1756–1849). A native of Baltimore County, Stansbury played an active role in public life during the American Revolution and after, serving as Speaker of the Maryland House of Delegates from 1805 to 1807. During the War of 1812, he held various commands. As brigadier general of the 11th Brigade, 3rd Division of the Maryland militia, he fought in the Battle of Bladensburg in August 1814 and the following month commanded a key position in the defenses of Baltimore. After the war, he represented Baltimore in the Maryland House of Delegates until retiring in 1823.

Capt. George Stiles (1760–1819). In 1808, following the *Chesapeake–Leopard* affair the year before, this son of a dry goods merchant from Harford County, Maryland, organized and commanded the First Marine Artillery of the Union of Fells Point in Baltimore. Some two hundred mariners and sea captains belonged to the company, which became Baltimore's most revered unit of citizen-soldiers for its service during the War of 1812. The company did more than any other military unit to prepare the defenses of Baltimore in 1813–14, and when the British actually threatened the city in 1814, Stiles's men daily manned the gunboats on the Patapsco River and later defended the heights of Hampstead Hill. Stiles's contribution to the defense of Baltimore was probably second only to that the Maj. Gen. Samuel Smith. "Without doing injustice to the great merits of others," said Hezekiah Niles in 1827, "Baltimore was more indebted to Capt. Stiles for her preservation than any other individual."[4] In 1816, Stiles was elected mayor of Baltimore, a position he held until his death three years later. He is buried in an unmarked grave at the Glendy Graveyard in Baltimore.

Brig. Gen. John Stricker (1759–1825). Born in Frederick, Maryland, Stricker served in his father's militia regiment during the Revolutionary War, attaining the rank of captain. By 1812, he had become a brigadier general and headed the 3rd Brigade of the Maryland militia. Although shirking his duty during the Baltimore riots of 1812 because he was reluctant to employ militia against his fellow citizens, he used his brigade to good effect in the Battle of North Point in 1814. American fire that day led to the death of Maj. Gen. Robert Ross and inflicted heavy casualties on the British force that was en route to Baltimore. After the war Stricker was a merchant who served as president of the Bank of Baltimore.

Maj. Gen. Nathan Towson (1784–1854). Born in Baltimore County, Towson served as the captain of a local artillery unit before the War of 1812. In March 1812, he was commissioned a captain in the 2nd U.S. Artillery. On October 9, he commanded a boarding party that captured the British brig *Caledonia* from under the guns of Fort Erie. Captured at the Battle of Stony Creek on June 5, 1813, Towson effected his escape and was then wounded in July 1813 during an attack on Fort George. At the Battle of Chippawa on July 5, 1814, the British named his gun battery "Towson's Lighthouse" for the constant light of fire coming from its guns. Towson also fought at the Battle of Lundy's Lane on July 25, 1814, and engaged in the defense of Fort Erie on August 15, 1814. Towson later served as paymaster general for the U.S. Army and was brevetted a major general.

Lt. John Adams Webster (1789–1877). Born in Harford County, Maryland, Webster served under Joshua Barney onboard the privateer *Rossie* early in the War of 1812. Securing a warrant from the U.S. Navy as sailing master, he subsequently commanded one of the U.S. Chesapeake Flotilla barges during the battles of St. Leonard Creek. Webster also commanded a contingent of flotillamen who acted as infantry to protect Barney's right flank at the Battle of Bladensburg. While he was retreating from the field, one bullet killed his horse, while another passed through the crown of his hat. Webster commanded the six-gun Fort Babcock battery during the Battle for Baltimore. He opened the first fire on the British flotilla of barges that sought unsuccessfully to outflank Fort McHenry in a night assault. During this engagement, Webster injured his shoulder while stopping one of his sailors—an Englishman—from sabotaging his powder magazine. This injury left Webster permanently disabled. After the war, Webster had a long and distinguished career as a captain in the revenue service. In this service he lost his left thumb in an encounter with pirates at Old Point Comfort, Virginia, and he commanded a squadron of revenue cutters during the Mexican War.

Maj. Gen. James Wilkinson (1757–1825). A native of Charles County, Maryland, Wilkinson served in the Revolutionary War, earning a brevet promotion to the rank of brigadier general in the Continental Army before his twenty-first birthday. Dogged by a reputation for intrigue and corruption, he was forced out of the army before the end of the war but returned in the 1790s and by 1796 had become the senior officer in the army, a position he still held when the war was declared in 1812. While holding this command, he served as a Spanish spy and took part in Aaron Burr's notorious western conspiracy of 1806. Unwilling to trust Wilkinson with a major combat command, the administration allowed him to languish in New Orleans after war was declared in 1812. But the following year local Republicans became so infuriated with his intrigues that Louisiana's two U.S. senators threatened to go into opposition if he were not transferred out of the state. Ordered to the Saint Lawrence River, Wilkinson was consumed by dysentery and thus watched from afar as his army was decisively defeated in the Battle of Crysler's Farm in November 1813. After a failed attempt to capture Lacolle Mill in Lower Canada in 1814, he was removed from command. In 1816, he published his *Memoirs of My Own Times,* a self-serving narrative of his military career. In 1821, he traveled to Mexico in pursuit of a Texas land grant. He died in Mexico City and was buried there.

Governor Levin Winder (1757–1819). The product of an influential family in Somerset County on the Eastern Shore, Winder served as an officer in the Maryland Line during the Revolutionary War. A Federalist, he was opposed to the decision to go to war against Great Britain in 1812. That fall the Federalist Assembly chose him to be governor, the first of three one-year terms that he served in this office. As Maryland's wartime governor, Levin was known to be against the war but busied himself with trying to provide for the defense of the state. After the British burned Washington in the summer of 1814, he played a role in rallying sentiment in Maryland for the defense of Baltimore. After the war, he returned to agricultural pursuits in Somerset County.

Brig. Gen. William H. Winder (1775–1824). Born in Somerset County, Maryland, Winder in 1802 moved to Baltimore, where he established a successful law practice. In 1812, he was appointed a lieutenant colonel in the U.S. Infantry. He took part in the campaign on the Niagara front in 1812 and (after being promoted to brigadier general) was captured at Stoney Creek in 1813 but released on parole. The following year, he negotiated a prisoner-of-war exchange with the British, but the United States refused to ratify the agreement because it did not cover all the prisoners held by each side.

In the summer of 1814, Winder was put in command of the newly created military district that embraced the nation's capital, in part because the government hoped for the cooperation of his uncle, Governor Levin Winder of Maryland. Not up to the command, Winder did little to prepare the defenses of Washington, and his force was routed in the Battle of Bladensburg, which left the road to the capital city open to the British. After the war Winder resumed his successful law practice and was a respected member of the community despite his disastrous military career.

What Role Did Virginia Play in the War of 1812?

With 974,600 people, Virginia accounted for 12.2 percent of the nation's population. Although its relative size in the Union was declining because immigration fueled population growth in the North, it was still the second largest state (behind New York), and its political culture produced four of the first five presidents as well as countless other statesmen who shaped the early republic. In the War of 1812, Virginians paid less in taxes and purchased fewer war bonds than people in other populous states, but the Old Dominion was the home state of the president (James Madison), the secretary of state and secretary of war (James Monroe), and one of the leading generals (Winfield Scott). Virginia also produced the Petersburg Volunteers, a unit of U.S. Volunteers outfitted with cockade hats that was one of the first units to reach the Canadian border in 1812.

The only deepwater access into the Chesapeake Bay was through the Virginia capes bounded by Cape Henry on the north and Cape Charles on the south. Lynnhaven Roads, sometimes incorrectly referred to as Lynnhaven Bay, which is a smaller inlet not suitable for larger ships, served as an important anchorage for the Royal Navy throughout the war. It was from here that the British fleet operated its blockade of the Chesapeake. Norfolk, due to the presence of the Gosport Navy Yard, was a significant military objective. In 1813, Norfolk was the most fortified city in the Chesapeake Bay, defended by four forts and numerous other earthworks such as gun batteries and entrenchments. When the U.S. frigate *Constellation* became blockaded within the Bay, it sought the safety of the defenses at Norfolk and at the same time aided its defenses.

Saltpetre was produced in western Virginia for making gunpowder, and the federal arsenal in Harpers Ferry and the Virginia Manufactory of Arms in Richmond both produced arms for the war effort. In addition, the Tarr Iron Furnace in western Virginia, now West Virginia, produced cannonballs for use during the Battle of Lake Erie in September 1813.

Virginia had a rich tradition of public service, and many prominent residents of the state played a significant role in the war.

Lt. Col. George Armistead (1780–1818). Born in Newmarket, Virginia, Armistead was one of five brothers who served in the War of 1812. Commissioned a 2nd lieutenant in the U.S. Infantry in 1799, Armistead transferred to the artillery two years later. By 1813, he had attained the rank of major, and that year he distinguished himself in the capture of Fort George, Ontario. Charged with taking the captured British colors to Washington, he was rewarded with the command of Fort McHenry. He ordered the large flag that flew over the fort, and he was in charge when the British tried to bombard the post into submission in 1814. The successful defense of Fort McHenry inspired Francis Scott Key to write the poem that eventually became "The Star-Spangled Banner." For his success Armistead was feted by the people of Baltimore and honored by the government with a brevet promotion to the rank of lieutenant colonel. Armistead retained command of Fort McHenry until his death, and the celebrated flag remained in his family until it was loaned to the Smithsonian Institution in 1907 and then donated to it as a gift in 1912.

James Barbour (1775–1842). Born in Orange County, Virginia, Barbour served for many years in the House of Delegates before being elected Speaker in 1809, a position he held for three years. In early 1812, the legislature chose him to serve as governor when his predecessor, George W. Smith, was killed in the great Richmond theater fire of 1811. Barbour continued as governor until December 1814, having served for three terms, the maximum allowed under Virginia law. A strong supporter of the war and an effective wartime leader, Barbour devoted much of his attention to the defense of the state, seeking to find a way to counter the growing number of British coastal raids. He endorsed laws to raise state armies in 1813 and 1814, but the first law was suspended when the federal government promised to station more regulars in Virginia, and the second was rendered moot by the end of the war. After the war, Barbour spent a decade in the U.S. Senate before serving as secretary of war under John Quincy Adams.

William Branch Giles (1762–1830). Born in Amelia County, Virginia, Giles was a longtime member of Congress, serving in the House or Senate almost continuously from 1790 to 1815. Although he was a Jeffersonian Republican who generally supported administration policies and had a reputation as a good political in-fighter, he openly feuded, first with Secretary of the Treasury Albert Gallatin and later with Secretary of State James Monroe. Although Giles voted for the declaration of war, he was frequently at odds with administration policies for waging the war. As a member of a small band of Senate Republicans known as the "Invisibles" or "Malcontents," he often joined the Federalist minority to kill administration initiatives. After briefly retiring at the end of the war, he returned to public life in 1816 and closed out his public career as governor of Virginia (1827–30).

Brig. Gen. John Pratt Hungerford (1761–1833). Born in Leeds, Westmoreland County, Virginia, Hungerford (whose middle initial is sometimes incorrectly given as "H.") was a lawyer who fought in the American Revolution and later served in the Virginia legislature. A brigadier general in the Virginia militia during the War of 1812, he commanded the 14th Brigade of the Northern Neck. Hungerford took part in the Battle of the White House, which grew out of an American attempt to harass a British naval squadron descending the Potomac River after plundering Alexandria. Hungerford also served as a member of the U.S. House of Representatives during the war. In the postwar years, he returned to the Virginia legislature.

Col. Thomas Sidney Jesup (1788–1860). Born in Berkeley County, Virginia, Jesup was commissioned a 2nd lieutenant in the U.S. Army in 1808. By 1812, he was a 1st lieutenant and served as adjutant general of Brig. Gen. William Hull's staff in the ill-fated campaign on the Detroit River. In 1814, he fought with distinction in the battles on the Niagara frontier. Severely wounded in the Battle of Lundy's Lane, he was rewarded with a brevet promotion to rank of colonel. He remained in the army after the war, ultimately achieving the rank of brevet major general. He served in the Seminole and Mexican wars and was the army's quartermaster general for forty-two years, from 1818 until his death in 1842. He died in Washington, D.C., and is buried in Arlington Cemetery.

Dolley Payne Madison (1768–1849). Born in North Carolina but raised in Virginia, Dolley Madison moved with her family to Pennsylvania when she was fifteen. As the president's wife from 1809 to 1817, she turned the White House into the center of Washington's social scene. More than anyone else, she invented the role of the First Lady. She also performed a signal service for the new nation in 1814 as the British approached the capital when she sacrificed her personal belongings to save a number of White House treasures, including a portrait of George Washington. Later, when the government returned to the city, Dolley Madison helped transform the Octagon House into the temporary headquarters of the executive branch of the government.

After her husband's retirement from the presidency in 1817, she served as host at Montpelier, and after his death, she closed out her days in Washington.

James Madison (1750/51–1836). Born in Orange County, Virginia, James Madison was a lifelong friend and collaborator of Thomas Jefferson and an accomplished student of Republican government. He helped democratize Virginia in the 1780s and was largely responsible for framing the U.S. Constitution and then securing the adoption of the Bill of Rights. As President Thomas Jefferson's secretary of state from 1801 to 1809, he was the chief architect of the restrictive system. As the nation's wartime president, he was not a strong leader. Although respectful of the rights of his domestic foes, he was unable to control his cabinet and his recommendations were frequently ignored by Congress. As a result, the war never bore his stamp even though Federalists sought to label the contest "Mr. Madison's War." He lived for more than twenty years after the war and was known as "the last of the Founders."

James Monroe (1758–1831). Born in Westmoreland County, Virginia, Monroe served in the American Revolution and held various public offices in the 1780s and 1790s. As the U.S. minister to Great Britain during Jefferson's presidency, he negotiated a treaty with William Pinkney in 1806 that the administration refused to ratify. Returning home, Monroe was alienated from the administration until just before the war, when he agreed to serve as President James Madison's secretary of state, a position he held from 1811 to 1817. He also served as secretary of war in 1814–15. Although Monroe never got the high-level combat command that he coveted, he reconnoitered the British landing at Benedict on the Patuxent River, and before the Battle of Bladensburg he weakened the American defensive position by redeploying some elements of the militia. Elected president in the quieter and less partisan period that followed the war, he was the last member of the Virginia Dynasty.

John Randolph (1733–1833). Born at "Cawsons" in Prince George County, John Randolph of Roanoke came from a distinguished Virginia family. A member of Congress from 1799 to 1813, Randolph served as the Republican floor leader until 1806, when he broke with the administration and went into opposition. Thereafter, he headed a small band of southern conservatives known as "Old Republicans" who thought that the regular Republicans had forsaken limited government and strict construction of the Constitution. In Congress, Randolph now voted with the Federalists, opposing first the restrictive system and then the War of 1812. Voted out of Congress during the war, Randolph was returned

to the body after the conflict and enjoyed a revival of his popularity as a spokesman for southern sectionalism.

Brig. Gen. Winfield Scott (1786–1866). Born on the family estate of Laurel Branch near Dinwiddie, Virginia, Scott joined the army as a captain of the artillery in 1808 and enjoyed a long and distinguished military career. Promoted to lieutenant colonel at the beginning of the War of 1812, he took part in almost every major engagement on the Niagara front from 1812 to 1814: Queenston Heights, the capture of Fort George, and the battles of Chippawa and Lundy's Lane. He was wounded so severely at Lundy's Lane that he was knocked out of the war. Although sometimes reckless on the battlefield, Scott was an accomplished trainer and tactician who knew how to whip raw recruits into reliable soldiers and then use them effectively in battle. Sometimes called "the hero of three wars," he also distinguished himself in the Mexican War (1846–48), and he devised the strategy for the Union in 1861 that ultimately won the Civil War.

Brig. Gen. Alexander Smyth (1765–1830). Born on the isle of Rathlin off the coast of Ireland, Smyth was brought to America by his parents and raised in Botetourt County in Virginia. Trained as a lawyer, he served for many years in the Virginia Assembly before being commissioned a colonel in the Virginia rifle regiment in 1808. In July 1812, he was promoted to brigadier general and published *Regulations for the Field Exercise, Manoeuvers, and Conduct of the Infantry of the United States,* which became a standard manual during the war. Smyth was ordered to the Niagara frontier in 1812 but offered only half-hearted cooperation to Maj. Gen. Stephan Van Rensselaer, the New York militia officer who had the overall American command in the theater. When Van Rensselaer resigned after an assault on Queenston Heights failed, Smyth succeeded him to the command. But Smyth declined to launch a major offensive, citing an insufficiency of boats to carry his men across the Niagara River to the Canadian side. With winter setting in, he left for home, and several months later was struck from the rolls of the army during a reorganization. After the war he served for several years in the Virginia House of Delegates and was elected to almost every Congress until his death. He died in Washington and was buried in the Congressional Cemetery.

Brig. Gen. Robert B. Taylor (1774–1834). After attending William and Mary College, Taylor set up a law practice in Norfolk and soon gained a reputation as one of the leading lawyers in the state. Although a Federalist who opposed the decision to go to war against Great Britain in 1812, he was commissioned a brigadier general in the state militia and held various commands during the War of 1812. As head of the Norfolk militia, Taylor played a central role in repulsing the British attack on Craney Island in 1813. After the war, he was promoted to major general, served on the board of visitors of the University of Virginia, and held a position as a state judge.

What Role Did Washington, D.C., Play in the War of 1812?

The 100-square-mile District of Columbia boasted 15,500 people in 1810, which was only 0.2 percent of the nation's total. The City of Washington accounted for a little over half the district's total. With 8,200 people, it was the 14th largest city in the nation. This small southern city was the center of federal activity during the war. Here the president recommended war preparations and war strategy, and here Congress adopted a war program and then passed the war bill. For the next thirty-two months, the president and his cabinet devised strategy and managed the war effort from Washington, while Congress met periodically to raise men and money and adopt other war-related legislation. The war began when the president signed the war bill into law in the White House on June 18, 1812, and it officially ended when he ratified the Treaty of Ghent in the Octagon House on February 16, 1815.

Also located in the federal district was the Washington Navy Yard and the Greenleaf Point Federal Arsenal, where arms and ammunition were stored. There were several war industries in Washington as well, most notably the Columbian Foundry, which made shot and cannon, and three rope walks, which made rope for the standing and running rigging of the U.S. warships as well as for other war-related purposes.

The nation's capital suffered a terrific blow when the British occupied it in August 1814. The British burned most of the public buildings and destroyed the federal arsenal, while American officials torched the navy yard and two warships under construction there and destroyed most of the bridges across the Potomac and Anacostia rivers. The British evidently missed the U.S. Marine barracks, for it survived the occupation intact.

Several residents of the federal district made notable contributions during the war.

Henry Foxall (1758–1823). A British-born iron-founder and lay minister, Foxall learned his trade in the mother country before migrating to Ireland in 1794 and then to the United States in 1797. After founding the Eagle Iron Works

in Philadelphia, he moved in 1800 to Georgetown, D.C., where he established the Columbian Foundry, which was one of the first in the United States to manufacture effective boring machinery. With an annual production capacity of three hundred heavy guns and thirty thousand shot, the Columbian Foundry over the next fifteen years manufactured an enormous quantity of long guns, carronades, mortars, gun carriages, and shot for the U.S. government. During the War of 1812, it was one of the principal suppliers of ordnance for both the U.S. Army and the U.S. Navy. After the war, Foxall sold his foundry and divided his time between England and the United States. His last public service was as mayor of Georgetown from 1821 to 1823.

Joseph Gales, Jr. (1786–1860). Born in England, Gales was brought to America by his father when he was nine. He acquired an education and learned the printing trade and shorthand from his father before moving in 1807 to Washington, where he worked with Joseph Harrison Smith on the *National Intelligencer.* Gales assumed control of the paper in 1810 but took on William W. Seaton as a partner in 1812. By transforming the paper from a tri-weekly into a daily, reporting the debates and proceedings in Congress, and publishing other government documents, the two men solidified the *National Intelligencer*'s reputation as the leading Republican paper in the country. Gales used the columns of the paper to support the War of 1812 and served as a private in the militia called out to defend Washington and other nearby communities. The British destroyed the press and other property belonging to Gales and Seaton when they captured Washington in 1814, but the paper resumed publication within a week. Although their own losses were large, the editors praised the British for generally respecting private property during the occupation. A longtime resident of the District of Columbia, Gales built his country estate—Eckington—two miles from his office and served as mayor of the capital city from 1827 to 1830. His most enduring legacy after the war was the publication of various collections of government documents—including the *Annals of Congress* and the *American State Papers*—which illuminate the history of the early republic.

Francis Scott Key (1779–1843). Born at Terra Rubra, Keysville, Maryland, Key established a law practice in Frederick before relocating to Georgetown in 1802. Well connected socially, he built a successful practice in the nation's capital. Key served in Capt. George Peter's Georgetown Artillery Company during the Battle of Bladensburg. Although a Federalist, he was asked after the Battle for Baltimore to intervene to secure the release of Dr. William Beanes, whom the British had captured and imprisoned on a warship. Joined by the U.S. agent for the exchange of prisoners, Key visited the British under a flag of truce and managed to secure Beanes's release. After witnessing the twenty-five-hour bombardment of Fort McHenry from his truce ship, which was anchored beyond the guns of the British fleet, Key was moved to write "The Defense of Fort M'Henry," later re-titled "The Star-Spangled Banner." It was an immediate hit and ultimately, in 1931, became the national anthem. Key continued to practice law after the war and in the 1830s served as U.S. district attorney for the District of Columbia.

William Thornton (1759–1828). Born in the Virgin Islands but educated in England, Thornton migrated to the United States in 1787. Although trained as a doctor, Thornton was a man of many talents who left his mark as both an architect and inventor. He designed the Capitol Building as well as several other buildings in Washington, D.C., including the Octagon House, which served as the temporary executive mansion after the White House was burned by the British in 1814. As superintendent of patents, a position he held from 1802 until his death, Thornton persuaded the British to spare the patent office from destruction.

Capt. Thomas Tingey (1750–1829). Born in England, Tingey served briefly as an officer in the Royal Navy before resigning in the early 1770s to go into the merchant service in the West Indies. After the American Revolution, he commanded American merchantmen until 1798, when he was commissioned a captain in the U.S. Navy. He was named superintendent of the Washington Navy Yard in 1803 and held this position during the War of 1812. The Washington yard was the nation's principal naval base during the war, and Tingey worked indefatigably building, repairing, and re-supplying warships. In August 1814, when the British marched into the city, Tingey burned the yard and two ships under construction there. Although the losses were heavy—estimated at more than $400,000—Tingey was acting in accordance with standing orders, and he was probably the last high-ranking U.S. officer to leave the city. After the war, he continued to serve as superintendent (as well as naval agent) of the Washington yard until his death.

What Was the War's Legacy in the Chesapeake?

The legacy of the War of 1812 in the Chesapeake was significant. Many people there had experienced firsthand the horrors of war. The British blockade disrupted trade, and British raids sometimes resulted in looting and arson. Many buildings in towns such as Washington, Havre de Grace,

Fredericktown, and Tappahannock had been burned, and other communities had experienced the indignity of enemy occupation and minor abuses of looting. At least one town, Hampton, Virginia, had experienced not only looting and arson but rape and murder as well. Some people who lost their businesses were unable to rebound. After the British burned the Principio Iron Furnace in Cecil County, the owner was forced to mortgage his wood, coal, and iron resources to reopen but ultimately had to sell off his mansion to pay his debts. Washington Bowie, George Washington's godchild, lost his shipping business and had to sell his Georgetown home, Bowie House, to pay his debts. These experiences were not unique. Many people who had sustained property losses in the war found it difficult to bounce back.

There were at least 160 military actions in the Chesapeake region, including 11 battles, 61 skirmishes, and 87 raids. (See appendix D for a complete list of these actions.) The suffering in the Chesapeake was not as widespread as it had been in the American Revolution or as it would be in the Civil War, mainly because it was restricted mostly to coastal areas. Still, it was bad enough. While other areas, most notably the Niagara region, had been the scene of significant campaigning and extensive property losses, no region in the United States suffered such immense losses as the Chesapeake (see endnote 1, introduction). These losses ran in the millions of dollars—this at a time when there was virtually no property insurance or government assistance programs (although the State of Maryland did give funds to the needy in Fredericktown and Havre de Grace).

Many Americans in southern Maryland, an estimated three hundred from St. Mary's County alone, suffered such damage from the depredations that they left the state, most moving to Kentucky. We do not have yearly population records for the Chesapeake counties, but between 1810 and 1820 the population of Charles Country dropped 3,745 persons, while that of Harford County declined by more than 5,000. Despite rapid population growth in many other parts of the country, the numbers in Calvert County and St. Mary's County remained flat during this decade. For Maryland as a whole, the white population in this period fell by 34,894 (although the black population actually increased by 1,698). Some areas took years to recover from the war, and the damage was visible for a generation or even longer. To this day, long-hidden walls in the White House still show scorch marks from the British burning.

People in the Chesapeake did not soon forget these depredations. Rear Admiral Cockburn and his men were long remembered as bandits, pirates, or barbarians. Many residents agreed with the assessment of Cockburn made in 1813 by the Baltimore magazine *Niles' Weekly Register:* "The wantonness of his barbarities have gibbetted him on infamy."[5] Even today, some residents in the area still speak of British operations in the Chesapeake with bitterness.

But if the war caused heart-rending losses in the Chesapeake, it also left a legacy of pride. The success of the privateers was long remembered, and today a replica of the original *Chasseur* has been built to keep that memory alive. Known as *The Pride of Baltimore II,* it was launched in 1988 and serves an educational purpose and sails the seas as a goodwill ambassador on behalf of Baltimore and Maryland. (The first replica, *The Pride of Baltimore,* tragically sank in the West Indies in 1986, taking with it four members of its crew.)

On September 12, 1816, the second anniversary of the Battle for Baltimore, the city council passed a resolution calling for the annual commemoration of the engagement, a commemoration that is now known as Defenders Day. By state legislation, this date in 1907 became a Maryland holiday. Maryland schools and banks closed and state employees were given the day off. Although the paid holiday was dropped in 1996, Defenders Day is still commemorated with reenactments at North Point and a wreath laying at the Battle Monument in Baltimore.

People in the Chesapeake may have suffered, but they also consider the war a success, an important step in forging a nation. The war in this theater produced two great national symbols. The bombardment of Fort McHenry gave special meaning to the garrison flag, which is now on display at the Smithsonian Institution. It also helped generate reverence for the national banner that had not existed before the war. In addition, the bombardment produced Francis Scott Key's poem, which eventually became "The Star-Spangled Banner," another important link to the war, one that was sung on countless occasions throughout the nation before becoming the national anthem in 1931. The flag and the song have been irrevocably bound together in the public memory ever since that fateful day that Fort McHenry survived the British attack.

For one group of people in the Chesapeake, the war was a defining moment of monumental proportions, for their lives were never the same afterward. Several thousand slaves escaped to British ships and British camps during the war, and many scouted and fought for the British. Those who survived left with the British, settling in Nova Scotia, the West Indies, or elsewhere in the British Empire. They had never been American citizens in any true sense of the word, and now they were British subjects. Identifiable remnants of this black diaspora survive today. In Nova Scotia, the residents of a section of Halifax called Africville, settled by African Americans after the War of 1812, were evicted and the town demolished in the late 1960s to make way for bridge and road construction. A sun dial monument marks the town site, and some descendants of the former slaves still live in the area. Similarly, there are people living in Trinidad today who trace their roots to the former slaves who left with the British. These people still call themselves "Merikans."

CHAPTER 3

Maryland Sites

ADDISON CHAPEL, also called "upper chapel" of King George's Parish or St. Matthew's Church, now St. Matthew's Anglican Catholic Church (intersection of 62nd Place and 5610 Addison Road, Seat Pleasant, Prince George's County). NRHP. The present church structure, at least the third built on the site and completed circa 1809, reportedly served as a temporary headquarters on August 24, 1814, when British troops passed here on Addison Road during their march on Washington. The chapel appears essentially as it did in 1814, although the pitch in the roof, visible in the brick gable ends, was changed in 1902. Francis Scott Key served here as one of the lay readers. Addison Chapel attained church status in 1919, was deconsecrated in 1990, and was acquired in 1991 by the Prince George's County Historical and Cultural Trust.

AETNA POWDER MILL SITE, also called Baltimore Aetna Gun Powder Factory, later called Battle Mills or Battleworks Powder Mill (Powder Mill Run, upstream from Gwynndale Avenue, near Powder Mill Park, in woods at terminus of Stonington Avenue, Howard Park, Woodlawn, Baltimore County). The Aetna Powder Mill began operations in 1812 and produced gunpowder for the defense of Baltimore. James Beatty owed the mill at the beginning of the war, but by July 1814 Joseph Jamieson had acquired it. The ruins of the dam and millrace can still be seen, but the area is heavily overgrown and littered with trash.[1]

<blockquote>

Baltimore Aetna Gun Powder
Factory.

The Powder of this Factory is warranted of the first quality . . . the quality of the Powder is such that it will give general satisfaction, and the price such as will induce those wanting this article to give him the preference; there is a quantity now on hand to which the works are daily adding more. (Baltimore *Federal Gazette,* July 5, 1814)

</blockquote>

ANCHORAGE (5667 Augustine Herman Highway [Route 213], Cecilton, Cecil County). PRIVATE. Jacob Jones (1768–1850) joined the U.S. Navy as a midshipman in 1799 and lived at the Anchorage, built in 1710. In 1835, he added the Georgian style addition with the paneled front door and fanlight. Jones commanded the U.S. sloop-of-war *Wasp,* built at the Washington Navy Yard,* which captured H.M. brig *Frolic* on October 18, 1812, in the Atlantic off Chesapeake Bay after a vicious fight that left both vessels disabled. On the same day in a second action the 74-gun H.M. ship-of-the-line *Poictiers* captured the crippled *Wasp.* Then a master commandant, Jones was exchanged and later commanded the recently captured H.M. frigate *Macedonian* and then the U.S. frigate *Constitution.* His home, the Anchorage, is now operated as a bed and breakfast. Originally buried in nearby North Sassafras Parish (now St. Stephen's Episcopal Church Cemetery), Commodore Jones was re-interred at the Wilmington and Brandywine Cemetery,* Wilmington, Delaware, where he was born in March 1768. A large 2007 addition detracts from the historic integrity of the Anchorage.

ANDREWS AIR FORCE BASE/BRITISH ENCAMPMENT SITE (near intersection of Patrick and Fechet avenues, Prince George's County). Military installation, access restricted. After camping at Upper Marlboro, the invading British troops took up the march again around noon, August 23, 1814. The exact location of their next camp was apparently where Old Marlboro Pike turned north following what today is called Fechet Avenue within the military base. Before the base was established in 1943, this area was known as the Meadows or Centreville. The British column rested only about two miles north of the American encampment at Woodyard* and about the same distance from the American encampment at Long Old Fields.* It was either at this bivouac or more likely during their march to this camp that Maj. Gen. Robert Ross and Rear Adm. George Cockburn

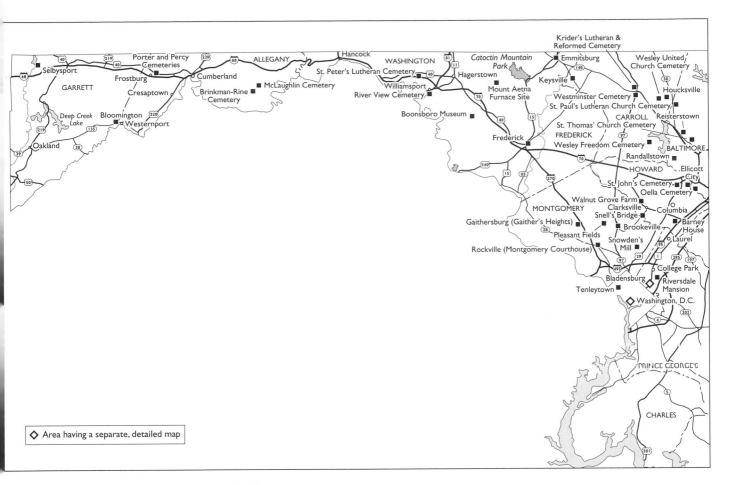

Maryland War of 1812 Sites, Western Maryland

Congress awarded Com. Jacob Jones this gold medal for his action during the *Wasp–Frolic* engagement. (Lossing, *Pictorial Field-Book of the War of 1812*)

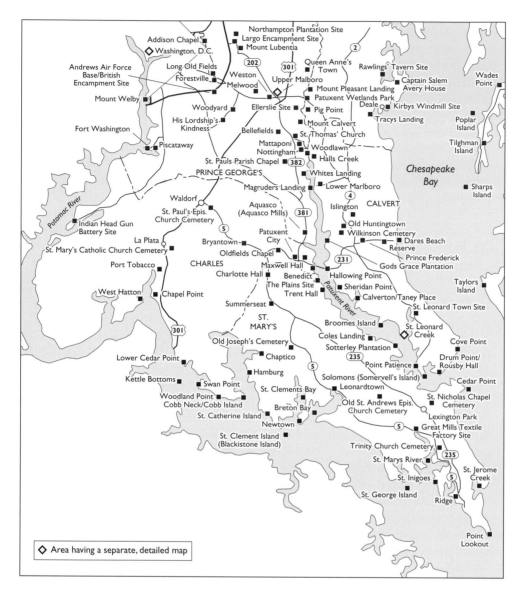

Maryland War of 1812 Sites, Southern Maryland

stopped at nearby Melwood* for dinner. Belle Chance, probably a corruption of Beall Chance, built prior to 1738, was located just west of this encampment site. The British advance guard probably occupied the grounds of Belle Chance at this time. It burned in 1913. The present Belle Chance is a concrete house where the commander of the Air Force's Systems Command resides. (See map, p. 29.)

ANNAPOLIS (mouth of Severn River, Anne Arundel County). NHD. Before war was declared, Secretary of the Navy William Jones dispatched the 58-gun U.S. frigate *President,* anchored off Fort Severn,* to search for a British warship that had boarded an American merchant ship seeking an alleged deserter. Capt. John Rodgers sailed *President* out of the Chesapeake Bay and on May 16, 1811, met the 20-gun H.M. sloop-of-war *Little Belt.* It is unclear who fired first, but most Americans considered the *Little Belt* affair just retribution for the *Chesapeake–Leopard* affair,* and it probably heightened war sentiment in the United States.

Annapolis became a military camp and served as the legislative center for the state government where issues relating to the defense of Maryland were debated.

The respective infantry companies of this city, are requested to meet at the state-house this morning at 9 o'clock, for the purpose of receiving their arms from the armory. (Annapolis *Maryland Republican,* June 20, 1812)

The British fleet blockaded Annapolis in April and again in July 1813. Two British officers scouted the Annapolis defenses without detection. Because of the threat of a British attack, the public records were moved from the state capital on April 19, 1813, to the relative safety of Upper Marlboro.* Upper Marlboro was later occupied by the British, but by then the records had been relocated to nearby Mount Lubentia.*

Our city was alarmed at an early hour on Friday morning last by the discharge of several cannon from the fort, and drums beating to arms—The alarm was caused by the arrival of several privateers, who reported that they had been pursued some considerable distance up the Bay by a part of the blockading squadron. Although the alarm was sounded at an hour when our citizens were slumbering in their beds, and they were summoned from them totally unconscious of the extent of their danger, they repaired to the place of rendezvous with a degree of promptness and alacrity highly honorable and meritorious. (Annapolis *Maryland Gazette and Political Intelligencer,* April 15, 1813)

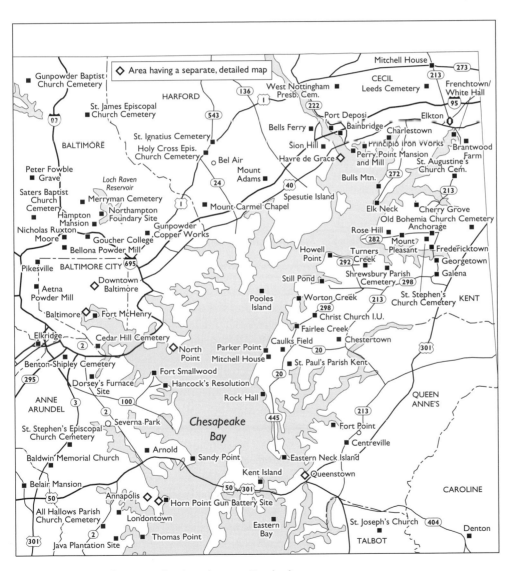

Maryland War of 1812 Sites, Central and Northeastern Maryland

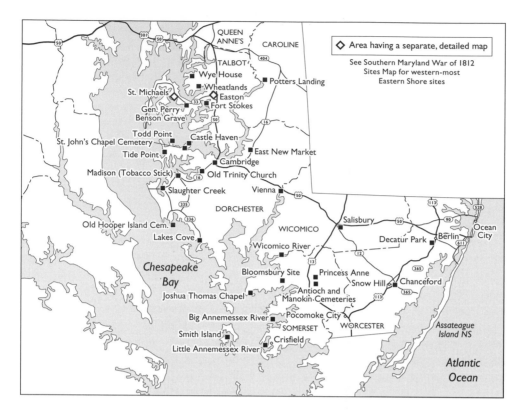

Maryland War of 1812 Sites, Southeastern Maryland

THE ENEMY . . . One frigate said to be [Rear] Admiral [George] Cockburn's is opposite the harbor [Annapolis], within about six miles of the city. We have expected an attack for several nights past, and the most strict precautions are taken to prevent a surpize, guards are posted in every direction, and the troops are on their posts from 2 till 6 o'clock every morning. A schooner [British] has been sounding the harbor for two days past. (Annapolis *Maryland Republican,* August 14, 1813)

Great alarm existed at Annapolis, Baltimore, &c.; troops were pouring in, and all was bustle and preparation. Annapolis has many natural advantages, and may readily be made a very strong place. The fears of the people in that quarter were strongly excited, and they have had many tedious marches, countermarches, &c.; and this is all the British appear to aim at, excepting the destruction of shipping, river craft, &c. (Boston *Columbia Centinel,* August 14, 1813)

The U.S. Chesapeake Flotilla put into Annapolis on April 17, 1814, during its cruise down the Chesapeake Bay to en-

gage the British at Tangier Island.* Annapolis was threatened in late August 1814 by Capt. Sir Peter Parker's naval squadron as part of a feint up the Chesapeake to keep the Americans guessing as to where the British were going to next attack and to tie down local militia from supporting Baltimore. After the British occupation of Washington, Judge Jeremiah T. Chase, chairman of the Annapolis Committee of Safety, endorsed a resolution to surrender the town if threatened by the British; the resolution did not pass (Alexandria, Virginia, and Charlestown, Maryland, did capitulate to the British).

I am much embarrassed about the situation of Annapolis: it cannot be defended against a serious attack by land and water, without a large force and many additional works. (Brig. Gen. William H. Winder to Secretary of War John Armstrong, July 16, 1814)[2]

Anapolis is the Capital of Maryland . . . perfectly open and liable to an attack. (Vice Adm. Sir Alexander F. I. Cochrane to First Lord of the Admiralty Viscount Robert Saunders Dundas Melville, July 17, 1814)[3]

Yet, on the same day another British officer made the following contradictory statement.

> Annapolis being fortified, a Station for Troops, and [is] not to be approached by our larger Ships on Account of the Shallowness of the Water, it is possible and probable the Occupation of it might cost us some little Time, which would of Course be taken Advantage of by the Enemy to draw together all the Force at his Command for the Defence of Washington. (Rear Adm. George Cockburn to Vice Adm. Sir Alexander F. I. Cochrane, July 17, 1814)[4]

As the British fleet under Vice Adm. Alexander Cochrane sailed up the Chesapeake Bay to attack Baltimore in the second week of September 1814, people in Annapolis, fearing an attack, fled the city in wagons loaded with their possessions.

> As we ascended the bay, alarm guns were fired in all directions; thus testifying the terror which the inhabitants of the surrounding country felt at the approach of the British arms . . . As we passed the picturesque town of Annapolis . . . we could plainly perceive the inhabitants flying in all directions. (Midshipman Robert J. Barrett)[5]

When the news of peace with England reached the Chesapeake on February 13, 1815, the citizens of Annapolis celebrated by brilliantly illuminating the statehouse with candles in the windows and cupola as well as in other buildings, firing cannons, ringing bells, and building grand bonfires.

Horn Point Gun Battery Site, also called Fort Horn (southeast side of Spa Creek, northeast end of Chester Avenue, Eastport). Near this site partially destroyed by erosion and now occupied by condominiums along Eastern Avenue stood a Revolutionary War-era gun battery that was also used during the War of 1812. Named Fort Horn, it stood ready to defend the harbor of Annapolis in case of a British attack. It was one of four fortifications (the others were forts Madison,* Nonsense,* and Severn*) near the mouth of the Severn River. Fort Horn was abandoned in 1866.

> under arms on the parade in the front of the State house, and shortly after the enemy's fleet had anchored off the harbor [at Annapolis], Gen. [?] Williams required ninety volunteers from the companies to defend the old fort on Horn Point, when considerably more than the number called for nobly stepped forward and immediately tendered their services. They were marched over in the course of the afternoon, and are now on duty . . . Yesterday at noon, when the [British] shipping were about weighing anchor to proceed up the Bay,

> 12 or 14 shots were fired from the battery on the Point, with the expectation of bringing them to an engagement, but John Bull [the British] thought proper to pocket the insult and sneak off without even answering them. (Easton *Republican Star,* April 27, 1813)

★ **Maryland Statehouse** (91 State Circle). NHL. The statehouse, the third to occupy this site, was begun in 1772 and completed in 1779. It is the oldest functioning statehouse in the United States. The wooden dome, the largest in the

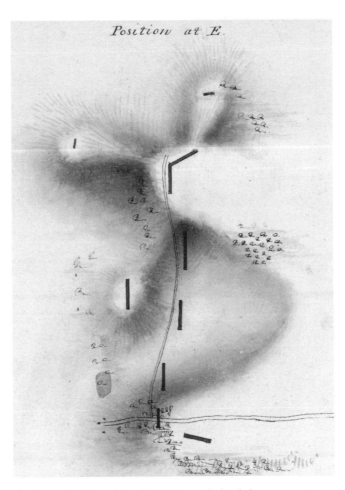

Sketch map showing position of British troops during their encampment on the evening of August 23, 1814. The road at the bottom is believed to represent a road that led west to the Alexandria ferry over the Potomac River and east to Upper Marlboro. The road to the north is believed to represent what was later called Old Marlboro Pike before Andrews Air Force Base was established. (1814 sketch map by Robert Smith, "Sketch of the march of the British army under M. Genl. Ross . . . "; courtesy of Bienecke Rare Book and Manuscript Library, Yale University)

United States, served as an observation station for British movements on the Chesapeake Bay.

> For near a week past there has been from 20 to 25 sail of the blockading squadron in sight of this city [Annapolis], plainly perceptible from the dome of the state house. (Annapolis *Maryland Republican,* August 7, 1813)

> Four of the enemy's ships were in sight last evening from the dome of the state-house, off Sharp's Island, about 15 or 20 miles below this city. It is conjectured here that an expedition has been sent to Cambridge as three of the original number are not to be seen [the British actually attacked Castle Haven* on the Choptank River]. (Annapolis *Maryland Republican,* October 22, 1814)

MARYLAND SILVER ROOM. Samuel Kirk and Sons, Inc., of Baltimore made the silver service on behalf of the citizens of Maryland to be presented to the U.S. armored cruiser *Maryland* in 1906. The new U.S. battleship *Maryland* received the silver service in 1921. The State of Maryland received the silver service upon the decommissioning of the battleship after World War II. Most of it is displayed in the Maryland Silver Room. Each Maryland county and Baltimore City contributed a piece to the service, each with representative historic scenes and symbols. Examples of War of 1812 depictions include:

Baltimore County and Baltimore City punch bowl
    bombardment of Fort McHenry
    birth of "The Star-Spangled Banner"
    Battle Monument*
Cecil County fish dish
    Kitty Knight House* saved from burning because of the stubborn stance of Miss Kitty Knight*
Harford County entree dish
    Rear Adm. George Cockburn's snuff box that he supposedly gave a young girl while she reportedly attempted to seek release of her captured father John O'Neill* at Havre de Grace
Kent County serving waiter
    Battle of Caulks Field* Monument
Prince George's County coffee platter
    Woodyard,* the site of an American encampment during the war
Montgomery County Ice Cream Platter and Knife
    Brookeville Academy,* where federal documents were stored to keep them out of British harm

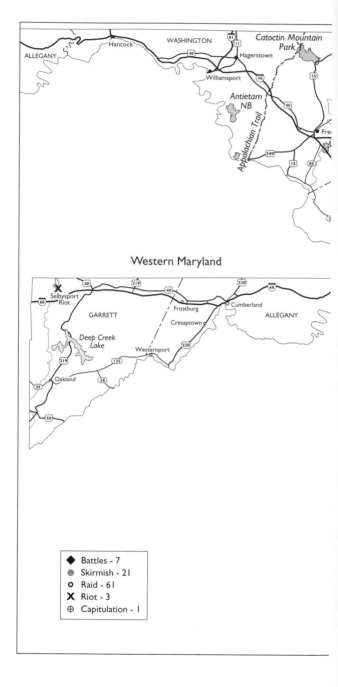

Western Maryland

Battles - 7
Skirmish - 21
Raid - 61
Riot - 3
Capitulation - 1

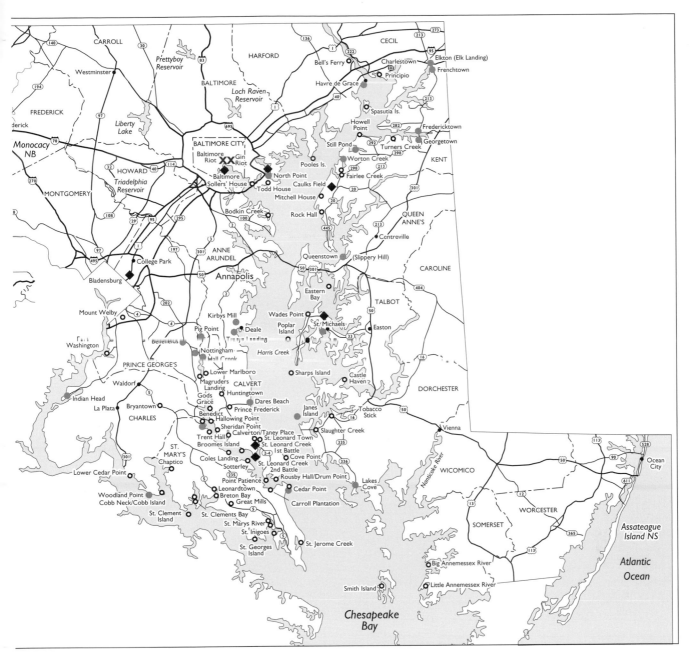

Maryland War of 1812 Battles, Skirmishes, Raids, Capitulations, and Riots

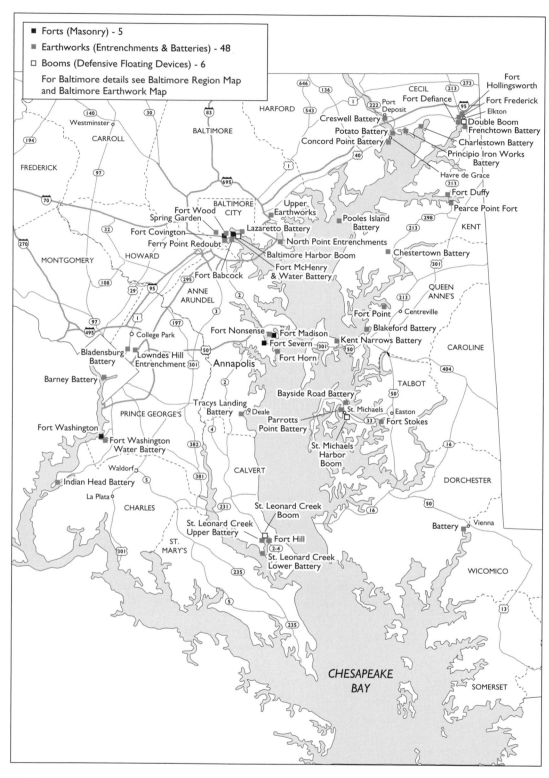

Westminster

CARROLL

FREDERICK

BALTIMORE

HARFORD

CECIL

Port Deposit

Fort Hollingsworth

Fort Defiance

Fort Frederick

Elkton

Double Boom

Frenchtown Battery

Creswell Battery

Potato Battery

Concord Point Battery

Charlestown Battery

Principio Iron Works Battery

Havre de Grace

Fort Duffy

Pearce Point Fort

KENT

MONTGOMERY

HOWARD

BALTIMORE CITY

Fort Wood

Spring Garden

Fort Covington

Ferry Point Redoubt

Upper Earthworks

Lazaretto Battery

North Point Entrenchments

Baltimore Harbor Boom

Fort McHenry & Water Battery

Fort Babcock

Pooles Island Battery

Chestertown Battery

QUEEN ANNE'S

Fort Point

Centreville

ANNE ARUNDEL

College Park

Fort Nonsense

Fort Madison

Fort Severn

Fort Horn

Blakeford Battery

Kent Narrows Battery

CAROLINE

Bladensburg Battery

Lowndes Hill Entrenchment

Annapolis

Barney Battery

PRINCE GEORGE'S

TALBOT

Bayside Road Battery

Tracys Landing Battery

Deale

Parrotts Point Battery

St. Michaels

St. Michaels Harbor Boom

Easton

Fort Stokes

Fort Washington

Fort Washington Water Battery

Waldorf

Indian Head Battery

La Plata

CHARLES

CALVERT

St. Leonard Creek Boom

St. Leonard Creek Upper Battery

Fort Hill

St. Leonard Creek Lower Battery

ST. MARY'S

DORCHESTER

Battery

Vienna

WICOMICO

CHESAPEAKE BAY

SOMERSET

Maryland War of 1812 Forts, Earthworks, and Booms (see map on p. 72 for details of Baltimore eastern defenses)

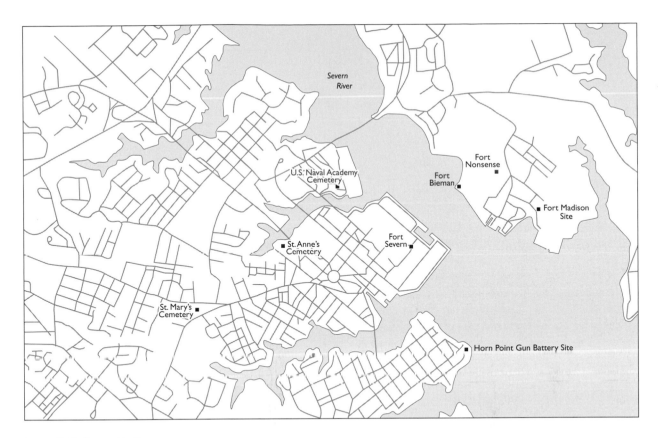

Annapolis Region and Defenses

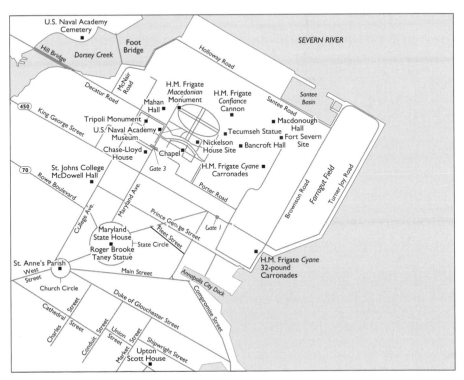

Annapolis

View from the dome of the statehouse circa 1855 showing the mouth of the Severn River, Chesapeake Bay, Kent Island, and Eastern Shore beyond. (Lithograph by Edward Sachse circa 1855, *View of Annapolis*; courtesy of The Maryland Historical Society)

Pinkney Farm Site (northeastern end of Monterey Avenue near intersection with Claude Street). The son of a Tory, William Pinkney* (1764–1822) lived at the Pinkney Farm. As U.S. attorney general, he wrote the bill declaring war in 1812 and as a major in the militia commanded the 1st Rifle Battalion in the defense of Baltimore. Pinkney is recognized by a plaque (now missing) on one of the Fort McHenry Memorial Trees and Markers.* Mrs. Ann Maria Rodgers Pinkney was in Havre de Grace* during the British burning of that town in 1813. A cenotaph for William Pinkney is located at Congressional Cemetery,* Washington, D.C.

St. Anne's Cemetery (Northwest Street, off Calvert Street). Near the northeast corner of St. Anne's Cemetery, which dates from 1692, is located a granite block monument to the Magruder family. The granite block came from the Col. Joseph Hopper Nicholson's home,* now gone, where a handwritten draft of Francis Scott Key's famous poem that

provided the words for "The Star-Spangled Banner" once was kept.

St. John's College (College Avenue, north of State Circle). Francis Scott Key* at age ten attended the grammar school of St. John's College, founded in 1696 as King William's School. On January 7, 1793, Key attended the French school before entering the college. Alexander Contee Hanson,* who also attended the school, became the founder and editor of the Baltimore *Federal Republican*,* whose editorials caused the Baltimore Riots* at the beginning of the War of 1812. Still another graduate was John Mercer,* a cornet in the U.S. Light Dragoons, who participated in the defense of Baltimore in 1814.

A plaque on a cannon located just to the northeast of McDowell Hall proclaims it is "of the type used in the defense of Baltimore in the War of 1812." It is probably one of thirteen cannons dredged out of Baltimore Harbor, possibly after the Baltimore fire of 1904, when many docks were rebuilt. Such guns were used as bollards (a post upon which to fasten mooring lines).

Taney, Roger Brooke, Statue (front of the Maryland statehouse). This statue is dedicated to Chief Justice of the Supreme Court Roger Taney,* who practiced law in Annapolis from 1796 to 1799. Taney married Ann Phoebe Charlton Key, sister of Francis Scott Key. In 1856, Taney wrote an account of the writing of "The Star-Spangled Banner" that first appeared in printed form as the foreword to a volume of Key's poems. Since Key himself did not elaborate on the writing of the poem, Taney's account is a valuable contribution. The statue of Taney, sculpted by William Henry Rinehart (who also did the bronze doors to the National Capitol) and dedicated December 10, 1872, was a gift of William Walters. It depicts Taney seated with his left hand resting on a book titled "THE CONSTITUTION." A duplicate of this statue stands at Mount Vernon, Baltimore.

U.S. Naval Academy (Severn River). NHL. The Naval Academy has numerous exhibits, monuments, and war relics related to the War of 1812.

BANCROFT HALL (opposite and east of Mahan Hall). Memorial Hall, within Bancroft Hall, serves as a shrine to the academy's most honored alumni. Here hangs a replica of the battle flag of Lake Erie that bears the words "Dont Give Up the Ship" (while proper punctuation would include an apostrophe in *don't*, no apostrophe is present on the flag). These words were supposedly uttered by the mortally wounded Capt. James Lawrence on June 1, 1813, when his ship, the U.S. frigate *Chesapeake*, fought the H.M. frigate *Shannon*. A banner with Lawrence's words was made at the order of Capt. Oliver Hazard Perry* and used by him on September 10, 1813, aboard the U.S. brig *Niagara* as a battle flag during his victorious action at Lake Erie. The original flag, exhibited at the U.S. Naval Academy since 1849, was withdrawn for conservation in 2002 and is scheduled to be re-hung in the U.S. Naval Academy Museum* upon completion.

On the right side of the replica flag is the 1959 painting *Battle of Lake Erie September 1813* by Charles Robert Patterson and Richard B. French. On the left is a portrait of Capt. James Lawrence by J. Herring after Gilbert Stuart.* In the same hall hangs a portrait of Capt. Oliver Hazard Perry by J. W. Jarvis.

CHAPEL (Blake Road east of Preble Hall near Gate 3). The chapel baptismal font is made of wood from the War of 1812-era U.S. frigate *Constitution*. Also in the chapel is David Glasgow Farragut's* prayer book and bible. At age nine and a half, Farragut became a midshipman and rose in rank to admiral, the first in the U.S. Navy. A beautiful stained glass window in the chapel dedicated to Farragut depicts his Civil War heroics. In the basement of the chapel in a small display case is the prayer book used by Francis Scott Key,* author of the words to "The Star-Spangled Banner."

H.M. FRIGATE *CONFIANCE* 24 POUNDER CANNON (north side of Bancroft Hall). This cannon, a war prize from the captured 36-gun H.M. frigate *Confiance,* was taken at the Battle of Lake Champlain on September 11, 1814. *Confiance* was struck no less than 105 times and 40 British sailors were killed and another 38 wounded. The cannon has a prominent dent on the muzzle from being struck by an American projectile during the battle.

H.M. FRIGATE *CYANE* 32 POUNDER CARRONADES (one carronade on the east side of Bancroft Hall and two others on the east side of the Armel-Leftwich Visitor Center). These war prize carronades from the H.M. frigate *Cyane,* Capt. Gordon Thomas commanding, were captured on February 20, 1815, by the U.S. frigate *Constitution* under the command of Capt. Charles Stewart.

Facsimile of Perry's blue battle flag with white letters "Dont Give Up The Ship." It is among the best-known American naval battle flags. At one time all midshipmen who entered the Naval Academy stood beneath this flag to take their oath. (Lossing, *Pictorial Field-Book of the War of 1812*)

FORTS SEVERN, NONSENSE, AND MADISON SITES. Fort Severn on the south side of Severn River, along with forts Madison and Nonsense on the north side of Severn River and a gun battery at Horn Point* on the south side of Spa Creek, defended Annapolis during the War of 1812. Fort Bieman, built during the Revolutionary War and located nearly opposite Fort Severn and west of Fort Nonsense on the north side of Severn River, may also have been used in the War of 1812.

Lt. Col. H. A. Fay, commander of forts Madison and Severn, complained that on several occasions he could row across the river at night, scale the walls of Fort Madison, and surprise the men on duty. Two British officers walked around the fort to ascertain troop and armament strength without detection.

> I may with safety give it as my opinion that Annapolis will face a very easy conquest (Two of my Officers walked round Fort Madison in the Night without being discovered.). (Capt. Sir Peter Parker to Vice Adm. Sir Alexander F. I. Cochrane, August 30, 1814)[6]

Judge Jeremiah T. Chase, chairman of the Annapolis Committee of Safety, pleaded with Lieutenant Colonel Fay not to fire on the British, fearing that provoking them would lead to an attack on Annapolis. Chase had written to Brig. Gen. William H. Winder on September 13, 1814, that "we are not capable of making any Resistance to the Enemy should he attack this place . . . the force at both Forts does not exceed Forty Regulars and many of those are unfit for Duty."[7]

> Lieutenant [Thomas?] Clark[e] has received orders from government to place this harbor in a complete state of defense. From this we infer, that it is the intention of government to man the forts with such as additional number of troops as the exposed situation of the city requires for its defense. (Annapolis *Maryland Republican,* March 25, 1812)

> About 1200 men, under Col's [Henry] Carberry and [?] Pickens, arrived in this city [Annapolis] from Fort Washington. We understand it is in contemplation immediately to entrench the peninsula in the rear of the city, and to post several pieces of cannon in the works to be well served with grape and cannister shot; if this is done, we may bid defiance to an invading force of 10,000 men in that quarter. A strong guard of several hundred men are ordered at Fort-Madison, and the commanding heights on the side of Severn, and Horn Point are to be defended to the last. (Boston *Columbia Centinel,* August 14, 1813)

FORT MADISON SITE (Severn River, under parking lot at the David Taylor Naval Ship Research and Development Center). Military establishment, restricted access. Fort Madison was built of masonry in 1808. It had a semi-elliptical face and circular flanks and was fitted for thirteen guns. A brick magazine and barrack for one company was also built. When Annapolis was blockaded by the British in April 1813, the guns of Fort Madison were supposedly fired hourly to reassure the citizens.

> information was given that the enemy were landing on Sandy Point, and surprised and taken part of the picket guard, and it was supposed intended an attack on Fort Madison. The alarm proved false, but it gave us peculiar pleasure to notice the promptitude displayed by the troops in the harbor. Although the alarm was in the middle of the night, many of the companies were formed, and on their post in from three to five minutes after the first gun was fired. (Annapolis Maryland *Republican,* August 21, 1813)

> Fort Madison, besides its exposed and defenceless situation, except from an approach direct by water, is so very unhealthy during the months of August and September, that it is not possible to keep a garrison in it . . . [its] guns will be exposed to certain capture if they are left there and will be turned against the town and Fort Severn, with decisive effect, unless we can find the means of making a substantial defence of the place. (Brig. Gen. William H. Winder to Secretary of War John Armstrong, July 16, 1814)[8]

> I have delayed dismantling Fort Madison, only because it will excite greater sensation and clamor, and by that means proclaim to the enemy that it . . . could not be, defended, and thus invite him to take possession of it. It would be impossible to dismantle it without making it public; and I have deemed it more expedient to risk the loss of the guns there, than by removing them, invite the enemy to take the place, which he may possibly abstain from while he supposed the place will be defended. (Brig. Gen. William H. Winder to Secretary of War John Armstrong, July 20, 1814)[9]

FORT NONSENSE (north side of Severn River, inside gate entrance to the Carderock Division of the Naval Surface Warfare Center, east of Church Street). Military establishment, restricted access. NRHP. A temporary earthwork, built circa 1810, probably protected Fort Madison* from a land assault. It could also have served as a lookout, as it was on the highest point in the Annapolis area. The earthworks were generally circular in shape with a diameter of roughly two hundred feet. They consisted of two arcs of earthen embankments and ditches and two gaps, which apparently provided ac-

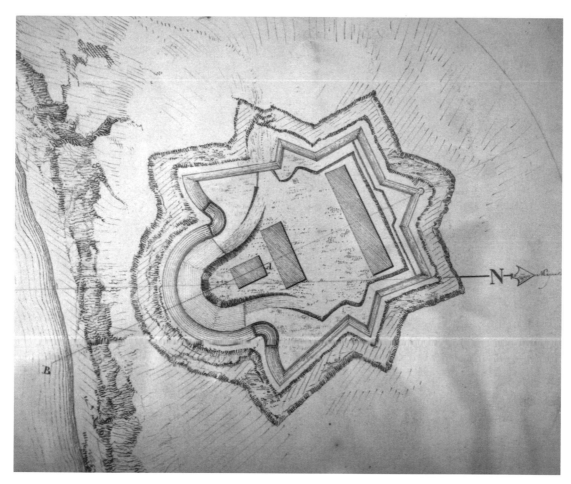

Fort Madison no longer exists but this 1819 plan illustrates the complexity of the fortification. (National Archives and Records Administration, Cartographic Section)

cess. The northern embankment has three embrasures, presumably for cannon facing away from the river. This suggests that the northern earthworks were built to protect the rear of Fort Madison. Archeological investigation suggests the southern earthworks were built earlier, possibly to defend the Severn River. Legend holds that the fort got its name because it was foolishly built out of artillery range of the harbor. Fort Nonsense is the only remnant of what was once a chain of forts to protect Annapolis.

FORT SEVERN SITE (south side of Severn River, originally Windmill Point, now within Academy grounds, near the northeast wall of Wing number 5, Bancroft Hall). The Fort Severn site is marked by two plaques and a stone monument set in the barrack wall to commemorate "Old Fort Severn,"

which protected the harbor of Annapolis during the War of 1812. Fort Severn consisted of a circular fourteen-foot-high stone wall on which were mounted twelve guns.

H.M. FRIGATE *MACEDONIAN* FIGUREHEAD MONUMENT (northeast of Preble Hall and northwest of Bancroft Hall on west end of green). This monument is a tribute to Capt. Stephen Decatur* and the crew of U.S. frigate *United States,* who on October 25, 1812, captured H.M. frigate *Macedonian.* The *Macedonian* was the only British frigate brought to America as a prize of war. The sculpture is a replica of the original figurehead depicting Alexander the Great and taken from *Macedonian.* Four 18 pounder cannon taken from *Macedonia* complete the monument designed by Baltimore native Edward Berge. A plaque on the monument describes the

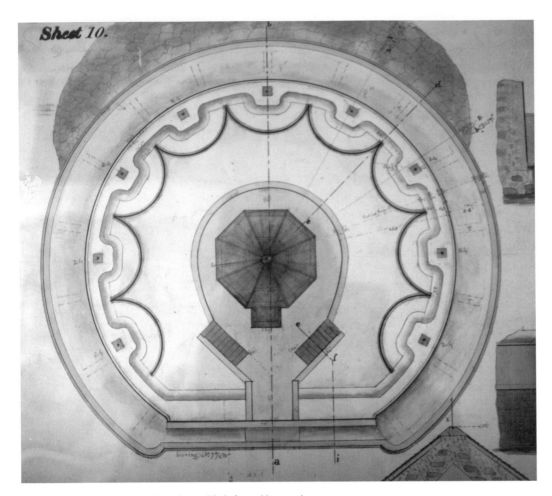

Fort Severn was built in 1808 and had changed little from this 1845 plan, the year it was demolished. (National Archives and Records Administration, Cartographic Section)

action. The U.S. Navy Trophy Flag Collection includes the flag from *Macedonian,* which was reportedly laid at the feet of Dolley Madison when it was presented to the American government during a presidential ball. This monument was located at the Gosport (Norfolk) Navy Yard* until 1875.

MACDONOUGH HALL (north of Bancroft Hall, east of Holloway Road). This hall is named for Capt. Thomas Macdonough (1783–1825), who commanded the American flotilla that won a major naval victory on September 11, 1814, in Plattsburg Bay, Lake Champlain, New York. The U.S. Navy Trophy Flag Collection includes the flag from Macdonough's flagship U.S. sloop-of-war *Saratoga.* In Government House, where the Maryland governor resides (State Circle, not open to the public except on special occasions), is a mirror with a

glass painting commemorating Macdonough's Lake Champlain victory.

MAHAN HALL (north end of Stribling Walk, opposite Bancroft Hall). Here are displayed some of the flags from the U.S. Navy Trophy Flag Collection. Of the thirty-four flags in the collection from the War of 1812, the following are on display in the main hall and main stairwell:

Jack from H.M. cutter *Landrail,* captured July 12, 1814, by American privateer schooner *Syren* of Baltimore in the English Channel.
Jack and pendant from H.M. frigate *Guerriere,* captured August 19, 1812, by the U.S. frigate *Constitution* about 750 miles east of Boston. It was during this

Congress awarded Com. Thomas Macdonough this medal for his naval victory at Lake Champaign. (Lossing, *Pictorial Field-Book of the War of 1812*)

Ensign from H.M. sloop-of-war *Levant*, captured February 20, 1815, by the U.S. frigate *Constitution* off Madeira.

Ensign from 34-gun H.M. frigate *Cyane*, captured February 20, 1815, by the U.S. frigate *Constitution*. (*Levant* and *Cyane* were captured on the same day by *Constitution*.)

Ensign from H.M. sloop *Peacock*, captured February 24, 1813, by the U.S. sloop-of-war *Hornet* off British Guiana.

Ensign from H.M. frigate *Macedonian*, captured October 25, 1812, by the U.S. frigate *United States* off Canary Islands.

Ensign from H.M. frigate *Confiance*, captured September 11, 1814, by the American squadron under command of Thomas Macdonough at Battle of Lake Champlain.

engagement that *Constitution* earned the nickname "Ironsides," which soon became "Old Ironsides."

Ensign from H.M. sloop-of-war *Penguin*, captured March 23, 1815, by U.S. sloop-of-war *Hornet* off Tristan da Cunha. (*See also* Price Shipyard Site.)

Ensign from H.M. sloop-of-war *Detroit*, captured September 10, 1813, by the U.S. squadron under command of Oliver Hazard Perry in the Battle of Lake Erie.

Ensign from H.M. brig *Reindeer*, captured June 28, 1814, by the U.S. sloop-of-war *Wasp* near Land's End, England.

Ensign from H.M. brig *Frolic*, captured October 19, 1812, by the U.S. sloop-of-war *Wasp* about five hundred miles east of Chesapeake Bay.

Congress awarded Capt. Charles Stewart, commander of U.S. frigate *Constitution,* a medal for his victories over H.M. frigate *Cyane* and H.M. sloop-of-war *Levant*. (Lossing, *Pictorial Field-Book of the War of 1812*)

After the victory of U.S. sloop-of-War *Hornet* over H.M. brig *Peacock,* Amos Doolittle engraved this cartoon depicting an immense hornet crying out "Free trade and sailors' rights, you old rascal" as it alights on the head of John Bull with the wings and tail of a peacock, which moans out "Boo-o-o-o-hoo!!!" after being stung in the neck. (Lossing, *Pictorial Field-Book of the War of 1812*)

I have the honor to convey to you (Secretary of Navy) the flags of his Britannic majesty's late squadron, captured on the 11th inst. By the United States' squadron, under my command. (Com. Thomas Macdonough to Secretary of Navy, Williams Jones, September 13, 1814; reprinted in Baltimore, *Niles' Weekly Register,* October 1, 1814)

NICHOLSON, COL. JOSEPH HOPPER, HOUSE SITE (near band stand on Chauvenet Walk). Col. Joseph Hopper Nicholson (1806–72), son of Judge Joseph Hopper Nicholson (1770–1817), Key's brother-in-law, occupied a home that stood on the south side of Scott Street near where the Chapel now stands, once parallel to Maryland Avenue. The original manuscript of Key's poem that eventually became "The Star-Spangled Banner" was kept here in a desk in Nicholson's house for many years. The plaque that marks this spot incorrectly claims the house belonged to Judge Joseph Hopper Nicholson. The house was owned by his son, who served as secretary of state of Maryland in 1838–39.

Peter Magruder, secretary of the Naval Academy, claimed that when Francis Scott Key had scribbled down the first draft of his poem that later became the national anthem, he showed it to his brother-in-law, who suggested alterations. Having made the alterations on a new copy, Key tossed the original in a wastebasket. Nicholson supposedly retrieved the copy and placed it in a pigeonhole in a desk at his home. When expansion of the Naval Academy required the destruction of the house, the furniture was removed. In 1890, a daughter discovered the draft poem in the desk. The manuscript was passed on to Rebecca Lloyd Shippens, Nicholson's granddaughter. This copy of Key's poem is now exhibited at the Maryland Historical Society.*

★ TECUMSEH STATUE, Tamanend Statue (Tecumseh Court, near southeast edge of green in front of Bancroft Hall). Tecumseh (Tecumtha), was a Shawnee chief who with his brother the Prophet in 1808 established a village called Prophet's Town near Lafayette, Indiana. Using this village as their base, the brothers headed a movement that encouraged their people to return to traditional Indian ways. Tecumseh formed a defensive confederacy of many American Indian tribes to hold their lands against the white man.

While he was away, Indiana Territory Governor William Henry Harrison led an expedition on November 7, 1811, against the village, destroying it after the fierce Battle of Tippecanoe. Tecumseh joined the British at the beginning of the War of 1812 and was killed on October 5, 1813, at the Battle of the Thames in Upper Canada. The Tecumseh Statue is the only known monument in the Chesapeake region that commemorates the role of American Indians in the War of 1812. Ironically, the "Tecumseh" monument is a bronze copy made in 1930 of the original circa 1817 wooden figurehead "Tamanend" from the 74-gun U.S. ship-of-the-line *Delaware,* built in 1820 at Gosport Shipyard,* Portsmouth, Virginia. The bronze replica was presented by the academy class of 1891. Tamanend was chief of the Delaware tribe; how it came to be known as the Tecumseh Statue is unclear. As a tribute to Tecumseh and in hope of good luck, it is painted with washable paint before every home football game as well as during the week that Navy plays Army and whenever there is a commissioning ceremony for midshipmen. Pennies are also traditionally placed on the monument for good luck before exams.

★ **TRIPOLI MONUMENT,** initially known as the Naval Monument (northwest side of Preble Hall). The Tripoli Monument, originally erected at the Washington Navy Yard,* is the oldest military monument in the United States and the first to be approved by U.S. Officers of the American Naval Mediterranean Fleet, who donated $3,000 for the design and construction of the monument to eulogize five American naval officers and one midshipman who in 1804 fell during the Tripolitan Wars. Largely through the efforts of Com. David Porter, Sr., it was erected in 1808 as Washington's first outdoor monument. The monument was reportedly mutilated by the British on August 25, 1814, although some accounts claim local citizens vandalized the monument in protest of the army's failure to protect the city. The monument, which was sculpted in 1806 by Giovanni C. Micali of Carrera Italian marble taken from the same quarry used by Michelangelo, was brought to the United States as ballast by the U.S. frigate *Constitution.* The monument consists of a rostral column crowned by a flying eagle. The column shaft is decorated with the bows of corsair vessels and the faces of Barbary pirates. On one side of the base on which the shaft rests is a sculptured basso-rilievo of Tripoli and its fortresses in the distance and the American fleet in the foreground. Benjamin Henry Latrobe added inscriptions to the other three faces, including the names of the officers who fell in the battle. Against Latrobe's wishes he also added an anti-British inscription insisted upon by Porter. The inscription, no longer present, blamed the British for the damage to the monument. At three corners of the base are half-life size marble allegorical figures representing History, Fame, and Commerce. (Some sources include Glory, which is represented by lamps, not a figure.) Although the monument was restored after it was damaged in 1814, there is speculation that the figures are not in their original positions. Damage included the loss of a gilded bronze pen clasped by History, a gilded palm held by Fame, and the forefinger of one statue. The caduceus (staff of an ancient herald) once held by Commerce disappeared sometime after 1927. The monument, originally built to be fifteen feet high, was raised on a large block of stone when moved to the western portico of the U.S. Capitol* in 1831. It was moved a second time to the Naval Academy in 1860.

The Barbary War Tripoli Monument, originally located at the Washington Navy Yard, was reportedly vandalized by the British during the War of 1812. (Lossing, *Pictorial Field-Book of the War of 1812*)

★ U.S. NAVAL ACADEMY MUSEUM (Preble Hall at northwest corner of Maryland Avenue and Decatur Road). Among the collections are prints, paintings, and artifacts relating to naval engagements during the War of 1812, including the original "Dont Give Up the Ship" flag and the bullet that killed Com. Stephen Decatur* in a duel in 1820.

AQUASCO MILLS SITE, later called Woodville and now Aquasco (near intersection of Brandywine [Route 381] and Doctor Bowen–Saint Marys Church roads, northwest of Benedict, Prince George's County). On August 20, 1814, about 10:00 a.m., at Aquasco Mills as well as at Butler's Mill, four miles from Benedict, Secretary of State James Monroe and a detachment of twenty-five to thirty dragoons from the District of Columbia reconnoitered the invading British fleet and army.

> I had a view of their ships but being at a distance of three miles, and having no glass, we could not count them . . . they are still debarking their troops [at Benedict], of the number of which I have not obtained any satisfactory information. The general idea also is, that Washington is their objective. (Secretary of State James Monroe, Washington *Daily National Intelligencer,* August 22, 1814)

Monroe ordered dragoons to be placed every twelve miles between Aquasco Mills and Washington to expedite communication. Later, British pickets were stationed within a mile of here on a high point between the mill and the river.

Brig. Gen. Leonard Covington (1768–1813), born October 30, 1768, at Covington's Fields (Mount Covington) in Aquasco, commanded the 3rd Brigade in Maj. Gen. James Wilkinson's unsuccessful invasion of Canada in 1813. Covington received a mortal wound on November 11, at the Battle of Crysler's Farm while attempting to capture some British artillery. His last words are reputed to be "Independence for forever!" He died on November 14, 1813, at French Mills, now Fort Covington, in Franklin County, New York. Originally interred in a mass grave somewhere in Fort Covington, in 1820 he was re-interred in a second mass grave at Sackets Harbor, New York. A cenotaph for Covington is located at Fort Covington Cemetery. Fort Covington,* Baltimore, which played a crucial role in defeating a British flanking night attack on Fort McHenry, is named after him.

AQUILA RANDALL OBELISK MONUMENT. *See* listing, North Point

At least twenty-one cities, towns, and counties in Alabama, Kentucky, Mississippi, Oklahoma, Texas, and Virginia are named for Brig. Gen. Leonard Covington. (*Memoir of Leonard Covington* by B. L. C. Wailes 1861; courtesy of C. Segert Wailes)

ASHLAND SQUARE. *See* Wells and McComas Monument, Baltimore

BAINBRIDGE (Susquehanna River, just south of Port Deposit and north of Perryville, Cecil County). The U.S. Naval Training Center established by President Franklin Delano Roosevelt in 1942 is named for Com. William Bainbridge, commander of the U.S. frigate *Constitution* and War of 1812 hero. Roosevelt credited Bainbridge with founding the first naval training school and expressed the wish that the standards established by him would be carried on by this center when it was activated on October 1, 1942. Deactivated on June 30, 1947, the Bainbridge Center had trained a total of 244,277 recruits by the conclusion of hostilities on V-J Day, August 14, 1945. Reactivated on February 1, 1951, because of the Korean conflict, the center consisted of four large camps, three of which are named after War of 1812 naval heroes with Chesapeake connections: John Rodgers,* Oliver Hazard Perry,* and Joshua Barney.*

William Bainbridge (1774–1833) succeeded Isaac Hull as commander of the U.S. frigate *Constitution.* On December 29, 1812, he encountered H.M. frigate *Java* off the coast of Brazil, where he received two wounds. The ship's wheel of the *Constitution* and much of the rigging of *Java* was shot away. *Java* ran alongside *Constitution* in an attempt to board it, but in close quarters it lost its foremast, main topsail, and then its mizzen-mast. *Java* surrendered. Bainbridge served as Com. Stephen Decatur's* second when Decatur was mortally wounded by Com. James Barron* in a 1820 duel. Bainbridge is buried at Christ Church Burial Ground,* Philadelphia.

BALLARDS LANDING. *See* Lower Marlboro

Congress awarded Com. William Bainbridge this medal for his capture of H.M. frigate *Java* while in command of U.S. frigate *Constitution.* (Lossing, *Pictorial Field-Book of the War of 1812*)

BALTIMORE CITY (Patapsco River). Baltimore was a leading seaport and builder and home of many Baltimore clippers (schooners). Known for their speed, these clippers, most constructed at Fells Point,* were often used as privateers. Baltimore was also the site of deadly pro-war riots in 1812 (*see* Baltimore Riot Sites). After the American defeat at the Battle of Bladensburg* and the British occupation of Washington,* the British set their sights on Baltimore. From this engagement came one of America's foremost icons—a poem that eventually became "The Star-Spangled Banner," inspired by the Fort McHenry garrison flag.

The British blockade of the Chesapeake disrupted ordinary maritime trade. The following account of the Baltimore–Queenstown packet exemplifies the problem:

we left Baltimore . . . down the Patapsco . . . near North Point, when we discovered plainly 3 large ships and several smaller vessels . . . above the mouth of Chester River . . . the Skipper . . . shifted his course and stood up the river . . . discerning nothing that could molest us . . . put again down the river, On our way this second time down, the [U.S. Navy] gunboat stationed some miles above North Point, got under way and stood up the river; had not proceeded far down the river than we discovered two row boats under North Point, about 15 miles distant . . . immediately put back again the second time up the river; after going on sometime we found the row-boats coming after us . . . they gained on us so fast that we were all convinced they were the enemy's barges . . . waved a signal to the gunboat just a head—finding she took no notice of us . . . exerted every nerve to prevent getting captured—vain struggle! . . . they fired several shot from musketry at us—we now found indeed that we were gone, though an hour before we had not the least idea but that we could make the fort [Fort McHenry] with all ease . . . the enemy came along side, boarded from two small barges containing 20 men each, and captured us, within five miles of the Fort of Baltimore . . . The officers who boarded, asked if the vessel was a packet, and upon being answered she was, they said, we need be under no apprehension, for that our person and private property should be respected. (John Meredith and William Bromwell, Easton *People's Monitor*, April 24, 1813; reprinted in the Annapolis *Maryland Gazette and Political Intelligencer,* April 29, 1813)

The British took the packet and its cargo as a prize.

Despite British threats on the city, many Baltimoreans fought for their country on the Canadian front: "our Company has reduced to 65 effective men out of all those brave fellow we started with. That their dicipline far exceeded any regulars I ever saw, that the British call us the Baltimore Blood hound. If we should meet with any of them we shall

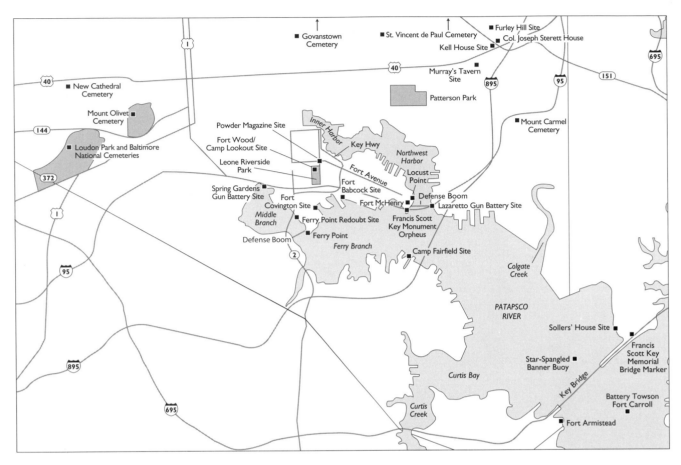

Baltimore City Region

Baltimore was the third largest city in America during the War of 1812. This illustration, the first contemporary panorama of the city, was produced 1810 looking south. Key: A. Fort McHenry. B. Federal Hill with its flagstaff and observatory. (Aquatint by J. L. Boqueta de Woiseri; courtesy Maryland Historical Society)

give a good account of them" (Thomas Warner, April 19, 1813).[10]

about to embark with my company, together with [Brig.] general [Zebulon] Pike's brigade, for the purpose of making a descent on the Canada shore . . . the result, which has been victorious and glorious to the American arms, although peculiarly unfortunate to me. We . . . debarked the forces about a mile above York [present-day Toronto], the capital of Upper Canada. Here we were met on the beach by about five hundred British regulars and two hundred and fifty Indians. We contended with them warmly for about an hour, when we succeeded in driving them before us, and made good our landing, with a loss of some brave officers, and about forty men killed and wounded. We then formed immediately, moved up to York, and when arrived just at the opening of the main street, the enemy sprung a mine upon us, which destroyed about eighty of his own men, and killed and wounded about one hundred and thirty of our men. This horrible explosion has deprived me of my leg, and oth-

erwise grievously wounded me. I was taken from the field, and carried on board the commodore's ship where my leg was amputated, and I am now likely to recover. Two of my company were killed at the same time, and four or five more of my brave fellows were severely wounded, now out of danger. We have taken the capital of the enemy, and about a million and a half worth of public stores and other property. We have killed and wounded about three hundred British and their savage allies, and taken prisoners about seven hundred men. We have taken from them also several vessels of war which were found in the harbor, and destroyed a 32 gun frigate, then on the stocks. (Capt. Stephen H. Moore, 1st Baltimore Volunteers, to his brother, Niagara, New York, May 5, 1813; reprinted in Easton *Republican Star,* May 25, 1813)

On April 16 and August 8, 1813, a Royal Navy squadron moved up the Patapsco River within sight of Baltimore, alarming the city and causing the forts to be manned, but no attack followed. These threats induced Fort McHenry

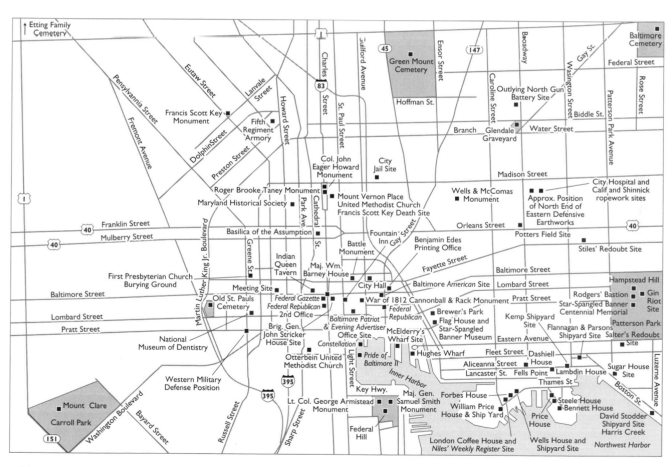

Baltimore City

commander Maj. George Armistead to commission two flags, a storm flag 17 by 25 feet and a garrison flag 30 by 42 feet. The latter was the subject of Francis Scott Key's famous poem a year later.

Local newspapers carried recruitment notices such as the following: "To Reputable Young Men Will be given a bounty of FORTY DOLLARS, and One Hundred and Sixty Acres of Land, for enlisting in the 3d Regiment of Artillery, by applying to Geo. Armistead, Maj., 3d Artillery" (Baltimore *Federal Gazette,* July 13, 1813).

Volunteers and militiamen poured into Baltimore to assist in its defense, among them, twenty-three-year-old James Buchanan, a militiaman from Pennsylvania who forty-two years later became the fifteenth president of the United States. False rumors of Baltimore's fall circulated in London. The London *Morning Chronicle* reported that Baltimore had not only surrendered but had "seceded from the Union and proclaimed itself neutral," and the London *Morning Post* reported that Maj. Gen. Robert Ross had scored "another brilliant victory."

Rations for the American troops were sparse and often spoiled. One veteran wrote about a mock funeral held for a rotted meat ration: "Two men went and dug a hole and for of them put straw bands round their hats as poll bearers and took the meet on two poles while the company marched after the drum beating a Dead March before and after they burned the meet they gave three cheers and Returned to their quarters" (1st Lt. Jacob Crumbacker [Crumbaker] to Solomon Crumbacker, October 19, 1835).[11]

Despite the threat of attack in 1814, Baltimoreans still found time for entertainment. The circus came to town with brilliant displays of horsemanship, including "The Mamaluke Manoeuvre." At Joseph Clarke's Market Space one could view the Mammoth Horse, said to be twenty hands high (that is, about six feet and six inches tall from hoof to shoulder), the largest horse ever produced in Europe or America. This horse and other animals could be seen for 25 cents. The Baltimore Museum (236 Market Street) had stuffed animals, including a twenty-foot-long snake, a shark, an alligator, two sea monsters, sucking and flying fish, and a lamb with two heads and five legs. The Peale's Museum and Gallery of Art (Holiday Street) offered "extra illuminations" (candles or torches) for Christmas and New Year's Eve. Dramas such as *The Robbers* and *The Exile* played at the theater.

The Royal Navy entered the Patapsco River on September 11, 1814. From here the British began their unsuccessful land and sea attack on the city.

Baltimorean account of possible British attack: our alarm guns were fired twenty minutes past twelve, since then the bells rang, drums beating, the houses generally lighted; we have all been up since that second. We know not the hour when we may be attacked. (Deborah Cochrane to Ruth Tobin of Elkton, September 15, 1814)[12]

The houses in the city were shaken to their foundations; for never, perhaps from the time of the invention of cannon to the present day, were the same number of pieces fired with so rapid a succession. (Baltimore *Niles' Weekly Register,* October 1, 1814)

ATTACK ON BALTIMORE. The British official (which is a truly British) account of the attack on Baltimore, is contained in London papers brought by the [Capt. Isaac] Chauncey. As usual, they magnify the force opposed to them for the purpose of lessening their defeat. Their own loss is stated to be 39 killed and 251 wounded; —that of the defenders of Baltimore (gravely asserted to consist of all the military force of the surrounding states, the advance consisting of 6 or 7000 men and the main body of 15 or 20,000! At from 5 to 600 killed and wounded, and 200 prisoners, making 1000 disabled from battle! But this, and the official accounts of the capture of Washington and the plundering of Alexandria, we shall publish as our limits admit. There were 40 Americans killed, 200 wounded, and 49 taken prisoners, by the British army, and 27 killed and wounded in the forts by the fleet. The British loss by land and water, was estimated at 6 to 700 killed, wounded and missing. The American force actually engaged (with the enemy) was 8185 men; the British advance consisted of between 5 and 4,000, and his whole force of 8 to 10,000. (Boston *Independent Chronicle,* November 5, 1814). (This paper overestimates the British strength, which is exactly what it accuses the British of doing for American troop strength.)

Rejoice, ye people of America! Inhabitants of Philadelphia, New York and Boston rejoice! Baltimore has nobly fought your battles! Thank God, and thank the people of Baltimore! ("A Republican paper of Boston," quoted in Baltimore *Niles' Weekly Register,* October 1, 1814)

I give you joy, my dear friend; after a tremendous conflict we have got rid of the enemy for the present. Baltimore has maintained its honor. It has not only saved itself, but it must tend to save the country by showing Philadelphia, New York and other cities how to contend against the enemy with spirit, bravery and unanimity, all of which have been shown in the memorable days and nights of the 12th, 13th and 14th of September 1814. (Pvt. George Douglas, Baltimore Fencibles, to a friend in Boston, September 30, 1814)[13]

The bombardment of Fort McHenry on September 13–14, 1814, led to the writing of the poem by Francis Scott Key that became "The Star-Spangled Banner."

When word of peace with England reached the City of Baltimore, Mayor Edward Johnson issued a proclamation on February 15, 1815, announcing the restoration of peace. A general illumination of window candles and torches followed.

A mass gathering of the citizens of Baltimore was held on April 10, 1815. The Baltimore Republican Committee sent a congratulatory address to President James Madison, who replied on April 22: "In the varied scenes which have put to the test the constancy of the nation Baltimore ranks among the portion most distinguished for devotion to the public cause. It has the satisfaction to reflect that it boldly and promptly espoused the resort to arms when no other honorable choice remained; that it found in the courage of its citizens a rampart against the assaults of an enterprising force; that it never wavered nor temporized with the vicissitudes of the contest; and that it had an ample share in the exertions which have brought it to an honorable conclusion."[14]

Contemporary cartoon "John Bull and the Baltimoreans" satirizes the British retreat from Baltimore. Gen. Robert Ross's death is depicted in the distant center with a militiaman in the woods to the left stating, "Now for this Chap on Horseback. There's a *Rifle Pill* for you—Thank a *quietus*." (1814 etching by William Charles; Library of Congress)

★ Armistead, Lt. Col. George, Monument (Federal Hill, bounded by Key Highway, Covington Street, and Warren and Battery avenues, overlooking Inner Harbor). Lieutenant Colonel Armistead,* commander of Fort McHenry, had four brothers who also served in the War of 1812; two were killed. Capt. Lewis Gustavus Adolphos Armistead, 1st U.S. Rifles, was killed on September 17, 1814, during a sortie from Fort Erie, in Upper Canada; Capt. Addison Bowles Armistead, born 1768, died on February 10, 1813, in Savannah, Georgia, while in the service.

The City of Baltimore erected the Armistead Monument, designed and sculpted by G. Metgerat, at City Spring on Saratoga Street in 1827. After years of neglect, the monument was dismantled in 1861 and placed in storage. In 1882, the marble cannons and flaming bomb were incorporated into a second monument located at Eutaw Place and dedicated on September 9, 1882. This monument was moved in 1886 to Federal Hill, where it was vandalized circa 1966; eight years later the monument was restored again.

In 1816, the citizens of Baltimore presented to Lieutenant Colonel Armistead a silver punch bowl in the shape of a thirteen-inch British mortar bomb supported by four silver American eagles as well as ten silver cups and an oval serving tray and ladle. Philadelphia silversmiths Thomas

The George Armistead monument consisted of a marble tablet flanked by two marble cannons surmounted by a flaming bomb. (Lossing, *Pictorial Field-Book of the War of 1812*)

The George Armistead monument can be seen through the arched passageway to the left of the gazebo in its original setting at City Spring. (Lossing, *Pictorial Field-Book of the War of 1812*)

Fletcher and Sidney Gardiner made the bowl and Capt. Andre E. Warner, 39th Regiment, Baltimore, made the ladle and cups. An engraving of Fort McHenry is on one side of the bowl, and on the opposite side is an inscription that reads as follows: "Presented by a number of citizens of Baltimore to Lt. Col. George Armistead for his gallant and successful defense of Fort McHenry during the bombardment by a large British force on the 12th and 13th of September when upwards of 1500 shells were thrown; 400 of which fell within the area of the Fort and some of them of the diameter of this vase." The Armistead bowl resides in the National Museum of American History,* Smithsonian Institution, Washington, D.C. A replica of this bowl is on exhibit at Fort McHenry.*

Baltimore *American and Commercial Daily Advertiser* Office Site, usually shortened to Baltimore *American* (approximately between 37 and 39 [then 31] Gay Street near Customs House at corner of Lombard and Gay streets). Fourteen-year-old Samuel Sands, a printer's assistant and later editor of the Baltimore *American Farmer,* printed as a handbill on September 17, 1814, the first copies of Francis Scott Key's poem "Defence of Fort M'Henry" (later renamed "The Star-Spangled Banner") at the Baltimore *American* newspaper office. The Baltimore *American* published the same poem in its newspaper on the morning of September 21, one day after the Baltimore *Patriot & Evening Advertiser* had published it. The newspaper ceased publication on September 13 and 14, as its employees were engaged in the defense of Baltimore.

Baltimore *Federal Republican* Sites (first office at corner of Gay and Water [then Second] streets; second office at 101 [then 45] South Charles Street). The *Federal Republican* newspaper, founded in 1808, editorialized against the war, declaring that "without funds, without taxes, without an army, navy, or adequate fortifications [this is] a war against the clear and decided sentiments of the nation."[15] These antiwar sentiments caused an angry mob on June 22, 1812, to raze the building. When publisher Alexander Contee Hanson remained defiant a month later, determined to distribute his newspaper in Baltimore from a fortified house at 101 (then 45 South) Charles Street, a mob rioted on July 27, 1812, outside the house. Taken to the local jail for their "protection," the Federalists were attacked by a mob that broke into the jail. One Federalist was killed and others were seriously injured (*see also* Baltimore Riot Sites; William Gaither II, a Federalist who was left for dead, lived at Pleasant Fields*).

It is our painful duty to record, that on Monday last [June 22, 1812], between eight and nine o'clock in the evening, a number of persons, citizens of Baltimore, armed with axes, hooks and other instruments of destruction, assembled at the office of the Federal Republican in Gay-street; a wooden building belonging to Mr. Robert Oliver, of this city, broke into the house, threw the types, printing presses, paper, &c. into the street, and destroyed them and leveled the house to its foundation. One of the persons thus engaged, while in the act of knocking out a window, fell with it into the street, and was killed on the spot. (Baltimore *Federal Gazette;* reprinted in the Annapolis *Maryland Gazette and Political Intelligencer,* July 2, 1812)

The outrage committed by the Mob of Baltimore-town on Tuesday last [July 28, 1812], equals, if it does not transcend, any act of enormity committed during the French revolution. ("The Friend of Justice" to Annapolis *Maryland Gazette and Political Intelligencer,* August 6, 1812)

Alexander Contee Hanson (1786–1819) was born in Annapolis, married Priscilla Dorsey, who inherited Belmont, home of Caleb Dorsey, iron master of Elk Ridge Furnace. Hanson studied law at St. John's College,* founded and became editor of the Baltimore *Federal Republican,* and despite his later antiwar beliefs served in 1808 as a lieutenant in the 39th Regiment, Maryland militia. Hanson is reputed to be buried in the Hanson Family Cemetery located at Belmont (Elkridge) although there is no gravestone marking his grave. This man should not be confused with his kinsman Alexander Contee Hanson (1840–57).

Baltimore National Cemetery/Cloud Capped Site (5501 Frederick Avenue, within Loudon Park Cemetery*). On the grounds of the Baltimore National Cemetery once stood Cloud Capped, a 1750 house greatly altered and enlarged into an Italianate villa, but torn down in 1937 to make space for the graveyard. Constructed largely from the villa's salvaged materials, the two-story Federal Revival superintendent's lodge is similar to one wing of Cloud Capped. From the towers of the original house one could see as far as Annapolis. According to local tradition, upon sighting the British fleet ascending the Patapsco River, a messenger was sent to warn the city but earlier messages had already been received from observation points such as Ridgely House* and Todd House,* located farther down the river.

Baltimore *Patriot & Evening Advertiser* Office Site, usually shortened to Baltimore *Patriot* (112 [then 54] South Street, nearly at intersection with Lombard Street [then Water

Street]). The Baltimore *Patriot & Evening Advertiser* was the first newspaper to print Francis Scott Key's poem although it was earlier printed as a handbill. Many accounts claim the Baltimore *American* was the first to publish the poem on September 21, but the Baltimore *Patriot* had already printed it the day before. The Baltimore *Patriot* closed during the hostilities in Baltimore from September 10 to September 19. One of the editors, Pvt. Isaac Monroe of the Baltimore Fencibles, 1st Regiment, Maryland Artillery, served at Fort McHenry during the bombardment. On September 17, 1814, Monroe wrote to a friend in Boston, "our morning gun was fired, the flag hoisted, Yankee Doodle played, and we all appeared in full view of a formidable and mortified enemy" (Boston *Yankee,* September 30, 1814).

Baltimore Riot Sites. When Alexander Contee Hanson, editor of the Baltimore *Federal Republican,* a Federalist newspaper in Baltimore, editorialized against the war, an angry mob of several hundred Republicans destroyed the wood-frame Gay Street building and its contents on the evening of June 22, 1812, only four days after war had been declared. Hanson remained defiant and reopened the paper a month later at a second Baltimore site on Charles Street, a three-story building surrounded by a brick wall, which the Republicans called "Fort Hanson." That evening, July 27, a mob of Republicans surrounded the office, but this time it was defended by fifty armed Federalists, including Gen. Henry "Light Horse Harry" Lee,* father of Robert E. Lee. The besieged Federalists fired a warning burst that first scattered the mob, but when the crowd, estimated to number about a thousand, again formed and pushed through the house doorway, the occupants opened fire, killing one and wounding several more. The mob threatened to fire a cannon loaded with grapeshot into the building but was deterred from doing so by Maj. William Barney. Finally, city officials arrived. They persuaded some twenty-five Federalists to surrender to protective custody and took them to the safety of the jail. On the way paving stones were hurled at the Federalists, hitting one in the face and almost knocking another down.

During the night of July 28, the Republican mob stormed the jail and beat and stabbed nine of the Federalist sympathizers as city officials stood by. One Federalist, stripped, tarred, feathered, and dumped in a cart, was clubbed as rioters pulled him through the city. At one point his feathers were set on fire. Women in the crowd reportedly chanted, "Kill the Tories." General Lee, who had eulogized George Washington, lost one eye while being beaten into a limp

and bloody mess; he never fully recovered from his injuries. Brig. Gen. James McCubbin Lingan, age sixty, died several hours after being beaten and stabbed in the chest despite his pleas for mercy. He is buried at Arlington Cemetery,* Virginia. "A scene of horror and murder ensued," the Maryland House of Delegates reported, "which for its barbarity has no parallel in the history of the American people, and no equal but in the massacres of Paris." In all one Federalist was killed and eleven others severely beaten. Hanson resumed publication on August 3, 1812, and shipped the papers to the Baltimore post office so they could be distributed by mail. The next day a mob gathered at the post office and threatened to tear it down to get at copies of the latest issue of the Baltimore *Federal Republican* inside. Mounted militia dispersed the mob.

Sites involved in the riots include the original *Federal Republican* office site (northwest corner of Gay and Lombard [then Water] streets); second office site (101 [then 45] South Charles Street); *Federal Gazette* office site; Brig. Gen. John Stricker's house site (where Sticker, commander of the 3rd Baltimore City Brigade, ordered Maj. William B. Barney and his squadron of cavalry to the scene of the second riot) (across from the dance hall at 15 South Charles Street); Maj. William Barney's house site (intersection of Charles and Baltimore streets); and the route taken by the Federalists to the jail (up Charles Street, right on Market, across Jones Falls, then left on High Street to outlying road leading to the jail). The jail site, located north of the northeast intersection of Buren and Madison streets, is the current site of the Maryland State Penitentiary, immediately north of the Baltimore City Detention Center.

> THE MASSACRE AT BALTIMORE. The history of Barbarians scarcely affords a parallel in perfidy and cruelty to the late transactions at Baltimore. Admonished by the manner in which our office was first destroyed, that no support to our rights was to be expected from the civil or military authorities, whose duty it was afford it; we had no alternatives but to prepare to defend ourselves, on the establishment of the paper on Monday. (Editorial of Alexander Contee Hanson, editor of the Baltimore *Federal Republican;* reprinted in Hartford *Connecticut Courant,* August 18, 1812)
>
> ANOTHER DARING OUTRAGE! . . . Yesterday the Federal Republican resumed its former circulation, and last evening the lawless mob made an attempt on the house, in Charles street . . . by breaking the windows and forcing the doors. The House was fortied and manned with the

Editor Mr. [Alexander Contee] Hanson; and thirty resolute volunteers, commanded by General [Harry] Lee. (Hartford *Connecticut Courant,* August 4, 1812)

Basilica of the Assumption, formerly the Roman Catholic Cathedral (Cathedral Street between Franklin and Mulberry streets). NHL. The cornerstone of the cathedral was laid on July 7, 1806, but the church was not dedicated until May 31, 1821, its completion delayed by the War of 1812. In a letter to Maj. Gen. Samuel Smith written prior to the British attack, Capt. Samuel Babcock suggested the then unfinished cathedral would make a good defensive point. If the American forces retreated from their defenses at Hampstead Hill,* the walls of this building were considered a second line of defense.

Battery Park. *See* Fort Wood/Camp Lookout Site, Baltimore

★**Battle Monument** (North Calvert between Fayette and Lexington streets). NRHP. Three guns reportedly mounted here at the former courthouse green on September 12, 1814, fired warning shots announcing the British fleet had arrived off North Point. Most accounts, however, claim the cannon were mounted on Federal Hill,* which was a more likely location. A year later construction began on the fifty-two-foot-tall Battle Monument, the first substantial war memorial built in the United States. J. Maximilian Godefroy, a French émigré, designed the monument. The cornerstone was laid September 12, 1815, the first anniversary of the Battle of North Point. A procession formed on Great York Street (now East Baltimore Street) and proceeded to Monument Square. The procession included a funeral car surmounted with a plan of the intended monument. Rembrandt Peale, one of Baltimore's foremost artists, assisted in the rendering. Six white horses escorted by six men in military uniform led the car guarded by the Baltimore Independent Blues, 5th Regiment. The architect and his assistants under the direction of Maj. Gen. Samuel Smith, Brig. Gen. John Stricker, Lt. Col. George Armistead, and Mayor Edward Johnson laid the cornerstone of the cenotaph monument. Deposited under the cornerstone were books containing the names of the subscribers who paid for the monument, the newspapers from the preceding day, U.S. gold, silver, and copper coins, and a copper plate on which was engraved the date and names of those who participated in the ceremony.

Upon the completion of the laying of the cornerstone, a detachment of artillery fired a federal salute. This was followed by the firing of minute-guns (distress guns fired every minute to signal mourning or distress such as during military funerals) and the ringing of the bells in Christ Church; all business was suspended for the day. Sculptor Antonio Capellano of Florence, Italy, executed the statue of Lady Baltimore, which was mounted in December 1925 on top of the monument. Lady Baltimore guides with her left hand a ship's rudder, the sign of navigation, and raises a laurel wreath of victory aloft in her right hand. She faces the field of battle. At her feet repose the National Eagle and a bomb symbolizing the attack on Fort McHenry. Depicted in relief at the base of the column on the south and north sides are, respectively, the Battle of North Point, the death of Maj. Gen. Robert Ross, and the bombardment of Fort McHenry. On carved ribbons wrapped diagonally across the monument and spelled out in copper lettering are the names of the men who fell in battle. The monument base consists of eighteen layers representing the eighteen states in the Union in 1815. The three steps at the base of the monument represent the three years of the war. An eagle stands atop each of the four corners of the base. A column rises from the base depicting bundled rods representing strength in union.

For many years, this was the site of the main commemoration of Defenders Day. "Old Defenders"—the survivors of the defense of Baltimore—were honored by military escorts and martial music. Many gravestones for these men bear the inscription "Defender of Baltimore." William Welsh, probably a fifer or drummer in the Washington Independent Blues at North Point, considered the last of the "Old Defenders," died in 1852 and is buried at Green Mount Cemetery.* President John Quincy Adams visited the monument in 1827 and raised a toast "to Baltimore, the Monumental City." This monument is depicted on the punch bowl given by Baltimore County and Baltimore City as part of the U.S. battleship *Maryland* silver service, which now is displayed at the Maryland statehouse* in Annapolis. The monument is also depicted on a memorial stone in the Washington Monument,* Washington, D.C., given by the City of Baltimore. During a storm in 1938, Lady Baltimore's upraised arm and the laurel wreath were blown off. J. Maximilian M. Godefroy, the designer of Battle Monument, also redesigned the defensive entrenchments on Hampstead Hill* after the battle to better defend the city in the event of a second British attack.

Brewer's Park Site (East Pratt Street, immediately west of the Flag House Museum). Because of its size, the American garrison flag for Fort McHenry was spread out by seamstress

Battle Monument was erected to commemorate those citizens who fell while defending Baltimore. In 1827, the monument became the official seal of the city. (Lossing, *Pictorial Field-Book of the War of 1812*)

Mary Pickersgill in the malt house of Eli Clagett's brewery. Two malt houses were located here, one paralleling Granby Road and the other just north of it. Brewer's Park featured the original foundations of the brewery and a partial reconstruction of one of the buildings. Pvt. Eli Clagett* served in Capt. David Warfield's Company, Baltimore United Volunteers, and was wounded at the Battle of North Point.

Camp Fairfield Site (Cromwell Marsh, south shore of Patapsco River, near south end of Baltimore Harbor Tunnel). At this camp was stationed the 36th Maryland Regiment under Col. Francis Hancock* as well as the Pennsylvania militia. Due to the low, marshy conditions here these units were removed to Baltimore City in October 1814.

Canton. *See* Harris Creek, Baltimore

City Hall (Fayette and Holliday streets). Access to City Hall is limited to those on official business.

THE STAR-SPANGLED BANNER MEMORIAL CENTENNIAL EAGLE (second-floor gallery off the rotunda). The Star-Spangled Banner Memorial consists of a bronze statue of an American eagle on a furled U.S. flag with laurel garland. The National Society United States Daughters of 1812 presented this plaque to the city in 1914 on the occasion of the centennial of the writing of the "The Star-Spangled Banner." Originally located in an alcove on the east front of City Hall, the plaque was moved inside to the rotunda in 1999 to better protect it. In a hall off the second gallery near Conference Room 1 is a replica of the Fort McHenry garrison flag. At one time the Association of the Defenders of Baltimore of the War of 1812 had its headquarters here at City Hall. Only one veteran was physically strong enough to attend the last dinner held on September 12, 1887, for the surviving members of the Association.

STAR-SPANGLED BANNER HOLLIDAY STREET THEATER MARKER (in front of City Hall, west side of War Memorial Plaza between East Fayette and East Lexington streets). The Patriotic Organization of Maryland erected a bronze plaque on June 14, 1941, to mark the site of the Holliday Theater, where on October 19, 1814, "The Star-Spangled Banner" was first sung in public. The War Memorial Plaza, built in 1923 and redesigned in 2005, now occupies the site of the theater, which burned in 1873. Here in 1858 was staged the play *The Boy Martyrs of Sept. 12, 1814, A Local Historical Drama in Three Acts* by local playwright Clifton W. Tayleure, which honored two young men who some believe shot Maj. Gen. Robert Ross just before the Battle of North Point. The Wells and McComas Monument,* Baltimore, was built in tribute to them but does not mention their role in the death of Ross because it was so widely disputed.

> In consequence of the universal call for the French inhabitants of New-York and Philadelphia for the *Marseilles Hymn,* which attracted overflowing houses, in both cities, of French and American Liberals, the *Marseilles Hymn* will be sung by the whole Company. The Tri-Colored Flag of France, will be displayed. The same Flag that was actually displayed at the attack of Baltimore, on the 13th and 14th September, 1814, will be displayed on the opposite side, by an American Tar, (Mr. Parker,) who will enter and dance a Naval Hornpipe. The Flags will wave, united with the Sprits of Washington and Lafayette. (Baltimore *Sun,* September 13, 1830)

Cloud Capped. *See* Baltimore National Cemetery

Constellation (Pier 1, 301 East Pratt Street). The first *Constellation* was the U.S. frigate *Constellation,* launched on September 7, 1797, at the David Stodder Shipyard on Harris Creek* and in service during the War of 1812. It received its name for the "new constellation of stars" on the American flag. The second *Constellation* is the sloop-of-war berthed at Pier 1, completed in 1854, although it may retain some timber from the original 1797 vessel. Some privateers such as Joshua Barney and David Porter, Sr., sailed from the Darley Lux Wharf (now Pier 1) during the War of 1812.

Federal Hill (bounded by Key Highway, Covington Street, and Warren and Battery avenues, overlooking Inner Harbor). NHD. A "marine observatory" and flag signal station to notify the city of ship arrivals was established on Federal Hill in 1795 by Capt. David Porter, Sr.

During the War of 1812, a military observation post, signal station, and one-gun battery occupied the heights. When the British threatened Baltimore in April 1813, the battery fired its guns to warn the citizenry.

> The British squadron . . . now in sight of the town, and have been signaled from the Observatory [Federal Hill]. (Baltimore *Federal Gazette,* April 17, 1813)

The glow of the burning of Washington on August 24–25, 1814, could be seen from Federal Hill. On September 12, 1814, the battery fired in quick succession three shots to inform Baltimoreans that the British had landed on North Point. One source suggests the cannons were fired from the site of Battle Monument,* but this seems unlikely.

> Yesterday morning, the British fleet were plainly seen from Federal Hill, and towards the afternoon they seemed to be working into the mouth of the Petapsco river . . . On firing alarm guns as signals of their approach, all the corps of ev-

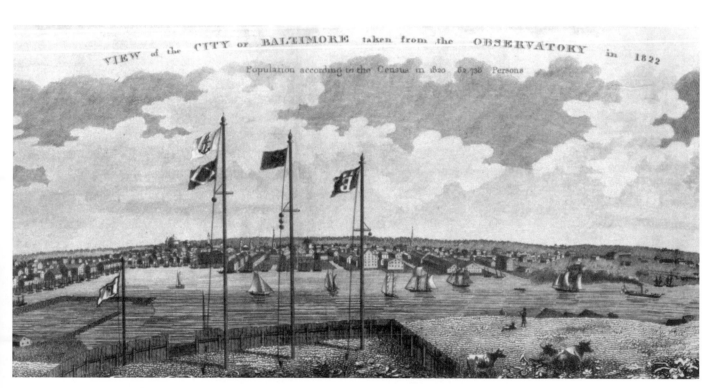

View of Baltimore looking north from Federal Hill. A bridge of scows built in 1814 (not shown in this 1822 view) between Fells Point (right opposite shore) and the shoreline at the east slope of Federal Hill (right near shore) provided a more direct line of communication and faster troop movement between Hampstead Hill, Ferry Point, and the Fort McHenry fortifications. (Detail from Thomas H. Poppleton, "Plan of the City of Baltimore 1822" [1852]; courtesy of Enoch Pratt Free Library, Central Library/State Library Resource Center, Baltimore)

ery description turned out with alacrity. (Baltimore *American,* September 12, 1814)

From here many citizens on September 13–14, 1814, watched the bombardment of Fort McHenry.

> The night of Tuesday [13th] and the morning of Wednesday (til about 4 o'clock) presented the whole awful spectacle of shot and shells, and rockets, shooting and bursting through the air. The well directed fire of the little fort [Wood] . . . checked the enemy on his approach, and probably saved the town from destruction in the dark hours of the night. The garrison was chiefly incommoded by the shells, which burst in and about the fort, whilst they had no bomb-proof shelter. As the darkness increased, the awful grandeur of the scene augmented. About one in the morning, the British passed several of their vessels above the Fort and near to town, but providently they were met by the fire of . . . marine battery. (Civilian account from Federal Hill, Salem *Gazette,* September 27, 1814)

> The attack on Fort McHenry, by nearly the whole British Fleet was distinctly seen from Federal Hill and from the tops of Houses which were covered with men, women and children. (Salem [Massachusetts] *Gazette,* September 27, 1814)

A monument to Lt. Col. George Armistead,* commanding officer at Fort McHenry during the Battle for Baltimore, was dedicated in 1886, and a monument to Maj. Gen. Samuel Smith,* officer in charge of the defense of Baltimore, was dedicated in 1918. A cannon dredged from the harbor and believed to date from the War of 1812 was placed on Federal Hill in 1959.

Sailing Master Leonard Hall, a member of the crew of the U.S. sloop-of-war *Ontario,* manned the gun battery, possibly single-handedly. The U.S. sloops-of-war *Ontario* and *Erie,* both built at Fells Point in 1813, were anchored off Fells Point* during the attack on Baltimore.

> On the night of the bombardment, not withstanding his [Leonard Hall] extreme indisposition bro't on by incessant labor and indifference to the symptoms of approaching illness, he insisted on remaining at the battery formed by himself on Federal Hill. (Baltimore *Patriot,* September 24, 1814)

The U.S. Navy later reported, "It is with deep regret that I inform you of the death of Sailing Master Leonard Hall of the *Ontario* who departed this life a few days since [the 22nd], after a short illness, occasioned by his excersions and nightly exposure, during the late preparation in the defense of Baltimore" (Capt. Robert T. Spence to Secretary of Navy William Jones, October 3, 1814).[16]

When Lt. Col. George Armistead died, minute-guns (distress guns fired every minute to signal mourning or distress) were fired from Federal Hill to punctuate his funeral ceremonies. Two shipyards operated along the shoreline below Federal Hill. In 1813, Andrew Descandes built the privateer xebeck (a fast three-masted slaver often rigged with lateen sails and used in privateering) *Ultor,* one of many vessels built here.

Fells Point (Northwest Branch and Fleet Street). NHD. Fells Point is named for William Fell, a ship's carpenter from England who in 1730 purchased a tract of land and established a shipyard there. Fells Point grew into an important ship-building center, where the fast and agile Baltimore clippers were built, many of which were used as privateers. The Baltimore clipper *Nonsuch* was the first privateer commissioned as a letter-of-marque during the war. Within four months of the beginning of the war, forty-two privateers sailed from Fells Point.

> By licensing private armed vessels the whole naval force of the nation is truly brought to bear on the foe; and while the contest lasts, that it may have the speedier termination, let every individual contribute his mite, in the best way he can, to distress and harass the enemy; and compel him to peace. (Baltimore *Niles' Weekly Register,* August 1, 1812)

> The private armed sch'r Surprize, Cathell [name of owner], of this port, has arrived at an eastern port from a cruize on the coast of Ireland; captured 6 brigs, 2 sch'rs and 1 ship, 2 of which she burned in sight of Baltimore harbor. (Baltimore *Federal Republican,* July 19, 1814)

During the American Revolution, the British first referred to Baltimore as "a nest of pirates." To punish Baltimore for its privateering industry and to destroy the shipyards there, the British in September 1814 mounted their attack on Baltimore. (*See also* Harris Creek, Baltimore, for information on the David Stodder Shipyard.)

> [This] nest of pirates [that is, Fells Point, Baltimore] would be shaken with weapons that shook the city of Copenhagen [Denmark]. (London *Evening Star;* reprinted in Baltimore *Niles' Weekly Register,* April 3, 1813)

On August 27, 1814, Capt. Thomas Boyle, captain of the Fells Point–built privateer *Chasseur,* captured the British brig *Marquis of Cornwallis* in the English Channel. The Marblehead, Massachusetts–born privateersman used the captured British ship as a cartel to carry an audacious proclamation to be posted at Lloyd's Coffee House in London:

BY THOMAS BOYLE, ESQUIRE

COMMANDER OF THE PRIVATE ARMED BRIG
CHASSEUR

Whereas, it has been customary with the admirals of Great Britain commanding small forces on the coast of the Untied States, particularly with Sir John Borlaise Warren and Sir Alexander Cochrane to declare the coast of the said United States in a state of strict and rigorous blockade, without possessing the power to justify such a declaration, or stationing an adequate force to command such a blockade.

I do, therefore, by virtue of the power and authority in me vested (possessing sufficient force) declare all the ports, harbors, bays, creeks, rivers, inlets, outlets, island and sea coasts of the United Kingdom of Great Britain and Ireland in a state of strict and rigorous blockade, and I do further declare that I consider the forces under my command adequate to maintain strictly, rigorously and effectually, the said blockade.

And, I do hereby require the respective officers, whether captain or commanding officers, under my command, employed or to be employed on the coast of England, Ireland and Scotland, to pay strict attention to this my proclamation.

And, I hereby caution and forbid the ships and vessels and every nation, in amity and peace with the United States, from entering or attempting to come out any of the said ports, harbors, bays, creeks, rivers, inlets, outlets, islands, or sea coasts, on or under any pretense whatever; and that no person may plead ignorance of this my proclamation, I have ordered the same to be made public in England. Given under my hand on board the *Chasseur.* By the command of the commanding Officer THOMAS BOYLE

J. B. STANSBURY, SECRETARY.[17]

A bridge of scows between Fells Point and Federal Hill allowed a more direct line of communication and troop movement between Hampstead Hill* and Ferry Point* and the Fort McHenry* fortifications. The U.S. Chesapeake Flotilla recruited volunteers at Fells Point.

Merchant Capt. George Stiles (1760–1819) organized in 1808 at Fells Point "The First Marine Artillery of the Union," an amphibious artillery unit of two hundred sea captains and seamen financed by the City of Baltimore. Of all the units in Baltimore, Maj. Gen. Samuel Smith considered this "most highly important corps" his "right arm" for Baltimore's defense. The "seaman's Corps" constructed the Lazaretto Gun Battery,* Fort Babcock,* and the shore batteries at Fort McHenry.*

The cloud gathers fast and heavy in the East, and all hands are called . . . you are therefore entreated to fall into our ranks. Many 18-pounders are already manned and many more fit for service; come and join as we give a long pull, a strong pull, and a pull altogether—and save the ship! (Capt. George Stiles,1st Marine Artillery of the Union, Baltimore *Patriot & Evening Advertiser,* July 20, 1814)

Capt. George Stiles also assisted Baltimore in its attempt to defend itself from British attack by offering to build a "Steam Battery," a floating gun barge propelled by a steam engine. The money needed to build the vessel—$150,000— was raised in Baltimore, and the hull was in frame when Robert Fulton, its designer, died on February 22, 1815. This, plus news of peace between England and the United States, caused construction to cease although $61,500 had already been expended.

BENNETT HOUSE (11 Fell Street). Here lived Charles Bennett, one of the many citizens of Fells Point and Baltimore who helped to defend Baltimore during the War of 1812.

DASHIELL HOUSE (corner of Aliceanna Street and Broadway). Here resided Capt. Henry Dashiell, commander the letter-of-marque schooner *Saranac.* The Dashiell home is now a restaurant.

FLANNIGAN AND PARSONS SHIPYARD SITE (bounded by Fountain and Fleet streets). William Flannigan and William Parsons built the U.S. frigate *Java,* which was not completed until after the war. The ordnance for *Java* was used at Fort Wood (Camp Lookout)* during the British attack of September 1814. Capt. Oliver Hazard Perry* in August 1815 assumed command of *Java.*

FORBES HOUSE (1624 Thames Street). Capt. James Forbes built this house with prize money from privateering during the Revolutionary War. During the War of 1812, he commanded a letter-of-marque blockade-runner and engaged in trade.

KEMP SHIPYARD SITE (Aliceanna and Washington streets). Thomas Kemp built the privateers *Rossie, Rolla, Comet, Patapsco, Midas,* and *Chasseur,* the latter made famous under the command of Capt. Thomas Boyle and referred to as the "Pride of Baltimore." Kemp also built the 5-gun U.S. sloop *Erie* and U.S. sloop *Ontario,* both launched in 1813, as well as gun barges for the Baltimore Flotilla and U.S. Chesapeake Flotilla.

The privateers Comet and Chasseur, of Baltimore, and other vessels belonging to this port, are doing a great business in the West Indies. It is stated that the former has taken nineteen prizes; one of which was a gun brig belonging to "his majesty." The latter has made six prizes, five of which she burnt, after divesting them of their valuable articles. (Baltimore *Niles' Weekly Register,* March 26, 1814)

LONDON COFFEE HOUSE, also called Merchant's Coffee House (northwest corner of Bond and Thames streets). The London Coffee House, built in 1771, operated here until 1804, when it became the Merchant's Coffee House. During the War of 1812, it became a center of political activity and the site where the Baltimore Committee for Vigilance and Safety met. Several other meetings were held here to discuss the defense of Baltimore. Here militia and seamen rallied in 1814 in defense of Baltimore.

NILES' WEEKLY REGISTER **OFFICE SITE** (next to London Coffee House, Bond Street [then South Street]). This news magazine operated next to the Merchant's Coffee House (London Coffee House*) at the northwest corner of Bond and Thames streets. Here were published many of the official military reports of the war as well as accounts by private citizens, providing an American viewpoint of the war.

PRICE SHIPYARD SITE (west end of Thames Street). Here in 1805 William Price built the U.S. brig *Hornet* (rebuilt and altered in 1811 to a ship-sloop) and in 1806 gunboats *No. 137* and *No. 138.*

WELLS HOUSE AND WELLS SHIPYARD SITE (southeast corner of Bond and Thames streets). The George Wells shipyard, which built the privateer *Virginia,* operated south of Wells's residence.

Ferry Branch (Middle Branch, Patapsco River). Fearing a second British attack after the Battle for Baltimore, Americans were prepared to sink ships to block any British naval advance up Ferry Branch. The weakness was exposed by the British barge probe during the night of the bombardment of Fort McHenry. Fort Covington,* Fort Babcock,* and Fort Wood* defended the city on Ferry Branch.

Ferry Point, also called Ferry Bar (Middle Branch, Patapsco River, near end of Peninsula Street [called Light Street on some maps] off Cromwell Street). On the west side of Ferry Point near the entrance to, and on Ridgely's Cove, is the site of Ferry Point Redoubt.* The 56th Virginia Regiment was stationed here in September and October 1814. Today Ferry

Point is occupied by Ferry Bar Park, but it is not maintained. After the bombardment of Fort McHenry, further defenses were prepared with a floating boom, which stretched across this cove entrance between Ferry Point and Moale's Point. A similar boom stretched between Fort McHenry and Lazaretto Point during the Battle for Baltimore.

Ferry Point Redoubt Site (side of Ferry Point and east side of Ridgley's Cove [Middle Branch], approximately at the end of Insulator Drive off Cromwell Street near the north side of Vietnam Veterans Memorial Bridge). This small redoubt protected Baltimore from a flanking maneuver around Fort McHenry. Broening Park (then called Moale's Point) on the opposite side of Middle Branch near the intersection of Hanover Street and Waterview Avenue provides a good view of this redoubt location along with the sites of forts Covington and Babcock.

Fifth Regiment Armory (bordered by Preston, Howard, Hoffman, and Bolton streets). NRHP. Dedicated in 1903, this fortress-like armory designed by Wyatt and Notting serves as the headquarters for the 175th Regiment of the Maryland National Guard, a direct descendant of Mordecai Gist's Baltimore Independent Cadets, organized in 1774. This unit reassembled in 1794 as the 5th Regiment of Maryland militia and fought in the battles of Bladensburg and North Point (Bladensburg is misspelled on the bronze plaque on the right entrance to the armory). The 5th Regiment, also known as the "Dandy Fifth," merged with the 1st and 4th Regiments during World War I to form the 115th Infantry. In 1940, it became the 175th Infantry. This regiment earned twenty-four battle ribbons between the Revolutionary War and the War of 1812. In the Brig. Gen. Bernard Feingold Museum, located in the armory, are several prints and reproductions of portraits of figures active in the War of 1812 as well as an original letter from Baltimore Mayor Edward Johnson to Gen. John Striker stating that the city approved the cost of having portraits made of Maj. Gen Samuel Smith, Brig. Gen. John Sticker, and Lt. Col. George Armistead for their services defending the city during the British attack. An oil portrait of Stricker is also on exhibit as well as shot fragments found along the shore of the Potomac River, possibly from the British attack in 1814 on Fort Washington* or White House Gun Battery.*

★ **First Presbyterian Church Burying Ground,** also called Western Burying Ground, Westminster Burying Ground, or Old Westminster Cemetery (West Fayette and Greene streets). At least twenty-five individuals who played a role in the War of 1812 are buried in this cemetery, which was established in 1786 (see appendix B). French émigré J. Maximilian M. Godefroy designed the Egyptian style gateposts on the west side of the cemetery. Godefroy is most noted for his design of Battle Monument,* but he also designed the tomb of Brig. Gen. Samuel Smith located here. Godefroy assisted in planning some of the outworks at Fort McHenry and other defenses of Baltimore in 1814.

The inscription on Gen. Samuel Smith's gravestone reads: "SAMUEL SMITH/LT. COL. U.S. ARMY / AMERICAN REVOLUTION / MAJ. GEN. U.S. ARMY/WAR OF 1812." There was no U.S. Army at the time of the American Revolution. Smith served as an officer in the Continental Army. At the time of the War of 1812, Smith did not serve as a general in the U.S. Army but as a major general of the Maryland militia taken into the service of the United States. Normally, a major general in the militia outranked a brigadier general in the regular army. Therefore, Brig. Gen. William H. Winder, the loser of the Battle of Bladensburg on August 24, 1814, technically outranked Smith. Winder expected to command all the troops as commander of the military district. But a committee of citizens led by Gen. John Eager Howard, who as a Federalist had been a bitter political rival of Smith, favored the militia general Smith. Other leading officers in Baltimore also backed Smith for the job. They included Brigadier General Stricker, who led the militia at the Battle of North Point; Capt. Robert Spence, chief of the Baltimore U.S. Naval Station; and Maj. George Armistead, commander of Fort McHenry. Finally, Winder's own uncle, Federalist Governor Levin Winder, sided with Smith against his nephew. Not surprisingly Acting Secretary of War James Monroe gave command to Smith. Smith had commanded the militia of Baltimore since 1781, when he had similarly stood ready to defend the city against a possible attack by the British.

David Poe, grandfather of poet Edgar Allan Poe, had served as a quartermaster in the American Revolution but the seventy-one-year-old also served as a private during the Battle of North Point. The remains of Edgar Allan Poe originally rested with his grandfather at the back of the churchyard, but in 1875 the poet's body was dug up and re-interred under a grand marble tomb. However, local tradition claims those digging up his body may have gone in the wrong direction and actually dug up the body of a militiaman who died of disease while serving on Hampstead Hill during the War of 1812. Whether this is true is unknown.

★ **Flag House and Star-Spangled Banner Museum** (844 East Pratt and Albermarle streets). NHL.

> The Military Gentlemen of Baltimore are respectfully informed that they can be supplied with Silk Standards & Cavalry and other colors of every description, finished in compleat order. (Baltimore *American,* July 30, 1807)

Mary, Pickergill's thirteen-year-old daughter Caroline, her nieces Margaret and Jane Young, her mother Rebecca Flower Young, and probably her servants helped to sew the 30 by 42 foot garrison flag as well as the fort's smaller 17 by 25 foot storm flag. A plaque mounted on the house proclaims the "Star Spangled Banner . . . floated over Ft. McHenry during the bombardment by the British September 13th and 14th 1814 and . . . inspired Francis Scott Key to write his immortal poem." The smaller flag, completed on August 13, 1813, is probably the flag that actually flew over Fort McHenry during most, if not all, of the bombardment. The practice at Fort McHenry to this day is to fly the smaller flag in inclement weather. The larger garrison was raised after the bombardment had ceased while the British fleet

Seamstress and businesswoman Mary Young Pickersgill (1776-1857) operated her shop at a 1793 Federal corner row house, now the Flag House. (Undated portrait by unknown artist based on 1850s photograph in collections of the Flag House; courtesy of Pickersgill Retirement Community, Towson, MD)

withdrew down the Patapsco River. The garrison flag cost $405.90.

While a plaque on the flag house correctly claims the flag was made here, because of its size the final flag assembly actually took place on the empty malt house floor of the nearby Eli Clagett's Brewery, once located next door on Lombard Street.

> the flag was made by my mother Mrs. Mary Pickersgill, and I assisted her . . . The flag being so very large, my mother was obliged to obtain permission from the proprietors of Claggett's brewery which was in our neighborhood to spread it out in their malt house. (Caroline Pickersgill Purdy, daughter of Mary Pickersgill, letter circa 1876 to Georgiana Armistead Appleton, daughter of Lt. Col. George Armistead, then owner of the flag)[18]

In the Flag House Museum are wool fragments of the Fort McHenry garrison flag, personal items belonging to Francis Scott Key, and military items from the War of 1812. Among the more interesting is a British cavalry saber reportedly kept by William Stansbury, who provided a cart and blanket to carry off mortally wounded Maj. Gen. Robert Ross at North Point*; an American cavalry saber belonging to William Houck* (Houk, Hauck?), reportedly of the 5th Maryland Regiment (there is a Capt. William Houk who served in the 6th Cavalry Regiment); and a spy glass used by Pvt. Thomas Bernard Todd at Todd House,* North Point.

Pickersgill lived in the house from 1807 until her death in 1857. She built an addition to the house in 1820. The City of Baltimore purchased the building in 1929 and removed a storefront window to restore the original facade. Other additions include a rear building added in 1953 and a museum addition in 2002.

Mary Pickersgill was related by marriage to Com. Joshua Barney and Brig. Gen. John S. Stricker. Pickersgill's uncle, John Young, married Mary Ann Bedford, whose sisters Ann and Martha married Barney and Stricker respectively. Caroline Pickersgill Purdy claims Barney and Stricker selected Mary to make the Fort McHenry flags. One account claims Mary also made the red, blue, and white flags used by Barney to identify his three divisions of the U.S. Chesapeake Flotilla.

Unconfirmed accounts claim Henry Lightner, drummer boy in the Washington Artillerists, stationed on the lower water battery of Fort McHenry during the bombardment of Fort McHenry, used the drum that his father had played during the Revolutionary War. Lightner may have played "Yankee Doodle" on the morning of September 14, 1814, when

the British warships withdrew to Old Roads Bay off North Point, Patapsco River, after the unsuccessful bombardment of the fort as the garrison flag was raised over the ramparts of Fort McHenry. It is fitting that Lightner is buried within view of Fort McHenry at Baltimore Cemetery* although there is no legible gravestone for him.

Henry Lightner (1798–1833) at the age of twelve served as a drummer boy at Fort McHenry. (Engraving, *Harper's Weekly,* September 25, 1880)

Henry Lightner's drum and drumsticks. (Engraving, *Harper's Weekly,* September 25, 1880)

Death of the Drummer Boy of 1812.— Mr. Henry Lightner, one of the old defenders, died . . . in the 85th year of his age. About six weeks ago he contracted a cold in attending a funeral of another of the old defenders and has since gradually declined in vital power. Mr. Lightner was a drummer boy in the war of 1812, and was in the Fort McHenry garrison during the bombardment . . . At the house of the deceased is the drum which his father used during the revolutionary war and which he used in the war of 1812. (Baltimore *Sun,* January 25, 1883)

Fort Armistead (Hawkin's Point, east end of Fort Armistead Road, immediately south of west end of Francis Scott Key Memorial Bridge [I-695]). This Spanish-American War-era fort is named for Lt. Col. George Armistead, who commanded Fort McHenry on September 13–14, 1814, during the bombardment. Fort Armistead consisted of four gun batteries, two of which are named for War of 1812 figures. Battery McFarland is named for Maj. Daniel McFarland of the 23rd Infantry, who died on July 25, 1814, at Lundy's Lane

in Upper Canada. Battery Winchester is named for Brig. Gen. James Winchester, who was captured at the Battle of Frenchtown on January 22, 1813.

Fort Babcock Site, also called Babcock Battery, City Battery, Fort Webster, Sailor's Battery, and Six Gun Battery (Middle Branch, Patapsco River, near intersection of I-95 and Key Highway). A small monument with cannon dedicated to Fort Babcock is located in front of the Gould Street Power Plant off McComas Street, but the actual site of the battery is slightly farther north, where I-95 now passes. Sailors of the U.S. Chesapeake Flotilla under the command of Sailing Master John Adams Webster* manned this gun battery consisting of a four-foot-high, semicircular-shaped breastwork reinforced with pine planking and mounting six 18 pounder cannons. A furnace for heating shot and an earthen powder magazine completed the battery. Webster and the flotillamen helped to turn back a British naval flanking attempt on Fort McHenry here in the early morning of September 14, 1814.

Alfred Jacob Miller painted this scene circa 1829 that depicts Fort Babcock as it probably appeared in 1814. (*The Battle of Fort McHenry;* Christie's Images)

about midnight I could hear a splashing in the water. The attention of the others was aroused and we were convinced it was the noise of the muffled oars of the British barges . . . Soon after I commenced firing. (Sailing Master John Adams Webster, commander of Fort Babcock)[19]

Fort Babcock, named after Capt. Samuel Babcock, of the U.S. Army Corps of Engineers, was also called Sailor's Battery for the forty-five to fifty flotillamen stationed here. Fort Babcock cannons are now reportedly mounted at Leone Riverside Park, site of Fort Wood/Camp Lookout* (Randall Street and Johnson Street, South Baltimore).

Fort Covington Site, also called Fort Wadsworth (Winans Cove, Middle Branch, Patapsco River, Port Covington, near end of Gould Street, near Baltimore *Sun* plant). Fort Covington was a brick and earthen-walled gun battery, located 1.5 miles on the west flank of Fort McHenry, commanded by Lt. Henry S. Newcomb and manned by eighty seamen from U.S. frigate *Guerriere.* This fort was originally named for Col. Decius Wadsworth, who supervised the construction of the fort, but it was later renamed for Brig. Gen. Leonard Covington* (1768–1813), a Marylander born at Aquasco who was mortally wounded on November 11, 1813, in the Battle of Crysler's Farm, Upper Canada. During the height of the Battle for Baltimore, seven of the Fort Covington 18 pounder guns were fired simultaneously, the recoil of which shattered the gun platform. Building materials used to construct the fort were sold at auction in 1832. Between 1903 and 1904, the Western Maryland Railroad Company built the Port Covington Rail Yard/Railhead facility, destroying part of the fort in the process. What was left of the fort disappeared with the extension of Cromwell Street and construction of the nearby Baltimore *Sun* plant. No monument marks the site.

> The enemy continued throwing shells, with one or two slight intermissions, till 1 o'clock in the morning of Wednesday, when it was discovered that he had availed himself of the darkness of the night, and had thrown a considerable force above to our right; they had approached very near to fort Covington, when they began to throw rockets; intended, I presume, to give them an opportunity of examining the shores; as I have since understood, they had detached 1250 picked men, with scaling landers [ladders?], for the purpose of storming this fort [McHenry]. We once more had an opportunity of opening our batteries, and kept up a continued blaze for nearly two hours, which had the effect again to drive them off. (Maj. George Armistead to Secretary of War James Monroe, September 24, 1814; reprinted in Baltimore *Niles' Weekly Register,* October 1, 1814)

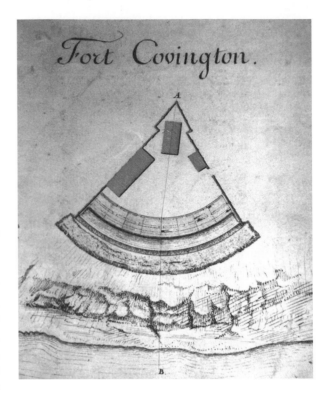

Fort Covington, completed in the spring of 1814, resembled a piece of pie with brick side walls ten feet high enclosing a brick barrack, brick guard house, powder magazine, and gun platform with ten 18 pounder naval guns. (1819 plan; National Archives and Records Administration, Cartographic Section)

Fort McHenry. Because of the significance and number of individual monuments here, Fort McHenry is not listed under Baltimore. *See* separate listing.

Fort Wood/Camp Lookout Site, also called Battery Park, Fort Look-Out, and Circular Battery (Middle Branch, Patapsco River, Leone Riverside Park, Randall and Johnson streets). Fort Wood gun battery overlooking Fort McHenry and commanded by Lt. George Budd of the U.S. sloop-of-war *Erie* was not completed prior to the British attack. It mounted seven 24 pounder naval guns intended for U.S. frigate *Java.* The cannons now at Fort Wood are reported to be from Fort Babcock* and were moved here in 1906. The fort also served as a military camp. This battery played an active role on September 13–14, 1814, in repulsing the British night flanking offensive. The camp site was long used as a observation post and thus named Camp Lookout. After the bombardment of Fort McHenry, Camp Lookout became

Fort Wood, named after Lt. Col. Eleazer Derby Wood, an artillery officer killed on September 17, 1814, leading a sortie from Fort Erie, Upper Canada. The federal government turned the property over to Baltimore City in 1854 for use as a park. Battery Avenue runs north and south, connecting Federal Hill and the gun battery site. Barney Street, named after Com. Joshua Barney, intersects the park on the west side. Several of the streets in the neighborhood are named after War of 1812 heroes. For an eyewitness account of the action at Fort Wood, *see* Federal Hill,* Baltimore. A second fort named for Lieutenant Colonel Wood is located in New York harbor and serves as the base for the Statue of Liberty.

> hire us your black Carpenters to work at the Fort at Camp-Look-out, in laying floors &c . . . the white Carpenters are all now on duty. (Minute Book of the Committee of Vigilance and Safety, September 15, 1814)[20]

Alfred Jacob Miller (1810–74), best-known for his paintings and sketches of the Indians and fur trappers of the Rocky Mountains, painted at least two scenes depicting the bombardment of Fort McHenry. Alfred was only four years old at the time of the battle. His father, George Miller, served as a private in Capt. John Berry's Washington Artillery stationed at Fort McHenry during the bombardment. Prior to his western travels and fame, Alfred painted or sketched the view from this site in 1828–29. His non-contemporary paintings correctly show forts Babcock and Covington. The site still offers a panorama of the harbor, although it is now somewhat obstructed by buildings that were not there when Miller executed his paintings. Miller's painting, *Bombardment of Fort McHenry Sept. 13–14, 1814,* is exhibited at the Maryland Historical Society.* A second painting, *The Battle of Fort McHenry,* is privately owned.

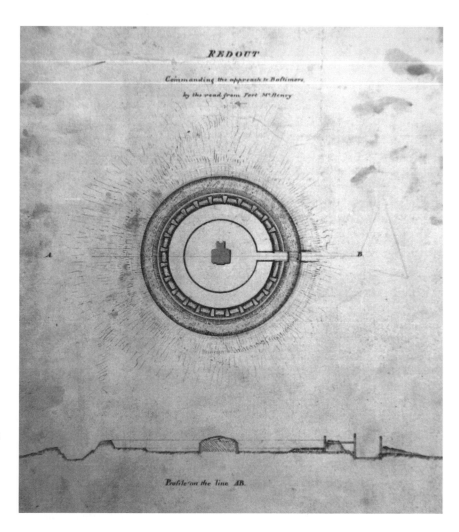

Fort Wood/Camp Lookout consisted of an earthen magazine enclosing an earthen circular redoubt, 180 feet in diameter, and an outer ditch and pine palisade. (1819 plan; National Archives and Records Administration, Cartographic Section)

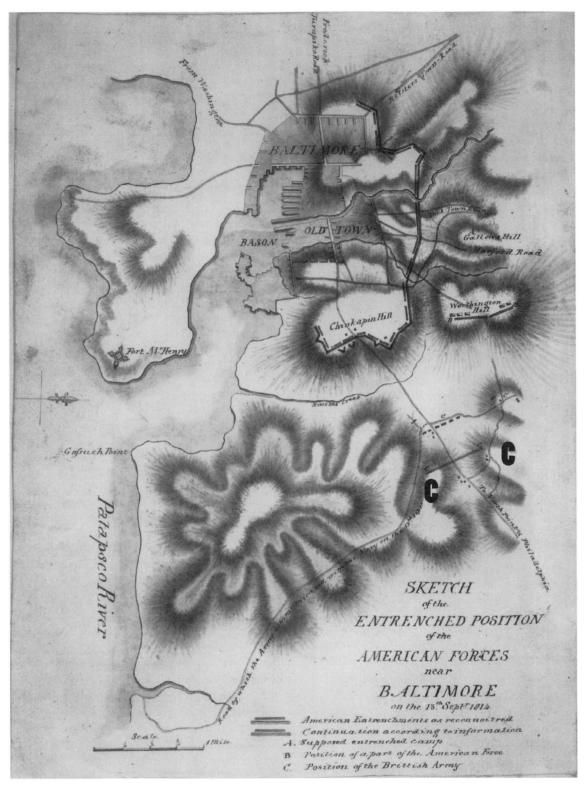

Sketch of the Entrenched Position of the American Forces near Baltimore on the 13th Sept. 1814. This colored British drawing shows Fort McHenry and the city's eastern defenses at Chinkapin or Hampstead Hill and Worthington Hill. A line marked "C" shows the British farthest advance to Baltimore. (Puteney Malcolm Papers; William L. Clements Library, University of Michigan)

Fountain Inn Site, also called Old Fountain Inn (northeast corner of Redwood and Light streets). On the evening of May 16, 1812, fifty of the leading citizens of Baltimore met here to petition Congress to declare war on Great Britain. One of the resolutions adopted claimed: "She [England] forcibly impresses our seamen, and detains them inhumanly in an odorous servitude—she obstructs our commerce in every channel . . . she has murdered our citizens within our own waters, and has made one attempt at least to dissolve the union of these States, thereby striking at the foundation of our government itself."

In August 1814, Fountain Inn hosted a ceremony honoring Oliver Hazard Perry,* hero of the Battle of Lake Erie and later commander of the newly launched U.S. frigate *Java* at Fells Point.

Some sources claim Francis Scott Key spent the night at Fountain Inn September 16–17, 1814, completing the poem that became the national anthem, but John Stuart Skinner, who was with Key, located the hotel "at the corner of Hanover and Market Street" (now Baltimore Street), which would mean that Key was at the Indian Queen Tavern.*

Furley Hall Site, also called Bowley House (near south side of Bowleys Lane, 150 feet east of Plainfield Avenue, near Herring Run Park). British soldiers reportedly occupied Furley Hall during their northward flanking maneuver in the late morning of September 13, 1814. This site marks roughly the northernmost extent of the British land movement during the Battle for Baltimore.

★ Hampstead Hill, also called Chinquapin Hill, now Patterson Park (bounded by Baltimore Street, Eastern, Patterson Park, and Linwood avenues). To defend the eastern approaches to Baltimore, American troops, private citizens, and slaves built a line of earthworks on three natural promontories of high ground at Hampstead Hill, Loudenslager's Hill, and Potter's Hill. These promontories reach an elevation of 80 to 120 feet at its northern end near where Johns Hopkins Hospital is now located and 40 to 80 feet in height at the southwest corner of Patterson Park. The earthworks, designed by Robert Cary Long and William Stuart, extended about a mile, stretching north from Belair Road south to Harris Creek, near the harbor. Hampstead Hill formed the heart of these defenses. All of those exempt from military duty including "free people of color" were requested to report to Hampstead Hill on Sunday morning, August 28, 1814, at 6:00 a.m. with "provision for the day" to assist the city in building defenses. Owners of slaves were requested

to send them to work as well.[21] (*See also* Rodgers's Bastion Cannon, Star-Spangled Banner Centennial Memorial, and War of 1812 Cannons, Baltimore.)

> Every American heart is bursting with shame and indignation at the catastrophe [at Washington]. All hearts and hands have cordially united in the common cause. Everyday, almost every hour, bodies of troops are marching in to our assistance. At this moment we cannot have less than 10,000 men under arms. The whole of the hills and rising grounds [Hampstead Hill] to the eastward of the city are covered with horse-foot and artillery exercises and training from morning until night. (Pvt. George Douglas, Baltimore Fencibles, to friend in Boston, August 30, 1814)[22]

Just east of Hampstead Hill, the British land advance reached its farthest penetration toward Baltimore on September 13, 1814.

> American account of looming British attack: On Tuesday the enemy appeared in front of my intrenchments, at the distance of two miles, on the Philadelphia road, from whence he had a full view of our position. He manoeuvred during the morning towards our left, as if with the intention of making a circuitous march and coming down on the Harford or York roads. Gens. [William H.] Winder and [John] Stricker were ordered to adapt their movements to those of the enemy, so as to baffle this supposed intention . . . This movement induced the enemy to concentrate his forces . . . in my front, pushing his advance to within a mile of us, driving in our videttes and showing an intention of attacking us that evening. I immediately drew Gens. Winder and Stricker nearer to the left of my intrenchments and to the right of the enemy, with the intention of their falling on his right or rear should he attack me; or, if he declined it, of attacking him in the morning. To this movement and to the strength of my defenses . . . I am induced to attribute his retreat, which . . . he was so favored by the extreme darkness and a continued rain that we did not discover it until daylight. (Maj. Gen. Samuel Smith, official report to Secretary of War James Monroe, September 19, 1814)[23]

> British account of American defenses: towards Baltimore, on approaching which, it was found to be defended by extremely Strong Works on every Side, and immediately in front of us by an extensive Hill on which was an entrenched Camp and great quantities of artillery, and the Information we collected added to what we observed, gave us to believe there were at least within their Works from 15 to 20,000 Men. (Rear Adm. George Cockburn to Vice Adm. Sir Alexander F. I. Cochrane, September 15, 1814)[24]

> We marched from Frederick Town . . . and arrived at Camp Hampstead . . . and we could not get tents until the Sunday

following and During that time we had to live in a rope walk; and the Second Night we lay there, their were alarm guns fired when we formed our company all under arms without a single cartrige and expecting an attack by the Enemy but in about an hour we found out that it was a false alarm and went to Rest; and on the Eleventh there was alarm guns fired again and in a short time the Enemy came in sight with about Twenty sail . . . On the night of the twelvth we lay about forty yards in the rear of the entrenchments on our arms all night without any sleep. Our men were permitted to let down some times but were roused very often as our piquots fired four or five times during the night . . . That night about eight thousand of the enemy's land forces lay within a mile and a half of us. We could see them at their fires and could hear the hogs squeal as they killed them in their camp. But about three o'clock in the morning when they found they could not silence our fort they threw some rockets down the bay as a signal for the land forces to retreat which they did in great haste and left some of their straglers behind wich were taken prisoners by our men next day. (Account of 1st Lt. Jacob Crumbaker [Crumbacker], September 2–13, 1814)[25]

we saw distinctly, across the water, the smoke of the battle in which the British commander, General [Robert] Ross, was killed. Orders were now received that we should march to meet the enemy. On our way, we met the wounded returning from the battle; and, passing the entrenchments [on Hampstead Hill], we halted for the night . . . Early next morning the bombardment of the Fort commenced . . . The following night . . . we lay so near them, that their encampment . . . appeared only a half mile distant. That was a fearful night . . . The roar of cannon and bombs . . . became fiercer and more tremendous. We lay on our arms; and three times we were alarmed by the signal of our sentinels, and put in order for battle. Just before day the firing ceased. All was still: and now the very silence rendered us uneasy. A question arose, in which our personal safety was deeply involved, whether the Fort [McHenry] had surrendered . . . At the first dawn, every eye was directed towards the Fort, to see whether the American banner still waved there; and when the morning mists had sufficiently dispersed, we were filled with exultation at beholding the stars and stripes still floating in the breeze. (Pvt. John Leadley Dagg)[26]

I think the handsomest sight I ever saw was during the bumbarding to se the bums [bombs] and rockets flying and the firing from our three forts[.] it was much handsomer at night than in the day[.] the firing continued four and twenty hours . . . I could see plenty of redcoats but could not get within musket shot of them. (Lt. John Harris to his brother William, September 27, 1814)[27]

Col. Arthur Brooke, commander of the British land forces, who succeeded Major General Ross after he received a mortal wound, saw this strongly fortified position for the first time from the second-story window of the Kell House.*

the capture of the town [Baltimore] would not have been sufficient to the loss which might probably be sustained in storming the heights [Hampstead Hill]. (Col. Arthur Brooke to Secretary of State for War and the Colonies Henry Bathurst, 3rd Earl Bathurst, September 17, 1814)[28]

The Gin Riot of 1808, a prelude to the War of 1812, took place on Hampstead Hill when Baltimoreans seized and burned gin from the ship *Sophia* that had been forced to pay British duties under the Orders-in-Council even though the goods were obtained in the Netherlands.

Samuel Carman, aster of the brig Sophia, of Baltimore . . . sailed . . . from Rotterdam, bound direct for this port of Baltimore; having on board . . . six pipes of gin . . . was boarded by an English gun brig, the commander of which ordered his vessel to England to pay duties on his cargo . . . at Harwich . . . was compelled, to pay *eight pence* sterling per gallon on said Gin—and the amount of pilotage, light money, tonnnage, &c. the same as if the said vessel had been bound for that port—and on payment thereof, license was given him to enable him to purse his voyage to Baltimore. (Easton *Republican Star,* November 4, 1808)

Sophia carried 720 gallons of Dutch gin, on which the import duty had been fully paid. However, this cargo caused a great excitement because it had paid "an infamous tribute" and at a Baltimore town meeting the gin was "condemned to the flames" in protest. Samuel Carman, the owner of the cargo, reluctantly agreed to allow the burning of his gin to escape the fury of the populace.

on the 4th of October, 1808, the houses were deserted, and city gave itself up to the declaration of the event. A monster procession was formed, which moved about two o'clock in the afternoon, and which was led by a beautiful barge on wheels, adorned with flags and streamers, and manned by masters of vessels. From her rigging floated flags eloquent with such patriotic inscriptions as "No Gag Bills," "No Stamp Act," "Bunker Hill Forever!" "No Tribute," "Liberty of the seas, Huzza!" This was followed by twelve hundred horsemen, preceded by a trumpeter, and the horsemen by a banner bearing the motto "God Speed the Plow." Next came more than four hundred sailors, with an American ensign and a white flag labeled "A proof that all the American seamen have not gone to Halifax," an allusion to the seizure of a number of the crew of the frigate "Chesapeake." After the sailors came a car bristling with national mottoes, followed by about five hundred citizens in platoons the width of the street; and after another vessel beautifully decorated came another large body of citizens, the whole procession marching to the patriotic and inspiring strains of "Yankee Doodle." The procession moved through the chief streets of the city, and arrived at Hampstead Hill, the place where the gin was to be destroyed, "at early candle-light." A general illumination [torches?] of the whole vicinity lighted up the scene; the citizens on horseback formed an immense circle, and the tributary gin was fastened to a sort of gallows in the center, to which was attached a flag inscribed "British Orders in Council." At length the fagots were kindled, and the proscribed liquor blazed in heaven amidst the discharge of cannon and the applause of fifteen thousand citizens met to show their love for independence, and to burn gin that had paid tribute to England.[29]

Wealthy merchant William Patterson, who served on the Committee of Supply for Maryland during the War of 1812, donated Hampstead Hill* to the city in 1827. Patterson is buried in the Patterson Family Cemetery, Baltimore.*

Harris Creek/Stodder Shipyard Site (Northwest Branch, Patapsco River, intersection of Luzerne Avenue and Boston Street, Canton). The U.S. frigate *Constellation,* the U.S. Navy's first frigate, was built in 1797 at the David Stodder* shipyard on Harris Creek. *Constellation* left Annapolis at the start of the war and attempted to reach the Atlantic, but encountered British vessels at the mouth of the Chesapeake Bay and thus sought the relative safety of the Elizabeth River near Norfolk, Virginia, where it was blockaded for the rest of the war. (*See also* Fells Point, Baltimore, for other shipyard locations.) The American line of defenses spanning Hampstead Hill (now Patterson Park) ended in Canton on the harbor just west of the mouth of Harris Creek. In late August 1814, owners of vessels moored at the city wharves were directed to move their vessels below Harris Creek "for the greater security" because of the ominous threat of a British attack.

George Roberts, an African American native of Canton, Maryland, served onboard Capt. Richard Moon's privateer *Sarah Ann* at the beginning of the war. H.M. frigate *Statira*

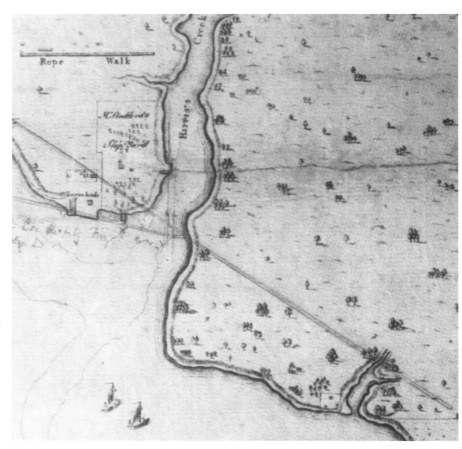

Stodder's Shipyard at mouth of Harris Creek. Note rope walk immediately to the north. (Detail from *Plan of the Town of Baltimore and its environs,* 1792 engraving by James Poupard of Philadelphia after drawing by A. P. Folie; courtesy of Enoch Pratt Free Library, Central Library/State Library Resource Center, Baltimore)

on September 13, 1812, captured *Sarah Ann* off the Bahamas. Six crewmen, including Roberts, were accused of being British subjects. Captain Moon denied that they were British, noting that George Robert had been born in the United States. The British placed these men onboard a ship headed for Jamaica and threatened to put them on trial. In retaliation the Charleston group of merchants who owned the *Sarah Ann* took twelve British prisoners and held them hostage. Roberts and the other American seamen were eventually released. Roberts later served as a gunner aboard Capt. Thomas Boyle's privateer *Chasseur*. Even though he had served most of the war at sea, he attended the parades of the "Old Defenders" of Baltimore and other military fetes. Local newspapers noted his death:

> Another Old Defender Gone—For a number of years past an aged colored man, named George Roberts, has been allowed to parade with the military of the city on all occasions of importance, and was generally mounted as servant to the major-general of the division. He died on Monday night, at the advanced age of ninety-five, at his residence, in Canton. Old George was among those who took up arms in defense of the city in 1814 . . . he never appeared on parade except in uniform and it was one of his highest aspirations to still be considered one of the defenders of his native city should the necessity have arrived to take up arms in its defense. The deceased was one of the crew under the command of Capt. Thomas Boyle, of this city, when Capt. Boyle declared the coast of Great Britain under blockade. He served during the war under several commanders, and generally at sea, and he had in the service many hairbreadth escapes. (Baltimore *Sun,* January 16, 1861)

Holliday Street Theater Site. *See* Star-Spangled Banner Holliday Theater Marker, City Hall, Baltimore

Howard, Col. John Eager, Monument (north end of Mount Vernon Place between 1 West and 1 East Madison streets). NHL District. This bronze equestrian statue, erected in 1904, primarily commemorates John Eager Howard's Revolutionary War achievements, including leading the Maryland Line on January 17, 1781, at the Battle of Cowpens, South Carolina. During the War of 1812, Howard, now a noncombatant general, proved to be a key member of Baltimore's Committee of Vigilance and Safety. He buried his political differences with Maj. Gen. Samuel Smith, a leading Republican, and worked with him to defend the city. Howard made the famous statement that during the defense of Baltimore he had four sons in the field and that he would rather see Baltimore in ashes and his sons weltering in blood than to see

the city captured by the enemy. When the Maryland legislature of 1890 refused to choose Howard as one of the two Marylanders to be granted statues in Statuary Hall in the U.S. Capitol, popular subscription defrayed the cost to the city for this monument that sits on property once part of his extensive estate. Howard County, formed from part of Anne Arundel County in 1851, and Fort Howard* at North Point are named after him.

Indian Queen Tavern Site (site of Mechanic Theater, southeast corner of Hanover and Baltimore [then Market] streets). Francis Scott Key spent the night of September 16–17, 1814, at the Indian Queen Tavern, where he completed his poem, "Defence of Fort M'Henry," later renamed "The Star-Spangled Banner." John Stuart Skinner,* who accompanied Key, claimed the poet stayed "at the corner of Hanover and Market Street," confirming Key stayed at Indian Queen Tavern and not at the Fountain Inn* as sometimes claimed. Francis Scott Key used the same tune as well as the words "star-spangled flag" in a song entitled "When the Warrior Returns" written in 1805 to honor Stephen Decatur* for his heroism during the Tripolitan War.

Kell House Site (approximately at athletic field southeast of Claremount School at 5301 Erdman Avenue). The British reportedly used Kell House as a headquarters on the evening of September 13 to the morning of September 14, 1814, during their advance toward Hampstead Hill.* Here from a second-story window, Col. Arthur Brooke, commander of the British land troops, and his aides reportedly observed the American forces and their strongly fortified position on Hampstead Hill. These earthworks very likely influenced Brooke to reconnoiter the city's northern defenses beyond the earthworks visible to him. The strength of these defenses and the failure of a night British naval flanking maneuver against Fort McHenry ultimately persuaded the British to withdraw. The topography of this area has been severely altered by road, railroad, and athletic field construction.

Key, Francis Scott, Death Site Plaque (wall of Mount Vernon Place United Methodist Church, 1 East Mount Vernon and 700 Washington Place). NHL District. Francis Scott Key died in a house that once stood on this site. Key was initially buried in Old St. Paul's Cemetery* before being finally interred in Mount Olivet Cemetery,* Frederick. A bronze plaque mounted in 1912 on the exterior wall of Mount Vernon Place United Methodist Church commemorates the house site where Francis Scott Key died in 1843.

Key (Francis Scott) Memorial Bridge (east side of I-695 bridge over the Patapsco River). This outer harbor bridge opened in 1977 to carry the Baltimore Beltway (I-695) across the Patapsco River. The bridge honors Francis Scott Key. A Maryland Historical Roadside Marker (north side of toll facility) says Key "was inspired to write the national anthem." Key was inspired to write a poem called "Defence of Fort M'Henry," the words of which became the lyrics of the national anthem in 1931.

★ **Key, Francis Scott, Monument** (Eutaw Place and West Lanvale Street). This impressive monument depicts Key returning from his British detainment standing in the bow of a small boat holding up his manuscript to an allegorical figure of Columbia on a four-columned marble canopy. Columbia proudly holds the Fort McHenry garrison flag. Gold-leafed tableaus on the base of the canopy depict the British bombardment of Fort McHenry on one side and the ramparts and cannons of Fort McHenry on the other. French sculptor Jean Marius Antonin Mercie, an 1868 recipient of the Prix de Rome, sculpted the monument, which was donated by tobacco importer Charles L. Marburg and erected in 1911. The monument originally had Key's birth date as 1779, but it has since been corrected to 1780. It was restored in 1998.

Key, Francis Scott, Monument (Fort McHenry) Orpheus. *See* Fort McHenry

Lazaretto Gun Battery Site, also called Gorsuch Point (Lehigh Cement Company silos now occupy the site at Lazaretto Point, end of Mertens Avenue). Lazaretto Gun Battery, located 600 yards across the Patapsco River opposite Fort McHenry, consisted of an earthwork mounted with three 18 pounder cannons on traveling field carriages. This battery was in service from 1813 to 1815.

> I hereby report to you that the Battery with tree [three] long eighteen pounders at the Lazaretto is fit for Service with one Hundred rounds and man'd agreeable to your orders Eight Barges up with long eight and four with long Twelves [guns] all with gunades Eighteens man'd and ready for Service. (Lt. Solomon Rutter to Com. John Rodgers, September 11, 1814)[30]

During the attack on Baltimore, Lt. Solomon Frazier commanded the battery manned by forty-five U.S. Chesapeake flotillamen. Lazaretto Point also served as the northern anchorage point for a defensive boom made of ships' masts chained together that stretched across the Patapsco River to Fort McHenry. Near here anchored eight armed barges of the Baltimore Flotilla and U.S. Chesapeake Flotilla under Lt. Solomon Rutter while offshore several vessels were sunk behind the mast boom to further hinder any British advance up river.

> orders were received that the Barges proceed to the wharves & take such vessels as were ballasted & could easily be sunk . . . it was deemed proper to take an ax & after careening the vessel, cut a hole in her bottom, let her right & sink. (Sailing Master Beverly Diggs, 1832)[31]

> The Barges and Battery at the Lazaretto under the command of Lieut. [Solomon] Rutter of the Flotilla kept up a brisk and it is believed, a successful fire during the hottest period of the bombardment. (Maj. Gen. Samuel Smith to Acting Secretary of War James Monroe, September 19, 1814)[32]

An additional 114 flotillamen protected the landward approach to the gun battery. During the night of September 12–13, 1814, several British landing barges reportedly attempting a diversion became separated from their force and mistakenly approached Lazaretto Point before realizing their error. The men at the battery detected them but, expecting a landing, sent a messenger for reinforcements instead of opening fire; by the time reinforcements arrived, the British barges had withdrawn. However, despite this widely held belief, it is possible that the British barges detected by the men at the battery were not attempting a diversion but were ascending Colgate Creek to communicate with the British land forces. Col. Arthur Brooke, acting commander of the British land troops, notified Vice Adm. Sir Alexander F. I. Cochrane, commander of the British naval forces during the night of September 13, that "Lasseto [Lazaretto] Point is most likely the place we shall be able to hold communication with you"[33] upon the successful taking of Baltimore.

A two-story brick building erected in 1801 as a "fever hospital," located a short distance to the north of the gun battery, served as headquarters of Capt. Matthew Simmons Bunbury's "First Marine Artillery of the Union" and later of the U.S. Chesapeake Flotilla. The hospital burned in 1835.

Half a mile northeast of Lazaretto Point in front of Rukert Terminal at 2021 Clinton Street is a cannon commemorating the Lazaretto Gun Battery. A plaque, like many others, claims Francis Scott Key was "inspired" to "compose our National Anthem." Rather, Key was inspired to write a poem that became the national anthem in 1931. This plaque sug-

View across Patapsco River showing Lazaretto Point at left, steamboat *Chesapeake* positioned in the passage between two moored gun barges and additional gun barges and sunken merchant ships on right. (Detail

from *An Eyewitness Sketch of the Bombardment of Fort McHenry,* date and artist unknown; courtesy Maryland Historical Society; see p. 116 for another detail of this watercolor)

gests the cannon on display was not used at the Lazaretto Gun Battery but came off a privateer and was subsequently used as a mooring bollard at Brown and Jackson wharves.

Com. Joshua Barney induced Lt. Solomon Frazier, a Revolutionary War veteran, popular mariner, and state legislator from the Eastern Shore, to resign his Maryland Senate seat and become a lieutenant of the U.S. Chesapeake Flotilla. Frazier recruited men from the Eastern Shore and commanded the blue division of the flotilla. He and a contingent of a hundred men were left behind at Pig Point* on the Patuxent River to scuttle the flotilla if threatened by the British. Frazier commanded the three-gun Lazaretto Gun Battery.

★ **Loudon Park Cemetery** (Wilkens Avenue [Route 372] near intersection with Southwestern Boulevard [U.S. Route 1]). Loudon Park, established in 1852, is Baltimore's largest public cemetery with more than 200,000 graves on 365 acres.

Here is buried Mary Pickersgill* (1776–1857), Baltimore's prominent "maker of ships colours and signals," who sewed the 15-star, 15-stripe, 30 by 42 foot Fort McHenry garrison flag. Near her grave is a marker erected in 1976 by the National Society United States Daughters of 1812 and the Star-Spangled Banner Flag House Association. At the entrance to the Garden of Military Honor is a monument to Mary Pickersgill and the words from the song, "The Star-Spangled Banner." A replica of the Fort McHenry garrison flag flies over the monument. (*See* appendix B for a list of War of 1812 veterans buried here.)

McElderry's Wharf Site, also referred to as Long Wharf (Pier 4, near the National Aquarium marine mammal pavilion off Pratt Street). Shortly after the Battle of Bladensburg, an ammunition laboratory began production of musket cartridges here for shipment as far away as Philadelphia and Washington.

★ **Maryland Historical Society** (201 West Monument Street). The Society possesses paintings, prints, and artifacts from the War of 1812, including the earliest known version of Francis Scott Key's poem, probably written at Indian Queen Tavern* the night after the bombardment based on notes taken aboard the flag-of-truce vessel September 15, 1814. This version was given to Judge Joseph Hopper Nicholson,* Key's sister's husband, who had it published. In the collections are Havre de Grace hero John O'Neill's* presentation sword and his daughter Matilda O'Neill's snuff box reportedly given to her by Rear Adm. George Cockburn. Another presentation sword is that of John Adams Webster,* a hero in the Battle for Baltimore. Also in the collections are portraits of Lt. Col. George Armistead, Maj. Gen. Samuel Smith, Brig. Gen. John Sticker, and Com. Joshua Barney, painted by the celebrated Rembrandt Peale under a commission by the City of Baltimore in 1816. Other paintings include *Troops Assembled on Hampstead Hill, Battle of North Point, near Baltimore, Sept. 12, 1814,* and Alfred Jacob Miller's *Bombardment of Fort McHenry Sept. 13–14, 1814,* sketched from Fort Wood/Camp Lookout.* One of the more interesting artifacts is a tin cup used by Samuel Gitting with the signatures of his comrades who served with him during the Battle of North Point. Ironically, the Maryland Historical Society demolished the house of Christopher Hughes Armistead and his mother Louisa, where "The Star-Spangled Banner" resided for many years in her care. The Society now occupies that site.

Meeting Sites for erection of works for the defense of the city. Believing that a second British attack was possible, the Baltimore Committee of Vigilance and Safety issued the following order three days after the Battle for Baltimore: "The inhabitants of the city and precincts are called on to deposit at the court-house, in the Third Ward; Centre Market, in the Fifth Ward; market-house, Fell's Point; riding-school, in the Seventh Ward; or take with them to the place required, all wheelbarrows, pick-axes, spades, and shovels that they can procure . . . with provision for the day" to assist the city in building defenses and "owners of slaves are requested to send them to work" on the days assigned in the several districts.[34]

Mount Clare, also called Mount Clare Mansion (Carroll Park, 1500 Washington Boulevard). NHL. On August 22, 1814, units of the Maryland militia marched past Mount Clare, to bivouac at Elkridge* and then on to Bladensburg to defend Washington against the British. Among the American militiamen was James Carroll, Jr., of Mount Clare who returned to Baltimore on the night of August 24 with dispatches of the American defeat at Bladensburg. From their house, the Carrolls could have seen the red glow in the southwestern sky from the burning of Washington. They could have also seen the British fleet in the Pataspco River on September 11, especially with a spyglass used at one of the upstairs windows. They certainly must have watched the bombardment of Fort McHenry from their hilltop vantage at Mount Clare.

Mount Clare served as the site of a National Encampment on May 14–30, 1841, attended by the surviving defenders of Baltimore, as well as troops from Virginia, Pennsylvania, and Washington. President John Tyler, Chief of Staff Gen. Winfield Scott,* and numerous other dignitaries reviewed the parade. An estimated ten thousand persons cheered when the Association of the Defenders of Baltimore of the War of 1812 entered the camp. The National Society of the Colonial Dames in America in the State of Maryland maintain Mount Clare Mansion.

Murray's Tavern Site (near intersection of Haven Street with Pulaski Highway [U.S. Route 40]). The British occupied positions near the John Murray tavern during their land advance on the afternoon and nightfall of September 13, 1814. After reconnoitering the city's defenses and learning of the fleet's failure to take Fort McHenry, the British troops withdrew during the night to their transport ships at North Point.* John Murray had two sons who served at the Battle of North Point: Francis served as ensign in Capt. Michael Peters's company, 51st Maryland Regiment, and Matthew served as a private in Capt. James Piper's United Maryland Artillery.

National Museum of Dentistry, also called the Dr. Samuel D. Harris Museum of Dentistry (31 South Greene Street). Exhibited here is a musket ball recovered from the Methodist Meeting House Site.* It was supposedly bitten down on by soldiers during surgery to help them endure the pain in an era before there were any anesthetics. (Hence, the source of the phrase "to bite the bullet.") This assumption apparently is based on the fact that it was recovered from the Meeting House, which served as a hospital after the Battle of North Point and that at least ten different tooth marks are present. However, a stick or leather strap that could not be accidentally swallowed seems more likely to have been used in such operations. Musket balls are known to have been chewed during marching and battles. Dr. James Haines McCulloh, barely out of his teens, having received his medical degree on July 17, 1814, attended to the British and American wounded here on September 13, 1814. It is possible he used this ball during his treatment of the wounded, but more likely the chewed ball is unrelated to medical procedures.

North End of Eastern Defensive Earthworks/City Hospital/ Calif and Shinnick Ropeworks Sites (between Washington and Wolfe streets at Monument Street). The extensive earthworks that protected Baltimore from a possible land assault from the east ended to the north on the high ground essentially where Johns Hopkins University Hospital is now located. Demolished shortly after the war, the north end of the Hampstead Hill fortifications consisted of two unnamed redoubts connected by earthworks; one was on the northwest end of the defenses located just south in the vicinity of the intersection of Monument Street and Broadway, while the other was on the northeast end of the defenses located near the intersection of Monument Street and Washington Avenue. A separate Northwest Gun Battery was located in the vicinity of the intersection of Broadway with Madison and Monument streets near the Kennedy Krieger Institute. This battery, along with the Outlying Northern Gun Battery,* provided an outer line of defense for any attack coming from the north. A potters field* as well as the Baltimore Public Hospital (bounded by Monument, Rutland, Broadway, and McElderry streets) occupied this site. One account says Quaker Joseph Townsend,* who operated the potters field,* helped bury the dead from the Battle of North Point. The Calif and Shinnick ropeworks, located a few blocks east of where Johns Hopkins University Hospital is located (bounded on the north by Monument, west by Collington, south by McElderry, and east by Milton streets), provided needed rigging for warships. (*See also* Hampstead Hill, Rodgers's Bastion/Gamble's Redoubt/Ramage's Redoubt Sites, Salter's Redoubt Site, Stiles's Redoubt Site, and Sugar House Site, Baltimore.)

Old St. Paul's Cemetery (between West Redwood and 700 West Lombard streets). NRHP. Open by appointment only. Old St. Paul's Cemetery, dating from 1800, is the third cemetery associated with St. Paul's Parish, established in 1692. At least twelve War of 1812 veterans are interned here although several are in unmarked plots (see appendix B). Here, in the Howard family vault Francis Scott Key laid from 1843 to 1866 before his re-internment at Mount Olivet Cemetery,* Frederick. Key's funeral was held at Old St. Paul's Church at St. Paul's and Saratoga streets. Mary Pickersgill,* the seamstress who made the Fort McHenry garrison and

storm flags, married her husband John on October 2, 1795, at Old St. Paul's Church.

Several acts of vandalism occurred in this cemetery during the 1960s. One of the worst involved the breaking into of the tomb of John Eager Howard,* removing the casket from the vault, and setting it on fire. After the fire department extinguished the flames, Howard's ceremonial sword was discovered in the mud.

Otterbein United Methodist Church, also called Old Otterbein Church (112 West Conway Street at Sharp Street). NRHP. This brick church, built in 1785–86, served as the mother church of the Church of the United Brethren. Tradition holds that the church bells, cast in Bremen, Germany, rang to announce the arrival and departure of the British in September 1814. Here on October 26, 1810, the future commander of Fort McHenry, Capt. George Armistead, wed Louisa Hughes, sister of Baltimore merchant Christopher Hughes, Jr. (1788–1846), who served as the secretary to the American Peace Commission at Ghent in present-day Belgium, in 1814. At the time, Armistead was a captain of Artillery and Engineers (appointed November 1, 1806) at Fort McHenry.

At least one clergy spoke out about the impending British attack on Baltimore when an unnamed minister at the Wilkes Street Methodist Church (Wilkes Street is now Eastern Avenue) dismissed the congregation (which included militiamen who had stacked their arms in front of the church) with the words, "May the God of Battles accompany you." (*See also* Thomas, Joshua Chapel for "Thou Shalt Not Kill" sermon and St. Thomas Chapel for Bishop Claggett boycott.)

Outlying Northern Gun Battery Site (vicinity of intersection of Broadway and Preston Street). This gun battery, located on the high ground commanding Bel Air Road, protected the American defenses from possible land attack from the north. Because the British never approached from this direction, the battery saw no action during the Battle for Baltimore. (*See also* Hampstead Hill, North End of Eastern Earthworks, Rodgers's Bastion/Gamble's Redoubt/Ramage's Redoubt Sites, Salter's Redoubt Site, Stiles's Redoubt Site, and Sugar House Site, Baltimore.)

Patterson Park. *See* Hampstead Hill as well as Rodgers's Bastion, Baltimore

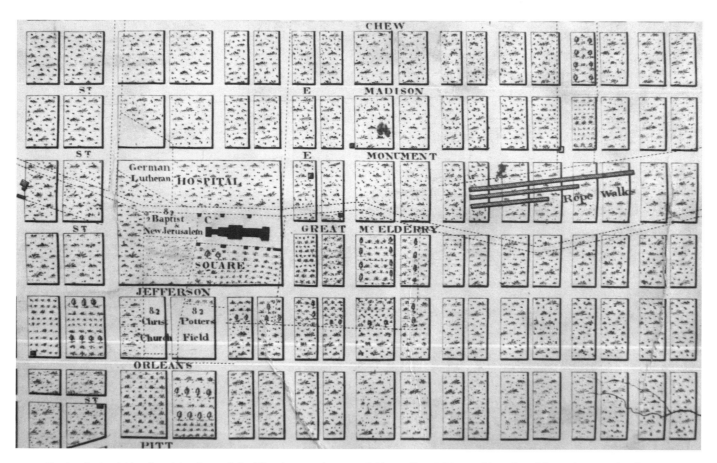

Two hundred and thirty-four sick and wounded soldiers from North Point and Fort McHenry received care at City Hospital during and after the Battle for Baltimore. In the potters field just south of the hospital, the unidentified dead were buried. The rope walks to the right of the hospital were burned by the Americans after the Battle of North Point to prevent their use as cover during the expected British attack on Baltimore. Many Baltimore citizens feared the smoke meant that the British were burning the city. (Detail from "This Plan of the City of Baltimore as enlarged & laid out under the direction of Commissioners appointed by the General Assembly of Maryland Citizens," 1818; courtesy of Enoch Pratt Free Library, Central Library/State Library Resource Center, Baltimore)

Potters Field Site (Johns Hopkins Hospital near southwest corner of Rutland [then Ann] and Jefferson streets). Americans killed in the Battle of North Point were laid in a circle behind the defensive earthworks on Hempstead Hill (now Patterson Park) for identification by their families. A dozen or more bodies not identified were buried in the potters field operated by Quaker Joseph Townsend. (*See* Methodist Meeting House Site, North Point, for another location of where Americans killed in the same conflict were buried.)

Powder Magazine Site (approximately at Key Highway and Anchor Street). Near this site a powder magazine served batteries such as Fort Wood/Camp Lookout* and Ferry Point.*

Pride of Baltimore II (Inner Harbor, Light Street). Because this vessel serves as a world ambassador to Baltimore it is not always at its berth. The *Pride of Baltimore II,* built in 1988, illustrates a typical Baltimore schooner, or clipper, used as a privateer during the War of 1812. This replica is based on the *Chasseur,* constructed at the Thomas Kemp Shipyard* in Fells Point and later made famous under command of Capt. Thomas Boyle.* Hezekiah Niles, editor of the Baltimore *Niles' Weekly Register* (April 25, 1815), referred to the *Chasseur* as the "pride of Baltimore" because of its success as a privateer. Many former crew from the *Chasseur* served in George Stiles's Marine Artillery during the Battle for Baltimore. (*See also* Fells Point, Baltimore, for further discussion of privateering.)

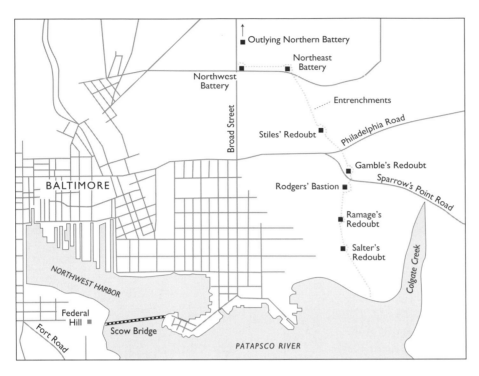

Baltimore City Eastern Defenses

Rodgers's Bastion or Bastion No. 5, also called de la Roche's Redoubt/Bastion No. 4, also called Gamble's Redoubt/and Ramage's Redoubt Sites (high ground along west side of Patterson Park, east of Patterson Park Avenue between Baltimore and Gough streets). An 1891 pagoda built near the end of Pratt Street and several War of 1812 cannons occupy the site of Rodgers's Bastion (Bastion No. 5), the contours of which are still discernable today. This fortification, commanded by Sailing Master George de la Roche and Midshipman Robert Fielding, consisted of two naval guns manned by twenty seamen from the U.S. frigate *Guerierre.*

> when we got to Baltimore, the Citizens had not determined to defend the townn[.] I believe had not Comodore [John] Rogers and crue arrived there as soon as the did the would have capitulated. (Lt. John Harris to his brother Dr. William Harris, September 27, 1814)[35]

The cannons mounted at the bastion site today were erected by the Society of the War of 1812 in 1906 and later refurbished as part of a Boy Scouts of America Eagle Scout Project. Reputed to have been used in the defense of Baltimore, they consist of 4 and 6 pounder cast iron guns, five mounted and a sixth buried in the ground with its barrel up. While these may be field cannon from the war, they are too small to be the principal cannon from this gun battery. Lt. Thomas Gamble with a hundred seamen and seven cannon commanded Bastion No. 4, located near the northwest corner of the park, vestiges of which may be discerned today. Because of the convergence of key roads here, 170 U.S. Marines were held in reserve behind this position, which was expected to take the brunt of the British land attack. Ramage's Redoubt (east-southeast of the intersection of Gough Street with Patterson Park Avenue), commanded by Sailing Master James Ramage, consisted of eighty seamen and five cannon, located to the south of Rodgers's Bastion. Grading for Gough Street Gateway in 1893 greatly altered the redoubt. (*See also* Hampstead Hill, North End of Eastern Earthworks, Outlying Northern Gun Battery Site, Salter's Redoubt Site, Stiles's Redoubt Site, and Sugar House Site, Baltimore.)

Salter's Redoubt Site (immediately west-southwest of intersection of Eastern Avenue and Bradford Street). Midshipman William D. Salter, of the U.S. frigate *Guerrire,* commanded Salter's Redoubt, consisting of twelve seamen and one cannon. If the British navy had succeeded in entering the Northwest Branch of the Patapsco River, this gun battery would have been susceptible to naval bombardment.

(See also Hampstead Hill, North End of Eastern Earthworks, Outlying Northern Gun Battery Site, Rodgers's Bastion/Gamble's Redoubt/Ramage's Redoubt Sites, Stiles's Redoubt Site, and Sugar House Site, Baltimore.)

★ **Smith, Major General Samuel, Monument** (Federal Hill, bounded by Key Highway, Covington Street, and Warren and Battery avenues, overlooking Inner Harbor). The Maj. Gen. Samuel Smith Monument, sculpted by Hans Schuler and erected by the National Star-Spangled Banner Centennial Commission, was originally dedicated on July 4, 1918, in Wyman Park. It was moved in 1953 to the Inner Harbor and then in 1971 to Federal Hill. Smith served as a captain in Gen. William Smallwood's Battalion of the Continental Line in 1776 and as a major and lieutenant colonel in the 4th Regiment in 1776–77. He received a wound while serving at Fort Mifflin, Pennsylvania, on October 23, 1777, and resigned from the army in 1779. Smith commanded the American forces defending Baltimore during the War of 1812. In the late 1790s, he built Montibello, where he lived for the rest of his life. Located east of Alameda and south of 33rd Street (east of Memorial Stadium and west of Lake Montibello), this house was torn down in 1907. Smith is buried at First Presbyterian Church Burying Ground in Baltimore.*

Spring Gardens Gun Battery Site (head of Ferry [Middle] Branch, Patapsco River, near the intersection of where I-395 crosses over Stockholm Street). Constructed in the spring of 1814 by James Mosher, superintendent of construction for the City of Baltimore, this small gun battery mounting three cannons defended the western approaches to the city in case the Royal Navy managed to get by the Middle Branch defenses of forts Covington* and Babcock.* Mosher, a veteran of the Revolutionary War and War of 1812, is buried at First Presbyterian Church Burying Ground in Baltimore.*

Star-Spangled Banner Buoy (Patapsco River, off Sollers' Point near the Dundalk Marine Terminal, just north of the Francis Scott Key Memorial Bridge). Access by water only. This decorative buoy, painted red, white, and blue, supposedly marks the spot near where Francis Scott Key observed the bombardment of Fort McHenry on September 13–14, 1814, and then wrote the poem that after his death became the national anthem. A buoy was first placed at this site during the centennial celebrations of 1914. Because of the lobbying effort of the Dundalk-Patapsco Neck Historical Society, the Maryland legislature authorized the placement of a temporary buoy again at this location during the 175th anniversary of the launching of the U.S. frigate *Constellation* in 1972 and permanently in 1979. The warships would have been at least two miles closer toward the fort while the British troop transports were anchored some four miles farther to the southeast in Old Roads Bay, near North Point.

Star-Spangled Banner Centennial Memorial (near Pagoda at Patterson Park, bounded by Baltimore Street, Eastern, Patterson Park, and Linwood avenues). This sculpture, created by J. Maxwell Miller, depicts two children who apocryphally

Rodgers's Bastion was still intact in the 1850s as shown in this drawing. Key: A. Fort McHenry with its garrison flag. (Lossing, *Pictorial Field-Book of the War of 1812*)

found a scroll while on their way home from school telling the story of how the national anthem came to be written. The sculpture served as the centerpiece of a float paraded in the 1914 centennial celebration before being erected at Patterson Park to commemorate the centennial of the writing of "The Star-Spangled Banner." Pupils of the Baltimore School System donated funds for the memorial.

Star-Spangled Banner Memorial Centennial Eagle. *See* City Hall, Baltimore

Star-Spangled Banner Holliday Street Theater Marker. *See* City Hall, Baltimore

Sterett, Joseph, House, also called Surrey Farm, Sterett's Mansion, and Fox Mansion (4901 Wilbur Avenue, near intersection of Federal Street, within Armistead Gardens housing development). An American courier from Todd House,* North Point, reported here to Col. Joseph Sterett the landing and advance of the British troops at North Point. The north end of the British line occupied this position on the afternoon and evening of September 13, 1814. British troops broke into Sterett's wine cellar and, after enjoying his wine and food, thanked him with a note. The once impressive Sterett House occupied a beautiful terraced slope overlooking the old Philadelphia Road (now Erdman Road). Numerous additions have significantly modified the original appearance of the house. Sterett served as a colonel in the Baltimore City militia in 1812 and captain in the Independent Company of militia in 1814 at the defense of Fort McHenry.

Stiles's Redoubt Site (near intersection of Fayette Street and Collington Avenue). This earthwork, under the command of Capt. George Stiles, formed part of the eastern defense of Baltimore. (*See also* Hampstead Hill, North End of Eastern Earthworks, Outlying Northern Gun Battery Site, Rodgers's Bastion/Gamble's Redoubt/Ramage's Redoubt Sites, Salter's Redoubt Site, and Sugar House Site, Baltimore.)

Stricker, Brig. Gen. John, House Site (15 South Charles Street). Brig. Gen. John Stricker, commander of the 3rd Baltimore City Brigade of Maryland militia, dispatched in July 1812 a squadron of cavalry under Maj. William B. Barney, son of Com. Joshua Barney, to end a pro-war riot at the *Federal Republican* newspaper office only a few houses north of Stricker's home. A truce of sorts was established until dawn the next day, when Stricker and Mayor Edward Johnson con-

vinced the Federalists to surrender into protective custody. That night a mob stormed the jail and severely beat most of the Federalists. (*See also* Baltimore Riot Sites, Baltimore *Federal Republican,* and First Presbyterian Church Burying Ground, Baltimore.)

Sugar House Site (immediately north of Hudson Street between South Post Street and South Milton Avenue). The Sugar House, demolished in the mid-nineteenth century, anchored the south end of the eastern defense of Baltimore. (*See also* Hampstead Hill, North End of Eastern Earthworks, Outlying Northern Gun Battery Site, Rodgers's Bastion/Gamble's Redoubt/Ramage's Redoubt Sites, Salter's Redoubt Site, and Stiles's Redoubt Site, Baltimore.)

Taney, Roger Brooke, Monument (north side of Mount Vernon Place). This statue is dedicated to Chief Justice of the Supreme Court Judge Roger Brooke Taney,* who wrote an account of the writing of "The Star-Spangled Banner" that first appeared in printed form as the foreword to a volume of Key's poems. Since Key himself did not elaborate on the writing of the poem, the account is a valuable contribution. The Taney statue is a copy of the original placed on the grounds of the Maryland statehouse,* Annapolis.

> [Francis Scott Key and John Stewart Skinner] paced the deck for the residue of the night in painful suspense . . . their glasses were turned to the fort, uncertain whether they should see there the stars and stripes, or the flag of the enemy. At length the light came, and they saw that "our flag was still there." (Roger Brooke Taney to Charles Howard, March 17, 1856)[36]

War of 1812 Cannonball and Rack Monument (sidewalk at 211 East Redwood Street). Michael Keyser, a successful iron merchant in Baltimore, erected this street side curiosity in 1863. The monument, knocked down in the 1904 Baltimore fire, was re-erected in 1906. The cannonball, actually a thirteen-inch British mortar shell, reportedly landed inside Fort McHenry.

★ Wells and McComas Monument (Ashland Square, Old Town Mall, East Monument and Aisquith streets). This impressive twenty-one-foot-tall obelisk monument commemorates Pvts. Daniel Wells and Henry Gough McComas, both members of Capt. Edward Aisquith's Sharpshooters, 1st Rifle Battalion, Maryland militia. While serving as part of Gen. John Stricker's advance guard, both were killed on September 12, 1814, during a skirmish preceding the Battle of North Point. Legend holds that Wells, age nineteen, and McComas, age eighteen, shot British Maj. Gen. Robert Ross, but there is no documentary evidence to substantiate the story. Nevertheless, they became known as the "boy heroes" of the War of 1812. Both were originally buried together in Second Baptist (New Jerusalem) Cemetery near Broadway where Johns Hopkins Hospital now stands. Their remains were later moved to Green Mount Cemetery,* where on September 10, 1858, they were exhumed for a second time and laid in state for three days at the Maryland Institute Building, Market Place. On the morning of September 12, 1858, on the anniversary of their death, their bodies were taken in a procession from Baltimore Street to Ashland Square and reburied. The base for a monument to them was not constructed until 1871 and the monument not completed until May 18, 1873.

On the occasion of the final burial of the two boys, a local poetaster who described himself as "one who was a little boy at the time of the Battle of Baltimore" composed a song entitled "Wells and McComas Funeral and Monument Song," to be sung to the tune of "The Star-Spangled Banner." One year later local playwright Clifton W. Tayleure wrote a play called *The Boy Martyrs of Sept. 12, 1814, A Local Historical Drama in Three Acts* in honor of Wells and McComas. The play was performed in Baltimore at the Holliday Street Theater* in 1858 to commemorate their reburial in Ashland Square. *The Boy Martyrs of Sept. 12* is a fictionalized telling of their alleged shooting of Maj. Gen. Robert Ross.

Western Military Defensive Position Site (near north side of intersection of Pratt and Green streets). A military force of unknown strength defended the city here from possible attack from the southwest.

BARNET FARM CEMETERY. *See* appendix A

BARNEY, COM. JOSHUA, MARYLAND HISTORICAL ROADSIDE MARKER (Patapsco High School, Wise Avenue, Dundalk, Baltimore County). Born at Baltimore, Joshua Barney (1759–1818) moved at the age of one to nearby Bear Creek, North Point, eight miles east of Baltimore. During the War of 1812, Barney commanded privateers as well as the U.S. Chesapeake Flotilla. During the Battle of Bladensburg, he was wounded and captured.

> Extract from the log-book of the privateer *Rossie,* Com. Joshua Barney commander: July 12th, sailed from Baltimore . . . July 21st, spoke ship Rising Sun, of Baltimore, informed her

of the war . . . July 23rd, was chased by a frigate; fired 25 shot at us; outsailed her. July 30th, chased by a frigate; outsailed her. July 31, took and burnt the ship Princess-Royal. August 1st, took and manned the ship Kitty; 2d, took and burnt the following: brig Fame, brig Devonshire, schooner Squid, and took the brig Brothers—put on board her 60 prisoners, and sent her to St. Johns [Newfoundland], to be exchanged for as many Americans. 3d, took and sunk the brig Henry and schooner Race-horse; burnt the schooner Halifax, manned the brig William (arrived) and gave the schooner Two Brothers to 40 prisoners, and sent them to St. Johns, on parole. 9th, took the ship Jeanie, after a short action; she mounting 12 guns; sent her for the United States.[37]

BARNEY HOUSE, also called Commodore Joshua Barney House or Harry's Lot (7912 Savage-Guilford Road, southwest corner of I-95 and Savage Road [Route 32], Savage, Howard County). NRHP. PRIVATE. Com. Joshua Barney lived in this circa 1760 house from June 1812 until April 1818. Barney retired here after being wounded, captured, and paroled on August 24, 1814, by the British after the Battle of Bladensburg. The house is now operated as the Commodore Joshua Barney House Bed and Breakfast and Historic Inn. The Commodore Suite is the largest guest room.

> Sir, . . . My wound is deep, but I flatter myself not dangerous; the ball is not yet extracted. I fondly hope a few weeks will restore me to health, and that an exchange will take place that I may resume my command, or any other that you and the President may think proper to honor me with. Yours respectfully, JOSHUA BARNEY. (Com. Joshua Barney to Secretary of Navy William Jones, August 29, 1814, written while he was recuperating from his wound at Barney House)[38]

BATTERY TOWSON, FORT CARROLL (island in Patapsco River southeast of Francis Scott Key Memorial Bridge [I-695], Baltimore County). PRIVATE. Best seen by boat, but views are also available from Key Bridge. Battery Towson is one of three Spanish-American War-era batteries built at Fort Carroll. The gun battery is named for Maj. Gen. Nathan Towson,* who served in the War of 1812 and the Mexican War. The citizens of Baltimore presented Maj. Gen. Nathan Towson with a gold sword and named a street near Fort McHenry after him. The three-story fort, never completed, was occupied during the Civil War and the Spanish-American War before being officially abandoned in March 1921.

BATTLE ACRE MONUMENT. *See* listing, North Point

BATTLE GROUND METHODIST EPISCOPAL CHURCH. *See* Methodist Meeting House

BATTLE MONUMENT. *See* listing, Baltimore

BATTLE OF THE ICE MOUND. *See* Taylors Island and Madison

BEALL-DAWSON HOUSE (Rockville, Montgomery County). *See* Rockville

BECKETT, CAPT. JOHN, GRAVESTONE. *See* Dares Beach

BELAIR (present-day Fairlee, Kent County). *See* Caulks Field

BELAIR, also called Belair Mansion or Moor's Field (12207 Tulip Grove Drive, off Laurel-Bowie Road [Route 197], Bowie, Prince George's County). NRHP. Benjamin Ogle II (1749–1809), governor of Maryland from 1798 to 1801, lived in this mansion during the War of 1812. On August 27, 1814, the family negotiated the sale of their horses to the British. In 1822, Henrietta Ogle successfully won compensation in the amount of $3,401 for slaves carried off by the British. The treaty ending the war forbid the British to transport slaves after the ratification on February 16, 1815. Benjamin and Henrietta Ogle are buried in the family cemetery located at the southwest corner of the property.

BELLE CHANCE. *See* Andrews Air Force Base/British Encampment Site

BELLEFIELDS, also called Bellefields Estate or Sim's Delight (intersection of 13104 Duley Station and Bellefield roads, off Croom Road [Route 382], Prince George's County). NRHP. PRIVATE. The central structure of Bellefields, built in the 1720s but altered in the twentieth century from its original appearance, was the home of Maj. Benjamin Oden. Brig. Gen. William H. Winder and his army, accompanied by Secretary of State James Monroe, came here from the Woodyard* encampment to intercept Maj. Gen. Robert Ross and his invading British troops. The farm is located "within half a mile of the junction of the roads from [Upper] Marlboro and the Woodyard to Nottingham" (Brig. Gen. William H. Winder, September 26, 1814).[39] If the British advance went north toward Upper Marlboro, they probably were headed to either Washington via an eastern approach or north toward Baltimore. If, however, they turned west, they probably were headed toward either Fort Washington or the City of Wash-

ington via a southern approach. As the British came to this fork about 8:30 a.m. on August 22, 1814, they saw American horsemen and swung west toward Bellefields to attack.

> set out for a skirmish; but, on approaching [Maj. Benjamin] Odin's, discovered that the enemy was also in motion. Question—what road he would take—that to [Upper] Marlborough or that to Washington? Decided to watch both. The enemy soon after taking the former, the General fell back on the Battalion's Old fields [Long Old Fields]. (Col. Allen McClane, August 22, 1814)[40]

> British account of skirmish: Our advanced people had some little affair with the enemy's Cavalry, in which no one was killed. (Lt. George Robert Gleig, August 22, 1814)[41]

The Americans withdrew toward Long Old Fields.* Maj. Gen. Robert Ross then halted his troops and reversed his course and marched north to Upper Marlboro. This confused the Americans, who thought the British were headed west toward either Fort Washington or the capital via a southern route.

Tradition holds that Major Oden gave his cattle to Brig. Gen. William H. Winder rather than hold them for selling to the British. These cattle, driven into the American encampment at Long Old Fields about 2:00 a.m. on August 23, 1814, alarmed the troops, who believed the British were attacking. Major Oden assisted other townsmen of Upper Marlboro* in guarding several stragglers and at least one deserter taken during the British withdrawal from Washington.

One of Maj. Oden's slaves, Frederick Hall, ran away from the Bellefields Plantation and on April 14, 1814, enlisted in the 38th U.S. Infantry as a private under the name of William Williams Hall. He was described as a "bright mulatto . . . fair enough to show freckles." He received his $50 enlistment bounty plus a private's wage of $8 per month. Hall served with the rest of his company in the dry moat of Fort McHenry during the bombardment of September 13–14, 1814, where his leg was blown off by a cannonball. He died two months later in the Baltimore Public Hospital. His story is known because Major Oden later tried to claim the bounty of 160 acres of land to which Williams's heirs were entitled for his military service. Congress denied the claim, saying that Oden had not tried hard enough to get his former slave back, even though he had advertised for his return.[42]

> Forty Dollars Reward
> For apprehending and securing in jail
> so that I can get him again,
> NEGRO FREDERICK;

Secretary of State James Monroe and Brig. Gen. William H. Winder reportedly observed the British advance from the upper window at Bellefields. (John. O. Brostrup 1936 photograph; HABS, Library of Congress)

Sometimes calls himself FREDERICK HALL a bright mulatto; straight and well made; 21 years old; 5 feet 7 or 8 inches high, with a short chub nose and so fair as to show freckles; he has no scars or marks of any kind that is recollected; his clothing when he left home, two months since, was home made cotton shirts, jacket, and Pantaloons of cotton and yarn twilled, all white. It is probable he may be in Baltimore, having a relation there, a house servant to a Mr. Williams, by the name of Frank, who is also a mulatto, but not so fair as Frederic.

Benjamin Oden
Prince George's County, may 12th
(Baltimore *American,* May 18, 1814)[43]

BELLONA GUNPOWDER MILLS SITE (near confluence of Jones Falls and Roland Run [now Lake Roland], on grounds of Robert E. Lee Park accessed by Hollins Avenue or Lakeside Drive, off Bellona Avenue [Route 25], Baltimore County). NHL District. The mill works were located on the east side of the lake, beyond the footbridge and the dam that are now located west of the parking lot. As early as the American Revolution, the Baltimore Committee of Observation had deemed that Baltimore should be self-sufficient in producing gunpowder, but it was not until the establishment of the Bellona Gunpowder Mills in 1801 that this need was fully met. The factory produced gunpowder used in the defense of Baltimore during the War of 1812. On May 11, 1813, Baltimore ordered 110 casks for packing musket cartridges; 20 additional barrels were ordered on July 28, 1813; and another 84 casks ordered on August 6, 1813, at $18 per cask. On June 12, 1814, Col. Decius Wadsworth, the chief ordnance officer of the War Department, ordered 200 barrels of gunpowder for Fort McHenry. That December, the Maryland General Assembly passed an act authorizing the incorporation of the company as the Bellona Gunpowder Company of Maryland. (*See also* Aetna Powder Mill.)

The E. I. du Pont Gunpowder Company* of Brandywine, Delaware, recognized Bellona Powder Mills as a competitor. At its peak, the Bellona Powder Mills employed fifty workers and is reported to have produced one-fifth of all the powder in the United States. In the course of its history, the establishment suffered numerous explosions. A series of violent explosions occurred in 1812 when a saltpeter shed caught fire and spread to adjoining structures. The factory closed in 1853. The ruins of most of the gunpowder works were visible as late as 1911, but have now been largely covered by the silt from Lake Roland, which was created in 1861. (*See also* Bellona Arsenal Site, Richmond, Virginia.)

GUNPOWDER
The Bellona Gunpowder Company offer for sale,
GUNPOWDER of various descriptions, and of a superior quality,
in half barrels, kegs, canisters and pound papers. Apply to
AARON R. LEVERING, Agent
No. 45, Cheapside
(Baltimore *Federal Gazette,* August 16, 1814)

The gunpowder mill is reputed to be named for Bellona, the daughter of part-owner James Beatty. She was said to have been born on the day that the Battle of Waterloo was fought. Since that battle took place on June 18, 1815, and the above ad with name "Bellona Gunpowder Company" dates from 1814, this story cannot be true. A more likely explanation is that the mill is named after the Roman goddess of war.

BELL'S FERRY, also called Smith's Ferry (Susquehanna River, Susquehanna State Park, end of Lapidum Road, off Level Road [Route 155], Lapidum, Harford County). After plundering Havre de Grace* on May 3, 1813, marauding British soldiers went to Bell's Ferry, where they rolled out a barrel of whiskey from John Stump's* warehouse, drank their fill, and then burned the warehouse along with five hundred barrels of flour and one of Stump's vessels.

BENEDICT (Patuxent River, Charles County). Benedict, established in 1683, was the site of two British raids in June 1814. It is also where the British landed when they marched on Washington in August 1814. The first raid occurred on June 15, 1814, when 160 marines and a detachment of 30 Colonial Marines (former slaves) landed without resistance despite the nearby presence of the Charles County militia under the command of Brig. Gen. Philip Stuart.

British account of raid: arrived at Benedict, here a Party of Regulars were station'd who fled on our approach, leaving several Musquets, Knapsacks, and Part of their Camp Equipage behind them, they also left a Six Pounder which was spiked—The Inhabitants deserted the Town and removed their effects—We found a Store containing about three Hundred and Sixty Hogsheads of Tobacco. (Capt. Robert Barrie to Rear Adm. George Cockburn, June 19, 1814)[44]

American account of raid: No buildings had been burnt at that place [Benedict], but many houses were much injured, the windows, doors, &c. having been destroyed. The Tobacco had been taken from the ware-house and carried off; except about 40 or 50 hogsheads, with which they had made a wharf to facilitate the shipping of the remainder. During their occupation of Benedict, small parties made incursions into the country for many miles round, plundering the deserted habitations. So fearless were they of interruption, that these parties did not think proper to encumber themselves with arms. (Baltimore *Federal Republican,* June 24, 1814)

The enemy at this moment were descending the Patuxent, with one more schooner than they ascended with, crowded with cattle and plunder. (Washington *Daily National Intelligencer,* June 20, 1814)

During the British occupation of Benedict, at least one barrel of poisoned whiskey was intentionally left for the British troops to drink.

American account of poison incident: I heard with astonishment and indignation, that a quantity of whisky had been by design poisoned, by an infusion of arsenic, and left in the town . . . I considered the American character as deeply implicated in this horrible deed, so inconsistent with humanity and the established usages of nations that its immediate disclosure was called for, lest its effects might produce the intended design, and thus give to our unfortunate situation a more desolating complexion. I determined immediately, under the sanction of a flag to return to the town, Dr. W[illiam Hatch]. Dent and Mr. [James] Brawner attended me. We . . . met with the commanding officer [Capt. Robert Barrie] [Dorsey having once previously talked with Barrie pleading to save the town from being burned] . . . I have heard with astonishment, that some person has most wickedly poisoned four barrels of whiskey [Dr. Dent, claimed only one barrel] and left them here . . . I have done this upon my own responsibility. I shall communicate it to my government, if that approves of it, it will be to me consolation; if not, I have the approbation of my own breast (Clement Dorsey to Brig. Gen. Philip Stuart, Annapolis *Maryland Gazette and Political Intelligencer,* June 23, 1814; reprinted from Washington *Daily National Intelligencer,* June 20, 1814) (It is interesting that Dorsey put up for sale a farm in the area that included a five-still distillery in January 1813; did this whiskey come from his previously owned still? The British complained of similar poisoning incidents on the Virginia side of the Potomac on August 9, 1814, at Nomini* as well as after their landing on September 12, 1814, at North Point.)

A second poison incident, or possibly a second version of the same incident, involved Charles Somerset Smith (1770–1831). British officers called at Mount Arundel, Smith's home. Smith received them by serving wine to which croton oil reportedly had been added, prepared from the seeds of *Croton tiglium,* also called Purging croton or Physic-nut, which is derived from a tree native to or cultivated in India and the Malay Islands. When taken internally, even in minute doses, croton oil causes much colic and diarrhea. It is said the officers became ill and remained at Benedict. Although some officers may have thought they had been poisoned, Smith would have been foolish to risk alienating his guests with such a trick. Most likely the British simply contracted one of the many ailments found in the Chesapeake during the "sickly season." Upon their return to Benedict after burning Washington, the British burned Mount Arundel.

The second British raid was successfully driven off circa 4:30 p.m., June 21, 1814, when the Maryland militia with the assistance of an artillery battery fired on a landing party from the 18-gun H.M. schooner *St. Lawrence.* This small skirmish resulted in five or six Royal Marines and sailors being captured and one sergeant killed.

British account of skirmish: I dispatched the St. Lawrence with the Launches and part of the Marines of the Frigate [Narcissus] up to St. Benedict, to load with the remaining Tobacco, after getting on board seventeen Hogsheads, the Party were surprised and attacked by several hundred Infantry and Cavalry, with four field Pieces, a Serjeant, four Marines and one Seaman, retreating to the Boats were cut off and made Prisoners, but I am happy to learn no lives have been lost, or any person wounded. (Capt. Thomas Brown to Rear Adm. George Cockburn, June 23, 1814)[45] (Despite Brown's claim, British Sergeant Mayo [also Mayeaux and Mahiou] was killed and apparently five or six taken prisoner.)

American account of skirmish: They [Americans] encamped . . . at Aquasco Mills,* 10 miles from Benedict, to wait the arrival of the baggage waggons; but on the following day, being advised of the enemy's ascending the river, they immediately repaired to arms, and arrived in sight of the town at half past 4 o'clock.—The British forces there consisted of large schooner [H.M. *St. Lawrence*], two barges and a smaller boat, lying immediately under the town. General Philip Stewart [Stuart], had under his command about thirty militia cavalry, forty mounted musket men, and some rifle men, and 150 militia infantry, which he had formed on the hill above. Immediately on their arrival an alarm gun was fired and the cavalry ordered to charge on a party of the enemy who had landed and approached the brink of the hill before they discovered the militia, when the cavalry rushed to the charge with a determination to cut them off . . . that they pursued single handed after the routed enemy. In this affair we regret to state that the brave, but unfortunate Mr. Francis Wise [*see* Oldfields Chapel, where he is reputed to be buried] was shot down by a serjeant [Sergeant Mayo] of marines, whose retreat he was intercepting. His death was immediately avenged by a young gentleman of this place who had volunteered his services on the occasion . . . The cavalry were exposed for 7 or 8 minutes to a heavy fire which though well directed was rather too much elevated.—"The Alexandrians," says our correspondent, "behaved like veterans." Remaining firm in their positions, while four or five very handsome fires were given from the two field pieces. The retreat as then made in order, and without precipitancy, under a heavy fire of 18 and 24 pounders. Five of the enemy were taken prisoners, and one killed. (Account from Alexandria, Virginia, dated June 24, republished in the Essex *Register* [Salem, Massachusetts], June 29, 1814)

Six British marines, made prisoners at Benedict on Tuesday last by our district dragoons, were escorted to this city [Washington] yesterday in a coach and committed to custody of the marshal. (Baltimore *Federal Republican,* June 23, 1814)

The District of Columbia militia under Brig. Gen. Walter Smith encamped here on June 21, 1814.

We came to this place on Monday night and after the Enemy had left it—a few of them, who had landed, being driven off that evening with some little loss . . . —They have now gone down the river. (Francis Scott Key to his mother Anne Carlton Key from his camp near Benedict, June 23, 1814)[46]

Benedict served as the temporary base for the U.S. Chesapeake Flotilla in early August 1814. Secretary of State James Monroe from about three miles distant at Aquasco Mills* reconnoitered the British fleet and troop strength about 10:00 a.m., August 20, 1814, and again the next morning. He counted twenty-three square-rigged British vessels lying below Benedict.

> I consider the Town of Benedict in the Patuxent, to offer us advantages for this Purpose beyond any other Spot within the Untied States.—It is I am informed only 44 or 45 Miles from Washington and there is a high Road between the two Places which tho' hilly is good . . . I therefore most firmly believe that within forty eight Hours after the Arrival in the Patuxent of such a Force as You expect, the City of Washington might be possessed without Difficulty or Opposition of any kind. (Rear Adm. George Cockburn to Vice Adm. Sir Alexander F. I. Cochrane, July 17, 1814)[47]

> I am informed by gentlemen of who have frequently travelled from this [Washington] to Benedict that there is a very good and direct road of 35 miles. Should the enemy dash for this place he will probably take this road. (Secretary of Navy William Jones to Com. Joshua Barney, August 20, 1814)[48]

The British landed at Benedict for a third time, but on this occasion their force was 4,370 strong and was intent on conducting major operations in Maryland and ultimately targeted Washington. Under the command of Maj. Gen. Robert Ross, troops began coming ashore on August 19 and continued through the late afternoon of August 20, 1814. They met with no resistance.

> The militia was in this part of the County appears to much opposed to fighting, thus officers can not get them to turn-out. (Clement Hollyday to Urban Hollyday, July 12, 1814)[49]

The British positioned three cannons on the hills west of Benedict. Along with pickets set up to two and a half miles inland, these cannon protected their encampment from possible American land attack. British warships protected the water approaches and east side of the encampment. The waters offshore and just below Benedict served as the main anchorage for British naval ships from August 19 to August 30, 1814, during the British invasion.

> [Benedict] is a small straggling place; the houses of which stand far apart from each other, and are surrounded by neat gardens, and apparently productive orchards. When we landed it [Benedict] was totally deserted by its inhabitants. The furniture however had not been removed, at least not wholly, from any of the houses, and not a few of the dairies were garnished with dishes of exquisite milk and delicate new cheese. (Lt. George Robert Gleig, 1833)[50]

Those British troops who had recently embarked from Bermuda had been held up in their ships for such a long time that upon landing at Benedict some were "lying at full length upon the grass, basking in the beams of a sultry sun, and apparently made happy by the very feeling of the green sod under them. Others were running and leaping about, giving

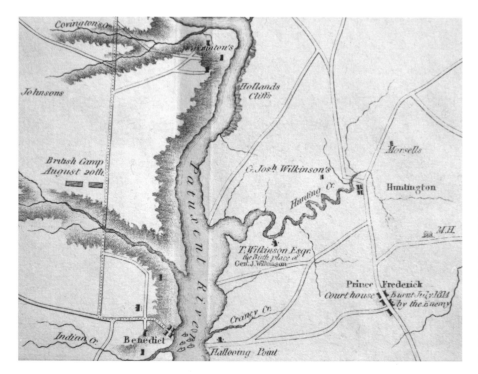

American 1816 map depicts British landing at Benedict from vessels offshore. The dotted line depicts the route taken by the British invasion troops to their first and second night encampments after departing Benedict. The first encampment is several miles north of that shown in a contemporaneous British map made in 1814 (see illustration on p. 171). Also depicted is the town of Prince Frederick, as well as Gen. James Wilkinson's birth place. (Detail of James Wilkinson map; Fort McHenry National Historic Monument collections)

(Right) British 1814 sketch map depicts the Patuxent River to the right and the village of Benedict and the British encampment immediately below the heights on both sides of what today is Route 231. (Lt. Robert Smith, 44th Regiment, "Sketch of the march of the British army under M. Genl. Ross from the 19th to the 29th Augt 1814"; courtesy Beinecke Rare Book and Manuscript Library, Yale University)

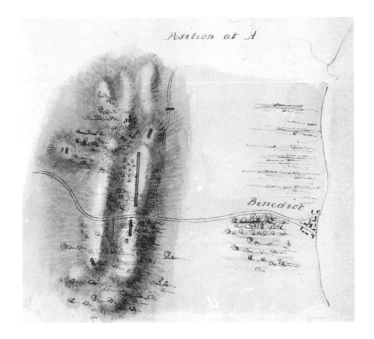

(Below) Present view of British encampment site looking east from heights toward Benedict and Patuxent River. (Ralph Eshelman 2005 photograph)

exercise to the limbs which had so long been cramped and confined onboard ship." (Lt. George Robert Gleig, 1833)[51]

West of Benedict on the Prince Frederick–Hughesville Road (Route 231), one can observe the hills where the British set up their piquets. The hill on the north side of the road, now covered in trees and occupied by a house, was the location of the British right flank of their defensive line, while the "mound" on the south side of the road, now occupied by a house, was the left flank of the British line. The British encampment of some four thousand men centered on the east slope of these hills on the north side of the road. Where the present road now crosses the hills, British light cannon were positioned facing westward.

This little army was posted upon a height which rises at the distance of two miles from the river. In front of a valley, cultivated for some way, and intersected with orchards; at the farther extremity of which the advanced piquets took their ground; pushing forward a chain of sentinels to the very skirts of the forest. The right of the position was protected by a farm-house with its inclosure and out-buildings, and the left rested upon the edge of the hill, or rather mound, which there abruptly ended. On the brow of the hill, and above the centre of the line, were placed the cannon, ready loaded, and having lighted fusees beside them; whilst the infantry bivouacked immediately under the ridge; that is, upon the slope of the hill which looked towards the shipping; in order to prevent their disposition from being seen by the enemy, should they come down to attack. But as we were now in a country, where we could not calculate upon being safe in rear, any more than in front, the chain of piquets was carried round both flanks, and so arranged, that no attempt could be made to get between the army and the fleet, without due notice, and time given to oppose and prevent it. (Lt. George Robert Gleig, 1821)[52]

Tradition claims that when the old Henderson Hotel was demolished in the late nineteenth century, shot was "dug out" of the old building frames. If this tradition is true, the shot is probably from the skirmish on June 21, 1814. More likely, the story grew out of a distortion of another tale about Minnie balls from the nearby American Civil War-era Camp Stanton. The claim of shot recovered from the old hotel may be a fabrication story to explain how the balls came to be recovered in Benedict.

After successfully capturing Washington, the British invasion forces returned to Benedict and re-boarded their ships and weighed anchor on August 29–30, 1814.

> Observed a great fire in the direction of Washington. (Log of H.M. ship-of-the-line *Albion,* 9:00 p.m., August 25, 1814, anchored on Patuxent River at Benedict)[53]

> By information received through the videttes and other means of intelligence recently organized, we learn, that the force of the enemy which retired from this place embarked on board his vessels at Benedict on Tuesday and that night; and appears to intend going down the river. (Annapolis *Maryland Republican,* September 3, 1814)

> The Persons named in the Margin having been found guilty of Robbery on shore, and as the Service will not admit of my immediately assembling a Court Martial for their Trial,—in order that the Inhabitants may be assured that their property will be protected from indiscriminate plunder. You are to cause the Persons to be taken onshore to the Village of

Benedict and there, in the presence of the Inhabitant whose House they robbed cause the Captains-Stewart to receive in the usual manner four Dozen Lashes, and the Gun Room Steward three dozen Lashes making the Boys who accompanied them and who acted under their directions witness this Punishment that they may be deterred from aiding such practices in future.—The Surgeon of the *Trave* is to attend to see that no more of this Punishment be inflicted at one period than the Parties can well bear. (Vice Adm. Sir. Alexander F. I. Cochrane to respective captains, August 25, 1814)[54]

> Read the Articles of War and punished Henry Farley (S) [Seaman] with 40 and Peter Anderson (M) [Marine] with 14 lashes for drunkeness, Michl Sullivan (S) with 18 lashes for neglect of duty, Wm. Smith (M) with 48 lashes for drunkeness and sleeping on his post, Jno. Sheridan (Arts) [Artillery] with 48 lashes and Henry Halls (M) with 36 lashes for drunkeness and violence. (H.M. ship-of-the-line *Albion* ship's log, Patuxent River at Benedict, August 21, 1814)[55]

BENSON, GEN. PERRY, GRAVE (east side of Station Road, first road to south just past Oak Creek Bridge, 0.2 mile south of St. Michaels Road [Route 33], near Newcomb, Talbot County). Gen. Perry Benson, commander of the militia forces that repulsed the British in the first and second attacks on St. Michaels on August 10 and 26, 1813, is buried here. His gravestone says he was wounded twice during the Revolutionary War and during the War of 1812 commanded the militia of Talbot, Caroline, and Dorchester counties. Benson lived at Wheatlands,* an estate near Easton, Maryland.

BIG ANNEMESSEX RIVER, also called Great Annemessex (between Manokin River to north and Little Annemessex River* to south, Somerset County). On May 19, 1814, a British vessel came into the Big Annemessex River, boarded an anchored vessel belonging to George Davey, and set it on fire. A ruse was used to make the British believe that the American troops present were stronger than they really were.

> Capt. [George] Davey immediately manned and sent off four canoe, the men in the canoes would have captured or had a brush with them [British] had not the alarm gun have been fired from the [H.M. brig] Jasseur [Jaseur], upon which they, the British, rowed off, though no without receiving a salute from the men aboard the canoes, as well as the militia who were collecting; Or, as others say, that Capt. Davey had that presence of mind to make the negroes march down opposite to them, with sticks shouldered as guns. The vessels not much injured. (Easton *Republican Star,* May 31, 1814)

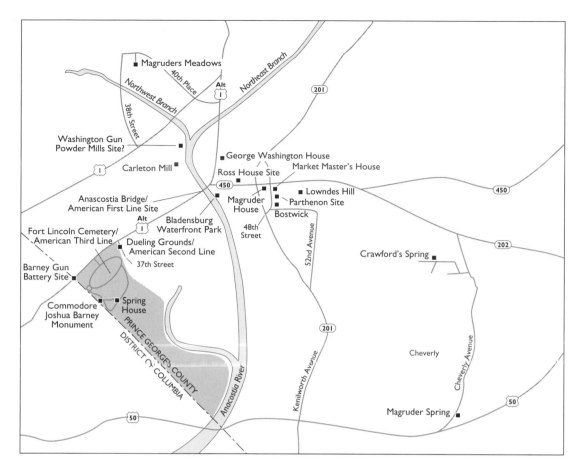

Bladensburg

BLACKISTONE ISLAND. *See* St. Clement Island

BLADENSBURG (Anacostia River, Annapolis Road [Route 450], Prince George's County). One of America's greatest defeats in the war occurred here on August 24, 1814, at the Battle of Bladensburg. Over 4,000 British forces, many veterans of the Napoleonic Wars, under Maj. Gen. Robert Ross, routed the American forces under Brig. Gen. William H. Winder consisting of approximately 6,000 largely raw militia, 1,000 regulars, 400 men from the U.S. Chesapeake Flotilla, and 114 marines. The battle took place at Bladensburg because it provided the nearest fordable point across the Eastern Branch of the Potomac River, now called the Anacostia River. Here British forces could march on Washington without crossing a bridge. The Americans had destroyed Stoddert's Bridge and East Branch Bridge, both farther down in the deeper section of the river. Brig. Gen. Tobias Stansbury and

his troops from Baltimore had been en route to the Washington Navy Yard when he learned the British were marching to Bladensburg. He reversed course and reached the bridge at Bladensburg, but instead of burning it, he placed his artillery and men at a position west or behind the bridge. Soon thereafter on the morning of August 24, 1814, Winder and his troops arrived from Washington.

The American forces hastily set up three defensive lines west of the river along the Bladensburg–Washington Road, where present-day Cottage City, Colmar Manor, and Fort Lincoln Cemetery are located. However, the American lines were too far apart to support one another or to provide cross firing positions. The British forces arrived about noon and attacked at about 1:00 p.m. Maj. Gen. Robert Ross is said to have surveyed the battlefield from the second floor of Parthenon* on Lowndes Hill,* from which he had a commanding view of the American positions. After a three-hour battle fought badly by both sides but especially by the Americans, the British outflanked and eventually routed the American first line, which collapsed into the second line, causing even greater confusion and leading to a general and disorganized retreat. Only the third line, manned by Com. Joshua Barney and his flotillamen and U.S. Marines, supported by five heavy naval guns, delayed the British advance by about thirty minutes before giving way. The British rested for two hours and then resumed their march on Washington, arriving about 8:00 p.m.

Dignitaries present during the engagement included President James Madison, Secretary of State James Monroe, Secretary of Navy William Jones, Attorney General Richard Rush,* and Secretary of War John Armstrong. For the first time in American history, the president as well as other high-ranking members of the government assumed an active role in the field in time of war directing troop movements. Many of the American defenders at the Battle of Bladensburg are buried at Congressional Cemetery.*

Brigadier General [William H.] Winder, has called into serviae 3000 of the drafted militia, to be stationed near Bladensburg. He has, also, authority from the Secretary of War, in case of exigency, to call in from the adjacent counties of Pennsylvania 5000 in addition; who are already in readiness to march at a moments notice. These, with Gen. [Tobias?] STANSBURY'S brigade, the Regulars and the Baltimore Volunteers, will form a force of 15,000 men, that can meet the enemy at any one point between Washington and Baltimore in a few hours. (Baltimore *Patriot;* reprinted in Annapolis *Maryland Republican,* August 13, 1814)

My dearest I have passed among the troops who are in high sprits and make a good appearance. The reports as to the enemy has varied from hour to hour, the last and probably best information is that they are not very strong and are without cavalry and artillery and of coarse they are not in a condition to strike at Washington. (President James Madison to Dolley Madison from Bladensburg, August 24, 1814)[56]

British account of American position: They [Americans] were drawn up in three lines upon the brow of a hill, having their front and left flank covered by a branch of the Potomac, and their right resting upon a thick wood and a deep ravine. This river . . . flowed between the heights occupied by the American forces, and the little town of Bladensburg.— Across it was thrown a narrow bridge, extending from the chief street in that town to the continuation of the road, which passed through the very center of their position; and its right bank (the bank above which they were drawn up) was covered with a narrow stripe of willows and larch trees,

whilst the left was altogether bare, low, and exposed. Such was the general aspect of their position as at the first glance it presented itself. (Lt. George Robert Gleig, 1847)[57]

There was not, in the whole space of their line, a single point where an enemy would be exposed to a cross fire. The troops were drawn up in three straight lines, like so many regiments upon a gala parade; while the guns were used as connecting links to a chain, being posted in the same order, by ones and twos, at every interval. (Lt. George Robert Gleig, 1821)[58]

American account of battle: If the militia regiments, that lay upon our right and left, could have been brought to charge the British, in close fight, as they crossed the bridge, we should have killed or taken the whole of them in a short time; but the militia ran like sheep chased by dogs. (Charles Ball, 1836)[59]

Second American account of battle: Superior numbers, however, rushed upon them [Americans], and made their retreat necessary, not, however, without great loss on the part of the enemy. (Brig. Gen. William H. Winder)[60]

British account of battle: Ross, however, did not hesitate in immediately advancing to attack [the Americans], although our troops were almost exhausted with the fatigue of the march they had just made, and but a small proportion of our little army had yet got up . . . in spite of the galling fire of the enemy, our troops advanced steadily on both flanks, and in his front; and as soon as they arrived on even ground with him, he fled in every direction, leaving behind him ten pieces of cannon, and a considerable number of killed and wounded; amongst the later Commodore [Joshua] Barney, and several other officers; some other prisoners were also taken, though not many owing to the swiftness with which the enemy went off, and the fatigue our army had previously undergone . . . that the Enemy, Eight thousand Strong, on Ground he had chosen as best adapted for him to defend, where he had time to erect his Batteries, and concert all his measures, was dislodged as Soon as reached, and a Victory gained over him by a Division of the British Army, not amounting to more than Fifteen hundred men. (Rear Adm. George Cockburn to Vice Adm. Alexander F. I. Cochrane, August 27, 1814)[61]

Second British account of battle: I think we shall have some promotion before our return to England—for if bullets do not give it the climate will . . . When I saw three field officers down and 8 or 9 others of the 85th sprawling on the ground, before we had been a quarter of an hour under fire, thinks I to myself, thinks I, by the time the action is over the devil is in it if I am not either a walking Major or a dead Captain. (Capt. John James Knox, November 23, 1814)[62]

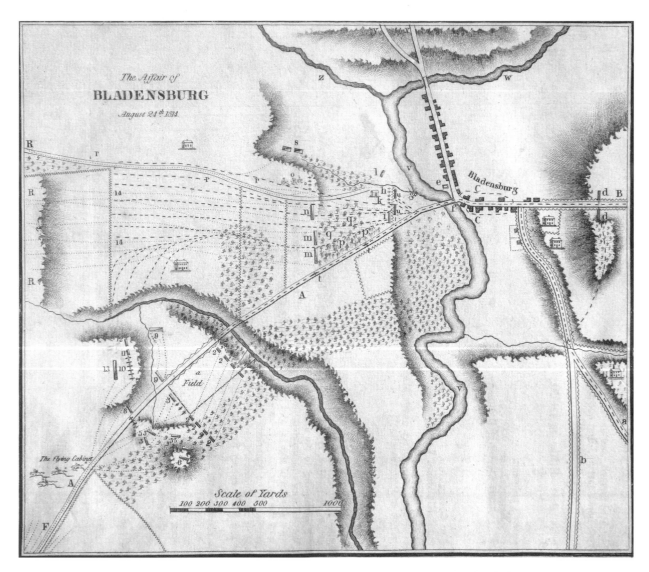

The Affair of
BLADENSBURG
August 24th 1814

American 1816 map depicts the Battle of Bladensburg. Note detail of the president and his flying cabinet in the lower left corner. Key: a. Route of British from Long Old Fields. b. Road by the ferry to Bladensburg. c. British column divided here with contingent of troops ascending Lowndes Hill while a flanking detachment continued directly into Bladensburg. d. British troops formed here and halted for twenty to thirty minutes while Gen. Robert Ross observed the American positions from the Parthenon house. e. Unoccupied fortified brick house. f. Bridge over Anacostia River. g. Stone mill later called Carleton's Mill. h. Baltimore Artillery battery of 6 pounders. i. Maj. William Pinkney's riflemen. k. Tobacco barn. l. Capt. John Doughty's rifle company. m m. Brig. Gen. Tobias E. Stansbury's Brigade. n. Lt. Col. Joseph Sterett's 5th Regiment. o. Capt. Benjamin Burch (Birch) Artillery. p p. Corn field. q q. Orchard. r r r. Road to Georgetown. s. Lt. Col. Lacint Lavall's 1st U.S. Dragoons. t t. Two pieces of artillery. u u. Where right column of British troops under Maj. (Francis F.?) Brown, 85th Regiment, first formed. v v. Eastern Branch (now Anacostia) of Potomac River. w. Northeast Branch. z. Northwest Branch. x. Turnpike road to Baltimore. y. Old road to Baltimore. A A. Turnpike to Washington City. B. Road to Governor's Bridge, Queen Anne, and Upper Marlboro by which the enemy retreated. C C. British advancing the attack. F. Retreat of the U.S. Marines, U.S. Chesapeake flotillamen, District of Columbia and Maryland militiamen, and Lt. Col. Lavall's U.S. and militia dragoons. - - - March of the British. ••• Retreat of American troops. R R R. Retreat of Baltimore and other militia units. 2 2. Left wing of British units under Col. William Thornton. 3. U.S. Marines under Capt. Samuel Miller at post and rail fence. 4. Com. Joshua Barney with battery. 5. First position of flotillamen. 3 3. Second position of U.S. Marines. 5 5. Second position of flotillamen. 22 22. Second position of Colonel Thornton. 6 6. First position of Col. William D. Beall with Maryland Militia. 6. Second position of Colonel Beall's militia. 8. Col. George Magruder's District of Columbia Militia. 9. Lt. Col. William Scott's 36th Regiment. 10. Maj. George Peter's Georgetown Artillery. 11. Capt. John Davidson's District of Columbia Militia. 12. Capt. John Stull's Rifle Company. 13. Col. William Brent's 2nd Regiment District of Columbia Militia. 14. Extent of British pursuit on the left. ("The Affair of Bladensburg August 24th, 1814," James Wilkinson 1816; Fort McHenry National Historic Monument collections)

Extract of report by Congressman Richard M. Johnson, from the committee appointed to inquire into the causes of the capture of Washington: [Brig. Gen. William H. Winder] harrassed and exposed the troops he had actually under his command to such an extent, as to incapacitate them from being as efficient as they otherwise would have been . . . arranged and commanded them with such miserable skill as to be beaten . . . that although some of the men did not act with bravery, but disorderly, there was a sufficient force on the ground, if it had been well arranged to have beaten the enemy; that the general is unfit for any important command, and that to him, principally, the enemy is indebted for his success of that day's. (Annapolis *Maryland Republican,* December 10, 1814)

The American rout, derided as the "Bladensburg Races," has sometimes been called "America's Darkest Hour." Although contemptuous of American militia, Maj. Gen. Robert Ross had nothing but praise for the flotillamen and U.S. Marines who had given the British the stiffest resistance that day.

Good God! How have we been disgraced? Our cursed militia have been coming in one, two, and three at a time, and all speak highly of their gallantry. (Capt. Joseph Hopper Nicholson to Secretary of Navy William Jones, August 28, 1814)[63]

An American battle flag was recovered from the battle-field and taken to England as a war prize.

I went to Cheslea Hospital . . . to church . . . all the Colours from different Nations which we have taken have been moved from White Hall to that and placed along the Aisles of the Church. What should I observe but the one that was found on the Battle Ground near Bladensburg. (J. Woods, 1836)[64]

The poem "Bladensburg Races," written by an anonymous American and produced as a parody of William Cowper's poem, "The Diverting History of John Gilpin," expressed a scornful view of the battle. The lines, "Sister Cutts and Cutts and I And Cutt's children three, Shall in the coach, and you shall ride O horseback after we," refer to Dolley Madison and her sister Mrs. Cutts and children fleeing the capital. Other verses are:

Armstrong and Rush, stay here in camp,
I'm sure you're not afraid—
Ourself will not return; and you,
Monroe shall be our aid.

And, Winder, do not fire your guns,
Nor' let your trumpets play
Till we are out of sight—forsooth,
My horse will run away.

Brig. Gen. William Henry Winder was captured at the Battle of Stony Creek on June 6, 1813, and imprisoned in Canada until early 1814. Nevertheless, on July 1, 1814, President James Madison appointed Winder commander of the newly established Tenth Military District, comprising the District of Columbia, Maryland, and Virginia between the Potomac and Rappahannock rivers. Winder scouted southern Maryland for potential camps from which his troops could be speedily employed to meet the British regardless of which approach they chose. However, he received little cooperation from Secretary of War John Armstrong. At Bladensburg the American troops were badly positioned, and the British assault led to confusion, panic, and a rout.

The British troops marched into Washington along the Bladensburg Road to Maryland Avenue. The victorious British army withdrew from Washington along the same route. The tired soldiers began passing through Bladensburg about midnight on August 25, 1814; some stragglers did not arrive until noon that day. To carry the wounded, about forty horses, ten or twelve carts and wagons, one ox cart, one coach, and several gigs had been gathered. This rag tag column was preceded by sixty or seventy cattle. About ninety British wounded were left behind.

The barrels of flour [taken from Washington] were arranged in the streets, the heads knocked in, and every soldier told to take some. Soldiers are greedy fellows, and many filled their haversacks. During a tedious night's march through woods as dark as chaos, they found the flour far from agreeable to carry and threw it away by degrees. If it had not been for the flour thus marking the track, the whole column would have lost its road. (Lt. Col. Harry Smith)[65]

When we reached the ground where yesterday's battle had been fought, the moon rose, and exhibited a spectacle by no means enlivening. The dead were still unburied, and lay about in every direction completely naked. They had been stripped even of their shirts, and having been exposed in this state to the violent rain in the morning, they appeared to be bleached to a most unnatural degree of whiteness. The heat and rain together had likewise affected them in a different manner; and the smell which rose upon the night air was horrible. (Lt. George Robert Gleig, 1847)[66]

The British left their men and horses unburied in the field of action. I saw many of them lying in and near the main road, and had them buried before I left. (Unnamed American officer, August 27, 1814)[67]

On our retreat to Benedict the pioneers were constantly at work cutting and clearing away the trees that had fallen across our road; the enemy could not have devised a surer mode of retarding our retrograde movements. (Capt. James Scott, 1834)[68]

Anacostia Bridge/American First Line Site (west end of bridge that carries Bladensburg Road [U.S Alternate Route 1]). Since it is dangerous to pull off here, visitors by automobile either park at Bladensburg Waterfront Park* and walk over the foot bridge to this site or continue by vehicle west and make a right (north) on 43rd Avenue and then right (east) on Bunker Hill Road. There is parking at the end of the road, and the west end of the bridge is only a short walk. The deployment of the American first line can be imaged from this location. Up the Anacostia River, one can see the forks of the Northwest and Northeast branches of the river. This fork, or *V,* in the river is mentioned in many of the contemporary accounts of the battle. Bladensburg Road continues southwest toward Washington. At a diagonal to the west (slightly off to the right) can be seen a berm built by

the U.S. Corps of Engineers in the 1950s to control floods. Just to the left of the berm is Bunker Hill Road, then called Georgetown Pike. Most of the retreating militiamen used this road as they fell back from the British advance. Georgetown Pike then ran into what today is Rhode Island Avenue, but it is now blocked by a railroad line. An American gun battery was located behind earthworks hastily dug by citizens of Washington between this road and Bladensburg Road approximately where a brick commercial building now stands. The actual bridge that crossed the river at this spot was a narrow wooden bridge capable of accommodating only three persons standing side by side.

★ **Bladensburg Waterfront Park** (Anacostia River, 4601 Annapolis Road [Route 450]). This park provides a good view of the bridge site where the British crossed and attacked the first line of the American defenses. Three War of 1812–related historic panels interpret the site.

This 1806 pencil watercolor depicts the bridge over the Eastern Branch (now Anacostia) from the northwest looking southeast. The buildings in the center stood essentially where the American first line was located. The buildings to the left depict the western edge of the village of Bladensburg. The sails and mast depict the port of Bladensburg. The bridge in this sketch is probably little changed from the bridge that the British crossed to attack the American defenders. (Benjamin H. Latrobe, *Sketch of Bladensburg, looking Northward* [actually southeastward]; courtesy Maryland Historical Society)

Bostwick (3901 48th Street). NRHP. Col. Thomas Barclay, British prisoner-of-war agent during the war, resided at Bostwick, built in 1746. He warmly welcomed the British.

> The Agent for British Prisoners of War [Col. Thomas Barclay] very fortunately residing at Bladensburg I have recommended the wounded Officers and Men to his particular attention and trust to his being able to effect their Exchange when sufficiently recovered. (Maj. Gen. Robert Ross to Secretary of State for War and the Colonies Henry Bathurst, 3rd Earl Bathurst, August 30, 1814)[69]

Carleton Mill Site, also Carlton, Penn Mill (north end of 43rd Avenue and Bunker Hill Road, Carleton Park, Cottage City). A grist mill (*see also* Washington Gun Powder Mills Site, appendix A), located on the battlefield along the road to Washington, was possibly used as a field hospital by the British after the Battle of Bladensburg. The mill, built in 1727, was owned by the family of Col. William Dudley Digges in 1814 although it has long been known for Henry L. Carleton, who purchased it in 1857. In ruins by the 1950s, the mill was demolished by the U.S. Army Corps of Engineers to control flooding. The mill dam was about 1.5 miles upstream in the center of what is now Brentwood. The appearance of the mill in 1814 is unknown. Two mill stones from Carleton Mill are incorporated into the private walkway at 3718 42nd Avenue at the intersection with Bunker Hill Road. Stones forming the wall around this property are said to be from the mill foundation.

> On arriving in the orchard near the mill, I directed the artillery to post themselves behind a small breast-work of dirt . . . the battery commanded the pass into Bladensburg, and the bridge south-westerly of the town. (Brig. Gen. Tobias E. Stansbury, November 15, 1814)[70]

The front facade of Bostwick is altered architecturally from its 1814 appearance by the addition of the porch and walled terrace. The British posted guards on the front steps and used the house as an office. (John O. Borstrup 1936 photograph; HABS, Library of Congress)

Carleton Mill as depicted in the 1850s with Bladensburg in the background. (Lossing, *Pictorial Field-Book of the War of 1812*)

Dueling Grounds/American Second Line Site (37th Avenue off Bladensburg Road [Alternate U.S. Route 1]). The American second line in the Battle of Bladensburg was located roughly at a popular dueling grounds. However, most of the action was located on the northwest side of Bladensburg Road, not on the dueling ground side. Tradition claims that over fifty duels took place here, although only twenty-six are documented. One duel was held during the war on March 12, 1814, between Lieutenants Hall and Hopkins. Another, which took place on March 22, 1822, grew out of the *Chesapeake–Leopard* affair in 1807 between Commodores Stephen Decatur* and James Barron.*

> A Duel.—We understand that a duel was fought on Saturday last, near Bladensburg, between lieut. [?] Hall and lieut. [?] Hopkins, both of col. [Henry] Carberry's regiment. At the second fire, lieut. Hopkins received the ball from his antagonist's pistol, in the breast, and expired immediately. (Baltimore *Patriot, & Evening Advertiser,* March 15, 1814)

Com. James Barron commanded the U.S. frigate *Chesapeake,* which surrendered to H.M. frigate *Leopard* off of the Virginia Capes in 1807. Barron was court-martialed and suspended during hearings presided over by Com. Stephen Decatur.* After years of exchanging rancorous letters, Barron challenged Decatur, who was mortally wounded in the duel. Gen. John Jackson, congressman from Virginia and brother-in-law of Dolley Payne Madison, was seriously wounded, but recovered, after a duel here in December 1809 with Joseph Pearson, a Federalist congressman from North Carolina. Also, Daniel Key, son of Francis Scott Key, was killed here in a duel in 1836.

Fort Lincoln Cemetery/American Third Line Site (3401 Bladensburg Road [Alternate U.S. Route 1], just northeast of Washington, D.C.–Maryland boundary). Fort Lincoln Cemetery, incorporated in 1912 and embracing 178 acres, stands essentially where the right flank of the American third line was located. Maj. George Peter's Georgetown Artillery was located on the northwest side of Bladensburg Road and the U.S. Chesapeake Flotillamen and U.S. Marines formed the center of the line near Bladensburg Road. These regulars offered the only effective American resistance during the battle. Com. Joshua Barney,* commander of the flotilla, had been stationed on the eastern branch of the Potomac River in what is now known as Barney Circle,* Pennsylvania Avenue, Southeast, Washington, D.C. (west side of John Phillip Sousa Bridge). Upon learning of the British approach at Bladensburg, Barney persuaded his superiors to grant him permission to join the fight. He and his men made a quick march to a position on Bladensburg Pike at the District line near Lincoln Cemetery. After displaying much courage, these troops were outflanked. Barney, now wounded, ordered his men to retreat. Shortly after, he was taken prisoner and paroled on the spot by the British officers in acknowledgment of respect. Capt. Samuel Miller, in command of the U.S. Marines, was also wounded although he managed to withdraw; Miller lost use of an arm for the rest of his life. All ten of Barney's cannons were captured and destroyed.

> When it was drawing towards 12 o'clock we could perceive heavy clouds of dust rising, and in half an hour more we saw the Yankeys drawn up the heights [present-day Fort Lincoln Cemetery area] above the village of Bladensburg. (Lt. George Robert Gleig, August 24, 1814)[71]

> Com. Joshua Barney's account of battle: I was informed the enemy was within a mile of Bladensburgh we hurried on, The day was hot, and my men much crippled from the severe marches we had experienced the preceding days. I preceded the men, and when I arrived at the line which separates the District from Maryland, the Battle began, I sent an officer back to hasten on my men, they came up in a trot, we took our position on the rising ground, . . . and waited the approach of the Enemy, during this period the engagement continued the enemy advancing,—our own Army retreating before them apparently in much disorder, at length the enemy made his appearance on the main road, in force, and in front of my Battery, and on seeing us made a halt, I reserved our fire, in a few minutes the enemy again advanced, when I ordered an 18 lb. to be fired, which completely cleared the road, shortly after a second and a third attempt was made by the enemy to come forward but all were destroyed, The enemy then crossed over into an Open field and attempted to flank our right, he was there met by three 12 pounders, the Marines under Capt. [Samuel] Miller and my men acting as Infantry, and again was totally cut up, by this time not a Vestige of the American Army remained except a body of 5 or 600 posted on a height on my right from whom I expected much support, from their fine situation, The Enemy from this point never appeared in force in front of us, they pushed forward their sharp shooters, one of which shot my horse under me, who fell dead between two of my Guns; The enemy who had been kept in check by our fire for nearly half an hour now began to out flank us on the right, our guns were turned that way, he pushed up the Hill, about 2 or 300 towards the Corps of Americans station'd as above described, who, to my great mortification made no resistance, giving

a fire or two and retired, in this situation we had the whole army of the Enemy to contend with; Our Ammunition was expended, and unfortunately the drivers of my Ammunition Waggons had gone off in the General Panic, at this time I received a severe wound in my thigh . . . Finding the enemy now completely in our rear and no means of defense I gave orders to my officers and men to retire. (Com. Joshua Barney to Secretary of Navy William Jones, August 29, 1814)[72]

L. O. Minear, former owner and president of Fort Lincoln Cemetery, established a tabular monument to Com. Joshua Barney located just east of the cemetery mausoleum. A historic marker is near this monument. Both contain errors. The actual site of Barney's gun battery was farther to the northeast on Bladensburg Road at the District of Columbia Line. That location has been called the brightest spot on Bladensburg Battlefield. The monument has the U.S. Marine Corps insignia on its front and states "Barney and his Marines." While Miller's marines were placed directly under the command of Barney during the engagement, Barney was also with his flotillamen, and he was a U.S. naval officer, not a marine. The marker claims Barney was in command of 500 men. Barney commanded about 450 flotillamen and about 100 marines. The marker claims the battle lasted four hours and "the overpowering numerical odds won out." The battle lasted only about three hours. While Barney and his men were outnumbered, the total American force was about six thousand, well over a thousand more than the British force.

The spring house (circa 1765) northeast of the Barney Monument is said to be the only structure surviving from the original farm located on this portion of the battlefield. Barney was probably treated here initially for his wounds. (*See* Ross House Site below, where Barney received additional medical treatment.) Near the cemetery spring house remains a section of an 1862 earthwork known as Battery Jameson, built to support nearby Fort Lincoln within the District of Columbia. These earthworks are not from the War of 1812. During the War of 1812, John Veitch II owned part of what today is Lincoln Cemetery. Veitch, commissioned a 1st lieutenant on June 27, 1812, served in the 34th Regiment, Maryland militia.

George Washington House/British Artillery Position Site, sometimes inaccurately called Indian Queen Tavern, which actually stood next door (4302 Baltimore Avenue [Alternate U.S. Route 1]). NRHP. Near the George Washington House, completed in 1765, the British established their artillery position consisting of one 6 pounder and two small 3 pounder cannon. The George Washington House is reputed to have cannonballs embedded in its walls from action during the battle but none are visible. This tradition is doubtful.

Lowndes Hill (Annapolis Road [Route 450] descends this hill heading west). American and later British forces encamped on Lowndes Hill. From the Parthenon* on this height, the British first observed the American defenses to the west on the opposite side of the Anacostia River. The Americans began digging earthworks on Lowndes Hill on August 22, 1814, to defend the road approaching from Upper Marlboro, but these were quickly abandoned when the troops withdrew back toward Washington.

We had a pleasant evening in camp near Bladensburg. Our tents were pitched on the slope of the hill [Loundes Hill] above the town on the eastern side of the river . . . we had leisure to refresh ourselves by a bath in the Eastern Branch . . . one o'clock [a.m.]—we were aroused by the scattered shots of our pickets, some four or five in succession, in the direction of the Marlborough road, and by the rapid beating of the long roll from every drum on the camp. Every one believed that the enemy was upon us, and there was consequently an immense bustle in getting ready to meet him. We struck a light to be able to find our coats, accoutrements, etc., but in a moment it was stolen away by some neighbor who came to borrow it only for a moment to light his own candle, and in the confusion forgot to return it. This gave rise to some ludicrous distresses. Some got the wrong boots, others a coat that didn't fit, some could not find their crossbelts. There was no time allowed to rectify these mistakes. I, luckily was all right, except that I sallied out in my pumps. We were formed in line and marched towards the front, perhaps a mile, and when we came to halt, we were soon ordered to march back again to camp. What was the cause of this sudden excursion and quick abandonment of it I never learned. But it was evident there was a false alarm. On our return march our attention was called to the sudden reddening of the sky in the direction of the low bridge of the Eastern Branch, by which the river road from Marlborough crossed to Washington. The sky became more lurid every moment, and at last we could discern the flames. A despatch which reached us when we got back to camp, and had just laid down again to sleep, brought us information that [Brig. Gen. William H.] Winder had crossed the bridge and then burnt it to impede the march of the enemy, who, in consequence, was forced to direct his march upon the Bladensburg road. (Pvt. John Pendleton Kennedy, August 23–24, 1814)[73]

a cloud of dust announced the advance of a body of troops [British] upon the upper road, and they soon showed themselves upon Lowndes' Hill, which they descended rapidly. (Maj. William Pinkney, November 16, 1814)[74]

I . . . had scarcely crossed the Bridge [Bladensburg], before the British were descending Lowndes Hill. (Capt. Henry Thompson to Brig. Gen. John Stricker, August 24, 1814, Ross Tavern, approximately 2:30 p.m.)[75]

Magruder House, also called Old Stone House, William Hilleary House, and Hilleary-Magruder House (4703 Annapolis Road [Route 450]). NRHP. PRIVATE. The stuccoed stone Magruder House dates from 1746. During the Battle of Bladensburg, British troops marched past Magruder's on their way toward the engagement at the Bladensburg bridge. Local tradition claims the only American civilian resistance at Bladensburg came from this house. Prince George's Heritage, Inc., acquired the dilapidated house in 1979, restored it, and now uses it as office space.

Magruders Meadows (Magruder Park, off Hamilton Street and 39th Avenue). This site, nicknamed Horse's Heaven, is said to be the burial site of horses killed during the Battle of Bladensburg. However, this location seems rather far from the battlefield to be a practical burial place.

Parthenon Site, also called War Park, Parthenon Heights, and Parthenon Manor (north of Bostwick House, intersection of Edmonston Road and Annapolis Road [Route 450]). Maj. Gen. Robert Ross reportedly surveyed the battlefield from the second floor of this house owned by Rev. John Bowie. The house was destroyed in 1941 for construction of a shopping mall. One account claims Ravenswood, located between 42nd Place and 43rd Avenue and Gallatin Street, Hyattsville, was the house where Major General Ross surveyed the battlefield. Both Parthenon and Ravenswood were at one time owned by the Bowie family, but the Parthenon, located on the slope of Lowndes Hill, is closer to the known British route and better located to serve as an observation point of the American defenses. Ravenswood was demolished in the 1950s, and St. Jeromes School now occupies the site. Parthenon was renamed War Park by Col. Thomas Bowie, nephew of Reverend Bowie, sometime after the battle. Colonel Bowie served in the 34th Regiment during the war.

Ross House Site, also called The Old Brick Hospital (corner of 46th Street and Annapolis Road [Route 450], where Ernest Maier store located). Dr. David Ross, Jr., bought the circa 1749 Ross House in 1793. It served as a hospital for treating wounded after the Battle of Bladensburg. Here Com. Joshua Barney* is believed to have been taken by the British for

Parthenon, built in 1769, would not have had in 1814 the extended porch as it appears in this early twentieth-century photograph. (Courtesy Prince George's County Historical Society)

Ross House was used as a temporary hospital after the Battle of Bladensburg. (Phillip Huntington Clark circa 1890 photograph "The Old hospital Bladensburg"; courtesy of Joseph S. Rogers)

further medical treatment after his initial treatment at the spring house. Among the at least eighteen wounded British officers treated here were two colonels, Lt. Col. William Wood and Col. William Thornton, Jr., and one major, probably Maj. Francis F. Brown, who died of his wounds.

> I strolled up to a house which had been converted into an hospital, and paid a hasty visit to the wounded. I found them in great pain, and some of them deeply affected at the thought of being abandoned by their comrades, and left to the mercy of their enemies. Yet, in their apprehension of the evil treatment from the Americans, the event proved that they had done injustice to that people; who were found to possess at least one generous trait in their character, namely, that of behaving kindly and attentively to their prisoners. (Lt. George Robert Gleig, 1847)[76]

The remains of six British soldiers are said to be buried in unmarked graves in Ross's former yard. Leonard C. Crewe, Jr., former chairman of the Maryland Historical Society, dismantled Ross House in 1957 and moved it to the Western Run Valley, Cockeysville, Baltimore County, where it was rebuilt and named Preservation Hill.

Washington Gun Powder Mills Site. *See* appendix A

BLAKEFORD (Queenstown Creek, Queen Anne's County). *See* Queenstown

BLOOMINGTON (near confluence of Savage River with Potomac River, Westernport Road–Pratt Street–Luke Road [Route 135], Garrett County). John G. C. Brant operated a gun factory on the Potomac River near Bloomington at a site called Brantsburg. In 1811, Brant received a contract to manufacture 2,375 muskets with bayonets for the government in anticipation of war with England. Wagons transported pig iron from Pennsylvania to Cumberland and then by flatboat to the factory. During the war, the William Shaw family and Notely Burnard provided black walnut logs for gun stocks. The muskets and walnut were transported on flatboats down the Potomac River to the Harpers Ferry Armory.*

BLOOMSBURY SITE (Little Monie Creek, near intersection of Deal Island Road [Route 363] and Oriole Back Road [Route 627], Somerset County). Governor Levin Winder (1757–1819) lived at Bloomsbury. As a Federalist, Governor Winder opposed the decision for war, but once war was declared he authorized the use of the Maryland militia to defend Washington and Baltimore. Winder's house no longer exists but a circa 1793 portrait of Winder by William Clarke held by the Baltimore Museum of Art depicts the home in the background. Governor Winder is believed to be buried at Bloomsbury although the exact location is unknown.

BODKIN CREEK. *See* Hancock's Resolution

BOONSBORO MUSEUM OF HISTORY (113 North Main Street, Boonsboro, Washington County). A carronade reportedly cast at the Mount Aetna Furnace,* Maryland, during the War of 1812 is exhibited on the front porch of the Boonsboro Museum. Of the several cannons on display, the 1812 gun is on the far south side of the porch (on the right as one faces the front door). The museum is open only by appointment.

BOWLINGLY. *See* listing, Queenstown

BRANTWOOD FARM, also called William's House (Williams Road, 0.5 mile east of intersection with Augustine Herman Highway [Route 213], Brantwood Golf Club, Cecil County). On the front lawn of the circa 1790 Brantwood farmhouse are either two separate cannons or two ends of an exploded cannon, reportedly dating from the Revolutionary War and used on April 29, 1813, during the skirmish at Frenchtown.* The cannon ends or cannons are stuck in the ground, one with the barrel up and the second with the barrel down, perhaps symbolic of war and peace. One legend holds that the cannon(s) were left behind when a gun carriage broke down during Maj. Gen. Sir William Howe's landing at nearby Elk Landing during the Revolutionary War. A newspaper photograph[77] of the cannon in 1991 shows the cannon tubes heavily leaning, indicating they have been realigned since then.

Revolutionary War-era cannon said to have been used in the defense of Frenchtown. (Ralph Eshelman 2002 photograph)

BREAD & CHEESE CREEK BATTLE MONUMENT. *See* Methodist Meeting House, North Point

BRETON BAY (off Potomac River, bounded by Newtown Neck on west and Medleys Neck on east, St. Mary's County). On August 2, 1814, the British conducted a raid on a large storehouse about two miles south of Breton Bay. The British sunk several fishing boats in Breton Bay in the fall of 1814.

> two small Schooners came up the Bay . . . & returned down the Bay, having in tow two captured Craft. I am informed these Picaroons have been as high up the [Potomac] River as Britans [Breton] Bay, & captured and destroyed several other vessels, exclusive of those they carried off. (Thomas Swann to Secretary of War James Monroe, December 19, 1814)[78]

BROOKEVILLE (Georgia Avenue [Route 97], Montgomery County). NHD. Brookeville, a quaint little town of narrow streets and older homes, consisted in 1814 of at least fourteen houses, two mills, a hide tanning yard, a blacksmith, a post office (Madison House*), and a private boys' school known as Brookeville Academy.* President James Madison and members of his cabinet spent the night and part of the next day at Madison House after fleeing Washington when the British occupied the city. Brookeville therefore calls itself the "United States Capital for a Day," although in actuality it was occupied for less than twenty-four hours over parts of two days, from about 6:00 p.m., August 26, to about noon, August 27, 1814.

Brookeville Academy (east side of High Street [Georgia Avenue extended] and south of intersection with Market Street). A Senate clerk and office messenger moved by wagon the executive proceedings of the U.S. Senate temporarily to Brookeville Academy from Washington to keep them safe from the invading British army. Many of the wall stones of the academy, established in 1808, contain graffiti, presumably penned by the students. The academy's original appearance was altered in 1848 when a second story was added.

Madison House, also called Caleb Bentley House (205 Market Street). PRIVATE. This Federal brick house (circa 1800) served as the temporary Executive Mansion. President James Madison, Attorney General Richard Rush,* Gen. John T. Mason, State Department Chief Clerk John Graham, their servants, and a guard of twenty dragoons occupied the house and grounds. Quaker storekeeper and postmaster Caleb Bentley and his wife Henrietta owned the Madison House, which took on this name after Madison stayed here. Henrietta's granddaughter claimed that Henrietta allowed the president to have refuge at their home even though it was against their principles to have anything to do with war. Mrs. Bentley gave her room to the president, and slept on the floor with her little daughter. Beds were spread in the parlor and the house was overflowing with the president's party. Grandmother's strongest impression of the experience was that the sentinels tramped around the dwelling all night, ruining rose bushes and vegetables. The president sat up late sending and receiving dispatches. Learning that the British had abandoned Washington, he ordered his cabinet to return to the city. The next morning on August 27, 1814, Secretary of State James Monroe met Madison at Brookeville. The Windsor chair Madison used while writing dispatches has been known since then as "the Madison Chair." It is part of the White House* collection. Henrietta Bentley was apparently a friend of Dolley Madison and may have visited her at the President's House.

While at the Bentley House, President Madison wrote to his wife, Dolley:

> My dearest: Finding that our army had left [Rockville] we pushed on to this place with a view to join it, or proceed to the City as further information might prescribe. I have just received a line from Col. [James] Monroe saying that the enemy is out of Washington & on retreat to their ships, and advising immediate return to Washington. We shall accordingly set out thither immediately. I know not where we are in the first instance to hide our head but shall look for a place on our arrival.[79]

Mrs. Margaret Bayard Smith, wife of Samuel Harrison Smith, president of the Bank of Washington and commissioner of revenue in the Treasury Department, and her two daughters, also fled to Brookeville. She described Brookeville in a letter to her sister on Wednesday before the president arrived:

> We received a most kind reception from Mrs. [Henrietta] Bentley, and excellent accommodation. The appearance of this village is romantic and beautiful, it is situated in a little valley totally embosom'd in woody hill, with a stream flowing at the bottom on which are mills. In this secluded spot one might hope the noise, or rumor of war would never reach. Here all seemed security and peace! . . . This morning [Thursday] on awakening we were greeted with the sad news, that our city was taken, the bridges and public buildings burnt, our troops flying in every direction. Our little army totally dispersed . . . Every hour the poor wearied and

The Madison House served as a refuge for President James Madison during the British occupation of Washington. (Postcard postmarked 1906; courtesy of Montgomery County Historical Society)

terrified creatures are passing by the door. Mrs. Bentley kindly invites them into rest and refresh. Major [Charles S.?] Ridgely's troop of horse all breakfasted in town.[80]

Friday morning Mrs. Smith visited Anna Maria Mason, a sick friend, about a mile away. That night she wrote:

The streets of this quiet village, which never before witnessed confusion, [are] now filled with carriages bringing out citizens, and Baggage wagons and troops. Mrs. Bentley's house is now crowded, she had been the whole evening sitting at the supper table, giving refreshment to soldiers and travellers. I suppose every house in the village is equally full. I never saw more benevolent people . . . The whole settlement are quakers. The table is just spread for the 4th or 5th time, more wanderers having just enter'd.[81]

Mrs. Smith apparently was not present at the Bentley House during the president's stay but wrote:

Just at bed time the Presd. had arrived and all hands went to work to prepare supper and lodging for him, his companions and guards,—beds were spread in the parlor, the house was filled and guards placed round the house during the

night. A large troop of horse likewise arrived and encamp'd for the night, beside the mill-wall in a beautiful little plain . . . The tents were scattered along the riverlet and the fires they kindled on the ground and the lights within the tents had a beautiful appearance. All the villagers, gentlemen and ladies, young and old, throng'd to see the President. He was tranquil as usual, and tho much distressed by the dreadful event, which had taken place not dispirited.[82]

BROOMES ISLAND (Patuxent River, south end of Broomes Island Road [Route 264], Calvert County). The British conducted a raid at Broomes Island on June 12, 1814, burning the home of John Broome VII (1775–1842), possibly because he raised and maintained a militia company at his own expense.

BRYANTOWN (intersection of Oliver's Shop Road and Waldorf–Leonardtown Road [Route 5], Charles County). NHD. The British reportedly conducted a poorly documented raid at Bryantown during the summer of 1814. The inhabitants could see the glow in the sky from the burning of Washington. At St. Mary's Catholic Church (Notre Dame Place, east off Oliver's Shop Road, 1.2 miles south of intersection with Leonardtown Road [Route 5]), established in 1793, is buried War of 1812 veteran Pvt. John Montgomery (not to be confused with Capt. John Montgomery, buried at Mount Carmel Church, Harford County).

BULLS MOUNTAIN (Northeast River, west side of Elk Neck, just south of Red Point, end of Boy Scout Road at Rodney Scout Reservation, Cecil County). The heights of Bulls Mountain served as an observation post from which the militia could see both the Upper Chesapeake Bay and the North East River to the north and west and the Elk River to the south and east.

BUTLER'S MILL. *See* Aquasco Mills

CALVERT MARINE MUSEUM (Calvert County). *See* Solomons

CALVERT MEMORIAL PARK. *See* Riversdale Mansion

CALVERTON, also called Calvert Town or Calvertown (Battle Creek, off Adelina Road [Route 508], Calvert County). PRIVATE. On July 16, 1814, H.M. frigate *Severn,* H.M. frigate *Brune,* H.M. bomb-vessel *Aetna,* and H.M. gun-brig *Manly* bombarded Calverton, the first county seat of Calvert County, and then raided it with three hundred British troops commanded by Capt. Joseph Nourse. Taney Place,* the home of Lt. Col. Michael Taney VI, commander of the Calvert County militia, eldest brother of Roger Brooke Taney,* overlooks this creek.

CAMBRIDGE (Choptank River, Dorchester County). There are several inaccurate stories dealing with a cannon once buried muzzle down in the ground to serve as a sidewalk marker at the courthouse on High Street. One story holds that the cannon was left by the British at Hooper's Island during the Revolutionary War. A second tradition claims the cannon was captured from the British at North Point and shipped to Cambridge by a man named Disney. The more probable interpretation is that the cannon was the "Becky Phipps" carronade taken by the local militia on February 7, 1815, from a captured British tender off James Island. The carronade was remounted at Taylors Island* in 1950 as a monument to what has been called the Battle of the Ice Mound.

Charles W. Goldsborough, Maryland congressman and later governor of Maryland, owned a farm at Horn Point, about two miles down the Choptank River from Cambridge. He reported the following incident:

our neighborhood had been alarmed by the arrival at Cambridge of 15 or 20 shallops, or baycraft, as we call them, seeking refuge from the British fleet, which was advancing up the bay and had then got as far as opposite to Hooper's Island. About that part of the bay they had taken 20 or 30 vessels of the above description and the fugitives . . . warned of their danger by some of their countrymen, who had escaped, came up Choptank all in a fleet together. The alarm was at once spread from Cambridge, throughout the neighborhood, as it was at the same time along the bay shore of the County by the appearance of the British squadron, and the flame and smoke of vessels which they burnt . . . on Thursday morning at 7 o'clock they were about two miles from Cambridge, directly opposite my farm at Horn's point, where they came to anchor. They remained in that reach of the river, a space of two or three miles, during Thursday and Friday, molested no one, made no attempt to land, never fired a gun, altho they saw the Banks of the river lined with militia, permitted Captn. R.[Robert] H. [Henry] Goldsborough and some of his troop and other officers to dine undisturbed in the house of Major Danl. Martin, directly on the river side, and within half a mile of the Brig, and on Friday evg. about sun-set got under way, and stood down the River, to the great Joy and relief of us all. (Charles Goldsborough to New York Congressman Harmanus Bleeker, April 2, 1813)[83]

CAMP EAGLESTON. *See* Sollers' House Site

CAMP HILL. *See* U.S. Naval Bureau of Medicine and Surgery, Washington, D.C.

CAPTAIN SALEM AVERY HOUSE (1418 East West Shady Side Road, east off Shady Side Road [Route 468], Shady Side, Anne Arundel County). Mounted along the waterfront of this museum is a cast iron cannon reputed to be a 6 pounder Revolutionary War-era gun. In the 1890s or 1900s, James Henry Nowell, captain of the Maryland Oyster Navy patrol schooner *Daisy Archer,* discovered the cannon in a shallow well while obtaining water at Fairhaven, Herring Bay, southern Anne Arundel County. He gave the cannon to his brother, Robert F. Nowell, who placed it on the lawn of his home in Shady Side. Circa 1967, the cannon was moved to the Shenton family home on West Shady Side Road and later donated to the Shady Side Rural Heritage Society, located at the Captain Salem Avery House. The cannon has no embossing or identification marks. It is possible that it may have been used unsuccessfully to defend nearby Tracys Landing* wharf on

October 27, 1814, although that cannon was reported to be a 9 pounder. The muzzle bore of the cannon is approximately 3.7 inches, which compares favorably with a 6 pounder. The bore for a 9 pound shot would be 4.2 inches. Where the cannon originally came from and how it ended up in the well at Fairhaven will probably never be known.

CASTLE HAVEN (Choptank River, north end of Castle Haven Road off Cambridge–Hudson Road [Route 343], near Lloyds, Dorchester County). On October 19, 1814, a British squadron comprising eighteen barges and a schooner entered the Choptank River. These vessels were observed from the dome of the Maryland statehouse.* At Castle Haven, troops landed and took poultry and cattle from a tenant at the farm of Dr. James Kemp. In March 1816, Kemp advertised the sale of his farm. He said it included a two-story brick house, "large barn, stable, carriage house and all other necessary buildings" (Easton *Republican Star,* March 12, 1816).

★ **CAULKS FIELD,** also called Battle of Moorefield, Moore's Field, and Arcadia (north side of Old Caulks Field Road, 0.33 mile northwest of its intersection with Tolchester Beach Road [Route 21], Kent County). On the night of August 30, 1814, the British landed approximately 260 troops near

Fairlee Creek at Parker Point.* Capt. Sir Peter Parker, commander of the British forces, called the maneuver a "frolic with the Yankees." The British advanced on an American encampment of approximately two hundred militiamen under the command of Lt. Col. Philip Reed. Under a moonlit night the British attacked the Americans at Caulks Field. Captain Parker was mortally wounded early on the morning of August 31. Parker had been previously conducting a feint up the Chesapeake Bay to make the Americans think the British were advancing on Baltimore and not Washington. With fifteen soldiers killed and another twenty-seven wounded, the British withdrew. They were unaware that the Americans were nearly out of ammunition. The Americans viewed the engagement as a victory and news of Parker's death may have helped buoy American morale during the Battle for Baltimore, less than two weeks later. The 1743 Caulk House, which overlooks the battlefield, belonged to Isaac Caulk (?–1837), who earlier had been a captain in the 21st Regiment under Lieutenant Colonel Reed. It contains mementoes of the battle, including a copy of a portrait of Sir Peter Parker.

British account of battle: An intelligent black man gave us information of two hundred Militia being encamped behind a Wood distant half a mile from the beach . . . On ar-

Sketch of the Battle of Caulks Field as drawn by Lt. Henry Crease within thirty-six hours of the action. Key: A. American militia camp is near where the Caulk House (not shown) still stands. B. Defile through which the British passed to reach the battlefield. A detachment of American troops fired on the British from the trees on right and withdrew to the American line. C. Position of the American line and artillery. (Courtesy National Archives United Kingdom, London)

riving at the Ground we discovered the Enemy had shifted his Position . . . of a mile farther . . . after a march of between four and five miles . . . we found the Enemy posted on a Plain, surrounded by Woods, with the camp in their Rear; they were drawn up in a line and perfectly ready to receive us; a single moment was not to be lost, by a smart fire and instant charge we commenced the attack, forced them . . . in full retreat, to the rear of their Artillery where they again made a stand, shewing a disposition to out flank us on the right; a movement was instantly made by Lieut. [Robert] Pearce's Division to force them from that Quarter, and it was at this time while animating his Men in the most heroic manner that Sir Peter Parker received his mortal wound which obliged him to quit the field and he expired in a few minutes. Lieut. Pearce with his Division soon routed the Enemy, while that under my Command gained and passed the Camp; one of the Field pieces was momentarily in our possession, but obliged to quit it from superior numbers; The Marines . . . formed our Centre and never was bravery more conspicuous. Finding it impossible to close on the Enemy from the rapidity of their Retreat, having pursued them upwards of a Mile I deemed it prudent to retire toward the Beach, which was effected in the best possible Order, taking with us from the field twenty five of our wounded, the whole we could find, the Enemy not even attempting to regain the ground they had lost. (Lt. Henry Crease, Acting Commander, to Vice Adm. Sir Alexander F. I. Cochrane, September 1, 1814)[84]

American account of battle: Orders were immediately given to . . . form on the rising ground about three hundred paces in the rear—the right towards Caulk's house, and the left retiring on the road, the artillery in the centre, supported by the infantry on the right and left . . . The head of the enemy's column soon presented itself and received the fire of our advance party, at seventy paces distance, and, being pressed by numbers vastly superior, I repaired to my post on the line; having ordered the riflemen to return and form on the right of the line. The fire now became general along the whole line, and was sustained by our troops with the most determined valor. The enemy pressed our front; foiled in this he threw himself upon our left flank . . . Here, too, his efforts were unavailing. His fire had nearly ceased, when I was informed that in some parts of our line cartridges were entirely expended, nor did any of the boxes contain more than a few rounds, although each man brought about twenty into the field.— The artillery cartridges were entirely expended. Under these circumstances I ordered the line to fall back to a convenient spot where a part of the line was fortified, when the few remaining cartridges were distributed amongst a part of the line, which was again brought into the field, where it remained for a considerable time, the night pre-

venting pursuit. The artillery and infantry for whom there were no cartridges were ordered to this place (Belle Air [now Fairlee]). The enemy having made every effort in his power, although apprized of our having fallen back, manifested no disposition to follow us up, but retreated about the time our ammunition was exhausted. (Lt. Col. Philip Reed to Brig. Gen. Benjamin Chambers, September 3, 1814)[85]

Thomas Dorris (also Doris or Douros) is believed to be one of the British troopers who was wounded during the battle. A sailmaker from Whitstable, England, Doris deserted to the American side.

On the American side there were three privates wounded, not supposed dangerously, and one taken prisoner. On the British one Master's Mate, one Midshipman, 3 privates killed, and 5 wounded left on the field of battle, two of them died of their wounds yesterday, one deserted. (Boston *Independent Chronicle,* September 12, 1814)

Lieutenant Colonel Reed thought the British were probably landing to raid Skidmore (also called Chantilly), a farm owned by John Waltham. (The house, now destroyed, was located off Laurel Point Lane.) The British passed Skidmore Farm both going to and coming back from the battle, but it was Reed's forces that the British sought.

On October 18, 1902, the Tolchester Steamboat Company steamer *Kitty Knight* arrived from Baltimore carrying eighteen guests, who were taken by carriage to the battlefield for the dedication of a monument. A lunch consisting of ham, oysters, bread, and coffee was served at the Caulk House. The monument was dedicated to the "victor and vanquished." It was restored by a local farmer, Charmayne Dieker, and the Colonel Reed Chapter of the 4-H Club in 1967 on the 153rd anniversary of the battle.

Local tradition holds that Sir Peter Parker was taken to the Mitchell House* after he was mortally wounded. This is based on a report after the incident that claims that "On their retreat they called at a house some distance from the field of battle and got a blanket and sheet, it is supposed to wrap Sir Peter in" (Baltimore *Federal Gazette,* September 7, 1814). It had been assumed by many that the house was the Mitchell House, but that house is not located along the known British route.

Later that morning Parker's right shoe was found. His name was written in it, and it was covered in blood. British Midshipman Frederick Chamier wrote years later that "it was the height of madness to advance into the interior of a country we knew nothing about, led by a black man [guide], whose sincerity in our cause was very questionable."[86] Parker's cousin Lord Byron wrote a poetic eulogy to his memory in 1815.

Lt. Col. Philip Reed is buried at nearby Christ Episcopal Church I.U.* (name of crossroads) near Worton; Brig. Gen. Benjamin Chambers is buried at nearby Chestertown Cemetery, Chestertown.* Sir Peter Parker's body was shipped back to London via Bermuda in a coffin filled with whiskey, and buried at St. Margaret's Church next to Westminster Abbey, London.

Among the text on the monument erected to Peter Parker at Westminster Abbey, London, it claims Parker "defeated an enemy, supported by cavalry & artillery, three times the number of his own force." The Americans were not directly supported by cavalry, the British slightly outnumbered the Americans, and the battle was at best a draw for the British, not a victory.

Dr. Peregrine Wroth wrote a poem commemorating the battle, entitled "The Battle of Caulk's Field." Kent County contributed a serving waiter that includes a depiction of the

Peter Parker, one of the Royal Navy's most promising young officers, was killed at the Battle of Caulks Field. (This sketch is based on John Hoppner's circa 1808-10 oil in the Greenwich Hospital Collection, National Maritime Museum, London; Lossing, *Pictorial Field-Book of the War of 1812*)

Caulks Field Monument to the U.S. battleship *Maryland* silver service made in 1906. It is now displayed at the Maryland statehouse.*

CEDAR POINT (confluence of Chesapeake Bay and Patuxent River, Patuxent Naval Air Test Center, St. Mary's County). Military establishment, limited access; area viewable by boat. The first naval skirmish in Maryland between the Royal Navy and U.S. Chesapeake Flotilla took place on June 1, 1814, off the shore of Cedar Point.

British account of skirmish: We wore round to Close the Enemy, who in his turn made Off and was ultimately chased into the Patuxent, where he arrived about Sunset . . . as the St. Lawrence & Boats rounded Cedar Point, the Flotilla opened its fire on us but at too great a distance to do execution, and as we were too feeble to attack the Flotilla. (Capt. Robert Barrie to Rear Adm. George Cockburn, June 1, 1814)[87]

American account of skirmish: off St. Jeromes [creek off Chesapeake Bay in St. Mary's County] we discovered a large ship underway, and that she had dispatched a number of Barges . . . the wind shifted to SW and squally, which brought the ship to windward of us and under a press of sail steering for point-look-out of course could cut us off from the Potomac, I then made the signal "for Patuxent," and was followed by a 74 [ship-of-the-line with seventy-four guns], the three schooners & Seven Barges, with a fresh wind, Squally & Rain (bad for my boats) at 4 PM we doubled round Cedar point in the mouth of this river, The barges in all sail, as the wind had hauled to the westward, & rowed up under the weather shore, The Scorpion [Barney's flagship, a block-sloop] worked in very well, but the Gun boats hung in the Rear, particularly Gun boat 137 (with provisions) The Enemies whole force very little astern, finding I must loose No. 137 or risk an engagement I brought the Scorpion, & gun-boat 138 to Anchor; sent men onboard 137 to Row & tow her in, the Tide & wind being against us, Signal'd my Barges to return and join me Imediately, at this moment No. 138 & myself opened a fire on the Large Schooner, who was leading in with a number of Barges, she Imediately bore up and got her boats ahead to tow her off; my Barges rowed down upon her and the other schooners and gave them a number of shot at long distance. We then gave up the chase, got under way with the Scorpion & gunboats and returned into port with all the flotilla, during the fireing, the enemy advanced a Barge which threw Rockets, but as they cannot be directed with any certainty they did no Execution, but I find they can be thrown further than we can our shot; and conclude from this Essay, this will be their mode of Warfare against the flotilla. (Com. Joshua Barney to Secretary of Navy William Jones, June 3, 1814)[88]

On June 3, 1814, the British burned Nicholas Sewall's home at Cedar Point, which had been used as a barracks by the local militia. They took his livestock and slaves, and then during a second raid on July 17, 1814, burned his warehouse. Earlier the British had burned Sewall's house during the Revolutionary War. (See Barney sketch showing Sewall house, Solomons.)

> I am just informed that the enemy landed last night at Cedar Point, carried off several Negroes and considerable stock, from a plantation belonging to Mr. Sewall. (Com. Joshua Barney to the Secretary of Navy William Jones, June 4, 1814)[89]

CENTREVILLE, originally called Chester Mill (head of Corsica River, Queen Anne's County). Centreville received its name because it was midway between Chestertown and Queenstown. Near here on the Corsica River, west of Centreville, an earthen fortification was constructed to protect the town from possible water attack. Fort Point,* as it was called, was never attacked and became a favorite picnic site on the Fourth of July. British troops under Col. Sir Sidney Beckwith skirmished with the 38th Regiment, Maryland militia, at Queenstown,* on August 13, 1813, after which the militia withdrew to Centreville.

> Eleven [British] deserters came into Centreville, and surrendered themselves, the day after the attack upon Queenstown[*]. (Baltimore Niles' Weekly Register, August 21, 1813)

Queen Anne's County Court House, constructed in 1796, is the oldest courthouse in continuous use in Maryland. It was built on Chesterfield, the ancestral home of Judge Joseph Hopper Nicholson. Francis Scott Key showed his handwritten poem, inspired by the bombardment of Fort McHenry,* to Judge Nicholson, his wife's sister's husband and commander of a volunteer company of artillerists at Fort McHenry. Nicholson had it printed. It is this handwritten copy of Key's poem that is believed to be the one now at the Maryland Historical Society.* Nicholson may have written the introduction and suggested the title for the poem as well.

After the news of peace with England reached Centreville, a public dinner was given there on May 24, 1815, at Samuel Chaplin's Hotel by the citizens of Queen Anne's County for their hero Lt. Col. Jacob H. Hindman. Hindman took part in various battles on the Niagara frontier from 1812 to 1814.

A slave named Nathan, belonging to Robert Gardner of Kent Island, having a "pert and lively look," was suspected of serving as a pilot for the British in their attack on Queen-

stown. He was arrested and put in the Centreville jail but escaped in February 1814. He likely joined the British and left with them at the end of the war. John Strachan (Stranhan), a resident of Centreville, was one of the four seamen taken by the British during the notorious June 22, 1807, Chesapeake–Leopard affair.* This incident brought the United States to the brink of war with England. Strachan had been previously impressed aboard H.M. frigate Melampus and afterward escaped and enlisted aboard Chesapeake.

> he [John Strachan] was pressed on board of the Melampus off Cape Finister [Cape Finisterre, Spain], to better his situation he consented to enter, being determined to make his escape when opportunity offered. He served on board the frigate two years. He is a white man, about 5 feet 7 inches high. (Easton Republican Star, August 4, 1807; see also October 6, 1807)

CHANCEFORD, also called Boxhaul and The Stanton Place (209 West Federal Street, Snow Hill, Worcester County). NHL. This Greek Revival home, known as Chanceford, was built between 1759 and 1792 and is reported to have served as a repository for the Worcester County government records during the War of 1812. Constructed of brick, Chanceford was considered safer than the wooden courthouse. It is now operated as a bed and breakfast.

CHAPEL POINT (overlooking Port Tobacco River, 8855 Chapel Point Road, near Bel Alton, Charles County). NRHP. St. Ignatius Catholic Church–St. Thomas Manor, founded in 1641, is situated on a ninety-foot hill overlooking the confluence of the Port Tobacco and the Potomac rivers. The U.S. Navy established an observation post at this strategic location to observe British ship movements on the Potomac River. Here citizens watched the British squadron advance up the Potomac in August 1814, which caused the officials of Alexandria* to capitulate. A British landing party also raided nearby Lower Cedar Point.*

CHAPTICO (head of Chaptico Bay, off Wicomico River, intersection of Maddox [Route 238] and Budds Creek–Deep Falls roads [Route 234], St. Mary's County). After landing at Hamburg,* British forces under Rear Adm. George Cockburn on July 30, 1814, marched to Chaptico and conducted a raid. The landing here, as well as landings at Lower Cedar Point* and Leonardtown,* were part of Cockburn's attempt to divert attention from his major objective, the capture of Washington via Benedict* on the Patuxent River—not the Potomac. At Chaptico many houses as well as the wharf and tobacco sheds were destroyed and the church was damaged. The British reportedly broke every pane of glass in the village.

★ **Christ Episcopal Church,** King and Queen Chapel. NRHP. Christ Episcopal Church was built in 1736 under the supervision of Philip Key, grandfather of Francis Scott Key. Several members of the Key family are buried in the Key vault, which is located immediately behind the church. The vault is identified only by "DEFAIS LE FOI." and the image of an eagle perched on a shield holding a key in its beak. During the British raid the church suffered damage to its marble floors when horses were reportedly stabled there. A raised wooden floor now covers the original damaged floor. In addition, the church organ was damaged and some grave vaults desecrated. The Maryland legislature approved a lottery in 1815 to repair the damage. Hence, most of the interior of the church dates from after 1814; however, the thick wooden front door with wooden lock appears to be original. The brick bell tower was added in 1913. The differences between the American and British accounts of this raid are striking.

British account of raid: passing the Night in the Boats I landed at daylight yesterday with the Marines about Three Miles below Chaptico, which Place we marched to and took Possession of without opposition. I remained all day quietly in Chaptico whilst the Boats shipped off the Tobacco which was found there in considerable quantity, and at Night I reembarked without molestation. I visited many Houses in different parts of the County we passed through, the owners of which were living quietly with their Families and seeming to consider themselves and the whole Neighborhood as being entirely at my disposal, I caused no further Inconvenience to [them], than obliging them to furnish Supplies of Cattle and Stock for the use of the Forces under my orders. (Rear Adm. George Cockburn to Vice Adm. Sir Alexander F. I. Cochrane, July 31, 1814)[90]

Second British account of raid: on 30th. We went 20 miles up the Wicomico River, there took possession of the Town of Chaptico—where some Ladies who had heard of our good behaviour at Leonards Town remained—and sang and played on the Piano. We took from thence 70 Hhds. of tobacco, some flour, & military stores but preserved their houses purchased from them stock and various articles of provisions. The men all fled, but the Ladies remained to see the wonderful [Rear] Admrl. [George] Cockburn and the British folks. (Capt. Robert Rowley's report to his superiors, August 1814)[91]

American account of raid: they [British] got about 30 hhds. [hogsheads] of tobacco and no other plunder, the inhabitants having moved all their property out of their grasp. Yet here they made a most furious attack on every window, door, and pane of glass in the village, not one was left in the whole . . . They picked their stolen geese in the church, dashed the pipes of the church organ on the pavement, opened a family vault in the churchyard, broke open the coffins, stirred the bones about with their hands in search of hidden treasure—all this in the presence of their worthy admiral. During all this havoc, not a man was in arms within fifteen miles of them, and they worked until ten o'clock at night, before they got the tobacco on board their vessels owing to the shallowness of the creek that leads up to Chaptico warehouse, they rolled more than half the tobacco one mile. [Brigadier] General [Philip] Stuart was encamped with the militia near sixteen miles from these free-booters; I presume he is waiting for a regular field action with the British. He has no confidence in our trees and bushes, as militia had in the revolutionary war. (Baltimore *Niles' Weekly Register,* August 14, 1814)

Second American account: I passed through Chaptico shortly after the enemy left it, and I am sorry to say that their [British] conduct would have disgraced cannibals; the houses were torn to pieces, the well which afforded water for the inhabitants was filled up, and, what was still worse, the church and the ashes of the dead shared an equally bad or worse fate. Will you believe me when I tell you that the sunken graves were converted into barbacue holes? The remaining glass of the church windows broken, the communion table used as a dinner table, and then broken to pieces. Bad as the above may appear, it dwindles into insignificance, when compared with what follows: the vault was entered and the remains of the dead disturbed. Yes, my friend, the winding sheet was torn from the body of a lady of the first respectability, and the whole contents of the vault entirely deranged! The above facts were witnessed by hundreds as well as myself, and I am happy to say, that but one sentiment pervaded our army. I immediately showed it to general Philip Stuart, lately commanding the American troops at that place, who read and declared it strictly true; that Cockburn was at the head of it; that they destroyed the organs; that judge Key's lady [relative of Francis Scott Key], who had been last put into the vault, was the person alluded to; that her winding sheet was torn in pieces, and her person wantonly exposed; and that his men were exasperated to desperation by this conduct. (Former Governor Robert Wright [1806–9], October 19, 1814)[92]

CHARLESTOWN (North East River, Cecil County). NHD. Like Alexandria,* Charlestown capitulated to the British on May 6, 1813, to prevent destruction of the town. A gun battery never used in defense of the town suffered from neglect, being washed down by heavy rains. A historical roadside marker (end of Conestoga Street at intersection with Water Street) near the location of the gun battery site claims the British destroyed the earthwork although no records have been uncovered to substantiate this claim. Two persons suspected of having supplied the British with provisions were arrested and sent to Brig. Gen. Benjamin Chambers at Charlestown.[93]

> I also had a Deputation from Charleston in the North East River, to assure me that that Place is considered by them as at your Mercy, and that neither Guns nor Militia Men shall be suffered there. (Rear Adm. George Cockburn to Adm. Sir John B. Warren, May 6, 1813)[94]

CHARLOTTE HALL, Cool Springs (St. Mary's County). Charlotte Hall served as the headquarters for the St. Mary's county militia in 1814. Secretary of State James Monroe visited here while reconnoitering the British landing at Benedict* and the British advance toward Washington in August 1814. Cadets from Charlotte Hall Military Academy were reportedly employed to help defend the nation against the British, but they are not known to have participated in any engagements. Only one building, the Old White House, survives from this period, erected as a classroom building and headmaster's residence in 1803 and restored in 1938. Just south (near the intersection of routes 6 and 236) is Dent Palace, site of the home of Dr. William Hatch Dent, who along with Clement Dorsey* and James Brawner warned the British at Benedict of a possible poisoning attempt.

> I have ordered on to Washington under an officer, who is directed upon his arrival to report himself to you, five prisoners and one deserter. The prisoners were taken on the 21 inst. by a detachment of Maryland militia under my command, aided by a squadron of horse from the district of Columbia under command of major [George] Peter. (Brig. Gen. Philip Stuart, Maryland militia, to the Secretary of War James Monroe, "Headquarters Charlotte Hall, June 23, 1814"; reprinted in Baltimore *Niles' Weekly Register,* July 2, 1814)[95]

CHEERY GROVE (southwest corner of intersection of Cherry Grove and Fingerboard roads, 1.6 miles west of intersection with Glebe-Pinewood Road, Cecil County). PRIVATE. Here lived and is buried Lt. Col. Thomas Ward Veazey, who served

in the 49th Regiment, Maryland militia, from 1810 to 1812 and who commanded Fort Duffy during the British attack on May 6, 1813, at Georgetown* and Fredericktown.* The historical roadside marker refers to Thomas Ward Veazey as colonel. In fact, he was only a lieutenant colonel.

CHESTERTOWN (Chester River, Kent County). NHD. The waterfront of Chestertown is lined with hansom homes of former merchantmen and ship owners. Chestertown, protected by an earthen gun battery that is now demolished, was never attacked.

Town Square (southeast side on medium between High and Cross streets). Immediately behind a sandstone memorial to the Kent County veterans of the Revolutionary War is a granite memorial to the veterans of the War of 1812. It simply says: "TO HONOR THOSE OF/KENT COUNTY/WHO FOUGHT SO VALIANTLY/DURING THE/WAR OF 1812."

Washington College (west side of Washington Avenue [Route 213], north of Chestertown center). Washington College, founded in 1782, boasts at least five alumni who fought at the nearby Battle of Caulks Field on August 31, 1814, including Judge Ezekiel Forman Chambers.* James Edmondson Barroll, another graduate, served as secretary and adjutant to the Troop of Horse in the Kent County militia.

Widehall (101 North Water Street). PRIVATE. Judge Ezekiel Forman Chambers lived at Widehall, built circa 1770. He commanded a company under Lt. Col. Philip Reed at the Battle of Caulks Field.* Ezekiel's father, Benjamin, served as a brigadier general in the War of 1812. Judge Chambers died at Widehall in 1866 and is buried in Chestertown Cemetery.*

Many members of the prominent Eastern Shore Nicholson family lived in Chestertown. This family did its part to help defend the country during the War of 1812. Joseph Hopper Nicholson sought a state commission in the militia but was barred from such service because he was a judge. As an alternative, he organized Nicholson's Fencibles, better known as the Baltimore Fencibles, a U.S. Volunteer unit. His uncle, Joseph H. Nicholson, Jr., served as a captain in the First Troop of the Queen Anne's True Republican Blues. His brother, James, served as a 2nd lieutenant in the horse troop of the same unit. A second brother, William, served as major of the 38th Infantry, Maryland militia. James Nicholson served as sailing master of U.S. gunbarge *No. 4* at Baltimore, which was assigned to the U.S. Chesapeake Flotilla.

He took part in the battles of St. Leonard Creek,* the Battle of Bladensburg, and the defense of Baltimore.

> We should have to fight hereafter, not for "free trade and sailor's rights," not for the conquest of the Canadas, but for our national existence. (Capt. Joseph Hopper Nicholson to Secretary of Navy William Jones, May 20, 1814)[96]

CHEVERLY (south of Bladensburg, Prince George's County). Cheverly is the site of Magruder Spring (also called Cheverly Spring, northeast corner of Columbia Park Road and Cheverly Avenue, south of Arbor Street) and Crawford's Spring (also called Crawford's Adventure Spring, northwest corner of Lockwood Road and Crest Avenue; the actual spring is located below in Cheverly Nature Park, west of Belleview Avenue, north of Lockwood Street, next to a large beech tree). The British reportedly used Magruder Spring, the water source for Mount Hope Plantation, during their advance on Washington and used Crawford's Spring on their return. While Crawford's Spring would have been along the British route and likely was used, the Magruder Spring location seems to be too far east for practical use. One British report mentions a stream but not a spring. A more likely watering spot would have been where Addison Road crossed Beaverdam Creek before I-295 and U.S. Route 50 disturbed the area.

> Numbers of men had already fallen to the rear, and many more could with difficulty keep up; consequently, if we pushed on much further without resting, the chances were that at least one half of the army would be left behind. To prevent this from happening, and to give time for the stragglers to overtake the column, a halt was determined upon, and being led forward to a spot of ground well wooded, and watered by a stream which crossed the road, the troops were ordered to refresh themselves. (Lt. George Robert Gleig, 1847)[97]

CHRIST CHURCH (Chaptico, St. Mary's County). *See* Chaptico

COLES LANDING (confluence of Coles Creek with Patuxent River, near end of Jones Wharf Road, off Three Notch Road [Route 235], Hollywood Shores, St. Mary's County). The British conducted several raids on the Patuxent, including one on June 18, 1814, at Coles Landing. Here Caroline Fenwick's house, previously occupied by militiamen of the 12th Regiment, was burned. As a result of these raids the Calvert County militia under Lt. Col. Michael Taney VI, eldest brother of Roger Brooke Taney,* was mustered but failed to stop the British depredations in the area.

COVE POINT (Chesapeake Bay, east end of Cove Point Road [Route 497], Calvert County). Restricted access. When the U.S. Chesapeake Flotilla sailed south to attack the British base established on Tangier Island,* it unexpectedly met a superior British naval force on June 1, 1814, off the mouth of the Potomac River and withdrew past Cedar Point* into the relative safety of the Patuxent River. During the engagement known as the Battle of Cedar Point, the British managed to separate a schooner and burn it just under Cove Point. Access to this point can be gained via a tour of the Cove Point Lighthouse, which is operated by Calvert Marine Museum, Solomons.*

> We wore round to Close the Enemy, who in his turn made Off and was ultimately chased into the Patuxent, where he arrived about Sunset . . . as the [H.M. schooner] St. Lawrence & Boats rounded Cedar Point, the Flotilla opened its fire on us but at too great a distance to do execution, and as we were too feeble to attack the Flotilla with the St. Lawrence and Boats, I endeavoured to tempt him to separate his force, by directing Lieutenant [George] Pedlar with the [H.M. ship-of-the-line] Dragon's Barge and Cutter, to Cut Off a Schooner under Cove Point, . . . and Commodore [Joshua] Barney allowed the Schooner to be burnt in the face of the Flotilla, without attempting a Rescue. (Capt. Robert Barrie to Rear Adm. George Cockburn, June 1, 1814)[98]

CRESWELL'S FERRY. *See* Port Deposit

DARES BEACH, also called Dare's Landing and Allnuts Landing (Chesapeake Bay, east end of Dares Beach Road [Route 402], Calvert County). On August 1, 1814, at or near Dare's Landing, a poorly documented skirmish took place between the Calvert County militia and a British landing party from H.M. gun-brig *Manly* and two gunboats from H.M. frigate *Severn*.

> I have proceeded twenty miles above Drum Point in H.M. Brig [*Manly*] . . . I landed with the troops about two o'clock the same day and found a Tobacco Store within a mile of the Beach, while the Seamen were rolling it [tobacco hogsheads] down we were attacked from a wood and a house a little way above us the Enemy's ferocious instantly returned by our Skirmishers and Captain Simson with the Marines rushed on to drive them out of the house & burnt it in five minutes there was not one of them to be seen having all retreated to the woods, they returned about an hour afterwards, but the instant we advanced they as quickly disappeared. Their numbers could not be quickly ascertained as never more than ten or twelve could be seen in one place but from the information I got from the Negroes I should suppose there were one hundred and forty of them and several

horsemen. We embarked without opposition at sunset with twenty Hogsheads of Tobacco after having burnt nine at the Store. I cannot speak in too high terms of the Steadiness and good conduct of the officers and men I had the honour to command and are happy to add that although exposed to a teasing fire from an Enemy who would only now and there be seen skulking among the trees and bushes we had not a Single accident. (Capt. Hugh Pearson to Capt. Joseph Nourse, August 3, 1814)[99]

The Militia are at last in Motion and on the Calvert Side have come as low down as the Court House [Prince Frederick*] hearing they had a guard over some Tobacco on the Bayside opposite St. Leonards Creek and a force differently stated from one to three hundred Militia in that neighbourhood I dispatched Captain [Hugh] Pearson in the [H.M. gun-brig] Manly with as many marines as I could conveniently send to Capture or drive away the Militia and bring off the Tobacco. (Capt. Joseph Nourse to Rear Adm. George Cockburn, August 4, 1814)[100]

At nearby Bayside Forrest is the grave of Capt. John Beckett, who attained the rank of captain in the 14th U.S. Infantry. On April 27, 1813, Beckett fought in the Battle of York (Toronto). He participated in the battles of Stoney Creek on June 6, 1813, and Crysler's Farm on November 11, 1813, and at Cook's Mills on Lyon's Creek, on October 19, 1814. At York he carried mortally wounded Brig. Gen. Zebulon Pike from the battlefield. After the war Beckett served in the Maryland House of Delegates and became the first Maryland state senator from Calvert County elected by popular vote. A copy of Beckett's 2nd lieutenant commission paper, dated July 23, 1812, and signed by President James Madison, is in the Calvert County Historical Society collections.

DECATUR, STEPHEN, PARK (intersection of Tripoli Street and Worcester Highway [U.S. Route 113], Berlin, Worcester County). Stephen Decatur Park commemorates the naval hero who served in the Tripolitan War (1801–5) and the War of 1812. Born in a nearby farmhouse on January 5, 1779, Decatur* moved to Philadelphia when he was only four months old. Decatur was a captain in the U.S. Navy during the War of 1812 and was killed on March 22, 1820, in a duel. Decatur's most notable quote comes from a toast he made after returning from the Barbary States at a dinner in Norfolk in 1815: "Our country! In her intercourse with foreign nations may she always be in the right; but our county, right or wrong!" This has often been shortened to "My country— may she ever be right, but right or wrong, my country."

DEEP FALLS (25040 Deep Falls Road [Route 234], near Chaptico, St. Mary's County). NRHP. PRIVATE. Dr. James Thomas (1785–1845), who lived at Deep Falls, which was built in 1745, served as a surgeon in the 45th Regiment, Maryland militia, in 1807 and as a major in the 4th Cavalry, Maryland militia, in 1814. He was brevetted a major general for his meritorious service. Dr. James also served as governor of Maryland from 1832 to 1836. He is buried in the family cemetery located among some trees east of the house. Deep Falls derives its name from the steep contour of the land at the back of the house.

DORSEY'S FURNACE SITE, also called Curtis Creek Furnace (south side of Furnace Branch off Curtis Creek, about 0.5 mile east of Ritchie Highway [Route 2], Anne Arundel County). John E. Dorsey established a furnace on Curtis Creek in 1759. Between April 12 and 16, 1813, this furnace supplied Baltimore with 80 6 pound shot, 80 4 pound shot, 85 French 36 pound shot, 386 French 18 pound shot, and 1,568 12 pound grape shot. In March 1814, the War Department contracted Dorsey to supply 300 tons of heavy shot (18 and 24 pounders), 10 ton of grape shot, and 60 traveling gun carriages. The furnace also supplied cannon for many of the barges in Com. Joshua Barney's U.S. Chesapeake Flotilla. Ordnance Road is named for this facility.

the Armament for them [eight barges built at St. Michaels*] is nearly ready, but I have been most cruelly disappointed in the delivery of the Guns (light 18 pounders) by Mr. Dorsey, he has trifled with us from the first, with promise from day to day, and it was but four days ago I was able to get from him the Guns, in fact, no dependence can be put, on his word. (Acting Mas. Com. Joshua Barney to Secretary of Navy William Jones, April 14, 1814)[101]

If her [U.S. frigate *Java*] lower battery is to be of the long 32's. of the new pattern (which will be the case if Mr. Dorsey can make them in time) and the spar deck battery of course of 32 pd. carronades, it will be necessary to attend to the Gun carriages in time. (Secretary of Navy William Jones to Capt. Oliver H. Perry, July 17, 1814)[102]

DRUM POINT (north side of the confluence of the Patuxent River with the Chesapeake Bay, off Rousby Hall Road, off Olivet Road [Route 760], Calvert County). PRIVATE, no public access. Best view is by boat. In the spring of 1813, at the mouth of the Patuxent River (probably Drum Point but could also be Cedar Point on south side of the river where the Nicholas Sewall* home was twice attacked), a fishery

One of the officers assisting the fatally wounded Gen. Zebulon Pike was Capt. John Beckett. This non-contemporary scene bears little resemblance to the fortifications at York and the town itself was out of sight to the east. (*Taking of York, and death of General Pike,* undated engraving; New York Public Library)

and planter's house were burned and cattle and twenty slaves carried off.

> There was but little property at the fishery that could be destroyed; but the enemy cut the seines to pieces, and, burned the sheds belonging to this place. They then marched up two miles into the country, burned the house of a planter, and brought away with them several cattle, that were found in his fields. They also carried off more than twenty slaves, which were never again restored to their owner; although, on the following day, he went on board the ship, with a flag of truce, and offered a large ransom for these slaves. (Charles Ball)[103]

The U.S. Chesapeake Flotilla took up anchorage under Drum Point circa May 31, 1814, on its way south to attack the British base at Tangier Island.* After unexpectedly meeting a large British squadron, the flotilla on June 1, 1814, withdrew into the Patuxent River. The British anchored H.M. frigate *Severn,* H.M. frigate *Brune,* H.M. gun-brig *Manly,* and three schooners across the mouth of the river to effect a blockade. H.M. ship-of-the-line *Dragon,* anchored under Drum Point, reported in its log on June 10, 1814, "heard the Report of Great Guns over the land N.N.W."[104] The sound came from a series of skirmishes known as the First Battle of St. Leonard Creek,* seven miles away. A contingent of militia under the command of Brig. Gen. Philip Stuart had

been encamped in the woods near Drum Point but left upon the arrival of the British fleet. Drum Point served as a watering place for the blockading British fleet from July to September 1814. In the space of a week more than ninety-nine tons of water was drawn there.

> [H.M. ship-of-the-line] Albion is completing her Water at Drum Point where I have established a most excellent Watering Place under the Guns of the Ship. (Rear Adm. George Cockburn to Capt. Robert Barrie, July 11, 1814)[105]

Drum Point also served as an anchorage and mustering point for the British invasion forces that ultimately landed at Benedict.* During a severe storm on July 25, 1814, a schooner serving as tender to H.M. frigate *Severn* capsized and one man drowned. Here lived Mr. Hopewell, a traitor who provided information about American troop locations and strengths. The British fleet again anchored under Drum Point on September 2, 1814, after safely re-embarking the troops who had successfully captured Washington. The British fleet again anchored under Drum Point at 6:20 a.m., September 18, 1814, after failing to take Baltimore. Wells were dug and provisions procured: "parties were sent on shore to dig wells in the sand, to which the boats resorted in great numbers for water. Cattle and sheep were likewise purchased from the natives; some of the flour which had

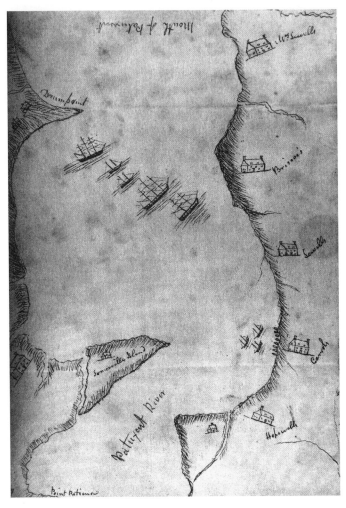

This August 1814 sketch by Com. Joshua Barney shows the British blockade at the mouth of Patuxent River off Drum Point. From left to right are the H.M. frigate *Brune,* two gunboats, H.M. frigate *Severn* and H.M. gunbrig *Manly.* Somervell (Somerville) Island is known as Solomons Island today. The Dr. William D. Somervell's house, the Nicholas Sewall house, and the Carroll house were all raided by the British. Barney's sketch shows three British schooners and eight barges raiding the Carroll Plantation. (National Archives and Records Administration)

been captured, was converted into biscuit, and every preparation seemed to be making for a long voyage" (Lt. George Robert Gleig, 1847).[106]

Rear Adm. Edward Codrington issued the following order to stem robbery and other offenses by the crews of the British ships:

> It has been represented to the Commander in Chief that plunder and Robbery has been committed on shore near Drum point upon even the poorest Inhabitants who have re-

mained quietly at their house under the faith of their property being respected; and that even women from some of the Transports have been guilty of enormities shocking to humanity.— It is therefore his positive order that no persons beneath the Rank of Field Officers and Captains of the Navy be allowed to go on shore except upon duty or by permission of a Flag Officer or the General— That no watering parties be permitted to go on shore before daylight or to remain there after dark, and that the guard stationed on the Hill to prevent straggling do not permit any persons whatever to go beyond the limits of their station without a pass; which pass the Officer is to countersign that he may know the persons in possession of it.— none of the Women are to be permitted to leave their ships.— A Commander will superintend the watering place for the day to see that order and regularity be observed beginning with the Senior— Boats will row guard at Night for the purpose of inforcing obedience to this order—. (Rear Adm. Edward Codrington to respective captains, September 3, 1814)[107]

The following day about 5:00 a.m. several men were flogged for drunkenness and two men hung for desertion. The British fleet weighed anchor 5:30 p.m., September 19, 1814, and departed the Patuxent, with one squadron sailing to Halifax with the remains of Maj. Gen. Robert Ross, who was killed at a skirmish prior to the Battle of North Point,* and another sailing to Bermuda bearing the body of Capt. Sir Peter Parker, who was killed at the Battle of Caulks Field.* The rest of the fleet was bound for Jamaica with troops that three months later would attack New Orleans.

DUELING GROUNDS. *See* listing, Bladensburg

EASTERN BAY (off Chesapeake Bay, south of Kent Island, Talbot County). The British conducted a raid on August 18, 1814, at Eastern Bay, capturing two small craft. Eastern Bay can be seen from the south end of Kent Point Road (Route 8).

> a ship, two schooners and a large sloop anchored off the mouth of the Eastern Bay in the evening two barges put off from them . . . captured a small boat and canoe, fired four guns, and after amusing themselves on the beach, returned to their vessels. (Easton *Republican Star,* August 23, 1814)

EASTERN NECK ISLAND (north entrance of Chester River, south end of Eastern Neck Island Road [Route 445], Kent County). John T. Durding, born in 1787 on Eastern Neck Island, served as a sharpshooter during the War of 1812. Lt. Col. Philip Reed,* commander of the 21st Regiment, Maryland militia, conducted a ruse on Eastern Neck Island to mislead the British on the size of his force. With the British encamped on Kent Island,* Reed directed his small force of cavalry to cross from the mainland at Trumpington Farm to Eastern Neck Island in full view of the British lookout-boats stationed at the mouth of the Chester River. By counter-marching and continually recrossing the river in a ferry scow the Americans hoped to make the British believe they had a much larger force. The ruse may have had some effect: "Running down the Eastern shore of Maryland on [August] 27th . . . I was surprized to observe the Enemy's Regular Troops and Militia in Motion along the whole coast" (Capt. Sir Peter Parker to Vice Adm. Alexander F. I. Cochrane, August 29, 1814).[108]

EASTON (Tred Avon River, Talbot County). NHD. Easton served as a center for military operations on the Eastern Shore of Maryland and therefore was considered a potential target of a British attack, although no such attack occurred. Fort Stokes* and two barges built by public subscription protected Easton from a possible water attack up the Tred Avon River.

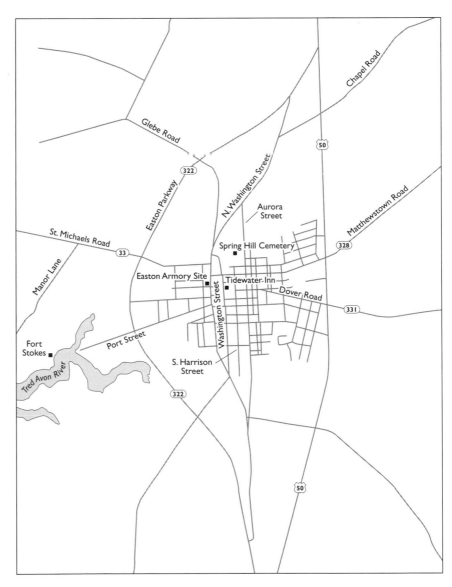

Easton

the town of Easton, being a place in which many of the public records are lodged, and in which too there is an armoury of the state, it is of importance that every protection and security, which can be afforded to it by either Government [federal and state], should properly be given. (Governor Levin Winder to Secretary of War John Armstrong, March 30, 1813; reprinted in Baltimore *Patriot,* May 22, 1813)

In a country so intersected by Rivers and Bays as ours, it is impossible to embody troops at all the points an enemy, having a naval superiority, may menace or assail. In this case it might be well to remove the armoury. (Secretary of War John Armstrong to Governor Levin Winder, April 13, 1813; reprinted in Baltimore *Patriot & Evening Advertiser,* May 22, 1813)

At least two prisoners captured from a tender of H.M. sloop *Dauntless* off James Island,* including Lt. Matthew Phibbs and a midshipman named Galloway, were sent to Easton, where they were given the freedom of the town. This caused so much concern among some of the citizens that Gen. Perry Benson,* who successfully commanded the defense of St. Michaels during two British attacks, ordered the prisoners taken by packet to Baltimore.

Several War of 1812 veterans came from near Easton: Capt. Robert Henry Goldsborough (1779–1836) of Myrtle Grove served in the 9th Cavalry, Independent Dragoons, Maryland militia, in 1813 and was promoted to major in 1814; William Hayward, Jr. (1787–1836) of Shipshead served in the 4th Regiment, Maryland militia, 1813–14; and Capt. John Leeds Kerr (1780–1844), buried at Belleville Cemetery (Spring Road) near Oxford Neck, served as a captain in the 4th Regiment, Maryland militia, and became division inspector of the 2nd Division in 1814.

American Legion Talbot Post 70 (29511 Canvasback Drive, east off Teal Drive, north off Dover Road [Route 331]). On the grounds of American Legion Talbot Post 70, formerly located on Dover Street, was mounted an 18 pounder carronade reportedly used at Fort Stokes.* The cannonade, named "Gentleman George," had been mounted on the courthouse grounds circa 1940. The Post plans to remount the carronade, now in storage, at its current location. A second cannon located at the Spring Hill Cemetery,* Easton, is also said to have been used at Fort Stokes but it is of post–War of 1812 vintage. While the 1812-era claim for the Spring Hill cannon can definitely be disproved, the carronade appears to be of the correct vintage, although its association with Fort Stokes remains unproven.

Easton Armory Site (east of courthouse green, which connects Washington and Harrison streets, where Courthouse Square Shops are located). The Easton Armory stood at this site until after 1900. It replaced an earlier powder magazine built on Magazine Alley. The 1812 armory occupied the public square behind the courthouse, where the Easton utilities building now stands. On June 9, 1861, a contingent of the 13th New York Regiment marched to Easton and seized arms to keep them out of the hands of Southern sympathizers. The cache included some muskets and cannon dating from the War of 1812. (*See also* Church Cove Park, St. Michaels.)

Carronade reportedly used at Fort Stokes in the defense of Easton. The fort was never attacked and the carronade never fired in anger. (Ralph Eshelman 2000 photograph)

Fort Stokes, also spelled Stoakes (North Fork of Tred Avon River, nearly opposite Easton Point at end of Port Street, off St. Michaels Road [Route 33]). PRIVATE. This fortification site can barely be seen from the end of Port Street looking across Tred Avon River. Fort Stokes, established about March 28, 1813, was built to defend Easton from an attack up the Tred Avon River. Located on Mr. Henry Hollyday's plantation, Ratcliffe Manor, Fort Stokes was named after James Stokes, a local shipbuilder and Methodist preacher whose shipyard workers largely built the earthen redoubt, which mounted six cannons behind breastworks and a structure built to house the fort's garrison. A contemporary account described the fort as "an embankment . . . thrown up, sufficient to effectually shelter 500 men, and entrench a score of pieces of artillery."[109] Although nearby St. Michaels was twice attacked in 1813, Fort Stokes never saw action but was manned when the British on October 19, 1814, raided up the Choptank River as far as Castle Haven.* After the war picnics were held at Fort Stokes. A cannonball from Fort Stokes is said to be located at the Alibi Club (1806 Eye Street) in Washington, D.C. (*See* American Legion Post 70, Easton, where a carronade reported to be from Fort Stokes was once was mounted.) Easton Point is where Capt. Clement Vickers,* who served at Fort Stokes, was originally buried. A private community is being developed at the site of Fort Stokes. The historic fort's earthworks are being preserved.

Tidewater Inn (101 East Dover Street). In the Hunter's Tavern dining room at Tidewater Inn is a series of sepia tone murals called *Historical Murals of the Eastern Shore* painted in 1951 by well-known Eastern shore artist John B. Moll. Two of them are War of 1812–related. *The Militia of St. Michaels, Maryland, preparing to repel the attack of the British Fleet during the War of 1812–15* depicts two traveling cannon being moved to the waterfront. The second smaller mural, partially obstructed by a partition, is titled *Taylors Island patriots capture the British ship Dauntless, aground off Parsons Creek—War of 1812–15*. The site of this capture was actually off James Point, James Island,* Little Choptank River; the capture was a tender from H.M. sloop *Dauntless,* not the *Dauntless* itself.

Union Tavern Site (corner of Washington and Goldsborough streets). Union Tavern or Public House, operated by Thomas Peacock, served as a popular militia rendezvous during the war. Peacock was reimbursed by the State of Maryland for providing $348.49 in provisions to the Talbot County Horse Troop in May 1813.

This two-story octagonal-shaped brick armory was built by the State of Maryland in 1811–12 and intended to serve the whole of the Eastern Shore. (Date and photographer unknown; courtesy Dr. Lawrence Claggett)

ELK NECK (peninsula between the Northeast River and the Elk River, south end of Turkey Point Road [Route 272], Cecil County). Local legend holds that the British landed on Elk Neck on April 28 or 29, 1813, resulting in a skirmish in which thirty British soldiers and three American brothers named Grace were killed and buried together in a crude grave at Turkey Point. The graves of the brothers were marked with rough stones, while those of the British were unmarked although the mounds of the graves were still visible as late as 1941. In 1995, State Terrestrial Archeologist Tyler Bastian investigated the site but failed to find any remains buried there. Furthermore, dispatches by Rear Adm. George Cockburn do not mention any men killed during a skirmish at Elk Neck. It is more probable that this skirmish, if it actually occurred, took place during the American Revolution when the British landed 15,000 troops to march on Philadelphia.

ELKRIDGE (Patapsco River, approximately southwest of Baltimore, Howard County). Units of the Baltimore militia camped at Elkridge on August 22, 1814, on their way to assist in the defense of Washington, D.C. In the cemetery of Melville Methodist Church (5660 Furnace Avenue), founded in 1777, War of 1812 veteran Sgt. William Earp is buried although there is no gravestone.

ELKTON, also called Head of Elk and Elk Landing (Elk River, Cecil County). When the British threatened Elkton in the spring of 1813, "a meeting of the people of the town and county was called, when not less than 200 convened at the court-house, and in a few minutes $1,000 was raised; a committee of three appointed; and on Saturday the ground laid out for three breast-works [forts Hollingsworth, Defiance, and Frederick]" (Baltimore *Patriot,* April 22, 1813).

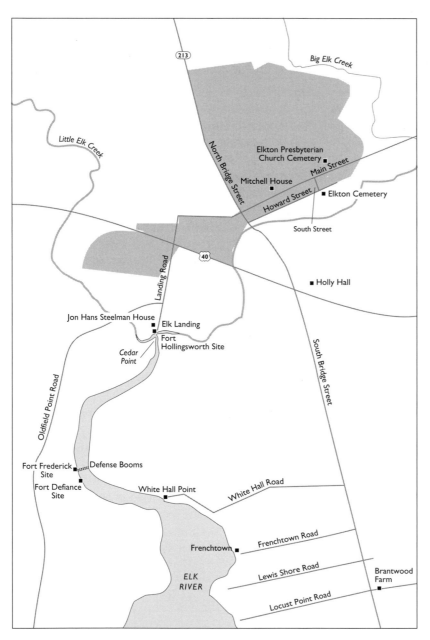

Elkton and Frenchtown Region

We have two forts [Defiance and Frederick] (tho small) and a chain across the river as an obstruction. An attack is more seriously apprehended by land and in this way we are as well prepared as the short term & the few troops I have heretofore permit. (Brig. Maj. James Sewall to Maj. Gen. Samuel Smith, May 7, 1813)[110]

On April 29, 1813, the American militia at Fort Defiance repulsed a British force of approximately 150 marines in at least 10 barges, saving Elkton and 30 bay craft from almost certain destruction.

American account of skirmish: the enemy made an attack . . . with 10 or 12 barges. From the extreme darkness of the night they succeeded in getting within a few yards of a small battery [Frenchtown?] before those who were stationed in it discovered them, when they opened a fire from a nine pounder charged with round shot & langrage, and supposed that considerable execution was done. There being but 14 or 15 men in the fort, and the enemy all around it, they spiked their cannon and retreated. Two small batteries [forts Frederick and Defiance?] placed in the town, with a few 6's in them, then opened their fire upon the barges, and in a few minutes compelled them to retreat with considerable precipitation, and they were seen about day-light towing a barge after them. It is not known what damage was done to the enemy, but it is supposed considerable fr. the great hurry with which they left the shore. (Alexandria *Gazette,* August 18, 1813)

The following year, on July 12, 1814, British barges attempted a surprise attack on Elkton but were again beaten off by an 11-gun battery. With more attacks likely, a contingent of 250 men from the Delaware Flotilla was sent with two cannon to reinforce the Elkton defenses.

American account of 1814 skirmish: Five barges were discovered on the river and about one o'clock they opened upon our view from behind a point, and point blank shot, say 1/2 a mile. We gave them in all eleven guns, so well directed, that they hastily put about and retreated down the river having fired but three at us, which did us no injury. (Brig. Gen. Thomas Marsh Forman to Martha Ogle Forman, July 12, 1814)[111]

Elkton was considered a possible landing place for a British land attack on Philadelphia; thus the Pennsylvania militia established a camp here. Elkton and St. Michaels* are the only places in the Chesapeake region known to have twice successfully repulsed British attacks.

Speech before the Pennsylvania militia who came to help defend Elkton: With a foe to contend with, who in our very infancy we have already humbled, we have nothing to dread if we are united.—Let us not be alarmed or discouraged by their plunder & burning, they will themselves become ashamed of the damned work and discontinue the brutal savage warfare. Let us act as virtuous citizens by banishing all party distinction until we have expelled the foe. To you, Gentleman officers and soldiers of the Pennsylvania militia in the name of the inhabitants of Elkton, I offer their warmest and most grateful acknowledgments. (Brig. Gen. Thomas Marsh Forman,* Elkton, May 22, 1813; reprinted in Easton *Republican Star,* June 8, 1813)

If Philadelphia is supposed to be an Object of greater Importance than the Places I have just mention'd [Baltimore, Washington, and Annapolis], I should deem the landing at Elkton the most advisable Mode of approaching it, as the intended Point of Attack would thereby be masked til the Army would be actually landed and on its March on the Road from Elton to Wilmington . . . this Movement need not prevent such Ships . . . from proceeding up the Delaware. (Rear Adm. George Cockburn to Vice Adm. Sir Alexander F. I. Cochrane, July 17, 1814)[112]

Judge Thomas J. Sample, although a fourteen-year-old boy at the time, later recounted what life was like at Elkton during the war:

I am an Elkton boy, . . . son of Captain John Sample [49th Regiment], . . . who served several years in the war of 1812, and was at Baltimore during the troubles there [account of June 26, 1880]; I was born on Nov. 4, 1800 . . . before the war we lived at the [Elk] Landing . . . My father . . . was captain of the company of infantry in camp Patapsco [Fort Covington], at Baltimore; and as my brother Samuel was in camp at Elk Landing, I had to be at home. I know that several times we— that is, my mother and brothers and sisters—had to flee to the country. We always went to our friend John Thompson's, in Delaware, about five miles . . . I don't remember how many times during the war we found that shelter, but several [account of September 3, 1881] . . . They burnt Havre de Grace. I saw distinctly the smoke ascending from that burning. It is almost sixteen miles, nearly due west, from Elkton . . . Often in the dead of night we would be aroused by the cry "THE BRITISH ARE COMING," and then we would have to seek shelter in the country [account of July 31, 1880] . . . There was a mud or earth battery built just below the old [Jon Hans Steelman] stone house which stood on the lower wharf [account of June 26, 1880] . . . There was a recruiting party in Elkton, the drummer of which, named Curtis, was the best drummer I ever heard . . . There was also a cavalry recruiting party here whose trumpeter, named French, exceeded any man I ever heard on the trumpet. Oh! I remember with great delight how delectable it was to be awakened almost daybreak by his trumpet notes, as he rode rapidly through the streets, sending forth such strains as he was wont to send forth to arouse me from a sweet sleep [account June 25, 1881] . . . After [Capt. Oliver Hazard] Perry's victory, our folks at Elkton made great preparations for an ox roasted whole, and all favorable to our side joined in the ovation. A day was appointed and a fine fat ox was procured and decorated with flags and ribbons, and accompanied by music. He was driven through the streets with this inscription on a large placard fastened to his horns: My horns, my hide, I freely give, My tallow and my lights, And all that is within me, too, For free trade and sailor's rights [account of August 14, 1880]; We could distinctly hear the booming of the cannon, during the bombardment of Fort McHenry, at Baltimore. (Elkton *Cecil Whig,* Judge Thomas J. Sample, "Recollections" and "Reminiscences," 1872 to 1881)[113]

Fort Defiance and Fort Frederick Sites (Fowlers Shore, west side of Elk River, east side of Oldfield Point Road, south of Elkton). PRIVATE. Two earthworks on the Elk River named Fort Defiance and Fort Frederick defended Elkton. At Fort Frederick, located about three hundred yards above Fort Defiance, a double chain stretched across the sixty-foot-wide river channel. The chains rested on the river bottom to allow passage of vessels but were raised by a windlass from within the fort to impede enemy vessels from moving up the river toward Elkton. Fort Defiance was the first fortification on the river below Fort Frederick. On April 29, 1813, Fort Defiance fired several shots at approaching British barges, forcing them to withdraw.

> The middle work [forts Defiance and Frederick] when finished, will mount seven cannon, one of them, a long 12 pounder, and its situation commands Frenchtown and Elkton. The channel can be swept the whole distance; it is 30 feet higher than the water, and the channel not 60 feet wide. An old vessel and a chain will be put across it. (Baltimore *Patriot,* April 22, 1813)

Fort Hollingsworth Site (east side of Elk River, south end of Landing Lane off Pulaski Highway [U.S. Route 40]). NRHP. This site is operated by the Historic Elk Landing Foundation. Fort Hollingsworth, under the command of Capt. Henry Bennett, served as the upper defensive earthwork on Elk River at Elk Landing.

> the ground laid out for three breast-works; one at Elk-Landing, one between the landing and Frenchtown, and one at Frenchtown. On Saturday [April 17] the first was nearly completed—300 feet of a semi-circle; and mounts five 6 pound cannon; the trench sufficient to contain 500 men—besides

this, at the landing, we have Captain [Zebediah] Snow's letter of marque [schooner *Atlanta*], with six cannon. (Baltimore *Patriot,* April 22, 1813)

On April 29, 1813, Fort Hollingsworth fended off a British landing party that had marched from White Hall Point* to Cedar Point opposite the fort. At the same time Fort Defiance repulsed a British barge probe up the Elk River.

When news of the Treaty of Ghent reached Elkton in February 1815, the citizens gathered at Fort Hollingsworth to celebrate. A frozen "clod" (a lump or chunk of earth or clay) was placed in one gun. When fired, it exploded, seriously injuring Capt. Ezekiel Forman Chambers.* (*See also* Rose Hill, for diary account of this incident.)

> There was a mud or earth battery built just below the old stone [Jon Hans Steelman] house which stood on the lower wharf. (Judge Thomas J. Sample, "Recollections" and "Reminiscences," Elkton *Cecil Whig,* June 26, 1880)

> There is no end to the warlike relics that have been lying concealed in the channel of the Elk River since the British army visited and destroyed Frenchtown . . . This week the dredgers exhumed a twelve-pound cannon ball, and a four-pound ball which has evidently been used as chain-shot and one end of what has been a twelve pound canister shot, from the channel of the river, a few hundred yards above Fort Hollingsworth, which were no doubt fired by the British upon that memorable occasion. (Elkton *Cecil Democrat,* April 28, 1881)

Holly Hall, also called Cecil Center (259 South Bridge Street [Route 213] near entrance to Big Elk Mall). NRHP. Brig. Maj. James Sewall, who commanded the Second Battalion at Fort Defiance during the repulse of the British probe up the Elk River on April 29, 1813, lived in the Federal style Holly Hall, built circa 1810. Sewall was buried in the brick family vault built into the slope west of the house in 1838. There is now a parking lot on the site, and it is unclear whether any of the graves were removed.

Mitchell House (131 East Main Street). NRHP. George Edward Mitchell* (1781–1832) was born at Mitchell House, built in 1769. Brevetted a colonel for his gallant conduct at Fort Oswego, New York, on May 5, 1814, Mitchell served in the 3rd U.S. Artillery.

White Hall Point (Elk River, end of White Hall Road, west off Augustine Herman Highway [Route 213], Cecil County). After their attack on Frenchtown,* the British on April 29, 1813, landed at White Hall Point, home of Frisby Hender-

The Jon Hans Steelman house, built circa 1700 and now in ruins, served as a tavern and an inn during the War of 1812. The earthworks forming Fort Hollingsworth were located immediately below this house. (E. H. Pickering 1936 photograph; HABS, Library of Congress)

son. From here they marched north across Cedar Point toward Elk Landing, defended by Fort Hollingsworth.*

ELLERSLIE SITE (6704 Chew Road, east off Blue Star Memorial Highway [U.S. Route 301], Prince George's County). PRIVATE. British soldiers stopped and rested at Ellerslie, site of a house and garden, during their return march from burning most of the public buildings at Washington. A later house dating from 1895 burned in 2008.

ELLICOTT CITY, then called Ellicotts Mills (Patapsco River, Howard County). NHD. After the Battle of Bladensburg, the American forces passed through Ellicott City on their way to defend Baltimore. Among the buildings that these troops passed are the Wayside Inn (4344 Columbia Road) and George Ellicott House (24 Frederick Road).

> the next day we encamped at Gaither's heights [Gaithersburg], thence to Ellicott's Mills, thence . . . towards Baltimore. (Col. William D. Beall)[114]

> a regiment of Virginia Militia under the command of [Lt.] Colonel [George] Minor is on its march to Ellicott's Mills

from Montgomery Court House [Rockville]. (Maj. Gen. Samuel Smith to General Singleton, August 27, 1814)[115]

Even after the Battle for Baltimore, militia were encamped in the Baltimore–Washington area because of fears of a second British attack. Two brigades of Virginia militia, for example, encamped from November 9 into December 1814 at Camp Crossroads, just outside of Ellicott City.

A 6 pounder cannon bearing a British crown is located near the entrance to the Howard County Courthouse on Capitoline Hill. It reportedly was captured at the Battle of Bladensburg. Since the British soundly routed the American forces, this is unlikely. Nevertheless, secondary source materials in the library of the Howard County Historical Society allege the Anne Arundel County militia captured the cannon during a lull in the battle. John Dorsey and Dr. Allen Thomas supposedly brought the cannon back to Ellicott City. While this story of capture may be correct, it seems more likely that the cannon was a trophy from the American Revolution, perhaps the Battle of Cowpens.

EMMITSBURG (north Frederick County). While Pennsylvania and Virginia were major producers of long rifles during the eighteenth and nineteenth centuries, Emmitsburg gunsmiths such as John Armstrong were noted for making some of the finest long rifles. The long rifle was properly called the "Pennsylvania rifle" and became known as the "Kentucky rifle" after a popular postwar song "The Hunters of Kentucky" had commemorated its use by Kentucky sharpshooters during the Battle of New Orleans.

The following Emmitsburg men joined the Maryland militia during the War of 1812, but their place of burial is unknown: Capts. Michael Sluss and Jacob Row and Pvts. Michael C. Adelsberger, Jesse Nusseur, Peter Remby, Felix B. Taney, and John Wetzel. Pvt. James Storm is buried at St. Joseph's Roman Catholic Church Cemetery* in Emmitsburg.

FAIRLEE CREEK (off Chesapeake Bay, Fairlee Public Landing Road, off Bay Shore Road, off Fairlee-Still Pond Road [Route 298], west of Fairlee, Kent County). PRIVATE. Henry Waller Farm, also called Big Fairlee and located on the west side of Fairlee Creek facing the Chesapeake Bay, was bombarded on August 28, 1814, by the Royal Navy under the command of Sir Peter Parker. (The original house, located near Fairlee Farm Lane, is gone; PRIVATE.) The Congreve rocket shell now on display at Fort McHenry* was fired at the Waller Farm. After the bombardment, a force of about a hundred troops raided the farm in retaliation for militia troops being posted there. The British burned every building on the farm, including the brick house, barn with attached granary, carriage house, brick dairy, corn house, two-story overseer's house, two slave quarters, and stacks of wheat in the fields.

> British account of raid: Early this morning we saw several militia men in full uniforms on the bank very near us, at ten a great many horsemen had collected round Genl. [James] Loyd's House [Big Fairlee], some dismounted, and came and reconnoitered the ship to drive them we fired a blank cartridge, at which they all but smashed their rumps; a shot was then fired, and they scampered off in style, but still a great many kept round the house. To dislodge them . . . some of Congreves Rockets . . . were well thrown afterwards, and some excellent shot from the 18 pdr . . . at five landed and . . . we then set fire to the house, which was nearly full of corn as well as ten outhouses and great quantity of corn in the ear . . . the Cavalry were latterly in three squadrons. I offered them Battle by advancing within one hundred yards of them, and giving them a sharp and galling fire for ten minutes which must have laid some of them low; they were extremely well

mounted—smashingly dress'd in Blue and long white feathers in their hats. Our fire completely routed them, at dusk no one was to be seen and we all embarked much pleased with our excursion; this is by far the finest part that I have seen in America. The house was elegant. (Lt. Benjamin George Beynon, August 28, 1814)[116]

American account of raid: On Sunday the 28th the enemy came on shore at the farm of Mr. Henry Waller, being on the Chesapeake Bay . . . and burnt his dwelling house, barns, all other out-houses, wheat in the granary and stack, and in short destroyed every thing by fire that they possibly could; his loss is estimated at eight or ten thousand dollars. (Annapolis *Maryland Gazette and Political Intelligencer,* September 7, 1814)

To secure reimbursement of his losses from the federal government, Henry Waller, Federalist, engaged Francis Scott Key as his attorney. Seventeen years later, after several petitions, Congress awarded Waller $7,000 in compensation.

> I have examined the proofs of Mr. Waller's claim before Congress . . . I am respectfully yours, FS Key. (Francis Scott Key to unidentified individual, December 27, 1831)[117]

On August 30, 1814, the British raided Great Oak Manor, which was built in 1762 and owned by James Frisby.* Although Frisby's wife persuaded the British to spare the house, they took poultry and four slaves, which the Frisbys later valued at $6,000. The British then landed at Farley, the farm of Richard Frisby (James's cousin), located on the south side of the creek. Located on a small bluff, it provided an excellent vantage point to monitor British movement. All the structures, valued at $4,450, were burned. It was one of Richard's three slaves or freed black that told the British of Lt. Col. Philip Reed's militia camp at nearby Belle Air (now Farilee). The British foray to this camp resulted in the Battle of Caulks Field. In 1838, Richard Frisby received $2,000 in compensation from Congress for his losses.

> we [British] saw several houses at the end of a large field, here we landed and marched up to it, we found some blacks who told us their masters were with the Cavalry, the house and nine considerable out houses [out buildings] besides ten rows of wheat were set on fire and burnt; while we were doing all this mischief a great many horsemen were close to us in the wood, they only made their appearance when we were imbarked—pulling out—a shot or two from the Barges soon dispersed them. (Lt. Benjamin George Beynon, August 30, 1814)[118]

FEDERAL HILL. *See* listing, Baltimore

FEDERAL REPUBLICAN. See listing, Baltimore

FELLS POINT. *See* listing, Baltimore

FERRY BRANCH. *See* listing, Baltimore

FERRY POINT. *See* listing, Baltimore

FLAG HOUSE AND 1812 MUSEUM. *See* listing, Baltimore

FORT BABCOCK. *See* listing, Baltimore

FORT COVINGTON. *See* listing, Baltimore

FORT DEFIANCE. *See* listing, Elkton

FORT DUFFY. *See* listing, Fredericktown

FORT HILL. *See* listing, St. Leonard Town

FORT HOLLINGSWORTH. *See* listing, Elkton

FORT LINCOLN CEMETERY. *See* listing, Bladensburg

★ **FORT McHENRY NATIONAL MONUMENT & HISTORIC SHRINE** (confluence of Northwest Harbor and Middle Branch, Patapsco River, east end of Fort Avenue, Locust Point, Baltimore City). NHL. Fort McHenry, originally named Fort Whetstone in 1776 for the point it is located on, was named in 1798 after James McHenry, then secretary of war. The star-shaped fort controlled the entrances to both the Northwest Branch and the Ferry Branch of the Patapsco River and thus served as the cornerstone of the water defenses of Baltimore. The present fort configuration dates from the late 1830s, not 1814. Postwar changes include the removal of the water batteries in 1829 and 1836, the raising of the bastions and ramparts, the addition of a second story to the barracks in 1829, and the removal of numerous pre-1814 structures located on the exterior of the fort. In addition, most of the guns date from after the 1814 conflict, including the big Rodman cannons, which are Civil War-era artillery. A partial reconstruction of the 1814 water battery was completed in 2005–6 and features two period 1809 French 36 pounder cannons. Six hundred yards across the narrows of the Northeast Branch from Fort McHenry to Lazaretto Point on the opposite side stretched a boom consisting of ships' masts laid end to end and fastened together by chains.

The garrison flag was raised at the fort at 9:00 a.m., September 14, 1814, as the Royal Navy sailed out of the Patapsco River. Because of the rainy, inclement conditions, the fort's smaller storm flag probably flew during most of the actual bombardment.

> We, Sir, are ready at Fort McHenry to defend Baltimore against invading by the enemy. That is to say, we are ready except that we have no suitable ensign to display over the Star Fort, and it is my desire to have a flag so large that the British will have no difficulty in seeing it from a distance. (Maj. George Armistead, commander of Fort McHenry, to Maj. Gen. Samuel Smith, 1813)[119]

During the twenty-five-hour bombardment (possibly forty-eight hours if one includes the range-finding shots fired by H.M. bomb-ship *Terror*), the British fired an estimated 1,800 explosive shells (bombs) while the fort's defenders were unable to reach the British fleet, which remained mostly outside the range of the fort's guns.

Prior to the Battle for Baltimore, Maj. George Amistead, commander of Fort McHenry, made a request for two ten-inch mortars located at the Greenleaf Point Federal Arsenal,* Washington, D.C. Although the mortars were sent, no shot, fuses, or carriages were included, rendering them unusable. Thus the fort did not have guns with sufficient range to match that of the British fleet. After the burning of Washington, federal officials, fearing a renewal of the attack on the capital, demanded that several cannons lent to Fort McHenry be returned. Maj. Gen. Samuel Smith, in charge of the defenses of Baltimore, replied that the government could have the guns but the carriages belonged to the city. As a result, the cannon were not removed.

> To the fleet the fort on the water was accordingly left, which by bombardment would, it was presumed, reduce it to ruins in a few hours . . . At last, when midnight was close at hand, a solitary report, accompanied by the ascension of a small bright spark into the sky, gave notice that the bombardment had begun. Another and another followed in quick succession. (Lt. George Robert Gleig, 1833)[120]

Marylander Maj. Gen. James Wilkinson,* former commander of the American forces on the Canadian front, said, "The defense of Fort McHenry was of no ordinary character, for the passive resistance of danger is the test of valor."[121]

> We were like pigeons tied by the legs to be shot at. (Capt. Joseph H. Nicholson, commander of the Baltimore Fencibles, to Secretary of War James Monroe, September 21, 1814)[122]

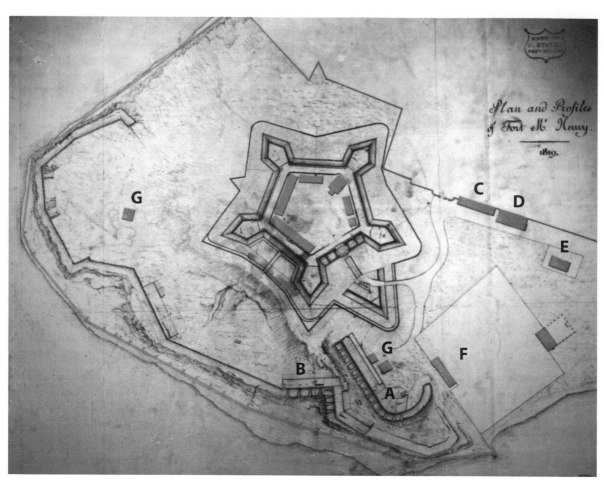

I do not feel able to paint out the distress and confution half as it was with us to se the wagons, carts and drays all in hast mooving the people, and the poorer sort with what they could cary and there children on there backs flying for there lives while I could see planely the British Sail which was ingaged in a severe fire on our fort for 24 Hours I could see them fire and the Bumbs lite and burst on the Shore at which explosion the hole town and several miles would shake—there bumbs waid upwards of 200 pounds which was throwd three miles, at least sum of them did not burst which I have seen in which there was Six pounds of powder for the purpose of bursting of them at this time we had our wounded fotch from the fort in to town with the wounded from the ingagement on land [Battle of North Point] below town a few mile[s] sum with there limbs broke and others with part of there limbs left behind, while two wagons were loaded with the dead. (Rev. James Stevens to his sister Julian Pernell, September 29, 1814)[123]

More than any other site, Fort McHenry has come to symbolize the U.S. experience in the War of 1812. The bombardment of the fort could be heard all the way to Elkton, Maryland, approximately forty-eight miles northeast of Baltimore. Judge Thomas J. Sample recalled that "we could distinctly hear the booming of the cannon, during the bombardment of Fort McHenry, at Baltimore."[124] A punch bowl given by Baltimore County and Baltimore City to the U.S. battleship *Maryland* as part of its silver service (and now on display at the Maryland statehouse* in Annapolis) depicts the bombardment of Fort McHenry. On exhibit in the fort's visitor center is a British 32 pounder incendiary Congreve rocket. This weapon inspired the words the "rockets' red glare" in "The Star-Spangled Banner," written by Francis

(Opposite, top) Plan of Fort McHenry showing its 1814 appearance. Note the brick-faced star fort and gun platforms along the Patapsco River outside the fort. Key: A. Upper Water Battery. B. Lower Water Battery. C. Gunhouse (1807). D. Storehouse (1807). E. Hospital (1814). F. Barracks and parade ground. G. Powder magazines. Other than the fort, only the foundations survive. (1819 plan; National Archives and Records Administration, Cartographic Section)

(Opposite, bottom) Detail of Fort McHenry depicting trees within the fort, the water batteries below and left, sunken ships and moored gun barges at left. The bulkhead-like linear structure along the shore are floating masts chained together and positioned by piles to prevent amphibious landings. The small structure above the water batteries is a hot shot furnace. While this drawing is considered accurate for its detail, the fort's garrison flag depicts an anchor in a circular star field. (Detail from *An Eyewitness Sketch of the Bombardment of Fort McHenry*, date and artist unknown; courtesy Maryland Historical Society; see p. 68 for another detail of this watercolor)

Scott Key. On or about September 17, 1814, every individual in the fort received a printed copy of Key's poem.

American account of the raising of the garrison flag (9:00 a.m., September 14, 1814): At dawn . . . our morning gun was fired, the flag hoisted, Yankee Doodle played, and we all appeared in full view of the formidable and mortified enemy, who calculated upon our surrender in 20 minutes after the commencement of the action. (Pvt. Isaac Munroe, Baltimore Fencibles, Fort McHenry, to editor, Boston *Yankee,* September 30, 1814)[125]

British account of the raising of the garrison flag: after bombarding the forts and harbor of Baltimore for twenty-four hours, the squadron of frigates weighed, without firing a shot, upon the forenoon of the 14th, and were immediately followed by the bombs [bomb-ships] and sloops of war. In truth, it was a galling spectacle for the British seaman to behold. And, as the last vessel spread her canvas to the wind, the Americans hoisted a splendid and superb ensign on their battery, and fired at the same time a gun of defiance. (Midshipman Robert J. Barrett, 1841)[126]

During the bombardment of Fort McHenry, a rooster reportedly climbed the parapet and seemingly crowed defiantly at the British. Tradition holds that one of the fort's defenders was so moved by the incident that he vowed he would treat the rooster to a pound cake if he lived to see Baltimore again. True to his word, he procured the promised cake the day after the bombardment. Similar rooster tales are told about the Battle of Trafalgar, October 21, 1805; the Battle of Lake Champlain, September 11, 1814; and at Parrott Point,* August 10, 1813, during the first engagement of St. Michaels, Maryland.

Jean Foncin, a Frenchman, redesigned the fortifications of Fort McHenry in 1799. He wrote Secretary of War James McHenry asking for a letter of reference. In the letter, he expressed hope that the fort would serve America well during its troubles with England. The letter was written in France on September 13, 1814, the day the British attack began on the fort. Ironically, during the Civil War the grandsons of Francis Scott Key and Lt. Col. George Armistead were imprisoned at Fort McHenry for siding with the South.

Armistead, George, Monument (near visitor center). The City of Baltimore Society of the War of 1812 donated this monument, which was designed to be a tribute to Lt. Col. George Armistead, the hero of Fort McHenry. Sculpted by Edward Berge, it was erected in September 1914. The inscription on the monument gives Armistead's year of birth as 1779, but it was actually 1780.

Armistead Headquarters (bottom floor of barracks near gunpowder house). Maj. George Armistead conducted the defense of Fort McHenry during the War of 1812 from this office. Here Armistead requisitioned the fort's garrison and storm flags made by seamstress Mary Pickersgill, both of which flew over the fort in September 1814.

British Bombs. Two British mortar shells are displayed at the fort—one in the visitor center and a second in the Maj. George Armistead headquarters. Capt. Frederick Evans, U.S. Corps of Artillery, second in command at Fort McHenry, took the first shell to his home in Columbia, Pennsylvania, after it fell harmlessly at his feet and failed to explode. The family donated the shell to the park in 1937.

The Armistead office example is a rare thirteen-inch carcass shell fired by the H.M. bomb-ship *Volcano* on September 13, 1814, during the night naval flanking assault on Ferry Branch. It is one of four carcass shells known to be fired that night to light the American shore defenses and to signal the beginning of the flanking attack.

Flag and Flag Staff Replica. In 1958, seven feet below the surface, archeologists discovered oak timber cross-braces that supported the original 1814 flag staff. An eighty-nine-foot-high replica flagstaff was installed in 1959 and then replaced in 1989. From this staff, a 30 by 42 foot replica garrison flag is flown, a tradition that continues to the present day, weather permitting. The original cross-braces are on display in the barracks.

Fort McHenry Memorial Trees and Markers (near the Francis Scott Key Orpheus Memorial). Between 1932 and 1933, thirty-five memorial markers and crab apple trees were placed in honor of heroes of the defense of Baltimore during the War of 1812. Several of the trees that died over the years were replaced in 2006.

Addison, Capt. William H.: THIS TREE DEDICATED TO CAPTAIN WILLIAM ADDISON WHO COMMANDED A COMPANY OF [U.S.] SEA FENCIBLES IN THE UPPER OUTSIDE BATTERY OF FORT MCHENRY DURING THE BRITISH BOMBARDMENT. PLANTED AND MARKED BY THE SOROPTIMIST CLUB OF BALTIMORE, SEPTEMBER 12, 1932.

Armistead, Lt. Col. George: THIS TREE DEDICATED TO [Lt.] COLONEL GEORGE ARMISTEAD COMMANDANT OF FORT MCHENRY DURING ITS BOMBARDMENT SEPTEMBER 13TH AND 14TH, 1814. PLANTED AND MARKED BY THE SOCIETY OF THE WAR OF 1812 IN MARYLAND, SEPTEMBER 12, 1932.

Barney, Comm. Joshua: THIS TREE DEDICATED TO COMMODORE JOSHUA BARNEY, U.S.N. AN ABLE BALTIMOREAN, WHO ORGANIZED AND COMMANDED THE BALTIMORE GUN BOAT FLOTILLA FOR COUNTER ATTACK AGAINST THE BRITISH FLEET IN THE CHESAPEAKE. PLANTED AND MARKED BY THE BALTIMORE CHAPTER NO. 7, NATIONAL SOJOURNERS SEPTEMBER 12, 1932.

Beeston, Thomas V.: THIS TREE DEDICATED TO THOMAS V. BEESTON PRIVATE IN THE WASHINGTON ARTILLERY OF BALTIMORE WHO WAS KILLED IN ACTION DURING THE BOMBARDMENT OF FORT MCHENRY SEPTEMBER 13, 1814. PLANTED AND MARKED BY THOMAS FOLEY HISKY, A RELATIVE, SEPTEMBER 12, 1932.

Berry, Capt. John: THIS TREE DEDICATED TO CAPTAIN JOHN BERRY WHO COMMANDED THE WASHINGTON ARTILLERY OF BALTIMORE IN THE UPPER OUTSIDE BATTERY OF FORT MCHENRY DURING THE BRITISH BOMBARDMENT SEPTEMBER 13 AND 14TH, 1814. PLANTED AND MARKED BY THE JUNIOR ORDER UNITED AMERICAN MECHANICS SEPTEMBER 12, 1932.

Bunbury, Capt. Matthew Simmones: THIS TREE DEDICATED TO CAPTAIN M. S. BUNBURY WHO COMMANDED A COMPANY OF SEA FENCIBLES IN THE UPPER OUTSIDE BATTERY OF FORT MCHENRY DURING THE BRITISH BOMBARDMENT SEPTEMBER 13TH AND 14TH, 1814. PLANTED AND MARKED BY THE JUNIOR ORDER UNITED AMERICAN MECHANICS SEPTEMBER 12, 1932. (This information appears to be incorrect. Prior to the battle, this entire ninety-three-man company of U.S. Sea Fencibles, a federal volunteer unit made up largely of U.S. Mariners, fell ill and was replaced by the U.S. Chesapeake Flotilla. Capt. Matthew Simmones Bunbury of the U.S. Sea Fencibles described the area of the fort as "One of the most sickly situations on the Patapsco.")

Clagett, Lt. L[evi].: THIS TREE DEDICATED TO LIEUTENANT L. CLAGETT OF THE BALTIMORE FENCIBLES WHO WAS KILLED IN ACTION DURING THE BRITISH BOMBARDMENT SEPTEMBER 13TH, 1814. PLANTED AND MARKED BY THE CITY OF BALTIMORE SEPTEMBER 12, 1932.

Clemm, Sgt. John: THIS TREE DEDICATED TO SERGEANT JOHN CLEMM OF THE BALTIMORE FENCIBLES WHO WAS KILLED IN ACTION DURING THE BRITISH BOMBARDMENT OF FORT MCHENRY SEPTEMBER 13TH, 1814. PLANTED AND MARKED BY THE CITY OF BALTIMORE SEPTEMBER 12, 1932.

Evans, Capt. Frederick: THIS TREE DEDICATED TO CAPTAIN FREDERICK EVANS WHO COMMANDED A COMPANY OF U.S. ARTILLERY WITHIN FORT MCHENRY DURING THE BRITISH BOMBARDMENT SEPTEMBER 13TH AND 14TH, 1814. PLANTED AND MARKED BY CITY OF BALTIMORE, 12 SEPTEMBER 1932. (Plaque missing.)

Fowler, Lt. Col. Benjamin: THIS TREE DEDICATED TO COLONEL BENJAMIN FOWLER WHO COMMANDED THE 39TH MARYLAND REGIMENT AT THE BATTLE OF NORTH POINT SEPTEMBER 12TH 1814. PLANTED AND MARKED BY THE SOCIETY OF THE WAR OF 1812 IN MARYLAND SEPTEMBER 12, 1932.

Frazier, Lt. John [Solomon]: THIS TREE DEDICATED TO LIEUTENANT JOHN FRAZIER OF CHESAPEAKE FLOTILLA WHO COMMANDED THE LAZARRETTO, A WATER FRONT BATTERY SUPPLEMENTAL TO FORT MCHENRY SEPTEMBER 13TH AND 14TH 1814. PLANTED AND MARKED BY THE SOCIETY OF THE WAR OF 1812 IN MARYLAND SEPTEMBER 12, 1932. (The correct name is Solomon Frazier.)

Hancock, Capt. Francis: THIS TREE DEDICATED TO CAPTAIN FRANCIS HANCOCK WHOSE COMMAND DISCOVERED THE ATTEMPT BY 1200 BRITISH MARINES TO SURPRISE FORT MCHENRY FROM THE REAR AND REVEALED THEIR BOATS TO ADJACENT BATTERIES BY LIGHTED FIRES ON THE OPPOSITE SHORE RESULTING IN REPULSE OF BRITISH SEPTEMBER 13TH 1814. PLANTED AND MARKED BY THE JAMES E. HANCOCK SOCIETY OF THE WAR OF 1812 IN MARYLAND SEPTEMBER 12, 1933. (According to one account, Capt. Francis Hancock's* company of the 22nd Regiment, Maryland militia, while patrolling in the vicinity of Wagner's Point, detected the British barge probe "and lighted a hayrick at Camp Fairfield, which threw [the British barges] into full view of the six-gun battery [Fort Babcock] and Fort Covington further up the river."[127] However, the credit for detecting the British barges is usually given to Sailing Master John Adams Webster at Fort Babcock.)

Heath, Maj. Richard: THIS TREE DEDICATED TO MAJOR RICHARD HEATH WHO COMMANDED THE BATTALION OF THE 5TH MD. REGIMENT THAT FIRST ENGAGED THE BRITISH ADVANCE AT THE BATTLE OF NORTH POINT WHERE THEIR COMMANDING [Maj.] GENERAL SIR ROBERT ROSS WAS KILLED SEPTEMBER 12, 1814. PLANTED AND MARKED BY THE 5TH MARYLAND REGIMENT. (*See* Old St. Paul's Cemetery, Baltimore, where he is buried. Ross is incorrectly referred to as Sir.)

Johnson, Edward: THIS TREE DEDICATED TO MAYOR EDWARD JOHNSON OF BALTIMORE, 1808–1816, WHO ORGANIZED THE RESOURCES OF THE PEOPLE OF BALTIMORE FOR THE DEFENSE OF BALTIMORE. PLANTED AND MARKED BY THE CITY OF BALTIMORE SEPTEMBER 12, 1932.

Key, Francis Scott: THIS TREE DEDICATED TO FRANCIS SCOTT KEY WHO WAS INSPIRED TO WRITE OUR NATIONAL ANTHEM THE STAR SPANGLED BANNER BY THE FLAG WHICH FLEW FROM FORT MCHENRY DURING ITS BOMBARDMENT SEPTEMBER 12TH AND 14TH 1814. PLANTED AND MARKED BY THE CITY OF BALTIMORE SEPTEMBER 12, 1932. (Key did not write the national anthem; he wrote a poem that after his death became the words for the anthem in 1931.)

Lane, Lt. Col. Samuel: THIS TREE DEDICATED TO COLONEL SAMUEL LANE COMMANDER OF A BATTALION OF [12TH U.S.] INFANTRY IN THE TRENCHES OF FORT MCHENRY DURING ITS BOMBARDMENT SEPTEMBER 13TH AND 14TH 1814. PLANTED AND MARKED BY THE CITY OF BALTIMORE SEPTEMBER 12, 1932.

Long, Lt. Col. Kennedy: THIS TREE DEDICATED TO COLONEL KENNEDY LONG WHO COMMANDED THE 27TH MARYLAND REGIMENT AT THE BATTLE OF NORTH POINT SEPTEMBER 12, 1814. PLANTED AND MARKED BY THE SOCIETY OF THE WAR OF 1812 IN MARYLAND SEPTEMBER12, 1932.

McDonald, Col. William M.: THIS TREE DEDICATED TO COLONEL WILLIAM M. MCDONALD WHO COMMANDED THE 6TH MARYLAND REGIMENT AT THE BATTLE OF NORTH POINT SEPTEMBER 12TH 1814. PLANTED AND MARKED BY THE SOCIETY OF THE WAR OF 1812 IN MARYLAND SEPTEMBER 12, 1933. (The 6th Regiment, Maryland militia, comprised of Baltimore County men, was held in reserve at the Battle of North Point, stationed at Cook's Tavern north of the battlefield.)

McHenry, Col. James: THIS TREE DEDICATED TO COLONEL JAMES MCHENRY SECRETARY OF WAR UNDER PRESIDENTS WASHINGTON AND JOHN ADAMS AND FOR WHOM FORT MCHENRY WAS NAMED IN 1798 WHEN IT WAS OFFERED TO THE FEDERAL GOVERNMENT. PLANTED AND MARKED BY THE FORT MCHENRY CHAPTER DAUGHTERS OF THE AMERICAN REVOLUTION, DISTRICT OF COLUMBIA, SEPTEMBER 12, 1932. (James McHenry named the fort after himself. He served as a surgeon on Washington's staff during the Revolution and was named the first secretary of war. *See also* Westminster Cemetery, Baltimore, where he is buried.)

Messenger, Charles: THIS TREE DEDICATED TO CHARLES MESSENGER GUNNER KILLED IN ACTION DURING THE BRITISH BOMBARDMENT SEPTEMBER 13TH 1814. PLANTED AND MARKED BY THE CITY OF BALTIMORE SEPTEMBER 12, 1932. (Charles Messenger was a crew member in Commodore Barney's U.S. Chesapeake Flotilla, assigned to service at Fort McHenry.)

Monroe, James: THIS TREE DEDICATED TO JAMES MONROE SECRETARY OF STATE, 1812–1816, AND THE ACTING SECRETARY OF WAR DURING THE BRITISH BOMBARDMENT SEPTEMBER 13TH AND 14TH 1814. PLANTED AND MARKED BY THE GENERAL SOCIETY OF THE WAR OF 1812 SEPTEMBER 12, 1933.

Newcomb, Lt. Henry S.: THIS TREE DEDICATED TO LIEUTENANT H.S. NEWCOMB OF BARNEY'S FLOTILLA WHO COMMANDED FORT COVINGTON A WATER FRONT BATTERY SUPPLEMENT TO FORT MCHENRY. PLANTED AND MARKED BY THE SOCIETY OF THE WAR OF 1812 IN MARYLAND SEPTEMBER 12, 1933. (Newcomb served on the U.S. frigate *Guerriere,* not the U.S. Chesapeake Flotilla.)

Nicholson, Capt. Joseph Hopper: THIS TREE DEDICATED TO CAPTAIN JOSEPH H. NICHOLSON WHO COMMANDED THE BALTIMORE FENCIBLES WITHIN FORT MCHENRY DURING THE BRITISH BOMBARDMENT SEPTEMBER 13TH AND 14TH 1814. PLANTED AND MARKED BY THE JUNIOR ORDER UNITED AMERICAN MECHANICS SEPTEMBER 12, 1932. (*See* Wye House, where he is buried.)

Pennington, Capt. Charles: THIS TREE DEDICATED TO CAPTAIN CHARLES PENNINGTON WHO COMMANDED THE BALTIMORE INDEPENDENT ARTILLERISTS IN THE UPPER OUTSIDE BATTERY OF FORT MCHENRY DURING THE BRITISH BOMBARDMENT SEPTEMBER 13TH AND 14TH 1814. PLANTED AND MARKED BY THE DAUGHTERS OF THE AMERICA, STATE OF MARYLAND SEPTEMBER 12, 1932.

Pinkney, Maj. William:* THIS TREE DEDICATED TO MAJOR WILLIAM PINKNEY, MARYLANDER WHO AS THE ATTORNEY GENERAL OF THE UNITED STATES, 1811–1814, WROTE THE DECLARATION OF THE WAR OF 1812, AND RAISED AND COMMANDED THE 1ST RIFLE BATTALION FOR THE DEFENSE OF BALTIMORE. PLANTED AND MARKED BY THE SOCIETY OF THE WAR OF 1812 IN MARYLAND SEPTEMBER 12, 1933. (Plaque missing.)

Rivardi, Maj. J. J. Ulrich: THIS TREE DEDICATED TO MAJOR J.J. ULRICH RIVARDI ARTILLERY ENGINEER EMPLOYED BY THE PEOPLE OF BALTIMORE IN 1794 TO DRAW UP THE PLANS FOR THE STAR BASTION FORT WITH UPPER AND LOWER BATTERIES. PLANTED AND MARKED BY THE WOMAN'S 20TH CENTURY CLUB OF BALTIMORE SEPTEMBER 12, 1932.

Rodgers, Comm. John: THIS TREE DEDICATED TO COMMODORE JOHN ROGERS [Rodgers meant] USN AN ENERGETIC MARYLANDER WHO FIRED FIRST SHOT OF WAR OF 1812 AND LATER ORGANIZED THE GENERAL ARTILLERY DEFENSE OF BALTIMORE. PLANTED AND MARKED BY THE SOCIETY OF THE WAR OF 1812 IN MARYLAND SEPTEMBER 12, 1932.

Rodmon, Lt. Solomon: THIS TREE DEDICATED TO LIEUTENANT SAMUEL [Solomon] RODMAN [Rodmon] WHO COMMANDED BARNEY'S MARINE ARTILLERY IN THE WATER BATTERY OF FORT MCHENRY DURING ITS BOMBARDMENT, SEPTEMBER 13TH AND 14TH 1814. PLANTED AND MARKED BY THE CITY OF BALTIMORE SEPTEMBER 12, 1932. (Rodmon's first name is Solomon, not Samuel, and his rank was sailing master, not lieutenant.)

Rutter, Lt. Solomon: THIS TREE DEDICATED TO LIEUTENANT S. RUTTER OF BARNEY'S FLOTILLA WHO COMMANDED THE BARGES THAT PROTECTED THE ENTRANCE TO THE HARBOR AS THE LEFT WING OF THE WATER BATTERY OF FORT MCHENRY. PLANTED AND MARKED BY THE SOCIETY OF THE WAR OF 1812 IN MARYLAND SEPTEMBER 12, 1932.

Smith, Maj. Gen. Samuel: THIS TREE DEDICATED TO MAJOR GENERAL SAMUEL SMITH U.S. SENATOR FROM MARYLAND 1803–1815 AND WHO COMMANDED THE CITIZEN SOLDIERS IN THE DEFENSE OF BALTIMORE. PLANTED AND MARKED BY THE STATE SOCIETIES CHILDREN OF AMERICAN REVOLUTION IN MARYLAND SEPTEMBER 12, 1932.

Sterett, Col. Joseph: THIS TREE DEDICATED TO COLONEL JOSEPH STERETT COMMANDED THE 5TH MD REGIMENT AT THE BATTLE OF NORTH POINT SEPTEMBER 12TH 1814. PLANTED AND MARKED BY THE 5TH MARYLAND REGIMENT SEPTEMBER 12, 1932.

Steuart, Col. William: THIS TREE DEDICATED TO COLONEL WILLIAM STEUART 38TH INF. U.S.A. COMMANDED A BATTALION OF INFANTRY IN THE TRENCHES OF FORT MCHENRY DURING ITS BOMBARDMENT SEPTEMBER 13TH AND 14TH 1814. PLANTED AND MARKED BY THE JUNIOR ORDER UNITED AMERICAN MECHANICS, STATE OF MARYLAND SEPTEMBER 12, 1932. (Tree missing.)

Stricker, Gen. John: THIS TREE DEDICATED TO GENERAL JOHN STRICKER WHO COMMANDED THE 3RD MARYLAND BRIGADE WHICH CHECKED THE BRITISH ARMY ADVANCE IN THE BATTLE OF NORTH POINT SEPTEMBER 12TH 1814, AND PREVENTED THE JUNCTION OF THE BRITISH ARMY AND NAVY OPPOSITE FORT MCHENRY. PLANTED AND MARKED BY THE NICLOLAS RUXTON MOORE SOCIETY, CHILDREN OF AMERICAN REVOLUTION IN MARYLAND SEPTEMBER 12, 1932.

Washington, George: THIS TREE DEDICATED TO GEORGE WASHINGTON PRESIDENT OF THE UNITED STATES, 1787–1797, WHOSE ORDER IN 1794 TO PREPARE FOR ANOTHER WAR AGAINST GREAT BRITAIN ENCOURAGED THE PEOPLE OF BALTIMORE TO BUILD THIS FORT AS DEFENSE OF THEIR CITY. PLANTED AND MARKED BY THE SOCIETY OF SONS OF THE AMERICAN REVOLUTION SEPTEMBER 12, 1932.

Webster, Lt. John Adams: THIS TREE DEDICATED TO LIEUTENANT JOHN A. WEBSTER, OF BARNEY'S [U.S. Chesapeake] FLOTILLA WHO COMMANDED FORT BABCOCK A WATER FRONT BATTERY SUPPLEMENTAL TO FORT MCHENRY, SEPTEMBER 12TH, 13TH, 14TH 1814. PLANTED AND MARKED BY THE SOCIETY OF WAR OF 1812 IN MARYLAND SEPTEMBER 12, 1933. (At the time of the Battle of Baltimore, Webster had the rank of sailing master in the U.S. Navy.)

Key (Francis Scott) Monument, Orpheus (west of fort near park entrance). In 1914, Congress funded this twenty-four-foot-tall statue, known as "Orpheus with the Awkward Foot," to mark the centennial of the writing of "The Star-Spangled Banner." Sculptor Charles H. Neithaus's design was selected from thirty-four submitted in a national competition. President Warren G. Harding delivered a speech during the unveiling ceremony on June 14, 1922, the first coast-to-coast radio broadcast by a president. Orpheus is depicted playing a lyre. The monument's marble base bears a medallion honoring Francis Scott Key, while the pedestal contains a time capsule filled with documents of patriotic and historical interest. In 1966, the statue was moved here from its original site near the fort's main entrance. Despite popular belief, the figure depicted does not bear any resemblance to F. S. Key.

Privateer Memorial (outside of main fort walls on southwest side). A small cannon dating from the era was erected to memorialize the privateers who not only harassed British shipping but brought in much needed supplies and funding to help pay for the War of 1812. This is the only known monument in the Chesapeake dedicated to this dimension of the war. The memorial plaque on the cannon is missing.

Water Battery Replica (between fort and Patapsco River shoreline). Thirty-two heavy cannon were mounted behind a defensive earthwork. A small section of the demolished earthwork has been re-created to illustrate its 1814 appearance. An interpretive panel discusses the importance of the gun battery and the type of guns that were placed here.

FORT MADISON. *See* Fort Severn, U.S. Naval Academy, Annapolis

FORT NONSENSE. *See* Fort Severn, U.S. Naval Academy, Annapolis

FORT POINT (south shore of Corsica River, end of Fort Point Road, off Corsica Neck Road [Route 304], west of Centreville, Queen Anne's County). PRIVATE. Fort Point, an earthen fort with a dry moat, high embankments, and redoubts for several cannon, was built to protect Centreville from an attack on the Corsica River. Neither the fort nor Centreville was ever attacked. Later the fort became a popular place for Independence Day celebrations, which included picnics, speeches, and gun salutes. Fort Point, although partially damaged by shoreline erosion, is among the best-preserved earthen fortifications in the mid-Atlantic region from the War of 1812. Because the fort is located on private property, it can be seen only from the water.

FORT SEVERN. *See* listing, U.S. Naval Academy, Annapolis

FORT SMALLWOOD (confluence of Rock Creek, Patapsco River and Chesapeake Bay, Fort Smallwood Park, Rock Point, northeast end of Fort Smallwood Road [Route 173], Anne Arundel County). Rock Point provides a splendid overlook of the mouth of the Patapsco River. Fort Howard Veterans Administration Hospital (under redevelopment), a tall brick building visible across the river at North Point,* is near the site where the British made their landing on September 12, 1814, prior to the Battle for Baltimore. Farther north is the Francis Scott Key Bridge,* near where British war ships bombarded Fort McHenry. Fort Smallwood dates from the Spanish-American period, not the War of 1812.

FORT STOKES. *See* Easton

★ **FORT WASHINGTON** (Potomac River, 13551 Old Fort Road off Indian Head Highway [Route 210], Prince George's County). NRHP. Fort Washington, originally named Fort Warburton after the estate on which it stood, was in 1809 completed and renamed to honor George Washington, who chose the defensive site in 1794. Both names were used during the War of 1812.

> Should proper works be erected on Digges's Point . . . at the junction of the Potomac and Piscataqua [Piscataway] Creek, it would not be in the power of all the navies of Europe to pass that place. (George Washington to Benjamin Stoddert, September 26, 1798)[128]

Fort Washington (Warburton), the earliest fortification built for the defense of Washington, offered a strategic location as the river channel narrows and swings close to the Maryland side, forcing ships to approach the fort bow on as they begin to pass up the river and then stern on after they pass. Only when directly opposite could a passing ship bring its guns to bear on the fort.

Lt. Theodore Maurice described the fort in 1815 as a small star-shaped earthwork with a circular gun battery in front. It mounted two 32 pounder, two 50 pounder, and nine 24 pounder guns. The fortification was based on the design of Fort Madison* near Annapolis (see p. 37). It was built at the ravelin (detached fortification with two embankments

projecting outward and forming a salient angle) adjacent to the 1898 Battery White that is located near the river outside of the walls of the main fort. A water battery closer to the shore mounted 18 pounder naval guns while behind the fort on the hill where the present stone fort is located was a brick octagonal blockhouse with six 18 pounder Columbiade guns. The British described the fort as a "most respectable defense," but Americans described it less confidently.

> the defense of the river depended on the sloop of war Adams, with a few small gunboats, and Fort Washington, a mere water battery of twelve or fifteen guns, bearing upon the channel in the ascent of the river, but useless the moment a vessel had passed. This work was seated at the foot of a steep acclivity, from the summit of which the garrison could have been driven out by musketry, but this height was protected by an octagonal Block house, built of brick, and of two stories altitude, which being calculated against musketry only, could have been knocked down by a twelve pounder. (Maj. Gen. James Wilkinson, 1816)[129]

> The mighty preparations made to resist this formidable over bearing force, is Fort Warburton, a mere pig pen with 13 guns mounted and a battery with seven guns more. (Baltimore *Federal Republican,* July 23, 1813)

In 1814, Fort Washington had a garrison of only forty-nine men under the command of Capt. Samuel T. Dyson, U.S. Army. Dyson ordered the fort blown up and the cannons spiked about 7:00 or 8:00 p.m., August 27, 1814, after a brief British bombardment by a squadron of six Royal Navy warships under the command of Capt. James Alexander Gordon. Dyson's decision allowed the British to take Alexandria* without the fort firing a single shot.

> if Washington (as I strongly recommend) be deemed worthy of our first Efforts, although our main Force should be landed in the Patuxent, yet a Tolerably good Diversion should at the same Time be sent up the Potowmac with Bomb Ships &ca which will tend to distract and divide the Enemy, amuse Fort Washington, if it does not reduce it, and will most probably offer other Advantages. (Rear Adm. George Cockburn to Vice Adm. Sir Alexander F. I. Cochrane, July 17, 1814)[130]

British account of fort's destruction: Fort Washington appeared to our anxious eyes, and to our great satisfaction it was considered assailable. A little before sunset the squadron anchored just out of gunshot, the bomb vessels at once taking up their positions to cover the frigates in the projected attack at daylight next morning, and began throwing shells. The garrison to our great surprise, retreated from the fort and a short time afterward Fort Washington was blown up, which left the Capitol of America and the popu-

A

This 1958 aerial view of Fort Washington shows the 1824 walled fort in the center and the Spanish-American War-era batteries located in the right foreground. Key: A. Approximate location of the 1814 fort, which is no longer extant. (Abbie Rowe 1957 or 1958 photograph; HABS, Library of Congress)

lous town of Alexandria open to the squadron without the loss of a man. It was too late to ascertain whether this catastrophe was occasioned by one of our shells or whether it had been blown up by the garrison, but the opinion was in favor of the latter. Still we are at a loss to account for such an extraordinary step. The position was good, and its capture would have cost us at least fifty men and more had it been properly defended. (Capt. James Alexander Gordon, August 27, 1814)[131]

American account of fort's destruction: The orders received from Brig. Gen. [William H.] Winder through Major [Robert G.] Hite, verbally, on the 24th inst. were, in case I was op-

pressed, or heard of an enemy in my rear, to spike our guns and make my escape over the river. The enemy approached by water on the 27th, and we had learnt that day through several channels that the enemy had been reinforced at Benedict 6000 [actually 4,370] strong, and that they were on their march to cooperate wish [with] the fleet, in addition to the force which left the city. Under all these circumstances, the officers under my command were consulted, and agreed it was best to abandon the fort and effect a retreat. The force under my command was thought not equal to a defense of the place. (Capt. Samuel T. Dyson to Secretary of War John Armstrong, August 29, 1814, Annapolis *Maryland Republican,* September 3, 1814)

Captain Dyson was placed under arrest and relieved of his command. He was afterward court-martialed, found guilty of abandoning his post and destroying government property. As a result, he was dismissed from the service.

> We were soon alarmed by a heavy cannonading, supposed to be at the Fort Warburton, and about 8 o'clock there was a most dreadful explosion. (Anna Marie Brodeau Thornton, August 27, 1814)[132]

> a smart cannonading commenc'd at, or from fort Washington, which continued from heavy Cannon till after 7 o'clock, during which it appear'd as if two or three severe explosions had taken place. (Capt. Thomas Tingey to Secretary of Navy William Jones, August 27, 1814)[133]

Endicott batteries were built at the fort in 1898 during the Spanish-American War. Two of them were named after War of 1812 heroes: Battery Decatur was named after Com. Stephen Decatur and Battery Many for Col. James B. Many, 3rd U.S. Infantry. The present fort bears no resemblance to the 1814 fortification.

With Fort Washington destroyed, the Americans erected batteries at White House* and Indian Head* to impede the British withdrawal back down the Potomac. Near Fort Washington the Americans unsuccessfully attempted to send fire-ships into the British squadron. (*See also* Mount Welby.)

> American account of a fire-ship attack on the British fleet September 4: The enemy's vessels dropt down the river from Alexandria on Friday night; and on Saturday com. Rodgers has possession of the unfortunate town. On Saturday two or three fireships were sent down to the frigates then lying off [Fort] Warburton, but did not take effect on them. The river was immediately covered with barges, thirty or forty in number, and these dangerous objects were towed out of the way of the vessels. The scene was witnessed from the high grounds of the city, and was very interesting—the river being covered with vessels and boats of almost every description. (Annapolis *Maryland Republican,* September 10, 1814)

FORT WOOD/CAMP LOOKOUT. *See* listing, Baltimore

FOUNTAIN INN. *See* listing, Baltimore

FOWBLE FAMILY CEMETERY. *See* appendix A

FREDERICK (south-central Frederick County). NHD. Frederick, located forty-four miles northwest of Washington, was considered safe from attack when the British occupied Washington. Hence, federal government funds and archives were temporarily stored here. U.S. Marine Lt. Col. Franklin Wharton and his paymaster took refuge in Frederick as did the Secretary of Treasury George Campbell and Secretary of War John Armstrong. One hundred and seven British prisoners were held in the county jail here although some accounts claim the Hessian Barracks* were also used. Another six British subjects of suspicious character were also held in custody.

The day after news reached Frederick of the defeat at the Battle of Bladensburg, Capt. John Brengle raised a company of about fifty men during a four-hour march through Frederick. Brengle's Company later served in the defense of Baltimore at Hampstead Hill.* Many of these veterans are buried in Mount Olivet Cemetery* in Frederick.

> At this place [Frederick], we have several hundred stand of arms, sent from the factory at Springfield [Massachusetts]. They at first appeared serviceable guns, highly burnished, but, upon personal inspection and trial, I find them very indifferent . . . A double charge I am convinced would burst half of them . . . Many of the balls not run to the calibre of the gun. These muskets cost the government sixteen dollars apiece; they have passed inspection, and have been issued as good serviceable guns! I do not know who are the inspectors for the Springfield factory. Such sir, are the arms with which we are to defend our county. (Philadelphia *General Aurora Advertiser,* June 30, 1812)

After the Battle of Bladensburg, an unnamed man who served as a British guide from Benedict to Upper Marlboro went to Frederick and mixed with the soldiers, making inquiries such as numbers and locations of troops. These were normal questions an American citizen might ask, but when he was recognized by one of the American officers who knew he had been with the British army, he was arrested as a spy. What became of him afterward is unknown.

Hessian Barracks, also called Frederick Barracks (242 South Market Street, on grounds of Maryland School for the Deaf). NRHP. Must make an appointment to visit inside the barracks. The stone Hessian Barracks, built in 1777–78, housed American troops during the War of 1812 and possibly British prisoners from the Battle of Bladensburg although most accounts claim the prisoners were taken to the county jail.

★ **Key, Francis Scott, Monument and Resting Place** (inside entrance of Mount Olivet Cemetery, 515 South Market Street). Francis Scott Key* and his wife and son, who had been buried twice before, were on October 1, 1866, re-interred in the family lot here with a simple gravestone. Key and his wife were moved to a crypt under the Key Monument in 1898. The monument, a gift of the Ladies Monument Association of Frederick, was designed by Alexander Doyle of New York City and executed by Pompeo Coppini, an emigrant from Italy. School children across the county contributed toward the cost of the monument. The central figure consists of a woman representing Columbia, the goddess of patriotism. She holds a staff in her right hand on which hangs the Fort McHenry garrison flag. On her left side is a teenage boy representing war, with his hand resting upon a sword. On her right is a young boy representing song or music, holding a lyre in his left hand and grasping the folds of the flag with his right hand. Beneath a bronze plaque is the seal of the state of Maryland. At the rear of the monument near the base is another bronze plaque bearing the words of the national anthem. On June 7, 1987, the Key Monument was restored and rededicated.

On the grounds of the cemetery just behind the monument is the Key Memorial Chapel, constructed in 1911 (open by appointment only). It contains the contents of the time capsule removed from the base of the Key Monument in 1998, including Key's bible, as well as memorabilia from the monument centennial dedication. The American flag flies continuously over Francis Scott Key Monument.

FREDERICKTOWN (Sassafras River, Cecil County). Rear Adm. George Cockburn burned Fredericktown and Georgetown* on May 6, 1813, after the militia offered resistance.

> in the name of God, gentlemen, for what purpose did I come here? I came here to fight and to defend the town, and I will do it, as long as I have a cartridge, or as a man will stand by me. (Lt. Col. Thomas Ward Veazey, Maryland militia, Easton *Republican Star*, June 1, 1813)

> American account of skirmish: The enemy still approaching gave three cheers, which was returned by the militia, and directly after, a volley from their small arms. The fire was immediately returned by the enemy, by a general discharge of grape, cannister, slugs, rockets, and musketry, which made such a terrible noise that one-half of the men

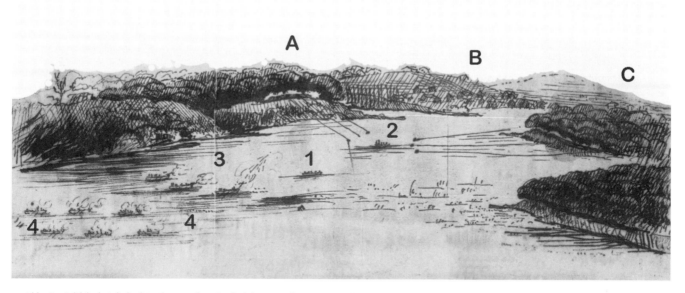

This 1813 British sketch depicts the attack on Fredericktown and Georgetown. Key: 1. Rear Admiral George Cockburn's boat. 2. Capt. Henry D. Byng's boat with 1st Lt. Frederick Robertson. 3. Launches with Congreve rockets. 4. Boats with Royal Marines. A. Fort Duffy. B. Georgetown. C. Fredericktown. Note that B and C are reversed; Fredericktown is actually on the north side (left) and Georgetown on the south side (right). The American battery on the left side of sketch is Fort Duffy and the battery on right side is Pearce Point Fort. North is to the left. (*Attack upon George & Frederick's towns by a detachment of boats from the R[ight] Honorable Sir. J.B. Warren's Squadron under Rear Admiral Cockburn in April 1813, Hon. Capt. Byng, Commanding*; Library of Congress)

shamefully ran, and could not be rallied again, whether it was from their political aversion to the present war, their dislike of shedding blood, or actually through fear, I cannot determine; but so it was that not more one half of the original number remained, to contend against the whole force of the enemy. This gallant little band resisted for near half an hour, in spite of the incessant fire of the enemy, until they were in danger of being surrounded, when they retreated in safety with the loss of but one man wounded. The enemy threw several rockets in the town (or rather village) and reduced the whole place to ashes, except two or three houses, saved by the entreaties of the women. Not satisfied with this destruction, they extended their ravage to the neighboring farm-houses, several of which were burned quite down. (May 14, 1813, Baltimore *American & Commercial Daily Advertizer*). (*See* Georgetown for British account of skirmish.)

Fredericktown consisted of a small tavern, a storehouse, three granaries, and seventeen houses. Ten victims reported the loss of dwellings, kitchens, meat houses, carriage houses, storehouses, and stables. Eight other owners reported the loss of furniture, clothing, and other property.

American eyewitness account of burning: Yesterday morning I witnessed a scene that surpasses all description. It was the little villages of George and Frederick towns, nearly all in flames. It would have excited sympathy in any human heart, except a savage, or still more ferocious Englishmen; and they you know are so much inured to villainy and destruction, that there is no mercy in their composition. It was [Rear] admiral [George] Cockburn himself, who led on the morn that tiger banditti, who committed the devastation. In the afternoon I repaired to the smoking, burning ruins, and found only a few houses standing, that had been spared at the entreaties of the women and aged; and these few, with one or two exceptions, nearly plundered of their all. Desks, bureaus, clocks, looking glasses, and such things as could not be carried off, were broken to pieces, and even beds cut open, the ticking taken off, and the feathers scattered to the winds. Even negroes cabins were reduced to ashes, or plundered of their scanty pittance of furniture and meat. (Washington *Daily National Intelligencer,* May 14, 1813)

In one building, belonging to John and James Allen, about a hundred barrels of sugar, casks of nails, barrels of pear ash, bales of hops, bolts of linen, trunks of dry goods, two large casks of tobacco, sails, and other articles were lost in the fire. The Allens put their loss at more than $8,000.

The inside works of the clock [from his house] they took on board the barge . . . Then my meat house, small granary, boat and fish house, containing fifty barrels of salt-fish; all my bacon, and one year's provision . . . My family Bible and the life of Washington [book] were taken away. Then the store was robbed of about $1200, on groceries; the heads of the liquor casks stove in, and mixed with molasses. (John Allen, 1813)[134]

all the vessels at the places [George-Town, in Kent, and Frederick-town in Cecil county, which are divided by the Sassafras river only,] were burnt, the militia dispersed with one killed; and notice given to Frederick-town to furnish immediately 12 bullocks [cattle], or the village would be laid in ashes . . . I open the letter at ten o'clock, to assure you, with sorrow, that both George-Town and Frederick-town were burnt down yesterday morning. This increasing wantonness seems most savage indeed. (Unidentified newspaper, Wilmington, Delaware, May 7, 1813; reprinted in the Annapolis *Maryland Gazette and Political Intelligencer*)

Only the tavern and seven dwellings survived the conflagration. Official estimate of losses among 30 inhabitants was placed at $15,871.07½. The Joseph Ward and John Ward farmhouses, about a mile from Fredericktown, and the Aguila Meeks house, about eight miles away (probably on Still Pond Neck), were also burned.

Fort Duffy, an earthwork built to defend the town, was destroyed circa 1985 during improvements at Skipjack Marina. A plaque dedicated to the men who defended the fort is located at the intersection of Duffy Creek Lane and Sassafras Street. It includes the names of thirty-six American defenders.

Col. [Thomas Ward] Veazey had for several days been assiduously employed in organizing a force to repel it [the British], but the militia did not turn out with as much alacrity, nor in such numbers as they have done. A small breast work was thrown up before the village of Frederick[town], upon which was mounted one small cannon, and about 70 or 80 militia was stationed in it, under the command of Col. Veazey, which was all the force that could be collected. (Easton *Republican Star,* June 1, 1813)

FRENCHTOWN SITE (Elk River, end of Frenchtown Road, west off Augustine Herman Highway [Route 213], south of Elkton, Cecil County). PRIVATE. Frenchtown during the War of 1812 consisted of a few dwellings, two warehouses, a tavern, outbuildings, and stables. Located on the original Baltimore–Philadelphia stage road, it became an important depot for military goods and agricultural produce. On April 29, 1813, following minor resistance by the local militia at Welsh Point, located about four miles below Frenchtown (at the confluence of Back Creek with Elk River), a British force of at least 150 Royal Marines landed from barges and

This 1806 watercolor depicts Frenchtown looking northward up the Elk River from the lower wharf on which the Americans established a gun battery in 1813. In the distance is the two-story Sewell's Tavern, also called the Frenchtown Tavern, built circa 1800, that stood until 1964, and the one-story frame Old Store House. The British burned the storehouse but the tavern survived. (Benjamin Henry Latrobe, *Rough sketch of French town, on Elk river, Cecil county Maryland*; courtesy Maryland Historical Society)

captured a gun battery built of logs defended in part by stage-drivers. The only reported casualty was one wounded British trooper. The British spiked the American cannons and destroyed a packet ship and four smaller vessels, along with a great quantity of flour, oats, army clothing, and other military equipment. Two storehouses and a fishery along with their contents estimated to be worth $300,000 were burned. Two cannon (or possibly separate ends of one cannon) reputed to be used at Frenchtown are located at nearby Brentwood Farm.*

> The work [gun battery] at Frenchtown mounts seven cannon. It is built on the east end of the wharf and commands the channel three miles down. (Baltimore *Patriot,* April 22, 1813)

> American account of skirmish: on the 29th day of April, 1813, about seven o'clock, A.M. a considerable British force, distributed into thirteen barges, commenced a hostile attack on a landing called Frenchtown . . . that some days previous thereto, a battery for five guns had been commenced on the wharf; but was in an unfinished state; that on the approach of the British force, eight or ten men collected and commenced firing from the battery, and stopped the advance of the barges for some time. The ammunition being expended, the barges then came on and a firing commenced of cannon shot at the battery and also at the dwelling house in Frenchtown. The British then landed on the wharf and immediately set fire to a new store house on the wharf, which at that time contained nothing but a large quantity of oats, the property of this deponent, and also a fishery adjoining the wharf was set on fire at the same time; after burning the said storehouse and fishery, a force of about two hundred and fifty marines . . . broke open the upper store house, which was that time full of goods, part of which was the property of the United States, and the remainder for different merchants of Baltimore, to the amount probably of fifty or sixty thousand dollars, and plundered and carried off part of the goods and set fire to the house and burnt it with

the remainder of the goods . . . the two store houses and fishery, together with the oats and property . . . sustained a loss of about three thousand dollars. (Alexander Kinkead's account, Annapolis *Maryland Republican,* November 20, 1813)

British account of skirmish: A heavy fire was opened upon our boats the moment they approached with its reach; but they [British forces] launched, with their carronades, . . . pulling resolutely up to the work, keeping up at the same time a constant and well-directed fire on it; and the marines being in the act of disembarking on the right, the Americans judged it prudent to quit their battery, and to retreat precipitately into the county, abandoning to their fate French Town and its depots of stores . . . the whole . . . consisting of much flour, a large quantity of army-clothing, of saddles, bridles, and other equipments for cavalry, &c . . . together with various articles of merchandise, were immediately set fire to, and entirely consumed, as were five vessels lying near the place. (Rear Adm. George Cockburn to Adm. Sir John Borlase Warren, April 29, 1813)[135]

Recollections from a then fourteen-year-old boy: I remember doing one day's work for my country at Frenchtown, helping to build a log battery on the wharf at that place by cutting and floating large trees from below there. The piratical bands from their [British] fleet afterward burnt several of Mr. Henderson's line of packets at Frenchtown. (Judge Thomas J. Sample, Elkton *Cecil Whig,* July 31, 1880)

Baltimore, May 1. FRENCHTOWN BURNT. The stage passengers from Philadelphia bring intelligence that two or three hundred of the enemy had landed below Frenchtown, and succeeded in burning a warehouse, containing 20 or 30,000 dollars worth of goods, two of the packets that ply between this [Baltimore] and Frenchtown, and some outhouses. A small garrison of a few men, stationed below the little town, retarded the operations of the British some time. (C.H.B. [Books], Washington *Daily National Intelligencer,* May 3, 1813)

GAITHERSBURG (central Montgomery County).

American troops camped at Gaithersburg on August 26, 1814, on their way toward Baltimore after retreating from Bladensburg via Georgetown, Tenleytown, and Montgomery Court House (Rockville). The exact location of the encampment is unknown but is believed to have been near a large oak tree that once grew along this road beside the railroad bridge in front of 5 North Frederick Street, where the Verizon switching station is now located.

the next day we encamped at Gaither's heights [Gaithersburg], thence to Ellicott's Mills, thence . . . towards Baltimore. (Col. William D. Beall, November 22, 1814)[136]

GAYLEARD CEMETERY. *See* appendix A

GEORGETOWN (Sassafras River, Kent County).

On the morning of May 6, 1813, Pearce Point Fort, on the Kent County side of the Sassafras River, and Fort Duffy, on the Cecil County side of the river, briefly defended Georgetown as well as Fredericktown* from a British attack. Georgetown consisted of a meetinghouse, Hastleton's Tavern, a cobbler shop, one or two merchant shops, a few old storehouses and granaries, and thirty houses. Of these, thirteen dwellings, stables and outbuildings, the cobbler's shop, the tavern, a granary, and a storehouse were destroyed. Furniture, apparel, musical instruments, books, and provisions were taken from another nine properties. After the raid, thirty of the town's residents petitioned the federal government for reimbursement for losses. While the Donlevys who lived at Montebello* did get some relief, it is not clear what if any restitution others may have received. The Maryland government gave some monetary relief to those who suffered at Fredericktown but gave nothing to the citizens of Georgetown.

British account of skirmish: having intercepted a small Boat with two of the Inhabitants . . . I sent forward the two Americans in their Boat to warn their Countrymen against acting in the same rash manner the People of Havre-de-Grace had done [who opened fire upon the British], assuring them if they did that their Towns would inevitably meet with a similar Fate [burning], but on the contrary, if they did not attempt Resistance no Injury should be done to them or their Towns, that Vessels and Public Property only, would be seized, that the strictest Discipline would be maintained, and that whatever Provisions or other Property of Individuals I might require for the use of the Squadron should be instantly paid for in the fullest Value . . . I soon found the more unwise alternative was adopted, for on our reaching within about a mile of the Town between two projected elevated Points of the River, a most heavy Fire of Musquetry was opened on us from about 400 Men divided and entrenched on the two opposite Banks, aided by one long Gun. The Launches and Rocket Boat smartly returned this Fire with good Effect, and with the other Boats and the Marines I pushed ashore immediately above the Enemy's Position, thereby ensuring the capture of his Towns or the bringing him to a decided action, he determined however not to risk the later, for the moment he discovered we had gained the shore, and that the Marines had fixed their Bayonets, he fled with his whole Force to the Woods, . . . the hot Fire we were under this Morning cost us five Men wounded one only however severely. (Rear Adm. George Cockburn to Adm. Sir John Borlase Warren, May 6, 1813)[137]

American account of raid: The British, with [Rear Adm. George] Cockburn at the head, proceeded to the village, and deliberately applied the flaming brand to the houses ... The ruin complete, the savages crossed to Georgetown, a village of about thirty houses in Kent county, where they, in a like manner, destroyed that place, with many houses in the vicinity. It is a satisfaction that some of the wretches paid the forfeit of their crimes—a good number of them were killed and wounded; nine in a single boat, about the whole loss is not known. The property destroyed is estimated at from seventy to eighty thousand dollars. (Baltimore *Niles' Weekly Register,* May 22, 1813). (*See also* Fredericktown for another American account of this skirmish.)

★ **Kitty Knight House** (14028 Augustine Herman Highway [Route 213]). The Kitty Night House (William Henry House) is one of ten or eleven houses that survived the British sacking of Georgetown. Kitty Knight is credited with saving the house by pleading with the British that an elderly lady occupied it. Miss Knight was renting the house during the attack and bought it in 1836. She lived there until her death in 1855. The William Henry House was later joined to the Archibald Wright House in what is now known as the Kitty Knight House Inn. Letters and writing samples from Kitty Knight, many written during the war, were at one time displayed in the house; their whereabouts today is unknown. In the sitting area is a twentieth-century mural depicting the attack of Georgetown and Fredericktown as well as a painting of Miss Kitty as a ghost at the door. A rocking chair now in the hall is said to have belonged to her. The original front door of the Henry House reportedly once showed damage from a British boarding ax.

Knight's grave is located several miles north at the historic Old Bohemia Church* near Warwick. As per her wishes, her tombstone reads "Miss Catherine Knight." The Kitty Knight House is depicted on a silver fish platter contributed by Cecil County to the U.S. battleship *Maryland* silver service set made in 1906 and now displayed at the Maryland statehouse* in Annapolis.

Montebello (nearly opposite Kitty Knight House Inn, east side of Augustine Herman Highway [Route 213]). PRIVATE. The Donlevys, who occupied Montebello that was built circa 1790, were fortunate in that their house was among the ten that survived the British attack but unfortunate in that their personal belongings such as clothing, musical instruments, and books were destroyed. They submitted a petition to the federal government for restitution amounting to $3,744.15 to cover their losses.

Other structures that survived the British burning include Valley Cottage (also called the Wallis House), a circa 1737 house located on the south side of Princess Way street (west of State Street); and the Archibald Wright House, a circa 1773 building located adjacent to the William Henry House and joined to it in 1928 to form the Kitty Knight House Inn. Just south of the Kitty Knight House Inn is the Presbyterian church. On this site a brick Presbyterian Meeting House survived the British raid but it was torn down in 1871 and replaced by the present structure.

GEORGE WASHINGTON HOUSE. *See* listing, Bladensburg

GODS GRACE PLANTATION SITE, also called Godsgrace (Patuxent River, end of Leitchs Road, off Stoakley Road, off Solomons Island Road [Routes 2/4], Calvert County). PRIVATE. James John Mackall lived at Gods Grace, where on July 17, 1814, British troops landed and took thirteen hogsheads of tobacco. From Gods Grace, the British marched to Huntingtown,* where they conducted a second raid.

[British] ascended as high as God's Grace, the property of the late George Mackall, when they debarked nearly 500 men, and demanded about 20 hogsheads of tobacco, belonging to Mr. Billingsley, the late tenant, and which they carried off, except three hogsheads, which they gave to an overseer or tenant of Doctor Bell's. (Baltimore *Federal Republican,* July 27, 1814)

I landed with the Marines . . . at a point about 3 or 4 miles above Benedict called Gods graces on the County of Calvert side and marched to Hunting town a distance of seven miles and destroyed a Store containing 130 Hogsheads of Tobacco, we returned by the same road, taking off from the Estate of Gods graces 13 Hogsheads of Tobacco. (Capt. Joseph Nourse to Rear Adm. George Cockburn, July 23, 1814)[138]

Commodore [Joshua] Barney . . . was seen with five of his Vessels at Anchor near Gods Graces by one of my boats. (Capt. Joseph Nourse to Rear Adm. George Cockburn, August 12, 1814)[139]

The British claimed that here or near Gods Grace Plantation Com. Joshua Barney had proposed "to get some people with Black faces & hands to [im]personate negroes begging to be taken off and to Surprise our Boat coming to fetch them" (Capt. Joseph Nourse to Rear Adm. George Cockburn, August 12, 1814).[140] If true, and that is doubtful, the plan was never carried out.

GOODWYN'S STEEPCHASE FARM. *See* Ridgely House, North Point

CORSUCH FARMHOUSE. *See* listing, North Point

CORSUCH POINT. *See* Lazaretto Point, Baltimore

GOUCHER COLLEGE (York Road [Route 146] south of intersection with Baltimore Beltway [I-695], Towson, Baltimore County). Epsom House (demolished, site between east side of Hoffberger Science Building and Kraushaar Auditorium of the Rhoda M. Dorsey College Center) was the home of Henry Banning Chew. A Revolutionary War cannon used during the War of 1812 was once mounted at a nearby federal powder magazine/armory located just north of Joppa Road at the intersection with Dulaney Valley Road. The cannon was brought to Epsom House as an ornament after the armory closed in the 1830s. Epsom Chapel was then built on the armory foundation. Epsom House burned in 1886, and the forgotten cannon was unexpectedly unearthed in 1953 during construction of the Julia Rodgers Library on the Goucher College campus. It was remounted there shortly after.

Unearthed about a hundred yards east of where it is now mounted, the cannon was probably cast at the Northampton Foundry* owned by the Ridgely family of Hampton Mansion.* Both the mansion and the foundry were located north of the armory. The site of the foundry now lies submerged below Loch Raven reservoir.

GRAHAM LANDING. *See* Lower Marlboro

GREAT MILLS TEXTILE FACTORY SITE, also called Clifton Factory (St. Marys River, Great Mills, St. Mary's County). In an unsuccessful attempt to develop cotton as an alternative crop to tobacco, a cloth factory was established at Great Mills in 1810. There were at least four mills located in this area. The St. Mary's County militia assembled at the factory on August 12, 1814, in an unsuccessful attempt to stem a British attack on the manufacturing complex located several miles inland from navigable waters. The mill was burned and the machinery for the factory was later moved to Savage Mills (Howard County) and Great Mills became a saw and grist mill.

> the Enemy had made a landing, by means of three schooners & 8 Barges at Carrols [Carrolls, on the Patuxent], and from Information it was supposed they intended the distruction of a Cloth manufactory belonging to Mr. Peter Goughf about

four miles from thence. (Com. Joshua Barney to Secretary of Navy William Jones, August 4, 1814)[141]

> We landed in various parts of this extensive Inlet [St. Marys River], and made some long Marches into the Country, particularly towards Sunset to a place they call the Factory of St. Mary's, where there is a building for Manufactoring Cotton, but (though Militia had certainly been formerly stationed at this Place for its defence) we did not meet with a Single Armed Person nor was one Musquet fired during the whole day. (Rear Adm. George Cockburn to Vice Adm. Sir Alexander F. I. Cochrane, August 13, 1814)[142]

> at a full trot we entered the village where the factory was placed . . . As the inhabitants had fled, with the exception of one or two old women, who disregarded us with all the vacancy of imbecility, we were blessed with a beautiful view of a "deserted village" . . . The houses were mere walls; the furniture was elsewhere: the population had flown, and a silence like that of the tomb prevailed. The crackling of the fagots, as the flames caught the factory, disturbed the repose: we most valiantly set fire to unprotected property, and, not withstanding the imploring looks of the old women, we like a parcel of savages as we were, danced round the wreck of ruin. (Capt. Frederick Chamier, 1839)[143]

GREEN MOUNT CEMETERY. *See* listing, Baltimore

GUNPOWDER COPPER WORKS, also called Hollingsworth and Company (10910 Harford Road [Route 147], 0.2 mile north of Factory Road, Baltimore County). PRIVATE. The Gunpowder Copper Works, owned by Baltimore merchant Levi Hollingsworth, operated along the Gunpowder Falls from circa 1812 to 1858 and from 1864 to circa 1866. This factory supplied copper sheathing, bolts, and nails for U.S. Navy vessels during the War of 1812. Much of the copper was shipped to Baltimore from Wales, and then hauled by ox cart to the copper works for rolling and fabrication.

Levi Hollingsworth served as a private in the 5th Regiment, Maryland militia. At the Battle of North Point on September 12, 1814, he was wounded in the left arm. He also invested in privateering vessels during the war. When Hollingsworth died in 1824, Isaac McKim, aide-de-camp to Maj. Gen. Samuel Smith* during the defense of Baltimore, took over the operation of the company. Apparently none of the period works survive except foundations. The spring house, built circa 1804, is said to be "restored" but appears to have been reconstructed. By the river, the mill race and ruins of other buildings are visible in the underbrush. The Gunpowder Copper Works was the only copper refinery in the United States south of Pittsburgh during the war and the second oldest copper works in the United States. The first, operated by Paul Revere near Boston, was established in 1801.

> [Levi Hollingsworth] went to England and studied thoroughly the rolling and refining of copper, and in 1814 built the Gunpowder Copper Works on the Gunpowder River, eleven miles north of Baltimore. Much of the machinery he brought from England with him, and the works were quite extensive, costing nearly $100,000. There were two sets of sheet rolls, two refining furnaces, and later, a cupola furnace for treating the slag, the power being furnished by water-wheel. The organization was somewhat bucolic, the men becoming farmers when business was slack, and rolling being apparently abandoned while the crops required attention. The copper itself came mostly in the form of bars or pigs of copper from the premises in the refining furnaces. (George Huntington Williams, 1880s)[144]

HAGER MUSEUM (110 Key Street, City Park off Prospect Avenue [U.S. Route 11], Hagerstown, Washington County). The Hager Museum contains collections related to the Hager House and Hagerstown, including a rare War of 1812 Maryland militia cavalry jacket that belonged to Sgt. Jacob Huyett of Capt. Jacob Barr's Cavalry Company, 1st District, Washington County. This unit served during the Battle for Baltimore. On the grounds of the museum is a cannon from Mount Aetna Furnace.*

HALL CREEK (Patuxent River, below Nottingham and above Lower Marlboro, Calvert County). Boat access only. On June 16, 1814, at the confluence of Hall Creek with Patuxent River, a U.S. Army Corps of Artillery unit of the 38th U.S. Infantry skirmished with British gun barges. Lt. Thomas Harrison, who was in command of the three-gun detachment, had crossed the Patuxent River at Nottingham in preparation to reinforce other units at St. Leonard Creek,* farther down the river, gathering in support of the U.S. Chesapeake Flotilla. At the urging of unarmed local citizens who reported marauding British troops in the area, Lieutenant Harrison lingered on the opposite shore just below Nottingham.* When they observed British barges moving up the Patuxent, they were able to drive them back with their cannon. This action saved Nottingham, which was otherwise unprotected from attack.

HALL'S LANDING (Queenstown Creek, Queen Anne's County). *See* Bowlingly Plantation, Queenstown

HALLOWING POINT (Patuxent River, east side of bridge carrying Hallowing Point Road [Route 231], Calvert County). On July 21, 1814, the British landed at Hallowing Point, where they destroyed the home and barn of Col. Benjamin Mackall and took twenty-one of his slaves. This action may have been taken because the house was being used by Lt. Col. Michael Taney VI, eldest brother of Roger Brooke Taney, as headquarters for his militia unit.

HAMBURG SITE (northeast shore of Wicomico River, Wicomico Shores, end of Army–Navy Drive, off Aviation Yacht Road, off Budds Creek Road [Route 234], St. Mary's County). On July 30, 1814, British forces under Rear Adm. George Cockburn landed at the small village of Hamburg and from here marched inland to raid Chaptico.* The British returned to Hamburg during the night, not reaching the safety of their fleet until 2:40 a.m., July 31.

> I landed at Hamburgh and examined in the course of the Evening the whole of the upper part of the River and passing the Night in the Boats I landed at daylight yesterday with the Marines about Three Miles below Chaptico, which Place we marched to and took Possession of without opposition . . . I visited many Houses in different parts of the Country we passed through, the owners of which living quietly with their Families and seeming to consider themselves and the whole Neighborhood as being entirely at my disposal, I caused no further Inconvenience to, than obliging them to furnish Supplies of Cattle and Stock for the use of the Forces under my orders. (Rear Adm. George Cockburn to Vice Adm. Sir Alexander F. I. Cochrane, July 31, 1814)[145]

HAMPSTEAD HILL. *See* listing, Baltimore

HAMPTON MANSION (535 Hampton Estate Lane, near intersection of Dulaney Valley Road [Route 146] and I-695, Baltimore County). NHS. Charles Carnan Ridgely (1790–1829), the second master (owner) of Hampton, also owned the nearby Northampton Foundry,* which supplied cannon to Baltimore privateers. Ridgely was commissioned a brigadier general in the Maryland militia in 1794 and served as a member of the Baltimore County Troop of Cavalry during the War of 1812. He also contributed a hundred barrels of flour worth $600 to Baltimore City to aid in the war effort. Two thirteen-inch British shells, one stamped with the British broad arrow, are located at the rear stair landing of the mansion. How these unexploded shells almost certainly from the bombardment of Fort McHenry ended up at Hampton is unknown. Ridgely is buried in the family vault at Hampton. The Ridgely family first lived at Ridgeley House,* North Point, which was used during the war as a signal station.

HANCOCK'S RESOLUTION (Bodkin Point near the mouth of Patapsco River, 2795 Bayside Beach Drive, Anne Arundel County). NRHP. Hancock's Resolution, built circa 1785, stands on what was then a four hundred-plus-acre farm. A second house on the farm was located on a high bluff overlooking the Chesapeake Bay near Appletree Road and Lake Drive. Capt. Francis Hancock,* who served with the 22nd Regiment, Maryland militia, during the defense of Baltimore, probably owned this second house, which burned down in 1931. Some sources credit Hancock with being the first to detect a British night flanking maneuver against Fort McHenry.* As early as the 1790s and as late as 1806, nearby Bodkin Point was used as an observation station to alert Baltimore merchants of the approach of their ships. A signal flag from Bodkin Point could have been seen at Ridgley House,* North Point, on the opposite shore of the Patapsco and that signal could then have been relayed to Federal Hill,* Baltimore. While Ridgley House and Federal Hill were part of a military signaling system in this era, no evidence has surfaced proving that Hancock's Resolution served in this capacity during the war.

The British entered Bodkin Creek and burned the schooner privateer *Lion* on August 24, 1814, the same day as the Battle of Bladensburg.

> A letter from Baltimore states, that the privateer schooner LION, commanded by Thomas Lewis, Esq. principal owner, had returned into L'Orient, in France, having on board about four hundred thousand dollars, taken from the enemy; besides having burnt from fifteen to twenty sail of British vessels. (Washington *Daily National Intelligencer*, December 16, 1813)

> The Enemy have several Gun Boats at Baltimore which have been twice driven in by His Majestys Ship, and on the 24th inst. Lieut. [William A.] Warre with two Boats burnt a Schooner in Narrows creek close to Bodkin point in face of these Gun Vessels. (Capt. Sir Peter Parker to Vice Admiral Sir Alexander F. I. Cochrane, August 30, 1814)[146]

While there is no public access at the waterfront to view this area and the mouth of the Patapsco River (which the Royal Navy entered on September 11, 1814), Fort Smallwood Park* offers a good vantage point.

HARRY'S LOT. *See* Barney House

HAVRE DE GRACE (Susquehanna River at confluence with Chesapeake Bay, Harford County). NHD. After a brief exchange of fire with the local militia in the dawn of May 3, 1813, a force of four hundred British troops in nineteen barges and supported by a rocket-vessel bombarded and occupied Havre de Grace.

British account of attack: I observed Guns fired and American Colours hoisted at a Battery lately erected at Havre-de-Grace . . . a warm fire was opened on the Place at Daylight from our Launches and Rocket Boat, which was smartly returned from the Battery for a short time, but . . . Captain [John] Lawrence . . . judiciously directed the landing of the Marines on the Left . . . Lieut. G[eorge]. A. Westphal . . . in the Rocket Boat close to the Battery . . . pulled directly up under the work and landing with his Boat's Crew got immediate possession of it, turned their own Guns on them, and thereby soon obliged them to retreat with their whole Force to the furthest Extremity of the Town, whither . . . they were closely pursued and no longer feeling themselves equal to the manly and open Resistance, they commenced a teasing and irritating fire from behind their Houses, Walls, Trees &c . . . soon succeeded in dislodging the whole of the Enemy from their lurking Places and driving them for Shelter to the Neighbouring Woods &c whilst performing which Service he had the satisfaction to overtake and with his remaining Hand to make Prisoner and bring in a Captain of their Militia—We also took an Ensign and some armed Individuals . . . setting Fire to some of the Houses to cause the Proprietors (who had deserted them and formed Part of the Militia who had fled to the Woods) to understand and feel what they were liable to bring upon themselves by building Batteries and acting towards us with so much useless Rancor, I embarked in the Boats the Guns from the Battery, and having also taken and destroyed about 130 Stand of small arms. (Rear Adm. George Cockburn to Adm. Sir John Borlase Warren, May 3, 1813)[147]

American account of battle: we were attacked by fifteen English barges at break of day. We had a small breastwork erected, with two six and one nine-pounder in it, and I was stationed at one of the guns. When the alarm was given I ran to the battery and found but one man there, and two or three came afterwards. After firing a few shots they retreated, and left me alone in the battery. The grape-shot flew very thick about me. I loaded the gun myself, without any one to serve the vent, which you know is very dangerous, and fired her, when she recoiled and ran over my thigh. I retreated down to town, and joined Mr. Barnes, of the nail manufactory, with a musket, and fired on the barges while we had ammunition, and then retreated to the common, where I kept waving my hat to the militia who had run away,

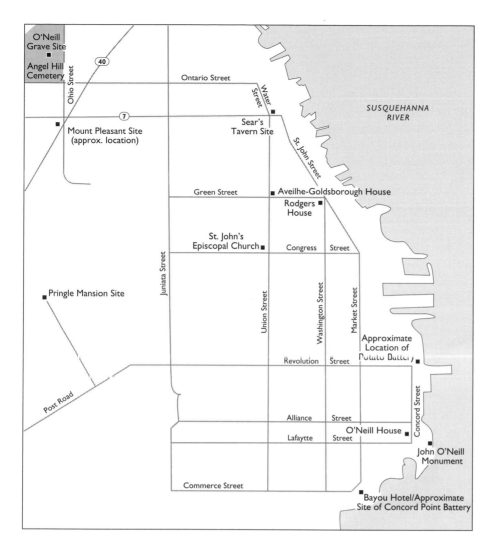

Havre de Grace

to come to our assistance, but they proved cowardly and would not come back. At the same time an English officer on horseback, followed by the marines, rode up and took me with two muskets in my hand. I was carried on Board the Maidstone frigate, where I remained until released, three days since. (John O'Neill's account, Baltimore *Niles' Weekly Register,* May 15, 1813)

Second American account of attack: On the report of guns we immediately jumped out of our beds; and from the top of the house could plainly see the [cannon] balls [could also have been Congreve rockets] and hear the cries of the inhabitants. We ran down the road, and soon began to met the distressed people, women and children half naked; children enquiring for their parents, parents for their children, and

wives for their husbands. It appeared to us as if the whole town was on fire. I think this act, committed without any previous warning, has degraded the British flag.

The enemy robbed every house of everything valuable that could be carried away, leaving not a change of raiment to one of ten persons; and what they could not take conveniently they destroyed by cutting in pieces or breaking to atoms . . . An officer put his sword through a large elegant looking glass, attacked the windows, and cut out several sashes. They cut hogs through the back, and some partly through, and then left them to run. Such wanton barbarity among civilized people, I have never heard of. (Eyewitness account dated May 7, 1813; reprinted in Baltimore *Niles' Weekly Register,* May 22, 1813)

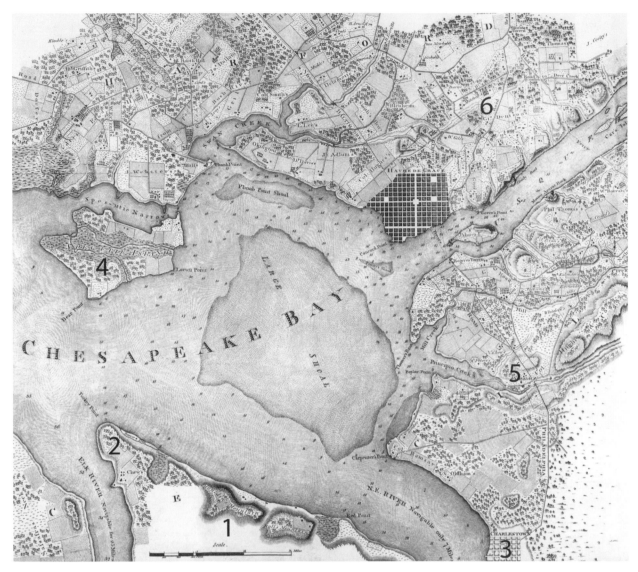

Detail of a 1799 map of the Upper Chesapeake Bay showing Havre de Grace. Key: 1. Bulls Mountain. 2. Elk Neck. 3. Charlestown. 4. Spesutie Island. 5. Principio Iron Works. 6. Sion Hill. ("A Map of the Head of Chesapeake Bay and Susquehanna River" by C. P. Hauducoeur 1799; courtesy of Enoch Pratt Free Library, Central Library/State Library Resource Center, Baltimore)

During the attack one British naval officer was wounded, while one American civilian, a Mr. Webster, was killed by a Congreve rocket.

a Congreve rocket . . . passed through the Battery and struck a man [Webster] in the back, when not a single vestige of him was to be found. This tremendous engine of death afterwards stuck the ground & forced itself full a mile into the country, tearing up everything in its way. (Capt. T. Marmaduke Wybourn, 1813)[148]

Of the town's sixty-two private homes, approximately forty were burned. The Maryland government provided $1,000 for the needy after the conflagration. At least one gunboat, *No. 7,* was built at Havre de Grace, but it is not known if it was used during the War of 1812.

Shortly after the raid, American satirist James Kirke Paulding (best known for his tongue-twister "Peter Piper picked a peck of pickled peppers") anonymously wrote a lengthy poem about the devastation of Havre de Grace called *The Lay of Scottish Fiddle: A Tale of Havre de Grace*. In it he wrote:

> Childe Cockburn carried in his hand
> A rocket and a burning brand,
> And waving o'er his august head
> The red-cross standard proudly spread,
> Whence hung by silver tonsil fair
> A bloody scalp of human hair.

During Fourth of July celebrations held throughout the state in 1813, many patriotic toasts were given, including the following: Commodore Rodgers (Havre de Grace native), "the noble Hero—May he revenge the fate of the Chesapeake" (referring to the *Chesapeake–Leopard* affair); and the brave [John] O'Neill, "Who has shewn to his adopted country what an emancipated Irishman can do" (Annapolis *Maryland Republican,* July 17, 1813).

Aveilhe-Goldsborough House (300 North Union Avenue). NRHP. The stuccoed brick Aveilhe-Goldsborough House, built in 1801, is one of the few homes that survived the burning of the town. Mary Goldsborough, Com. John Rodger's sister, lived here after 1816.

★**Concord Point** (Prospect Park, east end of Lafayette Street). Upon the elevation behind this point on which sits the Bayou Hotel Site* is the probable site of the Concord Point Gun Battery.* The monument and cannon erected in

1814 etching depicting the British raid on Havre de Grace. Rear Adm. George Cockburn is shown with his sword tip resting on the ground. Soldiers are pilfering private articles, shooting a hog, and burning private buildings. To the right a British officer is endeavoring to ride over two citizens. On the river is a barge with a coach that is probably the brass-studded chariot taken from Gideon Denison, Com. John Rodgers's father-in-law. A rocket-vessel is also depicted. ([William Charles] *Admiral Cockburn Burning & Plundering Havre de Grace on the 1st of June 1813. Done from a Sketch Taken on the Spot at the Time;* courtesy Maryland Historical Society)

1914 at Concord Point commemorate John O'Neill, who reportedly manned the Potato Gun Battery, which was located north of the Concord Point Lighthouse near the end of Bourbon and Fountain streets. This monument should be located farther north at the Potato Gun Battery Site.* For his bravery, O'Neill received a sword from the City of Philadelphia that can be seen at the Maryland Historical Society* in Baltimore. O'Neill apparently lived in a house on Washington Street between Fountain and Bourbon streets during the war. The respect for this man can be gleaned from the tax roll of 1814 when O'Neill's entry was recorded by the assessor as "List of property owned by the brave John O'Neal." This is the only known case in which the county assessor used this language.

One account claims John O'Neill's fifteen-year-old daughter, Matilda* successfully pleaded with Rear Adm. George Cockburn for the release of her father after he was captured during the attack. For her bravery, Cockburn supposedly gave her a gold-mounted tortoise shell snuff box, which can be seen at the Maryland Historical Society.* The snuff box is depicted on a silver entree dish contributed to the U.S. battleship *Maryland* silver service by Harford County, which can be seen at the Maryland statehouse.* Although the story is widely reported, actual documents indicate O'Neill was released on parole upon application of the magistrates of Havre de Grace. One contemporary report indicated a "Miss O'Neill" was among the town's committee members who visited the admiral under a flag of truce. She may very well have pleaded for her father's release then and received the snuff box, but if so she was far from alone.

The Maryland Historical Roadside Marker here claims there were "two small batteries on Concord Point." Only one gun battery was located at Concord Point; the other was the Potato Gun Battery located a few blocks farther to the north. A plaque on a cannon at Concord Point states that O'Neill served at the Concord Battery, but he was actually at the Potato Battery. It also says that O'Neill "was released from the British frigate Maidstone through the intercession of his young daughter Matilda," although she did not intercede on his behalf alone. Finally, the plaque claims that O'Neill served the guns of the battery "until disabled and captured." O'Neill was not captured at the gun battery but later in town, where he unsuccessfully attempted to rally the militia.

Concord Point Gun Battery/Bayou Hotel Site (south end of Market Street). PRIVATE. On the site of the former Bayou Hotel, which is now apartments, lies the probable site of the Concord Point Gun Battery, one of at least two earthworks built to defend Havre de Grace. Erosion of the bluff may have destroyed part or all of the original battery site.

Mount Pleasant Site (northwest of town near the intersection of routes 40 and 7). Col. Samuel Hughes, owner of the nearby Principio Iron Works,* lived here. After his furnace was destroyed by the British on May 3, 1813, he was forced to mortgage the wood, coal, ore, and iron at his furnace to raise the funds to reopen it the same year. But he never fully got out of debt and in 1823 was forced to sell Mount Pleasant. Daniel Mallory, his wife, and his child, traveling from Philadelphia, were awakened from their sleep by the cannon fire while staying at the Sears Tavern in town. Fleeing, they took refuge at Mount Pleasant.

> Just as the day dawned I was awakened by the report of heavy artillery. It neared with fearful rapidity. I had scarcely time to realize what it was, and our critical situation, when we were startled with a loud report in our room, accompanied with pieces of the wall flying in all directions! This was followed quickly with continuous showers of grapeshot, some entering through the upper part of the windows, cutting away the plaster over our heads, while others lodged in the roof. I ran to the window, but there was nothing to be seen but a few men without uniforms, behind a barn, who were evidently preparing to fight . . . My wife had no time to dress herself, or her infant. I threw her travelling dress over her shoulders, and in this deplorable condition we made our exit by the back door; and I believe we were the last that made their escape from this ill-fated house [Sear's Tavern]. The air seemed alive with congreve rockets, squirming and hissing about like so many fiery serpents. The hills were covered with flying, frightened, and haft-dressed people. (Daniel Mallory, 1842)[149]

O'Neill House, also called lighthouse keepers house (Concord Street, opposite lighthouse). For his heroism in the unsuccessful defense of Havre de Grace during the British raid, John O'Neill in 1827 was appointed by President John Quincy Adams as the first keeper of the newly built Concord Point Lighthouse. O'Neill retained this position and lived in the keepers house until his death in 1838.

William B. Barney,* son of Com. Joshua Barney* and hero during the First Battle of St. Leonard Creek, became a regional naval officer who was responsible for overseeing lighthouse construction. Having a warm spot in his heart for veterans of the War of 1812, he may have used his influence to secure the appointment of several veterans to serve as lighthouse keepers, a much sought-after government job

Several women, including the wives of Maj. William Pringle, Howes Goldsborough, and Com. John Rodgers, took refuge at the Pringle House during the British raid on Havre de Grace. This image shows the house as it appeared in the 1850s. (Lossing, *Pictorial Field-Book of the War of 1812*)

because of its steady income. At least two 1812 veterans became lighthouse keepers, including John O'Neill and Pvt. Samuel Cooper.* Cooper was present at the Battle of North Point and became keeper of Lazaretto Lighthouse, Baltimore, for twenty-five years. A third veteran, Capt. Solomon Frazier, commanded the Lazaretto Gun Battery* during the defense of Baltimore and later became the first keeper of the North Point Lighthouse, although in his case the appointment was probably more a result of his political connections than his war record.

Potato Gun Battery Site (between the east ends of Bourbon and Fountain streets near the intersection with Market Street where Tidewater Marina located). Potato Gun Battery, so called because of its shape, is one of two gun batteries built to protect Havre de Grave. Here is where John O'Neill heroically fought, not at Concord Point Gun Battery* as most accounts claim.

Pringle Mansion Site, also called Bloomsbury (area around Lewis Lane, off Post Road [Route 7]). Mark Pringle (1750–1819) built a six hundred-acre estate called Bloomsbury.

About two-thirds of the estate is now part of the incorporated town. The Pringle Mansion, a two-and-one-half-story five-bay brick house begun in 1808 and finished in 1812, was in 1863 called "the finest country residence in the state."[150] The grave of Maj. William Pringle was discovered in 1983 during construction of U.S. Route 40. He was hung at age sixty-eight by a Baltimore mob. Sgt. Elisha Lewis, a defender of Baltimore who served in Capt. Peter Pinney's Company, 27th Regiment, later owned Bloomsbury.

> The admiral himself was present at this work of destruction, and gave orders for it to his officers. Mrs. John Rogers , (wife to the commodore) Mrs. William Pinkney [Ann Maria, Rodger's sister] and Mrs. Goldsborough took shelter at Mr. Mark Pringel's. When a detachment was sent up to burn that elegant building Mrs. Goldsborough told the officer that she had an aged mother in it, and begged it might be spared. The officer replied that he acted under the admiral, and it would be necessary to obtain his consent. Mrs. Goldsborough returned with the officer and detachment, and obtained the permission that the house should be spared; but when she reached it, she found it on fire and met two men, one with a sheet, the other with a pillow-case crammed full, coming

out, which she could not then notice, but ran upstairs and found a large wardrobe standing in the passage all in flame. William Pinkney [apparently her son, William Jr.], who was with her, and two of the marines by great exertion saved the house; but some of the wretches, after that took the cover from the sofa in the front room and put coals in it, and it was in flames before it was discovered. (Eyewitness account dated May 7, 1813; reprinted in Baltimore *Niles' Weekly Register,* May 22, 1813)

A different version of the attempted burning of the Pringle Mansion comes from Benjamin Latrobe, who said that when the British went to the mansion, "Mr. Pringle met them with a white cloth hung on a staff and begged them to spare the women and children who had sought shelter with him. They suffered the house to stand."[151]

Rodgers House, also called Ferry House and Elizabeth Rodgers House (226 North Washington Street). NRHP. The 1788 Rodgers House is the oldest documented structure in Havre de Grace.

The enemy, however, set fire three times to Mrs. Rogers' house . . . but it fortunately each time was extinguished, though they defaced and mutilated much valuable furniture, broke the windows and doors and stole valuable clothing belonging to the ladies. (Rev. James Jones Wilmer, 1813)[152]

St. John's Episcopal Church (northwest corner of Union and Congress avenues). NRHP. St. John's Episcopal Church dates from circa 1805, but the present structure, built in 1809, is among the oldest surviving in the city despite the interior being gutted by fire in 1832. The British agreed to spare the church but destroyed the pews, pulpit, and windows. John O'Neill* served as a vestryman here.

They burst the doors, broke the window and sash, entered and beat the drum. One would [have] suppose . . . they would have shown some respect to this building, as it was called after their own name generally, "The English Church" . . . But it seems all sense of shame was lost, and every spark of grace was removed. (Rev. James Jones Wilmer, 1813)[153]

The Rodgers House as it appeared in the 1850s, was set on fire three times during the British attack. (Lossing, *Pictorial Field-Book of the War of 1812*)

The interior of St. John's Episcopal Church was damaged during the raid. This depiction illustrates the church as it appeared in the 1850s before the belfry was added circa 1884. (Lossing, *Pictorial Field-Book of the War of 1812*)

Not a house or shed is left standing, except an old church. (Benjamin Latrobe to Robert Fulton, May 4, 1813)[154]

The church at Havre de Grace . . . was not fired; but to shew their respect for "religion," [the enemy] assailed the house [of religion], and finding nothing to steal "magnanimously" attacked the window with brick-bats and stones, and demolished them. (Baltimore *Niles' Weekly Register,* May 8, 1813)

Sion Hill (2026 Level Road [Route 155]). NHL. PRIVATE. Glimpses of the house can be seen among a clump of mature trees on the south side of Level Road. This three-part brick house, begun in 1787 by Rev. John Ireland, became the home of Com. John Rodgers* (1772–1838), naval hero in War of 1812, when he married Minerva Denison, daughter of the second owner of Sion Hill. On October 21, 1806, the couple was married in the north parlor. Rodgers was in command of the U.S. frigate *President* when it engaged H.M. sloop-of-war *Little Belt* in 1811 and is credited with firing the first

shot of the War of 1812 when the *President* engaged H.M. frigate *Belvidera* in the summer of 1812. A popular bar-ballad saluted him as follows:

And Rodgers with his gallant crew,
O'er the wide ocean ride,
To prove their loyal spirits true,
And crush old Albion's pride.

[The British] set fire to everything, threw over the stages into the river, killed the horses in the stables, and then methodically burnt every house and shed in the village . . . The women and children fled to the woods . . . It is supposed that the circumstance of Commodore [John] Rodgers, being a native of Havre de Grace, this unmanly warfare is to be attributed. (Benjamin Latrobe to Robert Fulton, May 4, 1813)[155]

When the British burned Havre de Grace on May 3, 1813, Commodore Rodgers was at sea, but his wife and sister, Mrs. Ann Maria Rodgers Pinkney, wife of the U.S. Attor-

Sion Hill was spared burning by the pleading of prominent women in the village. (E. H. Pickering 1936 photograph; HABS, Library of Congress)

ney General William Pinkney* and their son William, were home. One account claims they approached Rear Adm. George Cockburn and convinced him to spare Sion Hill as well as some of the homes in town where elderly occupants lived. Cockburn insisted, however, on searching the house for important papers during which his men plunged a saber through the commodore's mahogany writing desk in hopes of finding a secret compartment. The British then reportedly took the desk with them. Ironically Rodgers retrieved the desk from a British ship he captured. This seemingly apocryphal story may actually be true as on September 26, 1813, Commodore Rodgers, in a fog off Nantucket, Massachusetts, captured the *Highflyer,* a Baltimore schooner that had been pressed into service in the Royal Navy. *Highflyer* was one of the vessels that the British used in support of the attack on Havre de Grace.

Cockburn coveted an elegant coach he saw and ordered it hauled aboard his vessel. This coach may have been the elegant brass-trimmed "chariot" that belonged to Rodgers's father-in-law Gideon Denion.

Commodore Rodgers was placed in charge of the naval defense of Baltimore in September 1814. He ordered the sinking of vessels in Baltimore harbor to impede any British naval attack. Rodgers' Bastion,* a key position in the defense of Baltimore, is named after Commodore Rodgers.

Commodore Rodgers unsuccessfully attempted to send fire-boats into the British squadron on the Potomac River near Alexandria. Between September 3 and 6, 1814, he also commanded the White House Gun Battery,* Virginia, which also unsuccessfully attempted to sink the British squadron as it withdrew down the river.

HAYWARD FAMILY CEMETERY. *See* appendix A

HESSIAN BARRACKS. *See* listing, Frederick

HOLLANDS CLIFFS (Patuxent River, above Deep Landing Road and south of Kings Landing Park, Calvert County). PRIVATE. On June 17, 1814, militia, possibly from the 36th Regiment, assembled along the bluffs of the Patuxent River to ambush a British raiding party as it descended the river after plundering Lower Marlboro.* Runaway slaves warned the British of the American presence and Royal Marines were therefore landed to flank them. While no Americans were found, a few shots were fired from the wooded heights as the British passed by the bluffs and down the river. Here the British burned a barn and tobacco belonging to a Mr. Morris.

HOLLY HALL. *See* Elkton

HONGA RIVER. *See* Lakes Cove

HORN POINT BATTERY. *See* listing, Annapolis

HOUSE OF HINGES, also called Brick Hotel (South Main Street [Route 16], fourth house south from intersection with Academy Street [only brick house in block], East New Market, Dorchester County). NHD. PRIVATE. 1st Lt. Anthony L. Manning, an officer in Capt. Richard Tootle's 10th Cavalry District, lived in this late eighteenth-century house. The house received its interesting name not from hinges on the house but large hinges on the door of a meat house located to the rear of the kitchen wing. The crossroad town of East New Market served as a supply center since before the American Revolution.

HOWELL POINT (confluence of Chesapeake Bay and Sassafras River, end of Howell Point Road, west off Still Pond Road [Route 292], Kent County). H.M. frigate *Maidstone* in late April 1813 bombarded the shore from Howell Point, causing havoc among the citizens of the area. This event probably occurred during the British raid at nearby Still Pond* on or about April 24, 1813.

> The Maidstone frigate lies so near Howell's point that she has thrown some of her shot a mile into the country. (Washington *Daily National Intelligencer,* May 10, 1813)

HUNTINGTOWN SITE, original town site (Hunting Creek, west of Solomons Island Road [Route 4] bridge over Hunting Creek, Calvert County). After landing at Gods Grace Plantation* on the Patuxent River, about 300 British troops marched nearly 7 miles to Huntingtown, where on July 17, 1814, they burned a warehouse and 130 hogsheads of tobacco. The flames spread to the rest of the town, destroying it. Huntingtown never fully recovered. The fire, coupled with siltation of the creek, induced residents to move the town approximately three miles to its present inland location. The town of St. Leonard,* St. Leonard Creek, was moved for similar reasons.

> British account of raid: landed . . . at a point about 3 or 4 miles above Benedict . . . and marched to Hunting town a distance of seven miles and destroyed a Store containing 130 Hogsheads of Tobacco. (Capt. Joseph Nourse to Rear Adm. George Cockburn, July 23, 1814)[156]

> American account of raid: A body of troops were landed at Huntingtown; some of the tobacco was carried off and the warehouse burnt. (Annapolis *Maryland Republican,* July 23, 1814)

> Second American account of raid: about 300 men landed just above and nearly opposite Benedict [Hallowing Point], deliberately commenced their march up to Huntington [Huntingtown], 7 miles off, burnt the warehouse, containing a considerable quantity of tobacco, and then returned without the least shadow of molestation. (Baltimore *Federal Republican,* July 26, 1814; reprinted in Philadelphia *United States Gazette,* August 3, 1814)

Buried in what is now a flower bed in the front yard of a private home about 1.2 miles southwest of Huntingtown is Maj. William L. Weems, who served in the 31st Regiment during the war.

INDIAN HEAD GUN BATTERY SITE (Potomac River, off Indian Head Highway [Route 210], on grounds of U.S. Naval Propellant Plant, Charles County). Restricted military base not open to public.

> This position (Say two hundred feet elevation above the river) is evidently the Gibraltar of the upper Potomack, and may be strongly fortified, to give certain security in the event of an increasing War. Its height is so relatively superior as to overlook the neighboring Country and render it difficult of access . . . From several prominent features of this height, an enemy's ship may be bombarded at various ranges. (William Tatham to Secretary of War John Armstrong, May 27, 1813)[157]

Here Capt. Oliver Hazard Perry erected a gun battery that on September 5, 1814, attempted to harass the British squadron as it withdrew down the Potomac River after the surrender of Alexandria.* The gun battery proving ineffectual, the British passed the point the following morning without further opposition. One American was wounded in the engagement. White House Gun Battery, under the command of Capt. David Porter, Jr., located farther up the Potomac on the Virginia side, had delayed the British squadron for several days, allowing Perry time to prepare his gun battery at Indian Head.

> American account of skirmish: The battery . . . at the Indian Head was of too small a caliber to make much impression on the Enemy as they descended the Potomak . . . A single 18 pounder, which arrived only 30 minutes before the firing began, ill supplied with ammunition, was the only Gun that could be of much service . . . The ammunition of the 18 pounder, and of the several of the sixes, being expended; and the fire of the Enemy from two Frigates [H.M. *Eurylus* and H.M. *Seahorse*], two sloops of war [probably the H.M. brig-sloop *Fairy* and H.M. dispatch *Anna Maria*], two Bombs [actually three, H.M.S. *Aetna,* H.M.S. *Devastation,*

and H.M.S. *Meteor*], one Rocket ship [H.M.S. *Erebus*], and several smaller vessels, being very heavy, it was thought advisable by General Stewart [Brig. Gen. Philip Stuart], Major [George] Peter and myself to retire a short distance in the rear. This was done in good-order, after sustaining their fire for more than an hour. (Capt. Oliver Hazard Perry to Secretary of Navy William Jones, September 9, 1814)[158]

British account of skirmish: they had two Batteries mounting from 14 to 18 Guns on a range of Cliffs about a mile extent under which we were of Necessity obliged to pass very close.— I did not intend to make the attack that evening, but the [H.M. rocket-vessel] Erebus grounding within Range we were necessarily called into action . . . the fire of the [H.M. brig-sloop] Fairy had the most decisive effect as well as that of the Erebus whilst the Bombs threw their shells with excellent precision; and the Guns of the batteries were thereby completely silenced by about 8. O'clock— At day light . . . they allowed us to pass without further molestation. (Capt. James Alexander Gordon to Vice Adm. Sir Alexander F. I. Cochrane, September 9, 1814)[159]

ISLINGTON SITE. *See* appendix A

JAMES ISLAND. *See* Madison

JAVA PLANTATION SITE, also called Contee Plantation or Sparrow's Rest (Contee Wharf Road, south off Muddy Creek Road [Route 468], near Collison Corner, Anne Arundel County). Near the end of Contee Wharf Road lie the brick ruins of Java Plantation, owned by John Contee, who on December 19, 1812, served as a 1st lieutenant in the U.S. Marine Corps onboard the U.S. frigate *Constitution* during its successful engagement of H.M. frigate *Java* off Bahia, Brazil. He resigned his commission on September 15, 1813. On January 28, 1830, the Maryland legislature presented Contee with a sword for his service. Local legend claims that Contee bought the property, including a 1747 plantation house, in 1828 with prize money received from the *Constitution*'s defeat of *Java*, and that he renamed the plantation for the captured vessel. (Interpretation about this plantation and legend can be found along the Java Plantation History Trail at the Smithsonian Environmental Research Center located at 647 Contee Wharf Road.)

JOHN ADAMS WEBSTER HOUSE. *See* Mount Adams

JOSHUA THOMAS CHAPEL. *See* Thomas, Joshua, Chapel

KENT ISLAND (bounded by Chesapeake Bay, Eastern Bay, and Chester River, Queen Anne's County). In the spring of 1813, the Queen Anne's County militia established a gun battery on the east side of Kent Island at the narrows between the island and the eastern shore. The militia abandoned the island in early August 1813, when it was occupied by a force of two thousand British troops who had previously occupied Point Lookout.* On August 6, 1813, the British erected their own gun battery at the narrows.

the enemy have taken possession of Kent Island, and that the inhabitants of every description have removed to the main land . . . From the circumstance of landing cannon on Kent Island, it appears to be the intention of the enemy to keep possession of it for some time; and certainly a more eligible situation could not have been selected for their own safety and convenience or from which to annoy us. The Island is separated from the main land of the eastern shore by a narrow strait, at one place not more than about 1-4 [one-quarter] of a mile broad, navigable only by boats or barges; their communication with the main land, will therefor be easily effected, and some of the finest and best stocked farms in this state are along the shores of the rivers Chester, Wye and St. Michael in their immediate vicinity. A part of their fleet is now visible from this city between the head of Kent Island and the mouth of our river. ("Commodore" [Captain] Charles Gordon, August 7, 1813; reprinted in Hartford *Connecticut Mirror,* August 16, 1813, and Hartford *Connecticut Courant,* August 17, 1813)

The enemy . . . have landed about 2000 troops upon Kent-Island, and taken possession of it. Several of their smaller vessels are stationed in the river which separates the island from the main, and they have several pieces of artillery planted to guard the only place in the river which is fordable. [Rear] Admiral [George] Cockburn headed the party which landed, and assured the few inhabitants that were remaining, that their property should be guarded with vigilance against any depredation, and themselves protected from violence. (Annapolis *Maryland Gazette and Political Intelligencer,* August 12, 1813)

Seven deserters . . . state that about 2500 or 3000 troops had been landed on Kent Island a few days before for the purpose of getting fresh provisions, &c. Their troops have not been so sickly as generally reported, but the deserters give it as their opinion that the majority of them will desert the first opportunity. (Annapolis *Maryland Republican,* August 14, 1813)

From August 6 to August 23, 1813, Kent Island served as a British base of operation for raids in the region. The British established their main camp at Jonathan Harrison's Belle

1814 map showing Kent Island, the narrows between the island and the Eastern Shore mainland, and the road to Queenstown. The American gun battery and later the British gun battery were located on the east side of the island at the narrows. (Mathew Carey, *Maryland*, 1814; courtesy Maryland State Archives)

Vue (Belleview) Plantation, later known as Sillen Plantation and now as Blue Bay Farm on the northwest side of the island. The British officers occupied Harrison's house, flying the Union Jack from its roof. Kent Island became a magnet for runaway slaves, some three hundred of whom found refuge here.

> a picturesque encampment formed about the centre of the island, in a beautiful spot resembling a gentleman's park. Here they constructed tents with the boughs of evergreen trees, which, being regularly placed and of equal size, formed a very pretty sight. A good-sized farmhouse on one side of the encampment served for the accommodation of the General and his staff. The ferry remained guarded by the marine artillery, with a couple of field-pieces and a howitzer, supported by some of the boats of the fleet . . . slaughtered sheep and quarters of beef that were suspended every morning from the trees, intermixed with a plentiful supply of geese, turkeys, fowls, &c. with heaps of vegetables . . . evinced that we had fallen on the land of "milk and honey." (Capt. James Scott, 1834)[160]

The British abandoned Kent Island on August 23, 1813, reportedly leaving graves of British troops who died of disease. Richard Ireland Jones of Kinnersley, Kent Island, who operated the ferry between Kent Island and Annapolis, was commissioned a captain in the 9th Cavalry and later appointed a major.

KETTLE BOTTOMS, now called Kettle Bottom Shoals (Potomac River, located just south of Wicomico River off Swan Point and Cobb Island, St. Mary's County). Kettle Bottoms is a series of shoals in the Potomac River. A British squadron ascended the Potomac River during August 1814 as part of a feint designed to keep the Americans guessing as to which approach they might take to Washington. Despite charting and setting buoys, the squadron encountered many difficulties at the shoals. Some of the larger vessels needed to be warped over the shoals (hauled by an anchor or kedge that had been drooped ahead by boat). This time-consuming and exhausting work continued with little interruption over five successive days. The total expedition lasted twenty-three days; each ship went aground at least twenty times and frigates were even obliged to remove their guns to lighten them over the shoals. The squadron faced these same perils during its descent. They also had to contend with fire-boats launched by their American foes and with artillery fire from American batteries at White House,* Virginia, and Indian Head,* Maryland.

> There are many shoals called Kettle Bottoms; none of the pilots know exactly where they lie. (1776 sailing chart directions)[161]

A Frigate, two schooners and eight or ten Barges ascended the Potomack yesterday— They have since been busily en-

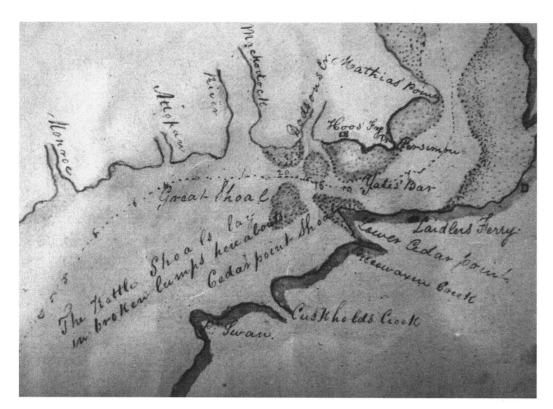

1813 map showing "The Kettle Shoals lay in broken lumps here abouts."
(Detail from "Plan of That Part of Potowmack River which applies to the
first Report on defencible Positions by William Tatham 24 May 1813";
National Archives and Records Administration)

gaged in sounding the River and marking the channel by a
chain of Buoys. The Frigate to day passed over the most difficult part of the Kettle Bottoms, which is the only obstruction in the navigation of the river, which could create any
serious delay to the Enemy's shipping. (Brig. Gen. Philip Stuart to Secretary of War John Armstrong, July 24, 1814)[162]

being without Pilots to assist us through that difficult part
of the River called the Kettle Bottoms, and from contrary
winds we were unable to reach Fort Washington until the
evening of the 27th.— Nor was this effected but by the sever-
est labour.— I believe each of the Ships was not less than
twenty different times aground and each time we were
obliged to haul off by main Strength,— and we were employed warping for five whole successive days, with the exception of a few hours, a distance of more than fifty miles.
(Capt. James Alexander Gordon to Vice Adm. Sir Alexander
F. I. Cochrane, September 9, 1814)[163]

KEY BRIDGE. *See* listing, Washington, D.C., and Baltimore

KEY MEMORIAL CHAPEL. *See* listing, Frederick

KIRBYS WIND MILL SITE, site of the "Battle of the Wind Mill"
(north side of entrance to Parker Creek, near south end of
Deale Beach Road, off Deale–Churchton Road [Route 256],
Deale, Anne Arundel County). Here on October 31, 1814,
American troops under Capt. John A. Burd of the U.S. Light
Dragoons repulsed a British landing force. Burd reported
that he and three of his men were wounded and nine horses
were killed. The British claimed two Americans were killed,
two were taken prisoner, and twenty horses were captured.
The British reported five of their own men missing. Brig.
Gen. William Madison, brother of President James Madison
and commander of the 1st Virginia Regiment, arrived with
his infantry after the skirmish. (*See also* Tracys Landing.)

American account of skirmish: the British again landed
yesterday morning at Deep Creek, and proceeded to Kirby's
Wind Mill, capt. [John A.] Burd, of the U.S. dragoons hav-

ing reconnoitered and ascertained the enemy's position, determined on an attempt to cut off his retreat back to his shipping. Capt. B. accordingly made a gallant charge, under severe fire from the enemy's cannon and musketry. But brig. general [William] Madison had not yet reached the scene of these operations, with his infantry from the camp near the Patuxent; and capt. Burd not being so well supported by his own men as he had expected, the charge was not successful. He, however made two prisoners. Capt. B. was severely wounded in the hand, narrowly escaped being himself taken. Our artillery is said to have galled the enemy while moving off in his barges. Another account says . . . that in the gallant attack made by capt. Burd, himself and three of his men were slightly wounded, and 9 horse killed. Loss of the enemy in killed and wounded unknown—we took five prisoners. (Baltimore *Niles' Weekly Register,* November 5, 1814)

Second American account of skirmish: I accompanied Capt. Burd to the spot where they [British] were debarked and drawn up in a line in a cornfield, protected in front by a creek, and on their right flank, where alone they could be approached, by a fence. Capt. Burd, after waiting for the infantry two hours, and seeing the enemy were beginning to reembark a mile below, consulted me, and I gave my opinion in favor of a charge which he immediately executed . . . the fire of the enemy was received, but passed unheeded; the fence thrown down, the line of the enemy in full flight; their men throwing down their arms and surrendering; when . . . some one in the rear cried "A retreat," and the dragoons gave way. Capt. Burd rallied part of them, and renewed his charge, but the enemy had now leisure to gain another fence, covered by a wood and kept up the hottest fire, separated from the force only by a fence, and the large proportion of the squadron not coming up, all the prisoners but two were lost, and two of the dragoons, whose horses were killed are missing; six were wounded and unfortunately Capt. B . . . was wounded by two balls in the hand, and thrown from his horse. (Col. John Francis Mercer* to Governor Levin Winder, October 31, 1814; reprinted in Boston *Patriot,* November 12, 1814)

British account of skirmish: proceeded to Parkers Point [Parkers Island has eroded away off present-day Long Point], with the Boats, and detachment of Royal Marines . . . on finding the Houses deserted, I made dispositions for driving in Cattle . . . On reconnoitreing, I perceiv'd the Enemy to be in considerable Force in Cavalry, therefore directed Captain [Nathaniel] Cole (Royal Marines) to bring up the Main Body, to support the advance, and the favorable position we had taken up, induced me to throw the Skirmishers forward, to entice the Enemy to make a Charge, which I am happy to say had the effect, but the steady and gallant reception, which I felt confident they would meet with from the Royal Marines, who threw in a destructive volley, put them to flight, leav-

ing two Killed, two Prisoners, and twenty Horses with their accoutrements &ca. &ca. in our possession, I only regret a body of Infantry (chiefly Militia) from eight Hundred, to one Thousand with field Pieces, supported this Squadron, in their attack, or I have not a doubt, from the gallant Intrepidity of the detachment, the whole destruction of this Squadron, consisting of one hundred & fourteen would have been effected. (Capt. Thomas Alexander to Capt. Robert Barrie, October 31, 1814)[164]

KITTY KNIGHT HOUSE. *See* listing, Georgetown

LAKES COVE (Honga River, end of Parks Neck Road, off Crapo Road [Route 336], near Crapo, Dorchester County). On January 12, 1815, a British tender and barge at Lakes Cove captured six American vessels bound for Norfolk. One American coaster was loaded with eighty thousand feet of planking. Lt. Washington Lake approached the British to ask if the vessels could be ransomed. The British officer in charge replied that if thirty bullocks (cattle) were delivered to him within five minutes he would spare the vessels. When Lake returned with fifteen to twenty militiamen, two of the vessels were already on fire. The militia fired upon the British and after driving them off put out the fires.

> Lieut. [Washington] Lake and Quartermaster Robert Hart, with the . . . militia, . . . commenced a brisk fire upon them from canoes and kept it up amungst a shower of grape and round shot from a 12 pounder, until they drove them off . . . the militia followed them in their canoes until their ammunition gave out, without the loss of a man in killed or wounded; they then returned and extinguished the fire on the vessels. (Charles K. Bryan to Brig. Gen. Perry Benson, Washington *Daily National Intelligencer,* February 25, 1815)

LAPIDUM. *See* Bell's Ferry

LARGO ENCAMPMENT SITE (intersection of Landover–Largo Road [Route 202] and Central Avenue [Route 214], Prince George's County). The British encamped at Largo the night of August 25–26, 1814, on their return march after burning Washington. (*See also* nearby Northampton Slave Quarters Archeological Site, where the British passed.)

LAZARETTO BATTERY. *See* listing, Baltimore

LEONARDTOWN (Breton Bay, St. Mary's County). A meeting was held at Leonardtown on April 3, 1813, to plan the defense of St. Mary's County.

The Alarm post for the Squadron of St. Mary's County is Leonard Town to which place every individual of our troop must repair on any given alarm or emergency (Col. F. Neuman to Capt. James Forrest, Leonardtown, July 11, 1812)[165]

On April 8, 1813, the commander of the 12th Regiment, Lt. Col. Athanasius Fenwick, informed Capt. James Forrest, commander of the Leonardtown Troop of Horse, that the enemy had landed at Point Lookout.*

the general [Philip Stuart] . . . immediately issued orders for the whole militia of Charles and St. Mary's counties to turn out en masse and to arrive at head quarters, near Leonardtown, to-morrow. (Unnamed man in Port Tobacco to his father in Alexandria, July 20, 1814; reprinted in Baltimore *Federal Republican,* July 26, 1814)

On July 19, 1814, about 1,500 British troops, divided into three forces, attacked Leonardtown. One force landed near Newtown* and marched inland to attack the town from the west; another approached by land from the east; and a third under Rear Adm. George Cockburn landed in barges at the Leonardtown waterfront on the south (south end of Washington Street). Although several men were seriously injured in a boating accident on their return to their ships, the British took Leonardtown without opposition. The British seized a small schooner, 70 hogsheads of tobacco, 20 barrels of flour, and 40 stands of arms left behind by the militia. Brig. Gen. Philip Stuart with about 250 militiamen was in the neighborhood at the time but did not think himself capable of challenging the larger enemy force.

British account of raid: I proceeded . . . up the Potowmac for the purpose of commencing by an attack on Leonard's Town, (the capital of St. Mary's County) where I understood the 36th. american Regiment to be stationed and much Stores &ca. to be deposited . . . I proceeded at Midnight up the Creek . . . At the dawn of Day the Marines were put on Shore at some distance from the Town, and I directed Major [George] Lewis to march round and attack it from the Land side whilst the Boats pulled up to it in Front. The Enemy however on discovering us withdrew whatever armed Force he had in the place and permitted us to take quiet Possession of it. I found here a quantity of Stores belonging to the 36th. Regiment and a Number of arms of different descriptions all of which were destroyed; A quantity of Tobacco, Flour, Provisions and other articles likewise found in the Town I caused to be shipped and brought away in the Boats and a Schooner which we took laying off it . . . not a musquet was fired at us nor indeed a single armed american discovered, in consequence of which conduct on part of the Enemy I deemed it prudent to spare the Town, which we quit-

ted in the Evening and returned to the Squadron without having sustained accident of any kind. (Rear Adm. George Cockburn to Vice Adm. Sir Alexander F. I. Cochrane, July 19, 1814)[166]

American account of assault: they landed, near Newtown, a heavy force, which marched to the right of Leonardtown, another to the left, and a third, commanded by [Rear] Admiral [George] Cockburn, landed at the warehouse, and took possession of Leonardtown. The two flank parties, reached the rear of the town a few minutes after the barges reached the landing. Their whole force in this expedition was estimated at about 1500 men. During their stay in the village, which was till about 2 o'clock, they [British] behaved with great politeness to the ladies, respected private property wherever the proprietors remained at home, destroyed about 100 bbls. of supplies belonging to col. [Henry] Carberry's [also Carbery] regt. the whole of Mr. [Robert B.] Haislip's store [valued at about $1,500 in merchandise], and the furniture, clothing and bedding of captains [James] Forrest and [Enoch J.] Millard, all of whom left town. They got possession of some muskets belonging to the state, which they broke to pieces, saying they were only fit to stick frogs with. Mrs. Thomson and Miss Eliza Key were very instrumental in saving the court-house, stating that is was sometimes a place of worship. (Annapolis *Maryland Gazette and Political Intelligencer,* August 4, 1814)

Second differing American account: I visited the town [Leonardtown] the next day [after the British raid]. Every housekeeper was plundered except one—to the Court House they did great injury; not a sash of glass but what they destroyed; much of the inside work cut to pieces, all the tobacco, about 70 hhds. carried off, and property belonging to individuals and the United States, to the amount of 4,000 dollars. Although [Rear] Admiral [George] Cockburn gave to some of the inhabitants a guard, yet his men plundered almost within reach of the guard's muskets. The admiral and his officers, I hear, conducted themselves politely to a Mr. Key and his daughter, and to most of the inhabitants; in this way they were honorably remunerated for the loss and destruction to their property—no houses were burnt. (Baltimore *Niles' Weekly Register,* August 14, 1814)[167]

The raid at Leonardtown was part of a series of raids along the Potomac River designed to divert attention from Rear Admiral Cockburn's plan to land an expeditionary force at Benedict* on the Patuxent River and capture Washington.

A Brigade Court-martial will assemble at Francis Abell's Tavern in Leonard Town . . . for the trial of Lieutenant Colonel Thomas Blakistone on charges exhibited against him by his commanding officer Colonel [Capt. James] Walker of the 45th Regiment. 1st charge—Disobedience of order . . . 2nd charge Violation of the Militia law of Maryland. (November 17, 1814)[168]

LITTLE ANNEMESSEX RIVER (off Tangier Sound, end of Crisfield Highway [Route 413], Somerset County). Although the city of Crisfield did not exist in 1813, the Little Annemessex River served as the principal means for the shipping of local goods. On April 6, 1814, several vessels from the Potomac River and Baltimore City area attempting to enter into the Pocomoke River were discovered by British warships, including a 74-gun man-of-war lying in Tangier Sound. The American vessels fled into the Big and Little Annemessex rivers for protection.

On Thursday the barges of the enemy went into Little Annemessex, and on that evening and the next morning burnt seven [vessels]. (Easton *Republican Star,* April 19, 1814)

The British removed several cannon from an armed vessel belonging to Isaac Atkinson of Baltimore and then burned it. In response to the British raid, on April 8 about 250 militiamen assembled about five miles to the northeast at Colbourn Creek, a tributary of the Big Annemessex River.* Anchored in the creek were fifteen vessels, two of which were loaded with timber for the "Navy Yard" (probably the Washington Navy Yard). If the British threatened, the vessels were to be scuttled, but to the relief of the vessels' crews, the British vessels entered the Pocomoke River instead.

LONDONTOWN (South River, 839 Londontown Road, off Mayo Road [Route 253], Anne Arundel County). NHL. Londontown served as a mustering center and encampment for the Anne Arundel County militia.

LONG GREEN CEMETERY. *See* appendix A

LONG OLD FIELDS ENCAMPMENT SITE, also called Oldfields, Old Fields, and Battalion Old Fields (near intersection of Donnell Drive and Marlboro Pike at Penn-Mar Shopping Center, Forestville, Prince George's County). The main north-south route from Bladensburg to a ferry crossing passed the Long Old Fields named for the worked-out tobacco fields there. Now known as Forestville, Long Old Fields once boasted five taverns, three ordinaries, a post office, a polling (voting) house, a horse race track, a tollhouse, an alms house, and a church. The American forces camped here on August 22–23, 1814, in anticipation of meeting the

invading British troops. Long Old Fields provided a good site for the American camp because it covered the main road to Washington only eight miles away, was located midway between it and Upper Marlboro, and permitted a speedy response to a British advance from any direction.

[Brig.] General [William H.] Winder retired by the Woodyard to a place called the Old Fields, which covered equally Bladensburg, the bridges on the Eastern Branch, and Fort Washington. (Secretary of State, James Monroe, November 13, 1814)[169]

Here about 4:00 p.m., August 22, 1814, Brig. Gen. William H. Winder encamped his troops of approximately 3,200 men, including cavalry, supported by 17 pieces of artillery. This force had fallen back from the Woodyard* in expectation of meeting the British troops of more than four thousand men supported by only two small field pieces and a howitzer and without cavalry.

The camp was as open all night as a race-field, and the sailors and militia were as noisy as if at a fair; you might hear the countersign fifty yards when a sentry challenged. I made up my mind that if Ross, whose camp I had reconnoitred in the evening, was a man of enterprise, he would be upon us in the course of the night, and, being determined to die like a trooper's horse, I slept with my shoes on. (Maj. Gen. James Wilkinson, night, August 22, 1814)[170]

About 2:00 a.m., August 23, 1814, Winder's tired and jumpy troops were roused by a false alarm as sentries mistook cattle driven into the camp for a British attack. Benjamin Oden of Bellefields* reportedly donated the cattle as a contribution to the war effort. Later that morning President James Madison and three cabinet members rode here from Washington to ascertain the situation at the encampment. The president inspected the troops about 11:00 a.m.

The President of the U States and heads of Departments are now in this camp, The enemy were last night at upper Marlbro', from which it is probable they will advance today toward Bladensburg. Our force is fast accumulating and we shall now retard and ultimately repel if not destroy the forces of the enemy whose numbers are various estimated but I believe does not exceed at most 5.000. (Secretary of Navy William Jones to Com. John Rodgers, August 23, 1814)[171]

I accompanied the President [Madison] to [Brig.] General [William H.] Winder's Camp, at the Old Fields, and passed the night in Commodore Barney's tent;—the Army of the enemy at Upper Marlborough eight miles distant. (Secretary of Navy William Jones to Congressman Richard M. Johnson, October 3, 1814)[172] at the Camp at the "Old Fields" . . . we were informed that the enemy was advancing upon us, The Army was put in order of battle and our position taken, my forces were on the right, flanked by the two Battaln. of the 36 & 38th. Regiments where we remained some hours, The enemy did not however make his appearance. (Com. Joshua Barney to Secretary of Navy William Jones, August 29, 1814)[173]

Winder feared that a night engagement would nullify his advantage in artillery. Hence, as darkness closed in on August 23, 1814, he ordered his troops to withdraw to the Washington Navy Yard. Some troops were stationed at the Eastern Branch bridge (now John Philip Sousa Bridge) across the Anacostia River (Eastern Branch of Potomac River) in case the bridge there needed to be destroyed. A gun battery (Barney Gun Battery*) was also established here to impede the expected British advance.

My reasons for not remaining at the Old Fields during the night [August 23, 1814] was, that, if an attack should be made in the night, our own superiority, which lay in artillery, was lost, and the inexperience of the troops would subject them to certain, infallible, and irremediable disorder, and probably destruction, and thereby occasion the loss of a full half of the force which I could hope to oppose, under favorable circumstances, to the enemy. (Report of Brig. Gen. William H. Winder)[174]

Maj. Gen. Robert Ross and his troops briefly rested in the early morning of August 24, 1814, at Long Old Fields on their way to Bladensburg. In what is District Heights today, one fork, Addison Road, ran northward toward Bladensburg and another, Marlboro Pike, ran westward toward the Eastern Branch bridge to Washington. Here Major General Ross pulled a second ruse (his first was at Bellefields*), first taking the west fork and then reversing himself and taking the north fork, as he had done along the road from Nottingham to Upper Marlboro.

various fields on each side of the high road . . . where smoking ashes, bundles of straw, and remnants of broken victuals were scattered about, indicated that considerable bodies of troops had passed the night in this neighbourhood. The appearance of the road itself, likewise, imprinted as it was with fresh marks of many feet and hoofs, proved that these troops could be no great way before us. (Lt. George Robert Gleig, 1821)[175]

LOUDON PARK CEMETERY. *See* appendix B

LOWER CEDAR POINT (Potomac River, end of Morgantown Road, off Rock Point Road [Route 257], Morgantown, Charles County). Rear Adm. George Cockburn conducted a series of raids along the Potomac River in July 1814, landing here as well as at Chaptico* and Leonardtown.* All of this was part of a campaign to disguise his plan to land an expeditionary force at Benedict* on the Patuxent River and ultimately capture Washington. Militia under the command of Brig. Gen. Philip Stuart succeeded in repulsing the British landing at Lower Cedar Point, but not before the warehouse caught fire, probably from a Congreve rocket.

the Enemy landed from 2 Schooners & 8 barges for the purpose of taking off the Tobacco from lower Cedar point Ware-House . . . I could not attack them with my Infantry as it would expose them to the rake of the Enemy's vessels and not assure to us the capture of the Enemy. So, I employed my Riflemen and artillery. With the later I drove them from the shore and then opened a fire upon the Schooners & Barges. I had but two light sixes [cannon], whilst the Enemy employed agt. us as heavy metal as 32 pounders. After an hour's firing, the Enemy hauled off, not a little damaged. But not before they set fire to the Ware-House, which I presume was done by a rocket, as they employed them against us. This affair demonstrates the wisdom of employing this species of force on the Banks of our Rivers—We can thus annoy the Enemy without fruitlessly exposing the lives of the men— (Brig. Gen. Philip Stuart to Secretary of War John Armstrong, July 24, 1814)[176]

When the British sent its diversionary squadron up the Potomac in August 1814, on the 21st they fired several canon shot at a guard house and mounted horseman on Lower Cedar Point.

LOWER MARLBORO, also called Graham or Grahame's Landing, and Ballard's Landing (Patuxent River, end of Lower Marlboro Road [Route 262], Calvert County). A British force of about 160 Royal Marines and a detachment of 30 Colonial Marines trained at Tangier Island* took Lower Marlboro without resistance after the militia and most townsfolk had fled. The British occupied the town from about 6:00 p.m., June 15, to about 8:00 a.m., June 16, 1814. Tobacco warehouses with 2,500 hogshead of tobacco valued at more than $125,000 were burned, a small schooner captured, and a civilian named J. W. Reynolds taken and later offered in trade for a Royal Marine the British believed had been captured by the Americans on June 21, 1814, at Benedict.*

British account of raid: I pushed on towards Marlborough where I understood there were several Stores of Tobacco and other property, and As Marlborough is near the Seat of Government [Washington] I thought an attack on this Town would be a sad Annoyance to the Enemy and oblige the Regulars and Militia to try their strength with us, but I was deceived as both Militia and Inhabitants made off to the woods and we were allowed to take quiet possession of a Town admirably situated for Defense, here we passed the night without molestation though only eighteen Miles from Washington, in the morning I loaded a small Schooner with Tobacco and having plentifully supplied ourselves with Stock, I burnt Tobacco Stores containing two thousand five hundred Hogsheads of this valuable Article and then Embarked. (Capt. Robert Barrie to Rear Adm. George Cockburn, June 19, 1814)[177]

American accounts of raid: They opened all the feather beds they could find, broke the doors and windows out and so tore the houses to pieces inside as to render them of very little value. (Baltimore *American & Commercial Daily Advertizer,* June 20, 1814)

I am sorry to inform you that the British have this forenoon BURNT the Tobacco Ware-Houses at lower Marlborough . . . they took a schooner (Capt. David's) and loaded her . . . near Lower Marlborough, they forced some negroes off with them—got some stock, poultry, &c. (Unnamed merchant, June 17, 1814, New York *Herald,* June 25, 1814)

A British officer and FIVE MEN marched three miles into the county and stole with impunity from a widow lady, thirteen slaves, and done considerable damage by the destruction of furniture, &c. at other places! (Annapolis *Maryland Republican,* June 25, 1814)

The farmers as well as all other persons residing on Patuxent . . . from Lower Marlborough to the mouth of the river, has been very much destructed by the enemy, they have burnt a considerable number of dwelling Houses, barns &c—at Benedict & Lower Marlborough they have not left a window sash, or a door standing in one of the buildings, Charles Gantt (in Calvert) has lost all his negroes & stock his house & furniture burnt, his wife was so much frightened she died in a very short time. About a 100 negroes & 4 white men & thirty were officers went to Mr. [Levin?] Ballards (near L. Marlborough) they plundered and took by force 14 negroes which were all the poor widow owned. They frequently marched 3 & 4 miles in the forested after negroes & stock. (Clement Hollyday to Urban Hollyday, July 12, 1814)[178]

The U.S. Chesapeake Flotilla was briefly stationed here after its escape from St. Leonard Creek* in late June 1814.

Local tradition claims a few British soldiers are buried here, although there is no firm evidence supporting the claim. At the ferry/steamboat landing, an interpretive panel provides information about Lower Marlboro and the surrounding area during the War of 1812.

Opposite Lower Marlboro and up river about one mile at Whites Ferry, is the site of the ferry-house where the British squadron halted for several hours midday on August 21, 1814. Rear Adm. George Cockburn met here with Maj. Gen. Robert Ross to discuss their joint operation. Upon completion of the meeting, the army continued its march to Nottingham,* while the squadron anchored for the night in the river at Lower Marlboro.

I endeavored to Keep with the Boats and Tenders as nearly as possible abreast of the Army under Major General [Robert] Ross that I might communicate with him as occasions offered, according to the plan previously arranged, and about mid-day yesterday I accordingly anchored at the Ferry House opposite Lower Marlborough where I met the [Major] General [Ross] and where the Army halted for some hours. (Rear Adm. George Cockburn to Vice Adm. Sir Alexander F. I. Cochrane, August 22, 1814)[179]

Charles Ball, a slave born in Calvert County circa 1790, was owned by Levin Ballard of Lower Marlboro. At about the age of twenty Ball was rented to a "man with epaulets on his shoulders" at the Washington Navy Yard. Ball worked as a cook under Com. Joshua Barney for the U.S. Chesapeake Flotilla during the First and Second Battles of St. Leonard Creek.* Ball was also present during the Battle of Bladensburg, where he said the militia "ran like sheep being chased by dogs."[180] After the war, Ball returned to Calvert County and was sold to a Georgia slave trader from whom he escaped. Returning to his family in Calvert County, he worked as a free black, saved money, and purchased a small farm near Baltimore. After ten years, he was enslaved again by his former master. On his third attempt, he again escaped, and at great risk returned to Baltimore for family members, but they had been kidnapped and sold south into slavery. Ball lived the rest of his life in Philadelphia as a free man. Charles Ball is probably a pseudonym; his real name unknown.

MADISON, then called Tobacco Stick (Madison Bay, Little Choptank River, north side of Taylors Island Road near intersection with White Marsh Road, Dorchester County). On February 6, 1815, eighteen crewmen from an H.M. sloop *Dauntless* tender pillaged the area of Madison, taking seven sheep from the farm of Moses Geohagan and burning several vessels. As the tender began its way back to the Patuxent River, it encountered considerable drift ice and so spent the night in the lee off nearby James Island, where on February 7, 1815, it became ice-bound. In response, Pvt. Joseph Fookes Stewart, a shipyard owner and planter in Capt. Thomas Woolford's detachment of the 48th Maryland militia, engaged the tender with a small group of militiamen. After Stewart's force launched a two-hour musket barrage on the British tender, the crew of twenty surrendered, including a lieutenant, a midshipman, thirteen crewmen, three Royal Marines, and a black man and woman. The British crew was detained in a house now demolished known as the John Hodson House, which served as the local jail and stood on the north side of Taylors Island Road (Route 16) about a mile from Madison. At least two of the prisoners, including its commander, Lt. Matthew Phibbs, were taken to Easton* and finally to Baltimore. This incident caused so much concern for the safety of the citizens in the area that a barracks was reportedly built on a lot near the home of George Jones. Militiamen were put on alert and encamped at a windmill at the upper end of town. The British tender was dismantled and the spoils of war sold at public auction. The tender's carronade was nicknamed "Becky Phipps" for the tender's captured black cook Becca (Becky) and the commander Lt. Matthew Phibbs (Phipps). Following this action, Stewart submitted a petition for prize money to Congress and on April 29, 1816, he and his comrades were awarded $1,800. The carronade was mounted at Taylors Island* about 1950 and made into a monument commemorating this skirmish. Madison is near the site of the last engagement of the war in Maryland, known as the Battle of the Ice Mound, named after a mound of ice used by Stewart's men during the engagement.

There is a mural by John Moll in Easton at the Tidewater Inn* entitled *Taylors Island patriots capture the British ship Dauntless, aground off Parsons Creek—War of 1812–15*. The site of the capture was actually off James Point, James Island, Little Choptank River; and the vessel captured was the tender of the *Dauntless,* not the *Dauntless* itself.

> American account of skirmish: found the tender . . . afloat between the body of the ice attached to the shore from the bay, and at about four hundred yards distance from the shore. They decried too, a mound of ice, which had been formed at about one hundred and fifty yards from the tender, by means of loose cakes floating in the mouth of the river, and accumulated by the force of the tide, in such a manner as to present a good breast work from whence the tender might be attacked, if the party should be able to make their way to it upon the ice . . . Upon the proposal of Joseph Stewart, and led on by him . . . made their way to the Ice Mound, and there commenced a fire upon the tender. Just as they arrived, the British had got their anchor on the bow and loosened their sails for the purpose of getting off. At the time of the first fire on the tender, there appeared but three men on deck, one of whom was shot through the neck, and fell, and the other two ran below. A fire of musketry was then commenced by the enemy from the hold of the tender, and was kept up by the party at the mound of ice, who cautiously watched for the appearance of any of the enemy above the hold, frequently firing at the tender and at a piece of canvas strung along the quarter rail, behind which it was apprehended some of the enemy might be screened. After an engagement kept up in this manner, for about two hours, suddenly the whole party of the enemy appeared upon deck and cried out for quarters, waving their handkerchief. Upon this, Joseph Stewart and his party immediately mounted their breast work of ice, and the said Stewart commanded them to come off without their arms, in their barge, which they did, through an opening in the ice, and were received into custody as prisoners, upon the ice, and were immediately marched ashore. (Pvt. Joseph Fookes Stewart, February 19, 1815; reprinted in Annapolis *Maryland Gazette and Political Intelligencer,* February 23, 1815)

MADISON HOUSE. *See* Brookeville

MAGRUDERS LANDING, formally called Hannah Brown's Landing and later Magruders Ferry (Patuxent River, end of Magruders Ferry Road, off Davis Shop–Croom Road [Route 382], Prince George's County). On June 17, 1814, the British conducted a raid at Magruders Landing, where they burned the Moil and Magruder warehouse, which contained hundreds of hogsheads of tobacco.

> the British have this forenoon BURNT the Tobacco Warehouses at lower Marlborough and Magruder's Ferry . . . It would have distressed you to see the tobacco at Magruder's burning, as I did, this evening. ELEVEN HUNDRED HOGSHEADS, nearly all consumed. (Unnamed merchant, New York *Herald,* June 25, 1814)

MARYLAND HISTORICAL SOCIETY. *See* listing, Baltimore

MARYLAND STATEHOUSE. *See* listing, Annapolis

MATTAPONI (11000 Mattaponi Road, south off St. Thomas Church Road, Prince George's County). PRIVATE. Mattaponi, constructed circa 1745, was altered in 1820 when one-story wings were added and the finishings on the central block changed. Here lived Robert Bowie* (1750–1818), governor of Maryland from 1803 to 1806 and 1811 to 1812. Bowie served as major general of the 1st Division, Maryland militia, in 1812. When British stragglers began stealing near Upper Marlboro on their way back to their ships after occupying Washington, Bowie was one of the citizens who seized several of the soldiers and placed them in jail at nearby Queen Anne's Town.* Upon learning of this incident, a contingent of British troops was sent back to Upper Marlboro* and seized Dr. William Beanes. It was Francis Scott Key's attempt to secure Dr. Beanes's release that led to the writing of "The Star-Spangled Banner." Bowie was born and died at Mattaponi and is believed to be buried in the family graveyard located in a field across the road south from the house, but there is no marker for him. Mattaponi is owned by the Catholic Church. The house can be seen from the parking area.

MAXWELL HALL (17388 Teagues Point Road, near Benedict, Charles County). NRHP. Maxwell Hall is not visible from the public road. It was built by George Maxwell during the mid-eighteenth century and sold in 1812 to Philemon Keech, a merchant from nearby Patuxent City. The British encamped at Patuxent City* near here on their first night, August 20, 1814, during their march from Benedict to Washington. Local tradition claims Maxwell Hall served as a temporary headquarters for the British during their march on Washington. The occupants of the house were ordered to the second floor while the British occupied the first floor. Contemporary maps suggest the British followed essentially Route 231, which bypasses Maxwell Hall. However, a road is known to have led from the plantation to a landing on Swanson Creek just off the Patuxent River, so it is possible some British troops, including sentinels and flanking forces, could have used the house or occupied the property, although no documentation supports this claim.

MELWOOD, also called Mellwood Park (11008 Old Marlboro Pike, near Upper Marlboro, Prince George's County). NRHP. PRIVATE. Melwood, built circa 1750 and raised to its present two-and-one-half-stories circa 1800, belonged to William and Ignatius Digges, sons of Col. William Dudley Digges of Warburton Manor, where Fort Washington* was built. During the War of 1812, the house was owned by Colonel Digges's daughter Mary and her husband, Thomas Sim Lee.* Their son, John Lee,* served as a colonel in the U.S. Army during the war. British forces marching to Washington encamped on the evening of August 23, 1814, to the west, approximately near the northeast corner of where Andrews Air Force Base* is now located. At the same time some American troops encamped about two miles northwest at Long Old Fields.* It was near Long Old Fields that American forces fired two or three rounds of artillery at the approaching enemy before withdrawing, the first artillery fired on the British in five days.

> British account of skirmish: Having advanced to within sixteen miles of Washington, and ascertaining the force of the enemy to be such as might authorize an attempt at carrying his capital, determined to make it and accordingly put the troops in movement on the evening of the 23rd. a corps of about 1200 men, appeared to oppose us, but retired after firing a few shot. (Maj. Gen. Robert Ross report; reprinted in Annapolis *Maryland Republican,* December 10, 1814)

> American reaction to British account: BRITISH LYING . . . Reader, you know how to form an estimate of British accuracy. The forces here magnified by [Maj.] gen. [Robert] Ross to 1200—were, Major [George] Peter's command, 110—Capt. [John J.] Stull's 105—and Capt. [John] Davidson's, 60—making in the whole 265 men—thus has the illustrious Ross, the second in command to [Duke of] Wellington, been guilty of two palpable lies, in a single dispatch to his government. (Annapolis *Maryland Republican,* December 10, 1814) (Major General Ross was not second in command to the Duke of Wellington. He was acknowledged to be a capable and even a brilliant brigade commander, but he had only been a major general for a year when he was sent on the expedition to the Chesapeake Bay.)

Tradition holds that several British officers, including Maj. Gen. Robert Ross, invited themselves for dinner with widow Mary Carroll Digges, who then occupied the house. American scout Thomas McKenny, possibly in company with Secretary of State James Monroe, observed that Major General Ross and Rear Admiral Cockburn slept in a small shed during the night of August 23–24, 1814, at the estate of Melwood. It is doubtful officers would sleep far from the safety of their encampment in enemy territory. Instead, it is more likely that officers may have napped or rested in a shed after having their dinner and while their troops passed on toward their encampment farther to the west near what today is Andrews Air Force Base.* Furthermore, Capt. James Scott wrote, "The army had taken up a position on rather elevated ground, in the centre of which, in a shepherd's hut, the General and Admiral had fixed their quarters" (Scott, 1834).[181] It is possible the shed or hut was on the Digges property but not necessarily near the house. While scholars such as Benson J. Lossing and Walter Lord claim

Maj. Gen. Robert Ross and Rear Adm. George Cockburn reportedly invited themselves for dinner here at Melwood. (John O. Brostrup 1936 photograph; HABS, Library of Congress)

the encampment on August 23 was at Melwood, contemporary British sketch maps suggest the encampment was a few miles west of Melwood.

METHODIST MEETING HOUSE. *See* listing, North Point

MITCHELL HOUSE (3370 Lewisville–Singerly Road [Route 213], at intersection with Telegraph Road [Route 273], Fair Hill, Cecil County). NRHP. PRIVATE. Dr. Abraham Mitchell of Elkton, a renowned physician during the Revolutionary War (*see* Mitchell House, Elkton), purchased this circa 1764 granite house in 1781. Col. George Edward Mitchell* (1781–1832) inherited the house from his father in 1817. During the War of 1812, Colonel Mitchell raised a company of volunteer militia and entered active military service, winning numerous citations for his efforts at Sacketts Harbor on Lake Ontario and on the Canadian frontier. He was commissioned a major of the 3rd Maryland Artillery on May 1, 1812, and lieu-

tenant colonel on March 3, 1813. He was transferred to the Artillery Corps on May 12, 1814, and then to the 3rd Artillery on June 1, 1814. Mitchell was brevetted colonel on May 5, 1814, for his gallant conduct at the defense of Fort Oswego, New York. He is buried at Congressional Cemetery,* Washington, D.C.

MITCHELL HOUSE (8796 Maryland Parkway, off Tolchester Beach Road [Route 21], Tolchester Beach, Kent County). PRIVATE. The main section of this house dates from 1825 although the earliest section is believed to date from 1743. It is claimed that after being mortally wounded at Caulks Field* Capt. Sir Peter Parker was taken to Mitchell House, now the Inn at Mitchell House, a bed and breakfast. A blanket was taken from a house to wrap Captain Parker in after the battle, but contemporary accounts do not specify which house it came from. Parker's body was taken directly to the British boats and never to any house. Furthermore, the Mitchell House is not along the route the British used to march from the battle and therefore is unlikely to be the house from which a blanket was taken.

However, Mitchell House is the site of an early morning British raid on September 3, 1814, during which Maj. Joseph Mitchell and his wife were roused from their bed and Mitchell's horses shot. Major Mitchell was taken prisoner as he was believed to be a commissary general for Maryland but was actually a militia contractor for Kent County. Mrs. Mitchell was permitted to visit her husband later that same day and the following day, bringing him fruit, butter, and cider. Some accounts claim Major Mitchell was sent as a prisoner of war to England and did not return until 1817.

MOORE, NICHOLAS RUXTON, GRAVE. *See* appendix B

MONTGOMERY COURT HOUSE. *See* Rockville

MOUNT ADAMS, also called The Mount (1912 Fountain Green Road [Route 543], Creswell, Harford County). NRHP. PRIVATE. Capt. John Adams Webster* (1787–1877) lived at Mount Adams, built in 1816. The squared columns were added to the house in the 1850s. Webster distinguished himself as an officer in Com. Joshua Barney's U.S. Chesapeake Flotilla and during the defense of Baltimore, where he commanded Fort Babcock. Twice wounded, Webster was presented with two swords for his service. The presentation sword given to Webster by the City of Baltimore is in the collections of the Maryland Historical Society.* A portrait of Webster hangs in the Harford County Courthouse at Bel Air. Webster was buried in the family graveyard located in a pasture about a mile north-northwest from the mansion and south of Mikara Court. Unfortunately, his gravestone is broken and partially buried in the ground, although a bronze plaque repeats the text of the gravestone.

> The flags at the City Hall and Custom House were displayed at half mast in honor of the memory of the deceased [Capt. John Adams Webster]. (Baltimore *American,* July 13, 1877)[182]

> The military service of the late Capt. Webster in aid of Fort McHenry and in the defense of Baltimore in 1814 was certainly of the highest importance and should be appreciated by every patriotic American. I will cause the flag of this fort to be half-masted and minute guns to be fired at noon tomorrow, the hour which you state has been appointed for Capt. Webster's internment. (Gen. William F. Barry, commander of Fort McHenry, July 6, 1877)[183]

Captain Webster's first sword was presented in 1816 by Baltimore luminaries; the inscription reads: May 11, 1816. To John A. Webster, later of the Chesapeake Flotilla. Sir, the citizens of Baltimore, with the most lively sentiments of gratitude to you and the brave men under your command during the attack of the British on the city . . . present you some testimony of it for your gallant and successful defense of the six-gun battery [Fort Babcock]. A second sword was presented by the State of Maryland in 1842. The inscription reads: Presented by the State of Maryland to Captain John A. Webster for his gallant defense of the battery committed to his charge during the memorable attack against the city of Baltimore September 12th, 1814. This sword was found in a pawnshop about 1908.

MOUNT AETNA FURNACE SITE, also called Antietam Furnace (not to be confused with the Antietam Iron Furnace), Black Rock Furnace, and Hughs Foundry (south side, near 21426 Mt. Aetna Road, Mount Aetna, Washington County). NRHP. PRIVATE. There are two iron furnace sites here. The first, called Antietam Furnace, began operation about 1761 (located behind Mt. Aetna Fire Department near the intersection of Crystal Falls Drive and Mt. Aetna Road). The second furnace site, called Mount Aetna Furnace, is located a few miles farther west and operated from 1808 to circa 1818. During the War of 1812, the Mount Aetna Furnace produced cannon for the U.S. Chesapeake Flotilla. At least five cannon from this furnace are known to survive: one at the Boonsboro Museum, one at Shafer Park in Boonsboro,* and one on loan to the Hager Museum* at Hagerstown. In the front yard of the house across the road from the Mount Aetna Furnace site is a fourth cannon set in the ground and fashioned into a light post. A fifth cannon, also in the front yard, has been mounted. Supposedly at least three more cannon and cannonballs are buried in the garden area of this house. These cannon show that the barrel bore was off center and thus the tubes were defective and discarded.

On March 7, 1814, owner Jonathan Brien put the furnace up for sale. An 1814 ad noted that the metal produced here also supplied Henry Foxall's Columbian Foundry* in Georgetown. There cannon and shot were produced for the U.S. Army and Navy and state militia during the War of 1812. The 15,000-acre Mount Aetna Furnace site contained stables for sixty-seven horses, warehouses, a hundred worker houses, a saw mill, a merchant mill, a mansion house, a blast furnace, a forge, and numerous other buildings. The ad also said "Forty negroes will also be sold who were millers, waggoners, shoemakers, etc." (Baltimore *Federal Gazette,* March 17, 1814).

MOUNT ANDREW SITE (east of Denton Bridge that carries Route 404 Business over Choptank River, Denton, Caroline County). Capt. Joseph Richardson was impressed into the service of the British Royal Navy. Impressment was one of the leading causes of the War of 1812. In 1835, Richardson built a three-story brick house named Mount Andrew, where he spent the rest of his life. He is buried in the graveyard of St. Elizabeth's Church (First and Franklin streets, Denton), established in 1831.

★**MOUNT CALVERT** (Patuxent River, 16800 Mount Calvert Road, Croom, Prince George's County). Mount Calvert is a Federal style plantation house built circa 1790. On the evening of August 22, 1814, while anchored off Mount Calvert aboard a tender from H.M. brig *Resolution,* Rear Adm. George Cockburn expressed satisfaction with "the complete destruction of this Flotilla [U.S. Chesapeake] of the Enemy which has lately occupied So much of our attention."[184] Here Cockburn disembarked a contingent of marines, marine artillery, and seamen to join the army at Upper Marlboro for the march on Washington. British naval forces occupied Mount Calvert until the return of the invading troops.

> I instantly sent orders for our Marine and Naval Forces at Pig Point to be forthwith moved over to Mount Calvert, and for the Marines, Marine Artillery, and a Proportion of the Seamen to be there landed, and with the utmost expedition to join the Army, which I also most readily agreed to accompany. (Rear Adm. George Cockburn to Vice Adm. Sir Alexander F. I. Cochrane, August 27, 1814)[185]

Following the British departure from the Patuxent River, Mount Calvert served as a U.S. Navy marshaling and transshipment area for materials salvaged from the scuttled U.S. Chesapeake Flotilla. The U.S. schooner *Asp* participated in these salvage operations during September and October 1814.

Lt. John Brookes of Capt. Richard L. Hall's Company, 34th Regiment, was commissioned a captain in the 38th U.S. Infantry on May 20, 1813. He owned Mount Calvert from 1835 to 1858.

MOUNT LUBENTIA (603 Largo Road, Prince George's County). NRHP. PRIVATE. Mount Lubentia (not visible from the public road), a 1798 Federal style home, served temporarily as the Prince George's county seat from June 25, 1814, until late August 1814, when British activity in the area threatened Upper Marlboro.* In addition to the public county records, the state records moved from Annapolis to Up-

per Marlboro for safekeeping were also temporarily stored here. Col. William Bradley Beanes,* Dr. William Beanes's half-brother, assisted in the movement of the records. Carts were hired at $7.00 each.

> Upon an alarm that the enemy was approaching the town of Upper Marlboro, the records and papers were removed by the Register of Wills and The Clerk of the County Court to a house [Mount Lubentia] in the possession of Dennis Magruder about eight miles from Upper Marlboro. (June 25, 1814)[186]

MOUNT PLEASANT (north side of Grove Neck Road [Route 282], 0.5 mile west of intersection with Sandy Bottom Road, Cecil County). NRHP. PRIVATE. Pass by only; no pull off. Dr. John Thompson Veazey,* who served in the defense of Fort Duffy during the May 6, 1813, British attack on Georgetown and Fredericktown lived at Mount Pleasant. The Maryland historical roadside marker at the entrance to Mount Pleasant gives the rank of Thomas Ward Veazey, who assisted in the defense of Fort Duffy, as colonel. Veazey was actually a lieutenant colonel.

MOUNT PLEASANT LANDING SITE (Patuxent River, approximately 2.0 miles above Hill Bridge, which carries Southern Maryland Boulevard [Route 4], Prince George's County). PRIVATE. John Weems in late August and September 1814 conducted salvage operations on the scuttled U.S. Chesapeake Flotilla from Mount Pleasant Landing.

★**MOUNT WELBY** (6411 Oxon Hill Road, Prince George's County). NRHP. Located at Oxen Hill Farm is Mount Welby, the circa 1811 home that belonged to Dr. Samuel DeButts, whose wife, Mary Welby DeButts, wrote letters to her sister describing Capt. James Alexander Gordon's British squadron advancing up the Potomac River and firing Congreve rockets, three of which landed near her home.

> I cannot express to you the distress it has occasioned at the Battle of Bladensburg we heard every fire (that place being not more 5 or 6 miles from us). Our House was shook repeatedly by the firing upon forts & Bridges, & illuminated by the fires in our Capitol. It was indeed a Day & night of horrors, the fleet debarkment from [Rear] Admiral [George] Cockburn's fleet lay directly before our House. The Capitulation of Alexandria & the result you must have seen in the Public papers. We left home for Loudoun (Virginia) while the British Vessels were in our River, passing in the ferry Boat close to them without being molested; you know not how it hurt me to think I was so near my Country men, & must look

Mount Lubentia served as temporary seat of government and housing for county and state documents when the Prince George's County seat of government at Upper Marlboro was threatened by British attack. (Circa 1883-88 photograph; HABS, Library of Congress)

These government document fragments were recovered from the attic of Mount Lubentia during restoration in the 1980s and 1990s. (Ralph Eshelman 2000 photograph)

upon them as Enemy, whom I should have rejoiced to have shown every attention to; we found three Rockets on our Hill evidently pointed at our House but fortunately did not reach it. (Mary Welby DuButts to Millicent Welby Ridgehill of Welbourne, March 18, 1815)[187]

To protect the rear of nearby Fort Washington,* Brig. Gen. Robert Young and 454 men were stationed at Mount Welby. These troops later joined the American forces defending the White House Gun Battery* in Virginia. From near here on September 4 and 5, 1814, Capt. John Rodgers launched fire vessels against the British squadron. (*See also* Fort Washington and Washington Navy Yard, Washington, D.C.)

American account of fire-ship attack: A fireship was sent down on Monday afternoon by com. Rodgers, which very nearly encountered one of the frigates of the enemy, but was grappled and towed out of the way by his barges. A torpedo [mine] was sent down on Monday evening, after the British fleet passed [David] Porter's battery [White House Gun Battery*], and exploded about 9 at night, with what effect is not yet known. (Annapolis *Maryland Republican,* September 10, 1814)

Second American account of fire-ship attack: proceeded down the Potomac with three small fire vessels under the protection of four barges or cutters, manned with about sixty seamen, armed with muskets, destined against two of the enemy's frigates and a bomb-ship, which lay about 2 1-2 miles below Alexandria . . . I have no doubt, would have succeeded in destroying two at least of the enemy's ships, had not the wind failed them sometime before, and particularly after they had reached the uppermost ship, within the range of musket shot . . . Of the enemy's boats, some were employed in towing off the fire-vessels, and the rest in pursuit of our four cutters . . . On the 4th inst. I had another fire vessel prepared, but it being calm, I ordered . . . the four cutters, to proceed with one of the remaining lighters . . . to attack the bomb-ship, which in the anxiety of the enemy to get below the temporary forts [White House Gun Battery* and Indian Head Gun Battery*] . . . had been left exposed to attack. (Capt. John Rodgers to Secretary of Navy William Jones, September 9, 1814; reprinted in Baltimore *Niles' Weekly Register,* October 1, 1814)

British account of fire boat attack: Contrary winds again occasioned us the laborious task of warping the Ships down the River in which a days delay early took place owing to the [H.M. bomb-ship] Devastation grounding. The Enemy took advantage of this Circumstance to attempt her destruction by three fire vessels and attended by five row Boats.— But their object was defeated by the promptitude and gallantry of Captain [Thomas] Alexander who pushed off with his own Boats and being followed by those of the other Ships chased the boats of the Enemy up to the town of Alexandria. (Capt. James Alexander Gordon to Vice Adm. Sir Alexander F. I. Cochrane, September 9, 1814)[188]

NEWTOWN (Breton Bay, end of Newtown Neck Road [Route 243], Newtown Neck, St. Mary's County). A detachment of British troops landed at dawn on July 19, 1814, at Newtown. From here they marched to take part in a coordinated raid on nearby Leonardtown.*

NORTHAMPTON PLANTATION SITE (10700 Lake Overlook Drive, off Lake Arbor Way, about 1.0 mile east of Landover Road [Route 202], near Largo, Prince George's County). The victorious British troops passed by Northampton Plantation, home of Samuel Sprigg, during their return march from burning Washington. The British encamped at Largo,* possibly on the plantation grounds. Only ruins of the plantation slave houses remain visible.

NORTHAMPTON FOUNDRY SITE, also called Northampton Iron Furnace, Northampton Iron Works, and Ashland Iron Company (Hampton Cove, north bank of Spring Branch, Patterson Run, Lock Raven Reservoir, about 2,500 feet east of Dulaney Valley Road [Route 146], southeast of intersection of Chapelwood Lane, Baltimore County). Northampton Foundry, owned by Charles Carnan Ridgely (1790–1829), second master of Hampton,* operated from 1760 until 1850. The foundry made camp kettles, cannons, grapeshot, and round shot ranging from two to eighteen pounds. The foundry was described as the best in the country and its cannon equal in quality of any yet made on the continent. The iron works supplied cannon to Baltimore privateers during the War of 1812. Fragments of a cannon were recovered from the testing area of the furnace in 1981 and deposited at the Baltimore County Historical Society. The stone remains of the foundry furnace are visible in Lock Raven Reservoir. A gated dirt road on the east side of Dulaney Valley Road just north of the intersection with Chapelwood Lane leads to the reservoir. About 0.5 mile east on this road are stone and brick ruins believed to be part of the furnace complex.

NORTH POINT (bounded by Patapsco River on south, Back River on north, and Chesapeake Bay on east, south end of North Point Road [Route 20], Baltimore County). North Point is named for Capt. Robert North, who established a trading company on the tip of this peninsula in 1793. The British fleet anchored in Old Roads Bay just off the point on

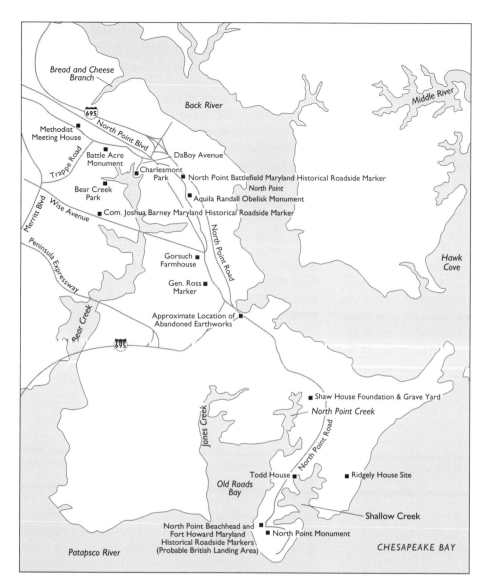

North Point Region

the evening of September 11, 1814, in preparation for their unsuccessful land assault on Baltimore. Approximately 4,500 troops began debarking about 3:00 a.m., September 12, 1814, and at about 8:00 a.m. began the fifteen-mile march toward Baltimore. Each man carried three days' provisions and eighty rounds of ammunition, twenty cartridges more than normal. Instead of the usual supply of clothing, the soldiers were allowed to take only one blanket, a spare shirt, and an extra pair of shoes. Hair brushes and other personal articles were to be shared. After the loss of Maj. Gen. Robert Ross in a skirmish at Godley Wood, just prior

to the Battle of North Point, and the failure of the naval attack on Fort McHenry, the British troops withdrew and on September 15 and 16, 1814, re-embarked. Each September during Defenders Day Celebration, the Battle of North Point is re-enacted at Fort Howard Park.

The "North Point Beachhead" Maryland historical roadside marker at the entrance to Fort Howard Veterans Hospital, at the end of North Point Road, claims Major General Ross was killed at the Battle of North Point. Actually Ross was killed in a skirmish prior to the Battle of North Point. A plaque behind the main hospital building at Fort Howard Veterans Hospital says "seven thousand troops" landed here from their fleet. The total number of British troops was closer to 4,500; these troops actually withdrew from the outskirts of Baltimore, not the North Point battlefield as claimed on the plaque. The text on the "Fort Howard" Maryland historical roadside marker at the end of North Point Road gives the first name of Lieutenant Colonel Harris as Davis, but his real name was actually David. The North Point Battlefield Maryland historical roadside marker (northeast side of Old North Point Road [Route 20], 200 feet east of Eleanor Terrace, 0.25 mile southeast of North Point Boulevard [Route 151]) claims the British army consisted of 7,000 troops; the true force was closer to 4,500 troops.

Five of the six Spanish-American War-era batteries at Fort Howard are named for War of 1812 veterans: Battery Clagett is named for Lt. Levi Clagett, who was killed in the defense of Fort McHenry; Battery Harris is named for Lt. Col. David Harris, who commanded a regiment of Baltimore artillery; Battery Key is named for Francis Scott Key, author of the poem that eventually became "The Star-Spangled Banner"; Battery Nicholson is named for Judge Joseph Hopper Nicholson, captain of the Baltimore Fencibles, U.S. Volunteers; and Battery Stricker is named for Brig. Gen. John Stricker, who commanded the 3rd Brigade, Maryland militia.

Abandoned and Unfinished Defensive Earthworks Site (near intersection of Delmar Avenue and North Point Road [Route 20], near Wells and McComas VFW Post, 6521 North Point Road). Along the North Point peninsula where it then narrowed to about a mile (Humphry Creek on the west, since filled, and Back River on the east) the Americans abandoned their uncompleted defensive earthworks to move to another choke point farther up the peninsula between the narrows of Bear Creek and Bread and Cheese Creek.

> Three miles from North point the enemy had entrenched himself quite across this neck of land . . . The enemy was actively employed in the completion of this work, deepening the ditch and strengthening it in front by a low Abbatis, —both which, however, he precipitately abandoned on the approach of our skirmishers, leaving in our hand some few dragoons, being part of his rear guard. (Col. Arthur Brooke to Secretary of State for War and the Colonies Earl Bathurst, 3rd Earl Bathurst, September 17, 1814)[189]

Battle Acre Monument (south side of 3100 block of Old North Point Road [Route 20], opposite intersection with Kimberly Road). Battle Acre Monument supposedly marks Brig. Gen. John Stricker's line of defense, specifically where the 5th Regiment, Maryland militia, was positioned on September 12, 1814, at the Battle of North Point. But General Stricker reported to Maj. Gen. Samuel Smith that his troops were located at the intersection of Trappe Road (then Long Log Lane) and North Point Road, which would mean Battle Acre was in front of the actual battle line. Battle Acre is more correctly in the vicinity of the log house occupied by Capt. Philip Benjamin Sadtler's Baltimore Yagers (light infantry) at the beginning of the battle. (The State of Maryland has recently purchased property near the intersection of Trappe Road and North Point Road to interpret the Battle of North Point. This site will be managed by the North Point State Park.)

A rough-hewn block of granite served as the cornerstone for the monument, which was laid on September 12, 1839, on the twenty-fifth anniversary of the battle. To celebrate the occasion the Fort McHenry garrison flag (Star-Spangled Banner) was spread for all to see. Remains of entrench-

(Opposite, top) Engraving circa 1814 of the Battle of North Point depicting a detail of the British positions. Key: I. British left flank. L. British artillery and rockets. M. British riflemen swarming American sharpshooters. O. Death of Major General Ross. ([Andrew Duluc], *First View of the Battle of Patapsco Neck*; courtesy Maryland Historical Society)

(Opposite, bottom) Battle of North Point viewed from behind the American line. Key: 1. Brig. Gen. John Stricker; 2. Aide-de-Camp George P. Stevenson; 3. Maj. James Calhoun; 4. Maj. William B. Barney; 5. Brig. Maj. Leonard Farleigh; 6. Maj. Gen. Robert Goodloe Harper; 7. John Buck, trumpeter; 8. Lt. Col. James Biays; 9. Maj. William Jackson; 10. Archibald Kerr, paymaster; 11. Adj. Lemuel G. Taylor; 12. Sgt. Maj. James Blair; 13. Capt. James Sterett's Hussars; 14. Capt. Jehu Bouldin and 1st Lt. Thomas Kell's troop; 15. Capt. James Horton's troop; 16. Capt. John Hanna's troop; 17. Lt. Col. Joseph Sterett's 5th Regiment; 18. Lt. Col. Kennedy Long's 27th Regiment; 19. Lt. Col. Benjamin Fowler, 39th Regiment; 20. Lt. Col. Henry Amey and 1st Maj. John Young, 51st Regiment; 21. Riflemen. 1st Lt. Gregorius Andre, mortally wounded; 22. Lt. Col. Richard Key Heath; 23. 2nd Maj. Standish Barry; 24. Adj. James Cheston; 25. John Montgomery's Artillery; 26. Maj. Samuel Moore; 27. Adj. Gen. James Lowrie Donaldson, mortally wounded; 28. Maj. Joseph Robinson; 29. Adj. Thomas Baltzell; 30. Maj. Jacob Steigers; 31. Capt. George Stiles artillery; 32. Maj. George Hennick; 33. Meadow and haystack; 34. House fired by Capt. Philip Benjamin Sadtler's company of Yagers; 35. Lt. John Reese and James M'Culloch, wounded; 36. Capt. Michael H. Spangler's Company of Volunteers from York, Pennsylvania; 37. Capt. Thomas Quantrill's Company of Volunteers from Hagerstown; 38 and 39. Capt. Baer and Frederick Metzger's companies from Hanover, Pennsylvania; 40. Head of Bear Creek; 41. British flankers; 42. British commanded by Col. Arthur Brooke wheeling into line. The rank and full names are corrected or added from Lossing's original key. (Lossing, *Pictorial Field-Book of the War of 1812*)

ments and a log hut bearing scars from cannonballs and musket balls were still present. A flotilla of seven steamboats left Baltimore for Bear Creek carrying dignitaries, among whom were two cabinet officers, two justices of the Supreme Court, the governor of Maryland, and at least three generals. Speeches and festivities were concluded with a national salute of artillery and infantry; the grand flag was then returned to Louisa Hughes Armistead at her residence in Mount Vernon, Baltimore. (*See* Maryland Historical Society, Baltimore.) Com. Joshua Barney's father may have owned or rented the property where the park is now located.

Dr. Jacob Houck, health commissioner of Baltimore County, conveyed the deed for Battle Acre to the State of Maryland for the sum of one dollar on the day before the ceremony. Houck annually hosted a diner for the North Point veterans at his nearby summer home called Houck's Pavilion. The monument, consisting of a square-shaped granite block with a bronze plaque mounted on the front (now missing) and a small cannon mounted on top, was not completed until the National Star-Spangled Centennial Celebration of 1914. Mrs. Reuben Ross Holloway was the driving force behind the effort to complete the monument. She also lobbied to get "The Star-Spangled Banner" designated our national anthem. The iron fence surrounding the acre was recycled from the Asylum for the Blind on east North Avenue, Baltimore, when that property was condemned. The park was last restored in 1962.

> The precession having formed around the foundation of the Monument, the venerable Major General [William M.?] McDonald, aided by a soldier of the Revolution, [Brig.] General T[obias]. E. Stansbury, Governor [William] Grason, [Brig.] General [Thomas Marsh] Forman, and others proceeded to the cornerstone, in doing which in its cavity an official list of all the officers and privates who were in the Battle of North Point and Fort McHenry, lists of the present members of the military corps of the city, the newspaper of the day, coins &c. and a feu de joie [firing of guns in celebration of joy] by the whole line of infantry. (Baltimore *American*, September 12, 1839)

Bear Creek Park (Park Haven Road, north off Gray Haven Road, south off Lynch Road, east off Trappe Road, south off Old North Point Road [Route 20]). Bear Creek Park provides a good view of the North Point battlefield. The British position is to the northeast and the American position to the northwest. The British withdrew their wounded by boat using Bear Creek. The 1839 delegation that celebrated the

dedication of Battle Acre traveled to the site by steamboat, landing at Bear Creek. (*See also* Battle Acre and Charlesmont Park, North Point.)

> On monday Brigadier General [John] Stricker took a good position at the junction of the two roads leading from this place to North Point, having his right flanked by Bear Creek and his left by a marsh. He here awaited the approach of the Enemy. (Maj. Gen. Samuel Smith to Acting Secretary of War James Monroe, September 19, 1814)[190]

Colgate Creek, also Colegate Creek (east-southeast of Fort McHenry and the northern entrance to Baltimore Harbor Tunnel near the east Baltimore City line, between Seagirt and Dundalk marine terminals). Colgate Creek was the third and northernmost water passage used by the British to communicate with and supply their troops during the land advance on September 13–14, 1814. (*See also* Sollers' House.)

Charlesmont Park (south end of Deboy Avenue, south off Old North Point Road [Route 20]). Charlesmont Park, located along Bear Creek, provides a good view of the North Point battlefield. On September 12, 1814, Brig. Gen. John Stricker positioned his right flank at the head of Bear Creek near Charlesmont Park. (*See also* Bear Creek Park, North Point.)

Gorsuch Farmhouse Site (just west of intersection of Wise Avenue and North Point Boulevard [Route 151]). The Robert Gorsuch farmhouse served as headquarters for American videttes (mounted sentinels) prior to the Battle of North Point. From here Brig. Gen. John Stricker on the night of September 11, 1814, sent his cavalry to reconnoiter the British advance. Maj. Gen. Robert Ross stopped here for breakfast the next morning and was killed soon after leaving the farm. (*See* Randall, Aquila, Obelisk Monument.) Ross died while being carried back to the fleet at a spot on North Point Road near the farm. The farm was burned by the British because American forces had occupied it. A golf course occupies the farm site today; the skirmish site is heavily developed.

The Maj. Gen. Robert Ross historic marker erected by the Patapsco Neck Historical Society and Patapsco Neck Bicentennial Committee (west side of North Point Boulevard, south of Wise Avenue) is located close to the Gorsuch Farm site (west of the marker). The marker first read General "Charles" Ross, and the name "Robert" was tacked over the incorrect name.

British account of Maj. Gen. Robert Ross's death: We had advanced about Five Miles . . . when the General and myself being with the advanced Guard observed a Division of the Enemy Posted at a turning of the Road, extending into a Wood on our Left, A sharp Fire was almost immediately opened upon us from it, and as quickly returned with considerable Effect by our advanced Guard which pressing steadily forward soon obliged the Enemy to run off with the utmost precipitation leaving behind him several Men Killed and Wounded; but it is with the most heartfelt sorrow I have to add that in this Short and desultory Skirmish my gallant and highly valued Friend the Major General received a Musquet Ball through his arm into his Breast, which proved fatal to him on his way to the Water Side for reembarkation— Our Country Sire has lost in him one of its best and bravest Soldiers. (Rear Adm. George Cockburn to Vice Adm. Sir Alexander F. I. Cochrane, September 15, 1814)[191]

A Relic Gone.—But few persons have ever gone down the North Point road, who have not had pointed out to them the large wild poplar tree, under which the British General [Robert] Ross, who commanded the troops, destined for an attack on Baltimore in 1814, drew his last breath . . . He fell by a shot fired from an ambush, and was removed from the advance to the tree in question. The old tree, after weathering thirty winters, since that occurrence, has at last fallen under the stroke of the woodman's axe. It was situated on the land of Mr. Vincent Green, who would not have had it cut down, but for the apprehension that the first hard blow would have thrown it across the road. We doubt whether there is to be found in the country, a tree, under which "confusion to the enemies of liberty," has been quaffed in full bumpers, more frequently than under "Ross Tree," as it has always been familiarily called. (Baltimore *Sun,* March 22, 1844). (A cane, reportedly made from wood from the tree under which Major General Ross was shot, is in the collections of the Maryland Historical Society.)

Maj. Gen. Robert Ross was buried with full military honors on September 29, 1814, on what was then English soil in St. Paul's Cemetery, Halifax, Nova Scotia. His gravestone reads in part "WAS KILLED at the commencement of an action which terminated in the defeat and Rout OF THE TROOPS OF THE UNITED STATES NEAR BALTIMORE." While the American forces retreated from the Battle of Bladensburg in panic, their withdrawal from the Battle of North Point was orderly.

The official coat of arms of the Ross family includes a "hand grasping a flag-staff broken in bend sinister [toward the left, suggesting disaster or misfortune], flowing the colors of the United States of America." Under the shield are the words "Maj. Gen. Robert Ross. Died August 4, 1814;

Major General Ross was mortally wounded near this spot. This 1816 romanticized print depicts him falling into the arms of another officer while a Congreve rocket passes overhead. ("The Death of General Ross, near Baltimore—As soon as he perceived he was wounded he fell into the arms of a Brother Officer"; Library of Congress)

Slain at Washington, in America, commanding his majesty's troops. His widow and descendants to be called ROSS OF BLADENSBURGH." Ross of course died at North Point on September 12, 1814, not at Washington; Bladensburg is misspelled.

Methodist Meeting House and Hospital Site, also called Battle Ground Methodist Episcopal Church and Bread & Cheese Creek Battle Monument (Old North Point Road and Perrins Lane, immediately north of Galilee Baptist Church [2440 Old North Point Road]). Brig. Gen. John Stricker's 3rd

Brigade of Maryland militia encamped from about 9:00 p.m., September 11, until the morning of September 12, 1814, at what was then called Godley Wood. Stricker may have actually stayed in the church. On the night of September 12–13, 1814, following the battle, Col. Arthur Brooke, Maj. Gen. Robert Ross's replacement, encamped here. The circa 1795 church served as a hospital after the engagement. When the church was remodeled in 1837 and again in 1858, hundreds of bullets were reportedly found in its frame. The church was demolished in 1921. A nearby log schoolhouse, demolished in 1927, also reportedly had numerous bullet holes. The Rev. Henry Smith, a Methodist circuit minister, visited the meeting house a few days after the engagement and remarked that the structure looked more like a slaughter-house than a house of worship. The meeting house became a place where veterans of the battle as well as other soldiers, politicians, and fraternal organizations gathered to commemorate the battle. A monument placed by the Patriotic Order of Sons of America in Maryland to commemorate the Methodist church and its role as a hospital in the Battle of North Point was dedicated in 1914 by the Star-Spangled Banner Centennial Committee. (*See also* Battle Acre Monument Site, North Point.)

British account of battle: [The Americans] gave way in every direction, and was chased by us a considerable distance with great Slaughter, abandoning his Post of the Meeting House situated in this Wood, and leaving all his Wounded and Two of his Field Guns in our possession. (Rear Adm. George Cockburn to Vice Adm. Sir Alexander F. I. Cochrane, September 14, 1814)[192]

Second British account of battle: The British soldiers moved forward with their accustomed fearlessness, and the Americans, with much apparent coolness, stood to receive them. Now, however, when little more than a hundred paces divided the one line from the other, both parties made ready to bring matters more decidedly to a personal struggle. The Americans were the first to use their small-arms. Having rent the air with a shout, they fired a volley, begun upon the right, and carried away regularly to the extreme left; and then loading again, kept up an unintermitted discharge, which soon in a great degree concealed them from observation. Nor were we backward in returning the salute. A hearty British cheer gave notice our willingness to meet them; and firing and running, we gradually closed upon them, with the design of bringing the bayonet into play . . . Volley upon volley having been given, we were now advanced within less than twenty yards of the American line; yet such was the denseness of the smoke, that it was only when a passing breeze swept away the cloud for a moment, that either force became visible to the other. It was not, therefore, at men's persons that the fire of our soldiers was directed. The flashes of the enemy's muskets alone served as an object to aim at, as, without, doubt, the flashes of our muskets alone guided the enemy. (Lt. George Robert Gleig, 1833)[193]

Methodist Meeting House, used by both the British and Americans as a field hospital, as it appeared in the 1850s. (Lossing, *Pictorial Field-Book of the War of 1812*)

Dr. James Haines McCulloh, Jr., barely out of his teens, received his medical degree on July 17, 1814, and was appointed U.S. Army garrison surgeon at Hampstead Hill. He left Baltimore traveling to North Point in search of his father, who was among the militia. At the Methodist Meeting House on September 13, 1814, he attended to the wounded of both British and American soldiers. In an era before anesthetics, a musket ball was given the patient to clench between his teeth to help endure pain. At least ten different individual tooth marks are present on a musket ball recovered from this site and now displayed at the Dr. Samuel D. Harris National Museum of Dentistry,* Baltimore. Some authorities claim that because a musket ball might be swallowed, surgeons were more likely to use a stick or a piece of leather.

> I was shewn the meeting house in which some of our wounded men lay—along with a few British—on not finding my father here—I instantly requested permission to go over the field of battle—which was granted one of the [British] surgeons accompanying me—on reaching the field of action—the surgeon promised me the use of some litters to bring the wounded in . . . In the course of a few hours I had the wounded brought in which were 28 in number—2 of these died in the course of the night after I had dressed them and extracted their balls one of which was a grape [shot]. (Dr. James Haines McCulloh, Jr. to Gen. Samuel Smith, September 14, 1814)[194]

At the Battle of North Point, where I accompanied my brother [Capt. George Steuart, 5th Regiment Infantry] and his company with my Father as Commissary, I found my little knowledge of surgery very useful. One of the soldiers had been shot through the thigh wounding the femoral artory, so with his cravat and a small stick I made a tournequet, arresting the flow of blood to place him in my wagon and bring him to the Md. Hospital. Here Surgeon Gibson received him and finally amputated the leg. (Richard Sprigg Steuart, age 17)[195]

The Night being fast approaching, and the Troops much fatigued, Colonel [Arthur] Brook determined on remaining for the Night on the Field of Battle, and on the morning of the 13th· leaving a small guard at the Meeting House to collect and protect the Wounded— We again moved forward towards Baltimore. (Rear Adm. George Cockburn to Vice Adm. Sir Alexander F. I. Cochrane, September 15, 1814)[196]

The meeting-house, a place of worship, the only building near the scene of battle, was converted into an temporary refuge for friends and foes. The temple of God—of peace and goodwill towards men—vibrated with the groans of the wounded and the dying. The accents of human woe floated upon the ear, and told a melancholy tale of ebbing tide of human life. (Capt. James Scott, 1834)[197]

Some of the soldiers killed during the Battle of North Point are said to be buried in the Methodist Meeting House yard but if grave markers were placed, none survive. (*See also* Potters Field Site, Baltimore, for another site where soldiers from this conflict were buried.)

North Point Road (road begins at Fort Howard and passes north through Edgemere, Charlemont, and Dundalk to the Philadelphia Road). The British marched from their landing near the tip of North Point to Baltimore along the North Point Road on September 12, 1814, and again during their withdrawal three days later.

> In most of the woods they [Americans] had felled trees, and thrown them across the road; but as these abatis were without defenders, we experienced no other inconvenience than what arose from loss of time, being obliged to halt on all such occasions till the pioneers had removed the obstacle. (Lt. George Robert Gleig, 1847)[198]

Randall, Aquila, Obelisk Monument (northeast side of 3970 Old North Point Road [Route 20], and 4000 Old Battle Grove Road, 200 feet east of Eleanor Terrace, 0.25 mile southeast of North Point Boulevard [Route 151]). The First Mechanical Volunteers erected a marble monument near here in July 1817 to commemorate the loss of twenty-four-year-old Pvt. Aquila Randall, a member of the Mechanical Volunteers, 5th Regiment, Maryland militia, who fell during a skirmish preceding the Battle of North Point on September 12, 1814. The only member of this unit killed in the skirmish, Randall died along with twenty-one other Americans as well as British commander Maj. Gen. Robert Ross. Some accounts claim Aquila Randall killed Major General Ross, but others credit American sharpshooters Pvt. Daniel Wells and Pvt. Harry McComas, both of whom died in the battle. The Wells and McComas Monument,* Baltimore, commemorates them. The Aquila Randall Obelisk Monument is among the first monuments ever erected on a battlefield in the United States. During the dedication, Benjamin C. Howard, the former commander of the Mechanical Volunteers, delivered a speech including the following lines: "It was here that the haughty General [Robert Ross] who declared he did not care if it rained militia atoned with his life for his opinion."

By 1944, the monument had suffered from neglect and the obelisk had fallen down. The monument was restored in

The Aquila Randall Monument as it appeared in the 1850s. (Lossing, *Pictorial Field-Book of the War of 1812*)

1945 by Eli Buniavas, a Croatian immigrant, who acquired the property. He spent $7,000 on the restoration. The monument was mounted on a wedding cake-like pyramid of five steps on an elliptical lawn 90 by 20 feet and surrounded by an iron fence. When Buniavas died in 1962, the executor of his estate offered a 21 by 26 foot parcel called the Monument Lot to the State of Maryland, but the offer was declined. In 1977, the new owner, a Mr. McClees, offered the monument to the Baltimore County Department of Recreation and Parks but this offer was also rejected. Because of nearby construction on July 20, 1977, the monument was moved and the fence and 1945 pedestal removed, thus giving the monument an appearance more similar to that in 1817. But it is still located on private property without a designated caretaker. At some point the monument was painted white with black letters. The original location of the monument was behind the house at 3995 North Point Road next to a large white oak tree that reportedly had no less than twenty musket balls embedded in it.

The monument includes the inscription "How beautiful is death, when earned by virtue." This quote is from Joseph Addison's drama *Cato: A Tragedy,* written in 1713, popular during the Colonial period.

On Monday last, "THE FIRST MECHANICAL VOLUNTEERS," one of the Companies attached to the Fifth Regiment erected on the spot where the advanced party under Major [Richard Key] Heath was engaged with the British forces, a MONUMENT to the memory of AQUILLA RANDALL, one of the members, who fell in that skirmish.

The company, headed by their commander, Capt. B[enjamin]. C[hew]. Howard, marched from town at an early hour; and having been joined on the ground, at eleven o'clock, by Col. [Richard Key] Heath, Lt. Col. Barry [John Berry?], Major [William] Steuart, and several other officers of the regiment, the ceremony of putting up the Monument was then commenced, and in a very short time completed under the direction of Mr. [Thomas] Towson (Lieut. of the Company)— Indeed, much commendation is due to this gentleman (and no less to Col. [Jacob] Small, who assisted in the design) for the style and good taste in which the Monument is executed. He has aimed at simplicity and neatness, and he had not been disappointed. (Baltimore *American,* July 28, 1817)

Maj. Richard Key Heath, 5th Regiment, Maryland militia, led the advance party of Brig. Gen. John Stricker's troops. His horse was shot out from under him, a second horse was badly wounded, and he himself sustained a contusion in his head from a musket ball.

Upon viewing the monument in 1832, a British army officer, Subaltern E. T. Coke, noted that Baltimoreans never allowed any honor to General Robert Ross and the British troops. Coke thought it unsporting for sharpshooters behind cover to pick off men in an open field. Who actually killed Ross is unclear; some evidence suggests he was shot by musketry during a skirmish-line discharge, not by sharpshooters in woods.

On October 16, 1826, President John Quincy Adams visited the battlefield. This was probably the first time a sitting president visited an American battlefield in an official capacity. President James Madison was present briefly during the Battle of Bladensburg but did not assume command. Adams noted that there were no other traces of the battle, although he was shown an oak tree in which it was said more than twenty of the enemy's musket balls had lodged. Adams picked up a dozen white oak acorns from under the tree to plant in Washington.

> The President [John Quincy Adams] left the City Hotel yesterday morning, about eight o'clock, accompanied by a number of citizens, on a visit to the Battle ground at North Point; and after an examination of the various points of this interesting spot, rendered additionally so by the explanations of those who had a personal share in the danger of the day. (Baltimore *American,* October 17, 1827)

Ridgely House Site, also called Sportmens' Hall, Steeple House Farm, and Goodwyn's [Goodwin's] Steeplechase Farm (near Shallow Creek at end of Bay Shore Road [instead of making turn to left (east), go straight] in edge of woods on left). A lookout station from the cupola on Ridgely House, built 1767 and destroyed by lightning in the late 1920s, was operated by Maj. Josiah Green in 1813 and 1814. (*See also* Todd House and Hancock's Resolution.) A blue jack (flag) signaled that the British were standing down the Bay, while a white jack signaled the enemy was coming up the Bay past Kent Island. A white jack was raised on Sunday morning, September 11, 1814, serving notice that the British fleet (consisting of some thirty vessels) was approaching Baltimore. When the signal was received in Baltimore that afternoon, three cannon shots were fired from Federal Hill* to notify the citizens of a possible attack.

> the House [Ridgely] [is] a very large Brick one, with a steeple like lookout place on top, from whence there is a most perfect view from North Point on one side, to and above Poplar Island on the other, and of the Bay in front, so that it would be next to an impossibility that any vessel or river boat could approach or pass without being observed. (Maj. William B. Barney to Brig. Gen. John Stricker, March 23, 1813)[199]

> man and despatch the barge belonging to the merchants, as low down the river as will enable her commander to see

The Ridgely House cupola was used as a lookout and signal station. (Photograph of painting from *Old Baltimore,* 1931; courtesy Dundalk Patapsco Neck Historical Society)

the top [cupola] of the Ridgley's house on North Point, and on observing her signal from the steeple, to hoist a flag of any find, fire a gun, and return to the Fort to note the signal hoisted. (Maj. Gen. Samuel Smith request to the Baltimore Committee of Vigilance and Public Safety)[200]

To monitor British naval movements and provide advance warning of possible attack, signal flags were flown between four leased Baltimore schooners named *Patapsco, Wasp, Comet,* and *Revenge,* as well as U.S. Navy gunboats and shore stations south of the Patapsco River.

Ridgely House was owned by Capt. Charles Goodwin, commander of the U.S. sloop-of-war *Erie,** built in Baltimore in 1813. He was ordered to Sackets Harbor.

Shaw House Site, also called Foulke Farmhouse (south end of Foulkes Farm Road, off North Point Road, near intersection with Millers Island Road). Capt. Thomas Shaw owned Shaw House, built circa 1800. British patrols brought a Mr. Nugent and two other militiamen to Shaw House after they had exchanged shots with them near where the Edgemere

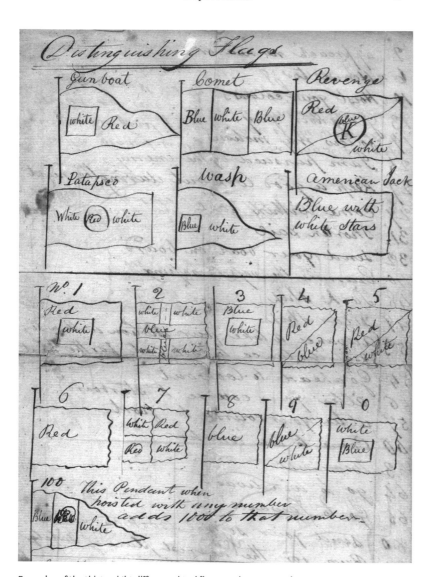

Examples of the thirty-eight different signal flags used to communicate between shore stations along Patapsco River, U.S. Navy gunboats, and Federal Hill. At night lanterns were used. (Capt. Charles Gordon, U.S.N., manuscript drawings; courtesy Maryland State Archives)

Shaw House as it appeared in the 1960s showing the upper windows, from one of which Eleanor Shaw reportedly jumped after the advances of a British lieutenant. (Photographer unknown; courtesy Dundalk Patapsco Neck Historical Society)

Senior Center is located today. Bethlehem Steel Company tore down the house in 1976, but the brick and stone foundation still survives.

Maj. Gen. Robert Ross and some of his men went to Shaw House, ordered the family upstairs, and took possession of the first floor. Local tradition holds that a British lieutenant met Eleanor, a daughter of Mr. Shaw, on the stairs and tried to kiss her; she broke away and jumped out from a second-story window. When Major General Ross heard of this incident, he supposedly punished the officer by sending him back to his ship.

Todd House, also called Todd's Inheritance (9000 North Point Road). NRHP. The Bernard Todd House served as the headquarters for Lt. Col. William McDonald, who commanded troops to prevent British landing parties at Patapsco Neck during the spring and summer of 1813. The house was also used as a signal house and horse courier station to report British movements in 1813 and 1814. A member of the Todd family reportedly served as one of the couriers. (*See also* Ridgely House Site, North Point.) Three mounted videttes were stationed at the house on September 11, 1814, to monitor the British landing at North Point. In retaliation for these activities, the British on September 12, 1814, burned the house and the outbuildings. The family lived in a granary for two years while the present house was built. In 1853, Bernard Todd's heirs received from the U.S. government $4,315, the appraised value of the burned property. A spyglass said to belong to Pvt. Bernard Todd, 1st Baltimore Hussars, is exhibited at the Flag House.*

The Maryland Historical Roadside Marker "Todd's Inheritance" claims the house was burned as the British withdrew from their unsuccessful assault on Baltimore, but the house was actually burned during the British march on Baltimore.

> From this [Todd] House there is a tolerable river view of the Bay, from the Bodkin [Point, Hancock's Resolution*] nearly across to Swan Point; Todds is a commodious two story frame house, with a large stable capable of accommodating in it and under its sheds at least thirty horses. (Maj. William Barney to Brig. Gen. John Stricker, March 23, 1813)[201]

Other North Point Sites

Lodge Farmhouse Site (between Jones and North Point creeks, near end of Lodge Farm Road, south off North Point Road, Chesapeake Terrace), the home of Capt. Sheppard Church Leakin, which burned circa 1960, reportedly contained the image of a Union Jack that had been artistically scratched into the plaster wall above the mantelpiece with a bayonet by one of the British troops. Leakin nearly lost his life while building earthworks overlooking the Philadelphia Road when a tree that had been cut down just missed him.

Trotten Farmhouse Site (Sparrows Point, now within the Sparrows Point Bethlehem Steele Plant), then the home of Sarah Trotten, from whom the British demanded the loan of a horse, cart, and some blankets. To Trotten's surprise, the British faithfully returned the borrowed items. The Trottens later learned that the cart had been used to convey the body of Maj. Gen. Robert Ross to a small craft for conveyance to fleet. The Trotten farmhouse was later used as the clubhouse of the Sparrows Point Country Club before burning down in 1954.

NOTTINGHAM (Patuxent River, east end of Tanyard and Nottingham roads, off Croom Road [Route 382], Prince George's County).

Nottingham, established in 1706, served during July and August 1814 as a naval base for the U.S. Chesapeake Flotilla.

> The town itself stands upon the banks of the Patuxent, and consists of four short streets, two running parallel with the river, and two others crossing them at right angles. The houses are not such as indicate the existence of much wealth or grandeur of the owners, being in general built of wood, and little superior to cottages; but around the village are others of a far better description, which convey the idea of good substantial farm-houses, a species of mansion very common in the United States. (Lt. George Robert Gleig, 1847)[202]

An artillery unit located just below at Hall's Creek* on June 16, 1814, prevented a British attack at Nottingham. When the local militia was mustered to respond to this threat, only six men appeared. Local farmer Clement Hollyday wrote Urban Hollyday on July 12, 1814, that "the militia was . . . much opposed to fighting, thus officers can not get them to turnout." He asked Urban to tell no one, for "It would give them [the British] a bad opinion of our part of the county . . . Nottingham has been & is now very sickly. The inhabitants has the flux & measles."[203]

> Furniture of all kinds removed from Nottingham—not a bed in the village . . . Last evening Col. [Decius] Wadsworth arrived at Nottingham, with two pieces of artillery, on his way to assist Com. [Joshua] Barney. Finding the barges of the enemy about halfway between Lower Marlborough and Nottingham he scaled his pieces—the enemy, on hearing the canon, advanced no farther. This no doubt saved the warehouse and other property there . . . The militia are collecting in considerable numbers, at Nottingham, but I trust the enemy will not again return. (Unknown individual to a merchant in New York City, June 17, 1814; reprinted in New York *Herald,* June 25, 1814)

Maj. John H. Briscoe of the St. Mary's County militia, stationed at the mouth of the Patuxent River, spotted the British fleet and sped to Nottingham, where he reported to Brig. Gen. William H. Winder that he saw several large British warships and five schooners, as well as three smaller craft that were being fitted out with two cannon each. Secretary of State James Monroe, acting as scout, first described the British strength as "not considerable," consisting of only three barges, but adds a P.S.: "Ten or twelve more barges in view. There are but two muskets in town [Nottingham], and a few scattering militia." Still later he writes, "Five o'clock. Thirty or forty barges are in view" (Secretary of State James Monroe to Brig. Gen. William H. Winder, August 21, 1814).[204]

Georgetown Dragoons passed through Nottingham about noon, June 20, 1814, on their way south to defend Benedict* but were unsuccessful in preventing the British landing.

> Yesterday at 4 A.M. a portion of our volunteers were ordered to March for Nottingham to assist in the defence of that place against the enemy . . . ascending the Patuxent . . . they have quietly taken off all the tob[acc]o at Benedict and . . . will attempt the same at L[ower] Marlboro & Nottingham, [Maj.] George Peters artillery company of 100 men & Stulls Rifleman & the squadron of Cavalry composed this detachm[en]t. (John Stull Williams to William Elie Williams, June 20, 1814)[205]

Nottingham was abandoned on August 21, 1814, after a brief skirmish between thirty U.S. Dragoons under Secretary of State James Monroe and British expeditionary forces under Maj. Gen. Robert Ross. Here the British troops made their second encampment in their march from Benedict to Washington. They remained here from about 6:00 p.m., August 21, to about 8:00 a.m., August 22, 1814. Thirty to forty British barges anchored offshore to protect the encampment. Major General Ross was reluctant to continue his march to Washington early on the 22nd, just as he was again at Upper Marlboro.

During the British advance toward Nottingham, reports were received that American riflemen were lurking in the woods preparing an ambush. The British increased their flanking patrols. Following is a humorous account of such an encounter:

I thought I could perceive something like the glitter of arms a little farther towards the middle of the wood. Sending several files of soldiers in different directions, I contrived to surround the spot, and then moving forward, I beheld two men dressed in black coats, and armed with bright firelocks, and bayonets, sitting under a tree; as soon as they observed me, they started up and took to their heels, but being hemmed in on all sides, they quickly perceived that to escape was impossible, and accordingly stood still . . . having arrived within a few paces of where they stood, I heard the one say to the other, with a look of the most perfect simplicity, "Stop, John till the gentlemen pass." There was something so ludicrous in this speech . . . that I could not help laughing aloud; nor was my mirth diminished by their attempts to persuade me that they were quiet country people, come out for no other purpose than to shoot squirrels. When I desired to know whether they carried bayonets to charge the squirrels, as well as muskets to shoot them, they were rather at loss to a reply; but they grumbled exceedingly when they found themselves prisoners, and conducted as such to the column. (Lt. George Robert Gleig, 1847)[206]

British account of skirmish: On our approaching the Town a few Shot were exchanged between the leading Boats and Some of the Enemy's Cavalry but the appearance of our Army advancing caused them to retire with precipitation. (Rear Adm. George Cockburn to Vice Adm. Sir Alexander F. I. Cochrane, August 22, 1814)[207] (The skirmish resulted in one American casualty.)

Second contrary British account: came in without the slightest opposition, to the town of Nottingham . . . completely deserted. Not an individual was to be seen in the streets, or remained in the house; while the appearance of the furniture, &c., in some places the very bread left in the ovens, showed

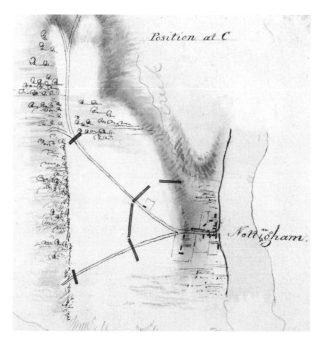

British 1814 sketch map showing the position of British troop deployment during their encampment at Nottingham. The bottom road leading to Nottingham is now called Tanyard Road. The upper road leading to Nottingham is now called Nottingham Road. The uppermost fork in this road shows Fenno Road branching to the right. It is this fork that the British used to march toward Upper Marlboro. The lower left fork is what today is called Candy Hill Road. (1814 sketch map by Robert Smith, "Sketch of the march of the British army under M. Genl. Ross . . .;" Beinecke Rare Book and Manuscript Library, Yale University)

that it had been evacuated in great haste. (Lt. George Robert Gleig, 1821)[208]

Nottingham served from August 21 to August 29, 1814, as a British rear guard encampment. Troops here saw the red glow in the sky on the night of August 25–26, 1814, from the burning of Washington. British vessels anchored here on August 27–29, 1814, and took on wounded soldiers and artillery from the Washington campaign as well as flour and tobacco.

A gun-brig, with a number of ships, launches, and long-boats, had made their way up the stream [river], and were at anchor opposite to the town. On board the former were carried such of the wounded as had been able to travel, while the latter were loaded with flour and tobacco, the only spoil which we found it possible to bring off. (Lt. George Robert Gleig, 1821)[209]

Two merchant vessels that operated between here and Liverpool, England, and belonging to Capt. Edward Griffin of Nottingham, were sunk by the British during their occupation of the town. In 1958, amateur divers discovered what they believed were the remains of Commodore Barney's U.S. Chesapeake Flotilla, but more likely they had found what was left of Griffin's vessels.

Robert Bowie, former governor of Maryland, died near Nottingham in 1818 at his home Mattaponi.* He was among the gentlemen and armed slaves who arrested some marauding British stragglers during their return from the burning of the capital. The British retaliated by seizing Dr. William Beanes and taking him to their fleet. John Stuart Skinner and Francis Scott Key went to the British fleet to seek Beanes's release. They were forced to remain with the fleet and thus observed the bombardment of Fort McHenry.

> to our no small surprise we saw our friend Dr. Bean[es] brought in as a prisoner. On enquiring into the cause we learned that as soon as our troops had left the village he had armed his slaves, and sallied forth cutting off all our stragglers. As soon as the General [Robert Ross] heard of it, he sent back our Cossacks [expert horsemen] who took him out of his bed, and brought him off a prisoner. (Lt. George Robert Gleig, August 28, 1814)[210]

> He [Beanes] was in the forward part of the ship among the sailors and soldiers. He had not had a change of clothes from the time he was seized; was constantly treated with indignity by those around him and no officer would speak to him. He was treated as a culprit and not as a prisoner of war and this harsh and humiliating treatment, continued until he was placed onboard the cartel. (Francis Scott Key)[211]

A historic marker (intersection of Tanyard Road and Watershed Drive) says, "During the Revolution the British camped here on Aug. 21, 1814." Of course the British landed in 1814 during the War of 1812, not the American Revolution. Located next to the old school near the north end of town is a interpretive panel that provides information on local activities during the War of 1812.

ODEN FARMHOUSE. *See* Bellefields

OLDFIELDS. *See* Forestville

OLDFIELDS CHAPEL, now called Oldfields Episcopal Church (0.7 mile west of intersection of Prince Frederick–Hughesville [Route 231] and Brandywine roads [Route 381], near Hughesville, Charles County). The present structure at Oldfields Chapel, established in 1753, dates from 1769 although altered from its original appearance. Local tradition claims that during the British march from Benedict to Washington, some British pickets camped on the grounds of this chapel.

Francis Wise, Alexandria Troops, killed during a skirmish on June 21, 1814, at Benedict is reportedly buried here but no marker for him was found.

> [Francis] Wise was buried to-day with the honors of war, by the Alexandria troop, at a church some mile off [from Benedict]. (One of Capt. Elias Boudinot Caldwell's men written at or near Benedict to a friend in Washington, D.C., dated June 23, 1814; reprinted in Washington *National Intelligencer,* June 24, 1814)

Two British soldiers, possibly victims of heat exhaustion during the march from Benedict, are reportedly buried in unmarked graves.[212] Most accounts claim the graves were located between two large oak trees that stood in front of the church where the parking area is now located; other sources claim the soldiers were buried on the right side of the walk leading to the sacristy (vestry).

OLD MIDDLETOWN CEMETERY. *See* appendix B, Gunpowder Baptist Cemetery

OLD ST. JOSEPH'S CHURCH. *See* appendix B, St. Joseph's Church

PARKER POINT (Chesapeake Bay, south of Farilee Creek, near Mendinhall Lake, off west end of Bay Shore Road, Kent County). PRIVATE. On August 28, 1814, the British conducted a raid on the John Waltham farm on Fairlee Creek.* During the night of August 30, 1814, approximately 260 troops landed here at Skidmore or Chantilly Farm, now called The Farm at Parker Point, to attack a militia encampment located farther inland. This engagement became known as the Battle of Caulks Field.* Unofficially this site has come to be known as Parker Point (not to be confused with Parker Point on the western shore of Anne Arundel County, where the Kirbys Wind Mill Site is located).

PARROTT POINT. *See* St. Michaels

PATTERSON PARK (BALTIMORE CITY). *See* Hampstead Hill, Baltimore

PATUXENT CITY (intersection of Prince Frederick–Hughesville Road [Routes 231] and Brandywine Road [Route 381], Charles County). The British began their march from Benedict to Washington about 4:00 p.m. on August 20, 1814, but because of the heat and the poor condition of the men, most of whom had been cramped onboard ships for weeks, there were many stragglers. After marching only about six miles, the troops camped at what today is known as Patuxent City. They were without shelter and got soaked by a violent thunderstorm that struck in the early evening of August 20.

> Our march to-day was . . . extremely short, the troops halting when they had arrived at a rising ground distant not more than six miles from the point whence they set out; and having stationed the piquets, planted the sentinels, and made such other arrangements as the case required, fires were lighted, and the men were suffered to lie down . . . during this short march of six miles a greater number of soldiers dropped out of the ranks, and fell behind from fatigue, than I recollect to have seen in any march in the Peninsula [Peninsular Campaign of Spain] of thrice its duration . . . The ground upon which we bivouacked . . . was a gentle eminence, fronted by an open and cultivated country, and crowned with two or three houses, having barns and walled gardens attached to them. Neither flank could be said to rest upon any point peculiarly well defended, but they were not exposed; because, by extending or condensing the line, almost any one of these houses might be converted into a protecting redoubt. The outposts . . . extended completely round the encampment, enclosing the entire army within a

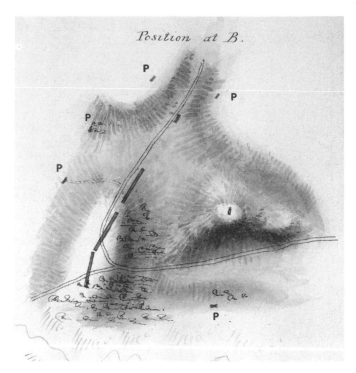

British 1814 sketch map showing the position of British troop deployment during their encampment at what today is Patuxent City. Prince Frederick Road runs east and west, and what today is called Brandywine Road runs north. Note the numerous piquet positions indicated by the letter *P* added to the original sketch. (1814 sketch map by Robert Smith, "Sketch of the march of the British army under M. Genl. Ross . . ."; Beinecke Rare Book and Manuscript Library, Yale University)

Photograph of the road conditions at Patuxent City circa 1917, probably little changed from those experienced by the British forces that encamped there in 1814. (*The Road to Washington,* 1919)

connected chain of sentinels; and precluding the possibility of even a single individual making his way within the line unperceived . . . The effect of the lightning [thunderstorm], as it glanced for a moment upon the bivouac, and displayed the firelocks piled in regular order, and the men stretched out like so many corpses beside them, was extremely fine. (Lt. George Robert Gleig, 1847)[213]

PATUXENT WETLANDS PARK (northeast side of bridge that carries Southern Maryland Boulevard [Route 4] over Patuxent River, Anne Arundel County). The scuttling of the U.S. Chesapeake Flotilla near Pig Point* under orders of the Secretary of Navy William Jones to prevent its capture took place on August 22, 1814, upstream from the river overlook at Patuxent Wetlands Park. This park is the closest public access point to the scuttling site. A historical roadside marker (now missing) claims a cutter, gunboats, and thirteen barges were found near the bridge in the early 1900s. In fact, only one positively identified vessel from the flotilla shuttled above the bridge has been identified and that was in 1980. In 1998, two additional flotilla vessels were identified in St. Leonard Creek.*

PEARCE POINT FORT. *See* Georgetown

PERRY CABIN. *See* listing under St. Michaels

PERRY POINT MANSION AND MILL (confluence of Susquehanna River and Chesapeake Bay, near end of Philadelphia Road [Route 7] on grounds of U.S. Veterans Hospital, Perryville, Cecil County). PRIVATE. The John Stump family owned the circa 1750 stuccoed brick Perry Point Mansion and stone mill. During their raids at nearby Havre de Grace and Principio Iron Works* on the upper Chesapeake in 1813, the British also burned a warehouse at Bell's Ferry* belonging to John Stump, while his home and gristmill at Perry Point survived. Stump sold grain from his mill to the British. Stump's wife, Mary Alicia, daughter of Col. George Edward Mitchell,* reportedly carried the news of the peace treaty of the War of 1812 from Fort Niagara to the British in Canada.

PIG POINT, originally called Wrighton, now called Bristol or Bristol Landing (Patuxent River, end of Wrighton Road, west off Southern Maryland Boulevard [Route 4], Anne Arundel County). No public access to waterfront. As a British squadron ascended the Patuxent River toward Pig Point on August 22, 1814, Rear Adm. George Cockburn sent a con-

tingent of Royal Marines under the command of Capt. John Robyns to advance on the village from the land side. This precaution turned out to be unneeded as the town offered no resistance.

On approaching Pig Point (where the Enemys Flotilla was said to be) I landed the Marines under Captain [John] Robyns on the left bank of the [Patuxent] River, and directed him to march round and attack on the Land Side, the Town situated on the Point to draw from us the attention of Such Troops as might be there for its defense. (Rear Adm. George Cockburn to Vice Adm. Sir Alexander F. I. Cochrane, morning, August 22, 1814)[214]

As the British squadron proceeded farther up the river to attack the U.S. Chesapeake Flotilla, the gun barges were scuttled. One gun barge survived when the powder failed to explode. Several merchantmen anchored behind the flotilla also survived.

British account of scuttling of flotilla: as we opened the Reach above Pig Point, I plainly discovered Commodore [Joshua] Barney's broad Pendent in the headmost Vessel (a large Sloop) [*Scorpion*] and remainder of the Flotilla extending in a long line astern of her. Our Boats now advanced toward them as rapidly as possible but on nearing them we observed the Sloop bearing Broad Pendent to be on fire, and she very soon afterward blew up, I now Saw clearly that they were all abandoned and on Fire with Trains to their Magaz[ines], and out of the Seventeen Vessels which composed this formidable and So much Vaunted Flotilla, Sixteen were in quick Succession blown to atoms, and the Seventeenth (in which the Fire had not taken) was captured . . . I found laying above the Flotilla under its protection Thirteen Merchant Schooner, Some of which not being worth bringing away I caused to be burnt, such as were in good Condition I directed to be moved to Pig Point. (Rear Adm. George Cockburn to Vice Adm. Sir Alexander F. I. Cochrane, morning, August 22, 1814)[215]

As the British were moving some of these merchant vessels to Pig Point, they were fired on by flotillamen, who were in turn captured by a British detachment put on shore. Some Americans on horseback also appeared but were driven off by Congreve rockets.

British account of skirmish: [American snipers fired upon the British ships from the nearby bluffs] Whilst employed in taking these Vessels a few shot were fired at us, by some of the Men of the flotilla from the Bushes on the Shore near us, but Lieut [James] Scott whom I landed for that purpose, Soon got hold of them and made them Prisoners . . . Some Horsemen likewise shewed themselves on the Neighbouring Heights but a Rocket or two dispersed them, and Captain [John] Robyns who had got possession of Pig Point without Resistance now Spreading his Men through the County the Enemy retreated to a distance and left us in quiet possession of the Town, the Neighbourhood, and our Prizes . . . A large quantity of Tobacco. (Rear Adm. George Cockburn to Vice Adm. Sir Alexander F. I. Cochrane, August 22, 1814)[216]

The prizes were loaded with the stores of tobacco taken there: "A large quantity of Tobacco having been found in the Town at Pig Point I have left Captain [John] Robyns, with the Marines, and Captain [Joseph] Nourse with two divisions of the Boats, to hold the place and Ship the Tobacco into the Prizes [captured vessels]" (Rear Adm. George Cockburn to Vice Adm. Sir Alexander F. I. Cochrane, August 22, 1814).[217]

PIKESVILLE (western Baltimore County). Local landowner Dr. James Smith named Pikesville for his friend Brig. Gen. Zebulon Pike,* who was killed April 30, 1813, during the American capture of York, present-day Toronto, then the capital of British Upper Canada. The American burning of the government buildings at York was one of the reasons cited by the British for the August 24, 1814, burning of the public buildings in Washington, D.C. Pike's Peak, Colorado, is also named for this American general and explorer of the West. The Pikesville Armory, begun in 1816 as a result of the War of 1812, served as the Confederate Veterans Home and still stands on the grounds of the State Police Barracks. The first commander of the armory was Lt. Nehemiah Baden, who served as assistant deputy commissary of ordnance during the War of 1812.

PISCATAWAY (near intersection of Piscataway [Route 223] and Floral Park roads, Prince George's County). To defend Fort Washington* from a possible land attack from the east, an American encampment was established at "Hatton's hill." Here Lt. Col. William Scott commanded about 330 men, including detachments of the 36th and 38th U.S. Infantry and a small detachment of light artillery.

On the 2d of August, I received orders to fall back with my detachment and take the most convenient position on the road from Piscatawa [Piscataway] to Washington, to defend the approach from below to Fort Washington . . . I accordingly took a strong position on Hatton's hill, about three miles in the rear of the fort. (Brig. Gen. Robert Young to the Committee of Congress)[218]

THE PLAINS SITE, also called Orphan's Gift (cemetery on north side of Allen Road, 0.2 mile from intersection with Golden Beach Road, 3.2 miles from "T" intersection with All Faith Church Road, and 2.5 miles from Waldorf–Leonardtown Road [Route 5], Golden Beach, St. Mary's County). Local tradition holds that the British fired upon the circa 1760 stuccoed brick plantation house known as The Plains and owned by the Sothoron family. Militia reportedly camped at the Plains in anticipation of the British landing at Benedict* but did not challenge the landing force. All that is left of this plantation is the cemetery.

PLEASANT FIELDS, also called Sundown Hills Farm, and Henry Chew Gaither House (4615 Sundown Road, west of intersection with Damascus Road [Route 650], west of Brookeville, Montgomery County). Henry Chew Gaither built this circa 1775 stone house, known as Pleasant Fields. Antiwar Federalist William Gaither II, born here October 1789, was severely injured and left for dead by a pro-war mob that attacked the office of the Baltimore *Federal Republic** in 1812. He recovered from his injuries and lived at Pleasant Fields until his death in 1834.

POINT LOOKOUT (point at confluence of Chesapeake Bay and Potomac River, Point Lookout State Park, south end of Point Lookout Road [Route 5], near Scotland, St. Mary's County). On March 25, 1813, U.S. Postmaster General Gideon Granger established an observation post here to monitor British activity on the Chesapeake Bay. Henry Weitz was appointed the first agent of the post, but he was replaced by Thomas Swann in June. In late spring of 1813, a British barge was sent to scuttle a grounded British ship off Point Lookout. But Elwiley (Wily) Smith and a party of ten or twelve men armed with "squirrel guns" fired on the barge from behind a fence, claiming that four of the British sailors were hit and that the barge retreated without completing its mission. On July 19, 1813, the U.S. Post Office began a daily express courier system between Point Lookout and Washington, D.C., to keep the capital informed of British fleet movements on the Bay. Point Lookout served as a staging area for the local militia in the early summer of 1813 until two thousand to three thousand British forces occupied the point between July 19 and July 27, 1813. The British used the point as a base for raids on St. Mary's County.

We anchored off Point Look-out, the entrance to the Potomac, and landed the troops; no resistance was offered, and the squadron and forces obtained a plentiful supply of the refreshment required. (Capt. James Scott, 1834)[219]

Scars from British cannonballs were said to be visible in the walls of The Plains until the home was razed in 1962. (Circa 1920s photograph from *The Chesapeake Bay Country,* 1938)

Our situation is extremely critical. From two to three thousand of the enemy are in complete possession of the point of land below the Ridge, which is two and half miles from Point Look Out. They have been five or six miles higher up procuring stock; and have now in Mr. Armstrong's corn field about 200 head of cattle, &c. Several of our most respectable inhabitants have been taken by the enemy . . . Many negroes have also been taken, some of whom have escaped and returned to their masters. Seven of the enemy's regulars have deserted, and are now with us. The whole fleet is yet lying off Point Look Out. What will be their next movement I know not. They have landed 6 pieces of artillery, and it is ascertained that they have on board rockets in abundance. (Capt. James Forrest, July 27, 1813; reprinted in Annapolis *Maryland Republican,* July 31, 1813)

Early on August 17, 1814, Thomas Swann, the forward observer at Point Lookout, sent a courier named Carmichael to warn Washington when he spotted the combined British invasion fleet moving up the Chesapeake Bay. The Americans had also established an observation base at Smith Point, Virginia, on the opposite side of the entrance of the Potomac River. They had detected the fleet the evening before.

Various rumors have been in circulation for two or three days past, relative to a large naval force which is said lately to have arrived in the bay. On Thursday last it was stated by an express from Point Look Out, that there were forty six sail in the bay, amongst which we understood there were several transports, bearing a large number of troops. (Annapolis *Maryland Republican,* August 20, 1814)

the enemy's fleet . . . making an aggregate of thirty three sail, anchored yesterday evening at half past 3 o'clock between Point No Point and the mouth of the Potomac, owning to the wind shifting to the southwest, which made it utterly impossible for them to proceed down. This morning at daylight the fleet all weighed anchor with a fine northwardly breeze and continued down; at 11 A.M. they were all out of sight below Smith Point Lighthouse. (Annapolis *Maryland Republican,* September 4, 1814)

it was a glorious and imposing spectacle to behold these noble ships standing up the vast bay of the Chesapeake, into the very heart of America; manned, too, with eager souls, panting for fame . . . The flags of three British Admirals, [Vice Adm. Sir Alexander F. I.] Cochrane, [Rear Adm. George] Cockburn, and [Rear Admiral] Poultney [Pulteney] Malcolm, were proudly flying at the mast-heads of their respective vessels [ships-of-the-line], the Tonnant, Albion, and Royal Oak. (Midshipman Robert J. Barrett, 1840)[220]

Benson J. Lossing reported in the 1860s that a monument erected at Point Lookout to commemorate events of the War of 1812 had been defaced. It is no longer present.

POINT PATIENCE (Patuxent River, about 1.0 mile north of Governor Thomas Johnson Memorial Bridge [Route 4], Calvert County). Military base, restricted access. Point Patience can best be seen by water or while passing west over the Governor Thomas Johnson Memorial Bridge. Point Patience is named for the patience it took to sail around this long point when sailing vessels were required to wait for favorable winds and tides. The British raided Point Patience on June 26, 1814, destroying the home of Dr. William D. Somervell. Here at about 8:00 a.m., June 26, 1814, the H.M. frigate *Loire,* damaged during Second Battle of St. Leonard Creek,* pulled back for repairs.

> This morning, at 4 A.M. a combined Attack of the Artillery, Marine Corps & flotilla, was made upon the Enemies two frigates [H.M.S. *Loire* and H.M.S. *Narcissus*], at the mouth of the Creek [St. Leonard], after two hours engagement, they got under way & made sail down the river, they are now warping round Point Patience. (Com. Joshua Barney to Secretary of Navy William Jones, June 26, 1814)[221]

Because of the difficulty of navigating around this point, Com. Joshua Barney suggested a gun battery be placed here to hinder British movement on the Patuxent River, but his recommendation was never acted upon.

> there is a fine point *below* this, called *Point Patience* where the river is very narrow not more than 200 yards wide. (Com. Joshua Barney to Secretary of Navy William Jones, June 20, 1814)[222]

During late July and August 1814, a squadron of Royal Navy ships rendezvoused here to take on water and coordinate raids along the Patuxent River.

> an express arrived from [Lt.] Colonel [Michael] Taney [VI], of Calvert county, requesting of [Brig.] Gen. [Stephen] West all the aid he could possibly afford, with information that the enemy had landed in considerable force at Point Patience—that they had horse and light artillery. (Baltimore *Federal Republican,* July 22, 1814)

> they [British] sent a detachment, 120 strong, to the interiour of the county, several miles from the river, pressed the citizens' carts, teams, and negroes, and compelled them to carry their own tobacco down to the shore. They have put that part of the county in such a complete state of subjection that the inhabitants are opposed to and in some cases,

positively forbid an armed American force from being stationed on their farms, knowing that no permanent security can be afforded them by the militia . . . Point Patience . . . is the place of general rendezvous for the enemy's fleet . . . The enemy took off great numbers of our negroes. (Baltimore *Federal Republican,* July 16, 1814; reprinted in Philadelphia *United States Gazette,* August 3, 1814)

> I have been laying down an Anchorage on the lower side & close to Point patience, it has this advantage, it is the narowest part of the river the point Projects, across the River so as to protect us from fire Vessels, In case of attack also, if he dare it, the point would bring up his point blank Shot, and ours being so much higher would reach him over it—we can also see a long way up the River & saves a long pull for our boats and there is a well upon the Point sufficient to keep up our Water. (Capt. Joseph Nourse to Rear Adm. George Cockburn, August 12, 1814)[223]

Just offshore of Point Patience an anchor was recovered in 1959 that had been lost on August 18, 1814, by H.M. troopship *Dictator,* which was transporting three companies of the 44th Regiment. The *Dictator* remained near this point until September 2, 1814, when the main contingent of the fleet returned downriver from Benedict with the victorious British troops who had captured Washington. This anchor is on exhibit at Mariner's Museum,* Virginia.[224]

POOLES ISLAND (Chesapeake Bay, approximately 1.5 miles off tip of Rickett Point, Gunpowder Neck, Aberdeen Proving Ground, Harford County). Military base, restricted access. On April 24, 1813, the British plundered the small settlement on Pooles Island and established a small gun battery there.

> The Enemy have landed at Pooles Island and taken everything from the Inhabitants; they have entered the mouths of all the Rivers above the mouth of the Patapsco and burned all the small Vessels. The Militia are on the alert, they have not yet landed on the Main. (Maj. Gen. Samuel Smith, April 21, 1813; reprinted in Baltimore *Niles' Weekly Register*)

The British used Pooles Island as a watering place as well as Cape Henry,* Drum Point,* New Point Comfort,* Point Patience,* St. Catherine Island,* and St. Clement Island.*

> Having reconnoitred Pool Island, and finding excellent water, two of the small prize schooners were converted into watering-vessels, and for a few days we were employed in replenishing our water. (Capt. James Scott, 1834)[225]

From Pooles Island and nearby Spesutie Island, the British staged raids on the upper Chesapeake Bay.

The enemy's force, consisting of one 74, three frigates, two brigs, two schrs. and a number of tenders and barges, are now lying from off Werton [Worton] to some distance below Pool's Island. They are on shore on Pool's Island every day, having got possession of it. (Washington *Daily National Intelligencer,* April 29, 1813)

The enemy passed this [Rock Hall] early in the morning up the bay, and proceeded above Pool's Island, where they anchored, and sent their barge out in all directions, both in the Western and Eastern Shores. (Baltimore *Federal Gazette,* July 15, 1814)

POPLAR ISLAND (Chesapeake Bay, approximately 3.0 miles east of Sherwood, Tilghman Neck, Talbot County). On April 16, 1813, William Sears, who leased on Poplar Island, began removing his personal effects due to British activity in the area. The British landed on the evening of April 18 and over the next day took cattle, sheep, lambs, pigs, and poultry.

American account of raid: the enemy had taken and killed about thirty head of black cattle, eighty-six head of old sheep and between twenty and thirty lambs, that they had killed three hundred breeding sows in their beds, whose pigs were found dead; and that they had taken off almost all his poultry, ALL he supposes they could catch. From his house (where he had left some of his worst furniture) they took off an old looking glass worth about four dollars and some newspapers in a file. They broke several locks and one door, and threw many things about the house. In a house on the island which had been occupied by James Sears, they broke his desk to pieces and threw about his furniture and other things; but the realtor does not recollect that any thing was taken away. (William Sears, June 22, 1813; reprinted in Annapolis *Maryland Republican,* November 20, 1813)

The British captured the sloop *Messenger* on November 11, 1814, off the north end of Poplar Island. Clement Vickers, captain of the sloop, gained a reputation from making weekly runs between Easton and Baltimore through the British blockade. Vickers was finally caught one day when the winds died and he was unable to evade the British.

Capt. Clement Vickers (or Vickars) assisted in the manning of Fort Stokes,* which protected Easton.* He also served in the defense of St. Michaels.* When Vickers's sloop *Messenger* was captured, he attempted to ransom both his vessel and its passengers. The British refused to give up the sloop but agreed to free those passengers who were not

members of the militia. Buried in the family cemetery at Easton Point, Vickers's body was removed and re-interred in 1965 at Woodlawn Memorial Park, Inc. (east side of Ocean Gateway [U.S. Route 50], 0.5 mile south of intersection with Plugge Road, near Easton) in an unmarked grave.

PORT DEPOSIT, then called Creswell's Ferry (Susquehanna River, Cecil County). NHD. A gun battery, erected by the citizens of Port Deposit, never fired a shot in defense of the town although on May 3, 1813, Bell's Ferry* (Lapidum) on the opposite shore of the Susquehanna River suffered a raid.

PORT TOBACCO (Port Tobacco River, near intersection of Port Tobacco Road [Route 6] and Chapel Point Road, Charles County). NHD. In 1813, Port Tobacco briefly served as a forward base of operations for the U.S. Potomac Flotilla. Several gunboats were stationed here as a reserve force. Port Tobacco also served as an observation point from which British activity on the Potomac River could be monitored.

You will please to proceed immediately to Port Tobacco, and after ascertaining the most suitable place for observation at Maryland point or Thomas's point, you will repair to that place, and during each day carefully watch with suitable glasses & note down what passes on the waters within the reach of your glasses, and send to this office by each mail a transcript of your journal. (Gideon Granger, Postmaster General to William Lambert, March 24, 1813)[226]

Fearful of a possible British raid on Port Tobacco, many residents fled during the summer of 1814: "the inhabitants of Port Tobacco are all packing up their goods and furniture and moving off from that place" (Baltimore *Federal Republican,* July 26, 1814).

The British considered landing their invasion force here—about equidistant to Washington as Benedict on the Patuxent—but chose Benedict instead. On July 26, 1814, Brig. Gen. William H. Winder visited Port Tobacco while scouting out possible encampment sites for his troops.

POTTERS LANDING, also called Potter Hall, Potters Mansion, Potter Town, and Williston Landing (Choptank River, about 5.0 miles south of Denton off Martin Lane, near intersection of Williston and Pealiquor roads, off Harmony–Denton Road [Route 16], Williston, Caroline County). NRHP. PRIVATE. Potter Hall, begun in 1730 and rebuilt to its present Georgian configuration in 1808, was expanded in the 1930s. It was the home of William Potter, lieutenant colonel in the

19th Regiment, Maryland militia, during the War of 1812. Potter's grave, originally located here, was moved to the Denton Cemetery.*

PRINCE FREDERICK (central Calvert County). On July 19, 1814, Prince Frederick, county seat of Calvert County, suffered a night raid after the British landed at Battle Creek* and marched nine miles without meeting much resistance from the local militia. The British burned the courthouse, the jail, the John Stuart Skinner home (The Reserve*), and a tobacco warehouse. After the war the county successfully petitioned the U.S. Committee of Claims for $3,000 to pay for the loss of the courthouse. The award was based partly on the testimony of Com. Joshua Barney, who said that the courthouse had been used as a hospital for the sick and wounded from the flotilla, that some prisoners and their guards were stationed there, and that some naval stores, including munitions, were deposited there. When these munitions were discovered, the British burned the courthouse. Because the jail apparently was never used by American troops, the county received no money for its loss. A circa 1969 mural in court room number 1 by local artist Robert Coffin (now deceased) depicts an American gun battery, camp, and gun barges during the Battle of St. Leonard Creek,* June 1814.

> British account of raid: I landed and marched nine miles to a place called the Court House in the County of Calvert denominated by the Americans a Town and where the Assizes [either court or place of weights and measures] are held—Burnt the Court House and Jail releasing one Black man confined for endeavoring to escape to us—returned by the same road and re-embarked every one by four o'Clock the same Evening. (Capt. Joseph Nourse to Rear Adm. George Cockburn, July 23, 1814)[227]

> American account of raid: The Calvert county court house had been burnt, and small parties plotted by negroes are marching through the country in different directions, committing almost every species of outrage. (Annapolis *Maryland Republican,* July 23, 1814)

> Second American account of raid: a detachment of Fifteen men from a British armed vessel, were a day or two ago, allowed to burn Calvert County Court House, and return unmolested to their vessels. (Washington *Daily National Intelligencer*; reprinted in Annapolis *Maryland Republican,* July 23, 1814)

> Excerpt of letter from a citizen of Calvert County expressing his rage at Com. Joshua Barney for bringing the war and its destruction to his homeland: I am sorry to see you . . . have such a mean opinion of the citizens of Calvert . . . to think that the militia could not fight . . . for the defense of old [Joshua] Barney who has been the means of ruining Calvert for if he had never of come in the Patuxent the British would never have thought nor had an idea that they could come as high as Lower Marlboro in the world but by his going down the Bay and giving them a challenge as it were he could not think they would let him return without following him up and he pitched on the Patuxent as a place of safety and as he knew Calvert St. Marys Charles and Prince George's County were all Federalist he thought it would be the means of making them all advocates of old [President] Jim [James] Madison but this has enraged them so that a great many that were in favor of him now are abusing him every day but I think when I tell you the mischief the British have done it will be enough to make you and every man abuse Jim Madison and old Barney in Hell . . . I will . . . tell you the damage that has been done since old Barney has been blockaded in (St. Leonard?) Creek in the first place they took R[?] Parran[,] S[?] Parran and Richard Parran overseer as prisoners while they were getting their stock off the river in the second place they burned John Pattersons [Pattison] dwelling house Barn and destroyed much of his stock in the third place they burned John Broome's [VII] house [Broome Island*] in the fourth place they burned every house John Mackall [Gods Grace Plantation*] had except the overseer house in the fifth place they came to Lower Marlboro tore and broke everybodys house to pieces and burned the ware house and all the tobacco took nearly all the poultry in town away took seventy sheep from Mr. Graham[e] [probably Patuxent Manor, Lower Marlboro*] took nearly all Mrs. Ballards negros and two of Mr. T. Blakes . . . and on the their return down they stopped at [Holland] Cliffts and burned Mr. Morris[?] Barns and some tobacco in it stopped at Benedict took nearly all the tobacco out of the ware house . . . stopped at Holland [Hallowing] Point[*] and burned Mrs. Mackalls barn burned a great many houses in St. Marys burned Dr. Sommersvilles' house . . . now after all this if you can yet think them right I must bid you adieu. (Thomas B. King, July 14, 1814)[228]

During their return to Battle Creek, the British took twenty slaves from Dr. Benjamin Williams's house.

The Reserve Site, also called Skinners Reserve and Trueman's Reserve (nearly opposite Calvert High School on south side of Dares Beach Road [Route 402]). PRIVATE. John Stuart Skinner* was born at the plantation known as The Reserve. Skinner rode to Washington to warn President

James Madison that British vessels loaded with troops were sailing up the Patuxent with the probable intention of attacking Washington. The British burned The Reserve on July 19, 1814, during their raid of Prince Frederick. The present structure, although still called "The Reserve," dates from after the conflict. Skinner and Francis Scott Key were sent by President Madison to seek the release of Dr. William Beanes; all were held onboard during the bombardment of Fort McHenry. Elizabeth Skinner married Joseph Wilkinson, whose two sons, James* and Joseph, both became generals in the War of 1812.

> Mr. [John Stuart] Skinner, the flag agent, is up, and says the enemy are landing at Benedict, their number 4,000. (London *Times,* September 28, 1814)

PRINCIPIO IRON WORKS, also called Principio Furnace and Cecil Furnace (Principio Creek, south side of Principio Furnace Road [Route 7], east of Perryville, Cecil County). NRHP. Principio Iron Works began operation in 1725 and by 1727 operated the first blast furnace and refinery forge in Maryland. Since at least 1796 Principio Iron Works produced cannon used by Maryland privateers and the U.S. Navy. In 1807, the furnace supplied 24 pounder long guns for the U.S. frigate *Constitution.* The complex in 1813 consisted of a blast furnace, two air furnaces, a boring mill capable of boring five cannon at one time, a stamping mill, a stone grist mill, managers and workmen's houses, coal house, stables, and a smith shop.

> We [defenders of Frenchtown and Elk Landing] yesterday [Tuesday, April 20] got 7000 weight of cannon balls from Cecil Furnace, to be returned if not used. (Baltimore *Patriot,* April 22, 1813)

> the Cecil or Principio Foundery . . . was one of the most valuable Works of the Kind in America, the Destruction of it therefore at this moment will I trust prove of much national Importance [to the British war effort]. (Rear Adm. George Cockburn to Adm. Sir John Borlase Warren, May 3, 1813)[229]

On May 3, 1813, the British destroyed a gun battery consisting of five 24 pounder cannons erected to protect the iron works as well as twenty-eight 32 pounder cannon ready to be shipped and eight other cannons and four carronades of different caliber. The British effectively destroyed the foundry and cannon boring machinery and burned the mills, coal houses, and the bridge across Principio Creek. The total loss to the owner was around $20,000. Rear Admiral Cockburn is reputed to have said the Americans knew better how to make guns than to use them. Col. Samuel

Hughes rebuilt the works the same year and on December 16, 1813, received a contract for forty 24 pounder cannons. But Hughes never recovered from his debts and was forced to sell his establishment.

> We understand that the cannon for the United States frigate Guerriere, are casting at Cecil Furnace, about 6 miles from the Susquehannah. It is not improbable that this Furnace is the object of the enemy's approach to that neighourhood. (Baltimore *Federal Gazette,* July 15, 1814)

QUEEN ANN, then called Queen Anne's Town (Patuxent River, south end of Queen Anne Bridge Road, southeast off Queen Anne Road, east of Bowie, Prince George's County). A detachment of U.S. Marines under the command of Capt. Samuel Miller crossed the Patuxent River here with three 12 pounder cannon on their way to St. Leonard Creek* to support the U.S. Chesapeake Flotilla blockaded by the British in June 1814.

> Lieutenant [Capt. Samuel] Miller with a detachment of about 110 Marines, with three light 12 pounders in complete order, set out this morning at day dawn to join you.— They will go by the way of Queen Ann's, as there are no means of passing the Artillery over the [Patuxent] river lower down. (Secretary of Navy William Jones to Com. Joshua Barney, June 12, 1814)[230]

In an effort to save the U.S. Chesapeake Flotilla from probable destruction by the British forces, Secretary of Navy William Jones on July 27, 1814, suggested carting the flotilla overland approximately six miles to the South River just below Annapolis. However, the plan was never carried out. Two fifty-foot class barges were able to ascend the Patuxent River to Queen Anne, where they were blown up in August 1814 to prevent capture. Private salvage operations on the scuttled U.S. Chesapeake Flotilla began in September 1814 and U.S. Navy operations began in November 1814. (*See also* Mount Calvert, Mount Pleasant Landing, and Pig Point.)

> I have had an officer and twenty five men at Queen Anns on the patuxent for several weeks, they have been very successfull in getting up the guns of the late flotilla, with a very considerable quantity of other valuable articles. (Com. Joshua Barney to Secretary of Navy William Jones, November 17, 1814)[231]

Several British stragglers and at least one deserter were arrested by townsmen near Upper Marlboro* during the British return march from Washington to Benedict. These stragglers were taken to Queen Anne, where it was thought safe from British reprisal. However, one soldier escaped. After he had informed his comrades, the British threatened to burn Upper Marlboro and held three civilians hostage pending the release of the remaining soldiers. With little alternative, John Hodges* of Darnall's Chance* released the captured soldiers. For this decision he was later tried for treason but found not guilty.

> The British have retired from Washington the way they came, except about five hundred men, who, it is said, have taken the road to Queen Ann, where there is a great quantity of Tobacco. (Philadelphia *American Weekly Messenger,* August 31, 1814)

QUEENSTOWN (Queenstown Creek, south-central Queen Anne's County). The British conducted a land and water attack on August 13, 1813, at Queenstown. The land contingent, consisting of about three hundred troops under the command of Col. Sir Thomas Sidney Beckwith, traveled along the Queenstown Road, now essentially Route 18. The Queen Anne's County militia under the command of Maj. William H. Nicholson, consisting of about 380 troops, were positioned to meet the attack. Fearing that he might get cut off by a British landing party to his rear, Nicholson withdrew his troops to Centreville after a series of brief skirmishes by about twenty of his pickets. One of the skirmishes took place at a "defile," probably the sunken road portion of Queenstown Road at Slippery Hill.* The British land forces were ordered to take the American advance picket station without firing a shot, but shots were mistakenly fired, alerting the American troops bivouacked closer to Queenstown. The British amphibious contingent (consisting of about three hundred men) was to land at Hall's Landing (Bowlingly*) on Queenstown Creek to cut off any American retreat. But because they became confused in the darkness, they landed instead at Blakeford.* This enabled the Americans to withdraw to Centreville. The skirmishing that took place west of Queenstown along a slope known as Slippery Hill has come to be known as the Battle of Slippery Hill.*

> American account of skirmish: soon . . . we observed by signal rockets, which were fired from the mouth of Queen's Town creek as well as from the column advancing from the ferry [Kent Narrows], that we were to have an attack from the water as well as the land side. About 10 minutes before 4 o'clock, not yet light, the enemy from his line upon the land side commenced a fire of rockets and round shot upon which, [Maj. William H.] Nicholson then hearing that a landing was effected at Hall's [Bowlingly], where we had posted no men, from the barges, and anticipating an immediate attack in the rear, ordered the artillery and infantry,

without firing to retreat, which was done in good order and without any loss. With the cavalry, I was posted in a very advantageous position to charge upon the right wing of the enemy, as soon as the action should commence in the center. By some neglect, I did not receive orders to retreat until some minutes had elapsed after the retreat of the infantry, etc., which the night, and observing the approaches of the enemy, prevented me from seeing. During this time, we were exposed to the whole and undivided firing of the enemy's artillery, who were not more than 200 yards from us, when we commenced a retreat which we maintained in good order without any loss, until we over took the infantry and artillery. The unevenness of the ground upon which the enemy worked his artillery alone prevented him from making sad havoc among us. They took possession of the town,

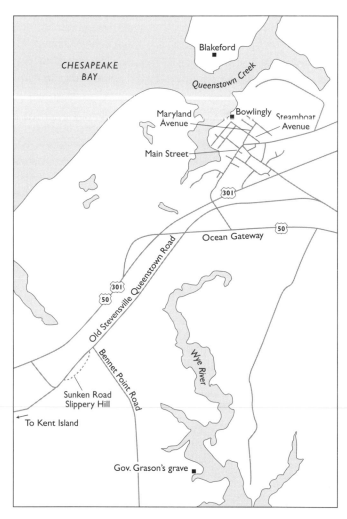

Queenstown Region

and held it for a few minutes, doing little other injury there than taking off a part of our stores of bread and bacon. (Maj. Thomas Emory, Easton *Republican Star,* August 17, 1813)

Second American account of skirmish: at 10 minutes before 3 o'clock of the 13th I was aroused by the quick approach of horsemen, and found them to be my Cavalry videts of the out posts, with the intelligence that the enemy was approaching in great force on the main road from Kent Narrows to Queen's Town . . . when an express arrived to me from Captains [Charles] Hobbs and [John D.] Taylor, with information that the enemy was advancing in such force, as to make it impossible that I could oppose them with mine; and that they expected to effect a safe retreat—This intelligence created great anxiety for the fate of my picquet guard, which was stationed about 2 miles in advance of Queen's Town, on the road by which the enemy was approaching—I immediately mounted my horse, and pressed forward toward my picquet—When I had advanced within 1.2 mile of the post, the firing commenced between them and the enemy—and the vollies of musquetry left me without hope that an individual of them was alive—I returned immediately to my main body . . . a fresh volley of musquetry . . . assured me that my picquet was not annihilated . . . I instantly sent the Adjutant onto meet them, and they arrived safely at our line, about 400 yards in advance of the enemy without the loss of a man, and only one very slightly wounded . . . About 4 o'clock, my cavalry videts . . . bringing . . . intelligence that a large number of barges were entering Queen's Town creek. In a few minutes after a signal rocket from the barges told me the news to be true; at the same moment, one of my guards stationed on the creek came with the information that they had formed their line across the mouth of Queen's Town Creek. The signal rocket was answered from the land side, and I instantly called in all my guard except three, out of twenty, stationed at Mr. [Richard] Hall's landing [Bowlingly] on the creek, who I left for the purpose of conveying intelligence to me of the enemy's approach; for I was firmly resolved to engage the enemy in my front, if it could be done without subjecting the force I commanded to certain capture. I had sent Major [Peregrine] Blake to take a view of the enemy on the water, who returned with the information that they had landed and that he was fired on by them. The force in my front was about 150 yards from us, and was plainly seen from both my left and right flanks. In this situation, I concluded, that nothing but a silent retreat could effect my escape. (Maj. William H. Nicholson to Lt. Col. Thomas Wright, August 16, 1813; reprinted in Easton *Republican Star,* August 24, 1813)

British account of skirmish: This was . . . a project devised for the surprise of some militia encamped at Queen's Town, . . . one battalion of marines with artillery was embarked in the night, to land high up in the bay and take their camp in reverse. The remainder of the troops, with two guns, were to pass the ferry [Kent Narrows] at midnight and march straight against the town, . . . This combination failed entirely; the boats with the detachment missed the landing point, and returned, and the officer with the advance guard, disobeyed [Lt. Col. Charles James] Napier's orders, which were calculated to capture the American out-post without a shot being fired. He had come suddenly upon an American vidette, and irresolutely suffered him to fire and gallop off. The vidette was followed by the picquet, which would otherwise have been surprised, and the English officer, in a disgracefully incapable state, ordered his men to fire, throwing himself on the ground; then the whole advanced guard commenced firing, which brought up [Col. Sir Thomas Sidney] Beckwith and Napier at a gallop to ascertain the cause. This done they ordered Captain [Frederick] Robertson to take command, and stop the firing, which they went to restore order in the rear; but the mischief had already spread there; for the men, seeing the road suddenly lighted up by the firing in the front, while reverberating sounds seemed to spread around, were panic-stricken, and in column as they were, fired right and left, shooting each other.

Beckwith ordered the band to play, and resumed the march, but at every turn the American patriots fired, and the panic returned. Then a fresh company was pushed in front, and Beckwith and Napier took the advance. Beckwith's horse was shot . . . At dawn Queenstown was reached, and a hundred American horsemen, were seen half a mile to the left, but being plied by Captain Robertson with some shots and rocket, fled; their infantry had previously gone off with two field guns. The enemy's captain of artillery [Capt. Gustavus W. T. Wright], who thus retired, had been a few days before received with a flag of truce, and on that occasion invited the British to fight, going so far as to offer single combat to Captain Robertson; he now fled without firing a shot though he might have used his guns effectually and safely, being beyond musquetry, and Beckwith had no cavalry. The projects of Sir J[ohn].[Borlase] Warren at whose entire disposal Beckwith and his troops were placed, were now exhausted, and he had done nothing. (Capt. Frederick Robertson)[232]

The home of Dr. Troupe (southwest side of intersection of Main and Wall streets) was among those that the Royal Marines sacked. Several valuables were taken, including a gold-headed cane. Later the British commander ordered many of the items returned.

Eleven deserters . . . surrendered themselves, the day after the attack upon Queenstown. (Baltimore *Niles' Weekly Register,* August 21, 1813)

At least some of the militiamen stationed at Queenstown apparently were not well fed or provided with proper sleeping quarters.

> stated publicly at Easton and on good authority that some of the troops at Queenstown had been quartered in a hen-house and that a Quarter-Master in Queen Anne's County had dealt out to the troops disastrous musty Indian meal in the husk when none but wheat flour or wheat bread was to be furnished by law. (Unnamed individual to Governor Levin Winder signed "Don't Give up the Ship"; reprinted in Easton *Republican Star,* September, 14, 1813)

British disruption of maritime commerce in the Chesapeake is illustrated by the following account of a Baltimore packet bound for Queenstown. It was captured on April 16, 1813, its cargo confiscated, and its passengers released after a thirty-seven-hour ordeal (for the beginning of this account, *see* Baltimore):

> Arrived at Queen's-Town at 12 o'clock on Saturday evening, the 17th, almost ready to kiss the ground for joy that we had got out of the enemy's clutches, and on land once more, safe and sound. From some of the prisoners put on board of us, we learned that the enemy had, during the time they were detained, destroyed upwards of 100 bay craft. (John Meredith and William Bromwell, Easton *People's Monitor,* April 24, 1813; reprinted in the Annapolis *Maryland Gazette and Political Intelligencer,* April 29, 1813)

Blakeford, also called Blakeford Shore, Blakefort, and Fort Hawkins (Queenstown Creek, south end of Blackford Farm Lane off Decoursey Thom Road). PRIVATE. On August 13, 1813, British barges mistakenly landed at Blakeford, instead of their intended objective Bowlingly* during their combined land and sea attack on Queenstown. Blakeford, built circa 1720, burned down in 1970. It was owned by Governor Robert Wright (1752–1826) during the War of 1812 and was named after a fort built to defend against possible Indian attack. Later it was used during the Revolutionary War and then the War of 1812. The earthworks survived at least until the 1950s.

> The governor [Robert Wright] having despatched his wife and daughter across the creek, and his two youngest sons round the head of the creek on horse back to aid in the fight, and particularly to the assistance of their brother [Captain] Gustavus [W. T. Wright], who commanded two pieces of artillery—he immediately loaded his straight rifle, sent off his carriage for his wife and daughter, mounted his famous Pocahontas, and gave his servant his rifle to run to the shore with it, that he might give the enemy a shot in their retreat,

which they were rapidly making; he got down in time to take long shots, but he fears without effect. It is a foul calamity on the governor's negroes, to impose they would defer to the enemy, as he declares he would much sooner trust his negro than such a contemptible creature as Poulson. The governor never left his farm. (Wilmington *American Watchman & Delaware Republican,* September 22, 1813)

Governor Wright supported the allocation of $30,000, $30 for each of 1,000 recruits, to encourage enlistment in the U.S. Chesapeake Flotilla, but this request was apparently never approved by the Maryland legislature. Fearing another British attack, Wright auctioned off his horses and cattle on November 18, 1813, to avoid their possible loss.

> To avoid their being stolen by the British—Will be sold at public sale . . . several full bred Mares, Colts, Geldings, and Fillies, among which are two good matches of Colts, both full brothers, also some other horses, and a number of young Cattle of both genders, of the Milk bread, equal to any in America. (Easton *Republican Star,* November 16, 1813)

Bowlingly, also called Hall's Landing, Neale's Residence in 1798, and The Ferry House from 1905 to 1914 (111 Bowlingly Circle, north of Maryland and Steamboat avenues). NRHP. PRIVATE. Richard Hall, owner of Bowlingly, lived at one of his inland properties during the war, allowing the local militia to use his Bowlingly home as headquarters. Cannon at various times were mounted on the creek bank at Bowlingly to protect Queenstown from a possible water attack, but none were apparently in place during the 1813 attack. On August 13, 1813, the British troops damaged the 1733 Georgian house after the militia fled. Damage included the destruction of interior doors, stairs, and wall paneling. In addition, the British took jewelry, broke furniture, and slashed family portraits.

> At [Richard] Hall's, the force that landed there under [Rear Adm. George] Cockburn, injured his house and furniture. (Maj. Thomas Emory, Easton *Republican Star,* August 17, 1813)

A short time previous to the appearance of the fleet before Queenstown my Father's [Richard Hall] health forced him to obtain a substitute [for militia duty] and to retire for a while from the army; accordingly, he with his family vacated our residence, situated about 1/4 of a mile from Queenstown, . . . on our leaving home our officers took possession of our house; but on the morning that the British fleet appeared in sight, Queenstown, our house and whole property were left to the mercy of the enemy. Our Army retreated . . . Every soul left Queenstown—and our negroes . . . The British . . . drove all the poultry and cattle, and took off what silver table and tea spoons, punch strainers, sugar, glass and china, that had been left for the use of our officers. They destroyed a valuable mahogany medicine case, inlaid with brass (which had been imported from England), breaking the bottles, and pouring the medicine over the floor. Cut open with their swords, large feather beds, strewing the feathers also on the floor and cutting the sackings around inside the cord, so that they could not be used again, and the mahogany bedsteads were cut to pieces, as with an axe-in this state we found our house, at their departure . . . The British were preparing to burn our houses, but desisted, at the earnest request of a person, who was greatly indebted to my Father, and who had rendered a signal favor to [Rear Adm. George] Cockburn . . . I have frequently heard my Father say, that his property and crops suffered much, on account of his negroes having been called frequently from their work, to aid our troops in removing baggage, ammunition etc., and placing and withdrawing cannon from our bank, (facing the river [Queenstown Creek]) and where I have frequently seen them placed, it being intended, as I often heard, to fire on the enemy from that point in case of a battle. I have also heard my father say, that the losses sustained by his property, during the war, induced or compelled him to sell his most valuable estate, and that he hoped and expected to be indemnified by Congress. (Sister M. Etienne Hall, December 10, 1862)[233]

Richard Hall was unsuccessful in getting reparations from Congress despite the fact that his house was used by the militia. The house remained unoccupied until Capt. James Massey, 38th Regiment and a participant in the Battle of Slippery Hill, purchased it in 1817.

There are two Maryland Historical Roadside Markers that refer to Bowlingly and the battle (north corner of Maryland and Steamboat avenues). One gives the date of the battle as August 2, 1813, and the second gives the date August 2–3, 1813. The battle actually took place August 13, 1813. One marker claims "Sir Charles James Napier" commanded a contingent of the British troops. Charles James Napier was a lieutenant colonel in the British army, who has been confused with his cousin Capt. Charles Napier Royal Navy, who later became an admiral.

Slippery Hill (high ground southwest of the intersection of Queenstown Road [Route 18] and Bennett Point Road, southwest of Queenstown). PRIVATE. Along the slope of this road, American videttes skirmished with British troops as they advanced on Queenstown. At least two British soldiers were killed as was Col. Sir Thomas Sidney Beckwith's horse.

the hogs have rooted up one [British soldier] that was buried [at Slippery Hill], and a horse was left dead in the road. (*Centreville Observer,* 1886–87)[234]

The "Earthworks," as they are sometimes referred to, are actually the remains of a sunken portion of the old road that led from the ferry at Kent Narrows to Queenstown. This defile made an excellent place for the Americans to fire upon the advancing British forces.

RANDALLSTOWN (southwest Baltimore County). Randallstown is named after the Randall family, which settled here circa 1719. Eight members of the family took up arms during the Battle for Baltimore. Best known is Lt. Col. Beal Randall, Jr., of Tobias E. Stansbury's 11th Brigade, who led a rifle battalion during the Battle of North Point. His brother, Capt. John T. Randall, commanded Company C. Others include Pvt. John C. Randall, Company B, 36th Regiment; Pvt. Nicholas Randall, Company D, 41st Regiment; and William Randall of the Baltimore Volunteers. Pvt. Aquila Randall,* killed during the Battle of North Point, is memorialized by name on Battle Monument* in Baltimore.

RAWLINGS' TAVERN SITE, also called Butler's Tavern (northeast corner of the intersection of Harwood Road and Solomons Island Road [Route 2], Harwood, Anne Arundel County). Located on the old ridge trail, the 1771 Rawlings' Tavern served as a meeting place for the officers of the 8th Brigade to prepare and organize the local militia in anticipation of war with England. A few rotten timbers from the tavern were extant as late as 1985.

Brigade Orders. The Colonels and Majors of the 8th Brigade are required to meet at the place known by the name of Rawling's Tavern, on West River, on Thursday, the last day of April next, at 11 o'clock A.M. in pursuance of orders issued by the brigadier general. William H. Marriott, Brigade Major, 8th Brigade. March 26, 1812. (Annapolis *Maryland Gazette and Political Intelligencer,* March 26, 1812)

RESERVE SITE. *See* Prince Frederick

RIDGE (southern St. Mary's County). Ridge was one of the courier post office stations along the route stretching from Point Lookout* to Washington. This service provided information on British fleet movements.

I have this moment ordered a daily express between this and the Ridge post office. It will leave that post office every day at 3 O.C. p.m. you will be careful on each day to send a letter for me at that office each day by 2 p.m. informing of every interesting event and reporting the state of things. (Postmaster General Gideon to Thomas Swann, Point Lookout, July 19, 1813)[235]

Yesterday at 9 a.m. I recd despatches by an express from my agent Thomas Swan at point Look Out stating that on Sunday the 18th a half past 4. p.m. a 74 gun ship and a 38 gun Frigate passed up the Potomack under full sail. (Postmaster General Gideon Granger to Secretary of War John Armstrong, July 21, 1813)[236]

Special agent Henry Wertz of Ridge reported that owners of the schooner *Sidney* furnished the enemy with flour and that several pilots from the neighborhood provided their services to the enemy at $6 per day.

RIDGELY HOUSE SITE. *See* listing, North Point

RINE, DANIEL AND HESTER ANN, GRAVE. *See* appendix B, Brinkman-Rine Cemetery

RIVERSDALE MANSION, also called Calvert Mansion (4811 Riverdale Road, Riverdale Park, Prince George's County). NHL. Baron Henri Joseph Stier built Riversdale, a stucco-covered five-part brick mansion, between 1801 and 1807. Rosalie Stier Calvert, "Mistress of Riversdale" and daughter of Stier, wrote in a letter in 1814, "We have been in a state of continual alarm."[237] Mrs. Calvert's husband, George, along with slaves from the plantation, helped bury the dead after the battle, and she and her husband became friends with some of the wounded British officers left behind at Bladensburg. Henry Clay, a War of 1812 War Hawk, was a frequent visitor to Riversdale. The history of the site during the War of 1812 is the subject of one interpretive panel in the visitor center.

At this time it is nearly impossible to send letters, and I begin this one without the least hope of being able to forward it for a long time. A fleet of two English ships of 74 cannon and six frigates close the entry to the Chesapeake and Delaware [bays] and do not allow the smallest boat to pass. (Rosalie Stier Calvert to Charles J. Stier, February 24, 1813)[238]

1827 lithograph showing the south portico from which the mistress of Riversdale, Rosalie Stier Calvert, observed "several cannonballs with my own eyes" during the Battle of Bladensburg. The battle was fought about two miles from the mansion. Rosalie probably saw Congreve rockets, which would have been more easily visible because of their smoky trails. (B. King from watercolor by Anthony St. John Baker; reproduced by permission of The Huntington Library, San Marino, California)

Among the wounded in our village [Bladensburg] there were Colonel [William] Wood, and a Major [Francis F.?] Brown, who stayed here two or three months and whose acquaintance we made. (Rosalie Stier Calvert to Charles J. Stier, December 27, 1814)[239]

Of the 100 hogsheads of tobacco that I bought for you in 1810, seven were in one of the warehouses which the British partially looted; they took five and left two. I hope the price we can get for the remainder will compensate you for this loss. (Rosalie Stier Calvert to Charles J. Stier, March 20, 1815)[240]

The burning of the public building in Washington is the best thing that has happened in a long time, as far as we are concerned, since this has finally settled the question of whether the seat of government would stay here. In the future they will no longer keep trying to change it, and as long as the union of states stands, the government will remain in Washington, despite the jealousy of Philadelphia, New York, and Baltimore. They are busy rebuilding the Capitol and all the buildings which were destroyed. I was quite calm during the Battle of Bladensburg because the only thing I feared was foragers, but we hardly suffered at all. (Rosalie Stier Calvert to Isabel van Havre, May 6, 1815)[241]

RIVERSIDE PARK. *See* Fort Wood/Camp Lookout, Baltimore

ROCK HALL (Swan Creek, southwest Kent County). On August 20, 1814, British forces under the command of Capt. Sir Peter Parker landed at Swan Creek from H.M. frigate *Menelaus* to raid Rock Hall. During a severe thunderstorm on August 24, 1814, H.M. tender *Mary* capsized at Swan Point and was lost along with one 32 pounder carronade, 150 cannonballs, 16 muskets, 16 swords, 16 bayonets, and all its gunpowder. This same storm dampened the flames of burning Washington.

ROCKVILLE, then called Montgomery Court House (south-central Montgomery County). NHD. On August 26, 1814, Brig. Gen. William H. Winder attempted with little success to regroup the scattered American troops at Montgomery Court House (intersection of Jefferson and Washington streets, twelve miles from the capital, now called Rockville) after retreating from Bladensburg via Washington and Tenleytown, in part using Falls Road (Route 189). Winder had expected to find food, tents, and other supplies sent by a quartermaster's wagon train, but it had gone off to Virginia instead. Winder and his troops left at approximately noon, marching out the Baltimore Road.

Good God! How have we been disgraced? Our cursed militia have been coming in [to Baltimore] one, two, and three at a time, and all speak highly of their gallantry. (Capt. Joseph Hopper Nicholson to Secretary of Navy William Jones, August 1814)[242]

President James Madison and his party, who planned to meet Brigadier General Winder at Montgomery Court House, arrived at 6:00 p.m. on August 26, 1814, but found Winder and his troops had already left so they continued on to Brookeville. From Courthouse Square at the intersection of Jefferson and Washington streets, then the main cross roads in town, one can nearly follow the route President James Madison used by traveling east on Jefferson Street (which becomes Veirs Mill Road [Route 586]), then northeast on Norbeck Road (Route 28), and finally north on Georgia Avenue (Route 97) to Brookeville. President Madison would have actually traveled north on First Street and then east on Baltimore Road to Norbeck Road, but these connections are no longer possible due to railroad and new road construction.

George Graff, a farmer who lived three miles north of Montgomery Court House, became a 2nd lieutenant in Capt. Henry Steiner's Frederick Artillery, 9th Brigade. Graff provided his own uniform and musket and purchased a cannon for his unit. His servant, Shadrach Nugent, probably a slave, claims he kept Graff's canteen filled with whiskey during the Battle for Baltimore. Nugent reportedly earned his freedom at this battle.

Beall-Dawson House (103 West Montgomery Avenue). NRHP. Owned by the Montgomery County Historical Society. The area around the Federal style Beall-Dawson House, built by Upton Beall, served as an encampment during the American retreat from Bladensburg. Beall, an officer in the local militia, is buried at Rockville Cemetery. Timbers stacked for use in the construction of the house were reportedly taken by the militia and used to fuel their campfires.

RODGERS'S BASTION. *See* Hampstead Hill, Baltimore

ROGER BROOKE TANEY HOUSE/FRANCIS SCOTT KEY MUSEUM. *See* listing, Frederick

ROSE HILL, also called Chance or Wheeler's Point (1110 Grove Neck Road, Cecil County). NRHP. PRIVATE. There is no public access to Rose Hill, and it cannot be seen from the public road. Here lived Brig. Gen. Thomas Marsh Forman, a Revolutionary War veteran who in September 1814 com-

"The Conspiracy against Baltimore, or The War Dance at Montgomery Count House" is a Republican cartoon lampooning the Federalists. Alexander Contee Hanson, who owned a home here, is depicted with devil horns overlooking his friend and legal advisor Robert Goodloe Harper, seated with a harp. To their right is Capt. Richard J. Crabb with a crab ornamenting his *chapeau de bras* (hat). Farther to the right is

Charles J. Kilgour with a bull's head symbolizing the "bull-headed" insistence of continuing to publish antiwar editorials. To the left of the cartoon is a Federalist war dance with Gen. Henry "Light Horse Harry" Lee (center left) wearing a *chapeau de bras*. (1812 engraving; courtesy Maryland Historical Society)

manded a brigade of militia from Cecil and Harford counties at Hampstead Hill during the defense of Baltimore. During his service at Baltimore, Forman and his newly wedded bride, Martha Ogle Brown Forman, exchanged letters. Both are buried in the family graveyard. The following excerpts from the diary of Martha illustrate the precautions taken to protect household possessions and what life was like married to a military man.

> July 10 [1814]. The General was sent for by express to come to Elkton under an impression that the British were landing. July 11. Sent our trunks containing plate, linen, and valuable to Middletown, Delaware, to the care of Mr. Joseph Robert, merchant. July 13. Sent our furniture to Mr. [James] Morgan. August 27. My Husband left me to take command of Brigade at Baltimore . . . February 14 [1815] . . . Capt. Chambers [Ezekiel Forman] was badly and dangerously wounded by the bursting of a Cannon which he had fired at Elkton at the celebration of Jackson's Victory and the News of the peace with Great Britain. (Martha Ogle Brown Forman, 1814–15)[243]

ROUSBY HALL (Patuxent River, near end of Rousby Hall Road [Route 760] on the south side, southern Calvert County). PRIVATE. Col. James Fitzhugh lived at Rousby Hall. It was bombarded and burned in 1780 by the British during the Revolutionary War because Fitzhugh's father (William) refused to provide provisions. The second house may also have been damaged by the British during the War of 1812 because James was a militia officer. The present house dates from circa 1818. The custom house, still standing but now altered, survived the 1780 and 1814 raids. There is evidence of burning on the interior beams. On June 9, 1814, the British landed at nearby Rousby Hall Creek, today called Mill Creek, and destroyed several watercraft.

ST. CATHERINE ISLAND, also St. Catherine's, St. Katherine('s) Island, and Cheseldine('s) Island (confluence of Wicomico and Potomac rivers, St. Mary's County). The British sank wells on St. Catherine Island on July 21, 1813, to obtain water during their raiding activities on the Potomac River.

Wells were also sunk at St. Clement Island,* Drum Point,* Cape Henry,* New Point Comfort,* Point Patience,* and Pooles Island.*

ST. CLEMENT BAY (off Potomac River, St. Mary's County). In July 1814, St. Clement Bay served as an anchorage for Rear Adm. George Cockburn during his raids on the lower Potomac River. On July 23, at the head of St. Clement Bay, the British captured four schooners, destroyed a fifth, and burned a house from which shots had been fired. On August 27, 1814, near the mouth of St. Clement Bay, about 1,200 marines and 40 sailors landed at the John Kilgour farm, where 20 head of cattle, 21 sheep, poultry, and some vegetables were taken. For this food, the British paid $305 in silver. Rear Admiral Cockburn remarked to Kilgour that "he [Cockburn] should respect private buildings, unless fired on by the militia from them; that he should take no citizens unless found in arms; that reinforcements had arrived that morning; and that he should immediately pay Washington a visit" (Annapolis, *Maryland Gazette and Political Intelligencer,* August 4, 1814).

> British account of raid: the Boats and Tenders went up St. Clements Creek [Bay] . . . with the Marines and marine artillery to examine the Country on its Shores—The Militia shewed themselves occasionally but always retreated when pursued, and our Force returned to the Ships in the Evening without casualty of any sort having Captured four Schooners and destroyed another which had taken shelter in the upper part of the Creek. The Inhabitants in this Neighbourhood having remained peaceably in their Houses I did not permit any Injury to be done to them, excepting only at one Farm from which two musket shots were fired at my Gig [ship's boat], where we therefore landed and destroyed the Property. (Rear Adm. George Cockburn to Vice Adm. Sir Alexander F. I. Cochrane, July 24, 1814)[244]

> American account of raid: [Rear] Adm. [George] Cockburn landed with 1200 Marines on the 23rd. near St. Clement's Bay—His object plunder. He consoled the suffering Individual, whom he had stripped of his property, by an assurance that He should not visit him again, as the reinforcement so long expected, had arrived and He should proceed on against Washington. (Brig. Gen. Philip Stuart to Secretary of War John Armstrong, July 24, 1814)[245]

ST. CLEMENT ISLAND, also called Blackistone Island (Potomac River, St. Mary's County). NHD. Access by boat from Colton Point. From July 19 to July 21, 1813, British forces landed on St. Clement Island and sank wells for water dur-

ing their raiding activities up the Potomac River. Wells were also sunk at nearby St. Catherine Island.* On November 2, 1813, the British raided the island. The following year the British reoccupied the island and used it as a watering place and harvested timber to build barges. It was from St. Clement Island that Rear Adm. George Cockburn with about 1,200 marines and 40 sailors landed at the John Kilgour farm at the mouth of St. Clement Bay.*

> on the 16th [December 1814] a British tender . . . gave chase to an oyster boat in the neighborhood of Blackstone's Island. A boat was manned from the tender with an officer and 4 men, armed with muskets and cutlasses, which got within gun shot of the oyster boat and fired several guns at her, which struck different parts of the vessel.—The owner . . . made for a small creek, and advised a young white man who was with him . . . to take his ducking gun . . . and go ashore, and secret himself till the boat should come near a point which he was endeavoring to make, and then fire into it. The young man kept himself snug until the boat came within about 50 yards of him, when he fired with such effect as to wound the officer and 3 men—they all immediately fell flat and bellowed out lustily for quarters. The young man loaded his gun again and ordered them to push the boat ashore and surrender, which they did, and after having secured their arms, (3 muskets and 2 cutlasses) and being joined by his companion, they marched them to where some militia were stationed . . . and delivered them up to the commanding officer who sent them under guard to Washington. The oyster boat arrived here yesterday, and proceeded onto Washington with her prize. (Baltimore *Federal Republican,* December 29, 1814)

ST. GEORGE ISLAND (confluence of St. Marys and Potomac rivers with St. George Creek, south end of Piney Point Road [Route 249], St. Mary's County). The British occupied St. George Island on July 19, 1813, and then returned on November 1, 1813. For ten days they occupied the island. Accounts claim that during this occupation the British burned every house, fence, and even pastureland. They also took slaves and cut down most of the large trees for use as masts and spars. After three days of pillaging, the militia finally appeared on the mainland and fired on a British ship's boat positioned at the narrows to prevent possible desertions.

> Last Wednesday I visited St. George's Island, viewed with affliction the great devastation made by the English in their last visit to the place. From the face of things they could have had no other view than to completely destroy the whole of the property. They have burnt every house . . . They had cut down 25 or 26 large oaks, all white oak excepting two or

three. The stocks of nearly all of them were carried off . . . They burnt as much of the fencing as they could, as also the marshes. (Father Francis Neale to Father John Grassi, president of Georgetown College, November 1813)[246]

On August 11, 1814, the British returned to the island. They sank wells for water and again used the island as a base for repairs and operations on the lower Potomac River.

[St.] George's Island in the Potowmac . . . affords plenty of Wood & Water. (Rear Adm. George Cockburn to Vice Adm. Sir Alexander F. I. Cochrane, April 2, 1814)[247]

Early this morning I went to St. George's Island and got dreadfully bit by flies, every ship almost has a party on shore cutting down Fir trees etc. etc. which are very large. (Lt. Benjamin George Beynon, October 1, 1814)[248]

completed the refitment of the Squadron and Transports under my orders and assembled them at [St.] Georges Island in the Potowmack. (Rear Adm. Pulteney Malcolm to Vice Adm. Sir Alexander F. I. Cochrane, October 7, 1814)[249]

I have a Tender up this River [Potomac] Havannah has one up the Rapahannock and Dauntless (who is stationed from Point Lookout to Annapolis) has one up the Patuxent, and you may rely Sir that every exertion shall be used by myself and the Ships under my Orders for the Annoyance and Destruction of the Enemy's Trade in the Rivers within the Capes of the Chesapeake. (Capt. John Clavell to Rear Adm. Sir George Cockburn, "His Majestys Ship Orlando at [St.] Georges Island," January 16, 1815)[250]

By January 25, 1815, the British had evacuated St. George Island.

ST. INIGOES MANOR SITE AND ST. IGNATIUS ROMAN CATHOLIC CHURCH (St. Inigoes Creek, southwest end of Villa Road, off Point Lookout Road [Route 5], St. Inigoes, St. Mary's County). NRHP. St. Inigoes Manor (priest house) and farm, located near the Jesuit Mission built in 1785 (now St. Ignatius Roman Catholic Church), supplied food to Georgetown College (now Georgetown University). The priests of the mission were panic stricken when the British came raiding up the Potomac River in the spring of 1813. Much of the mission's food stores was taken to the cellars of parishioners for safekeeping. On November 5, 1813, a raiding party captured three vessels after driving off the local militia. The St. Inigoes Manor and farm was looted on October 31, 1814, by a British boat crew from H.M. sloop *Saracen*. Sheep and cattle were taken as well as sacraments from the chapel in the priests' house. Ironically, the sacraments may have

been moved here from the mission for safekeeping after the previous British raid. Total loss was estimated at $1,033.70.

American account of raid: The Sacred Vestments thrown and dragged here and there, the vessels consecrated to the service of God prohaned, the holy Altar stripped naked, the tabernacle carried off and the most adorable Sacrament of the altar borne away in the hands of the wicked. (Brother Joseph Mobberly to Rev. John Grassi, October 31, 1814)[251]

Second American account of raid: The most wanton, and unprovoked destruction of private property, that has recently occured in the lower end of this County, was committed at Priest Ransaw's in the neighborhood of St. Inigoes, on Tuesday last. A marauding party of fifteen men belonging to a Brig off St. Georges Island, (supposed the [H.M. brig-sloop] *Jasseur* [*Jaseur*] Capt. [George E.] Watts) robbed him of all his household furniture, as well as his wearing apparel including his watch &c. &c. Such articles as they could not conveniently carry off, and by which they could not be benefitted, was destroyed in the most shamefull manner: amongst which was an Alter, that after they completely pillaged of its ornaments, they also destroyed. (Thomas Swann to Secretary of War James Monroe, November 7, 1814)[252]

Brother Joseph P. Mobberly convinced Lt. William Hancock, the British officer in command, to stop the pillaging of the manor and its private chapel. On November 18, 1814, Capt. Alexander Dixie, commander of *Saracen*, sent Lieutenant Hancock under a flag of truce with a letter of apology to the priests and other inhabitants of St. Inigoes, acknowledging the robbery and restoring various articles taken. He also gave Mobberly a bill to the government of England for £22.6.9 sterling and a gold piece valued at $9.00. Lieutenant Hancock was apparently sent back to England for disciplinary action.[253] Soon after Brother Mobberly moved many items to an unoccupied hut in the woodlands for protection. The manor house and farm were located farther to the east of the church inside what today is the Webster Field Annex of Patuxent Naval Air Station and is off limits to the public.

ST. JEROME CREEK (off Chesapeake Bay, St. Mary's County). On June 1, 1814, the British attempted to take an American sloop commanded by a Captain Baker that entered St. Jerome Creek to evade capture. Baker joined two inhabitants on shore who all began firing their muskets on the British barge. The British abandoned their pursuit after two of their men were supposedly killed.

American account of skirmish: Capt. Baker, of the sloop Swallow, of Baltimore, being chased into St. Jerome's creek, by a British barge, with 16 men, with small arms and a 4 pounder in her bow, left his vessel, and being joined on the shore by two of the inhabitants, having four muskets in all, commenced a fire upon the enemy, and though he had got possession of the sloop, compelled him to abandon her, with the loss of two killed, one of them supposed to be an officer. (Baltimore *Niles' Weekly Register*, April 23, 1814)

On July 4, 1814, the 74-gun H.M. ship-of-the-line *Albion* anchored off St. Jerome Creek and sent parties ashore to re-provision the ship. Six bullocks, sheep, and geese were taken from Jenifer Taylor, John Walsh, and the widow Locker. The British later returned under a white flag and paid Taylor and Locker for what they had taken. Since John Walsh was not present he received nothing.

ST. JOHNS COLLEGE. *See* listing, Annapolis

ST. JOHN'S METHODIST CHURCH (Deal Island, Somerset County). *See* Thomas, Joshua, Chapel

ST. LEONARD CREEK (off Patuxent River, Calvert County). The U.S. Chesapeake Flotilla, blockaded in St. Leonard Creek by a squadron of British vessels, fought a series of skirmishes known as the First Battle of St. Leonard Creek from June 8 to 10, 1814, and the Second Battle of St. Leonard Creek on June 26, 1814, the largest naval engagement ever fought in Maryland waters.

American account of First Battle of St. Leonard Creek (June 8, 1814): at 5 A.M. yesterday, we perceived One ship, Brig, two schooners, & 15 Barges coming up the Patuxent the wind at East, I got the flotilla under way and moved up the Creek about 2 Miles, and moored in line abreast across the channel & prepared for action, at 8 A.M., the Enemies Barges came up the creek, the ship &c. anchored at the mouth of the Creek, a Rocket barge was advanced upon us, we fired several shot to try the distance, which fell short, whilst their Rockets passed over us in every direction, finding myself exposed in such a situation I got my barges (13 in number) under way leaving the Scorpion [flag ship] & gunboats at Anchor, and rowed down upon them when they precipitately fled from their position behind a point, sailed and Rowed off with all their means—we pursued them until near the Shipping, fired several shot among them, when we returned to our moorings; In the afternoon they came up again, Again threw Rockets, and were again pursued out of the Creek, but this time they were more successfull, as One Rocket fell onboard of [gunbarge] No. 4 . . . killed one man, set fire to a barrel of musket carthridges, the explosion of which very much injured three men . . . The Militia under

[Lt.] Col [Michael] Taney [VI] are on the alert. (Com. Joshua Barney to Secretary of Navy William Jones, June 9, 1814)[254]

Account of American heroism during the First Battle of St. Leonard Creek (June 8, 1814): One of the enemy's [Congreve] rockets fell on board of one of our barges, and, after passing through one of the men [one of only three Americans to die from a British rocket during the entire war in Maryland], set the barge on fire—a barrel of powder, and another of musket cartridges, caught fire and exploded, by which several of the men were blown into the water, and one man very severely burned—his face, hands, and every uncovered part of his body, being perfectly crisped. The magazines were both on fire, and the commander of the boat, with his officers and crew, believing that she must inevitably blow up, abandoned her, and sought safety among the other barges. At this moment Major [William B.] Barney, who commanded the cutter 'Scorpion,' . . . hailed his father [Com. Joshua Barney] and asked his permission to take charge of the burning boat . . . Major Barney immediately put himself on board, and by dint of active labor in bailing water into the boat and rocking her constantly from side to side, he very soon succeeded in putting out the fire and saving the boat, to the very great delight, as well as astonishment of the Commodore. (Com. Joshua Barney, 1832)[255]

Second American account of First Battle of St. Leonard Creek (June 9, 1814): On the evening of the 9th, the enemy moved up with twenty barges, having received more force from the 74 [ship-of-the-line *Albion*], at the mouth of the Patuxent. I met them, and after a short action drove them until dark, and returned to my anchorage. Yesterday they made a bold attempt; about 2 P.M. they moved up with twenty-one barges, one rocket barge, and two schooners in tow. On making their appearance, we went down on them; they kept up a smart fire for sometime, and seemed determined to something decisive. But they soon gave way and retreated; we pursued them down the creek. At the mouth lay the eighteen gun schooner, she attempted to beat out, but our fire was so severe, she ran ashore at the entrance, and was abandoned. We still pursued, until the razee [armed vessel that has had its upper deck cut down] and brig opened upon us a brisk fire, which completely covered the schooner and the flying barges, &c. We must have done them considerable damage. (Com. Joshua Barney to Secretary of Navy William Jones, June 11, 1814)[256]

Third American account of First Battle of St. Leonard Creek (June 10, 1814): the Large schooner [18-gun H.M. *St. Lawrence*] was nearly destroyed, having several shot through her at the water's edge, her deck torn up, Gun dismounted, and main-mast nearly cut off about half way up, & rendered unserviceable . . . The commodore's boat [Barrie's armed gig]

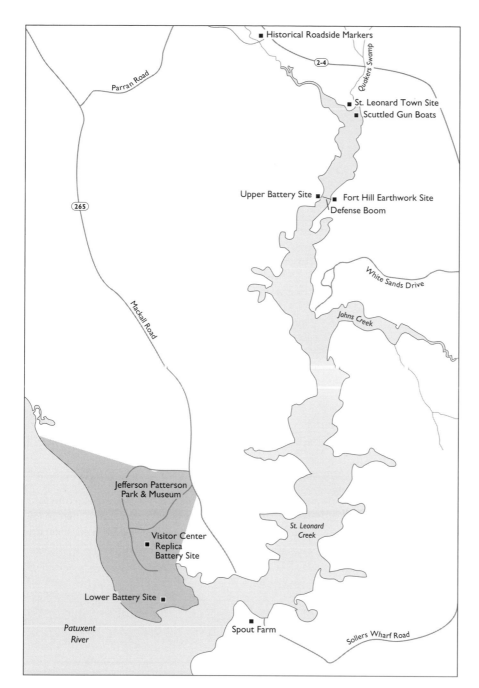

St. Leonard Creek

was cut in two, a shot went through the <u>Rocket</u> boat, One of the small schooners carrying the two 32 pounders had a shot which raked her from aft, forward; the boats generally suffered. (Com. Joshua Barney to Secretary of Navy William Jones, June 13, 1814)[257]

In an effort to draw the U.S. Chesapeake Flotilla out of its well-defended position in St. Leonard Creek, the British conducted raids up and down the Patuxent River.

American account of British raids on St. Leonard Creek: the enemy landed about 300 men one mile above St. Leonard's

Creek, and set fire to the dwelling house and tobacco house of Mr. Patterson [James John Pattison], which were entirely consumed, and attempted to set fire to his barn, but failed in consequence of a precipitate retreat before the fire was properly kindled. (Annapolis *Maryland Republican,* June 18, 1814)

Com. Joshua Barney reported that Pattison "would not suffer a man to go on his place for its defense, but declared he would shoot the first man that attempted to do so, rather trusting the enemy than the protection of the militia. This statement was made to me immediately after his declaration, and soon after his house was burnt, which could have been defended with ease, had not Mr. Pattison prevented it."[258]

Second American account of the British depredations on St. Leonard Creek: It is painful for me to pronounce to you the Loss of Tom and Abraham [slaves] who have taken themselves of with the Enemy Now lying In our river [Patuxent], with out any Cause whatever, the other Two boys I Do not aprehend much Danger of going tho there's No telling from apearances as there is not Less 40 gone from this County and Daily going. Our situation here is painful In upstream [?] the British are in full position [?] of the Lower part of our County they travel Daily in Every Direction below St. Leonard and oblige the Inhabitants to yoke their oxen and haul from their Barns hhds [hogsheads] of tobacco, and at the same time take whatever provision they may think proper— you no Doubt would ask for the militia But I asure you there is But Little Chance for our febal force to resist the strength of the Enemy at this time is said to be 11 ships and several schooners—as for assistance from government we have no expectation for we are Intirely Deserted—We are now left at the mercy of the Enemy—when the floitla Lay here Every Defense that Could be made In his Defense by the Inhabitants were made so soone as she [?] was relived [?] we were Emmidiately Left to Defend our selves worn out and fatigued with a hard time of Duty harassed out of our Lives with the Cares of our farm—bodys moving in Every Direction—The genral government had at that time a Considerable force here and was Cut [?] Emmediately of and from the state we are Equaly Neglected . . . our Dwelling is now within the Limits of the Kitchen. (James J. [John] Pattison to William Dalrymaple [?], July 17, 1814)[259]

American account of Second Battle of St. Leonard Creek (June 26, 1814): This morning at 4 AM a combined Attack of the Artillery, Marine Corps, & flotilla, was made upon the Enemies two frigates [H.M. frigate *Lorie* and H.M. frigate *Narcissus*] at the mouth of the Creek, after two hours engagement, they got under way & made sail down the river, they are now warping round Point Patience, and I am moving up the Patuxent with my flotilla, my loss is Acting-Midshipman [George] Asquith Killed & ten others killed & wounded. (Com. Joshua Barney to Secretary of Navy William Jones, June 26, 1814)[260]

British account of Second Battle of St. Leonard Creek (June 26, 1814): at daylight the Enemy opened a Battery of Five Guns on the two Ships [H.M. frigate *Lorie* and H.M. frigate *Narcissus*] under my Command, from the high land, forming the Entrance of [St.] Leonards Creek, on the Larboard hand, at point blank Shot, it being covered with Wood, we were only enabled to fire at where the smoke issued from, shortly after the Flotilla came down rounded the point and opened a well directed fire on both Ships, but from the warm reception they met with were soon obliged to retreat. I had previously to this sent the Launches of the Ships, with a boat fitted for Rockets to flank the battery, when I soon had the satisfaction to observe a light explosion to take place, and the Battery to cease fireing. But judeing we might be harrassed by the Battery again opening on us and the Ships having been frequently hulled, and part of the Riging Shot away, I thought it most prudent to weight and drop down the River . . . in hopes the Flotilla might be induced to follow, but on its falling calm had the mortification to observe them rowing down the Creek, and up the River, the whole consisting of One Sloop [*Scorpion*] and Eighteen Row Boats [mostly gun barges], One of them [gunboat] we observed, to be obliged to return to the Creek, which I imagine had sustained so much injury as to prevent her accompanying the rest . . . only person wounded is the Boatswain of the Narcissus who has lost a leg. (Capt. Thomas Brown to Rear Adm. George Cockburn, June 27, 1814)[261]

American account of the result of the Second Battle of St. Leonard Creek: Barney aided by a land force under col Wadsworth has forced his way out of St. Leonard's Creek, though he is yet contained in the Patuxent from which he may make his escape more easily. (Baltimore *Niles' Weekly Register,* July 2, 1814)

The secretary of navy, William Jones, suggested the flotilla be carted overland to the Chesapeake Bay to escape the blockade, but Com. Joshua Barney, commander of the flotilla, wisely pointed out that spies would probably notify the British, who could threaten the gunboats by anchoring their warships off the Bay shore. On July 2, 1814, the British raided the town of St. Leonard at the head of St. Leonard Creek.

First Ladies of St. Leonard Creek—Margaret Mackall Smith, born September 21, 1788, at St. Leonard Creek, probably where Jefferson Patterson Park and Museum is now located, became the wife of Zachary Taylor, who served as a captain in the U.S. Army during the War of 1812 and became the twelfth president of the United States. Louisa Catherine Johnson, born in London, lived on a farm near the entrance of St. Leonard Creek. She married John Quincy Adams in 1797, a member of the delegation that negotiated the peace treaty at Ghent (modern-day Belgium), ending the War of 1812. Adams later became the sixth president of the United States. On January 8, 1824, Louisa held an anniversary ball in honor of Gen. Andrew Jackson and his victory at the Battle of New Orleans. Thus there are two first ladies with ties to St. Leonard Creek and the War of 1812.

★ **Jefferson Patterson Park and Museum** (near south end of Mackall Road [Route 265], off Broomes Island Road [Route 264], Mackall). NHD. On this property, U.S. Army troops were mustered to support the U.S. Chesapeake Flotilla. Soldiers, marines, and flotillamen erected a gun battery during the Second Battle of St. Leonard Creek. James John Pattison,* who owned property here, lost two slaves, who fled to the British side. On March 26, 1814, John Stuart Skinner,* who also owned property here, was commissioned purser of the flotilla. He made a Revere-like ride to warn the capital of the approach of the British in August 1814 and served as agent for exchange of prisoners. He accompanied Francis Scott Key to seek the release of Dr. William Beanes,* whom the British had taken to their fleet. From his flag-of-truce ship, Key witnessed the bombardment of Fort McHenry. On June 11, 1814, the British burned Skinner's St. Leonard property. They also burned his birth place, The Reserve,* during their July 19, 1814, raid on Prince Frederick. Several War of 1812 interpretive panels and a replica naval gun battery are located at Jefferson Patterson Park and Museum.

Fort Hill Site (east side of St. Leonard Creek, off Planters Wharf Road, east off Saw Mill Road [Route 765]). PRIVATE. Elements of the 36th U.S. Infantry and U.S. Marines established an encampment here to protect the U.S. Chesapeake Flotilla's left flank and to control water access above the creek narrows. Overlooking the creek and St. Leonard Town,* Fort Hill, a semicircular earthwork about thirty feet long and up to three feet high, served as a lookout point. The Fort Hill earthworks were destroyed when a house was built on the site in the 1970s. A small one-gun battery was located on the opposite shore. It was destroyed when another house was built in 1980. Between these two defensive

points, a floating boom blocked access to the flotilla home base at St. Leonard Town.

> I have also erected a small battery, (1. 24 lb. Carronade), at the mouth of the branch [opposite Fort Hill] where the Scorpion & Gunboats lay, and have also drove piles across the Creek, with a Boom, so that, should the force increase we have little to fear from an Attack by boats, no matter how numerous. (Com. Joshua Barney to Secretary of Navy William Jones, June 13, 1814)[262]

St. Leonard Town Site (near head of St. Leonard Creek, driveway south off Solomons Island Road [Routes 2 and 4]). PRIVATE. The U.S. Chesapeake Flotilla established its base here during the St. Leonard Creek campaign of June 1814. On June 26, 1814, the Americans scuttled two gunboats here. Just west of the town was Fort Hill.* After the flotilla escaped into the Patuxent River, on July 2, 1814, the British destroyed several vessels and structures in the town, including a storehouse and tobacco warehouse owned by John Ireland, a house (used as a hospital by the U.S. Chesapeake Flotilla) and a tobacco warehouse owned by Mary Frazier, and a kitchen owned by Hezekiah Cobreth.

> Captain [Thomas] Brown with the Marines of both Ships landed about two miles up the Creek & proceeded for the Town [St. Leonard] while the boats under the orders of my first Lieutenant Wm. Gammon pushed up—but little opposition was made by musquetry, two of the Gun Boats of the Flotilla were found drawn up and scuttled which were with several other Vessels destroyed . . . a large Store of Tobacco was also destroyed. (Capt. Joseph Nourse to Rear Adm. George Cockburn, July 4, 1814)[263]

The British attacked St. Leonard Town a second time on August 19, 1814, taking eighty hogsheads of tobacco, some flour, military clothing, and several stands of arms.

Spout Farm, also called Parran Farm, and Nutt's Cliffs (southwest end of Sollers Wharf Road). PRIVATE. Some sources claim the earliest part of Spout Farm dates from the late eighteenth century, while other sources say the earliest surviving section of the house dates from 1828. The present house was significantly modified in 1928. The John Parran family lived here during the war. In the cove by Spout Farm, Com. Joshua Barney concealed his U.S. Chesapeake Flotilla and ambushed a British reconnaissance barge.

> American account of action near Spout Farm (June 10, 1814): about 10 AM. A Gig came in, and rowed up under the points untill she got within good gun shot, she then discovered us

but our round shot was very near destroying her, I saw two Oars cut off and was told, two men fell over board, or jumped over, Several bodies of dead men have floated ashore in the creek and River since the 10th inst. (Com. Joshua Barney to Secretary of Navy William Jones, June 20, 1814)[264]

British account of action near Spout Farm (June 10, 1814): the Water was too shoal to admit of even Jaseur [38-gun frigate] . . . and the St. Lawrence [18-gun schooner] had grounded early in the Morning, and was still ashore, every exertion was made to Anchor the Loire [38-gun frigate] and Jaseur at the Mouth Of the Creek, so as to Pen the Flotilla within it . . . I found him [Barney and flotilla] most advantageously Anchored about six miles from the [St. Leonard Creek] entrance . . . [on the 10th] he [Commodore Barney] quitted his position and Chased the Boats [British barges and launches] nearly to the Entrance of the Creek . . . the Enemy was so cautious of exposing himself, that he kept under the Trees of the Starboard Point [assumed to be the south or right side of St. Leonard Creek as the British looked up the creek] of entrance, out of sight of the Loire and Jaseur except from their Mast heads . . . a Party of Royal Marines . . . reach their station on the starboard point Of the Creek, over the position the Enemy had been firing from . . . and chased him to his former Anchor where he lay secure defended by strong parties of Regulars and Militia, stationed on each side of the Creek behind the Trees. (Capt. Robert Barrie to Rear Adm. George Cockburn, June 11, 1814)[265]

Commodore Barney accused John Parran of being a British spy. Charges were never pressed because Attorney General Richard Rush* doubted that a civilian court would convict Parran. Some claim that because the British did not burn Spout Farm, Parran must have been a spy. However, Morgan Hill Farm was spared, even after American forces had camped there.

Yesterday a Gentleman of this County by the name of [John?] Parren (a Violent Fed[eralist]) who lives at the mouth of the creek, came up, and said that himself & Brother had been taken and carried onbd.; That he had been landed from the Commodore, to inform the inhabitants that if they remained at home quietly, they should not be molested, but if on landing he found their houses deserted he would burn them all, as he had done the house of a Mr. Patterson [James John Pattison], and the Barn of Mr. [John Stuart] Skinner, (our Purser), he also said he had, promised the Commodore after having given such information to return onboard in the evening, he had the Impudence to come where the flotilla lay, and then into the Camp of Major Stewart [Brig. Gen. Philip Stuart?], where I found him, and on his declaring to me it was his intention to return onboard the Enemy in the

Evening, I had him arrested and have him now under guard. (Com. Joshua Barney to Secretary of Navy William Jones, June 13, 1814)[266]

ST. MARYS RIVER (off Potomac River, St. Mary's County). The British conducted three raids on the St. Marys River. On August 11–12, 1814, British troops under Rear Adm. George Cockburn raided homes and the Great Mills Textile Factory.*

British account of first raid: Anchored . . . at the Entrance to St. Mary's Creek [River], and the Marines . . . being embarked in the Boats during the Night . . . I proceeded followed by the [8-gun H.M. bomb-vessel] Aetna and Tenders into St. Mary's Creek— We landed in various parts of this extensive Inlet, and made some long Marches into the Country, particularly towards Sunset to a place they call the Factory of St. Mary's [Great Mills Textile Factory*], where there is a building for Manufactoring Cotton, but (though Militia had certainly been formerly stationed at this Place for its defence) we did not meet with a Single Armed Person nor was one Musquet fired during the whole day, the Inhabitants of this State appearing to have learnt that it is wiser for them to submit entirely to our Mercy than to attempt to oppose us in Arms—They very readily complied with whatever Directions I gave for the line of Conduct they were to adopt, and the Supplies they were to furnish to our Force. (Rear Adm. George Cockburn to Vice Adm. Sir Alexander F. I. Cochrane August 13, 1814)[267]

On September 27, 1814, British forces under Rear Adm. George Cockburn and Maj. Gen. Robert Ross again conducted raids along St. Marys River.

American account of second raid: to day we captured a barge and 15 prisoners, and killed or wounded three men at Port[o] Bello, a place on St. Mary's river. Of us, none were hurt except one a little by his horse falling . . . we dashed on at a full speed charge. When we reached the enclosure near the house . . . we found two barges and the English in them pushing off as hard as they could. I ordered them to surrender, at finding them not disposed, we commenced a brisk fire upon the outmost boat. At the same time some of us rushed into the water and laid hold of the nearest, which we brought to shore. In the other when we commenced a fire, they held up their hands and begged for mercy, at the same time were pushing off and some pretending to push in. I was deceived and they managed to get out of musket shot. I ordered the men to jump in the other boat and pursue them which was eagerly obeyed, but soon found my men were only soldiers, not sailors. Out of the first boat we got ten prisoners. Of the one that got off three were got, two fell over board and one the [word unintelligible]. We picked up the five others along the shore and three returning with their plunder on two horses . . . Prisoners Captured. 5 seamen; 2 artillery men; 1 sergeant; 6 regulars; 1 steuart all of the [H.M. ship-of-the-line] Diadem. Total 15 prisoners. Three killed or wounded. (Annapolis *Maryland Republican,* October 8, 1814)[268]

On November 6, 1814, the British raided St. Marys River for a third time. Five barges proceeded as far as St. Inigoes Creek* and took possession of two schooners loaded with wheat and a sloop loaded with flour, all bound for Baltimore. After unloading the prizes, the schooners were burned.

ST. MICHAELS (Miles River, western Talbot County). NHD.

St. Michaels is one of only two towns in Maryland that twice successfully defended itself from British attacks. (The other was Elkton.*) The first engagement, better known as the "Battle of St. Michaels," took place at twilight on August 10, 1813, and from it the village become known as the "town that fooled the British."

American account of skirmish: the enemy made an attack on that place [St. Michaels] with 10 or 12 barges. From the extreme darkness of the night they succeeded in getting within a few yards of a small battery [Parrott Point] before those who were stationed in it discovered them, when they opened a fire from a nine pounder charged with round shot & langrage, and supposed that considerable execution was done. There being but 14 or 15 men in the fort, and the enemy all around it, they spiked their cannon and retreated. Two small batteries placed in the town [Mill Point and Dawsons Wharf], with a few 6's in them, then opened their fire upon the barges, and in a few minutes compelled them to retreat with considerable precipitation, and they were seen about day-light towing a barge after them. It is not known what damage was done to the enemy, but it is supposed considerable fr. the great hurry with which they left the shore. (Annapolis *Maryland Gazette and Political Intelligencer,* August 19, 1813)

British account of skirmish: I proceeded with the division of Boats . . . up the St. Michael's [Miles] river. We advanced along Shore close to the Town of St. Michaels, and were discovered by the Enemies Patrol who fired on us, a few minutes after a Battery [Parrott Point] mounting Six Twelve and Six pounders gave us a round of Grape and Cannister, when we immediately landed I got possession of the Battery and drove the Enemy into the Town after Spiking the guns; Splitting the Carriages and destroying the Ammunition and Stores, I reembarked with the loss of only two wounded; by this time the Enemy had collected in considerable numbers,

and commenced firing from two field pieces [Mill Point and Dawsons Wharf] in the Town. The destruction of the Battery being complete, and not a Vessel to be seen, I deemed the object of the enterprise fulfilled, and returned on board with the Boats. (Lt. James Polkingthorne to Capt. Henry Baker, August 10, 1813)[269]

A boom and three gun batteries defended at St. Michaels: an earthwork at the entrance to the town at Parrott Point* and traveling cannons set up at Dawsons Wharf* and Mill Point* within the harbor. Both the Americans and the British claim to have spiked the cannons at Parrott Point. It appears one cannon was spiked by the militia before fleeing, and the British spiked the remaining three cannon after taking the gun battery. The cannons at Dawsons Wharf and Mill Point drove the British back to their boats, after which the H.M. sloop *Conflict,* positioned out of reach of the American guns, bombarded the town. There is a mural by John B. Moll in the Tidewater Inn* entitled *The Militia of St. Michaels, Maryland, preparing to repel the attack of the British Fleet during the War of 1812–15,* depicting the two traveling cannons being moved to the waterfront.

A second engagement took place at St. Michaels on August 26, 1813, when a British force of approximately 2,100 men landed at Wades Point,* about six miles from town. One detachment of about 300 troops headed south to attack a militia camp near Harris Creek, while the main body, consisting of about 1,800 men, headed east toward St. Michaels. At a narrows bounded by Porter Creek on the north and Broad Creek on the south, about 1.5 miles west of St. Michaels, the British met an American force five hundred strong supported by cavalry and artillery. After a few shots were fired, the British withdrew. The detached British force near Harris Creek captured fourteen militiamen who had fled to their homes. They were paroled the next day.

Gen. Perry Benson* commanded the forces that repulsed the British in the first and second attacks on St. Michaels. The first engagement is often referred to as the "Battle of St. Michaels," although only a few score Americans took part in it. The second action, which involved hundreds of men on each side, is little known and has no common name. The first engagement is more correctly termed a skirmish, while the second engagement is more correctly termed a battle (see appendix D).

American account of second engagement: about day-light the enemy was discovered by our videts stationed at Col. [Hugh] Auld's point [Wade Point], to be landing from upwards of 60 barges—They immediately moved in column

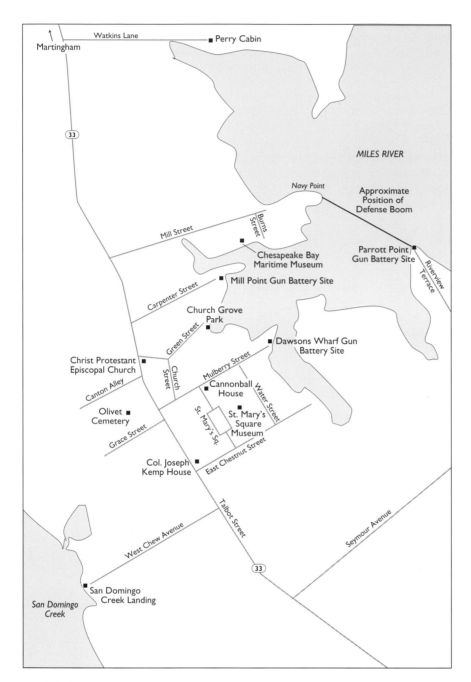

St. Michaels

about two miles toward our camp at this place [St. Michaels]. They then posted a picquet of men in advance, within four miles of us—They had two field pieces, and a number of rockets on the road, in rear of the picquet. At the same time we discovered three schooners and a brig beating up the river, crowded with troops, evidently with all intentions of cutting off our retreat, and destroying this place, should we march down to attack them . . . A flag from one of the schooners landed and informed several persons on the water, that the British troops would land in a few hours, and if they would remain in their houses, their property should not be injured. The vessels, after grounding several times, came to anchor. After this, [Rear] Admiral [George] Cockburn, at the head of 300 men, marched below in search of a militia company stationed there; the greater part of whom made their retreat across Harris's creek . . . Fourteen were afterwards taken at their own houses. They burnt two small vessels, and plundered the inhabitants of clothing, &c. to a large amount. From information received that morning from five seamen who deserted after landing, their force on shore was 300 under [Col.] Sir [Thomas] Sidney Beckwith. At six, P.M. they re-embarked, taking with them the 14 prisoners, whom they released the next day on parole. (Gen. Perry Benson, *Easton Star,* August 29, 1813)

St. Michaels, a well-known ship-building center that produced privateers, was a prime target for attack. Among the successful privateers built here are the *Surprise,* which captured 43 prizes; the *Caroline,* which captured 30; the *Lawrence,* which captured 22; and the *Fairy,* which took 4 British prizes worth $67,500. Altogether, 28 Talbot County vessels, many St. Michaels built, operated against British shipping during the war. Perry Spencer built at least 8 barges for the U.S. Chesapeake Flotilla but the exact location of his yard is unknown.

I am of opinion that the Barges now building at St. Michaels had better be armed with a long 12 pr. [powder] instead of a heavy 18. and a 32 pd. carronade instead of a 24—they will be equally formidable, the two Guns will balance each other and the Barges will row lighter. (Secretary of Navy William Jones to Acting Mas. Com. Joshua Barney, February 18, 1814)[270]

four of the new barges from the Eastern-shore [St. Michales] are here, and Col. [Perry] Spencer the builder, will be here (if Weather permits), with four more this week. (Acting Mas. Com. Joshua Barney to Secretary of Navy William Jones, April 4, 1814)[271]

The boats . . . building on the Eastern Shore, are completed, and now in the care of their able and experienced commander, Commodore [Joshua] Barney . . . Mounting so heavy metal, and presenting so small a mark to the enemy's fire, they are specially adapted to the service for which they possess so great advantages . . . The carpenters, to the number of thirty five, who had been engaged in completing the boats on the Eastern Shore . . . entered the service, and took in charge the vessels they had been building. (Easton *Republican Star,* April 19, 1814)

St. Michaels is known as "the town that fooled the British" from a legend that suggests that during the first skirmish Americans hung lanterns from the tops of buildings and trees and on mastheads of vessels in the harbor to induce the British to fire over the town. In actuality, the bombardment took place in early morning light, so the British would have been able to see the town even with the overcast conditions that morning. Furthermore, in the official report by Gen. Perry Benson he wrote that several homes (such as the Cannonball House*) were hit, suggesting the British were not fooled. Finally, the story of the lanterns did not surface until many years after the war.

On August 11, 1934, St. Michaels celebrated the centennial of the War of 1812 with bands, fireworks, and the dedication of a cannon at St. Mary's Square.* Maryland Governor Charles Goldsborough was present for the activities.

Cannonball House (200 Mulberry Street, near southeast corner of St. Mary's Square). NRHP. PRIVATE. The Cannonball House, built circa 1805 by shipwright William Merchant, was struck on August 10, 1813, by a cannonball during the British bombardment. A cannonball reportedly penetrated the roof of this house, then rolled across the attic and down the staircase, frightening Mrs. Merchant, who was carrying her infant daughter downstairs at the time.

Chesapeake Bay Maritime Museum (Navy Point at end of Mill and Cherry streets). The Chesapeake Bay Maritime Museum includes a small exhibit on the War of 1812. Among the exhibits is an engraving showing the privateer *Rossie,* commanded by Joshua Barney, taking the British mail packet *Princess Amelia* in 1812. The museum and the Inn at Perry Cabin, located north of the museum on the waterfront, were once part of the Perry Cabin Farm, owned by Samuel Hambleton, U.S. Navy purser during the War of 1812. Hambleton named the point where the museum is centered Navy Point.

Christ Protestant Episcopal Church (intersection of Talbot and Green streets). Christ Protestant Episcopal Church was founded in 1672, although the present structure, the third at this location, dates from 1878. American troops reportedly occupied an earlier frame structure that served as the church during the first engagement of St. Michaels. During a reconstruction of the church in 1814, muskets left behind during or shortly after the skirmish were said to be discovered under the floorboards.

Church Cove Park (foot of Green Street). Two replica War of 1812 6 pounder cannons were mounted at Church Cove Park in 1975. The original cannons were donated to the town in 1813 by Jacob Gibson* as a peace offering after a mischievous prank. On April 17, 1813, he had disguised his boat to look like a British naval vessel and had approached St. Michaels via San Domingo Creek (now Back Creek), frightening the town's inhabitants. At the beginning of the American Civil War, federal troops from the arsenal at Easton* confiscated the cannons.

Dawsons Wharf Gun Battery Site (foot of Mulberry Street at Town Dock Restaurant). A two-gun battery commanded by Lt. John Graham was positioned on shipwright Impy Dawson's wharf.

Kemp, Col. Joseph, House (412 Talbot Street). PRIVATE. Col. Joseph Kemp built the Georgian style house in 1805–7. He commanded the Saint Michaels Patriotic Blues of the 26th Regiment, Maryland militia. During the first engagement of St. Michaels, he led a cavalry patrol along San Domingo Creek (now Back Creek). Kemp is buried at Olivet Cemetery.*

> Ordered that the treasurer of the Western Shore pay to Thomas Haddaway and Joseph Kemp Fifty-eight dollars and thirty-three cents and one-third cent for sawing 3500 feet of pine planks for the batteries at St. Michael's by order of General [Perry] Benson. (January 17, 1814)[272]

Mill Point Gun Battery Site (foot of Carpenter Street at Two Swan Inn). A two gun-battery commanded by Capt. Clement Vickers was positioned at the end of Mill Point.

Parrott Point Gun Battery Site (south side of entrance to harbor, northwest end of Riverview Terrace, off Seymour Avenue). A defensive boom was erected across the harbor mouth from Parrott Point. A four-gun battery erected at Parrott Point fired two shots before being captured by British troops who landed before sunrise in eleven barges. Although the British were driven away by the Mill Point* and Dawson Wharf* gun batteries, they spiked the cannons at Parrott Point before leaving. (Withdrawing militia may have spiked one.)

> the trunnions were knocked off the guns, and a shot enveloped in wet cloth was rammed tight home into the chambers,—a plan generally adopted by us, whenever it was inconvenient to ship off the artillery that fell into our power. (Capt. James Scott, 1834)[273]

Capt. William Dodson commanded the Parrott Point gun battery. He later commanded one of the U.S. Chesapeake Flotilla barges and participated in the Battle of Bladensburg.

Dodson is buried at Olivet Cemetery,* St. Michaels. In May 1813, the ladies of St. Michaels presented to Captain Dodson a flag on which were embroidered the names of the officers. The following words were said during the presentation:

> The ladies of St. Michael's . . . wishing to express the high sense of gratitude they feel to the gentlemen, for their prompt exertions in erecting a fort for the common defense; and also in some degree to testify their zeal for liberty and honor of their beloved country, have prepared a flag at their own expense, made it with their own hands, and do most respectfully present the same to you, and through you to them for the use of said fort—having entire confidence the same will not be disgraced for want of patriotic zeal and preserving bravery which always inspires the breast of people enlightened and free. (Easton *Republican Star,* May 25, 1813)

Perry Cabin, also Perry's Cabin, now called Inn at Perry Cabin (east end of Perry Cabin Drive). Samuel Hambleton* (1777–1851), born in Talbot County, served as a U.S. Navy purser and aide-de-camp to Capt. Oliver Hazard Perry* during the September 10, 1813, Battle of Lake Erie. He was wounded in this battle. Some sources credit him with suggesting "Don't Give Up the Ship" on Perry's flag, which was made by seven women in Erie, Pennsylvania. The flag is now in the U.S. Naval Academy Museum.* Hambleton retired in 1816 to Perry Cabin, an estate named after his former commander. The original north wing of the Inn at Perry Cabin is said to resemble Perry's cabin on his flagship, the U.S. brig *Niagara.* This original structure, now part of a restaurant/hotel complex, is but a small part of a greatly expanded structure.

Oliver's brother, Com. Matthew Calbraith Perry, is best remembered as commander of the East Asia Squadron expedition to Japan and negotiator of the Treaty of Kanagawa in 1854. But he was also aboard the U.S. frigate *President* when it engaged H.M. sloop-of-war *Little Belt* on May 18, 1811, and he served under Com. John Rodgers* during the War of 1812. Later, Matthew Perry supervised the construction of the navy's first steam frigate, U.S.S. *Fulton* II, launched in 1837.

St. Mary's Square (between Mulberry and East Chestnut streets). A public market house built on St. Mary's Square in 1805 was reportedly used to store the cannons used in the defense of St. Michaels. During the early morning of August 10, 1813, the houses and churches that bordered the square billeted militia. Of the two cannon mounted on the square, one is said to be a Revolutionary War cannon and the smaller 6 pounder cannon is said to have been used in the defense of St. Michaels during the War of 1812. This cannon was dedicated in 1913 by the Centennial Commission on the 100th anniversary of the battle.

St. Michaels Museum (St. Mary's Square, between Mulburry and East Chestnut streets). In the St. Michaels Museum is a model depicting the town during the war and showing the location of Parrott Point gun battery and the floating "boom" across the harbor mouth. There are also mementoes of the St. Michaels 100th Anniversary Committee of the "Battle of St. Michaels." Among the exhibits are three "Flash Backs" by Patrick M. Reynolds that appeared in the comic section of the Sunday *Washington Post* featuring St. Michaels in the War of 1812: "The Two Shot Battle" (which refers to the claim that only two shots were fired from Parrott Point gun battery before it was abandoned by the militia), "The Town that Fooled the British," and "The Cannonball House."

San Domingo Creek, also called Back Creek (west end of West Chew Avenue). On April 17, 1813, Jacob Gibson* approached St. Michaels in a boat disguised as a British naval vessel with a red bandana tied to its masthead. This prank so frightened the inhabitants that women and children were sent to the country and the militia assembled. Upon learning of the prank, citizens were so furious that Gibson donated two cannon to the town as a peace offering. Replicas of these cannon are mounted at Church Cove Park.*

ST. PAUL'S PARISH KENT (7579 Sandy Bottom Road, Sandy Bottom, west of Chestertown, Kent County). The present structure of St. Paul's Parish Kent, established in 1692, dates from 1713. Glazed bricks on one gable end of the nearby vestry house bear the date "1766." Local tradition asserts that the church served as barracks during the war and that wounded soldiers from the battle at nearby Caulks Field* were treated here and the dead buried at St. Paul's. A survey of the grounds conducted by the University of Delaware's Center for Archaeological Research in 1992 failed to find any supporting physical evidence.

ST. PAUL'S PARISH CHAPEL, also called St. Paul's Episcopal Church (northwest of Baden–Naylor and Horsehead roads, just east of Brandywine Road [Route 381], Baden, Prince George's County). NRHP. St. Paul's Parish Chapel dates from 1733–35, with alterations made in 1769, 1793, 1857, 1882, and 1921. On August 21, 1814, a small detachment of British troops reportedly passed by this chapel while protecting the left flank of the main British column three miles farther east on Croom Road (Route 382) en route to Nottingham. Local tradition claims the marble baptismal font, sent from England in 1752, was knocked over and damaged by the British patrol. It was repaired with copper bands. Although the British did employ flanking units, this site seems too far away from the known British route to have been used for any purpose.

ST. THOMAS' CHURCH, also called Page's Chapel (intersection of St. Thomas Church and Croom [Route 381] roads, Croom, Prince George's County). NRHP. As the British invasion force advanced toward Upper Marlboro,* it passed St. Thomas' Church, located just south of the intersection of Duley Station and Croom roads. Here the British conducted a feint, first turning west toward Bellefields,* Woodyard, and possibly Fort Washington,* and then doubling back and heading north to Upper Marlboro.* Brig. Gen. William H. Winder, commander of the Washington defense, mentions this chapel several times in his correspondence, once as the place where he planned to meet Lt. Col. Frisby Tilghman with his cavalry.

> intelligence was brought that the enemy was moving on from Nottingham in force toward the Chapel. I immediately proceeded, . . . to gain an observation of the enemy, and came with in view of the enemy's advance about two miles below the Chapel. The observation was continued until the enemy reached the Chapel. (Brig. Gen. William H. Winder, September 26, 1814)[274]

The 1745 colonial cruciform chapel was modified by the addition of an east chancel in 1859; the tower was added in 1888; and a small northeasterly sacristy was added in 1905. During the 1850s, stained glass windows were installed in reconfigured gothic-arch windows and decorative vergeboards applied to the gable eaves.

Many War of 1812 figures worshiped here. Maj. Benjamin Oden, owner of nearby Bellefields, purchased pew no. 1; William Beanes (presumably Dr. William Beanes, not his half-brother William Bradley Beanes) purchased pew no. 7 on the southeast square nearest to the communion; and Governor Robert Bowie* purchased pew no. 7 on the northwest square. Local tradition claims seven British soldiers are buried in unmarked graves on the north side of the chapel near the Berry family plot.

President James Madison declared in 1812 that the third Thursday in August be observed as a fast day of prayer and humiliation on account of the recent declaration of war. Bishop Thomas John Claggett* ordered church services throughout the Diocese of Maryland and called for repentance, fasting, and reformation so that the nation might be spared divine vengeance. On the presidential fast day the following year, Bishop Claggett instructed his followers to ignore the boycott of such services as proposed by antiwar newspaper editors in Maryland and the District of Columbia: "Trusting that a call thus sanctioned by God, by the Church and by the Civil authority, will not be lightly regarded. I do direct and require the members of the said Church to repair to their respective parish churches on that day."[275] (See also Otterbein Church, Baltimore, for Rev. Jacob Gruber's quote against King George III; and Deal Island for Joshua Thomas's "Thou Shalt Not Kill" sermon.)

> Day of National Humiliation. The President of the United States has appointed THURSDAY, the 9 day of September next, to be observed throughout the U. States, as a day of Public Humiliation and Prayer. (Baltimore *Patriot,* July 24, 1813)

SANDY POINT (Chesapeake Bay, off Ocean Highway [U.S. Route 50], Sandy Point State Park, Anne Arundel County). On August 11, 1813, seven British deserters came ashore at Sandy Point.

> THE ENEMY. The greater part of the enemy's force is now lying off and a little way above Sandy Point. Seven deserters came on shore at Sandy Point on Wednesday morning last from one of the enemy's ships on the bay. (Annapolis *Maryland Republican,* August 14, 1813)

1st Lt. Baptist Mezick (1773–1863), who served in Capt. George Stiles's 1st Marine Artillery of the Union, lived at Sandy Point. His home still stands within Sandy Point State Park. Mezick was buried at Glendale Graveyard,* Baltimore, but no gravestone is known to survive.

> Obituary: Death of an Old Ship Master.— We regret to record the death of Captain Baptist Mezick, one of the oldest shipmasters out of the port of Baltimore. He died on Sunday last at his farm on Sandy Point, Chesapeake Bay, at the advanced age of 90. Captain Mezick for many years commanded some of the first vessels sailing from Baltimore, and was widely known and highly esteemed as an experienced and successful navigator . . . he retired to his beautiful residence on the banks of the Chesapeake, where, surrounded by his family—with the roar of the breakers sounding on his ear— he quietly breathed his last . . . As a mark of respect to the deceased the flags of the shipping in port were at half-mast yesterday. (Baltimore *Daily Gazette,* March 18, 1863)

SELBYSPORT (intersection of Friendsville Addison and Old Morgantown roads, 2.3 miles north of Friendsville, Garrett County). A short unpaved road provides access to the Youghiogheny River. When lake levels are low, the stone abutments of a former bridge that carried Old Morgantown Road over the Youghiogheny River are visible. A good overview of the area can be had from the Maryland Welcome Center just east on I-68. Legendary hunter Meshack (also Meshach) Browning, commissioned a captain (sergeant according to some accounts) in the 50th Regiment, Maryland militia, mustered his men at Selby's Port, then a flourishing river port at the head of navigation on the Youghiogheny.

Because Browning was an antiwar Federalist, members of the Republican Party resented him and instigated a political fracas near a bridge over the Youghiogheny River. Years after the affair, Browning wrote of his experience:

> These formed two lines on both sides of a [mill] tail-race . . . , about twenty on each side, determined to attack and beat me as I should pass the bridge. Many passes were made at me, but the cowards would run as soon as they struck. Let me turn my face which way I would, it met somebody's fist. Let them beat away; but once in a while I would get a chance at one who would be exposed, and give him a good send. This happened about the middle of November [1812], and I was not able to carry firewood till the first of May following.[276]

Tradition claims Browning won the fracas, but he was so badly injured that it ended his military career.

SHARPS ISLAND SITE (former island in Chesapeake Bay, Talbot County). On April 12, 1813, the British raided Sharps Island, owned by Jacob Gibson, seizing his livestock, for which they paid $225. Although Gibson later donated the money to the state and national governments, he was nevertheless accused of trading with the enemy. On April 17, Gibson tied a red bandana to his mast and pretended to be a British barge and sailed toward St. Michaels. The prank so outraged the citizens that he sought to make amends by donating two cannons, which were used on August 10, 1813, in the defense of the town. (See Church Cove Park, St. Michaels.)

> At the mouth of Choptank lies an Island of some extent and value, called Sharp's Island, owned by one Jacob Gibson, a violent democrat, [who] . . . happened to be . . . on his Island, in the ful possession and exercise of sovereign power, at the Time the British arrived. It was said he went for the purpose of removing his property to a place of safety. They [British] landed and took possession of them and his Island . . . and saved him the trouble of removing his stock as they slaugh-

tered and appropriated to the use of his Majesty's fleet such of his Beeves and Hogs and Sheep as were fit for that purpose. These however they honorably paid him for. He . . . made an acquaintance with Admiral [John Borlase] Warren, whom he represents as the most perfect Gentleman he ever saw. The Admiral invited him to take coffe with him on board of his ship . . . on which occasion he represents himself to have been treated with the most polite attention and to have had much free political conversation with the Admiral and his officers . . . The Admiral . . . assured him that no depredations would be committed on the land, nor any molestation of personal property further than to procure provisions which they would honestly pay for . . . In return for the Admiral's politeness, the Citizen gave him an invitation to dine with him the next Day on his Island. The invitation was accepted and he treated Admiral Warren to a barbecued pig dressed in the best style of our electioneering cookery . . . the Admiral gave a protection . . . for his Island and all the property of every sort upon it, another protection or license to remove his crop of wheat, which was on Hand, and which they did not touch, off to any place except Baltimore, and a passport for him to carry across the Bay a young lady from the western shore, then a visitor at his house, and also his daughter, who wished to accompany her friend upon her return home. (Charles Goldsborough to Congressman Harmanus Bleeker, April 2, 1813)[277]

Despite Congressman Goldsborough's claim of a British protective document, the British conducted a second raid on the island while he was away at St. Michaels.

On Saturday the 16th, the enemy's barges landed on Sharp's island, and swept the island of the remnant of stock left last year; they have taken off every hoof except 3 or 4 cows. The owner has lost from that island 60 cattle, 94 sheep, 40 of which were mingled with the merino, 50 hogs and 3 valuable young negroes, 2 men and 1 woman. They have left a compensation of $300 in government bills, which no one will buy, and $104 in specie. (Baltimore *Niles' Weekly Register,* April 30, 1814)

Jacob Gibson, a wealthy eccentric, owned several estates in Talbot County, which he named after Napoleonic victories. They included Marengo, Austerlitz, and Friedland, although another carried the name Waterloo for Napoleon's defeat. Jena, another Napoleon victory, was a house owned by Perry Spencer, a friend of Gibson, who probably suggested the name.

SHAW HOUSE. *See* listing, North Point

SHERIDAN POINT (Patuxent River, southwest end of Sheridan Point Road, off Adelina Road [Route 506], Calvert County). PRIVATE. On July 16–17, 1814, the British bombarded and then raided Sheridan Point, burning the home of Dr. John Gray because it was occupied by Calvert County militia under the command of Lt. Col. Michael Taney. A petition to Congress for reimbursement for damages reported the following values: dwelling house ($1,000), four slave houses ($400), two tobacco barns ($1,000), overseer's house ($200), corn house ($150), two out buildings ($200), 600 bushels of oats ($300), 300 bushels of wheat ($600), crop of corn ($600), 26 head of cattle ($264), 50 head of sheep ($100), 40 hogs ($86), and furniture ($150). The total loss was $5,050. The present house dates from after the raid.

We cooked our rations in the houses [Sheridan Point]; we occupied them eight or ten days . . . until the British landed their force under a heavy fire of cannon; they drove us out of the houses; and on the same day we left the building they set fire and destroyed the whole of them, and every thing on the farm. (John Smith, April 3, 1839)[278]

I was manager to Doctor John Gray on his farm . . . at the time the British army made an attack . . . on seeing our light infantry posted there, they . . . commenced a heavy fire from their fleet at our light horse [cavalry], who retreated behind a hill. On landing, they took me prisoner, and treated me very roughly . . . They then fired several hundred balls at the hill, in the mean time landing their men and giving them orders to scour the pines . . . They searched the houses, and finding a canteen, one of their soldiers placed it on a bayonet, and raised it in the air, saying to one of their officers, "We have found them out; their militia has been stationed here" . . . Finding, in one of the barns, some prime cedar timber, they ordered their men to take it on board their ships; they likewise carried off a large crop of oats, wheat, and corn, saying it would do for their cows on board; also, all the vegetables, and the stock of cattle, sheep, and hogs. (William G. Jones, July 3, 1837)[279]

SHOAL CREEK SITE. *See* Cambridge

SHOWER, JACOB, GRAVE. *See* appendix A

SION HILL. *See* listing, Havre de Grace

SLAUGHTER CREEK (off Little Choptank River, east side of Taylor's Island, Dorchester County). On August 2, 1814, the British took as a prize one schooner and burned five other large schooners on Slaughter Creek.

The Vessels were burnt in this river in a Creek called Slaughters Creek. (Capt. Joseph Nourse to Rear Adm. George Cockburn, August 4, 1814)[280]

SMITH ISLAND (bounded by Chesapeake Bay on west, Kedges Straits on north, and Tangier Sound on east, Somerset County). The British provisioned at Smith Island in 1814. An unknown Englishman, said to be a veteran of the War of 1812, is reported to be buried on the grounds of the former Pittcraft (Pitchcroft) Plantation but the grave is no longer marked.

> the next cluster of Islands which are called *Smith's,* and of which perhaps you may also think it right to take possession after you commence operations, but at present it is too much out of the way for me to make other use of than sending in occasionally to it for small Supplies of Stock. (Rear Adm. George Cockburn to Adm. Sir John B. Warren, April 13, 1814)[281]

SNELL'S BRIDGE ENCAMPMENT SITE (Patuxent River, Ashton Road/Clarksville Pike [Route 108], Howard and Montgomery counties). On August 26, 1814, American troops encamped at Snell's Bridge as they marched from Washington to Baltimore after their retreat from the Battle of Bladensburg. It is unknown on which side of the river the troops camped.

> When the forces arrived at Snell's bridge, on the upper branch of the Patuxent, I had concluded that, if the enemy was, as we had still reason to believe, proceeding to Baltimore, that it would be most advisable for me to proceed directly thither. (Brig. Gen. William H. Winder, September 26, 1814)[282]

> On arriving at the capitol, I understood that the city had been abandoned . . . encamped that night at Tenly Town, about three miles back of Georgetown. The next day they marched to Montgomery court-house, and on the 26th August to Snell's Bridge [Patuxent River], on the road to Baltimore. (Sgt. John Law, November 10, 1814)[283]

Secretary of State James Monroe reportedly visited the encampment. The next day the troops reached Baltimore. The bridge carried Clarksville Pike over the Patuxent River. The pike was then a major road between Montgomery Court House (now Rockville) and Ellicott City. About fifty yards upstream (northwest) of the modern 1928 concrete arch bridge on the Montgomery (or southwest) side of the river is a stone bridge abutment. It is not certain if this abutment dates from the 1814 bridge, but it does mark the location of that earlier bridge. Here bridge support piles can be seen in the middle of the river.

SNOWDEN'S ENCAMPMENT SITE. *See* appendix A

SOLLERS' HOUSE/CAMP EAGLESTON SITE (also called Sollers Point Farm, north side of confluence of Patapsco River and Bear Creek, Baltimore County). An encampment of more than four hundred militiamen was established here by Maj. Gen. Samuel Smith by August 1813, as it was considered one of four primary landing spots for a possible British attack on Baltimore. On September 11, 1814, in anticipation of the British attack on Baltimore, Maj. Beale Randall and Capt. Benjamin Wilson occupied the Sollers' House at Sollers' Point while their troops (about four hundred) occupied the barn and outbuildings. The next day the British spotted uniformed troops here and fired rockets and cannon on the farm. The American troops fled. The following evening (September 13, 1814) the British landed just north of Sollers' Point and burned the Frederick O'Brien and then the Sollers' farms. In 1827, Juliet Eliza Sollers petitioned Congress for restitution of losses, which included a brick dwelling and kitchen, brick barn and stable, brick cider and spinning house, log granary, frame carriage house, and fencing, all valued at $9,475. Her petition was denied on grounds that while her farm had been occupied by U.S. troops prior to the attack, no troops were present during the British raid. The British used the adjacent Bear Creek to support their land troops during their march on Baltimore from North Point. (*See also* Colgate Creek, which was also used to support the British land troops.)

SOLOMONS, also called Solomon's Island, referred to as Somervell's Island during War of 1812 (Patuxent River, southern Calvert County). The Calvert Marine Museum, located at Solomons, exhibits artifacts recovered from one of the vessels of the U.S. Chesapeake Flotilla scuttled on August 22, 1814, above Pig Point* on the Patuxent River, as well as an electric map of the British invasion route up the river. On August 13, 1814, the British raided Carroll Plantation, located nearly directly across the Patuxent River near Mill Stone Landing (end of Mill Stone Landing Road, St. Mary's County). A Maryland Historical Roadside Marker for Solomons Island (west side of Route 2 at bridge onto island) claims "in the war of 1812, Commander Joshua Barney's flotilla sailed from here to attack British vessels on Chesapeake Bay." The flotilla was anchored under Drum Point at the mouth of the Patuxent River about May 31, 1814, not what is called Solomon's Island today.

the Enemy had made a landing, by means of three schooners & 8 Barges at *Carrols* [Carrolls]. (Com. Joshua Barney to Secretary of Navy William Jones, August 4, 1814)[284]

SOTTERLEY PLANTATION (Patuxent River, east end of Sotterley Gate Road [Route 245], St. Mary's County). NRHP. Sotterley, built at least by 1717, was owned by George Plater V, but because he was only in his teens, his uncle, Col. John Rousby Plater,* served as his guardian. Sotterley was a mustering site for militia coming to the aid of the U.S. Chesapeake Flotilla. Some of these forces crossed the Patuxent River to join other U.S. troops on June 10, 1814. The British landed near Sotterley and attacked an estimated three hundred militia, who quickly fled.

How shall I express to you the feelings of shame that consume me, when I inform you the sight of a British barge alone is sufficient to put to flight every man in our neighbourhood? What, what must be the opinions of our enemies of such conduct! I blush for my countrymen! (Unnamed daughter to Col. John Rousby Plater, quoted in Capt. James Scott, 1834)[285]

Colonel [John Rousby] Plater . . . told the [Rear] Admiral [George Cockburn] that he had done his utmost to bring forward his regiment (militia) to beat him back, but that they had deserted him, and he surrendered himself a prisoner, feeling he was entirely at his mercy. This candour at once gained the favour and protection of Admiral Cockburn, and the most rigid orders were issued, and sentinels placed around, to secure the premises from molestation or injury. The gallant Colonel himself remained at perfect liberty . . . For his conduct, Colonel Plater was held up by democratic portion of the republican press as something akin to a traitor. (Capt. James Scott, 1834)[286]

Despite the reported assurance of protection proclaimed on June 14, 1814, by Rear Admiral Cockburn, the British opened an ineffective bombardment on the plantation, burning a tobacco warehouse and a house formerly occupied by the militia. In addition, at least thirty-nine slaves belonging to Colonel Plater escaped to British vessels.

a flag of truce was sent to the St. Mary's side of the Patuxent [opposite St. Leonard Creek near Sotterley] to demand cattle, with a threat that they would destroy the houses if they were not furnished, the demand we understand was not complied with, & in the evening eleven barges were sent over, but no houses were destroyed; a few shot were fired onshore by the enemy, but it is uncertain what damage was done. By a gentleman who left St. Leonards . . . we learn that 17 barges went to the opposite side of the river that evening;

that several shots were fired, and some houses destroyed; amongst others it was expected a warehouse near Col. Plater [of Sotterley], for the storage and inspection of tobacco was burnt. (Annapolis *Maryland Republican,* June 18, 1814)

On the 13th. Captain [Thomas] Carters party was landed on the South Side of the River [Patuxent] to oppose three hundred Militia collected near the House of Mr Prater [Plater], but the Enemy aware of our Intentions fled into the Woods— On the 14th. We again landed on the South Side, and burned a Tobacco Store and a House which the Soldiers had occupied. (Capt. Robert Barrie to Rear Admiral George Cockburn, June 19, 1814)[287]

four of Col. [John Rousby] Plater's negroes went over to the enemy; and at 10 A.M. the next day, the enemy commenced a cannonade of his house, but without effect. (Baltimore *Federal Republican,* June 24, 1814)

the people on either side of the Patuxent are in the greatest alarm and consternation many are moving entirely away from both Calvert & St. Marys, and I think in a short time they will be nearly deserted, those that remained at home all their Slaves have left them and come to us, last night 39 Men Women and Children came from Colonel Plater's. (Capt. Joseph Nourse to Rear Adm. George Cockburn, July 23, 1814)[288]

SPESUTIE, also Spesutia Island (Chesapeake Bay, U.S. Army Aberdeen Proving Ground, Harford County). Military base, restricted access. Robert Smith, brother of Baltimore's Maj. Gen. Samuel Smith, lived on Spesutie Island. As secretary of the navy from 1801 to 1809, Smith oversaw the U.S. Navy, which gave a good account of itself during the war. Smith changed the sailors' rum ration to rye whiskey. On April 23, 1813, the British seized Spesutie Island, carrying off a number of Smith's cattle and hogs. Spesutie Island was used as a base of operations during the British harassment of the upper Chesapeake Bay in the spring of 1813 when Havre de Grace,* Fredericktown,* Georgetown,* and Principio* were attacked.

The enemy have just taken possession of Specuci island, and have killed and destroyed a number of cattle and hogs. The barges and men could be plainly seen from this place [Havre de Grace], with glasses, passing along the shore: two schooners and brig have come to anchor near the Eastern Shore, abreast of the island. (Washington *Daily National Intelligencer,* May 11, 1813)

The British occupied Spesutie Island again in July 1814.

I . . . saw a shooner [schooner] near Spesutia a Frigate above Pools Island & a schooner below. 150 men since landed on Spesutia & have again gone down the Bay. (Henry Lee Williams to William Elie Williams, July 13, 1814)[289]

SPOUT FARM. *See* listing, St. Leonard Creek

SPRING GARDENS BATTERY. *See* listing, Baltimore

SPURRIER FAMILY CEMETERY. *See* appendix A

STAG TAVERN SITE. *See* appendix A

STAR-SPANGLED BANNER BUOY. *See* listing, Baltimore

STERETT, JOSEPH, HOUSE. *See* listing, Baltimore

STILL POND (Still Pond Creek, just south of Sassafras River, Kent County). There is no public access with a good view of this creek other than by boat. A British raid in April (probably April 24) 1813, at Still Pond was repulsed by the local militia. (*See also* Howell Point and Worton Creek, nearby sites of other British raids.)

> On Saturday they made an attempt to land at the mouth of Still Point [Creek], but were repulsed by the force collected on the shore; the firing could be seen and heard from Stoney Point [just south of Spesutie Island, Harford County, western shore of Chesapeake Bay]. (Washington *Daily National Intelligencer*, April 29, 1813)

STRICKER, BRIG. GEN. JOHN, HOME. *See* Baltimore Riot Sites, Baltimore

SUMMERSEAT (26655 Three Notch Road [Route 235], Mechanicsville, St. Mary's County). The Clement Dorsey (1778–1848) family lived at Summerseat, a Georgian plantation house destroyed by fire in 1874. The property is now called Summerseat Sanctuary, Inc. A major in the Maryland militia from 1812 until 1818, Dorsey in 1812 collected all arms belonging to the State of Maryland located in Charles County. A graduate of St. John's College,* Dorsey married Dicandia Smith, owner of the Benedict farm, where on August 19–20, 1814, the British encamped. He warned the British at Benedict* of a potential poison attempt. Clement Dorsey is buried in the family graveyard, located northwest of the present house.

TANEY PLACE (Battle Creek, south end of Adelina Road [Route 508], Calvert County). NRHP. PRIVATE. Taney Place is the birthplace of Roger Brooke Taney,* brother-in-law and law partner of Francis Scott Key and chief justice of the U.S. Supreme Court from 1836 to 1862. A Federalist, Taney supported Alexander Contee Hanson and his *Federal Republican* newspaper, whose editorials against the war led to the Baltimore Riots of 1812. During the War of 1812, Michael Taney VI, Roger's eldest brother, lived at Taney Place and served as a major and then lieutenant colonel of the 31st Regiment, Calvert County militia. Com. Joshua Barney had little good to say about Lieutenant Colonel Taney, stating that he "has never done anything [to assist], nor do I believe would, if in his Power."[290] Barney protested that the Calvert County militia was "to be seen everywhere but just when they were wanted—wherever the enemy appeared they disappeared." Barney even charged "Old Major Taney" with supplying horses to a British raiding party that burned Prince Frederick,* the county seat.[291] On July 20, 1814, upon their return from raiding Prince Frederick, the British looted and destroyed much property at Taney Place. Some accounts suggest that because Taney's house was spared burning he must have cooperated with the British. Even if true, this did not stop the British from liberating some of Taney's slaves. (*See also* Calverton.)

TAYLORS ISLAND (bounded by Chesapeake Bay on west, Little Choptank River on north, and Slaughter Creek on east and south, Dorchester County). On the east side of Taylors Island is a monument dedicated to the Battle of the Ice Mound. It consists of the "Becky Phipps" carronade captured on February 7, 1815, from a British tender to H.M. sloop *Dauntless* after becoming stuck in ice at nearby James Island.* (*See also* Madison.) The 12 pounder carronade was mounted here about 1950 and refurbished in 1999. It was fired to celebrate political elections until it exploded during President Woodrow Wilson's election in 1912. The DAR marker at the monument (north side of Taylors Island Road, Route 16, west side of Slaughter Creek bridge on Taylors Island*) has several mistakes. The carronade was captured in 1815, not 1814. Pvt. Joseph Fookes Stewart is referred to a captain. While he may have been captain of a nonmilitary vessel, there is no documentation that he held that rank in the militia. The carronade was nicknamed "Becky Phipps" for the tender's captured black cook Becky and the commander Lt. Matthew Phipps. The cook's name was actually "Becca" and the commander's name was "Phibbs." "Becca Phibbs" was corrupted to "Becky Phipps."

In the nearby Aaron Farm Cemetery* is buried Elijah Tall, who is said to have single-handedly put a British barge to flight by firing at it. It is known that Tall received compensation from the government for the capture of another vessel during the War of 1812.

THOMAS, JOSHUA, CHAPEL (Deal Island, Deal Island Road [Route 363], Park's Grove, Somerset County). The Greek Revival Joshua Thomas Chapel, built in 1850, is named after Rev. Joshua Thomas,* known as "the Parson of the Islands" and the "shouting preacher." Thomas was illiterate and stammered during ordinary speech but became articulate and moving when giving a spiritual sermon. While living on Tangier Island,* Virginia, Thomas preached his famous fiery sermon "Thou Shalt Not Kill" to the departing British troops, predicting their defeat at the Battle for Baltimore. Reverend Thomas moved to Deal Island in the 1820s. His grave is located near the chapel door on the south side so he can hear the Sunday sermons. Also in the cemetery is the grave of Corp. Jacob Webster, who served in Capt. William White's Company, 23rd Maryland Regiment.

Deal Island, called Devil's Island during the War of 1812, is where eighty British troops under the command of Capt. James Watts from H.M. brig-sloop *Jaseur* landed on April 20, 1813, for provisions, including poultry and cattle. During this landing, Corp. Thomas Riley deserted, providing information on the strength of forces and position of the British fleet.

> eighty men from the Jaseur brig, under the command of Capt. [James] Watts, were debarked at Devil's Island, (mouth of Menokin) one of who, to wit, Thomas Riley, a native of Carlisle in the north of England, who occupied the place of ship's corporal, effected his escape. (Baltimore *Federal Republican,* May 3, 1814)

THOMAS POINT (north side of confluence of South River and Chesapeake Bay, Thomas Point Park, end of Thomas Point Road, off Arundel on the Bay Road, off Bay Ridge Road, Anne Arundel County). A British sloop-of-war became grounded at Thomas Point Shoal in May 1813, about one and a half miles offshore from Thomas Point. American plans were made to erect earthworks and a hot shot furnace to destroy the vessel, but the plan was abandoned because it was too difficult to secure the men and ordnance needed for the job. It was also too easy to cut off any American force that ventured up this narrow peninsula.

> a British sloop of war . . . ran aground on Thomas's Point, about seven miles from this city [Annapolis], and about a mile and a half or two from the shore. Several persons . . . were under an impression that if a few pieces of cannon were conveyed to the point, with hot shot, she might be easily destroyed. This being represented to the governor [Levin Winder], he took a horse, and in company with several military gentlemen rode immediately down to see whether it were practicable to destroy her or not . . . it was his opinion that it must be done with such sacrifices and uncertainty of success that he should not be justified in commanding or authorship the attempt. There was neither breast work to protect soldiers from the enemy fire, nor any conveniences for heating ball. Not withstanding . . . there were some who differed in opinions with the governor, and thought breast-work might be thrown up under cover of the night, and balls heated at a log-house at a very considerable distance, and her destruction would be certain. Could it have been effected, the triumph would have been glorious to us, but there were other difficulties . . . She [sloop-of-war] was accompanied by Statira, a large frigate, and by hoisting signals of distress, several other vessels hove in sight, coming to her assistance . . . Even admitting a probability of success, it would have required a much larger force than could have been spared from the city to prevent surprise, or being cut off by the enemy's barges, at the narrow isthmus which connects the point with the main land, the only retreat in case of a necessity for it. Had troops been marched from Annapolis for this purpose, and accident of the kind above alluded to occurred, the city itself would have fallen a prey of the enemy, being previously drained of its defences. (Annapolis *Maryland Gazette and Political Intelligencer,* May 13, 1813)

During the summer of 1814, the British captured a Cambridge packet boat off Thomas Point.

> On Saturday morning a frigate and four schooners, with several barges of the enemy made their appearance between Poplar Island and Kent Point, where they remained principal part of the day, captured off Thomas Point another of the Cambridge Packets, and in evening moved up the bay, supposed for water. (Easton *Republican Star,* July 12, 1814)

TILGHMAN ISLAND, also called Choptank Island (north side of confluence of Choptank River with Chesapeake Bay, south end of Tilghman Island Road [Route 33], Talbot County). The British occupied Tilghman Island in the spring of 1813. In October 1814, the British landed troops, built barracks, and seized nearly a hundred head of cattle. The island was abandoned before the end of the month.

> the enemy have landed from their squadron about 1000 men and built two houses for barracks, on Tilghman Island. He

states they are well supplied with cattle, having nearly 400 head [later reports corrected this number to a hundred]. We apprehend they have done much mischief in the neighborhood. (Annapolis *Maryland Gazette and Political Intelligencer,* October 27, 1814)

The enemy in the Chesapeake have taken possession of Tilghman's Island (about 30 miles below Annapolis) with the apparent view of fixing winter quarters there. The force in the neighborhood consists of 4 ships, 1 brig and two schooners. (Baltimore *Niles' Weekly Register,* October 29, 1814)

the enemy having landed a considerable number of his troops on Tilghman's Island . . . commenced the erection of extensive Barracks.—This is a much more advanced position, as well as a safer and more comfortable harbor than he possessed at the Tangiers [Tangier Island*]. He is now within sixty miles of Baltimore. (Alexandria *Gazette,* November 9, 1814)

TOBACCO STICK. *See* Madison

TODD HOUSE. *See* listing, North Point

TODD POINT (north end of Todd Point Road, north off Hudson Road [Route 343], west of Cambridge, Dorchester County). PRIVATE. Naval hero Lt. Com. John Trippe was born in 1785 at Todd Point. He is best remembered for his gallant fight of the Barbary pirates with Com. Steven Decatur* in 1804, but he also played a role in an episode in the run-up to the War of 1812. On June 24, 1809, when Trippe was in command of the U.S. schooner *Vixen,* his ship was fired on by the H.M. sloop *Moselle,* whose commander mistook the American vessel for a French ship. When Trippe was summoned aboard the *Moselle,* he refused, cleared the decks for action, and demanded an explanation. The British commander, realizing his error, responded with an apology. This was one of several naval confrontations that increased Anglo-American tension before the War of 1812. (*See also* Sion Hill, Havre de Grace, for another example.) On July 9, 1810, Trippe died at sea. Four U.S. naval ships have carried his name; the first was the U.S. sloop *Trippe,* which was commissioned in 1812 and distinguished itself in the Battle of Lake Erie.

TRACYS LANDING (Herring Bay off Chesapeake Bay, Town Point, Anne Arundel County). PRIVATE. Some accounts call the engagement that took place here the Battle of the Windmills, but that skirmish occurred four days later at nearby Kirbys Wind Mill.* The U.S. Chesapeake Flotilla* used the tobacco warehouse at Tracys Landing as a temporary stor-

age depot during the spring of 1814. On July 25–26, 1814, the local militia under Capt. Thomas R. Simmons established a gun battery at Town Point, at the request of Capt. Jacob Franklin by order of the governor. The battery was located on John Scrivener's property, probably on or near a knoll on which now sits the 1860 home known as Acceptance, at the end of Leitch Road. On October 27, 1814, one of the last skirmishes in Maryland was fought when 250 to 300 British troops landed at Tracys Landing and defeated a band of local militiamen armed with a 9 pounder cannon. (*See* Captain Salem Avery House, where this cannon is possibly located.) During the time of the attack Simmons and most of his men were posted at Baltimore. The battery was either unmanned or abandoned as tobacco hogsheads were hastily rolled from the warehouse and placed in front of it as a temporary breastwork.

The British approached the fortification in their barges, in such an overwhelming force, that all the men but some 6 or 8 retreated. The battle commenced—the station was gallantly defended by lt. [John] Scrivener—his canon was well plied—and when the match gave out, in his zeal to repel the enemy, he laid the pan of a musket on the touch hole of the cannon and fired her in that way—standing too near the gun carriage the recoil of the gun ran over his foot—they were compelled to retreat through an open field, nearly half a mile, all the while exposed to the fire of a fleet of barges. All the men could run but poor Scrivener, who hobbled away as well as he could with his lacerated foot, the blood running over the top of his shoe almost at every step.[292]

The British carried off large quantities of tobacco and destroyed the warehouse and at least two dwellings. In 1836, a petition was submitted for damages of several structures burned by the British during the skirmish, but in 1842 a congressional Committee of Claims denied it on the grounds that the owners could not prove the loss was because of U.S. military usage. The claims were made by James Tongue, $1,837.78 for loss of his tobacco warehouse; John Scrivener, $3,840 for loss of his dwelling house and attached outbuildings; and William Hodson (deceased), $3,968.39 for loss of his dwelling house, store, windmill, and outbuildings.

THE ENEMY . . . landing at Town Point, Tracy's Landing . . . were fired on by the fort, containing one nine pounder, and garrisoned with five men. After two fires, the enemy's force, one schooner and seven barges carried the Fort. They then landed between 250 and 300 men, and after gallantly repulsing five Americans, had a sufficient stock of modesty on hand to give ONLY three cheers! . . . We are informed by an eye witness, that there were but 11 rounds of cartridge in the fort—that the first and second fires were effected with a fire chunk, and the third attempt, flashed. Shortly after landing the enemy commenced plundering the tobacco house, and were seen late in the evening near the house of a Mr. [James] Tongue. When our informant left the neighborhood of Tracy's Landing, Capt. [Jacob] Franklin had about 70 men, and no doubt by 10 o'clock yesterday, had 200—and intended giving them battle. (Annapolis *Maryland Republican,* October 29, 1814).

On the 27th October [the British] crossed the Bay [from Tilghman Island] and came ashore at Tracy's Landing, and soon went to work carrying off tobacco, &c . . . demolishing the houses. But they remained not long—a small party of militia appeared and the robbers fled to their vessels. (Baltimore *Niles' Weekly Register,* October 29, 1814)

TRENT HALL (Patuxent River, northeast end of Trent Hall Road, off New Market Turner Road [Route 6], St. Mary's County). PRIVATE. Some five hundred British troops landed at Trent Hall in July 1814, and marched inland in pursuit of tobacco and other property belonging to a Mr. W. Kilgour. Overwhelmed by sheer numbers, the militia fled.

a detachment of about 500, exclusive of sailors, landed from the Patuxent shipping near Trent Hall. The sailors were armed with boarding pikes and cutlasses (for the cavalry). They ascended into the country in quest of a quantity of tobacco, and other property belonging to Mr. W. Kilgour, which he had removed about three miles to a Mr. Alvey's, as a place of safety. The property was in a barn and covered with Alvey's wheat, this they deliberately removed for some time; they at length became tired and rolled out four hogsheads of tobacco, which they gave Alvey as an equivalent for the remaining wheat and a saddle they took from him—the barn was then burnt with all the tobacco. They then under the direction of a negro of Mr. Kilgour's, who had gone to them, patiently selected the bacon and other things . . . They found eight hogsheads of tobacco concealed in the woods near the water, which they carried off with a great deal of stock. Mr. Kilgour's loss is ruinous. As soon as [Brigadier] General [Philip] Stuart received intelligence that the enemy were landing, he moved with his whole force in pursuit of them. He arrived at High Hill where he saw the enemy's barges prepared to cover the retreat of the men over the plain, and a frigate with her broadside ready for the same object. He could not receive any intelligence of the course they had taken till it was disclosed by the smoke ascending from Alvey's barn. To get between them and their shipping must necessarily have exposed his force to a galling fire from their shipping, and give their infantry the advantage of a high commanding situation; to get in their front, as to

annoy them in their retreat, he must have taken a circuitous route of seven miles. Independent of all this, his force was much inferior to that of their's; he therefore returned to his encampment. (Baltimore *Federal Republican,* July 27, 1814)

TURKEY POINT. *See* Elk Neck

TURNERS CREEK (off Sassafras River, just west of Shrewsberry Neck, Kent County). In May 1813, a British raiding party came up the Sassafras River to attack Georgetown and Fredericktown. The British landed at the mouth of Turners Creek and forced John Stavely to accompany them and serve as a pilot. After burning Georgetown and Fredericktown on May 6, 1813, the British returned to Turners Creek to obtain supplies at the John Lathim property and also to return their reluctant guide. Turners Creek can be seen at the boat ramp, end of Turners Creek Road, off Lambs Meadow Road (Route 298), in Turners Creek Park.

UPPER MARLBORO (Western Branch of Patuxent River, east-central Prince George's County). Upper Marlborough was established in 1706. Because two towns on the Patuxent River were named for the first Duke of Marlborough, one became Upper Marlboro and the other Lower Marlboro.*

American commander Brig. Gen. William H. Winder lodged at Upper Marlboro on July 8, 1814, while scouting for an appropriate encampment for his troops.

From what I have seen and learned, it appears to me that there cannot be found a place of tolerable convenience with reference to the objects of defence, for an encampment, except in this neighborhood. Two places near here offer many conveniences: the one, two and a half miles on the Western branch and the road to Bladensburg, which I have seen [Long Old Fields*]; the other, about five miles on the road to Washington and Piscataway, near the Woodyard[*], which I shall examine today. (Brig. Gen. William H. Winder to Secretary of War John Armstrong, July 16, 1814)[293]

During a second visit on July 15–16, 1814, Winder learned by express courier that a British force had arrived and was advancing up the Patuxent River. Upper Marlboro served as an assembly point for the U.S. Army in August 1814. On August 22, 1814, after abandoning their boats above Pig Point,* Com. Joshua Barney and nearly four hundred U.S. Chesapeake flotillamen passed through Upper Marlboro, where they joined Brigadier General Winder's troops marching toward Long Old Fields.* Here later that same day Adm. Sir George Cockburn and approximately 400 marines and sailors who had debarked at Mount Calvert* on the Patuxent

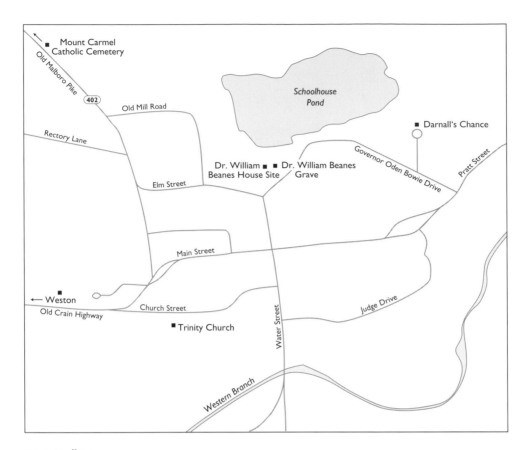

Upper Marlboro

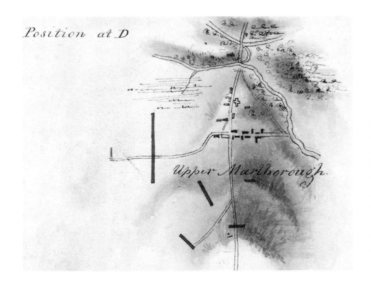

British 1814 sketch map showing the deployment of the British troops when they were encamped at Upper Marlboro. This sketch is not oriented with north at top of map. Main Street runs top (northeast) to bottom (southwest) and Water Street is the cross road running to the right (southeast) terminating at the Western Branch of the Patuxent River. Water Street becomes Old Mill Road and Old Marlboro Pike to the left (northwest). British troops encamped along what are today Old Crain Highway and Old Marlboro Pike to the west and southwest of the village. (1814 sketch map by Robert Smith, "Sketch of the march of the British army under M. Genl. Ross . . ."; Beinecke Rare Book and Manuscript Library, Yale University)

River joined Maj. Gen. Robert Ross and approximately 4,400 British regulars who had debarked at Benedict.* The combined force encamped here from August 22 to noon August 23 during its march to Washington. (*See also* Melwood.)

> several bodies of the enemy's horse occasionally showing themselves, and what appeared to be the rear-guard of a column of infantry evacuating [Upper] Marlborough, as our advance entered. There was, however, little or no skirmishing, and we were allowed to remain in the village all night without molestation. (Lt. George Robert Gleig, 1821)[294]

> Came in at one o'clock to a nice village called [Upper] Marlboro, where we bivouacked in a large green field. Got plenty of fowls and for once ate a hearty dinner undisturbed. Chose a snug situation with some trees, where we brought some hay, and passed the night very comfortably. (Lt. George Robert Gleig, August 22, 1814)[295]

> The village itself lies in a valley formed by two green hills; the distance from the base of one hill to the base of the other may be about two miles, the whole of which was laid out in fields of corn, hay, and tobacco; whilst the slopes themselves were covered with sheep, for whose support they furnished ample means . . . the houses are scattered over the plain, and along the sides of the hills, at considerable intervals from one another, and are all surrounded by orchards and gardens, abounding in peaches and other fruits of the most delicious flavour. To add to the beauty of this place, a small rivulet makes its way through the bottom, and winding round the foot of one of these ridges, falls into the Patuxent, which flows at its back. (Lt. George Robert Gleig, 1847)[296]

After capturing Washington, the British returned to Upper Marlboro, encamping here from late afternoon August 26 to early morning August 27. Lt. George Robert Gleig, British 85th Regiment, reported that near here many slaves offered to serve as either soldiers or sailors, if given their liberty, but Maj. Gen. Robert Ross refused, probably fearing they would delay the march back to the ships. The Maryland State records were moved here from Annapolis during the war for protection. Ironically, Annapolis was never attacked while Upper Marlboro was occupied by British troops. By this time, however, the public records had been moved again to nearby Mount Lubentia.*

Beanes, Dr. William, House Site (Academy Hill, 14518 Church Street [Elm Street]). Dr. William Beanes's home site is located on the property of the Office of the Sheriff, the former site of the Marlborough Academy, Upper Marlboro High School (1921), and Upper Marlboro Elementary School. British officers used Dr. Beanes's home as a headquarters during their occupation of the town. On the night of August 22, 1814, Maj. Gen. Robert Ross reportedly had dinner with Beanes. Rear Adm. George Cockburn met here with Ross on the morning of August 23, 1814, to persuade him to attack Washington despite the lack of cavalry and adequate artillery.

> I proceeded by Land . . . to Upper Marlborough, to meet and confer with Major General Ross as to our further operations against the Enemy, and we were not long in agreeing on the propriety of making an immediate attempt on the City of Washington. (Rear Adm. George Cockburn to Vice Adm. Sir Alexander F. I. Cochrane, August 27, 1814)[297]

Dr. William Beanes,* a Federalist, loathed President James Madison's administration, although in 1812 he was commissioned a lieutenant colonel in the 2nd Maryland Cavalry District, Prince George's County. Beanes and Major General Ross became acquainted during the British occupation of Upper Marlboro.

> Walked up into the village where I procured some tea and sugar, and got a bottle of milk from a gentleman of the name of Dr. Bean [Beanes]. He remains quietly in his house, has his property respected and does not seem inimical to us. (Lt. George Robert Gleig, August 23, 1814)[298]

But Ross became furious when Beanes later jailed some British stragglers and a deserter, believing Beanes had betrayed him. On July 25, 1855, Beanes's house burned.

> I am going to the morning to Balt^e. to proceed in a flag-vessel to Genl [Robert] Ross. Old D^r [William] Beanes of [Upper] Marlboro' is taken prisoner by the Enemy, who threaten to carry him off—Some of his friends have urged me to apply for a flag & go & try to procure his release. I hope to return in about 8 or 10 days, though it is uncertain, as I do not know where to find the fleet. (Francis Scott Key to his mother Anne Carlton Key, September 2, 1814)[299]

30 DOLLARS REWARD

Was taken from my plantation, near this place, by the British, on the 22d August last. One black mare . . . For this mare I will pay $10—at the same time was taken, one young mare and three mules—for which I will pay five dollars each . . . all three branded on the thigh with a perpendicular mark, with two branches on each side it, resembling a tree. W. B. BEANES. (Baltimore *Federal Republican,* November 22, 1814; this is William Bradley Beanes, half brother of Dr. William Beanes)

★ **Beanes, Dr. William, Grave** (immediately east of the house site, on hilltop at the corner of Elm Street and Governor Oden Bowie Drive). Dr. William Beanes's* grave, located in what was probably the former garden of his home, was restored in 1914, partially from contributions from Prince George's County public school children during a centennial celebration sponsored by the National Star-Spangled Banner Centennial Commission. The inscription on a plaque on Beanes's grave claims Key wrote the national anthem when inspired by the defense of Fort McHenry. Key wrote a poem that after his death became the words to the national anthem in 1931. This plaque and a Maryland Historical Roadside Marker (Route 4, both north and south sides off ramp to Water Street) both omit the fact that John Stuart Skinner, U.S. agent for prisoner exchange, was also present and that both negotiated the release of Beanes.

Darnall's Chance (14800 Governor Oden Bowie Drive). Darnall's Chance, built 1741–42, was remodeled in 1857 and restored to its original appearance in 1986. When a detachment of British troops returned to Upper Marlboro to retrieve soldiers incarcerated by local citizens, John Hodges, who lived here from 1800 until 1825, reluctantly released them from the nearby Queen Anne* jail. For his actions, Hodges was tried for treason. Defended by William Pinkney, attorney general of Maryland in 1805 and attorney general of the United States in 1811–14, Hodges was found not guilty. In Darnall's Chance is a small diorama on the second floor depicting Dr. Beanes, John Stuart Skinner, and Francis Scott Key observing the bombardment of Fort McHenry.

Trinity Church (14515 Church Street). Anglican Bishop Thomas John Claggett* established Trinity Church in 1810. The present structure dates from 1846 and 1896. Parish records confirm that British soldiers entered the church and tore pages from the parish register book.

> The Parish Register reads: No meeting from 21st May 1814 to 27 March 1815 owing to the situation into which the country was thrown by the invasion of the British army in August . . . Several leaves here and some other parts of this book were torn out by some of [Maj. Gen. Robert] Ross's soldiers who found the book in the Church where it put for safe keeping. To their eternal disgrace be it recorded, John Read Magruder, clerk of the vestry.[300]

Weston (6601 Old Crain Highway, south of Upper Marlboro). PRIVATE. Weston, a three-story brick Georgian house built circa 1820 by Thomas Clagett VI, replaced a 1713 house, which had burned during the Revolutionary War. The present house configuration dates from the late 1830s. Clagett served as a private during the War of 1812 and was wounded in the arm. He is buried in the family cemetery on a tree-covered knoll visible from Old Crain Highway.

U.S. NAVAL ACADEMY. *See* listing, Annapolis

VIENNA (Nanticoke River, east end of Marsh Road [Route 731], Dorchester County). Vienna, established as an official port of entry in 1768, was never attacked during the War of 1812, although British barges came up the Nanticoke River within sight of the town. To protect Vienna, a gun battery was built, but its location is in dispute. One source claims the battery was located at the "saw-mill wharf." A saw mill was located near the east end of Race Street, but it is unclear if a saw mill wharf was located here in 1814. Local tradition claims a breastwork was built from ship ballast at the south end of Water Street near where the Nanticoke Manor House now stands. A granite wall between the customs house and Nanticoke Manor House is claimed by some to be the remains of a breastwork, but more likely it is just a retaining wall. The high ground at the south end of Water Street is the more logical location for a gun battery.

Richard Crafus, an African American sailor born in Vienna, was captured onboard the American privateer *Raccoon* off Bordeaux, France, on March 6, 1814, and made a British prisoner at Dartmoor Prison. There he dominated Cell Block 4, largely populated by African Americans. He earned the nickname "King Dick" and taught his fellow prisoners to box and wrestle. After the war, he changed his name to Richard Seavers and became a leader of the African American community in Boston.

WADES POINT, then called Auld's Point (Eastern Bay, northwest end of Wades Point Road, Talbot County). On August 26, 1813, the British landed 2,100 men at Wades Point. While 300 of these troops sought out militia reported to be in the area, the remaining force of 1,800 attempted a second unsuccessful attack against St. Michaels.* The British troops retreated when the road they used passed through a thick woods occupied by five hundred militia supported by cavalry and artillery. Lt. Col. Hugh Auld, Jr. (1767–1820), a member of the family for which Auld's Point (also called Wades Point) is named, served in the 26th Regiment, 12th

Maryland Brigade. Auld was also present during the first engagement of St. Michaels and is buried at Arlington National Cemetery.*

> American account of landing: about day-light the enemy was discovered by our videts stationed at Col. Auld's point [Wade Point], to be landing from upwards of 60 barges—They immediately moved in column about two miles toward our camp [St. Michaels] . . . They had two field pieces, and a number of rockets on the road, in rear of the picquets. At the same time we discovered three schooners and a brig beating up the river, crowded with troops, evidently with all intentions of cutting off our retreat, and destroying this place, should we march down to attack them . . . [Rear] Admiral [George] Cockburn, at the head of 300 men, marched below in search of a militia company stationed there; the greater part of whom made their retreat across Harris's creek—Fourteen were afterwards taken at their own houses . . . they re-embarked, taking with them the 14 prisoners, whom they released the next day on parole. (Brig. Maj. Solomon Dickinson, Easton *Republican Star,* August 31, 1813)

WASHINGTON GUN POWDER MILLS SITE. *See* appendix A

WEBSTER, JOHN ADAMS, HOUSE. *See* Mount Adams

WELLS AND MCCOMAS MONUMENT. *See* listing, Baltimore

WELSH POINT. *See* Frenchtown

WHEATLANDS (Miles River, southeast end of Wheatlands Road, south off Miles River Road, 0.9 mile southwest from intersection with Marengo Road, east of Easton, Talbot County). PRIVATE. Here lived Gen. Perry Benson,* commander of the American militia during the attacks on St. Michaels on August 10, 1813, and August 26, 1813. The central portion of Wheatlands dates from the late eighteenth century with the hyphens and wings added later. It is said General Benson enjoyed hosting his guests in his large Revolutionary War tent on the lawn of his house overlooking the Miles River. He served simple military fare and copious libations. General Benson is buried in the Benson family cemetery* at nearby Royal Oak.

WHITE HALL POINT. *See* listing, Elkton

WHITES LANDING (Patuxent, east end of Whites Landing Road, off Croom Road [Route 382], Prince George's County). PRIVATE. No turnaround or public access. Whites Landing served as a temporary base for Com. Joshua Barney's U.S. Chesapeake Flotilla after it escaped from St. Leonard Creek.* Here at the ferry-house at midday on August 21, 1814, the British halted for several hours while Rear Adm. George Cockburn, commander of the British squadron, met with Maj. Gen. Robert Ross, commander of the British army. The army then continued its march toward Nottingham along a road that has been in existence since at least 1739, while the fleet anchored in the river for the night about a mile above Lower Marlboro.*

> the British with a number of barges were as high as Lower Marlbourough. [Com. Joshua] Barney lies at White's Landing, about two miles above Lower Marlborough. (Baltimore *Federal Republican,* July 22, 1814)

WICOMICO RIVER (off Chesapeake Bay, forming boundary between Wicomico and Somerset counties). There are two Wicomico rivers, one off the Potomac on the western shore and this one on the Eastern Shore. The British conducted raids along the lower portions of this Wicomico River during the spring of 1814.

> the British squadron (1 ship, 1 brig and 2 schooners,) . . . sent six barges into Wecomico, it being foggy they were not discovered until they landed. They carried off a variety of articles belonging to the farm houses there, and wantonly destroyed all the furniture; set fire to a small house, where in was a loom. They did not discover any vessels in the creek; before the militia could collect, they were off. (Baltimore *Niles' Weekly Register,* March 26, 1814)

On April 9, 1814, a British raid was driven off by the local militia.

> The schooner Buzzi, a bay trading vessel, capt. Jarvis, was chased into Wicomico, on the 9th by a tender and several barges. Capt. [James] Dashiel[l], with 25 men of his artillery company and a 6 pounder came to his rescure. They had several fine raking shots at the enemy; several men were seen to fall, and oars floated on shore. The Englishmen retreated in great haste. (Baltimore *Niles' Weekly Register,* April 30, 1814)

WILKINSON FAMILY CEMETERY (field overlooking Hunting Creek, near 1445 Mallard Point Road, off Leitchs Road, off Stoakley Road, off Solomons Island Road [Route 2/4], east of Prince Frederick, Calvert County). PRIVATE. The Wilkinson family owned Gods Grace* (also Godsgrace) and Stoakley, located on the south side of Hunting Creek. The family cemetery is located on private property and is not accessible to the public. Two of the Wilkinsons, James and Joseph, became generals during the War of 1812. Maj. Gen. James Wilkinson* (1757–1825), a soldier and adventurer, was born on Hunting Creek. He joined the Continental Army at age nineteen and within a year served as adjutant to Gen. Horatio Gates. During the War of 1812, Wilkinson received the rank of major general and was placed in command of the American forces in Louisiana and Alabama and then in command of the forces on the Canada border, where on November 11, 1813, he was defeated in the Battle of Crysler's Farm. While waiting in Washington for an inquiry into his defeat, he offered his services for the defense of Washington, but his offer was declined.

WOODLAND POINT (Potomac River, east end of Potomac View Road, south off Woodland Road [also called Woodland Point Road], south off Swan Point Road, west off Rock Point Road [Route 257], Cobb Neck area, Charles County). PRIVATE. During the night of July 16, 1813, British troops landed near the home of Henry Hamersley [Hammersly], Jr., at Woodland Point. The raid was successfully repulsed by about 140 poorly equipped militiamen under the command of Maj. Luke F. Matthews, aided by Secretary of State James Monroe and a small troop of horse from Washington commanded by Capt. Elias B. Caldwell. During the skirmish Capt. James Neale was killed and Dr. Walter Hanson wounded. It was reported that five British soldiers, including an officer, were also killed. The next morning the British fired seven or eight cannon shot from one of their frigates at the home of Hamersley but without effect.

> Our numbers amounted now to about 140 men, officers included; of those, 60 or 70 had no guns—some who had guns, were only provided with one of two cartridges, and some of the guns so totally unfit for service, as not to be got off . . . About half past eleven, we were alarmed by the general cry that the enemy were landing . . . I ordered the whole battalion to form and advance to the bank; and on reaching the bank, the enemy were discovered by Capt. John Matthews and his company, who immediately commenced a brisk and active firing, which lasted about 10 minutes, when the enemy were repulsed & retreated with great precipitation to their barges and shipping. (Maj. Luke F. Matthews's report; reprinted in Washington *Daily National Intelligencer,* July 21, 1813)

> The ships anchored off a farm owned by Mr. Hammersby [Henry Hamersley]. When Mr. Hammersby saw the troops coming ashore, he invited them to his house for refreshment. They visited for several hours and on leaving thanked

him kindly and promised that his place should not be disturbed. In almost every other house in the same section everything was lugged off that could be moved. Feather beds, pillows, etc., were taken to the windows and doors, ripped open with bayonets and the feathers scattered to the winds. The poultry was shot down, the fruits and vegetables carried away and every outrage that could be perpetrated marked their passage through the neighborhood. Fortunately women, children, servants, horses, etc., had been sent into the interior of the country and silver and other valuables secreted in some places of safety. Coming back down the river they fired several times into Cobb Neck and only a few years since large cannon balls were still lying about in the yards of some of the residences. They were of immense weight and children could roll but not lift them. (Account of Sister Mary Xavier Queen, 1899)[301]

Such plundering caused many to question why the local militia could not do more to protect their homes, as expressed below:

> Charles County Patriotism. We understand that it is deemed treason to fire a gun on the Maryland side of the Potomac, lest the British should take offence at it, and punish the dastardly wretches for permitting their honors to be uselessly alarmed.—What degeneracy! What baseness? What infamy! Cowards?—cast your eyes on the opposite side of this river [Virginia], and see men who you dare not imitate, rushing at a moments warning, to the shore, in defense of all men should hold dear on earth—driving the cowardly foe from their land, and chastising his insolence for daring to pollute their soil. Lilly livered poltroons, can you not be kicked into the common feelings of men? Will you quietly permit an overbearing enemy, as pusillanimous as yourselves, to drive and destroy you, without daring to resist.—Wretches! You have become the bye word of contempt, the mere laughing stock of your countrymen. Wretches! (*Washington City Gazette*; reprinted in Annapolis *Maryland Republican,* 1814)

WOODYARD SITE, also called Woodyard Plantation and Darnall's Delight (north side of intersection of Woodyard [Route 223] and Rosaryville roads, Woodyard, Prince George's County). NRHP Archeological Site. Woodyard is the site of Darnall's Delight, built prior to 1711 and later called Woodyard. Located at the strategic crossroad leading to the capital and Fort Washington, Woodyard was owned by Richard E. West. In July, Brig. Gen. William H. Winder visited Woodyard and reported that it would make a good encampment because any troops there would be within two hours' travel of the Patuxent or Potomac rivers. On August 21, 1814, Woodyard served as a mustering site for Winder's troops. Shortly after 8:00 p.m., August 21, 1814, Secretary of State James Monroe joined the troops here. The next day Com. Joshua Barney and most of his U.S. Chesapeake Flotillamen joined Winder's troops and then marched with them to Long Old Fields.*

> The enemy are advanced six miles on the road to the Wood Yard, and our troops retiring. Our troops were on the march to meet them, but in too small a body to engage. General [William H.] Winder proposes to retire till he can collect them in a body. The enemy are in full march for Washington. Have the material prepared to destroy the bridges. You had better remove the records. (Secretary of State James Monroe to President James Madison, night of August 22, 1814)[302]

> arrived at the Woodyard much about the time [Maj. Gen. Robert] Ross arrived at Nottingham . . . Had we moved a day sooner, or even somewhat faster, and carried with us the regulars only, we might have struck a fine blow—capturing or killing the whole of Ross's party . . . set out for a skirmish; but, . . . discovered that the enemy was also in motion. Question—what road he would take—that to Marlborough or that to Washington? Decided to watch both. The enemy soon after taking the former, the General [William H. Winder] fell back on the Battalion's [Long] Old fields. (Col. Allen McClane, August 22, 1814)[303]

Woodyard burned in 1867. Francis Scott Key* served as the Richard West family attorney, while Dr. William Beanes* served as the family physician. West asked Key to assist in the release of Dr. Beans after he was taken by the British. This is why Key was with the British fleet during the bombardment of Fort McHenry* on September 13–14, 1814. Richard E. West is buried in an unmarked grave at Woodyard.

WORTON CREEK (off Chesapeake Bay, north of Rock Hall, Kent County). The British in April 1813 bombarded Simon Wilmer's home, Airy Hill, on Worton Creek. The location of Airy Hill is unknown. Worton Creek can be seen from several public boat ramps.

> The enemy's force, consisting of one 74, three frigates, two brigs, two schrs. and a number of tenders and barges, are now lying from off Werton [Worton Creek] to some distance below Pool's Island. (Washington *Daily National Intelligencer,* May 10, 1813)

> a ship of war passing down the bay . . . commenced a bombardment on S[imon]. Wilmer's house, . . . and after firing 15 shots at the house, 6 of which lodged in the wall and two passed thro the house, they landed at Mr. [George] Medford's a few miles above Mr. Wilmer's. (Washington *Daily National Intelligencer,* April 29, 1813)

From here the British moved about two miles up the Chesapeake Bay to Plum (Plump) Point and circa April 27, 1813, landed at George Medford's home, where cattle were killed and the smoke house, hen-house, and sheep-pen looted. (*See also* Howell Point.)

> Last week a party of the enemy landed at Mr. George Medford's, at Plump Point, in Werton [Worton], and robbed his meat-house, hen-house and sheep-fold; they even went into the kitchen, stole the kitchen furniture and took his negroes' weekly allowance of meat. They also killed several of his cattle—while they were thus employed an express was sent for the militia, a party of whom arrived in time to prevent the enemy from carrying off the cattle which they had killed; the militia fired on the barges as they left the shore, and it is thought some of the enemy were killed. (Washington *Daily National Intelligencer,* May 10, 1813)

A second raid at Worton Creek on July 11, 1814, was repulsed by about twenty locals using duck guns and muskets and led by war veteran Lt. Col. Philip Reed.

> four of their [British] barges entered Warton [Worton] creek.—This being reported to col. Reed, (an old seventy-sixer,) [referring to his Revolutionary War service] who happened to be on a visit in the neighborhood, he borrowed a musket and hastily collected about 20 armed with duck guns and muskets, they formed an ambuscade, and when the largest barge had fairly passed, opened a certain fire upon them. They had four deliberate rounds at the enemy before he escaped; which he did with all possible haste—for though he rowed 24 ours [oars] when he entered the creek, he could man but 4 when he went out of it. (Baltimore *Niles' Weekly Register,* July 16, 1814)

> A small body of our men reached Worton Creek . . . in time yesterday evening to save much devastation in that quarter, they attacked the advanced barge of four, that was prodding up the Creek, and just in the act of taking Mr. Graves' craft and granery, full of wheat; killed 15 or 16 out of 20, and forced the whole of them to leave the Creek and return to their shipping, not a man of ours was hurt. (Baltimore *Federal Gazette,* July 15, 1814)

WYE HOUSE, also called Lloyds House (Lloyd Creek and Wye East River, private drive north off Bruffs Island Road, Talbot County). NHL. PRIVATE. Wye House was the home of Edward Lloyd IV, known as Edward the Magnificent because of his great wealth. Lloyd also owned Chase-Lloyd House. Judge Joseph Hopper Nicholson* (1770–1817) (not to be confused with his son Joseph H. Nicholson, who is buried at St. Anne's Cemetery, Annapolis) married Rebecca Lloyd of

Annapolis and is buried at Wye House. Nicholson formed an artillery company called the Baltimore Fencibles in 1813 and served in the defense of Fort McHenry in September 1814. He helped obtain the promotion for Lt. Col. George Armistead, commander of Fort McHenry, and is said to be responsible for having Francis Scott Key's poem published. After learning of Napoleon's defeat in the spring of 1814, Nicholson wrote on May 20, 1814, to the Secretary of Navy William Jones that "we should have to fight hereafter, not for 'free trade and sailors rights,' not for the conquest of the Canadas, but for our National existence."[304] Also buried here is Edward Lloyd (1779–1834), who was commissioned a lieutenant colonel in the 9th Cavalry, Maryland militia, in February 1812.

ZION REFORMED CHURCH. *See* listing, Hagerstown

CHAPTER 4

Virginia Sites

During the War of 1812, what today is West Virginia (established in 1863) was part of Virginia. Thus a few sites in West Virginia are included here. Barbour County, West Virginia, is believed to be named for James Barbour,* "the war governor" of Virginia (1812–14) and secretary of war during John Quincy Adams's administration (1825–28). Jackson County, West Virginia, is named after Andrew Jackson, hero of the Battle of New Orleans and seventh president of the United States.

ALDIE (southeast corner of John Mosby Highway [U.S. Route 50] and Meetinghouse Lane, Loundon County). PRIVATE. Aldie can be seen as a drive-by only. This community took its name from the home of Charles Fenton Mercer (1778–1858), a brigadier general in the War of 1812. The Mercer house stands on a hill in a grove of oak trees on the north side of John Mosby Highway near the center of town. Mercer held commissions as major in command at Norfolk, lieutenant colonel of the 5th Virginia Regiment, inspector general of Virginia militia, aide-de-camp to Governor James Barbour of Virginia, and brigadier general in command of the 2nd Virginia Brigade. He is buried at Union Cemetery* at Leesburg.

ALEXANDRIA (Potomac River, below Washington D.C.). British naval forces occupied Alexandria from August 28 through September 3, 1814, after the city capitulated to a British squadron. Commanded by Capt. James Alexander Gordon,[1] the squadron consisted of the 36-gun H.M. frigate *Euryalus*, the 38-gun H.M. frigate *Sea Horse*, the 18-gun H.M. rocket-vessel *Erebus*, the 8-gun H.M. bomb-vessel *Aetna*, the 8-gun H.M. bomb-vessel *Devastation*, the 8-gun H.M. bomb-vessel *Meteor*, and the 2-gun H.M. schooner/dispatch-ship *Anna Maria*.

The Alexandria Committee of Vigilance, despairing of its situation, recommended to the Alexandria Council Committee: "That, in case the British vessels should pass the fort [Washington], or their forces approach the town by land, and there should be <u>no sufficient force</u> on our part, to oppose them, with any reasonable prospect of success, they should appoint a committee to carry a flag to the officer commanding the enemy's force, about to attack the town, and to procure the best terms for the safety of persons, houses, and property, in their power."[2]

When the British squadron threatened Alexandria, the city's Common Council ordered the following:

The forts erected for the defence of the district having been blown up by our men, [U.S. regular troops], and abandoned without resistance, and the town of Alexandria having been left without troops or any means of defence against the hostile force now within sight, the Common Council of Alexandria have with reluctance been compelled, from a regard to the safety of the inhabitants, to authorize an arrangement with the enemy, by which it has been stipulated that, during their continuance before the town, they shall not be molested. No superior power having, in this emergency, appeared to defend or direct, the Common Council has considered itself authorized, from extreme necessity, to make the above stipulation; they, consider it binding on themselves and on the nation, require a faithful observance of it from all the inhabitants of the town. (Thomas Herbert, president of the Alexandria Common Council, August 28, 1814; reprinted in Baltimore *Niles' Weekly Register,* September 10, 1814)

Prior to the occupation of Alexandria by the British, six hundred small arms were destroyed and two cannon, the only artillery in the city, were removed to prevent their capture. The Americans also burned the long bridge joining Washington with the Virginia shore and scuttled twenty-one vessels in the port. In order to keep their city from being plundered or possibly burned, members of the Alexandria Council Committee reluctantly accepted Captain Gordon's terms of capitulation outlined below:

The town of Alexandria (with the exception of public works) shall not be destroyed, unless hostilities are commenced on the part of the Americans, nor shall the inhabitants be molested in any manner whatever, or their dwelling-houses entered, if the following articles are complied with:—

Article 1. All naval and ordnance stores (public and private) must be immediately given up.

Article 2. Possession will be immediately taken of all the shipping, and their furniture must be sent on board by the owners without delay.

Article 3. The vessels which have been sunk must be delivered up in the state they were in on the 19th of August, the day of the squadron passing the Kettle Bottoms.

Article 4. Merchandise of every description must be instantly delivered up, and to prevent any irregularities that might be committed in its embarkation, the merchants have it in their option to load the vessels generally employed for that purpose, when they will be towed off by us.

Article 5. All merchandise that has been removed from Alexandria since the 19th inst., is to be included in the above articles.

Article 6. Refreshments of every description to be supplied the ships, and paid for at the market price by bills on the British government.

Article 7. Officers will be appointed to see that the articles Nos. 2, 3, 4, and 5, are strictly complied with, and any deviation or non-compliance, on the part of the inhabitants of Alexandria, will render this treaty null and void. JAMES A. GORDON, Captain of His Majesty's Ship Sea-Horse.[3]

In exchange for the acceptance of these terms, the British agreed not to invade private dwellings or to molest the citizens of Alexandria. The British did not insist on the enforcement of Articles 3 and 5. They did, however, carry away as prizes three ships, four brigs, ten schooners, and three sloops. They burned one sunken ship that they could not raise. They also captured a gunboat from the Washington Navy Yard mounting a long 18 pounder cannon and a 32 pounder carronade that had been sent to Alexandria for safekeeping. The British confiscated about 16,000 barrels of flour, about 1,000 hogsheads of tobacco, 150 bales of cotton, as well as wine, sugar, and other articles, all amounting to upwards of $5,000 in value.

It is impossible that men could behave better than the British behaved while the town was in their power, not a single inhabitant was insulted or injured by them in their person or houses. (Alexandria Mayor Charles Simms to his wife Nancy Simms, September 3, 1814)[4]

In what terms can we express our indignation against the conduct of the citizens of Alexandria? Thanks be to the Al-

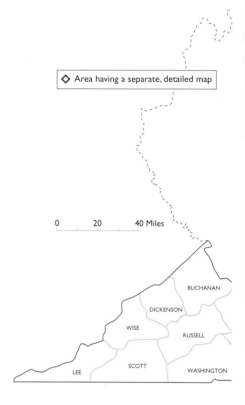

◇ Area having a separate, detailed map

0   20   40 Miles

BUCHANAN

DICKENSON

WISE

RUSSELL

LEE   SCOTT   WASHINGTON

mighty God: that this degraded town no longer forms a part of the state of Virginia [this portion of Virginia had been deeded as part of the Nation's Capitol and later returned to Virginia]. (Richmond *Enquirer,* August 31, 1814)

The degrading terms dictated by the Commander of the British squadron below Alexandria, to the civil authority of that town, connected with the offer of the townsmen, before the squadron had even reached the fort [Washington], to surrender without resistance, and their singular submission to [Rear] Admiral [George] Cockburn whilst he was in this city, have everywhere excited astonishment and indignation. (Washington *Daily National Intelligencer,* September 1, 1814)

Brig. Gen. John Pratt Hungerford* in command of the 14th Brigade of the Northern Neck Virginia militia was or-

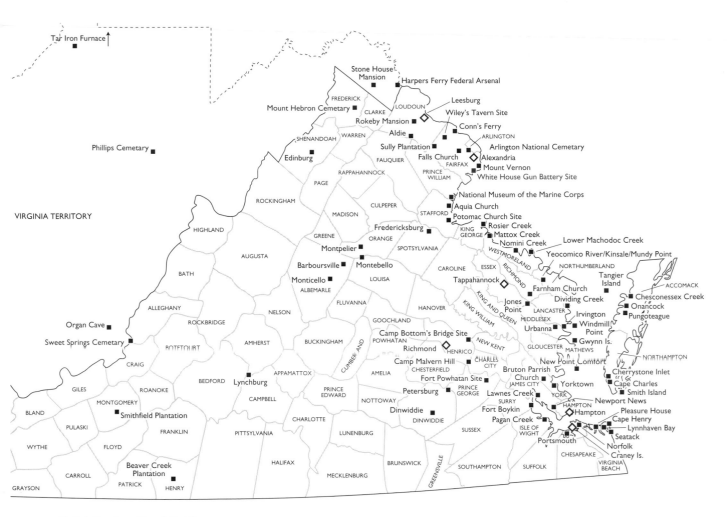

Virginia Territory War of 1812 Sites

The map shows the following labeled sites:

Tar Iron Furnace

Stone House Mansion

Harpers Ferry Federal Arsenal

Leesburg

Mount Hebron Cemetary

Wiley's Tavern Site

Rokeby Mansion

Conn's Ferry

Aldie

Phillips Cemetery

Sully Plantation

Arlington National Cemetary

Edinburg

Falls Church

Alexandria

Mount Vernon

White House Gun Battery Site

National Museum of the Marine Corps

VIRGINIA TERRITORY

Aquia Church

Potomac Church Site

Rosier Creek

Fredericksburg

Mattox Creek

Lower Machodoc Creek

Nomini Creek

Yeocomico River/Kinsale/Mundy Point

Montpelier

Tangier Island

Barboursville

Montebello

Tappahannock

Chesconessex Creek

Monticello

Farnham Church

Onancock

Dividing Creek

Pungoteague

Jones Point

Irvington

Organ Cave

Camp Bottom's Bridge Site

Urbanna

Windmill Point

Sweet Springs Cemetery

Richmond

Gwynn Is.

Camp Malvern Hill

New Point Comfort

Cherrystone Inlet

Bruton Parrish Church

Fort Powhatan Site

Cape Charles

Petersburg

Yorktown

Smith Island

Smithfield Plantation

Dinwiddie

Lawnes Creek

Newport News

Fort Boykin

Pleasure House

Lynchburg

Pagan Creek

Hampton

Cape Henry

Lynnhaven Bay

Beaver Creek Plantation

Portsmouth

Seatack

Norfolk

Craney Is.

dered to Washington, but when he arrived within ten miles of Alexandria a delegation attempted to stop him and his troops from entering the city for fear it would interfere with their planed capitulation to the British. Hungerford stated he was ordered by the War Department and had no choice but to resist the enemy. However, shortly thereafter he received new orders to encamp on Shuter's (Shooters) Hill* just to the west of Alexandria.

U.S. Naval officer Capt. David Porter, Jr. (1780–1843) reportedly put on civilian clothing to reconnoiter the occupied town. At a warehouse near the intersection of Princess and Union streets, Captain Porter spotted a young British lieutenant, John West Fraser, and a squad of men rolling out barrels of flour. Porter grabbed Fraser by his neck scarf and would have abducted him had not the scarf given away.

British account of the David Porter incident: An enterprising [America] midshipman [actually captain] thought it would be fine fun to carry off an officer; and . . . dashed into the town on horseback . . . came boldly down to the boats, and seized a midshipman [lieutenant] by the collar. The fellow was strong, and attempted to get him on his horse. The youngster, quite astonished, kicked and squalled most lustily; and after being dragged a hundred yards, the American was obliged to drop his brother officer. This operation . . . created a considerable alarm; the men retreated to the boats, and prepared their carronades, and were with difficulty prevented from firing. This occurrence soon found its way to the mayor, who came off in great alarm for the town. Captain [James Alexander] Gordon, with great good humour, admitted his apology, and treated it . . . as a midshipman's spree; but recommended that proper precau-

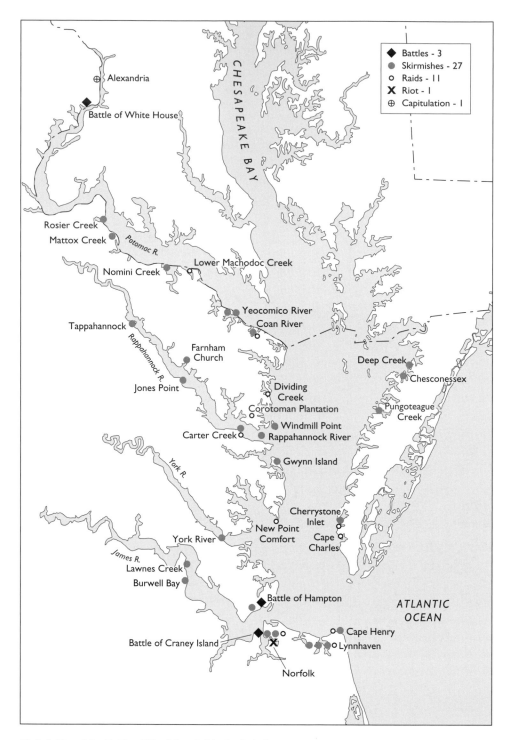

Virginia War of 1812 Battles, Skirmishes, Raids, Capitulation, and Riot

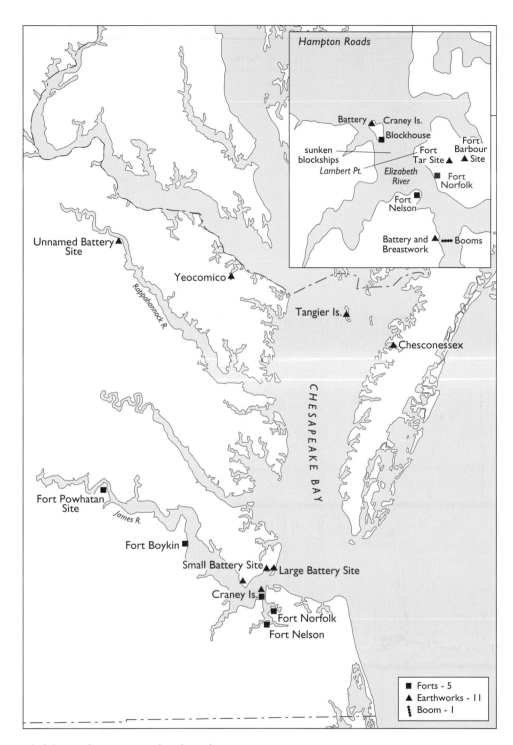

Hampton Roads

Battery

Craney Is.

Blockhouse

sunken
blockships

Fort
Tar Site

Fort
Barbour
Site

Lambert Pt.

Elizabeth
River

Fort
Norfolk

Fort
Nelson

Battery and
Breastwork

Booms

Unnamed Battery
Site

Rappahannock R.

Yeocomico

Tangier Is.

Chesconessex

CHESAPEAKE BAY

Fort Powhatan
Site

James R.

Fort Boykin

Small Battery Site

Large Battery Site

Craney Is.

Fort Norfolk

Fort Nelson

■	Forts - 5
▲	Earthworks - 11
⸸	Boom - 1

Virginia War of 1812 Forts, Earthworks, and Booms

Alexandria Region

tions should be taken as a repetition . . . might lead to the destruction of the town. (Capt. Charles Napier, commander of H.M. frigate *Eurylaus*)[5]

American account of incident: Capt. [David] Porter, Lieutenant [Mas. Com. John O.] Creighton and Lieutenant [Midshipman Charles T.] Platt naval officers rode into Town like Saracens and seized on a poor unarmed Midshipman [John Fraser] a mere strapling, and would have carried him off or killd him had not his neck handerchief broke. This rash act excited the greatest alarm among the Inhabitants of the Town, Women and children runing and screaming through the Streets and hundreds of them layed out that night without Shelter. I immediately prepared a message to Commodore [Capt. James Alexander Gordon] explaining the manner and circumstances of this insult and sent it on board . . . while I was preparing the message One of the Captains [probably Capt. Charles Napier] rushed into the parlour with the strongest expressions of rage in his countenance

bringing with him the midshipman who had been so valiantly assaulted by those Gallant Naval Officers, I explained to him by whom the outrage was committed, that the Town had no control over them; and ought not be held responsible for their conduct, and I was at that time preparing a message of explanation to the Commodore he said it was necessary that it should be explained, after which his fury seemd to abate and he went off, before Mr. Swann [attorney] and Mr. Lee [former member of the Alexandria Common Council] got on Board the Signal of Battle was hoisted and all the Vessels were prepared for action when Mr. Swan and Mr. Lee made their explanation & the Commodore said he was satisfied and ordered the signal of Battle to be annulld thus the Town was providentially preserved from destruction, by the accidental circumstance of the midshipmans neck handkercief giving way for had he been killd or carried off, I do not believe the Town could have been saved from destruction. (Mayor Charles Simms to Nancy Simms, September 3, 1814)[6]

At the time I took possession of Alexandria, there were 1500 pounds of fresh beef lying on the wharfs ready to be delivered to the boats of the enemy's ships, which were then only 2½ or 3 miles below the town, and I mention this to show the state that place was in at the time. (Capt. John Rodgers to Secretary of Navy William Jones, September 9, 1814; reprinted in Baltimore *Niles' Weekly Register,* October 1, 1814)

Even after the British had retired twenty miles down the Potomac River, Alexandria officials did not raise the American flag until Capt. John Rodgers threatened to fire on the town if they did not consent to his hoisting the American colors. Dolley Madison told friends that the Alexandrians should have let their town burn rather than accept such humiliating terms. Charlestown,* Maryland, is the only other town in the Chesapeake known to have capitulated to the British. The chairman of the Annapolis Committee of Safety recommended that the Maryland capital city surrender if threatened by attack, but his resolution did not pass, and Annapolis was never attacked.

King Street Waterfront. Near the end of King Street at Union Street (then the original waterfront), the British loaded the goods taken from Alexandria. John Fitzgerald's warehouse on the southeast corner of King and Union streets as well as three warehouses on the north side of the 100 block of King Street all date from before the war and are little altered. The Chequire House, built 1797 and located at 202 King Street, and Gilpin House, built 1798 and located at 208 King Street, are typical merchants' houses of the time, consisting of

"Johnny Bull and the Alexandrians" is a cartoon satirizing the capitulation of Alexandria. The Bull demands all the flower and tobacco except Porter and Perry (beer and a pear cordial), a punning reference to the otherwise victorious American naval officers who ironically were unsuccessful in opposing the British during their withdrawal down the Potomac River. Local residents plead for mercy on the grounds that they were always friendly to the British, even trading with them when it was outlawed by the embargo. (1814 etching by William Charles; Library of Congress, Prints and Photographs Division)

shops on the ground floor and living quarters above. In 1812, Francis Peyton exhibited wax figures, including those of George Washington and Stephen Decatur,* at his house located at the intersection of King and Patrick streets.

Lee, Henry "Light Horse Harry," House (611 Cameron Street). PRIVATE. Henry "Light Horse Harry" Lee,* his wife, and their five children, including Robert E. Lee of Civil War fame, lived in this 1796 built house from 1810 to 1811, when they moved to 607 Oronoco Street. Henry Lee, a Federalist, defended the printing office of the Baltimore *Federal Republican* newspaper during the Baltimore Riots* of 1812 and sustained serious injuries from the enraged and drunken mob. Lee remained an invalid until his death. He is buried at Lee Chapel and Museum,* Virginia.

Other prominent Alexandria citizens include Brig. Gen. Robert Young (629 King Street), who served in the 2nd Regiment District of Columbia militia during the war; Charles Simms (229 South Pitt Street), who served as mayor during the war; Charles McKnight (607 Prince Street), who commanded the Alexandria Blues during the Battle of the White House*; Ferdinando Fairfax* (208 North Royal Street), who offered timber and stone for construction of the White House Gun Battery*; and Brig. Gen. William Summers (312 Queen Street), who served in the District of Columbia militia during the war.

Long Bridge Site (approximately where the railroad bridge and 14th Street bridge cross the Potomac River). A bridge connected Alexandria with Washington. The Virginia side of the bridge was approximately due east of the Pentagon, north of Gravelly Point. The Maryland side of the bridge extended toward the northeast to about where the U.S. Bureau of Engraving and Printing is located at 14th Street. Much of the water that it crossed has since been reclaimed with land fill.

Because of a severe August 25 storm, the chains that operated the draw span of the long bridge buckled, and the draw could not be raised. In response, the Americans on the Virginia side burned the bridge while British forces fired on them from the Washington side. To prevent any surprise attack by these American forces, the British burned their side of the bridge as well. The Americans abandoned the Virginia side of the bridge upon the arrival of the British squadron at Alexandria.

A blind woman with her children, believing the whole of Washington was on fire, ran onto the burning bridge toward Alexandria. Three British soldiers risked their lives to whisk the family to safety.

a woman, blind, poor creature, with alarm at the supposition that the whole town was to be fired, ran on to the bridge with her children in order to escape. Three of the Johnnies who had just set fire to the under part of the bridge, called to her to stop; but the more they called the faster she ran. They sprang after her, and whilst one seized and brought off in safety the poor panic-struck mother, the others did the same by the children. And thus was this family protected by enemies at the risk of their lives; whilst multitudes of their own countrymen were flying from a handful of British troops, weak as children from fatigue, with scarcely anything but their courage to make them formidable. (Sir Edward Codrington, 1875)[7]

Lyceum (201 South Washington Street). The 1839 Creek Revival Lyceum houses exhibits focusing on Alexandria. A small exhibit on the War of 1812 includes a carronade recovered from the shoreline of the Potomac River near its confluence with Hunting Creek. It is possible this gun was scuttled to keep it out of British hands prior to the British occupation of Alexandria. Also on display is a sword and scabbard made by John Gaither of Alexandria. On the knuckle guard of the sword are the initials of Lt. C. I. Queen, who served in the 36th Regiment. This regiment participated in the Battle of Bladensburg* and was present during the defense of Fort McHenry.*

Muster Site (area north of Oronoco and North Washington streets). This area was used by troops for training purposes during the French and Indian War, the Revolutionary War, and the War of 1812. In 1755, at age twenty-three, George Washington drilled here with Gen. Edward Braddock.

Shooter's Hill/George Washington Masonic National Memorial, then called Shuter's Hill (highest hill overlooking Alexandria, site of George Washington Masonic National Memorial, off King Street). Brig. Gen. John Pratt Hungerford, who commanded the Virginia militia in the Northern Neck of Virginia, was ordered by the War Department to encamp on Shooter's Hill, just outside of and overlooking Alexandria. When the British withdrew from Alexandria, President James Madison, Secretary of Navy William Jones, Brig. Gen. John Hungerford, and U.S. Navy Capt. David Porter, Jr. met at Shooter's Hill to plan countermeasures for attacking the British as they descended the Potomac River. Here the plans to erect batteries at White House* on the Virginia shore and Indian Head* on the Maryland shore were made. Inside the George Washington Masonic National Memorial on the balcony of the George Washington Museum is a banner carried by the Alexandria Independent Blues during the War of 1812.

AQUIA CHURCH (2938 Jefferson Davis Highway [U.S. Route 1] at intersection with Garrisonville Road [Route 610], Garrisonville, Stafford County). This church, built in 1757 on the site of an earlier church, possesses a communion silver service given in 1739. A Virginia Historical Highway Marker perpetuates the tradition that the silver service was buried during the American Revolution, the War of 1812, and the Civil War to protect it from marauding armies. While there is no documentation of the British ever being in the immediate vicinity of Stafford or Garrisonville, the citizens felt threatened on many occasions and may have buried the silver for safekeeping.

★**Arlington National Cemetery** (off George Washington Parkway, Arlington). The remains of fourteen unknown soldiers and sailors of the War of 1812, uncovered during a construction project at the Washington Navy Yard* in 1905, are buried at Humphreys Drive, section 1, lot 299, near the Swamp Oak Tree. The site, originally dedicated by the Daughters of American Colonists, was also dedicated in April 1976 by the National Society United States Daughters War of 1812. The monument says the Treaty of Ghent was ratified February 15, 1815. The Senate unanimously approved the treaty on February 16, and the president signed off on the agreement later that day, thus completing the ratification process. Ratifications were exchanged with the British the next day.

ASH LAWN-HIGHLAND (1000 James Monroe Parkway [Route 795], southwest off Thomas Jefferson Parkway [Route 53], south of Charlottesville, Albemarle County). James Monroe, who served as secretary of state and secretary of war during the War of 1812, lived at Ash Lawn-Highland for twenty-four years. Monroe was compelled to sell the property for financial reasons and moved to Oak Hill.* Ash Lawn-Highland is operated by the College of William and Mary, Monroe's alma mater.

BARBOURSVILLE (Orange County). During the War of 1812, Capt. William Brumfield raised a cavalry company in Orange County. On the grounds of the Barboursville Vineyards (17655 Winery Road, 0.2 mile west off Route 777, 0.2 mile south off Route 678, 0.6 mile east off Route 20) are the ruins of Governor James Barbour's house and the Barbour family cemetery where he is buried. Governor Barbour viewed the war as the

only means by which to end British threats to American sovereignty. He sought to prepare Virginia for war. Barbour's father had trained the Orange militia, and his son was well aware of the inadequacies of Virginia's militia. Thus, on January 27, 1812, he addressed the General Assembly and sought appropriations for training and arming a stronger militia. Barbour toured the tidewater region from April 21 to May 10, 1812, to form a plan for the defense of Virginia against the British. For his energetic service during the conflict, Barbour thereafter was known as "the war governor."

BEAVER CREEK PLANTATION (south side of Beaver Creek, 1300 Kings Mountain Road [Route 108], north of Martinsville, Henry County). PRIVATE. Lt. Col. George Hairston (1750–1827) lived at Beaver Creek Plantation. The present Greek Revival house built in 1837, with later additions, replaced the original 1776 house where Lieutenant Colonel Hairston lived. He fought during the Revolutionary War at Guilford Court House and Eutaw Springs and was commissioned a lieutenant colonel in the 64th Virginia Regiment on May 6, 1793. On March 24, 1813, Lieutenant Colonel Hairston was among those mobilized into the 5th Virginia Regiment, which was stationed at the rear of Fort Norfolk.* Three swords belonging to family members once hung in the library: one from the Revolutionary War, one from the War of 1812, and one from the Civil War. The War of 1812 sword belonged to General Hairston, who obtained the rank of general after the war and is buried in the family cemetery on the grounds of Beaver Creek Plantation. The path to the cemetery is lined with boxwood trees planted in 1813 to 1816. The property now serves as the headquarters for Bank Services of Virginia, Inc.

BELLONA ARSENAL. *See* listing, Richmond

BENVENUE. *See* listing, McLean

BLANDFORD CHURCH CEMETERY. *See* listing, Petersburg

CAMP BOTTOM'S BRIDGE SITE (Williamsburg Road [U.S. Route 60] bridge over Chickahominy River, Henrico County). PRIVATE. A militia camp was established here from late August to early December 1814 because of the British threat on Richmond. This camp, occupied by the Virginia 1st Brigade under Brig. Gen. William B. Chamberlayne, was located in concert with Camp Carter* about two miles to the west. The forces located at these camps could thwart any British movement up the Williamsburg Road or from landings on the York River across the Peninsula. Camp Bottom's Bridge was probably located on the west side of the Chicka-hominy River, slightly to the south, where old Williamsburg Road crossed the river.

CAMP CARTER SITE (near intersection of Old Williamsburg and Meadow roads [Route 156], Antioch, Henrico County). PRIVATE. This camp in concert with Camp Bottom's Bridge* located about two miles to the east could thwart any British movement up the Williamsburg Road or from landings on the York River across the Peninsula.

CAMP HOLLY SPRINGS SITE (near intersection of Camp Holly Drive and Turner Road, New Market Heights, Henrico County). PRIVATE. This is one of several camps established to protect Richmond from British attacks. Lt. Col. John Hartwell Cocke commanded the troops here as well as Camp Malvern Hill.* The Diamond Springs Bottling Company occupies the site today.

CAMP MALVERN HILL SITE, also called Camp Hill (Malvern Hill Farm, Malvern Hill Lane, off New Market Road [Route 5], south of Glendale, approximately 12.2 miles southeast of Richmond, Henrico County). PRIVATE. Malvern Hill is a high bluff overlooking the James River. It is best known for its role during the American Civil War, but that action actually took place farther north on Carters Mill Road near the intersection with Willis Church Road. Malvern Hill Farm was the site of a Virginia militia encampment during the War of 1812. A battery was erected on this hill but no earthworks are known to survive.

CAPE CHARLES (Chesapeake Bay, west end of Stone Road [Route 184], lower Northampton County). The British made a raid at Cape Charles on March 10, 1813, boarding a grounded schooner and taking five turkeys before the local militia drove off the enemy. It is assumed the raid occurred here and not at Cape Charles Inlet or Cape Charles Island, which are farther south at the mouth of Chesapeake Bay because the British only the day before raided nearby Cherrystone Inlet,* also known as Cheriton. Good views of Chesapeake Bay can be had along Bay Avenue and from the pier at the corner of Bay and Mason avenues.

CAPE HENRY (confluence of Chesapeake Bay and Atlantic Ocean, north off Shore Drive [U.S. Route 60], Virginia Beach). U.S. military installation. Cape Henry was an important landmark for the entrance of Chesapeake Bay, dis-

tinguished by the Cape Henry Lighthouse, completed in 1792. The British conducted a raid on the Cape Henry Lighthouse on February 14, 1813, taking meat from the keeper's smokehouse. The raid was described in the following humorous account:

> British valor and discipline. A band of veterans from Admiral [John Borlase] Warren's squadron landed at the lighthouse on Cape Henry and with the most undaunted heroism attacked the pantry and smoke house of the keeper, captured his hams, mince pies and sausages, leaving not a link behind!—after when they effected their retreat in the greatest good order and regularity to their ships, with flying colors, without the loss of a ham! So much for British heroism and discipline—HUZZA! "England expects every man to do his duty!" This gallant and brilliant smokehouse exploit was achieved on the 14th inst. (Wilmington *American Watchman & Delaware Republican,* February 24, 1813)

> The enemy, contrary to his own interest, (a rare occurrence with citizens of the United States,) had extinguished the light on Cape Henry: this gratuitous act saved us the trouble of "dowsing the glim." (Capt. James Scott, 1843)[8]

Cape Henry served as the southern end of the blockade of the mouth of the Chesapeake Bay. (*See* New Point Comfort for a discussion of how Baltimore clippers attempted to run the British blockade at the mouth of the Bay.)

> arrived off Cape Henry. The day we made the land the Dragon [H.M. ship-of-the-line] was sent in chase of two schooners, and succeeded in capturing both: they were commanded by officers in the American navy, who had been stationed off the Chesapeake for purpose of warning off their countrymen from entering the bay: they were beautiful pilot-schooners and provided invaluable as tenders, to which purpose they were immediately converted. (Capt. James Scott, 1834)[9]

Cape Henry served as a watering area for the British blockading fleet.

> The [H.M. ship-of-the-line] Plantagenet, 74 [guns], has for some days past been lying off Cape Henry Light-House, near enough in shore to protect the landing of her men, who were sent on shore to procure water.—The enemy had sunk wells for this purpose on the Cape Point, where there is excellent water, and every day visited them in their barges, supplying themselves with water and plundering the inhabitants. (Baltimore *Patriot,* July 19, 1813)

About fifty local militia positioned themselves among the sand dunes to ambush a watering party in the early morning of July 14, 1813.

At half past 5 this morning, a barge, full of men from the ship [H.M. ship-of-the-line *Plantagenet*], was seen rowing towards the shore. They landed about 6 o'clock, and all hands proceeded to the wells, where they received a full fire from the militia, who, until that moment were concealed from their view by the sand-hills. The enemy were panic struck. They threw down their arms, and ran in confusion to their boat. Some were cut off in their running, and those who reached the boat immediately laid themselves down in her, and durst not shew their heads . . . and were all taken prisoners. The enemy's force consisted of 3 lieutenants 16 seamen, and 9 marines; and they had three marines killed, and 1 lieut. 2 seamen, and 2 marines wounded. We had not a man injured. As the barge could not be moved without exposure to the guns of the 74, a piece of cannon which was in her bow, and whatever else that could be detached from her, were taken out and she was scuttled. (Baltimore *Patriot,* July 19, 1813)

The prisoners were taken to Hampton.* In revenge the British bombarded Pleasure House.* On June 15, 1813, a second British landing took place at Ragged Island Lake Plantation near Cape Henry and destroyed a corn mill after the owner refused to provide sheep and oxen. When a small contingent of militia arrived, the British bombarded the plantation, destroying a second mill.

Captain [Frederick] Hickey, commanding the British ship [sloop], Atalante, sent a boat on shore a few miles to southward of Cape Henry, and made a demand of some fresh provision, accompanying the demand with a threat, that if it was not compiled with, he would burn a wind-mill, belonging to the citizen at whose house the boat landed—the demand was not complied with, and . . . destroyed the wind-mill. (Norfolk *Public Ledger,* July 19, 1813)

On December 20, 1813, the Maryland privateer armed schooner *Tartar,* under the command of Capt. Edward Veazey out of Wicomico River, carrying 999 barrels of flour, ran aground on Cape Henry. Six crewmen froze to death, among them apparently two black sailors named Perry Sullivan and Henry James.

Strong gales prevented enemy from getting to her [schooner *Tartar*] and Captain landed its crew and few stores. On 22nd being calm, enemy in barges to take her, but militia on shore fired upon them and kept up a battle just out of musket shot; finally burnt her cargo and ship. (Norfolk *Herald,* December 24, 1813)

We the undersigned, Officers of the private armed schooner Tartar of Baltimore, return our sincere thanks to Captain Lemuel Cornick of Princess Ann for his humane and generous conduct towards us when cast away on Cape Henry. (Norfolk *Herald,* January 4, 1814)

In 1805, a commission recommended that the U.S. Navy support Robert Fulton's new invention, the "torpedo" (water mine). In the summer of 1813, Secretary of Navy William Jones gave encouragement to Elijah Mix, who worked with Capt. Charles Stewart of the U.S. frigate *Constellation,* to use a mine to blow up H.M. ship-of-the-line *Plantagenet* off the Chesapeake capes. Mix rowed near *Plantagenet* in an open boat named *Chesapeake's Revenge* and dropped a torpedo into the water, hoping it would drift into the vessel and explode. Despite several attempts, Mix was never successful, although on July 24 a torpedo exploded so near *Plantagenet* that it caused a cascade of water to fall on its deck. The British referred to these mines as "Powder Machines."

It was like the concussion of an earthquake attended with a sound louder and more terrific than the heaviest peal of thunder. A pyramid of water 50 feet in circumference was thrown up to the height of 30 or 40 feet . . . on ascending to its greatest height, it burst at the top with a tremendous explosion and fell in torrents on the deck of the ship which rolled into the yawning chasm below. (Washington *Daily National Intelligencer,* August 2, 1813)

While the "torpedo" attempt in the Chesapeake failed, a second attempt off New London, Connecticut, was more successful. There a "torpedo" blew up a small British vessel, inflicting a number of British casualties and producing much acrimony between the two countries.

CARTER CREEK. *See* Irvington

CHRIST CHURCH (Irvington). *See* Irvington

CHAIN BRIDGE AND PATTERSON MILL SITE, also called Little Falls Bridge (Potomac River, Chain Bridge Road [Route 123], Arlington County). A small parking area is located on the east side of 41st Street at the intersection with North Glebe Road. A trail along Pimmit Run is located on the west side of North Glebe Road just to the north of the parking area. The trail runs under Chain Bridge to a foundation ruin of what is believed to be the Patterson Mill, which was located near the confluence of Pimmit Run with the Potomac River.

On August 23, 1814, Stephen Pleasonton* led a contingent of twenty-two wagons loaded with government documents (including the Declaration of Independence) packed in coarse linen bags to an unoccupied grist mill belonging to Mr. Edgar Patterson, situated a short distance on the Virginia side of the Potomac beyond Chain Bridge, two miles above Georgetown. There were three mill complexes in the area at the time, but two were owned by the Adams family. Patterson mill is believed to be located closest to Chain Bridge. Barges from the navy yard were ordered here to save them from British destruction. In addition, wagons of gun powder were removed from the navy yard and taken to a barn belonging to a man named Dulany, about nine miles above the city. The exact location of this barn is unknown. The following day, Dolley Madison crossed Chain Bridge on her way to Rokeby Farm* to escape the advancing British army.

CHERRYSTONE INLET,

CHERRYSTONE INLET, also called Cheriton after the community there (Chesapeake Bay, north of town of Cape Charles, lower Northampton County). On March 9, 1813, a British tender and barges carried out a raid on Cherrystone Inlet, taking two cows belonging to a Mr. Savage. The British also seized a cargo of flour from one schooner and burned another. The 27th Regiment of Northampton County militia under the command of Lt. Col. John Cropper were able to recapture the prize schooner. The following day the British conducted a raid at nearby Cape Charles.* The general area can be viewed from the end of Cherrystone Road (Route 663).

The British attacked American schooners in Cherrystone Inlet and Kings Creek (immediately south on the north side of Cape Charles municipality) circa September 21, 1813. Five boats from the H.M. ship-of-the-line *Dragon* and H.M. frigate *Lacedemonian,* supported by the H.M. brig *Mohawk,* moved toward the schooners before dawn, but their approach was discovered and the militia assembled. The British set fire to the schooners before being driven off, but the militia were able to extinguish the flames and save the vessels.

Their force at this time was about a Hundred Riflemen which covered themselves behind Trees, Sand Hills, and every where they could shelter themselves. Independent of this Force they have two Field Pieces, one of which was abandoned and it is thought dismounted—the Launch was stationed to keep clear and secure the entrance of the Creek, whilst the other Boats were employed in bringing down the Vessels, and after towing them down for nearly two miles exposed to a heavy fire of Musketry from both sides of the Creek. I am sorry to say that there was not sufficient Water to get them over the Bar—the [H.M. brig] Mohawk at this time also took the ground, and upon which it was found necessary to set fire to the vessels in our possession—Their

Cargoes consisted of Corn and Potatoes—By this time the Enemy had collected from two to three Hundred Men who were driven from one position to another whenever they came within the reach of our fire. (Capt. Samuel Jackson to Capt. Robert Barrie, September 23, 1813)[10]

CHESCONESSEX CREEK, also Chesconnessex and Chessenessix (off Pocomoke Sound east of Watts Island, northwest of Onancock, Accomac County). In consequence of the British establishment of a base on Tangier Island,* a militia camp was established here as well as at Onancock* and Pungoteaque* creeks. Here on June 21, 1814, an eleven-man crew from H.M. ship-of-the-line *Albion,* anchored off Tangier Island, transferred a lieutenant to Watts Island. Once completing their task, the crew members deserted at Chesconessex. Lt. Col. Thomas M. Bayly described the deserters as between the ages of twenty and thirty years. The Americans sent the deserters to Baltimore by land.

The Battle of Chesconessex, more correctly a skirmish, took place on June 25, 1814. The local militia, alerted to a possible British threat because of the earlier attack on Pungoteague Creek,* established a small earthwork with a 4 pounder cannon at Camp Chesconessex, which was located on the northeast side of the creek. A separate detachment of men was positioned on the opposite side of the creek in temporary pine barracks. About five hundred British troops, including about fifty Colonial Marines, approached by barge with muffled oars under the cover of darkness in the early morning. Sentinels sounded the alarm about 2:45 a.m. Capt. John G. Joynes ordered thirty-two militiamen to form behind the breastwork eighty yards behind the landing location. Both sides exchanged fire while additional barges attempted to land troops on the American left to cut off any escape. Captain Joynes ordered a retreat to some nearby woods. His men then scattered. By sunrise, Captain Joynes had again gathered his troops and returned to the camp, but the British had already withdrawn to their ships, which were still visible offshore. The British had taken cannon, baggage, and public stores and had burned the barracks as well as a house belonging to a man named Salisbury. This was the last major engagement on the Virginia Eastern Shore.

the Enemy had established another Post and Battery at a place called Chissinessick immediately abreast of Watts' Island I determined on destroying it, which was ably and gallantly accomplished by the Boats of the this Ship the Dragon, and Endymion . . . who brought off with them another Six Pounder Field Piece after destroying the Work and burning the Guard Houses &c. &c. in its Vicinity. (Rear Adm. George Cockburn to Vice Adm. Sir Alexander F. I. Cochrane, June 25, 1814)[11]

The area of the battle can best be seen by boat although the general area can be viewed from the public boat ramp located at the end of Southside Road (Route 655) and along Crystal Beach Road (Route 782), South Chesconessex.

COAN RIVER (off Potomac River, below Yeocomico River and above Smith Point, Northumberland County). After attacking an American battery erected at the mouth of the Yeocomico River,* British troops on August 7, 1814, continued to the head of Coan River in several barges, where they captured three schooners and some tobacco and burned several houses.

American account of action: they sent three barges up near the head of the creek, and within two miles of Northumberland courthouse, for the purpose of taking three schooners anchored in their view: they were met by a company of Lancaster militia, who drove them back, and cut away their colours; but the appearance of ten other barges filled with men obliged our militia, who had not been reinforced, to retreat, which they did in good order, and without any personal injury; the British troops then took possession of the three schooners—landed on both sides of Cone [Coan], and burned all the houses they could find, some of which, the property of James Smith, postmaster at Northumberland courthouse, cost upwards of six thousand dollars. (William Lambert to Secretary of Navy William Jones, August 12, 1814)[12]

The British conducted a second raid on Coan River on October 4, 1814; their target was Northumberland Court House (now called Heathsville). Although two schooners were destroyed, the British met resistance from the militia. British casualties were one killed (Capt. Richard Kenah) and two wounded. An American account claims two Englishmen were killed and four taken prisoner. American casualties were one wounded.

American account of action: from 900 to 1000 of the enemy landed at Black point,—marched from thence, and took possession of Northumberland courthouse,—stayed about two days, and pillaged the inhabitants of that place and its vicinity, of negroes, provisions, &c. (William Lambert to Secretary of Navy William Jones, October 13, 1814)[13]

British account of action: a body of the Virginia Militia stationed near to the Northumberland Court House might be surprised for which purpose a detachment . . . was landed half an hour before daylight . . . at Black point Six Miles up the Coan River and one Mile from the Court House.—They immediately advanced on the Enemy who after firing a few Rounds from the Woods, retreated, his Guns having been removed a short time before on the Sentinels discovering our Boats . . . after pursing them five Miles and finding very little probability of coming up with their Guns as they had left their Ammunition and every other encumbrance on the Road and dispersed by various intricate passages that lead through thick woods on the Country returned to Black point . . . joined . . . with the First Regiment which had been landed at Mundy point three Miles up the Yocomico . . . the 2nd Battalion of Royal Marines was landed at Ragged point both . . . were near to parties of the Enemy who always escaped into the woods. (Rear Adm. Pulteney Malcolm to Vice Adm. Sir Alexander F. I. Cochrane, October 7, 1814)[14]

CONN'S FERRY (Potomac River, Riverbend Park, near east end of Potomac Hills Street, east off Jeffery Road [Route 1268], east off River Bend Road [Route 603], Fairfax County). This ferry, established by 1790, provided a crossing of the Potomac River above the Great Falls. President James Madison and his entourage traveled from Wiley's Tavern* to Conn's Ferry on August 26, 1814, to cross the Potomac River into Maryland, where they attempted to meet up with the American troops at Montgomery Courthouse (Rockville,* Maryland). The exact location of the ferry crossing is unclear, but it was probably near the boat ramp in the park. The river, however, is wider and deeper today than it was in 1814 due to the construction of an aqueduct dam.

COROTOMAN PLANTATION SITE. *See* listing, Irvington

CRANEY ISLAND (west entrance to Elizabeth River, Portsmouth City). U.S. military installation, restricted access. Craney Island, shaped like a painter's pallet and covering about thirty acres, was just a few feet above water. It was separated from the mainland on the northwest side by a shallow channel called the Thoroughfare, which was fordable at low to mid-tide. A temporary bridge over Craney Island Creek connected the west side of the island to Stringer's Farm on the mainland. The British attacked this fortified and strategic location on June 22, 1813, but shallow flats that extended north into Hampton Roads for nearly two miles prohibited large war vessels from supporting the British amphibious assaults. Hence the larger British warships did not play much of a role in the engagement. The Elizabeth River channel to the east was protected by American gunboats. Because of extensive land filling, Craney Island today bears no resemblance to the island in 1813. The U.S. Navy fuel depot and U.S. Army Corps of Engineers occupy the site today.

Craney Island served as the first line of defense for Norfolk, Portsmouth, Gosport Navy Yard, and the U.S. frigate *Constellation*. In addition, forts Norfolk* and Nelson* on opposite sides of the Elizabeth River served as a second line of defense. Despite its important position, the Carney Island defenses were not completed when attacked. An unfinished blockhouse mounting two 24 pounder and one 18 pounder cannon was built on the southeastern point of the island and commanded the ship channel at the mouth of river. A small battery mounting four 6 pounders was also erected on the northwest point of the island.

> It is much to be regretted that a strong work has not been erected on Crany Island . . . a small work for eight or ten guns made sufficiently high to prevent an escalade or surprize; the Narrows piered and secured with strong booms and chains; should that have been done, the Gun Boats well manned and stationed above the booms, it appears to me we might bid defiance to their [British] operations by water. (Capt. Charles Stewart to Secretary of Navy William Jones, March 22, 1813)[15]

On June 22, at 9:00 a.m., an estimated force of 2,400 British troops made a landing at Hoffleur's Creek on the mainland about two and a half miles west of Craney Island, debarking from about 60 barges and 2 schooners. It appeared the British would attack the island either across the Thoroughfare or across Craney Island Creek. The island was defended by a U.S. regiment of infantry and various militia units. These troops were positioned on the north and western side of the island, but the cannon were located on the opposite (southeast) point of the island. The heavy guns—seven pieces in all—were hastily moved to the north end. British troops meanwhile were delayed by unexpectedly deep waters at Wise's Creek, which was located between their landing place and the Thoroughfare. British artillery and Congreve rocket fire had no effect. American return fire from the battery and a gunboat inflicted casualties on the British and damaged the slave quarters at the George Wise farm that the British were using for cover. The British then withdrew beyond the artillery range.

About 11:00 a.m., almost simultaneously with the bombardment, an estimated 50 barges from the British fleet with a force of approximately 1,500 troops, including about 600 Independent Foreigners (Frenchmen), began approaching the north end of Craney Island in 2 columns. Capt. John M. Hanchett, illegitimate son of King George III, is reported to have led one column seated in the stern of Adm. John Borlase Warren's twenty-four-oar barge *Centipede* holding an open umbrella over his head. Five American guns now turned on the approaching boats. The lead boat grounded about two hundred or three hundred yards from shore in thick mud, making an amphibious landing here nearly impossible. Captain Hanchett's column turned parallel to the island and moved westward toward the second column. A cannonball smashed through the barge, wounding several men, including Hanchett. The British then began to withdraw. A detachment of militia was summoned to wade out and seize the barge and take prisoners. A terrier dog was found sitting on a bow cannon. The American guns ceased their fire so as not to harm the militia, while additional men without orders waded out into the water to get better shots at the departing enemy. British accounts claim one boat with thirty Independent Foreigners had capsized and the French soldiers were massacred by these wading Americans.

> American account of attack: their fire, which was so well directed that the Enemy were glad to get off, after sinking three [British accounts claims only two] of their largest boats, one of which called the Santapee [*Centipede*], Admiral [John Borlase] Warrens boat, fifty feet in length, carrying seventy five men, the greater part of the Crew were lost by sinking; twenty Soldiers & Sailors were saved & the boat haul'd up . . . the troops that were landed fell back in the rear of the Island & Commenced throwing rockets from Mr. [George] Wise's house, when Gun Boat 67 throw'd a few shot over that way, they dispersed & went back; we have had all day deserters from the Army coming in, I have myself taken in twenty five and Eighteen prisoners belonging to the Santapee [*Centipede*]; the Officers of the [U.S. frigate] Constellation fired their 18 pounder more like rifflemen than Artillerists, I never saw such shooting and seriously believe they saved the Island yesterday. (Capt. John Cassin to Secretary of Navy William Jones, June 23, 1813)[16]

> British account of attack: I directed the Troops . . . to be landed upon the Continent . . . but upon approaching the Island, from the extreme Shoalness of the Water on the Sea Side, and the difficulty of getting across from the Land: as well as the Island itself being Fortified with a Number of Guns & Mens from the Frigate [*Constellation*], and Militia; and Flanked by Fifteen Gun Boats: I considered . . . the difficulty of their passing over from the Land . . . would cost more Men than the numbers with us would permit: as the other Forts [Norfolk and Nelson] must have been Stormed before the Frigate and [Gosport] Dock Yard could be destroyed; I therefore ordered the Troops to be Re-embarked.

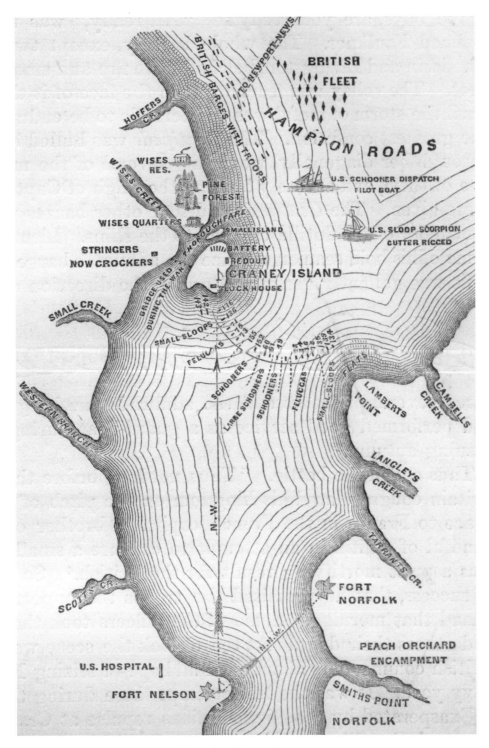

Sketch of Battle of Craney Island showing location of forts and batteries and position of American and British vessels. (Lossing, *Pictorial Field-Book of the War of 1812;* based on map now in Library of Congress by James Travis, a soldier in the U.S. Army at Norfolk during the war)

I am happy to say the Loss in the above affair has not been considerable, and only two Boats Sunk. (Adm. Sir John Borlase Warren to First Secretary of the Admiralty John W. Croker, June 24, 1813)[17]

The greater part of the prisoners are French soldiers (taken prisoners in Spain) whom the wretched fare of British prison ships had driven into the service of the enemy. (Washington *Daily National Intelligencer,* June 28, 1813)[18]

The British held their position at Wise's Plantation until after sunset, when they withdrew by barge to their ships but not before killing some sheep and hogs and burning several dwellings, including that of George Wise. There were no American battle casualties, although after the attack a sentinel guarding the powder magazine died when he lit his pipe and the magazine exploded. British casualties were three killed, sixteen wounded, and sixty-two missing. After the attack, Craney Island was further fortified by a two-story hexagonal brick block house and two brick magazines, but it escaped further attack. Thus ended the first and only attempt to take Norfolk,* Portsmouth,* the U.S. frigate *Constellation,* and the Gosport Navy Yard.*

DEEP CREEK. *See* appendix A

DINWIDDIE (southwest of Petersburg, Dinwiddie County). Gen. Winfield Scott* (1786–1866), a distinguished War of 1812 hero, was born near here at Laurel Branch (see below) and had a law office in town. For his heroism Scott was voted a gold medal by Congress on November 3, 1814. Winfield's brother Lt. Col. James Scott also served in the War of 1812.

When H.M. frigate *Leopard* attacked U.S. frigate *Chesapeake* off the Virginia Capes on June 22, 1807, President Thomas Jefferson issued a proclamation in response to the heightened tensions prohibiting all British warships from entering American rivers and harbors. Winfield Scott enlisted as a private in the Petersburg cavalry and shortly thereafter was instrumental in capturing two British officers and six seamen who landed at Lynnhaven Bay* while their fleet was anchored off shore. (*See* Norfolk and Fort Norfolk for more discussion about the *Chesapeake–Leopard* affair.)

Laurel Branch Site (I-85, south of Dinwiddie) PRIVATE. Laurel Branch, the home of Winfield Scott, is reputed to have been destroyed when I-85 was constructed. It stood

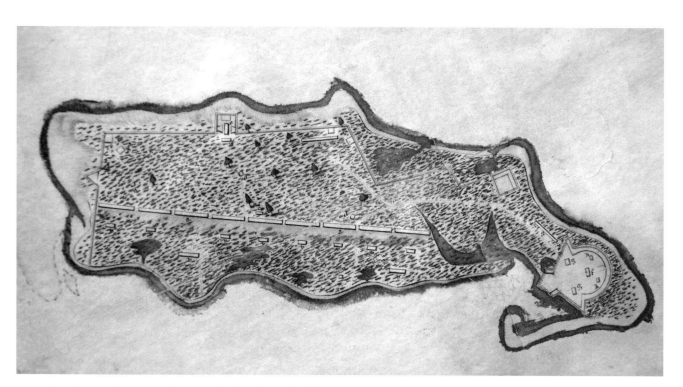

The defenses of Craney Island as surveyed in 1819. (National Archives and Records Administration, Cartographic Section)

Ruins of the brick magazine built on Craney Island after the initial attack as it appeared in the 1850s. (Lossing, *Pictorial Field-Book of the War of 1812*)

Ruins of brick magazine built on Craney Island after the initial attack as it appeared in the 1850s. (Lossing, *Pictorial Field-Book of the War of 1812*)

near Laurel Branch, which runs into Stoney Creek. Laurel Branch Farm (0.2 mile northeast off Gatewood Road [Route 656], 0.3 mile south off Boydon Plank Road [U.S. Route 1]) is part of the original land grant but not the home where Scott was born.

DIVIDING CREEK (off Chesapeake Bay, south of Great Wicomico River, northeast of Kilmarnock, Northumberland County). The British raided Dividing Creek on October 7, 1814.

> fifteen ships and nine schooners anchored off the mouth of Dividing Creek, in Northumberland,—sent five barges filled with men, who were plundering the inhabitants of negroes, stock, &c. and had burned a valuable house, the property of a capt. [?] Hughlett . . . Having no force to rely on but the militia, much injury to the people of Lancaster and Northumberland was apprehended . . . ten negroes had lately gone off to the enemy from the lower part of Northumberland, and fourteen from Richmond county, out of which last five number have been taken, and committed to gaol. (William Lambert to Secretary of Navy William Jones, October 13, 1814)[19]

EDINBURG (south of Winchester, Shenandoah County). Philip Grandstaff (1764–1832) operated a gun factory here that supplied arms during the War of 1812. His 1787 two-story log house and circa 1810 brick office are located on the east side of Stony Creek (nearly behind VFW Post 2447; 108 Creekside Lane, west off Stony Creek Boulevard [Route 675], north off Old Valley Pike [U.S. Route 11]). The exact location of a boring mill used for making gun barrels is unclear. It was apparently located either near Philip's home between the railroad and Old Valley Pike or near where the 1848 mill is still standing on the north side of Old Valley Pike at the intersection with Massey Farm Lane. Philip and George Grandstaff are among the better known gunsmiths who lived in Edinburg.

> In October, 1813, Philip Grandstaff made application to the Court for permission to erect a dam on Stony Creek (probably at Edinburg), for working a sawmill, carding machine and boring mill [used in making guns].[20]

FALLS CHURCH (Fairfax County).

Falls Church (115 East Fairfax Street). NRHP. This Georgian style church was built 1767–69. Francis Scott Key was a lay reader here. The church yard served as a muster site for Col. George Minor's 60th Regiment, Virginia militia.

Minor (Minor's) Hill (near intersection of Rockingham and Powhatan streets, Arlington County). Minor Hill, situated on the highest elevation in the area, was named for Col. George Minor, who lived here. Colonel Minor, commander of the 60th Regiment of Virginia militia, took his troops to Washington, but because of bureaucratic delays in receiving arms, the men remained in the city and thus missed the Battle of Bladensburg.* Although a story circulated that President James Madison had stayed the night of August 24, 1814, at Minor's home, in fact he and his entourage had only briefly stopped here. However, Dolley Madison did stay there the nights of August 26–27 after spending her first night in Virginia at Rokeby Farm* and her second night at Wiley's Tavern.*

Wren's Tavern Site (400 East Broad Street). Washington Navy Yard clerk Mordecai Booth arrived at Wren's Tavern about midnight August 24/25, 1814. A traveler there claimed President James Madison was less than a mile way. Another report said Madison was at Minor Hill* approximately two miles to the north. Still other reports claimed the president was at Salona.* All of these reports could have been accurate because all the places mentioned were on the route believed to have been taken by the president, although there is no authoritative account of the president's precise movements that night. President Madison did briefly stop here the next morning, but soon left for Salona looking for his wife Dolley.

FARNHAM CHURCH, also called North Farnham Church (231 North Farnham Church Road [Route 692], Farnham, Richmond County). This Anglican church, built in 1737 and apparently abandoned by 1814, served as a mustering site for the local militia. When the British raided the Rappahannock River in December 1814, slaves informed them of the presence of militia at Farnham Church. Landing at Morattico, Lancaster County, the British marched about seven miles inland and attacked the militia on the morning of December 6, 1814. There were no British casualties, although twelve marines and soldiers got "beastly Drunk" and "in consequence lost in Wood and left behind."[21] American casualties included Capt. Vincent Shackleford, seriously wounded in the leg, and artillerist William Garland, wounded in the shoulder, both of whom were taken prisoner and paroled. Thirteen militiamen were reported missing. (*See also* Jones Point, where a simultaneous skirmish took place.)

at daybreak on the 6th I landed . . . about three hundred and Sixty Bayonets.—On approaching the Shore, a party of the Enemy's Horsemen were observed reconnoitring our motions, from some Slaves who joined us, I was informed that the Enemy had a Force of Six hundred Militia with two Field Pieces assembled at Farnham Church distant near seven Miles from the place of landing, and that a few hours before daybreak a Party also consisting of about Six hundred had marched on our right, expecting we should land in Lancaster County: the Slaves volunteering to be our Guides I determined to attack the Party at Farnham before those Marched to Lancaster County could be apprized of our intentions . . . on our March we had frequent views of the Enemy's reconnoitring parties, and when within a Mile and half of Farnham the Skirmishers discovered part of his Force drawn up across the Road, which is narrow, and on each side closely Wooded; on a little Hill in the rear of his Troops he had stationed his Field Pieces, and from them he fired several ineffectual Shot. The Enemy . . . frequently hailed us to advance . . . the Light Division was directed to amuse the Enemy in front and on his right, while the Main Body penetrated the Wood on his left, with the intent to gain the Rear . . . so thick was the Wood that we were frequently obliged to crawl through it . . . when we advanced to Charge the Enemy . . . altering his line formed on the cross road near the Church protected by some Houses . . . they allowed us to approach within Musket range, without firing a Short . . . meantime the Light Troops gallantly advanced on the Enemy's right, who finding himself outflanked on our charging over the hedge, gave us a volley and fled; the pursuit was continued with great zeal, but the Enemy's superior speed and knowledge of the Country enabled him to escape into the Wood, and the Light Troops could only secure one Field Piece, the Horses of which with five others had been Shot.

While the Main Body of the Troops were halted at the Church, I dispatched . . . Marines . . . with part of the new raised Colonial Corps [former slaves called Colonial Marines] to release a number of Slaves . . . confined about two Miles from the Church . . . fell in with several parties of the Enemy, but succeeding in releasing about Twenty Negroes, several of whom . . . found in the Woods handcuffed round the Trees . . . A store containing Spirits I directed to be burnt, the Inhabitants had previously abandoned the Town and removed most their effects. (Capt. Robert Barrie to Rear Adm. George Cockburn, December 7, 1814)[22]

Over seventy slaves, twenty-eight of whom belonged to Edward Sanders, were reported lost during the British attack at Farnham. The average assessed value of each slave was $450, for a total of $31,500.

The Virginia Historical Roadside Marker at the site claims that bullet holes from this engagement can be seen in the church walls, but none are now visible. There are a few holes from imperfection in the brick, which may be misidentified as bullet holes, or possibly the bullet holes were repaired during the 1924 restoration.

FORT ALBION. *See* Tangier Island

FORT BOYKIN, also called Fort at Rock Wharf (James River, Fort Boykin Historic Park, 7410 Fort Boykin Trail [Route 705], Mogarts Beach, Smithfield, Isle of Wight County). In 1623, this site was chosen by the early Jamestown colonists to be a point of defense. It was known as the Castle or Fort Warraskoyack, and strategically located on a forty-five-foot height bounded on the north side by a deep natural ravine, on the south and west side by gentle slopes, and on the east by a steep bank of the James River where the channel runs close to the shore along a bend in the river, making enemy ships vulnerable to cannon fire. It was refortified during the Revolution and renamed for Maj. Francis Boykin of the Continental Army. As a consequence of the *Chesapeake–Leopard* affair* in 1807, the fort was again strengthened into a five-pointed star (local legend claims seven-pointed star)-shaped earthwork and log palisade called Fort at Rock Wharf. Francis Marshall Boykin II (1806–63), son of Lt. Col. Francis Marshall Boykin, a War of 1812 veteran and grandson of Maj. Francis Boykin for whom the fort was named, owned the property after the War of 1812. The land on which the fort was located was never federal or public property until the site was donated to Virginia in the late 1970s. The 29th Virginia militia from the fort repelled a British landing party at Rock Wharf located five hundred yards to the west. This strategic spot was fortified yet again during the American Civil War by the Confederates. The significant earthworks seen today date from that era. The 1812 fort included barracks, a powder magazine, a well, and six gun positions. The present configuration of the fort dates from the Civil War era, although the south exterior wall and possibly one gun emplacement wall may in part date from the War of 1812. Erosion along the river bank has destroyed some of the War of 1812-era earthworks. The fort is owned by the State of Virginia and operated by the Isle of Wight Public Recreation Facilities Authority. A small interpretive shelter is located at the entrance to the fort.

The British ascended the James River* in July 1813, raiding and plundering along the way. Just to the west at Rocks Plantation (7431 Boykin Lane, PRIVATE), also known as Edward Bennett's Plantation, on Burwell Bay, the British

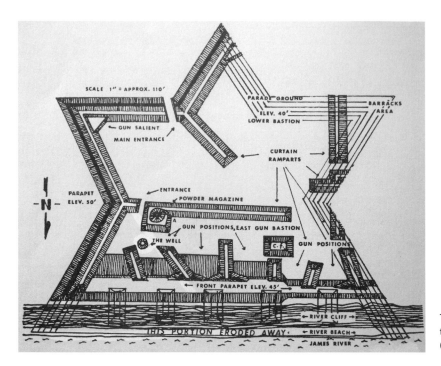

This sketch of Fort Boykin, based on conjecture, was prepared by the late Floyd Painter. (Courtesy of the artist)

attempted a landing on July 2, 1813, but were driven off by militia under the command of Capt. David Dick and Capt. Charles Wrenn of the 29th Regiment. Rocks Landing development now occupies the Rocks Wharf area.

> 3 barges from the frigate then laying off the mouth of Pagan Creek, full of men, went up the creek [James River?] as far as the rocks [Fort Boykin], (about three miles below Smithfield) they were fired upon by a small detachment of militia, (from 12 to 15) and after returning their fire for about ten minutes, decamped. None of our men were injured, though the balls flew around them like hail. An attack on Smithfield was hourly expected; they have, however, respectable force at that place. But even if they should succeed in getting possession of it, they will find nothing but bare walls, as every article of value is removed, and all the inhabitants, except those under arms, have left the town. (Washington *Daily National Intelligencer,* July 9, 1813)

FORT POWHATAN SITE (James River, Hood's Point, Fort Powhatan Gun Club, near north end of private road at north end of Fort Powhatan Road [Route 656], off Wards Creek Road [Route 614], near Burrowsville, Prince George's County). PRIVATE. Fort Powhatan, located at the narrowest width of the James River between Hampton and Richmond, was considered a strategic position in the defense of Richmond. This position was fortified during the Revolutionary War

and was called Hood's Battery. In the wake of the *Chesapeake–Leopard* affair* in 1807, the federal government purchased eight acres here and developed plans for a fort. Construction began the following year, and by 1814 there were in place twenty-two guns, including thirteen in the masonry fort and the others in a lower water battery. Barracks, officers quarters, magazine, hospital, "ravine," and two blockhouses were included in the plan. Because the river possessed many turns above this point and was not sufficiently deep beyond here to allow ships to ascend very far, this fortification was not considered a high priority by the U.S. Corps of Engineers despite strenuous pleas by Governor Barbour and other Virginia politicians to upgrade the fort. Nevertheless, units of the 35th U.S. Infantry were garrisoned here during much of the war. Sickness was a major concern and many died. The fort site is overgrown in dense forest. A brick magazine and significant earthworks including dry moat are present, but it is believed most if not all of these remains date from the Civil War era.

When the British sent a raiding party up the James River* in early July 1813, there was concern Fort Powhatan and possibly even Richmond* might be attacked.

> vessels [British] are positively all that are in the [James] River from James Town to Hoods [Point]. (Richmond *Enquirer,* July 6, 1813)

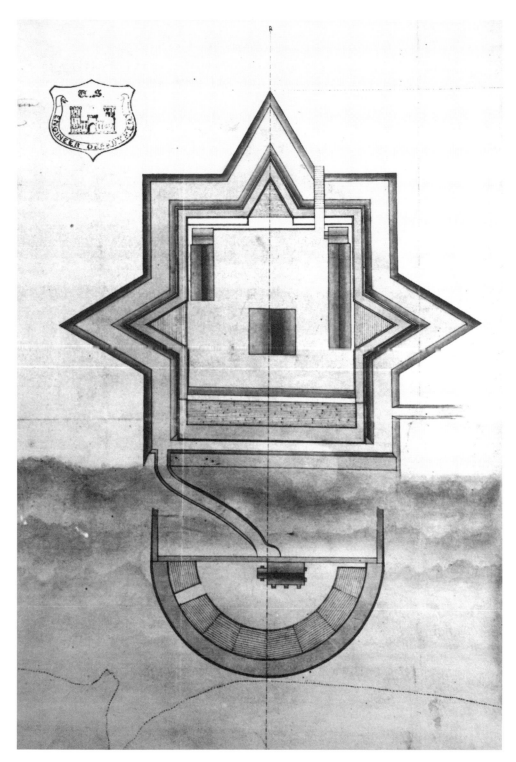

Fort Powhatan consisted of a two-story brick and earthen fortification as shown in this 1819 plan. (Plan by Elijah Brown; Library of Virginia)

Enemy frigates at mouth of Pagan Creek [off James River] intention to take fort at Hoods. (Richmond *Enquirer,* July 9, 1813)

Despite this concern nothing was done to strengthen the position, as revealed in a letter written nearly a year later.

I beg to call attention and solicit your aid, in opening the eyes of the Executive to the defenceless and dangerous situation of Fort Powhatan. There are upward of seven hundred Kegs of Powder, besides all the Guns and other public property at the Fort, and only twelve men, and several of them sick, to guard it. If our enemy knew the situation of this place, they would most certainly destroy it; and as the Citizens of Richmond must feel equal interest with ourselves in protecting this place, I trust you'll lose no time in communicating the same to the Executive, and make known the results. (Mayor Edward Pegram, Jr., Petersburg, to Maj. Thomas Wilson, June 30, 1814)[23]

FREDERICKSBURG (Rappahannock River, Spotsylvania County). On December 4, 1814, the British sent a small force up the Rappahannock River to assess the feasibility of attacking Fredericksburg. Capt. Robert Barrie decided not to pursue such an attack because the river was so narrow, it was late in the season, and militia were being mustered to meet the British. This was a wise decision as the militia under Lt. Col. Richard E. Parker, commander of the 111th Regiment, Westmoreland County militia, established a battery of four cannon on the bluffs of the river near the Westmoreland–Richmond County line, southeast of Leedstown, which could have played havoc on the British squadron.

James Monroe, secretary of state (1811–17) and secretary of war (1814–15), lived in Fredericksburg from 1786 to 1789. He practiced law in an office that still stands on Charles Street (immediately north of Masonic Cemetery*) and now serves as the James Monroe Museum (908 Charles Street). He is buried at Hollywood Cemetery, Richmond.

The Sentry Box is a late eighteenth-century home (133 Caroline Street, near east end of Dixon Street) located on the south side of town that is reputed to have been used as a lookout for enemy ships ascending the Rappahannock River during the War of 1812 and the Civil War.

GWYNN ISLAND (mouth of Piankatank River, east end of Old Ferry Road [Route 633], Matthews County). Near midnight March 10, 1813, some American vessels taking up anchorage just under Gwynn Island were hailed by an armed schooner. Two different accounts of this incident illustrate how difficult it can be to interpret such encounters. The first account

shows the perspective of the American privateer schooner *Fox* under the command of a man named Vial that was approached by the H.M. pilot schooner *Lottery.* Vial hailed the British vessel and when he got an unsatisfactory answer opened fire. The *Lottery* returned fire, and after a two-hour engagement the *Fox* stood up the Bay.

hailed a second time, and desired them to send their boat on board, suspecting strongly from the answer given that they were British, fired, which was immediately returned; shortly after observed a schr. and launch (carrying an 18 or 24 pound carronade) who all opened a destructive fire upon us, particularly the launch, whose grape did great injury to our sails, rigging, &c.—She was silenced; being dark could not see whether she sunk or not, after sustaining the action near two hours cut the cable and stood out, as we passed the schooner gave her a broadside when the main mast went over, then stood up the bay. The Fox had one shot in her hull, her sails, &c. much cut, had five men badly wounded, and capt. V[ial]. very much so in the face, she has put back to repair damages. (Baltimore *Niles' Weekly Register,* March 13, 1813)

The second account is from the perspective of Mas. Com. Arthur Sinclair, commander of the U.S. Schooner *Adeline* (renamed *Asp**). It is interesting that Vial makes no mention of any U.S. Navy vessels involved in the engagement, while Lieutenant Sinclair makes no mention of any privateer. This might indicate that there were two such engagements, although this seems unlikely.

at midnight made a harbour under Gwins Island . . . After having anchored in a line across the Channel with two gunboats in company . . . I was hailed from an armed Schooner [H.M. schooner *Lottery*], within us, to know who we were—I informed him, and upon requiring to know who he was, he went to quarters immediately and ordered my Boat onbd. him . . . I fired a musket a head of him, which he instantly returned with a Broadside of Round and grape with a constant fire of small arms—Being well assured, from this conduct that it was one of the Enemies Schooners, I opened a fire on her from this vessel and in 15 or 20 minutes silenced her—I now ceased firing and desired the nearest gunboat to hail him and know if he had struck to us, and who he was—He made no reply but immediately renewed the Action—I then ordered a genl. fire from all the vessels, and in about the same length of time silenced him a second time—He acted, upon our ceasing our fire, precisely as he had before done, and it was now half an hour before he was a third time silenced . . . I was now in the act of sending an officer on board him to take possession, when I discovered he had made Sail and was endeavouring to escape under cover of darkness of the night—I immediately cut my cable and made sail after him, but after a running fight of half an Hour, his great superiority of sailing and the extreme darkness of the night effected his escape. (Mas. Com. Arthur Sinclair to Secretary of Navy William Jones, March 11, 1813)[24]

The British schooner sank while attempting to reach the British fleet at New Point Comfort.*

HAMPTON (Hampton River off James River). Little England Farm,* then on the outskirts of Hampton, was home of the Barron family, which served in the navy during the Revolutionary War, the War of 1812, and the Civil War. James Barron* (1789–1851) commanded the U.S. frigate *Chesapeake* during the infamous encounter with H.M. frigate *Leopard* on June 22, 1807. The British demanded that Barron permit a search for suspected deserters. When Barron refused, the *Leopard* opened fire, killing three and wounding eighteen, including Barron. Four American crew members were taken. For this unwarranted attack, the British government

ultimately apologized, and returned the two surviving men and agreed to pay an indemnity (although it was apparently never paid). Barron was court-martialed and sentenced to five years' suspension without pay for neglecting on the probability of an engagement to clear his ship for action. An exchange of correspondence between Barron and Com. Stephen Decatur,* who served on the court martial board, resulted in Barron killing Decatur in a duel. The impressment of American sailors—typically from merchant vessels rather than a warship like in this incident—was one of the leading causes of the War of 1812.

Because communication was slow, news of the declaration of war was not widely known by the middle of 1812. Such was the case when H.M. schooner *Whiting* anchored at Hampton on July 8, 1812. While the British commander Lieutenant Maxey was coming ashore, an American privateer under the command of Capt. John Carraway seized the warship.

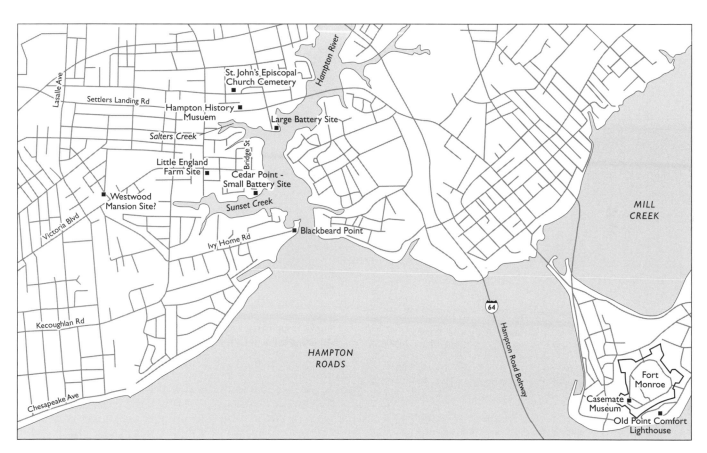

Hampton Region

his Britannic majesty's sch'r Whiting, Lieut. Maxey (detained by the Dash privateer) was conducted to Hampton Roads by the revenue cutter Gallatin, captain Edward Herbert. The crew of the Whiting was given in charge to capt. H. with orders to deliver them up to their commander at the very place where they had been taken [Hampton], which was done, and lieut. Maxey was then ordered to quit the waters of the United States with all possible speed. (Baltimore *Niles' Weekly Register,* August 29, 1812)

Soon after their abortive attempt to take Craney Island* on June 22, 1813, the British on June 25, 1813, attacked Hampton. While the British fleet bombarded an American camp defended by two batteries on the Little England Farm* southeast of Hampton, some two thousand British troops landed two miles west of Hampton on the James River near

Newport News just before daylight. They then marched along Celey's Road to attack Hampton from the rear opposite the waterfront. At the same time British barges approached from the waterside at Blackbeard Point.* Maj. Stapleton Crutchfield, in command of the 450 American forces, believing that the waterborne attack was only a feint, fired upon the barges from his four-gun battery, but he moved the bulk of his forces north to defend against the British land attack. Near the head of the west branch of Hampton Creek, where Celey's Road joins Yorktown Road, the Americans held back the British advance about three-quarters of an hour before their lines gave way and the militia fled into the thick woods. Artillerymen protecting a bridge spiked their canon and fled. During the confusion, British troops landed at Hampton from barges. Outflanked and outnum-

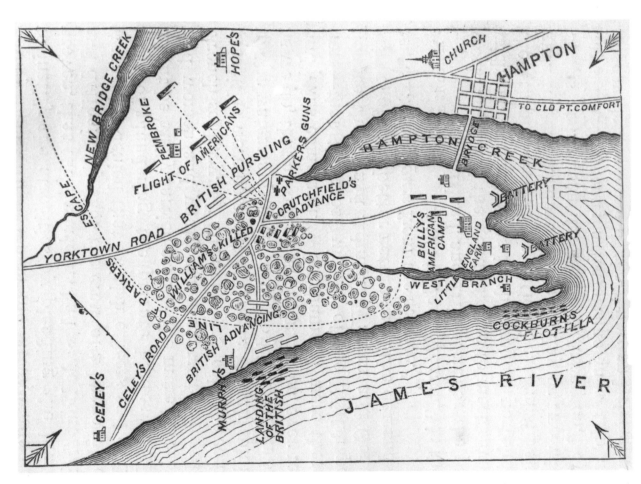

Sketch of the Battle of Hampton showing the locations of Celey's Road; site of death of Lt. Col. Richard Williams; Pembrooke or Westwood Mansion, where Williams was buried; Little England Farm; and the large (upper) battery and the small (lower) battery. Blackbeard Point is not identified but is the lowermost point at the entrance to Hampton Creek where Cockburn's Flotilla is located. (Lossing, *Pictorial Field-Book of the War of 1812*)

bered, the American forces escaped to the north. The British occupied Hampton for ten days, destroying all ordnance and commandeering supplies for their ships. British casualties were 5 killed, 33 wounded and 10 missing; among the killed was Lt. Col. Richard Williams.* American casualties were 7 killed, 12 wounded, 11 missing, and 1 taken prisoner. Several of the missing had apparently fled to their homes.

> American account of action: I am sorry to inform you the Enemy succeeded in Hampton yesterday morning, after a very obstinate resistance, and no doubt great loss on both sides; the Enemy landed several hundred Troops near Newportnews at 4 A.M. marched round, commencing the Action with their Rockets, while the barges forty in number entered the Creek, so few troops tho I believe brave as Ceazer [Caesar] did not exceed five hundred, were overpower'd by numbers, and the Rockets thrown in such way as to confuse them; from the best information we can receive the Inhabitants had flown and little or nothing left in town but the shells of houses. (Capt. John Cassin to Secretary of Navy William Jones, June 26, 1813)[25]

> British account of action: landed half an hour before day light . . . about two miles to the westward of the town . . . With a view to turn the enemy's position our march was directed towards the great road leading from the country into the rear of the Town . . . to engage the enemy's attention . . . armed launches and rocket boats to commence a fire upon their batteries this succeeded so completely that the head of our advance guard, had cleared a wood and were already on the enemy's flank before our approach was perceived. They then moved from their camp to their position in the rear of the town and here they were vigorously attacked . . . a detachment . . . push'd thro' the town and forced their way across a bridge of planks into the enemy's Encampment, of which, and the batteries, immediate possession was gained—In the mean time some Artillery men stormed and took the enemy's remaining field force . . . Lieut. Colonel [Richard] William will have the honor of delivering to you a stand of colours of the 68th Regt. James City Light Infantry, and one of the 1st Battn. 85th Regt. (Col. Sir Thomas Sidney Beckwith to Adm. Sir John Borace Warren, June 28, 1813)[26]

> HAMPTON TAKEN . . . About 5 o'clock the British made an attack by land and water upon Hampton. One party landed about 5 miles above that place, while another proceeded directly by water . . . the firing was kept up for 1 hour and 45 minutes when it ceased . . . the barges row into the creek and land at Hampton. The firing from the fort ceased with that of the musketry. We cannot state what became of the troop stationed there, but is to be hoped they have escaped. The force was as we understand, between 6 and 800. Two houses were set on fire by the rockets. (Washington *Daily National Intelligencer,* June 29, 1813)

The British victory at Hampton was tainted by the pillaging, murder, and rape committed by members of two Companies of Independent Foreigners who participated in the attack. These companies consisted of French deserters and prisoners from the Peninsular War. The British claim these men were spoiling for revenge for the loss of thirty Independent Foreigners during the Battle of Craney Island.*

> American account of plundering: That the town and country adjacent, was given up to the indiscriminate plunder of a licentious soldiery . . . In many houses not even a knife, a fork or a plate was left . . . The church was pillaged and the plate belonging to it was taken away . . . The wind-mills in the neighborhood were stript of their sails. The closets, private drawers and trunks of the inhabitants were broken open and scarcely any thing semed to be too trifling an object to excite the cupidity of those robbers. (Baltimore *Patriot,* July 23, 1813)

> American account of atrocities: The enemy took possession of Hampton . . . During their stay, their conduct exhibited deeds of infamy and barbarity which none but British savages could have been so callous and lost to the tender feelings of human nature. They pillaged the place of every article they could convey . . . they murdered the sick and dying and committed the most hard and cruel insults to the defenseless young ladies. From such nefarious enemies good Lord deliver us, is the prayer of your affectionate sister. (Margaret Ann Bonyer to Sally Wyatt Bibb, June 30, 1813)[27]

> British acknowledgment of unacceptable behavior: It is with great Regret I am obliged to entreat your Attention to the Situation & Conduct of the Two Independent Companies of Foreigners embarked on this Service . . . Their Behavior on the recent Landing at Hampton . . . dispersing to plunder in every direction; their brutal Treatment of several Peaceable Inhabitants, whose Age or Infirmities rendered them unable to get out of their Way . . . and whose Lives they threatened . . . I take the Liberty of submitting to You, the necessity of their being sent away as soon as possible. (Col. Sir Thomas Sidney Beckwith to Adm. Sir John Borlace Warren, July 5, 1813)[28]

American newspapers spread many stories of the atrocities committed during the British occupation of Hampton, but one story of the death of a very sick and aged man named Kirby whose wife was also shot in the hip and the family dog reportedly killed is far from credible.

> A Mr. Kilby, near Hampton was dying in his house in the arms of his wife, when the British troops approached, and

one of them cooly pulled out his pistol, shot poor Kilby and the ball lodged in the hip of the wife. "Expect no quarter," said an officer to his friend here. (Washington *Daily National Intelligencer,* July 2, 1813)

Kirby, who for seven weeks or more had been confined to his bed, and whose death the savages only a little hastened, was shot in the arms of his wife . . . go to his wounded wife and hear her heart-rendering tale. (Baltimore *Patriot,* July 23, 1813)

Benson J. Lossing visited this widow in 1853 and wrote the following: "her version of the story was that, with vengeful feelings, the soldiers chased an ugly dog into the house, which ran under Mr. Kirby's chair, in which he was sitting, and, in their eagerness to shoot the dog, shot the aged invalid, the bullet grazing the hip of Mrs. Kirby. Mrs. Kirby always considered the shooting of her husband an accident."[29] Thus the shooting appears to be accidental despite the claims of the contemporary American press.

On November 6, 1814, thirteen barges and one tender from the British blockading squadron overwhelmed the American schooner *Franklin.* There were no American casualties; British casualties are unknown. All the American crew members were taken prisoner, treated well, and exchanged within a month.

discovered two Boats with Sails & oars coming . . . for me, and a Schooner close in with the Land, apparently with a view to cut me off, continued my course, the two Barges, coming up very fast, and about 9 oclock engaged me to windward, their first fire I returned immediately, they bearing down upon me keeping up a brisk fire with their Mustketry and one of them with a brass eighteen [cannon] in her bow, but finding their situation rather warm, took in their sails and row'd round my Stern where I had a Carronade for their reception, and after a desperate attempt to board me, one on my Stern the Other on my Quarter were compell'd to Sheer off . . . they however made Sail and retreated under a warm fire untill out of grape [shot] distance . . . the Tender firing as She came up, the first Boats finding they had reinforcements from every direction renew'd the attack finding my retreat cut off . . . I then made a feint to go on Shore . . . the wind dying away enabled them to wear me in every direction . . . finding myself compleatley surrounded, opposed to a force nearly nine times my own and no possibility of escape, I thought further resistance would be wanton sacrifice of the lives of the men under my Command— I gave the painful order for the Ensign to be hauld down. (Sailing Master Thomas S. Hamersley to Capt. Charles Gordon, November 8, 1814)[30]

Blackbeard Point (west side of mouth of Hampton River, east end of Ivy Home Road). PRIVATE. This site is presently an abandoned seafood house/restaurant posted with "no trespassing" signs. When British barges appeared on June 16, 1813, off Blackbeard Point, they were discovered by an American patrol, which sounded the alarm. American leaders believed this was only a feint, and although a battery located near the mouth of Salters Creek fired on the barges, the majority of the American troops who were encamped at nearby Little England Farm* were ordered to defend against a possible British landing two miles west on the James River near Newport News.

intelligence was received from the videts stationed on the shore, fronting Hampton Roads, that the enemy were landing from their barges in considerable force, some little distance above Blackbeard's Point. (Boston *Columbian Centinel,* July 7, 1813)

Fort Monroe (north side of confluence of James River and Chesapeake Bay, south end of NcNair Drive [U.S. Route 258]). Fort Monroe was began in 1819 to beef up American coastal defense, which had been far from adequate during the War of 1812. Completed in 1834, the fort is named for James Monroe, who served as secretary of state and of war during the War of 1812 and later became the fifth president of the United States (1817–25). Several officers who later served at Fort Monroe took part in the War of 1812. Among them are John Walbach, Abraham Eustis, Charles Gratiot, and Walker K. Armistead. René Edward DeRussy, one of the engineers who built the fort, and John E. Wool, commander of the fort, fought at the Battle of Plattsburgh (September 11, 1814). U.S. Army base Fort Eustis, located near Newport News, is named after Brig. Gen. Abraham Eustis, who commanded Fort Monroe. One or more of these men may have brought the siege mortar from Plattsburgh to Fort Monroe, where it is on display at the Casemate Museum.*

CASEMATE MUSEUM (northwest interior casement of fort). Among the artifacts related to the War of 1812 is the flag of the 3rd Regiment, U.S. Artillery, which includes ribbons for the unit's participation at the Battle of Chippawa (July 5, 1814), the Battle of Lundy's Lane (July 25, 1814), and the Battle of Fort Erie (August 15, 1814), all in Upper Canada. An eight-inch siege mortar, made at the Woolwich Arsenal in England, was captured by the Americans at Fort George, Canada, in May 1813. It was used in the defense of Plattsburgh, New York, on September 11, 1814. This mortar was kept as a trophy and is believed to be among the original armaments of the fort.

OLD POINT COMFORT LIGHTHOUSE (north side of Fenwick Road). The Virginia Historical Roadside Marker (Fenwick Road, at Fort Monroe, near Old Point Comfort) claims that "During the War of 1812, the tower was used as a lookout by a British invasion force while they attacked Washington." This text is misleading as the British used the lighthouse tower as an observation station in 1813, not specifically during their attack on Washington in 1814.

On March 8, 1813, a schooner was attacked and taken by a British naval force.

> A small black schooner with one gun, supposed from Baltimore, was attacked on Monday morning off Old Point Comfort by 13 boats, after fighting them for some time was overpowered and carried. (Baltimore *Niles' Weekly Register*, March 13, 1813)

In early July the British landed in twenty barges about two miles above Old Point Comfort and established an encampment of "50 tents."[31]

Hampton History Museum (120 Old Hampton Lane). This museum contains a small exhibit about life in Hampton during the War of 1812. Artifacts include a musket made by Archibald Rutherford in 1810, one of seventy-five delivered to the Hampton Volunteer Rifle Company. This one was taken as a war trophy to England by the British after their attack on Hampton. On the musket barrel is stamped "115 REGT VA MA ELIZABETH CITY."

Little England Farm Site (area around 4400 Victoria Boulevard). Little England Farm was a five hundred-acre estate located a short distance southwest from the 1813 town limits of Hampton. Here the James Barron family lived. The American encampment and two batteries were located on the Little England Farm.

LARGE BATTERY SITE (north mouth of Salters Creek, approximately south end of King Street). The total armament between the two batteries was 4 6 pounders, 2 12 pounders, and 1 18 pounder. Of the 7 guns, 4 were located here and 3 at the small battery.

SMALL BATTERY SITE (Cedar Point, north mouth of Sunset Creek [West Branch], south end of Cedar Point Drive, south off Bridge Street).

St. John's Episcopal Church (100 West Queens Way). This parish, founded in 1610, is the oldest Anglican parish in America. The present structure, the fourth, was completed in 1728; the belfry was added in 1762. The British are said to have used the cemetery grounds as a slaughterhouse for the butchering of cattle taken from the inhabitants of

1852 view of Hampton Creek from Hampton, looking south toward Little England Farm, the home of Com. James Barron. Key: 1. Large battery. 2. Small battery. 3. Blackbeard Point. (Lossing, *Pictorial Field-Book of the War of 1812*)

Hampton. A historic marker on the grounds of the church proclaims that the walls that surround the church "have suffered during the Revolutionary War, the War of 1812 and the War between the states."

Westwood Mansion Site (near Old Pembroke Church Site, also called Third Parish Church, northeast intersection of West Pembroke and Patterson avenues, Lincoln Park area). Lt. Col. Richard Williams of the Royal Marines was killed during the attack of Hampton, June 26, 1813, and was buried in the gardens of John S. Westwood's mansion.

HARPERS FERRY FEDERAL ARSENAL SITE (at confluence of Potomac and Shenandoah rivers, West Virginia). In 1796, President George Washington selected Harpers Ferry as the site for a new United States Arsenal and Armory. Construction began in 1799. Some of the rifles used in the War of 1812 were manufactured here, others were made at small communities such as Edinburg,* Virginia, and Emmitsburg,* Maryland.

IRVINGTON (off Rappahannock River, bounded by Carter Creek on the west and Eastern Branch on the east, Lancaster County). The 92nd Virginia Regiment under Lt. Col. John Chewning, Jr., repulsed a British landing at Chewning Point, on Carter Creek, April 4, 1813.

> The British landed at capt. [Lt. Col. John] Chowning's [Chewning, Jr.], robbed his plantation, took work oxen from the ploughs, pillaged the house, and broke open Mr. C's desk. (Alexandria *Gazette*, April 12, 1813)

On April 18 and April 22, 1814, the British again raided Carter Creek, causing heavy damage to private property including Corotoman.*

> On the 18th instant four British barges passed up the river to Carter's Creek, where they captured two schooners, one the "Felicity," belonging to that Creek and the other the "Antilope," Hughes, of Baltimore with 250 barrels of flour on board. They also took some sheep. It was Election and court day, of which they were supposed to be apprized, and they met no opposition.—On the 22d, . . . the same number of barges passed up to Carter's Creek, and took some negroes. They were fired at by five or six militia. (Baltimore *Patriot*, May 4, 1814)

The next day the British raided Windmill Point.*

Christ Church (southwest intersection of Christ Church [Route 646] and Gaskins roads, north of Irvington). In the

Westwood Mansion, shown here as it appeared in 1850s, was used by the British as a headquarters during their occupation of Hampton. (Lossing, *Pictorial Field-Book of the War of 1812*)

church museum is an exhibit that includes information on Corotoman, including artifacts and a drawing of how the plantation might have appeared.

Corotoman Plantation Site (Orchard Point at west entrance to Carter Creek, Weems). PRIVATE. Corotoman Plantation was owned by Robert "King" Carter. The plantation house, completed in 1725, burned in 1729. One surviving structure from the plantation stood until the 1970s. It had been plundered by the British on April 4, 1814. Only the foundation of the manor house, partially outlined by plantings, survives. On April 22, 1814, the British landed and removed sixty-nine slaves from the adjoining plantations of Joseph C. Cabell and Charles Carter.

JAMES RIVER (navigable from its mouth at Hampton Roads to Richmond). In April 1813, a group of escaped slaves seeking freedom rowed to a ship on the James River inquiring if it was British. The captain and crew of the American privateer reportedly said they were British, luring the slaves onboard. The slaves asked for arms to assist their comrades, who were planning a massacre of their masters. After divulging the details of this plan, the slaves were seized and incarcerated in the Williamsburg jail. What happened to them thereafter is unknown.

In July 1813, a British naval force ascended the James River and conducted a series of raids. (*See* the following listings for additional specific actions: Fort Boykin, Lawnes Creek, and Smithfield.)

> The [British] schooners proceeded up as high as Cabin-Point Creek, and sent ashore detachments of men at several seats on both sides of the river to plunder . . . and took off as many beeves as their barges would carry; others were landed at different points in Surry county, where they succeeded in laying the inhabitants under contribution for supplies of fresh provisions, and not content with that, they disfigured the houses, destroyed the furniture, and committed numberless excesses, unauthorized by the usages of civilized warfare. (Washington *Daily National Intelligencer,* July 9, 1813)

> We [British] landed in several places up James's river, and obtained supplies and intelligence, nightly, of what was going on in the neighbourhood . . . We very soon established an understanding with some of the inhabitants in the immediate vicinity of the river, who willingly met our views and cared for our safety when landed . . . Our means of security were afterwards greatly increased by the assistance of the negroes. (Capt. James Scott, 1834)[32]

After the Battle for Baltimore, the British fleet withdrew down the Chesapeake Bay to the James River, where it was met by an American schooner carrying the wounded British troops left behind at Bladensburg.*

> When we reached the James River, we anchored, and were joined by an American schooner bearing a flag of truce. She brought with her Colonel [William] Thornton, Lieut.-Colonel [William] Wood, with the rest of the officers and men who had been left behind at Bladensburg, Maryland. (Lt. George Robert Gleig, 1847)[33]

JONES POINT (Rappahannock River, end of Butylo Road, off Tidewater Trail [Route 17], Butylo, King and Queen County). While the main body of British troops operating on the Rappahannock were attacking militia at Farnham Church,* Capt. John Sheridan commanded a smaller British force in an attack on militia on the opposite side of the river at Jones Point. During the evening of December 6, 1814, two British deserters absconded with a barge and landed at Jones Point. They informed the militia that the British planned to attack Urbanna* next. Thirty-eight militiamen concealed themselves near the barge in hopes the British would try to retrieve the vessel. On the morning of December 7, 1814, several British barges approached and were ambushed by the militia. When more barges appeared, the militia, now low on ammunition, withdrew. Casualties from this engagement are unknown.

KINSALE. *See* Yeocomico

LAUREL BRANCH SITE. *See* Dinwiddie

LAWNES CREEK (James River, east side of Gravel Neck, forming the boundary between Surry and Isle of Wight counties). In June and July 1813, barges, brigs, and a schooner entered the James River, destroying several vessels and plundering the neighborhood. Off Lawnes Creek, July 6, 1813, a skirmish took place between the local militia and a British raiding party.

> Several of the enemy's vessels, in descending the river, came to, opposite the mouth of Lawn's Creek, in which there was several vessels; two of which they captured and burnt . . . one detachment [of militia] which moved down in the night, and yesterday morning early a warm engagement, for a short time, took place between the enemy and a few . . . militia, who had volunteered & crossed Lawn's Creek . . . About twenty-three or four, exclusive of officers, were opposed to seven barges and other vessels. One of the schooners being

aground, every effort was made by them to save her; and not withstanding the fire from one of their brigs and other vessels, they were compelled to set fire to her, and she was burnt —After which all the barges (seven in number) were compelled to retreat. During the engagement several of the enemy were seen to fall and one of them has floated on shore. The militia received no injury whatever. (Washington *Daily National Intelligencer,* July 16, 1813)

The enemy made no attempt to land but got the tender [schooner] aground, about two hundred yards below Lawn's creek. Twenty nine of our troops crossed the creek, and beat the enemy off from the tender; and the barges came from the brigs to their assistance. The enemy commenced a heavy fire from the brigs and boats on our men, but without effect. The enemy lost two killed and several wounded. At 11 A.M. the enemy set fire to the tender . . . and proceeded down the river. (Capt. Benedict to Mayor Thomas Wilson of Richmond via Lt. Col. John Hartwell Cocke, Washington *Daily National Intelligencer,* July 16, 1813)

LEESBURG (Loudoun County, northern Virginia). Although Leesburg was thirty-five miles from Washington, citizens there observed a shimmering red light over the city during the British occupation. Rumors circulated that the British had burned every building in the capital: "news reached us, that British vessels were ascending the Potomac . . . I was therefore compelled . . . to become a soldier. With hasty preparation I joined the march; and, the first night, lodged in a hay loft near Leesburg. From this point we saw the light of the burning capitol, which the British had fired the day before" (Pvt. John Leadley Dagg).[34]

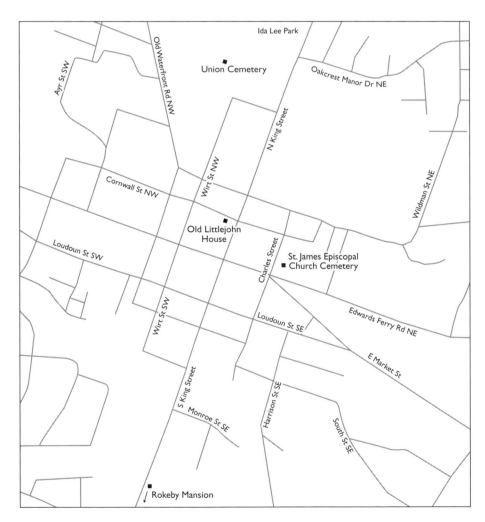

Leesburg

Old Littlejohn House (11 West Cornwall Street). NRHP. PRI-
VATE. When the British threatened the nation's capital,
twenty-two wagon loads of national documents, including
the Declaration of Independence, the Articles of Confederation, and the Constitution, much of George Washington's
correspondence, and many congressional and State Department records, were taken from Washington to Edgar
Patterson's abandoned gristmill on the Virginia side of
the Potomac River across from Columbian Foundry* near
Chain Bridge* at Pimmit Run. Because this location was
too near the foundry, a likely British target, the documents
were next moved to the Old Littlejohn House* and then to
Rokeby Mansion.*

Rokeby Mansion (west side of Gleedsville Road [Route 650],
1.0 mile south of intersection of King Street [U.S. Route 15],
south of Leesburg). NRHP. PRIVATE. Rokeby Mansion cannot be seen from the public road. Rokeby Mansion was built
in 1757 by Charles Binns II, first clerk of the circuit court of
Loudoun County. Binns probably stored court records here
in a fireproof basement room.

> I proceeded with them [documents] to the town of Lees-
> burg, a distance of 35 miles, at which place an empty house
> was procured, in which the papers were safely placed, the
> doors locked, and the keys given to the Rev. Mr. [John] Little-
> john, who was then, or had been, one of the collectors of the
> internal revenue. (Stephen Pleasonton to Brig. Gen. William
> H. Winder, August 7, 1814)[35]

Much of the original Georgian character of Rokeby Mansion was changed in 1836, when Benjamin Shreve, Jr., then
the owner, removed the clipped gables, remodeled the windows, and replaced the interior trim. The manor was enlarged in 1886 with a rear addition. The house was restored
to its original appearance in 1958.

LEWINSVILLE PRESBYTERIAN CHURCH. *See* listing, McLean

LOWER MACHODOC CREEK (off Potomac River, west side of
Coles Neck, Westmoreland County). On July 26, 1814, the
British conducted a raid on Lower Machodoc Creek, where
they burned six schooners and took a hundred head of cattle. Good views of the creek can be had along Tidewell Road
North and Tidewell Road South, off Erica Road (Route 626),
north off Cople Highway (Route 202).

> proceeded to the Head of the [Lower] Machodick River in Vir-
> ginia where I burnt Six Schooners, and the Marines having
> at the same time marched over the Country on the banks of

This brick arched storage chamber in the basement of Rokeby Mansion
is where some of the federal documents were ultimately housed until it
was deemed safe to return them to Washington. (Ralph Eshelman 2001
photograph)

that River without opposition. (Rear Adm. George Cockburn
to Vice Adm. Sir Alexander F. I. Cochrane, July 31, 1814)[36]

LYNNHAVEN BAY (near mouth of Chesapeake Bay, Virginia
Beach City). When the British referred to Lynnhaven Bay
they usually meant Lynnhaven Roads, which is the mouth
of the Chesapeake Bay north of Lynnhaven Bay. It was from
here that the British fleet operated its blockade of the mouth
of the Chesapeake Bay. Lynnhaven Bay served as an important anchorage for the Royal Navy throughout the war. Near
Lynnhaven in October 1813, a voluntary association of white
men attacked a group of escaped slaves seeking to join the
British, killing five or six and wounding others.[37]

> You are . . . to make a point of having always at least *two* Frig-
> ates in Lynnhaven Bay, as well the more effectually to secure
> the Blockade of that General Entrance, as to prevent as far
> as may be possible the practicability of the Enemy's Frigate
> [U.S. *Constellation*] now at Norfolk getting out to Sea unob-
> served. (Rear Adm. George Cockburn to Capt. John Clavell,
> December 13, 1814)[38]

Though the blockade was relatively effective, some
American privateers and warships slipped through.

> In spite of our utmost endeavours the Enemy's Clippers con-
> tinue to pass us every Northerly Wind. The Armide [H.M.
> frigate] chased one 120 miles going ten and eleven knots
> without being able to come up with her. (Captain Robert
> Barrie to Adm. Sir John B. Warren, November 14, 1813)[39]

None of our [British] vessels had yet ascended the bay: the enterprising inhabitants of Baltimore wisely took advantage of this circumstance, by sending their letters of marque and privateers down in the neighbourhood of New Point Comfort[*], there to wait for one of the severe northeast gales that frequently blow at that period of year. During the dark nights, six and eight at a time would endeavour to push by the squadron lying in Lynhaven Bay. Our sloops-of-war and frigates would slip on these occasions in chase; but, if the clippers succeeded in getting outside the Capes, they dispersed, and some were sure of escaping: it, however, frequently occurred that they ran aground on Cape Henry[*], and were of course destroyed by us . . . No less than four or five beautiful American clippers, from two hundred and fifty to three hundred tons, were lost one night inside Cape Henry. (Capt. James Scott, 1834)[40]

Pleasure House Site (near intersection of Lookout and Pleasure House roads, near the southern end of the Chesapeake Bay Bridge-Tunnel). Pleasure House was a popular tavern and place for entertainment: "It [Pleasure House] is a suitable lounge for Gamblers, tipplers, & those gentry of pleasure who love idleness, lack of discipline, & temporary convenience, in preference to their countries safety" (William Tatham to Governor James Barbour, May 17, 1812).[41]

After the *Chesapeake–Leopard* affair* off the Virginia Capes on June 22, 1807, William Tatham (1752–1819) was employed by President Thomas Jefferson to establish an observation post near Pleasure House to observe British activities at Lynnhaven Bay and the mouth of the Chesapeake Bay. During the War of 1812, the post was reactivated by February 1813 and an observation tower was constructed to increase the range of visibility from this strategic position. Virginia militia units were also stationed here.

Possibly as revenge for the capture of men at Cape Henry on a watering detail, a British force of between 100 and 150 troops landed at Lynnhaven Bay on September 21, 1813, and attacked the Pleasure House, which was defended by a militia company and 10 to 12 cavalry. The house and guard house were burned. So, too, apparently was an unnamed mansion at Church Point located at the north entrance to Thoroughgood Cove south of Pleasure House Creek.

It appears that the enemy were guided by some persons who was very well acquainted with the country, as his advance towards the house was extremely judicious, and rendered a retreat on our part very difficult. While one party proceeded along the shore in the rear of the house, another took a course through a field which led them into the lane in front—The centinels gave the alarm and Capt. [Richard L.] Lawson roused his few companions and formed them in order of battle, but it was impossible for him to make a stand the enemy pressing upon him in solid columns at two different points, threatening to overwhelm him by dint of numerical force, resistance was vain, and duty as well as prudence made it necessary for him to retreat. Of the detachment under Captain Lawson, only 27 were fit for duty; the troopers as they could not prepare them selves in time, were unable to render assistance—two of them had their horses killed under them. We lost 6 men, viz. 3 troopers and 3 infantry, who mistaking the enemy for their own party went in among them and were taken prisoners—There were none killed or wounded on either side. (Richmond *Virginia Argus,* September 27, 1813)

A flag of truce from the squadron came ashore at the Pleasure House on Friday to land prisoners. (Wilmington *American Watchman & Delaware Republican,* February 20, 1814)

Sailing Master Joseph Middleton, stationed at the Pleasure House observation post, reported on August 15, 1814, the arrival of a formidable British fleet consisting of at least twenty-two vessels coming into the Chesapeake Bay. Middleton immediately sent a dispatch by horseman to Norfolk. To the relief of the military and citizens of that city, the convey of ships sailed past Norfolk up the Chesapeake. Middleton could not have known that the troops being brought by this fleet would spearhead the invasion of Maryland and the capture of Washington.

MACCLESFIELD ESTATE SITE, also Macklesfield (intersection of Old Macklesfield Road and Macklesfield Court, south of Smithfield, near Carrollton, Isle of Wight County). A militia camp was located on the Macclesfield estate. Here was located the home of Col. Josiah Parker (1751–1810), hero of the Revolutionary War. Fearful of British hostilities beginning with the *Chesapeake–Leopard* affair of 1807, tradition claims that Colonel Parker was deliberately buried in the nearby family cemetery without a gravestone to protect his remains from possible British degradations.

MCLEAN (Fairfax County)

Benvenue (6800 Churchill Road [Route 687]). PRIVATE. This house was acquired by Com. Thomas Catesby Jones* in 1830. Jones reportedly named the house after the Louisiana plantation where he recovered from a wound received during an engagement at Lake Borgne prior to the Battle of New Orleans. Jones was captured and held prisoner at Bermuda until February 1815, when he was exchanged.

Lewinsville Presbyterian Church Cemetery (1724 Chain Bridge Road [Route 123]). This church began informal meetings in 1812 but was only officially established by Rev. William Maffitt with the guidance of Com. Thomas Catesby Jones (1790–1858) in 1846. Jones delayed the British at Lake Borgne prior to their attack on New Orleans in 1815. Commodore Jones returned the young deserter Herman Melville from the Sandwich Islands (Hawaii) to the United States in 1843. Melville modeled "Commodore J" after him in *Moby Dick*. His twin brother Roger (1780–1852) also served in the War of 1812 and later served as adjutant-general of the army from 1825 to 1852. Thomas's son Catesby Roger Jones commanded the *Virginia* (*Merrimac*) during its famous engagement with the *Monitor* in the Civil War. Reverend Maffitt owned Salona,* where President James Madison stayed after fleeing from Washington just before the British occupation.

Salona (private driveway at 1214 Buchanan Street, south off Dolley Madison Boulevard [Route 123]). NRHP. PRIVATE. Salona, built circa 1804 by Rev. William Maffitt (1739–1020), cannot be seen from a public road. President Madison spent the night of August 24, 1814, here after first stopping at Minor Hill* and Wren's Tavern,* while Dolley stayed at nearby Rokeby Farm,* home of her friends Richard and Matilda Lee Love.

MATTOX CREEK (off Potomac River, just below Colonial Beach, Westmoreland County). A small British schooner supported by barges entered Mattox Creek on July 19, 1813, but withdrew after firing on a company of light infantry under the command of Capt. Henry Hungerford. Mattox Creek can be seen from the James Monroe Highway (Route 205) bridge.

MINOR HILL. *See* listing, Falls Church

MONROE, JAMES, BIRTHPLACE SITE (James Monroe Highway [Route 205], Monroe Hall, southwest of Colonial Beach, Westmoreland County). The house in which James Monroe was born and raised is no longer standing but there is an effort to establish the James Monroe Birthplace Park, which will include a reconstruction of the Monroe family home, outbuildings, and visitor center. Monroe served as secretaries of state and war during the War of 1812.

MONTEBELLO (Spottswood Trail [Route 33], 3.0 miles west of Gordonsville, Orange County). PRIVATE. Zachary Taylor, a veteran of the War of 1812 , is best known for his fighting during the Mexican War and serving as the twelfth president of the United States. Taylor was born at Montebello on November 24, 1784; however, there is some dispute over which house on this property he was born in. During the War of 1812, Taylor gained a reputation as a talented military commander. As commander of Fort Harrison on the Wabash River, near present-day Terre Haute, Indiana, he successfully defended against a British-inspired attack by about five hundred Native Americans on September 4–16, 1812. The defense of Fort Harrison has been called the first American land victory of the War of 1812. For his effort, Taylor was brevetted to major on October 31, 1812.

MONTICELLO (931 Thomas Jefferson Parkway, Charlottesville, Albemarle County). The Petersburg U.S. Volunteers* stopped at Monticello in the fall of 1812 on their way to Fort Meigs, Ohio. Accounts, such as those in the Richmond *Enquirer, November 20, 1812, and the Niles' Weekly Register,* November 28, 1812, claim the entire company was entertained by Thomas Jefferson. However, other accounts (notably the Federalist Richmond *Virginia Patriot,* December 8, 1812, and September 21, 1813) differ.

> We drew up, in military array, at the base of the hill on which the great house [Monticello] was erected. About half way down the hill stood a very homely old man, dressed in plain Virginia cloth, his head uncovered, and his venerable locks flowing in the wind . . . But how we were astonished when he advanced to our officers and introduced himself as Thomas Jefferson! The officers were invited in to a collation, while we were marched off to the town, where more abundant provisions had been made. (Alfred M. Lorrain, 1862)[42]

> As a singular instance of the small reliance that can be put . . . on newspaper paragraphs I here subscribe an extract from my son's letter, who joined the Petersburg Volunteers . . . we . . . went three miles out of our way to gratify Mr. Jefferson's curiosity; and our expectations were highly raised, for we all expected to see and partake of every thing the house could afford, as having met the most bountiful treatment elsewhere; but we were all disappointed and horrified; though hungry, thirsty and tired, we got neither meat nor drink; not even water. We had a distance view of Mr. Jefferson and house. (Richmond *Virginia Patriot,* December 8, 1812)

> Jefferson sent them away without help, insulting them horrendously. This, while he keeps some British prisoners of

war at his house as they eat and carouse free and far from war. (Richmond *Virginia Patriot,* September 21, 1813)

Uriah Phillips Levy (1792–1862) owned Monticello from 1834 to 1863. Although court-martialed six times and dismissed from the U.S. Navy three times, he became the navy's first Jewish captain and later its first Jewish commodore. During the War of 1812, Levy served as a supernumerary sailing master on the 18-gun U.S. brig *Argus.* The *Argus* captured or destroyed at least fifteen British ships. Levy was placed in command of the prize merchant-ship *Betsey,* but this vessel was captured by H.M. sloop-of-war *Pelican* the next day. Levy spent the next sixteen months in Dartmoor Prison. He abolished flogging in the U.S. Navy, which led to the approval of a congressional anti-flogging bill in 1850. An admirer of Thomas Jefferson, Levy purchased Monticello eight years after Jefferson's death, refurbishing it and even increasing its acreage. Years before Mount Vernon was restored, Levy can be credited with saving Monticello; he was possibly "the first American to act upon the idea of preserving a historic dwelling."[43] A bronze statue of Thomas Jefferson located in the rotunda of the U.S. Capitol* was presented by Uriah Levy. This is the only privately funded statue in the Capitol. The Jewish Chapel at the U.S. Naval Academy that opened in 2005 is named for Uriah Levy.

MONTPELIER (11407 Constitution Highway [Route 20], Montpelier Station, Orange County). Here lived and were buried James and Dorothea (Dolley) Madison.* President Madison* served as the fourth president of the United States and chief executive throughout the War of 1812. Dolley Payne Madison* was responsible for saving important state papers and the portrait of George Washington from certain burning by the British. The gravestone for President Madison was erected in 1856 and that for Dolley about 1858. On the grounds of Montpelier was Bloomingdale the boyhood home of Governor James Barbour.*

MOUNT PLEASANT (James River, Swanns Point, off Swanns Point Road [Route 610], Surry County). PRIVATE. Nicholas Faulcon and his wife Polly bought Mount Pleasant in 1808 from Col. John Hartwell Cocke, brother of Polley. Colonel Cocke served in the Virginia militia, which was activated for federal service during the War of 1812 for the invasion of Canada. He also commanded camps Holly Springs* and Malvern Hill* beginning in May until about July 1813, when Richmond was no longer threatened by attack. In a British raid on June 29, 1813, the plantation suffered considerable damage, including smashed windows, doors, and furniture. Some accounts claim escaped slaves from the plantation played a role in the raid, possibly as Colonial Marines. While Faulcon suspected that his neighbor's slaves may have aided the British, it is unlikely slaves participated in the actual raid. This was very early in the war for runaway slaves to have been organized by the British as part of their raiding parties. The Battle of Pungoteague* on May 30, 1814, is regarded as the first use of trained slaves in combat by the British. In a letter to his brother-in-law on July 24, 1813, Faulcon wrote his slaves told him that the house would be totally destroyed if they did not supply the English with geese, chickens, and the like.

Destruction of Mr. Faulcon's property at Mt. Pleasant extensive. 35 sheep taken; slave aided no doubt . . . British deserted by name of Dodd said they had come up for water and provisions. (Richmond *Enquirer,* July 6, 1813)

MOUNT VERNON (Potomac River, south end of George Washington Memorial Parkway, Fairfax County). At 5:00 p.m., August 26, 1814, British warships ascended the Potomac to Alexandria, passing Mount Vernon, home of George Washington. Each ship lowered its foretopsails in salute and bands played Washington's march.[44]

Mount Vernon,—the retreat of the illustrious Washington,—opened to our view, and showed us, for the first time since we entered the Potomac, a gentleman's residence. (Capt. Charles Napier, August 26, 1814)[45]

The British squadron assembled near here in preparation for descending the Potomac and passing the White House* and Indian Head* gun batteries.

The British squadron (assembled at Mr. Marshall's Point [Maryland side] and a little below Mount Vernon) began to move downwards about two o'clock on Monday at the pitch of high tide and a most favorable fresh wind at N.E. The preceding ship was the Commodore [Capt. Charles Gordon] in the Sea Horse frigate of 38 guns with the first division of the prize craft. (Boston *Weekly Messenger,* September 16, 1814)

MUNDY POINT. *See* Yeocomico River

NANESMOND RIVER (off James River, Suffolk City).

Hills Point Fort Site (west side of Nanesmond River, Brock Point, near Reids Ferry). A gun battery was located here to protect the town of Suffolk from possible water attack up the Nanesmond River.

Pembroke (Pembroke Lane, east off Goodwin Boulevard [U.S. Route 10]). This early eighteenth-century five-bay house is reported to have been attacked and the interior burned during a British raid, but little is known about this incident.

NATIONAL MUSEUM OF THE MARINE CORPS (18900 Jefferson Davis Highway, Triangle, Prince William County). Part of the Marine Crops Heritage Center, this museum has presently only a few exhibits that deal with the War of 1812, although a future gallery, to be called "From the Halls of Montezuma: 1775–1865," will include more coverage on the role the Marine Corps played in the war. Even now, some information can be gleamed from the timeline exhibit. An 1810 shako (tar bucket type hat) plate marked "MARINES" is on display.

NEW POINT COMFORT (north confluence of Mobjack Bay with Chesapeake Bay, end of Lighthouse Road [Route 600], south off New Comfort Highway [Route 14], Matthews County). On the boardwalk of the New Point Comfort Natural Preserve Area are interpretive panels telling the history of the region and presenting some details on the War of 1812. The boardwalk also provides excellent views of the area. The New Point Comfort Lighthouse, completed in 1804, was apparently used by the British as a lookout station. American privateers stood near New Point Comfort waiting for severe weather to run the British blockade at the mouth of the Chesapeake Bay (*see* Lynnhaven Bay).

New Point Comfort was one of many watering places used by the British. Others include St. Catherine Island,* St. Clement Island,* St. George Island,* Drum Point,* and Kent Island,* all in Maryland, and Cape Henry* in Virginia.

> I am in great Hope that we shall find enough [water on islands in the Middle Chesapeake] by digging a number of Wells, and if they should at any time fail us unexpectedly, our Watering place at New Point Comfort is so near as to make this a matter of less moment. (Rear Adm. George Cockburn to Vice Adm. Sir Alexander F. I. Cochrane, April 2, 1814)[46]

> Wells were sunk near the light-house, and a plentiful supply obtained; we were only reminded of the enemy's presence by an occasional shot from his field-pieces, whenever he fancied a boat within reach of them. (Capt. James Scott, 1834)[47]

On March 17, 1814, a skirmish between about fifty British troops and Virginia militia took place.

> near New Point Comfort . . . had the pleasure of seeing one of the handsomest skirmishes I ever witnessed . . . The fire commenced equally severe on both sides for about fifteen minutes, when the enemy was compelled to take shelter under the cover of some sand hills. At this moment a barge came to their assistance and commenced a fire from a 12 pound cannon, which was returned from a concealed six; which was continued with great warmth for a few minutes, when she had to make the best of her way to the beach, being in a sinking condition, having several shot through her . . . although . . . his [Capt. Frederick Weedon] horse shot down . . . we lost not a man. (Richard *Virginia Patriot,* March 30, 1814)[48]

The British burned the lighthouse keeper's dwelling and oil vault, shattered the lantern glass, and removed the window frames and door from the tower.

NEWPORT NEWS (James River, northwest of Norfolk)

Mariners' Museum (100 Museum Drive, south off J. Clyde Morris Blvd. [Avenue of the Arts], south off Warwick Boulevard [Route 312]). Among the exhibits is an anchor from H.M. troop-ship *Dictator* recovered from the Patuxent River in the 1950s. *Dictator* was one of the transport ships that took part in the British invasion of Maryland in August 1814. The anchor is the Chesapeake Bay Gallery.

Virginia War Museum (9285 Warwick Boulevard). Among the War of 1812 artifacts on exhibit here are the uniform of Greenleaf Dearborn, an officer during the war; a circa 1878 oil painting depicting the Battle of Lake Erie; a circa 1812 guard officer's coatee worn by Moses Myers (1752–1835), active in the Norfolk Junior Volunteers; circa 1812 knee breeches and trousers wore by members of the Myers family; and a wooden canteen used by George Schrader of Norfolk during the war.

NOMINI CREEK, Nomini Ferry (off Potomac River, west of Lower Machodoc Creek, and east of Popes Creek, Westmoreland County). The British received intelligence in July 1814 that a unit of militia with field artillery, stores, and vessels had assembled at Nomini Ferry on Nomini Creek. At noon on July 20, three divisions of British boats proceeded to Nomini Ferry but H.M. sloop-of-war *Thistle* and its tenders were unable to provide support because the creek was too shallow. A small British force was landed by barge on the militia's flank, while the main force landed at the wharf.

his Knowledge of the Country and his advantage in Cavalry enabled him to baffle all my endeavors to bring him to Action, though I succeeded in overtaking a few of his Stragglers in the Woods and in making them Prisoners, after following him therefore into the Country between four and five Miles. (Rear Adm. George Cockburn to Vice Adm. Sir Alexander F. I. Cochrane, July 21, 1814)[49]

The British spent the night at Nomini Ferry and left the next morning, taking tobacco and cattle and destroying storehouses and buildings. While descending the creek, the British saw movement along the shore.

scarcely had we landed here before a heavy Volley of musquettry was discharged at us by the Enemy, but the advance Guard of Marines dashing into the woods after them, soon dispersed them and I saw no more of them, Every thing in this neighbourhood was therefore all destroyed or brought off. (Rear Adm. George Cockburn to Vice Adm. Sir Alexander F. I. Cochrane, July 21, 1814)[50]

The militiamen claimed that they hid their field artillery in the woods, while the British insisted that it was simply abandoned. The British freed about 135 slaves, seized a schooner, a large ferry, and fifty hogsheads of tobacco, and took two American prisoners. British casualties were one killed and four wounded; American casualties are unknown.

Soon after landing at Nomini Ferry, a British officer discovered at the house of a Mrs. Thompson spirits set out with glasses all around. Fear of poisoning, however, kept the British from sampling the whiskey.

The house . . . had evidently been their headquarters . . . The . . . largest room on the ground floor appeared as if it had been the scene of a carousing party, from the number of glasses, bottles of liquour, &c. that graced the whole length of the table . . . I fortunately observed that the glasses had not been used, and the full bottles created a painful suspicion that the wine and liquor might be poisoned, which, but for the recent transaction at Benedict [Maryland], would not have crossed my mind . . . sent to the surgeon of the [H.M. ship-of-the-line] Albion for examination, and found to contain a very large quantity of arsenic. (Capt. James Scott, 1834)[51]

While Lt. James Scott claims arsenic was discovered in at least one bottle, contemporary reports do not confirm this statement. Lt. Col. Richard E. Parker of the American militia claims he "had drunk of the spirits but a few moments before the British came up, and that it was impossible it could have been poisoned."[52]

A second British raid occurred on October 4, 1814, when a battalion of Royal Marines again landed at Nomini Bay at the mouth of Nomini Creek. This was part of an effort to locate militia rumored to be in the area. Simultaneously, another contingent of troops landed at Coan River to attack Northumberland Court House.*

Nomini Church, also called Nomini Episcopal Church, then called Mount Holly Church (3589 Cople Highway [Route 202]). This brick church, built circa 1852, replaced an earlier church constructed on the opposite side of Nomini Creek called Mount Holly Church. The British absconded with the communion silver service during their raid here July 21, 1814 (see Lower Machodoc Creek). The original site is private property. Good views of Nomini Creek can be had from the Route 202 bridge.

NORFOLK (east side of confluence of Elizabeth and James rivers). Off the Virginia capes on June 22, 1807, occurred the famous *Chesapeake–Leopard* affair.* H.M. frigate *Leopard* hailed U.S. frigate *Chesapeake* and insisted it muster its crew. Com. James Barron,* commander of the *Chesapeake,* refused, whereupon the British opened fire, killing three Americans and wounding eighteen others, including Commodore Barron. After firing only one shot, *Chesapeake* struck its colors. Four crewmen from the *Chesapeake* were accused of being British deserters and taken prisoner. The *Chesapeake* sailed back to Norfolk with its mortified officers and crew. A public meeting was held in Norfolk, and it was resolved that no intercourse of any kind was to be had with the British squadron then in the area; thus no pilots or water were to be provided and no supplies were to be sold to any British ships.

Citizens donated a fund for the families of the men who had been killed. Robert McDonald, one of the wounded sailors, died on June 27, 1807, bringing the death toll in this incident to four. In the harbor the American vessels displayed their colors at half mast, while artillery fired from shore. An estimated four thousand citizens gathered on Market Square and formed a long procession, which marched to the beat of muffled drums to the First Christ Church on Church Street.

As news of the *Chesapeake–Leopard* affair spread, Americans everywhere became outraged. A mob destroyed British naval property in Norfolk. The mob spared the British Consul Col. John Hamilton's residence* only because of his personal popularity. Similarly, the British consul's house in New York City needed to be protected. Governor William

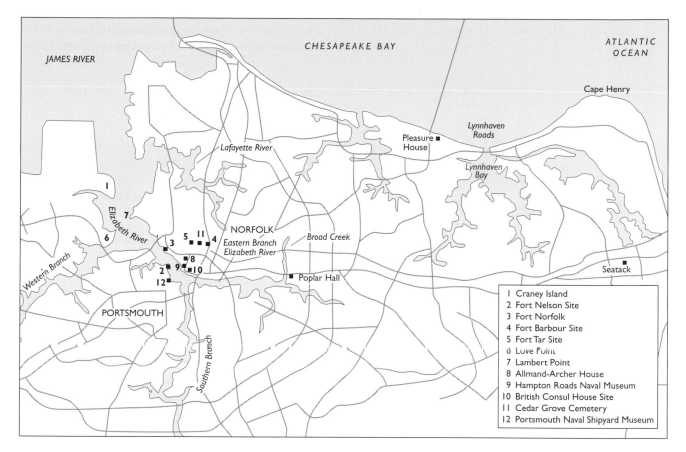

Norfolk and Portsmouth Region

Map legend:
1. Craney Island
2. Fort Nelson Site
3. Fort Norfolk
4. Fort Barbour Site
5. Fort Tar Site
6. Love Point
7. Lambert Point
8. Allmand-Archer House
9. Hampton Roads Naval Museum
10. British Consul House Site
11. Cedar Grove Cemetery
12. Portsmouth Naval Shipyard Museum

H. Cabell ordered detachments of militia to the Hampton Roads area to prepare for a possible British attack. Although the British formally apologized for the incident in 1811, emotions ran high, fueling the war movement.

On February 3, 1813, upon approaching the mouth of the Chesapeake Bay, U.S. frigate *Constellation,* under command of Capt. Charles Stewart, sighted a British squadron. Captain Stewart wisely sought the protection of forts Norfolk and Nelson, which defended Norfolk, Portsmouth, and the Gosport Navy Yard. Although now blockaded in the river for the duration of the war, the *Constellation* was an added enticement for the British to attack Norfolk, but *Constellation* also provided additional men and cannon for protection.

> Stood out to Sea, but when off Cape Henry were chased back by four British frigates. Ran up and moored the frigate [*Constellation*] between forts Norfolk & Nelson in Elizabeth River for the defences of Norfolk, being blockaded by the British Squadron. (Capt. George de la Roche, February 3, 1813)[53]

> From the first I was desirous of avoiding this place [Hampton Roads], satisfied that our chance of getting to sea, would be rendered difficult, as the Enemy possesses, no doubt, the earliest information from their Agents here. We had not been twenty fours in the [Hampton] Roads before they were apprised of it. (Capt. Charles Stewart to Secretary of Navy William Jones, February 5, 1813)[54]

On February 8, 1813, the Baltimore letter-of-marque, *Lottery,* under the command of Capt. John Southcomb, sailed for the Atlantic bound for Bordeaux with sugar, coffee, and logwood. A lookout onboard the H.M. frigate *Maidstone* sighted the schooner. A two hundred-man British force in nine boats led by Lt. Kelly Nazer intercepted *Lottery,* which first attempted to flee but when overtaken defended itself with its six 12 pounder cannon and later by hand-to-hand combat. *Lottery* ultimately succumbed to superior numbers. Captain Southcomb died of his wounds, and nineteen of his twenty-eight crew were either killed or wounded. The

British suffered thirteen casualties. *Lottery* became the first Royal Navy prize taken in the Chesapeake. On February 16, 1813, the British fired minute-guns (cannons fired every minute as signal of distress or mourning) in salute to the gallant Captain Southcomb as he was being transferred to shore for burial. The British blockade of the Chesapeake had begun in earnest.

The British attempted a barge attack on U.S. frigate *Constellation* on March 20, 1813, during ebb tide when the frigate's stern would be facing downriver. British barges heading toward the frigate got within two miles before strong contrary winds forced them to withdraw. Still, two pilot schooners, manned by *Constellation*'s crew, were captured off Cape Henry* and later used as British tenders.

To protect Norfolk, Portsmouth, Gosport Navy Yard, and the U.S. frigate *Constellation,* forts Barbour,* Nelson,* Norfolk,* and Tar* were placed on alert and blockships (hulks) were sunk in the Elizabeth River channel off Lamberts Point.*

the town [Norfolk] embraces two peninsulas, one lying on the [Elizabeth] river varying in breadth from three to six hundred yards, a [Smiths] creek makes up on the east & one [Newtons Creek] on the west; which approach each other within 400 yard. The neck of land between theses creeks unites it to the outer and larger peninsula. Our line of defence to protect the town must necessarily be on the neck of the outer peninsula, which is much larger and less secured

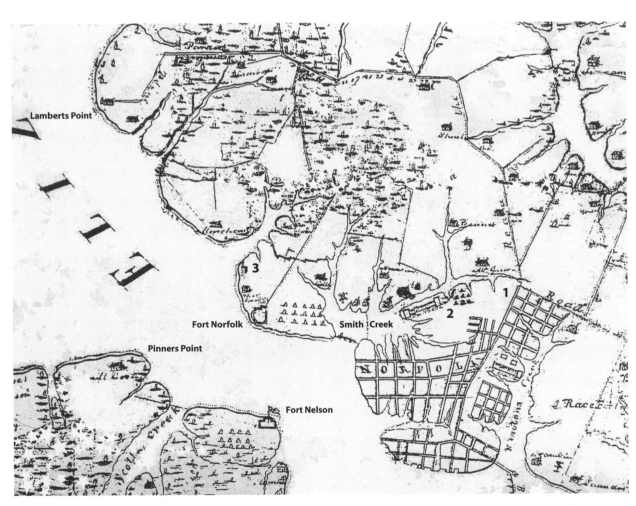

Sketch map circa 1813 showing the location of forts Nelson and Norfolk and adjacent encampments (designated by tents) on Elizabeth River. Key: 1. Fort Barbour. 2. Earthwork and encampment near at Fort Tar. 3. Earthwork near Fort Norfolk. Some labeling added for clarity. (Detail of

"Map of the Country contiguous to Norfolk Taken by actual Survey under the direction of Brigadier Gen'l Robt. B. Taylor"; National Archives and Records Administration)

by nature than the other. (Brig. Gen. Robert B. Taylor to Secretary of War John Armstrong, March 21, 1813)[55]

Our port is so completely blockaded, that nothing can go in or out. Three ships of the line and two frigates are in Hampton Roads and their boats are constantly in motion. The Constellation and the gunboats are now between our forts. Our channel has been obstructed by sinking three vessels; two more will be sunk, and then no vessel can pass drawing more than 16 feet.—We feel no apprehension of an attack on our harbor by ships. The enemy might attempt to and in the night and assail our forts; which is the only possible way of annoying us at present—and it would not find expedient at least until the talked of brigade of marines arrive from England. (Anonymous, March 18, 1813; reprinted in Baltimore *Patriot,* March 22, 1813)

The Chesapeake Blockading Squadron . . . about eleven sail of British ships had arrived at the mouth of Black River [Back River?]; and that the residue were in sight. He expresses his fears that all communication with Norfolk would be cut off. The whole number of the British vessels in the Chesapeake are about 30—the troops including marines, about 2500. (Massachusetts *Spy* [Worcester *Gazette*] September 15, 1813)

About 4:00 a.m., on June 20, 1813, the becalmed H.M. frigate *Junon* at the mouth of the Elizabeth River, with no other British ships within three miles of it, was attacked by fifteen American gunboats under the command of Capt. Joseph Tarbell. Without a breeze the *Junon* was at the mercy of the gunboat flotilla, which pummeled it for about forty-five minutes before a breeze allowed the frigate to get underway. When the wind picked up, the H.M. frigate *Barossa* and H.M. frigate *Laurestinus* came to the aid of *Junon,* forcing Captain Tarbell to withdraw from the action. American casualties were one killed (Master's Mate Thomas Allison) and six wounded. The Americans also had two boats damaged. British casualties consisted of one killed and three wounded.

American account of action: the Flotilla commenced a heavy gawling fire on a Frigate [*Junon*] at about three quarters of a mile distance . . . the frigate . . . was certainly very severely handled for I heard the Shot distinctly strike her . . . Our loss is very trifling Mr. [Thomas] Allinson Masters Mate . . . kill'd . . . by an Eighteen pound ball which past through him & lodged in the Mast . . . two men slightly injured by splinters. (Capt. John Cassin to Secretary of Navy William Jones, June 21, 1813)[56]

British account of action: our loss is one Marine killed and three Seamen wounded, and one Seaman killed by the ex-

ploding of a Gun after the Enemy withdrew, Several shot in our hull and some of the standing and running rigger cut. (Capt. James Sanders to Rear Adm. George Cockburn, June 20, 1813)[57]

Tradition holds that in Norfolk on April 4, 1816, at a testimonial dinner held in his honor, after his triumphant return from the Barbary States, Com. Stephen Decatur said, "Our country! In her intercourse with foreign nations, may she always be in the right, but our country right or wrong." But, according to the Norfolk *American Beacon,* April 5, 1816, and the Norfolk *Gazette & Public Ledger,* April 6, 1816, Decatur said: "Our country! In her intercourse with foreign nations, may she always be in the right, and always successful, right or wrong." After dinner and numerous toasts the guests sang a two-verse song written especially for the occasion to the tune "To Anacreon in Heaven," the same melody used by Francis Scott Key for "The Star-Spangled Banner."

Allmand-Archer House (327 Duke Street). NRHP. PRIVATE.
The Allmand-Archer House, said to be the oldest standing house in Norfolk, was built in the 1790s by Matthew Heary, who sold it in 1802 to Harrison Allmand, a Norfolk merchant who was known as "Old Gold Dust" because of his great wealth. The Allmand-Archer House served as the headquarters for the American forces during the War of 1812.

British Consul House Site (118 Main Street). Here lived British Consul Col. John Hamilton, whose house was saved from destruction by an angry mob only by his popularity after the *Chesapeake–Leopard* affair* on June 22, 1807. The structure was demolished during city development in the twentieth century. It is now occupied by TownPoint Garage.

Fort Barbour Site (near intersection of Princess Anne Road and Church Street). This earthen redoubt was east of Church Street and south of Princess Anne Road, and in consort with Fort Tar,* both connected by breastworks, defended against a possible land attack from the north and east. Fort Barbour is named after James Barbour, the war governor of Virginia.

The Town of Norfolk is made a peninsula by Smith's Creek on the one hand and Newton's creek on the other. The heads of these creeks are distance about 60 yards and the intermediate space is partly occupied by a line of entrenchments called Fort Barbour. (Capt. Sylvanus Thayer to Brevet Brig. Gen. Moses Porter, May 16, 1814)[58]

British Consul House in Norfolk as it appeared in 1865. (Lossing, *Pictorial Field-Book of the War of 1812*)

Fort Norfolk (Elizabeth River, 803 Front Street). NRHP. This important War of 1812-era fort is occupied by the U.S. Army Corps of Engineers. Tours can be arranged through the Norfolk Historical Society. Forts Norfolk and Nelson* were located at "The Narrows" on the Elizabeth River and served as the second line of defense after Craney Island.* Like Fort Nelson on the west side of the river, Fort Norfolk was originally constructed during the Revolutionary War. The present asymmetrical and oddly shaped Fort Norfolk, with two bastions, was begun as part of a national defense effort in 1794. The *Chesapeake–Leopard* affair* in the Atlantic off Cape Henry* on June 22, 1807, caused the citizens and military to upgrade the fort, and by July 1808 it was reported to be "in excellent order" and mounted nine 18 pounder cannon. It mounted twenty-seven 24 pounder and two 9 pounder cannon in March 1813. Fort Norfolk is one of the best preserved examples of pre-1812 fortifications to survive largely unchanged.

Fort Tar Site (Fort Tar Lane, northwest off Saint Pauls Boulevard, north of intersection with Virginia Beach Boulevard). This fort, a small earthen redoubt, was located south of Armistead's Bridge over Glebe Creek. In consort with Fort Barbour,* both connected by breastworks, defended against a possible land attack from the east.

Hampton Roads Naval Museum (second floor of Nauticus, One Waterside Drive). This excellent museum has a small War of 1812 exhibit that includes a model of U.S. gunboat *No. 135*, which was employed in the Elizabeth River during the Battle of Craney Island.* A second gunboat model, *No. 2*, was designed by Com. James Barron.* Also on display is a piece of wood from the U.S. frigate *Chesapeake*, which was captured by H.M. frigate *Shannon* after mortally wounded Capt. James Lawrence supposedly uttered the words, "Don't give up the ship." Taken as a prize to England, *Chesapeake* was broken up in 1820, and its timbers were used to build a mill that still stands in Wickham. This *Chesapeake* wood fragment was obtained from that mill.

Lamberts Point (Elizabeth River, Lamberts Point Terminal). No public access. Lamberts Point was 2,500 yards distant across the Elizabeth River from Craney Island* and made a good cross fire position. Just off shore of the point vessels were sunk to keep British warships from approaching Norfolk. Gunboats were arranged in a semicircle between Lamberts Point and Craney Island to further protect the city and U.S. frigate *Constellation*. A four-gun battery at Lamberts Point could control the Elizabeth River channel that bends around it, compelling ships to remain for some time under the fire of this position. Many troops, including the 35th U.S. Infantry and militia, were stationed here.

Poplar Hall (Broad Creek, 400 Stuart Circle, west end of Poplar Hall Drive, west off Military Highway [U.S. Route 13]). NRHP. PRIVATE. Poplar Hall was built by Thurmer Hoggard between 1761 and 1767. During 1813, three unfinished vessels being built at Hoggard's shipyard on Broad Creek were burned and Poplar Hall broken into.

OAK HILL (James Monroe Highway [U.S. Route 15], 2.0 miles north of Gilberts Corner intersection with John Mosby Highway [U.S. Route 59], Loudoun County). PRIVATE. Only distant views of the house can be seen from the highway. James Monroe (1758–1831), the fifth president of the United States, began the construction of Oak Hill between 1820 and 1823 and lived here following his presidency until 1830, the year before he died. Monroe's wife and daughter were buried here until re-interred near his grave at Hollywood Cemetery,* Richmond.

OLD POINT COMFORT LIGHTHOUSE. *See* Hampton

ONANCOCK (head of Onancock Creek, Market Street [Route 179], west off Charles Lankford Memorial Highway [U.S. Route 13], Accomac County). In consequence of the British establishment of a base on Tangier Island,* a militia camp was established here as well as at Chesconessex* and Pungoteaque* creeks. At 7:00 a.m. on May 30, 1814, a small British force appeared at the mouth of Onancock Creek. Some accounts claim the British barges had become lost during the night while others claim they were a diversion for a larger attack on nearby Pungoteague* Creek. Regardless, the brief cannon exchange caused Lt. Col. Thomas M. Bayly, commander of 2nd Virginia Regiment, to rush to Onancock only to discover the enemy had withdrawn and were now entering Pungoteague Creek.*

On or about August 12, 1814, the British again planned to attack Onancock with a force of some two thousand troops. Lieutenant Colonel Bayly set up his headquarters in Onancock and assembled as many militiamen as he could. Only a 4 pounder brass cannon was available as two other 4 pounder cannon had already been captured at Pungoteaque and Chesconessex.* The British approached Onancock by barge about 2:00 a.m. While the militia heard their oars they never saw them. For some unexplained reason, possibly a warning that the militia were prepared for their attack, the British returned to their ships without landing.

ORGAN CAVE (417 Masters Road [Route 63], south of Roncevorte, Greenbrier County, West Virginia). Organ Cave preserves an impressive thirty-seven saltpetre leaching hoppers, including fragments of at least three that date from the War of 1812. The remaining are from the Civil War period. Saltpetre (potassium nitrate) was used in the making of gunpowder and may have been mined here as early as the American Revolution. The date 1704 is inscribed on the wall in a saltpetre-producing area of the cave. During the War of 1812, the market price for saltpetre was between 75 cents and $1.00 per pound, making good nitre caves extremely valuable. An estimated 250 caves in the United States were mined during the Revolution, the War of 1812, and the Civil War. During the War of 1812, saltpetre was mined from caves in Indiana, Kentucky, Tennessee, and Virginia (including present-day West Virginia). Mammoth Cave, Kentucky, is perhaps the best known.[59] It is unclear how many Maryland and Virginia caves were mined for saltpetre during the War of 1812, although Thomas Jefferson mentions that there were several caves in Virginia with saltpetre

potential.[60] However, the following Virginia caves in addition to Organ Cave are believed to have been mined during the War of 1812: Haynes Cave, Monroe County; Trout Cave and/or New Trout Cave, Pendleton County (both now West Virginia); Madison Cave, Augusta County; and an unnamed cave near Natural Bridge, Rockbridge County, Virginia. Grand Caverns, Augusta County, has been open to the public sporadically since 1806 and legend holds it was mined during the War of 1812, but no documentary evidence supporting this claim has been found.

Organ Cave is open for public tours, but the "1812 Room" can only be visited by making a strenuous guided "wild cave" tour, which involves much crawling. Only fragments of the original 1812 saltpetre hoppers survive. However, Civil War-era hoppers in excellent condition and on display on the public tour give one an idea of what the 1812 hoppers might have looked like. The name Henry Cadiz is inscribed on the walls about 0.5 mile beyond the "1812 Room." Cadiz is believed to have contracted with E. I. du Pont to supply saltpetre for making gunpowder. Tradition holds that the saltpetre was dragged by sled to the entrance of the cave and then shipped to nearby Union. From here it was probably transported to E. I. du Pont's Gunpowder Company*

Fort Norfolk as it appeared in 1853. (Lossing, *Pictorial Field-Book of the War of 1812*)

near Wilmington,* Delaware, where gunpowder was made and then shipped to places like Fort McHenry.*

PAGAN CREEK. *See* Smithfield

PETERSBURG (Appomattox River, northeast Dinwiddie County). The Petersburg Volunteers fought at Fort Meigs, Ohio, in 1813. This U.S. Volunteer unit was raised under an act of February 1812. A public meeting was held at the courthouse on September 8, 1812, and a committee of eleven was appointed to raise funds by public subscription to finance the creation of the unit. A resolution was adopted:

> That the town of Petersburg will ever hold in high remembrance those Noble & Patriotic young men, who, unmindful of every other consideration, save love of country, have volunteered their services to retrieve the reputation of the republic, so shamefully, ignominiously and disgracefully sullied by the imbecile (if not treacherous) conduct of General [William] Hull" [referring to Brigadier General Hull, commander of the "North Western Army," who was bluffed into surrendering Detroit, August 16, 1812]. (Richmond *Virginia Argus,* September 17, 1812)

The Volunteers were described as "not the dregs of society, culled from the by-lanes & alleys of the town; but of the flower of our youth and the best blood of our country . . . they have left the caresses of friends, and the soft repose of their private life, to treat the snows of Canada and the inhospitable wilds of the Savage" (Richmond *Virginia Argus,* October 12, 1812).

On October 21, 1812, the Volunteers assembled at Centre Hill (the old historic section of Petersburg on the hill above the Appomattox River near Courthouse Avenue and Adams Street). There Benjamin Watkins Leigh* presented a flag made by the "fair hands" (women) of Petersburg. En route to Canada via Richmond, they were followed by carriages filled with ladies. The Volunteers marched down Sycamore Street and across the Pocahontas Bridge over the Appomattox River, where a small cannon saluted them from a schooner. They were present at the siege of Fort Meigs in May and June 1813 and remained in service until October 1813.

Petersburg is reputed to have been named "The Cockade City of the Union" by President James Madison when the Petersburg Volunteers visited Washington during their return from Fort Meigs, Ohio, where they had distinguished themselves in 1813. Their leather cockade hats supposedly prompted President Madison to make the statement. In reality the Petersburg Volunteers returned in several groups, taking many different routes to Petersburg, although some

soldiers may have stopped in Washington. The sobriquet may have been conferred when Capt. Richard McRae, the unit's commander, visited Washington in July 1814. However, the appellation "The Cockade of the Union" seems to have first appeared in a toast on July 4, 1838, and then showed up several times in the press between 1843 and 1848. The term "The Cockade City" does not appear until after 1850. The Cockade Monument, also known as the Petersburg Volunteers Monument, is inscribed "Cockade City of the Union," but it was not erected until 1857. Thus it is unclear who coined the phrase or when it was first used.

Just within the southern city limits of Petersburg near the intersection of Crater Road South (U.S. 301) and Rives Road (Route 629) once stood the Alexander Belsches House. Lt. Alexander Belches distinguished himself during the August 19, 1812 engagement between U.S. frigate *Constitution* and H.M. frigate *Guerriere.* For his service the State of Virginia presented a sword to him.

Central Park, then known as Poplar Lawn (northeast corner of Sycamore and Filmore streets). The Petersburg Volunteers mustered and drilled on this green at the beginning of the War of 1812. A granite monument commemorating this site is located near the northwest corner of the park. When the Petersburg Volunteers returned to Petersburg after defending Fort Meigs, festivities honoring the company were held January 8, 1814. Guns were fired at Centre Hill, and after appropriate salutes, the company proceeded to Poplar Lawn. A band played and patriotic songs were sung. A dinner and a ball followed. Poplar Lawn was decorated with flags, among which was a war-worn banner from Fort Meigs.

★ **Old Blandford Church and Cemetery** (319 South Crater Road [U.S. Route 301] and Rochelle Lane). Blandford Church was erected in 1735, abandoned, and then restored in 1882. In 1901, it became a memorial chapel to Confederate veterans. Within the 18-acre cemetery dating from 1702 are buried Revolutionary War, War of 1812, and Civil War veterans. A replica of the uniform, including the famous cockade hat, is on display in the church reception center. A monument was erected over the grave of Capt. Richard McRae in 1856 to honor him and the Petersburg Volunteers. The 10-foot obelisk monument features an American shield surmounted by an American eagle gilded with 23 karat gold and surrounded by an ornate cast iron fence incorporating into its design an eagle with spread wings, the U.S. shield, cockade hats, muskets, swords, powder horns, belts, a bullet pouch, a drum, and cannonballs. At each corner is a post in the form of a battle axe. On top of the fence are seventeen stars representing the states of the Union at the time of the war. The monument was damaged during the Federal cannonading of Petersburg during the Civil War, but it was later restored by the Cockade City Garden Club. The gilded eagle was stolen several years ago and later found in a pawn shop in Richmond. A replica now surmounts the obelisk, while the original is on display in the reception center at Blandford Church.

> In granting a discharge to this Patriotic and Gallant Corps, the General feels at a loss for words adequate to convey his sense of their exalted merits. Almost exclusively composed of individuals who had been nursed in the laps of ease, they have for twelve months, borne the hardships, and privations of Military life in the midst of an inhospitable wilderness, with a cheerfulness and alacrity which has never been surpassed. Their conduct in the field has been excelled by no other corps, and whilst in Camp, they have set an example of Subordination and Respect for Military Authority to the whole Army. The General requests Captain M'Rae, his Subalterns, Non-Commissioned Officers and privates, to accept his warmest thanks. (Acting Assistant Adj. Gen. Robert Butler, October 17, 1813, reprinted in Richmond *Enquirer,* November 16, 1813)

PLEASURE HOUSE. *See* Lynnhaven Bay

PORTSMOUTH (west side of confluence of Elizabeth and James rivers). Portsmouth was never attacked during the war, although it was an attractive target because the Gosport Navy Yard and U.S. frigate *Constellation* were both located there. The American success in the Battle of Craney Island* on June 22, 1813, spared Portsmouth from occupation or destruction.

William "Billy" Flora, a free black man and citizen of Portsmouth who lived at the corner of Washington and King streets, fought against the British during the American Revolution, and is said to have joined the American forces again during the War of 1812. Because of his advanced age, he probably did not participate in any actual combat.

Ball House (213 Middle Street). This house served as a barracks during the War of 1812.

Fort Nelson Site, originally called Fort at Portsmouth (Elizabeth River at Hospital Point, Portsmouth Naval Hospital). Military, restricted access. Robert MacDonald, one of the wounded crew members from the U.S. frigate *Chesapeake,* was taken here for treatment after the infamous *Chesapeake–Leopard* affair* of June 22, 1807. MacDonald died several days later and a huge crowd assembled for his funeral in Norfolk.*

Forts Nelson* and Norfolk,* located at "The Narrows" of the Elizabeth River, served as the second line of defense after Craney Island.* Fort Nelson was named for Thomas Nelson, who served as both general and governor (1781) of Virginia. The original triangular-shaped fort, built at Tucker's Mill on a point that then extended over a thousand feet into the river, consisted of earthworks begun in 1776 but mostly destroyed by the British after they captured it in 1779. Like Fort Norfolk on the east side of the river, Fort Nelson was rebuilt as part of a national defense initiative in 1794. The irregular triangular-shaped fort utilized some of the original earthworks and mounted thirty-three cannon in March 1813. To strengthen this position the U.S. frigate *Constellation* was anchored nearly opposite Fort Nelson with her broadside facing north toward Craney Island about four miles distant.

Gosport Navy Yard, now called the Norfolk Naval Shipyard (about 0.5 mile up Elizabeth River from Portsmouth). U.S. military base, restricted access. The British established Gosport Navy Yard in 1767. When the Revolution began, Virginia confiscated the property and operated the yard. The federal government purchased the yard from Virginia in 1798. During the Civil War, the name of the yard was changed to the Norfolk Navy Yard and in 1945 to Norfolk Naval Shipyard. "Portsmouth" was not used in the yard's name because the navy yard at Portsmouth, New Hampshire, already carried that name. The U.S. frigate *Chesapeake* was built here between 1794 and 1799. War of 1812 hero Stephen Decatur commanded Gosport Navy Yard from 1805 to 1807. When the war began, there were only twenty-one gunboats to protect the lower Chesapeake Bay tidewater region. When *Constellation* became blockaded here, Capt. Charles Stewart, its commander, placed several gunboats on each side to protect the frigate from boarding and to provide flanking fire.

> In the present state and probable continuance of the Blockade, the prospect of your getting to sea is not only hopeless but it would be temerity to make the attempt. (Secretary of Navy William Jones to Capt. Charles Gordon, April 15, 1814)[61]

After the British attack on Craney Island* and Hampton* in 1813, a series of defensive booms, a breastwork outside the yard, and a battery inside the yard were built to further defend them against a future attack.

> I have a range of heavy Booms, well chaind & Anchord in the Narrows . . . The Battery for the defense of the Navy Yard will evidently be formidable, as it will Command the only pass to the Yard, about 300 yards spaced between the heads of two Creeks or Branches which lead up on either side of Gosport and effectually enclose both. (Capt. Charles Gordon to Secretary of Navy William Jones, September 20, 1814)[62]

> I was resolved to erect a battery inside of the yard, which is finished with Six eighteen pounders, pointing West to SW and two thirty two pounders from SW to South, long Guns,

the battery is made of timber . . . also four twelve pounders at the gate way. (Capt. John Cassin to Secretary of Navy William Jones, September 16, 1814)[63]

Portsmouth Naval Shipyard Museum (2 High Street). While this museum focuses on the history of America's oldest shipyard, it features a few War of 1812 artifacts, including a smooth bore .69 muzzle-loading flintlock musket made at the Virginia Manufactory of Arms,* Richmond, based on U.S. models 1812 and 1816. While made after the war, it illustrates the common issue musket used by the Virginia militia during the war.

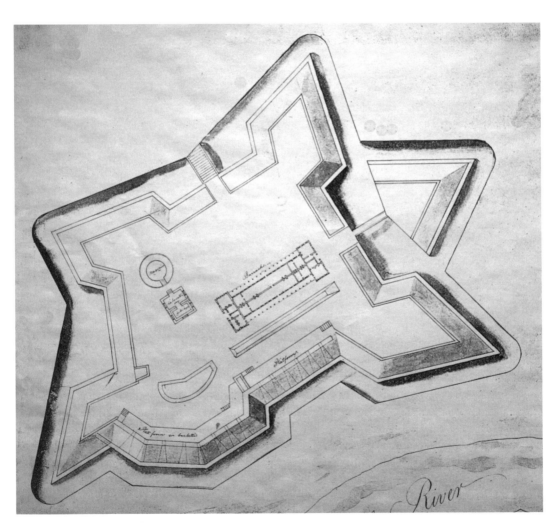

Fort Nelson as it appeared in 1798. (National Archives and Records Administration, Cartographic Section)

POTOMAC CHURCH SITE. *See* appendix A

PUNGOTEAGUE CREEK (off Pocomoke Sound, end of Harborton Road [Route 180], southwest of Onancock, Accomack County). In consequence of the British establishment of a base on Tangier Island,* a militia camp was established here as well as at Onancock* and Chesconessex* creeks. The Battle of Pungoteague, or Rumleys Gut, took place May 30, 1814. Here the Colonial Marines, British-trained former slaves, saw their first action. Approximately five hundred British troops in eleven barges and launches entered Onancock* Creek about 7:00 a.m. before turning south into Pungoteague Creek. The militia, who occupied two pine plank barracks roughly twenty-feet-square built near the entrance to the creek, could not effectively fire on the British when they landed on the opposite side of the creek because their gun powder was so poor. Maj. John Finney and Lt. Thomas Underhill assembled some militia on the opposite shore, who soon came under fire from British cannon and Congreve rockets. The Americans returned fire with a 4 pounder Revolutionary War cannon. The British troops rushed the American line. About this time Capt. Isaac Smith then arrived with twenty more militiamen who took up a position in a pine woods to the right of the enemy. A general fire ensured upon both sides. By about 8:00 a.m. the militiamen withdrew to a thick woods on their left after spiking their cannon. Col. Thomas M. Bayley, commander of the 2nd Regiment, arrived on the field with a thousand additional militia and with more on the way. The British withdrew after a bugle call from one of their barges. At least six British troops were killed, including one member of the Colonial Marines as well as a midshipman named Frazier, who was buried on Tangier Island; another fourteen were wounded. No Americans were killed, although two were wounded, Ezor Kellom seriously so. During their hasty retreat, the British dropped furniture taken from the John Smith house. The British burned the American barracks.

> about sunrise, eleven British barges, containing four or five hundred men, effected a landing on Pungoteague Creek, near the house of a Mr. [John] Smith, where was stationed a guard of 50 or 60 men, who fought bravely for half an hour, and retreated, with the loss of one piece of artillery. The enemy took possession of Smith's house, and plundered him of every thing.—At 1 o'clock about 1000 militia and volunteers assembled, attacked the enemy at Smith's house, who made their escape, and got on board their barges in a few minutes; one of the enemy was found dead on the shore, and a great deal of blood all the way from the place of attack down to the place of embarkation—an officer's sword was also found, so that it is probable they went off many of them with sore bones. On our part only two were wounded.—If the artillery had been up in time, the enemy must have been cut to pieces. (Baltimore *Federal Republican,* June 10, 1814)

> The enemy used his 18-lb., 12-lb., 4-lb. cannister and grape shot and Congreve Rocketts with great profusion, but without effect. He soon landed from eight barges and Launches one quarter of a mile from Major [John] Finney and Lieutenant [Thomas] Underhill, and gave three cheers; put about 30 negroes [Colonial Marines] in full uniform in front and rushed upon the Major, receiving and giving a continued fire. (Lt. Col. Thomas M. Bayly to Governor James Barbour, May 31, 1814; reprinted in Philadelphia *United States Gazette,* July 2, 1814)[64]

> The Conduct of our new raided Corps, the Colonial Marines, who were for the first time, employed in Arms against their old Masters on this occassion, and behaved to the admiration of every Body. (Rear Adm. George Cockburn to Vice Adm. Sir Alexander F. I. Cochrane, June 25, 1814)[65]

The only public place to view Pungoteague Creek is at the end of Harborton Road (Route 180) at the Harborton Landing public boat ramp. The entrance to Underhill Creek can be seen to the northeast across the creek and the area of Rumsey's Gut still farther to the northeast. Waterhouse Point is downcreek on the same side of the ramp but is not visible. Closer views can be had only by boat.

Tradition claims the British attack on Pungoteague was in retaliation for the American seizure of the *Hiram,* an American schooner from New York, which had been captured and anchored off Tangier Island. On its mast the British nailed charts to guide British ships into the harbor. Militia from the 2nd Regiment in April 1814 reportedly took advantage of a strong northwest gale to sneak up to the schooner, cut the cables, and allow it to drift ashore between Nandua and Pungoteague creeks.

RAPPAHANNOCK RIVER (off Chesapeake Bay). Late on April 2, 1813, Lt. James Polkingthorne, with 105 troops in five boats, sighted the American privateers *Dolphin, Racer, Lynx,* and *Arab,* which were headed toward the mouth of the Rappahannock River. Polkingthorne chased them by rowing fifteen miles before catching them the next day, drawn up in a line. When the British attacked, the captain of the *Arab* ran it ashore and set it on fire but the British extinguished the flames and refloated it. The *Lynx* lowered her colors when a British pinnace came alongside. The *Racer* was boarded and, after a sharp resistance, its guns were turned on the

Dolphin and it was finally boarded. In total, 219 men and 31 guns were captured. The *Lynx* and *Racer* became British tenders that participated in the attack on Elkton,* French-town,* Fredericktown,* and Georgetown,* Maryland. The Rappahannock River skirmish resulted in sixteen American and thirteen British casualties. American newspaper accounts of the engagement claimed several British barges were sunk and a fisherman brought up many British bodies in his net three days later. But the following British account presents a very different story:

> On the second [April], when abreast of New Point Comfort [*] we gave chase to five vessels, four of which were large schooners . . . they took shelter in Rappahannock river . . . anchored at mouth off Windmill Point[*], and the boats of the squadron were despatched in pursuit . . . We continued in chase all night; at daylight the enemy was discovered at anchor, but, on perceiving us, immediately weighed and formed in line of battle . . . The stars and stripes were floating proudly at their peaks . . . their guns were run out, and all prepared to receive us . . . on getting well within gun-shot, the whole of the enemy's vessels opened their broadsides upon us . . . In half an hour four large vessels under sail, with every preparation for battle, mounting thirty-one guns, manned with two hundred and nineteen men, forming a whole of upwards twelve hundred tons, were attacked in open day and captured by five boats with one twelve-pounder carronade and one hundred and five men. (Capt. James Scott, 1834)[66]

RICHMOND (head of navigation on James River). On September 1, 1812, the War Department asked Virginia to provide 1,500 armed militia for the North Western Army in Ohio. This request grew out of the surrender of Detroit to the British on August 16. The control of Lake Erie and the Michigan Territory was at stake. Governor James Barbour put out a call for volunteers from the various militia units of the state. One of the units to respond was the Petersburg Volunteers.* In late June 1814, British ships ran up the James River raiding some plantations but were primarily seeking to replenish their fresh water supplies. Nevertheless, exaggerated reports caused citizens of Richmond to fear an attack was eminent. Before calm could be restored, plans were underway to remove the women and children, public records, and bank specie from the capital.

By mid October 1814, nearly 11,000 troops were present for the defense of Richmond. They were in a number of camps, including Camp Malvern Hill, Camp Holly Springs, Camp Carter, Camp Mims, Camp Fairfield, Camp Mitchell's

Springs, and Camp Bottoms Bridge. While the exact location of most of these camps is unclear, Camp Malvern Hill* was located 12.2 miles southeast of Richmond on heights near the James River,* and Camp Holly Springs* was 9.8 miles east of Richmond. Camp Bottoms Bridge* was just east of the Henrico–Charles City line on the old Richmond–Williamsburg road. Camp Carter* was two miles west. Fort Powhatan* on the James River also defended Richmond.*

Bellona Arsenal Site (south side of James River, between 3901 and 4400 block on north side of Old Gun Road [Route 673], north off West Huguenot Road [Route 147], just west of Richmond City limits, Chesterfield County). PRIVATE. The early history of this arsenal is unknown, but Maj. John Clarke and noted Richmond lawyer William Wirt established a weapons factory here in 1810. It was probably in operation during the War of 1812 although Bellona Arsenal was not established here until 1816. Immediately on the north side of Old Gun Road at the Bellona Arsenal Site is a gun mold and cannon retrieved from the James River. Immediately behind these artifacts can be seen the remains of several brick buildings. The artifacts and structures are believed to date from after the War of 1812. The history of the area is reflected by the names of Arsenal Hills and Arsenal Road; the house opposite the arsenal site is called the Foundry. (*See also* Bellona Gunpowder Mills Site, Maryland.)

Virginia Manufactory of Arms Site (James River, Tredegar Street at foot of 5th Street). The Virginia legislature authorized the construction of an armory to manufacture weapons for the state in 1797. Built in 1801, the Virginia Manufactory began production the following year. Virginia was the only state after the Revolutionary War to arm its own forces entirely with locally made weapons. Other states depended upon federal armories at Harpers Ferry,* Virginia (now West Virginia), or Springfield, Massachusetts, or on private contractors such as the one at Edinburg,* Virginia. The Virginia armory closed in 1821. The manufactory consisted of a boring mill and a two-and-a-half-story *U*-shaped structure where the manufacturing of arms took place. This complex later became the Richmond Manufactory.

In the Richmond National Battlefield Civil War visitor center (Tredegar Street, second floor) are three models of the Tredegar area. The early industries model shows the location of the Virginia Manufactory in relation to the Tredegar Iron Works established in 1836. The stone foundations near the intersection of 5th and Tredegar streets may represent the remains of the Virginia Manufactory. A model 1817

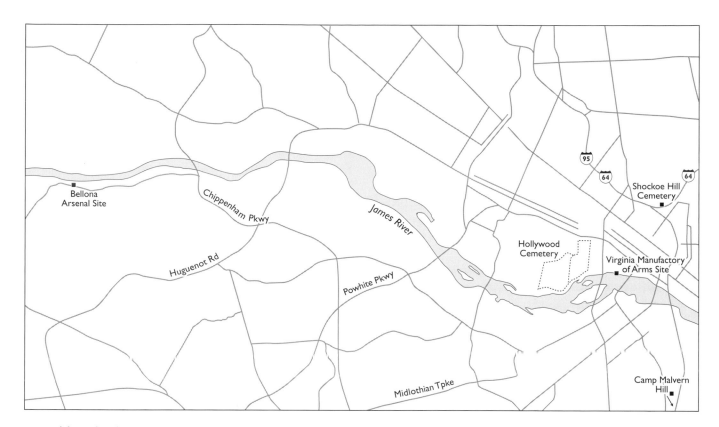

Richmond Region

muzzle-loading flintlock musket made here is exhibited at the Portsmouth Naval Shipyard Museum.*

On March 20, 1813, Lt. Col. John Cropper, 2nd Regiment, Accomack County, wrote Governor James Barbour that 18,000 cartridges that had been sent from Richmond in June 1812 appeared to date from the Revolutionary War and "are good for nothing except the bullets . . . paper and powder have mouldered to fine dust."[67]

ROKEBY MANSION. *See* Leesburg

ROKEBY FARM SITE (near 830 Chain Bridge Road [Route 123], Fairfax County) PRIVATE. The original Rokeby Farm house was completed in 1813 but apparently burned shortly after and was rebuilt circa 1820. The property is near Rokeby Farms Stables. James Monroe briefly stopped at Rokeby Farm while looking for the president. He stayed only long enough to have a quick meal. After securing the removal of some public records and the portrait of George Washington, Dolley Payne Madison fled from the capital to Virginia via Dunbarton House* and Chain Bridge* to Rokeby Farm, where she spent the night of August 24, 1814. From a window she could see a red sky from the fires the British set in Washington. Ironically, the Rokeby Farm was owned by Richard and Matilda Lee Love, daughter of Federalist Ludwell Lee, a scion of the Virginia Lee family and a political opponent of James Madison. Matilda was a niece of Henry "Light Horse Harry" Lee.* Rokeby Farm was named by Matilda after a poem by Sir Walter Scott.

ROSIER CREEK, also Rozier Creek (off Potomac River, just above Colonial Beach, Westmoreland County). On July 18, 1813, the British attempted to land on Rosier Creek but were repulsed by the local militia under the command of Lt. Col. Richard E. Parker. Parker and his men were part of the 111th Regiment that established a camp near the creek. Rosier Creek can be seen from Shellfield Lane off James Monroe Highway (Route 205) south of Colonial Beach.

SALONA. *See* listing, McLean

SCOTT COUNTY (southwest Virginia). Scott County was formed in 1816 from portions of Russell and Lee counties in tribute to Gen. Winfield Scott (1786–1866). Born at Dinwiddie,* Scott was arguably the most accomplished soldier in the U.S. Army prior to the Civil War. He served as a lieutenant colonel in command of the regulars at the Battle of Queenstown on October 13, 1812, when Maj. Gen. Stephen van Rensselaer returned to the American side of the Niagara River. Scott, after rallying the troops, was forced to surrender. After being exchanged, Scott was promoted to colonel of the 2nd Regiment of Artillery. Scott was in the lead boat in the first wave of vessels that attacked Fort George on May 27, 1813. He was also the first to enter the fort, where he extinguished a burning trail of gunpowder leading to the magazine. Scott also captured the fort's colors. President James Madison promoted him to brigadier general in March 1814. He retired in 1861 after serving forty-seven years as an officer. (*See* chapter 3 for a fuller account of Scott's War of 1812 accomplishments.)

SEATACK (area around intersection of Virginia Beach Boulevard and North Birdneck Road, Virginia Beach City). Seatack was reportedly named because it was the target of British naval fire and was where troops came ashore during an unspecified attack in the War of 1812. The isolated stretch of beach became known as "Sea Attack" and was gradually shortened to "Sea tack," and finally "Seatack."

SMITHFIELD (James River, Isle of Wight County). The British ascended the James River* in early June and July 1813, raiding and plundering along the way. Among their targets was Smithfield on Pagan Creek, which they attacked on June 26, 1813.

> SMITHFIELD ATTACKED . . . three of the enemy's barges attempted to enter Pagan Creek, but were resisted by a detachment of militia, and after exchanging fourteen shot without effect on either side, the enemy retired. On the same evening, a frigate and a brig, attended by a number of barges anchored in sight of Smithfield . . . ; the enemy is using every effort to take sounding of the Creek up to Smithfield and an attack is hourly expected there; but from the precautionary measure adapted by Majors [Charles] Ballard of the Infantry and Byrd [possibly Capt. John A Burd, U.S. Light Dragoons] of the cavalry, he will be meet with a warmer reception than he anticipated. (Richmond *Virginia Argus,* July 1, 1813)

About four miles south of Smithfield (14477 Benn's Church Boulevard [Route 10]) is the Old Brick Church (St. Lukes Church), built circa 1632 and restored in 1887. Virginia militia are reported to have bivouacked here during the War of 1812.

SMITH ISLAND (bounded by the Atlantic Ocean on the east, Smith Island Inlet on the south, Smith Island Bay on the west, and South Bay on the north, east of Virginia Eastern Shore Peninsula, on north side of entrance to Chesapeake Bay, Northampton County). The British procured provisions on Smith Island as early as 1807 during the so-called Douglas War caused by the *Chesapeake–Leopard* affair.* The islanders reportedly encouraged such encounters when the British offered to pay for their plunder. During the spring of 1813, the British again provisioned on Smith Island, shooting cattle and sheep and seining for fish.

> The sheep in this [Smith] island were of a peculiar, fine breed, in great numbers, and perfectly wild. The mode of catching them was too complicated . . . our only alternative was to approach and shoot them like deer. Their flesh . . . fully equalled English mutton. (Capt. James Scott, 1834)[68]

STONE HOUSE MANSION (east side of Route 9/19, 0.4 mile southwest from intersection of Route 9, Shaw Spring, approximately 5 miles southeast of Martinsburg, Berkeley County, West Virginia). Stone House Mansion is a two-story house dating from 1757. Two War of 1812 veterans lived here at different times. Lt. David Hunter (unit unknown) was killed at the Battle of Crysler's Farm, September 11, 1813, when struck by cannister shot. Here also lived Capt. Henry St. George Tucker,* who served with a Troop of Cavalry at Alexandria from August 26 to September 23, 1814, and at Camp Holly Springs* from February 6 to March 1, 1815.

SULLY PLANTATION (3601 Sully Road [Route 28], Chantilly, Fairfax County). Access from northbound Sully Road only. Sully Plantation was built 1794 by Richard Bland Lee, brother of Henry "Light Horse Harry" Lee* and uncle of Robert E. Lee. Sully served as Richard B. Lee's country home until 1811, when it was sold to his second cousin, Francis Lightfoot Lee. Richard B. Lee was appointed by President James Monroe to adjudicate claims arising from property losses during the War of 1812. He was originally interred at Congressional Cemetery,* but his remains were moved to Sully in 1978. The cemetery is located just northwest of the main house.

TANGIER ISLAND (Chesapeake Bay on west and Pocomoke Sound on east, Accomack County). The British established a temporary base on Tangier Island soon after arriving in the lower Chesapeake Bay on April 11, 1813. On about April 8, 1814, some fifty British troops landed on Tangier near Zachariah Crockett's house and took cattle, pigs, and sheep, paying what they saw proper. On April 14, 1814, the British landed some two hundred troops and developed a base called Fort Albion on the southern end of the island, close to a deep water anchorage required for their large 74-gun ships-of-the-line. Ideally situated for control of the central Chesapeake Bay, Tangier Island was surrounded by shallows and other islands, making it difficult to attack. Yet it offered easy access to the Potomac and Patuxent rivers and upper Chesapeake Bay. Fort Albion was fitted with barracks, which provided shelter for over a thousand men. Because of the success of the British raids, especially on the Potomac River, several of the barracks and other buildings were used to temporarily store plunder until it could be shipped out.

Two redoubts about three hundred yards apart and mounted with eight guns defended the base.

I consider under all the Circumstances that Tangier Island (particularly the end of it which I have occupied) though perhaps not without its inconveniences, is far better adapted for the purposes you contemplated than any other in the Chesapeake, and though I have no doubt the Moschettos [mosquitoes] will be numerous in the Summer time, yet I do not think it probable they will be much worse here than at the other Islands, and as we clear the Ground from the underwood they will I think be likely to quit us for the other places where there is this necessary shelter for them from the Wind when blowing fresh, particularly the Sea Breeze to which the Southern end of this Island is fully exposed. (Rear Adm. George Cockburn to Vice Adm. Sir Alexander F. I. Cochrane, May 9, 1814)[69]

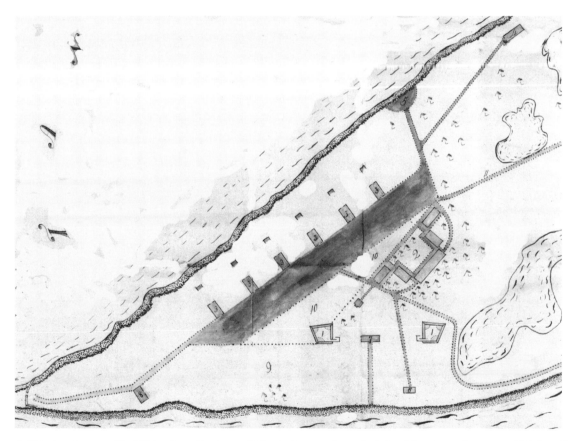

British circa 1814 map of Fort Albion. Key: 1. Two trapezoidal redoubts (bottom center). 2. Officers barracks (near center). 3. Privates barracks (possibly used by the Colonial Corps, six in total, with doors on each end, probable three-sided out houses to northwest of each barrack). 4. Hospital (end of path to northeast). 5. Fish market (end of path to north). 6. Garrison barracks (end of path to south). 7. Garrison store-house (end of path from lower shore to north). 8. Guard house along path to southwest. 9. Parade grounds. 10. Gardens. 13. Burial ground beyond image to lower left. 14. Public store beyond image to middle right. (Water colored pen and ink *Plan of the Island of Tangier in Chesapeake Bay*; courtesy National Library of Scotland)

But conditions at Tangier Island were far from ideal, as suggested by comments made by British deserters.

> the crews there are very sickly with the flux, the water being brackish and bad—that they had been for 2 months on short allowance of food, but had lately obtained a supply from Bermuda. That the fort at Tangier had only three sides done, each side 250 yards long, and mounting eight 24 lbers, and about 18 24 lbers just received by the [H.M. frigate] Endymion; that it is to be the H. Q. [head-quarters] for the Commander in Chief—that gardens are laid out in the Island, vegtables of all kinds growing, a hospital to contain 100 sick, a Church, and 20 houses and laid out into streets. (Lt. Col. Thomas M. Bayly to Governor James Barbour; reprinted in Baltimore *Patriot,* July 9, 1814)

> Sent a boat to attend the punishment of a Seaman belonging to Endymion for desertion. Sold Dead man cloathes. (Ship-log of H.M. brig-sloop *Jaseur,* June 22, 1814, at "Tangier Road")[70]

The British occupation of Tangier Island had a significant impact on the life of the inhabitants. Local vessels were numbered to keep track of their movements, and passports were required to leave the island. Those who managed to get a passport to leave the island were treated with suspicion by Americans on the mainland.

> being informed that the enemy had registered every man upon the Island, numbered their boats and canoes and would permit no one to leave the Islands without passports, with orders to return, and considering these men thus situated would give the enemy all the information they could, I ordered all persons coming from the Islands to be detained. (Lt. Col. Thomas M. Bayly to Governor James Barbour, Baltimore *Federal Republican,* May 6, 1814)

Rev. Joshua Thomas* frequently preached to the British officers and men at the Camp Meeting Grove, located near the fort. Here on the eve of their departure for Baltimore in September 1814, Reverend Thomas reportedly gave his "Thou Shalt Not Kill" sermon and predicted the British failure in attacking that city.

Almost seven hundred former slaves took refuge on Tangier Island, and about two hundred were taught to use arms and enlisted into the Colonial Marines. These troops saw their first action at Pungoteague Creek.* Tangier Island was abandoned by the British in early 1815. Several British, including a midshipman named Frazier who was killed at Pungoteague Creek, were buried in a cemetery the British established there. Because of erosion, the fort and its cemetery are now under water.

As the ponderous men of war piped to weigh anchor for the last time, we were all gathered on the beach to return their waving farewell. (Rev. Joshua Thomas, 1861)[71]

All ordnance, stores, and materiels that could be salvaged were removed.

> you are to bring with you all the Ordnance and Stores of every description from Tangier Island, as by the Treaty such things only as were captured <u>thereon</u> are to be left, and the Commander in Chief desires in particular that on no account a Single Negro be left, except by his own request, if he joined you prior to the Ratification of the Treaty which took place at 11 PM of the 17th. February, the Commander in Chief also wishes you to take down the Barracks &ca. erected by us on Tangier, and to bring the Materials with you if you can manage it, and whenever you have so evacuated this Place and brought every thing from it, you are to repair with the Ships under your Orders to Bermuda. (Rear Adm. Sir George Cockburn to Capt. John Clavell, March 10, 1815)[72]

TAPPAHANNOCK (Rappahannock River, Essex County). Tappahannock retains many structures dating from before the War of 1812, including the custom house (1720), the old debtors' prison (1769), the clerk's office (1808), and the Meriwether Ritchie House (1706). The last two structures are located on the corner of Prince and Cross streets. Rappahannock River can be seen at the end of Prince Street, where the British loaded tobacco and flour during their raid here on December 2–3, 1814.

In late November 1814, Capt. Robert Barrie received information "that the Regiments of Virginia militia, lately stationed on the Banks of the Rappahannock, had been for several days passed disbanded for the Winter and that most of the Troops belonging to the distant parts of the State were already returned to their homes."[73] Taking advantage of this intelligence, Captain Barrie planned an attack on Tappahannock to "annoy the Enemy by obliging him to reassemble his Militia, and by landing in different parts of the River, keep his Troops constantly on the alert, which in this Country at this advanced season of the year is most harassing Service."[74] The attack of approximately five hundred troops, including some fifty Colonial Marines (made up of former slaves), took place on December 2, 1814, and ended the next day. The outnumbered local militia withdrew to nearby hills when the British landed. Congreve rockets forced the militia to retreat farther. The British burned the custom house and jail. They also burned Lawrence Muse's large granary. The following day the county court house and a second jail were torched.

Non-contemporaneous illustration depicting Rev. Joshua Thomas preaching to the British army on Tangier Island, 1814. (*The Parson of the Islands,* 1861)

American account of raid: all the houses had been pillaged of everything; except some fine pieces of furniture. Some furniture they carried off, other of the most valuable broken to pieces, all the beds, their furniture, etc. which were left, taken off, except in one house, where the beds were ripped open, the feathers left on the floor, but the ticking carried off, the glass in the windows of many houses entirely broken. (Lt. Col. Archibald Ritchie to Governor James Barbour, Richmond *Enquirer,* December 6, 1814)

Second American account of raid: landed here . . . were three companies, of about 50 each, of negroes [Colonial Marines] in uniform and apparently well trained, commanded by white officers.—They were said to be Virginia & Maryland negroes, trained at Tangier Islands[*]— . . . The plundering of the Enemy has been confined [to the] bay Shores of inconsiderable amount, & on a few plantations . . . There has been much wanton destruction of private property here [Tappahannock]—in breaking windows & furniture—and one deed of damnation has been performed which out does all their former atrocities— The family Vault of the Ritchies was broken open and the Coffins searched— I have seen the shocking spectacle— (Brig. Gen. John Hartwell Cocke to Governor James Barbour, December 4, 1814)[75]

British account of raid: we observed a considerable body of Troops drawn out with their Field Pieces . . . proceeded with the Boats abreast of the Town [Tappahannock], and when within Grape Shot commenced our Fire, which the Enemy

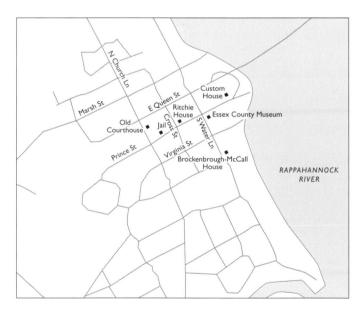

Tappahanock

did not return and observing them abandoning the Town ... the Inhabitants with the exception of two had entirely deserted the Town, and removed all their effects except about forty hogsheads of Tobacco and some Flour. The Enemy in his haste to abandon the Town left behind him a Stand of Colours, several Musquets, Bayonets, and a quantity of Ammunition and Camp Equipage ... the Enemy, being in sight drawn up on a Hill, about a Mile and a half above the Town ... Rockets ... fell among the Enemy who soon retreated into the Wood behind the Hill, wishing to entice him to attack us in the Town, I caused to be set on fire the Custom House and a Jail, but as he envinced no disposition to quit his fastness, I embarked the Troops at Sunset, and at daylight on the 3rd. I again landed and completed Shipping the Flour and Tobacco; in the course of the day, a second Jail and the Court House was consumed without molestation from the Enemy though he frequently shewed himself with increased Force. (Capt. Robert Barrie to Rear Adm. George Cockburn, December 7, 1814)[76]

Second British account of raid: We first took the town of Rappahannock [Tappahannock], driving the enemy out of it, who ran away so fast that they dropped their colours, which we took. On one side of them, under the American eagle, was this motto, "Death or victory"; on the other, "Down with the tyrants." However, they were "scared" from death and ran away from victory. (Vice Adm. William Stanhope Lovell, 1879)[77]

British account of plundering: We were particularly desired not to land; but seeing boots and shoes walking into a captain's gig,—half a butcher's shop in another, the cockswain of a third with two geese dangling to his hands—we became hungry from fancy, and impatient under our restrictions; and therefore edged near the beach, and landed in the vicinity of a large house which belonged to one Doctor Bolingbroke [Austin Brockenbrough?]. In about five minutes the house was turned out of the windows, and every man carried off some of the property. A large staircase clock was clapped upon a few geese at the bottom of the boat to keep them quiet; then came a bundle of books and some cabbages, a feather-bed, and a small cask of peach brandy. The boat was soon deeply laden, and we all re-embarked, like good boys. (Capt. Frederick Chamier, 1850)[78]

A Virginia Historical Highway Marker (Richmond Road [Route 360]) entitled "Historic Tappahannock" states "The British Admiral Cockburn shelled the town, December 1, 1814." While the town may have been shelled December 1, the raid took place on December 2 and 3.

Brockenbrough-McCall House (South Water Lane near intersection with Virginia Street). PRIVATE. This home, built 1763 and owned by the Brockenbrough family during the War of 1812, was hit by cannon fire during the British attack on Tappahannock, shattering a black marble mantel that has since been reassembled. One account mentions the plundering of the Bolingbroke House. It is possible this was the Brockenbrough house, the name having been corrupted over time.

Custom House (109 Prince Street). PRIVATE. This structure, which reportedly dates from 1760 or before, was used at one time as the custom house. The bank of the Rappahannock River was nearly adjacent to this house at that time. The British reportedly burned this structure, but either the damage was slight or this structure was built later.

Essex County Museum (218 Water Lane). Among the exhibits is a cavalryman's saber dating from the War of 1812.

Jail (Prince Street). There were as many as four jails in Tappahannock, and two of them were supposedly burned by the British. The exact location of the jails that were burned is unclear. The Treasurer's Office now occupies a building then referred to as the "debtors' jail." It is located on the north side of Prince Street just west of the intersection with Church Lane.

Old Courthouse, later the Beale Memorial Baptist Church (202 Church Lane). This 1729 structure served as a courthouse until 1848, when the court was moved to its present location on Prince Street. The courthouse was burned by the British. Some accounts claim the walls of the old structure were used in the new courthouse, while others claim the original building was a total loss. A church tower was added to the structure when it served as the Beale Memorial Baptist Church.

TARR IRON FURNACE (north side of Kings Creek Road at intersection with Patricia Avenue, 1.8 miles east of Country Road [Route 2], near Weirton, Hancock County, West Virginia). In the 1790s, Peter Tarr established this iron furnace, the first blast furnace west of the Alleghenies. In addition to making skillets, kettles, grates, and other household items, it produced cannonballs used on September 10, 1813, during the Battle of Lake Erie. The stone furnace was reconstructed in 1868.

URBANNA (west side of Urbanna Creek at confluence with Rappahannock River, north end of Urbana Road [Route 227], Middlesex County). The inhabitants of Urbanna became frightened when the British on April 2, 1813, conducted a raid on the Rappahannock River above Urbanna, taking vessels and burning several inland properties.

> The British are in Rappahannock, and six of their barges were sent on Saturday last above Urbana , to take two privateers said to belong to Baltimore, and two letters of marque. (Alexandria *Gazette,* April 12, 1813)[79]

The citizens of Urbanna became alarmed again on December 6, 1814, when two British deserters informed the militia that British troops intended to burn and loot the town. The militia was called out, but the attack never took place.

A Scottish factor store (1766), which serves as the town's visitor center and museum, and the custom house (private) line Pettyman's rolling road to the waterfront. A good view of Urbanna Creek can be had from the Urbanna Road (Route 227) bridge south of town. Urbanna retains much of its eighteenth-century charm.

VIRGINIA WAR MUSEUM. *See* Newport News

WATTS ISLAND (Tangier Sound, east of Tangier Island, Accomack County). The British occupied Watts Island in June 1814, cutting timber there for ship spars and for stakes needed in their fortification on Tangier Island.*

WHITE HOUSE GUN BATTERY SITE (bluffs along Potomac River between Dogue Creek and Gunston Cove, Fort Belvoir Army Base, approximately 4.0 miles below Mount Vernon,* Fairfax County). Military base with restricted assess. White House is named for a large white painted fishing house once located on the beach and used as a navigational landmark along the Potomac River. In 1775, George Washington recommended batteries be placed here because the Potomac River channel confined ships to within three hundred yards of the shore.

> The face of this bank is in some places, a hundred feet high, the surface stone bare . . . It has great advantages from the circumstance of a deep channel . . . within pistol shot of the free stone heights, and not more than three hundred yards wide . . . the act of quarrying stone, for other works, may be made to economize the labour of erecting batteries, and other powerful works of defence. (William Tatham to Secretary of War John Armstrong, May 27, 1813)[80]

An American gun battery consisting of three 18 pounders, two 12 pounders, six 6 pounders, and two 4 pounders was hastily erected here in early September 1814. Two mortars and a 32 pounder cannon, which could have provided much needed range and destructive power, were not readied in time. From September 2 through September 5, 1814, Capt. David Porter, Jr.,* fired canon and the militia fired muskets on the British warships as they worked their way down the Potomac after the capitulation of Alexandria.*

The White House Gun Battery Site stretches along the steep bluffs of the Potomac River just north of the White House site. A small parking area located immediately south of the intersection of Fomey Loop and Fairfax Circle provides access to a Potomac View Trail. Immediately to the east the Belvoir Mansion Site (0.3 mile down the trail) can be seen a linear entrenchment along the bluff top. Two gun battery depressions can be found farther down the slope on a point flanked by two deep ravines. These depressions are believed to date from the War of 1812. Near the south end of the Potomac View Trail loop are several interpretive panels, one of which deals with the War of 1812. Near here are the remains of two long trenches that may be related to the war. Additionally, there is another possible gun battery depression connected to what appears to be entrenchments located on the southwest side of the trail. If these are indeed military earthworks, they would have protected the landward side of the White House Gun Battery site. Over 150 artifacts, including dozens of 13-inch and 10-inch mortar shells, one with its wooden plug still intact, have been recovered from this area. (Please remember it is illegal to pick up or disturb and artifacts on government property.)

Acting Secretary of War James Monroe visited this battery several times during the battle. This action was the first American military action after the British burning of Washington. American losses were twelve killed and seventeen wounded, while British losses were seven killed and thirty-five wounded. (*See also* Indian Head Gun Battery and Mount Welby, where additional activities to impede the British took place.)

> The battery erected at the white house under the command of Com: [David] Porter, promises to embarrass, if not impede the progress of the enemy down the bay. (Secretary of State James Monroe to Com. John Rodgers, September 2, 1814)[81]

> A terrible cannonading from about 12 o'clock till after sunset with very little interruption. (Anna Marie Brodeau Thornton, September 5, 1814)[82]

Non-contemporaneous sketch of White House gun battery suggesting its appearance in 1814. (Pen and ink sketch by William Bainbridge Hoff, date unknown; Naval Historical Center)

This morning a bomb vessel from off Alexandria anchored, out of reach of our cannon shot, off the White House . . . where a body of our men are stationed, and amused them for some hours with throwing bomb shells at them, which however had no other effect than to accustom the militia to disregard this sort of annoyance. (Washington *Daily National Intelligencer,* September 3, 1814)

Com. [David] Porter has hoisted a large flag over his battery, on which is inscribed, in sufficiently legible characters "FREE TRADE and SAILORS' RIGHTS." Who does not echo the sentiment? (Annapolis *Maryland Republican,* September 10, 1814)

The Americans fought under a white flag, bearing the words "Free Trade and Sailors" Rights,' and behaved remarkably well—but their efforts were useless. (Sir Charles Napier, 1862)[83]

American account of skirmish: 2 o'clock, the enemy's squadron discontinued the bombardment which had been kept up with little intermission, for three days, weighed anchor, and stood down the river, commencing a heavy fire on the battery, and across the neck of land through which the militia were compelled to march to its assistance . . . finding our little battery inefficient to impede the progress of the vessels, after having long gallantly defended it, and considering a longer contention with such a superiority of metal a wanton sacrifice of blood, ordered the battery to be evacuated and his men to retire, which they did. The two largest of the enemy's vessels, then anchored; one just above, and the other just below the battery, and commenced a most galling cross fire of round shot, grape, canister, &c . . . Notwithstanding the dreadful cross fire of every species of mis-

sive, by the enemy, to which they were exposed, without a possibility of returning the fire (the most trying of all situations) not a man under my command offered to move, until orders to that effect was given . . . Our whole loss was eleven killed, and seventeen or eighteen wounded. (Brig. Gen. John P. Hungerford to Acting Secretary of War James Monroe, September 6, 1814)[84]

British account of skirmish: The [eight-gun H.M. bomb-vessel] *Meteor* and the [H.M. brig-sloop] *Fairy* assisted by the *Anna Maria* despatch boat, a prize gun Boat, and a boat belonging to the [H.M. frigate] *Euryalus* with a howitzer, had greatly impeded the progress of the Enemy in their works, notwithstanding which they were enabled to encrease their battery to eleven guns with a furnace for heating Shot.— on the 3d the wind coming to the North west the Aetna and the [H.M. rocket-vessel] *Erebus* succeeded in getting down to their assistance and the whole of us with the prizes were assembled there on the 4th, except the [H.M. bomb-vessel] *Devastation,* which in spite of our utmost exertion in warping her, still remained five miles higher up the River.— This was the moment when the Enemy made his greatest efforts to effect our destruction.— The *Erebus* being judiciously placed by Captain [David E.] Bartholomew in an admirable position for harrassing the workmen employed in the trenches, was attacked by three field pieces which did her considerable damage before they were beaten off . . . On the 5th . . . the [H.M. frigates] *Seahorse* and *Euryalus* anchored within short Musquet Shot of the Batteries whilst the whole of the prizes passed betwixt us and the shoal, the Bombs, the [H.M. brig-sloop] *Fairy,* and [H.M. rocket-vessel] *Erebus* firing as they passed and afterwards anchoring in a favourable position for facilitating by means of their fire the further removal of the Frigates. At 3 PM having completely silenced the Enemy's fire, the *Seahorse* and *Euryalus* cut their Cables, and the whole of us proceeded to the next position . . . [Indian Head Gun Battery] taken up by the troops. (Capt. James Alexander Gordon to Vice Adm. Sir Alexander F. I. Cochrane, September 9, 1814)[85]

On September 4–5, 1814, Com. John Rodgers sent fire-vessels down the Potomac toward the British squadron, but the vessels did no damage because the wind had shifted and the British were able to fend them off.

American account of event: September 5 . . . Com. [John] Rodgers, on Sunday evening, proceeded down the river with four barges, well manned;—when he came within two miles distance, seven barges full of men were sent to meet him.—The barges manoeuvred within gun shot of each other till nine or ten o'clock at night, when a very warm firing of musquetry and large shot commenced between them, which lasted 15 minutes, and ended in the repulse of the British barges with much loss. A barge was found on shore in the morning, with swords, &c. in it; and at least one barge was destroyed. On our part two or three men only were hurt, Com. [John] Rodgers yesterday joined the batteries under Com. [David] Porter. (Annapolis *Maryland Republican,* September 10, 1814)

British account of event: The cool and steady conduct of midshipman John Moore, of the [H.M. frigate] Seahorse, in towing the nearest fire-vessel on shore, while the others were removed from the power of doing mischief by the smaller boats of the [H.M. bomb-vessel] Devastation, is spoken of in high and just terms of commendation by captain [James Alexander] Gordon. (William James, 1826)[86]

William Fairfax served as collector of customs of the south Potomac Naval District for the Crown from 1734 to 1741. He built the manor house Belvoir about 1741. It burned in the late eighteenth century. Ironically, the ruins of this house, built by a British agent and located just behind the American battery site, were destroyed by British cannon fire from the passing fleet. Ferdinando Fairfax, who had inherited Belvoir, lived at the White House during the war. He served as a citizen volunteer during the battle and offered stone from his quarry and timber from his grove to build the batteries and defenses.

Mr. Ferdinando Fairfax and several other citizens and officers of the Militia and Volunteer Companies ably hearing of my destination volunteered their services on the occasion and ably supported me throughout the arduous and fatiguing Enterprise. (Capt. David Porter, Jr., September 7, 1814)[87]

I authorize you . . . the use of my freestone quarries . . . free of cost . . . I allow you to take from my woodland . . . timber and wood. (Ferdinando Fairfax)[88]

WILEY'S TAVERN SITE. *See* appendix A

WINDMILL POINT (Fleets Island, north entrance to Rappahannock River, end of Windmill Point Road [Route 695], Westland, Lancaster County). The lookout at Windmill Point on Fleet's Island reported on April 23, 1814, that the British landed near North Point, about two miles northwest, and took a boat and other possessions from the owner. A detachment of the 92nd Regiment of Lancaster militia posted in the vicinity fired across a nearby creek and drove the British back to their ship. A good view of the waterfront can be had from the end of Windmill Point Road (there is a turn-around but no parking).

WREN'S TAVERN. *See* Falls Church

YEOCOMICO RIVER (off Potomac River, above Coan River, forming boundary of Westmoreland and Northumberland counties). On the morning of July 14, 1813, H.M. brig *Mohawk* and H.M. sloop *Contest* spotted the American schooner *Asp** and sloop *Scorpion* sailing out of the Yeocomico River into the Potomac River. The *Scorpion* was able to sail up the Potomac but the *Asp,* a poor sailor facing head winds, took refuge up Yeocomico River. The waters were shallow so the British vessels anchored their ships and dispatched two cutters to chase the American schooner. A fierce engagement ensured. British casualties consisted of two killed and six wounded; American casualties were ten, including at least one killed (Midshipman James Butler Sigourney,* commander of *Asp*) as well as some missing. There were two U.S.N. destroyers named after Sigourney, DD-81 commissioned in 1918 and DD-643 commissioned in 1943. There are good views of Yeocomico River from the end of Mundy Point Road (Route 621) north off Cople Highway (Route 202) and from where the Kinsale–White Point Road (Route 203) bridge crosses the river just northeast of Kinsale.* American and British accounts of the engagement vary considerably. The Virginia Historical Highway Marker (Cople Highway [Route 202], 4.8 miles northwest of Callao) claims the engagement of the *Asp* took place on June 14, 1813. It actually took place in July.

American account of action: we were obliged to cut our cable, we were attacked by 3 boats well manned and armed we continued a well directed fire on them and after a short time they were compelled to retreat and obtain a reinforcement about an hour after we retired we were attacked by 5 boats we continued doing the same as before but having so few men we were unable to repel the enemy, when they boarded us they refused giving any quarters, there was upwards of fifty men on our decks which compelled us to leave the vessel, as the enemy had [possessed] it they put her on fire and retreated, a short time after they left her we went on board and with much difficulty extinguished the flames. (Midshipman Henry McClintock to Secretary of Navy William Jones, July 19, 1813)[89]

Second American account of action: Capt. Liggany [Midshipman James Butler Sigourney], the commander of the schooner, was basely murdered, after the enemy boarded, when there were but three men on the deck, one of whom asked for quarters, which was refused! And Mr. M'Clintic [Midshipman Henry McClintock] the midshipman and the other man jumped overboard & succeded with several others in making their escape through a shower of balls from their musketry. The body of Liggany was found on board, and was to be buried yesterday with the honors of war. The schooner was left on fire; but through the vigilance of some of our men who repaired to her, it was extinguished, and exertions are making to save the guns, &c. (Baltimore *Patriot*, July 19, 1813)[90]

British account of action: The Enemy had hauld the Schooner within her own width of the Beach, under the protection of a large Body of Militia and placed her in a position with a spring on her Cable to bring all the guns to bear on the two boats. On their approach, a heavy & tremendous fire opened from the Schooner and the Shore . . . she was carried by Boarding in a few minutes . . . In consequence of the Asp being three or four miles up the Creek, and the Channel extremely difficult and narrow, with a wind right and a vast number of Troops advancing toward the Beech, I deem'd it prudent to set her on fire. (Commander James Rattray to Adm. Sir John Borlace Warren, July 14, 1813)[91]

At daybreak on August 3, 1814, the British in twenty barges attacked a two-gun battery under the command of Captain William Henderson at Mundy Point (sometimes incorrectly called Monday Point) on the Yeocomico River. The battery consisted of an earthen mound fronted by logs and ditched at the rear. (A second battery was located at Thicket Point on the east side of the entrance to Yeocomico River.) American artillery fire beheaded a Royal Marine in the lead boat and killed two additional British soldiers after they reached the shore. Expending almost all their ammunition, the American defenders withdrew.

a round shot came in over the bow of the boat, and regularly enfiladed us, taking off the poor marine's head that sat facing me amidships on the after thwart. At that precise instant I was in the act of piking up one of the cutlasses, and as I raised my head I received in my face part of the poor fellow's brains. (Capt. James Scott, 1834)[92]

The American battery was destroyed, one cannon captured, and several homes in the area, including that of one Captain Henderson, burned. Henderson's loss was valued at $6,045. American casualties were two officers wounded, one of whom later died; British casualties were three killed and four wounded, one of whom later died. During this engagement, which has come to be known as the Battle of Mundy Point (although it was little more than a skirmish), the British learned that Brig. Gen. John Pratt Hungerford was in force at nearby Kinsale,* farther up Yeocomico River. Nearly opposite Kinsale, Maj. Henry Blackwell had taken up a position at Oyster Shell Point. The British found Hungerford's force at Kinsale, where a second engagement took place.

American account of action: proceeded up Yeocomico to Kinsale, which they totally destroyed, together with several other houses for seven or eight miles on both sides of the road leading from thence to Richmond courthhouse; they were then checked in their progress by a detachment of artillery under the command of capt. [William] Henderson, but that small party were forced in a short time to retreat with the loss of their piece of artillery . . . the fortunate arrival of a considerable number of our militia from some of the upper counties prevented a farther incursion into Richmond, on the edge of which, the enemy burned the houses of capt. Henderson. (William Lambert to Secretary of Navy William Jones, August 12, 1814)[93]

British account of action: We here found more resistance from the Enemy than usual he having collected in great Force to oppose, but . . . after forcing the Enemy to give way, followed him Ten Miles into the Country, capturing from him a Field Piece, and burnt in Route several Houses which had been converted into Depôts for Militia Arms, Ordnance Stores &c . . . afterwards . . . we proceeded [to Kinsale] and though the Position of the Enemy had there taken was extremely strong he had only time to give us an ineffectual Volley or two of musquettry before our People gained the height, when he again retired with precipitation and we saw no more of him, we then shipped off without further molestation the Stores found at Kinsale, and having burnt the Store Houses and other Places and Two old Schooners, and having destroyed two Batteries, we embarked again . . . with us Five Prize Schooners, a large quantity of Tobacco, Flour

&ca., a Field Piece, five Prisoners and the Horses of [Brig.] General [Robert] Taylor and his Son, the former of whom being wounded was unhorsed and only escaped being taken by the Thickness of the Wood and Bushes into which he run. (Rear Adm. George Cockburn to Vice Adm. Sir Alexander F.I. Cochrane, August 4, 1814)[94]

the [British] vessels . . . then proceeded up Yeocomico River; the consequence was soon very obvious, several large fires were distinctly observed; which continued to burn during the day, and appearenlty originated from houses and vessels. The large neck of woods, lying between the Rivers Cone [Coan] and Yeocomico, was immediately fired upon the enemy's landing, which burnt till Thursday night, and then was fortunately extinguished by the rain. In the morning . . . the squadron left Yeocomico, accompanied by four captured shcrs [schooners]. (Baltimore *Patriot,* August 15, 1814)

American casualties were eight killed and five taken prisoner; four British suffered wounds, three severely.

Kinsale Museum (440 Kinsale Road, Kinsale). Here is a noncontemporary watercolor painting of the engagement at Kinsale, July 14, 1813.

Yeocomico Church (1233 Old Yecomico Road, 1.3 miles east from intersection with Sandy Point Road [Route 604], 2.2 miles north of intersection with Oldhams Road [Route 203], north of Kinsale and south of Tucker Hill). This church was built in 1706 on the site of a framed church built in 1655. The original high-backed pews were apparently destroyed by the British when they used it as a barracks. The lectern and walnut communion table survive.

YORK RIVER (off Chesapeake Bay, north of James River, forms parts of boundaries of Gloucester, York, King and Queen, and New Kent counties). During the foggy night of June 12, 1813, the Revenue Service cutter *Surveyor,* under the command of Capt. Samuel Travis, was captured by three boats from the H.M. frigate *Narcissus.* Travis had sent out the cutter's boat to patrol the surrounding waters, and it exchanged musket fire with one of the British boats, but

neither vessel suffered any harm. The British boats next approached the cutter from such a direction that its six 12-pounder carronades could not be brought to bear upon them. An estimated fifty British troops swarmed onto the *Surveyor* and were met by volleys of musket fire. After fierce hand-to-hand combat, Travis surrendered to Lt. John Cririe (Crerie), the British officer in charge. British casualties were three killed and seven wounded; American casualties were six wounded.

Lt. John Cririe returned Capt. Travis's sword the next day with a note that reportedly said: "Your gallant and desperate attempt to defend your vessel against more than double your number . . . excited such admiration, on the part of your opponents, as I have seldom witnessed, and induced me to return your sword you so ably used, in testimony of mine."[95]

In command of seven gunboats and two schooners, Capt. Joseph Tarbell pursued two British brigs in the York River in December 1813, but no details of the chase are known.

YORKTOWN (York River, York County).

Grace Episcopal Church (east side of Church Street, north off Main Street). Below the wall of the churchyard behind the church lies a stone plaque that claims the "English Navy" burned the church in 1814. There is no evidence that the British were ever in Yorktown during the War of 1812, although a fire on March 3, 1814, destroyed several buildings, including a church. The British did use this church as a magazine and destroyed pews and windows during the American Revolution 1781 siege of Yorktown.

York Hall (301 Main Street, between Ballard and Church streets). Here on the lawn is a monument to the veterans of York County. It includes veterans from Bacon's Rebellion, the Revolutionary War, the War of 1812, the Civil War, and the two world wars. The names of veterans from the War of 1812 are Tyler Crockett, Carter H. Longst, James Martin, Amiger Parsons, and Aaron Tennis.

CHAPTER 5

The District of Columbia and Other Sites Related to the Chesapeake

The ten-mile square comprising the District of Columbia was carved out of Maryland and Virginia. Washington, D.C., did not appear like a proper capital city in 1814. With a population of some eight thousand inhabitants, one-third of whom were slaves, the city took up only a small part of the hundred square miles set aside for it. Georgetown and Alexandria were in the new district, as was the new capital, Washington.[1] The U.S. Capitol building was far from finished. It had no central core or dome; only the House and Senate wings were completed (not the same wings as so identified today). The lawn of the President's House served as a pasture for sheep. The roads were unimproved and thus usually either muddy or dusty.

Secretary of War John Armstrong was convinced the British would not target Washington because it had little military value. Only the navy yard, arsenal, and rope walks were of military consequence. Armstrong failed to appreciate the morale value the British might gain from capturing the city. Local citizens expressed alarm at the lack of defense for the city.

The citizens complain loudly of the defenceless state of the district—Armstrong is suspected and cursed by almost every person here. Deputations have been sent to the President both from this city and Georgetown—they have declared to the President their total want of confidence in Armstrong, and demanded in strong terms that steps be immediately taken to place the district in a state of defence. (London *Times,* September 23, 1814)

General Orders
Adjutant-General's Office, Head-Quarters, Military District No. 10, Washington City, August 20, 1814.

Soldiers! The enemy threaten the capital of your country, and are now pressing towards it with a force which will require every one to do his duty, without regard to sacrifices and privations. The zeal and promptitude evinced by those in the field, with the reinforcements which are rapidly pressing to your aid, afford the fairest promise that the enemy will receive the just chastisement of his temerity.

On August 20, 1814, a 10:00 p.m. curfew was imposed. All unauthorized persons had to be off the streets or be arrested.

On Sunday [August 21], the public offices were all engaged in packing and sending off their books . . . On Monday, this business was continued with great industry . . . The specie was removed from all the Banks in the district . . . on Tuesday [August 23] . . . all the books and papers were sent off, and the citizens generally left the place. (Boston *Independent Chronicle,* September 5, 1814)

NOTICE. All-able-bodied Citizens remaining here, and all free-men of color, are required to convene to-morrow morning at 6 o'clock precisely, at the Capitol—and from thence to proceed to a site near Bladensburg, to throw up a breastwork or redoubt, deemed important by the Commanding General, for the defense of our city. Those who cannot attend in person, will please send substitutes. Shovels, spades and pick-axes, will be furnished on the spot. Each man must take his provisions for the day with him. (Mayor James H. Blake, Washington *Daily National Intelligencer,* August 24, 1814)

Due to Mayor Blake's call to action, a battery earthwork was hastily established by the citizens of the District of Columbia on the west side of the Bladensburg bridge.

The British occupation of the capital was probably the lowest point of the war for the United States and the highest for the British. As the British advanced on Washington at sunset on August 24, 1814, they could see a red glow to the southeast of the city, where the Washington Navy Yard* had already been torched to keep its ships and supplies out of British hands. The British themselves burned many of the public buildings, including the U.S. Capitol* and the President's House (White House).* A few private buildings were also burned, including the rental house that once belonged

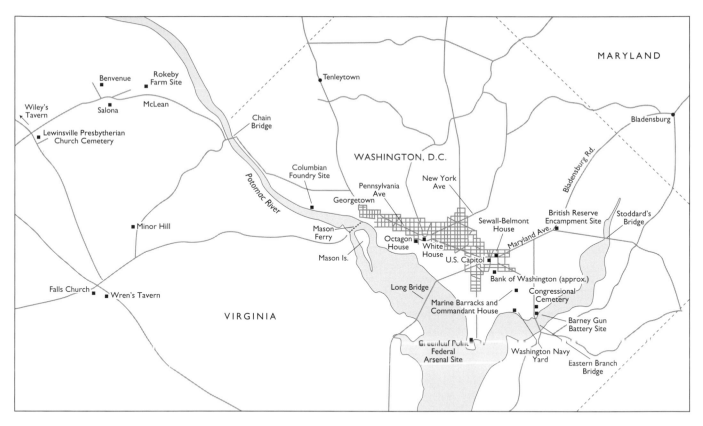

Washington, D.C. Region

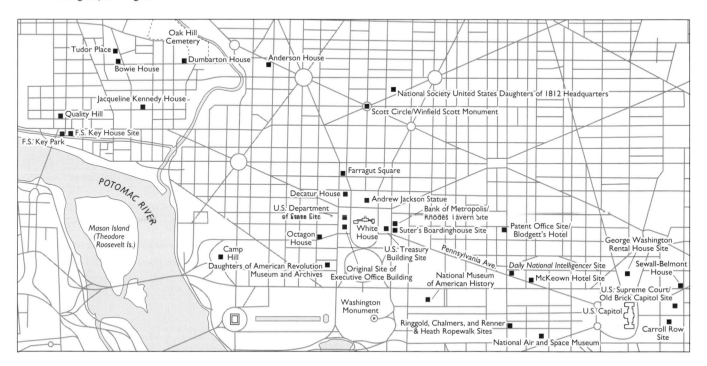

Washington, D.C. Downtown Area

to George Washington* on the brow of Capitol Hill, then called Jenkins Hill; a large hotel belonging to Daniel Carroll; and the three rope walks. All told, lost property value was estimated at $1.5 million.

American account of the approach of the British: We were roused on Tuesday night by a loud knocking,— on the opening of the door, Willie Bradley called to us, "The enemy are advancing, our own troops are giving way on all sides and are retreating to the city. Go, for Gods sake go." He spoke in a voice of agony, and then flew to his horse and was out of sight in a moment. (Margaret Bayard Smith, August 1814)[2]

British account of the taking of Washington: I have the honour to Communicate to your Lordship that on the night of the 24th Instant after Defeating the Army of the United States on that day the Troops under my Command entered and took possession of the City of Washington. (Maj. Gen. Robert Ross to Secretary of State for War and the Colonies Earl Henry Bathurst, August 30, 1814)[3]

British account of the burning of Washington: On taking Possession of the City we also set fire to the Presidents Palace [White House], the Treasury, and the War Office, and in the morning Captain [John] Wainwright went with a Party to see that the Destruction of the Navy Yard was Complete, when he destroyed whatever Stores and Buildings had escaped the Flames of the preceding Night—A large quantity of Ammunition and ordnance Stores were likewise destroyed by us in the [Greenleaf Point Federal] Arsenal, as were about Two hundred pieces of Artillery of different Calibers, as well as a Vast quantity of small Arms. Two Rope Walks [actually three: Tench Ringgold, John Chalmers, and Renner & Heath] of a very extensive Nature, full of Tar, Rope, &c. Situated at a considerable distance from the Yard were likewise set Fire to and consumed, in short Sir, I do not believe a Vestige of Public Property, or a Store of any kind which could be converted to the use of the Government, escaped Destruction; the Bridges across the Eastern Branch and the Potomac were likewise destroyed. (Rear Adm. George Cockburn to Vice Admiral Sir Alexander F. I. Cochrane, August 27, 1814)[4]

Second British account of the burning of Washington: It would be difficult to conceive a finer spectacle than that which presented itself as they [British troops] approached the town. The sky was brilliantly illuminated by the different conflagrations; and a dark red light was thrown upon the road, sufficient to permit each man to view distinctly his comrade's face. Except the burning of St. Sebastian's, I do not recollect to have witnessed at any period of my life a scene more striking or more sublime. (Lt. George Robert Gleig, 1821)[5]

American reaction to burning of Washington: Whereas the enemy by a sudden incursion have succeeded in invading the capital of the nation, defended at the moment by troops less numerous than their own, and almost entirely of the militia; during their possession of which, though for a single day only, they wantonly destroyed the public edifices having no relation in their structure to operations of war, nor used at the time for military annoyance; some of theses edifices being also costly monuments of taste and of the arts, & others depositories of the public archives, not only precious to the nation as the memorials of it origin and its early transactions, but interesting to all nations as contribution to the general stock of historical instruction and political science. (Proclamation by President James Madison, September 3, 1814)[6]

WASHINGTON, August 30, THE FATE OF WAR has befallen the city of Washington, It was taken by the enemy on Wednesday the 25th inst. and evacuated by them in the course of Thursdry night, after destroying the interior and combustible part of the Capitol, of the President's house, and of the public offices. (Brig. Gen. John P. Hungerford, August 31, 1814; reprinted in Annapolis Maryland Republican, September 3, 1814)

The destruction of the public property at Washington, is an event deeply to be regretted by every American. The Twenty-Fourth of August, Eighteen Hundred and Fourteen, will be a memorable era in History,—inasmuch as on that day the Capital of the country, the pride and boast of America, was leveled with the dust; and presents at this time nought to the eye, save stupendous and melancholy ruin. (Annapolis Maryland Republican, August 27, 1814)

Horror! Horror! Horror!—How shall we depict to our readers without our cheeks being tinged with the blush of shame and confusion, when we inform them the spot bearing the hallowed name of the deliverer of this country, has been polluted by the footsteps of British myrmidons! All—all is lost; the army is dispersed, the Capitol in flames, &c. &c.— Nought can obliterate or wash away the indelible stain by British blood. (Unnamed "southern paper" quoted by Capt. James Scott, 1834)[7]

British account of the withdrawal from Washington: It was about eight o'clock at night when a staff-officer, arriving upon the ground, gave direction for the corps to form in marching order. Preparatory to this step, large quantities of fresh fuel were heaped upon the fires, while from every company a few men were selected who should remain beside them till the pickets withdrew, and move from time to time about, so as their figures might be seen by the light of the blaze. After this, the troops stole to the rear of the fires by twos and threes; when far enough removed to avoid observation, they took their place, and in profound silence, began their march. (Lt. George Robert Gleig, 1833)[8]

On February 14, 1815, the Treaty of Ghent reached the capital. The Senate and president signed off on it two days later, thus officially bringing the war to an end. Celebrations in the capital city, already underway, now took on an official character. The capital was decked out in patriotic splendor with the Stars and Stripes flying beside the Union Jack at city hall. At 7:00 p.m. a gun salute was fired, and the city was illuminated by the synchronized lighting of candles and oil lamps in the homes. Everyone, Republicans and Federalists alike, was relieved that the war was now over.

ANDERSON HOUSE. *See* The Society of the Cincinnati Museum listing, Washington, D.C.

BANK OF THE METROPOLIS/RHODES TAVERN SITE (northeast corner of 15th and F streets, NW). The building housing Rhodes Tavern, constructed in 1799, was used by the Bank of the Metropolis from 1814 to 1836, by the Riggs Bank from 1840 to 1845, and by the Washington Stock Exchange from 1881 to 1884. After the British destruction of the public buildings, Congress debated moving the capital to Philadelphia, but the offer of loans from the Bank of the Metropolis to rebuild these structures helped tip the balance for remaining in Washington, D.C. Two plaques commemorat-

British satirical cartoon in 1814 speculates that President Madison has fled to Elba to join Napoleon to the amusement of the Federalists he abandoned. (S. W. Fores, "The Fall of Washington or Maddy in full flight"; Library of Congress, Prints and Photographs Division)

ing Rhodes Tavern, demolished in 1984, are mounted on the wall of the present structure.

As the British proceeded down Pennsylvania Avenue to burn the President's House, they threatened to burn the Bank of the Metropolis as well. Mrs. Sarah Sweeny, the bank's cleaning woman, convinced Rear Adm. George Cockburn to spare the building by claiming that a poor widow owned it and that renting it out was her only source of income. For saving the bank, the owners gave her $100.

BANK OF WASHINGTON SITE (New Jersey Avenue, SE). Dolley Payne Madison had packed several boxes in a wagon to be delivered to the Bank of Washington for safety.

> Two messengers, covered with dust, come to bid me fly; but here I mean to wait for him [President Madison] At this late hour a wagon has been procured, and I have had it filled with plate and the most valuable portable articles, belonging to the house. Whether it will reach its destination, the "Bank of Maryland," or fall into the hands of British soldiery, events must determine. (An after-the-fact re-creation by Dolley Payne Madison to her sister Lucy Payne Todd of an event that took place approximately 3:00 p.m., August 24, 1814)[9]

Believing the government kept its money in the Bank of Washington, Maj. Gen. Robert Ross ordered it to be burned but countermanded the order when Dr. James Ewell* pointed out that the bank was private property. An alternate version of this story holds that a British naval officer pointed out that the flames from burning the bank would most certainly engulf the adjacent private properties. Rear Adm. George Cockburn then ordered the bank building pulled down but desisted when Dr. Ewell pointed out that it was private property. Since Ross and Cockburn were usually together during the British occupation of Washington, both could have played a role in the story. The bank survived, but whether Ross or Cockburn played a role in preserving it is unclear.

BARNEY GUN BATTERY SITE (west side of John Philip Sousa Bridge [then called Eastern Branch Bridge] which carries Pennsylvania Avenue across Anacostia River, Barney Circle area, extreme south end of Congressional Cemetery, SE). During the night of August 22–23, 1814, Brig. Gen. William H. Winder established a temporary headquarters near here at a Dr. Hunter's to be near the navy yard. Winder also ordered the Eastern Branch Bridge prepared for destruction so the British could not use it.

During the night, a boat, containing eight barrels of powder, was stationed underneath the bridge . . . with orders to blow it up on the approach of the enemy. About sunrise . . . we were shortly ordered to pull down the rails of the neighboring fence, and place them on the bridge, in order that it might be effectually burnt, in case the explosion of gunpowder should not succeed in preventing the enemy from passing it. For the same purpose, the toll house was ordered to be pulled down, and the planks placed on the bridge. (Sgt. John Law, November 10, 1814)[10]

The 1,500-foot-long Eastern Branch Bridge was destroyed as a precaution. A good view of this area can be had from Congressional Cemetery.*

> When on my way, I saw a portion of the Eastern Branch Bridge Blown, into Splintery fragments, in the Air. (Captain's Clerk Mordecai Booth to Capt. Thomas Tingey, August 24, 1814)[11]

Before the Battle of Bladensburg, Com. Joshua Barney and his flotillamen were stationed at Eastern Branch Bridge to protect the lower crossing of the Anacostia River to Washington. Barney established a battery (presumably on the hill now part of Congressional Cemetery) and persuaded his superiors to let him abandon this position when it became clear the British were heading toward Bladensburg. He quickly marched his force to Bladensburg, arriving just as the battle began on August 24, 1814.

> it was understood the enemy were advancing towards the Eastern Branch Bridge Commodore [Joshua] Barneys artillery being planted on the hill in front of the Bridge and Materials placed under the Bridge ready to explode and destroy it should the enemy approach. (Secretary of Navy William Jones, August 24, 1814)[12]

I found Commodore [Joshua] Barney employed, by order of the General [William H. Winder], in planting his Battery on the Hill, near the head of the Bridge. He was charged to defend that pass and to destroy the Bridge, on the appearance of the Enemy; for which purpose scows and Boats, with combustible materials, were placed under the Bridge ready to explode. At this time the enemy was apparently advancing on the road to the Bridge; but shortly after advice was received that he had turned off on the road towards Bladensburg, about six miles from that place;—General Winder set off for Bladensburg, leaving Commodore Barney, with his Seamen and Marines in charge of the Bridge.

It was soon observed that a very efficient part of the force had been left to destroy the Eastern Branch Bridge, which could as well be done by half a dozen men, as by five hundred. The subject was discussed by the President, Heads of

Departments, and Com. Barney, which resulted in the order for his immediate and rapid march, to join the Army near Bladensburg, which he reached, just in time to form his men for Battle. (Secretary of Navy William Jones to Congressman Richard M. Johnson, October 3, 1814)[13]

BOWIE HOUSE (3124 Q Street, NW). Bowie House was built by Washington Bowie, George Washington's godchild, who lost his shipping business and had to sell this home as a result of trade disruptions caused by the War of 1812.

BRITISH RESERVE ENCAMPMENT SITE, Old Circus Grounds Site (former Graceland Cemetery site, intersection of Maryland Avenue, Bladensburg Road, and 15th Street, NE). The invading British column rested here after making an exhausting march and fighting the battle at Bladensburg in temperatures that approached a hundred degrees. The bulk of the army remained here to serve as a reserve and to defend the rear while detachments entered and burned Washington.

> General [Robert] Ross . . . did not march the troops immediately into the city, but halted them upon a plain in its immediate vicinity . . . [then later] having advanced as far as the plain, where the reserve had previously paused, the first and second brigades halted; and, forming into close column, passed the night in bivouack . . . [then later during the British withdrawal] it was not long before we reached the ground which had been occupied by the other brigades. here we found a second line of fires blazing in the same manner as those deserted by ourselves; and the same precautions, in every respect, adopted, to induce a belief that our army was still quit. (Lt. George Robert Gleig, 1821)[14]

Later this area became known as the old circus grounds.

CAMP HILL. *See* U.S. Naval Bureau of Medicine and Surgery listing, Washington, D.C.

CARROLL ROW SITE (site of Library of Congress, southeast corner of East Capitol and 1st Street, SE). Demolished in 1887 for construction of the Library of Congress, Carroll Row was located across from the U.S. Capitol on the northeast corner of 1st and A streets (before A Street was cut off for the new library building). It consisted of five houses. The north end was a hotel where in 1809 the inaugural ball for President James Madison was held. The south end was occupied by Dr. James Ewell, a prominent Washington physician who wrote *Planter's and Mariner's Medical Companion* in 1807, and his family. Rear Adm. George Cockburn and

Maj. Gen. Robert Ross chose this residence as their headquarters. Believing the enemy would treat him and his family with more compassion if he were tending to the sick, Dr. Ewell had already taken his family to the home of a sickly neighbor who lived a few doors away.

As the Ewell family watched the capital burn that night, British soldiers came to the house for food. Confused by the light of the fire, Dr. James Ewell feared his own home was on fire. When he returned to his house, he found it occupied by British officers. Local tradition holds that upon hearing that the doctor had a wife and two daughters, Major General Ross offered to take up residence in another home, but the doctor demurred, apparently realizing Ross's presence would ensure its safety. Ewell spent the night at the neighbors' house and offered Ross his own bed. The next morning the doctor returned to his house and found a British soldier there who suddenly fell to the road in convulsions. When a British sergeant ordered Ewell to fetch him some water, the doctor instructed a black man to get the water. When he returned with a pitcher, the sergeant reportedly shouted to the doctor to give him a cup. At this time Major General Ross appeared, grabbed the sergeant by the collar, and scolded him for speaking rudely to a man who was kind enough to help one of his sick comrades. Ross apologized for the insolence of the sergeant and thanked Ewell. Later, Dr. Ewell treated British soldiers who were wounded when the Greenleaf Point Federal Arsenal* blew up.

COLUMBIAN FOUNDRY SITE, also called the Columbia Foundry or the Foxall Foundry (Foundry Branch, near south end of Foxall Road between Potomac and C&O Canal, within Chesapeake & Ohio Canal National Historical Park). Henry Foxall operated the foundry from 1808 to 1849. Mount Aetna Furnace* supplied iron to this foundry. In 1808, the Columbian Foundry supplied 32 pounder carronades for the U.S. frigate *Constitution*. During the War of 1812, this foundry was the leading manufacturer of ordnance for the U.S. government. A shot tower produced lead ball ammunition, and Foxall also manufactured the Columbiad here. This was a short, heavy, and exceptionally powerful cannon, which may have been named after the foundry.

Henry Foxall (1758–1823), a Methodist minister and mayor of Georgetown, prayed that his foundry be spared when the British invaded. When it survived, Foxall paid for the construction of a Methodist Church at 14th and G streets. The present and third Foundry Methodist Church stands at 1500 16th Street, NW. To keep the archives of the Department of State from being burned they were taken

Carroll Row, built in 1805, consisted of a three-and-one-half-story brick structure divided into town houses. Rear Adm. George Cockburn and Maj. Gen. Robert Ross used the south end unit (right) as their tempo-rary headquarters during the British occupation of Washington. View is southeast from the dome of the U.S. Capitol. (Circa 1880 photograph detail; Library of Congress, Prints and Photographs Division)

first to Edgar Patterson's* abandoned gristmill near Chain Bridge,* across the river from the Columbian Foundry. But because the foundry might be a British target, the records were moved to Old Littlejohn House* in Leesburg, Virginia, and then to Rokeby Mansion,* outside Leesburg.

CONGRESSIONAL CEMETERY. *See* appendix B

DAUGHTERS OF THE AMERICAN REVOLUTION MUSEUM AND ARCHIVES (1776 D Street, NW). NRHP. The DAR headquarters, museum, and library are located in the original 1903 built section of Memorial Constitution Hall. The bullet extracted on August 24, 1814, from Joshua Barney, commodore of the U.S. Chesapeake Flotilla, after the Battle of Bladensburg, is in the Society's collection. It is mounted on a silver pendant that reads "In defending Washington this British bullet terminated the life of Joshua Barney." Barney died on December 1, 1818, when his war wound flared up. A belt buckle, officer's epaulets, ring, and miniature portrait of Barney are among the exhibits featured here. The DAR

Library is a good source for genealogical information on participants in the War of 1812.

DECATUR HOUSE (748 Jackson Place, NW). NRHP. Com. Stephen Decatur,* a U.S. Navy War of 1812 hero, lived in the 1817 Decatur House, the first private house built on the site then known as "President's Square," but today known as Lafayette Square, immediately north of the White House. Decatur achieved fame as commander of the U.S. frigate *United States* when on October 25, 1812, he captured the H.M. frigate *Macedonian*. Decatur was later awarded $30,000 in prize money. This was the only British frigate brought to America as a prize of war (*see also* Macedonian Monument*). With the *United States* blockaded in New London, Connecticut, Decatur in May 1814 took command of the U.S. frigate *President* at New York City. He attempted to sail to the open sea but ran aground at Sandy Hook because of a piloting error. Although he freed his ship, Decatur on January 15, 1815, was captured by three British frigates. Decatur died in a basement-room of Decatur House from a wound received in a duel with Capt. James Barron* at the Bladensburg Dueling Grounds* on March 22, 1820.

In Decatur House is the sword that the Commonwealth of Virginia presented to Decatur in recognition of his capture of H.M. frigate *Macedonian.* Benjamin Henry Latrobe* designed Decatur House as well as the gate house and commandant's house (Tingey House*) of the Washington Navy Yard,* and Baltimore's Basilica of the Assumption.* He also served as architect for the rebuilding of the U.S. Capitol after the British burning.

DUNBARTON HOUSE, also called Bellevue (2715 Q Street, NW, Georgetown). NRHP. Dolley Madison fled the President's House (White House*) to the 1805-built Dunbarton House accompanied by Charles Carroll, who owned this property. Here Dolley received a message from her husband, requesting her to meet him the next day at Wiley's Tavern,* a Virginia inn about sixteen miles northwest of Georgetown near Great Falls. Dolley stayed here only until late afternoon before traveling by carriage across the Potomac River at Chain Bridge to the relative safety of Virginia. President Madison left Washington by horseback via the ferry near present-day Key Bridge. Dunbarton House, then called Bellevue,

Pendant with musket ball that ultimately took Com. Joshua Barney's life when the wound it inflicted flared up in 1818. (Lossing, *Pictorial Field-Book of the War of 1812*)

became the home of War of 1812 hero Com. John Rodgers* sometime before 1820.

> Our kind friend, Mr. [Charles] Carroll, has come to hasten my departure [from the President's House], and is in a very bad humour with me because I insist on waiting until the large picture of Gen. [George] Washington is secured. (An after-the-fact re-creation by Dolley Payne Madison to her sister Lucy Payne Todd of an event that took place after 3:00 p.m., August 24, 1814)[15]

EASTERN BRANCH BRIDGE. *See* Barney Gun Battery Site, Washington, D.C.

EXECUTIVE OFFICE BUILDING, ORIGINAL SITE, also called the Southwest Executive Building (northwest quadrant on south side of Pennsylvania Avenue and East Executive Avenue [closed to traffic] where the Eisenhower Executive Office Building now sits; nearly a duplicate of the original Treasury Department building on the east side, NW). The original 1800 brick Executive Office Building, including the offices of Secretary of State James Monroe and Secretary of War John Armstrong, was burned about 8:00 a.m. on August 25, 1814, by the British. Here President James Madison's brother-in-law, Richard Cutts, superintendent general of military supplies, maintained an office. Before the burning, government clerks had removed the department's documents and prized standards and colors seized from British troops during the Revolutionary War. (*See also* U.S. Treasury Building, Washington, D.C.) The postwar Navy and State Department buildings were replaced by the present Eisenhower Executive Office Building, constructed 1871–88.

Stephen Pleasonton (1777–1855), a State Department clerk, supervised the saving of the most important documents, including the U.S. Constitution, the Declaration of Independence, George Washington's resignation letter as commander of the Continental Army, and the unpublished journals of Congress, by putting them in coarse linen sacks and hurrying them by cart to Edgar Patterson's abandoned gristmill on the Virginia side of the Potomac River near Chain Bridge* two miles north of Georgetown. Because this location was close to the Columbian Foundry,* a likely British target, the records were reloaded into wagons obtained from nearby farms and taken to Rokeby Mansion,* near Leesburg, Virginia, and stored in a vacant vault protected by iron bars and door. (*See* illustration on page 243; *see also* Patent Office Site listing for a similar effort to save documents.)

Earlier, while scouting British movements near Benedict, Maryland, Secretary of State James Monroe had sent a courier to the State Department suggesting, "You had better remove the records" (Secretary of State James Monroe to President James Madison, Woodyard, 9:00 p.m. August 22, 1814).[16]

While packing the documents Pleasonton was chided by Secretary of War John Armstrong,* who insisted there was nothing to fear as the British would surely not attack Washington.[17] These documents are preserved today at the National Archives (7th Street and Pennsylvania Avenue, Washington, D.C.).

FARRAGUT SQUARE (near intersection of 17th and I Streets, NW). Farragut Square is named after Adm. David Glasgow Farragut* of Civil War fame, who fought as a midshipman onboard U.S. frigate *Essex* during the War of 1812. *Essex* sailed into the Pacific during the war to harass British whaling ships while protecting American ones. The *Essex* was captured by two British warships on March 28, 1814, near Valparaiso, Chile. Farragut later criticized Capt. David Porter, Jr.,* for surrendering to the British. Farragut's sword, which he had onboard the *Essex,* is on display at the U.S. Navy Museum,* Washington Navy Yard. The Farragut Monument in the square commemorates Farragut's Civil War exploits and includes mortars cast from the propeller of U.S. sloop-of-war *Hartford,* on whose deck in 1864 he reportedly uttered the famous words "Damn the torpedoes, full speed ahead." The monument, sculpted by Vinnie Ream, was dedicated on April 25, 1881. Within the granite base of the monument is a box with documents relating to Farragut's career.

GREENLEAF POINT FEDERAL ARSENAL SITE (point between fork of Washington Channel and Anacostia River, U.S. Army Fort McNair, SW). Military installation with restricted access. The Greenleaf Point Federal Arsenal, established in 1794 near the National Defense University (NRHP), once called the National War College, consisted of several magazines and buildings. Here gunpowder was tested to meet government standards. (*See* Washington Gun Powder Mills, Bladensburg.) Cannon batteries were established here and across the river at Windmill Point in July 1813 to defend the Washington Navy Yard.* The arsenal was destroyed on August 25, 1814, by the British. During the burning an accidental explosion killed twelve soldiers and wounded thirty. From the body of one of the British soldiers, the Americans recovered a copy of the order in which the British regiments were to be landed at Benedict* in Maryland. This document is now in the manuscript department of the Maryland Historical Society,* Baltimore.

American account of explosion: The magazine at Greenleaf's Point was destroyed (partially only) and the guns spiked on Thursday. In a dry well belonging to the barracks our soldiers had thrown many barrels of powder for concealment. After exploding the magazine, the British soldiers threw casually into the well one or two of their matches, which communicated to the powder deposited there. The effect was terrific. Every one of his soldiers near was blown into eternity, many at a greater distance wounded, and the excavation remains an evidence of the great force of this explosion. (Annapolis *Maryland Republican,* September 3, 1814)

British account of explosion: One of the artillery-men most unfortunately dropped a lighted port-fire into the well, which, with a magazine about twenty yards distant, full of shells, charged and primed, blew up with the most tremendous explosion I ever heard. One house was unroofed, and the walls of two others, which had been burnt an hour before, were shook down. Large pieces of earth, stones, bricks, shot, shells, etc., burst into the air, and, falling among us (who had nowhere to run, being on a narrow neck of land, with sea [bounded by Washington Channel and Anacostia River] on three sides), killed about twelve men and wounded above thirty more, most of them in a dreadful manner. I had the good fortune to escape with whole skin and bones, but somewhat bruised. The groans of the people almost buried in the earth, or with legs and arms broke, and the sight of pieces of bodies lying about, was a thousand times more distressing than the loss we met in the field that day before [at the Battle for Bladensburg]. (Account of unnamed officer published in the London *Morning Post,* October 7, 1814)

Prior to the Battle for Baltimore, Maj. George Armistead, commander of Fort McHenry, requested that the large mortars located at the Greenleaf Point Federal Arsenal be sent to the fort. Although the mortars were sent, no shot, fuses, or carriages were included. The weapons were therefore unusable. It was for this reason that Fort McHenry did not have guns of sufficient range to respond to the British fleet's long-range artillery barrage. After the burning of Washington, the government demanded that several cannon from Fort McHenry be returned to the capital. Gen. Samuel Smith, commander in chief of the defense of Baltimore, shrewdly replied that the government could have the cannon but the carriages belonged to the city. Hence, the cannon stayed put.

On the parade grounds of Fort McNair, near the flag staff, is a cannon reportedly captured during the Battle of Lundy's Lane by the U.S. Infantry. This is one of seven cannons captured, but due to lack of horses only this one was removed, and the British retook the remaining six the next morning.

★**JACKSON, MAJ. GEN. ANDREW, STATUE** (center of Lafayette Square, bounded on north by H Street, east by Madison Place, south by Pennsylvania Avenue, and west by Jackson Place, just north of White House, NW). Lafayette Square NHD. The Andrew Jackson Monument is dedicated to U.S. President and War of 1812 hero Maj. Gen. Andrew Jackson for his defeat of the British on January 8, 1815, at the Battle of New Orleans. The equestrian sculpture, dedicated on January 8, 1853, the 38th anniversary of Jackson's victory at New Orleans, depicts him doffing his cocked hat on a rearing horse. This was the first equestrian sculpture cast in the United States. Clark Mills designed the stature, which was cast from melted bronze taken from British cannons captured at the Battle of New Orleans. The four 870-pound cannons at the base of the statue were captured from the Spanish when the United States occupied Florida prior to the signing of the Adams–Onis Treaty in 1819; they are named El Egica, El Aristo, El Apolo, and Witza. Lafayette Square, then called President Square, served as an American encampment during the War of 1812 and for a brief time as a British camp during their occupation of Washington.

KENNEDY, JACQUELINE, HOUSE (3017 N Street, Georgetown, NW). Maj. George Peter, who organized the "Flying Artillery" of the District of Columbia militia during the War of 1812, lived in what today is known as the Jacqueline Kennedy House. On August 21, 1814, Peter's Company briefly skirmished with the British at Nottingham,* Maryland, when the latter were marching on Washington. Peter is buried at Oak Hill Cemetery,* Washington.

KEY, FRANCIS SCOTT, MEMORIAL BRIDGE/MASON FERRY SITE (carries U.S. Route 29 across Potomac River, NW). NRHP. To the west, nearly opposite this bridge, lived John Mason, who owned a farm on Mason Island, today called Theodore Roosevelt Island.* After destroying Fort Washington,* the American force there retreated to Mason Island. Mason operated a ferry across the Potomac where Key Bridge is located today. President Madison fled to Virginia via this ferry on the night of August 24, 1814, and rode by horseback to Falls Church.* He and his entourage spent most of the night and the next day on horseback, occasionally looking back to observe the red sky of the burning capital.

If at intervals the dismal sight was lost to our view, we got it again from some hill-top or eminence where we paused to look at it. (Attorney Gen. Richard Rush to John S. Williams, July 10, 1855)[18]

The Francis Scott Key Memorial Bridge, built for $16 million in 1923, became a memorial to Key, but only after the National Society United States Daughters of 1812 convinced Congress to allow them to place a tablet on the east balustrade of the structure. The ceremony, held on April 21, 1924, took place fifteen months after the bridge had been completed. The original tablet was removed when the bridge was widened, and on April 20, 1957, a new marker was dedicated. It was refurbished in September 1993 by the Daughters of 1812. Francis Scott Key's home was located near the northeast end of the bridge. (*See also* Key House, Washington, D.C., and Francis Scott Key Bridge, Baltimore.)

KEY, FRANCIS SCOTT, HOUSE SITE, also called Key Mansion (34th and M Street [then 3516-8 M Street, also called Falls or Bridge Street], NW). Francis Scott Key's home (opposite Key Park) and adjacent (west side) one-story law office occupied this site from 1805 to 1828. Key served from June 19, 1814, to July 1, 1814, as a lieutenant and quartermaster in the Georgetown Light Artillery. Key and his wife, Mary Tayloe Lloyd Key, watched the conflagration of Washington from their home the night after he had served as aide to Brig. Gen. Walter Smith of the D.C. militia, during the Battle of Bladensburg.* It was here that Richard E. West of Woodyard,* Mary's brother-in-law, came to seek Key's assistance in freeing Dr. William Beanes, who on August 26, 1814, had been seized by the British in Upper Marlboro.* As a result, Key found himself with the British fleet during the bombardment of Fort McHenry. This inspired him to write the poem that eventually was titled "The Star-Spangled Banner," which became the national anthem in 1931. Key moved to another house near Third and C streets in 1828, when construction of the Chesapeake and Ohio Canal cut across the back of his property and threatened to destroy his solitude. A subsequent owner removed the gabled roof and added a store front on the first floor. In 1948, the M Street house was demolished in order to connect Whitehurst Freeway with Key Bridge.

Under the leadership of Francis Scott Key-Smith, a direct descendant of F. S. Key, the Francis Scott Key Memorial Association sought to buy the Key House in 1908 but lacked the funds. In 1931, the District of Columbia Historical Society spearheaded a second attempt to buy the building, but

Over the years, the Key House (now demolished) has been used for many purposes: a flag factory, an ice cream parlor, and an awning shop. As shown here, it was simply a tourist attraction. (Circa 1896 photograph; HABS, Library of Congress)

this attempt also failed. Mr. Key-Smith noted that most of the original building had been destroyed in late 1912 and early 1913, leaving only the south wall and a portion of original east wall intact. The house was acquired by the National Park Service, but because of the Great Depression, no funds were authorized to restore it. In 1947, Congress authorized $75,000 for the construction of a replica Key House. Bricks and lumber from the post-Key structure were numbered and stored around the city, some under Key Bridge. But the money was never authorized because President Harry S. Truman pocket-vetoed the bill. Much of the building material was either lost or stolen. This prompted the jibe that "anyone can lose a house key but only Uncle Sam could lose Key's house." A rafter end from the house is exhibited at the Flag House* in Baltimore.

★ **KEY, FRANCIS SCOTT, PARK, STAR-SPANGLED BANNER MEMORIAL** (34th and M [then called Falls or Bridge Street] streets, NW). Key Park is near the site of the circa 1803 house that became Francis Scott Key's home and adjacent one-story law office. (*See* Key House, Washington, D.C.) This small park, featuring interpretive plaques about Francis Scott Key, was dedicated on September 14, 1993.

MCKEOWN HOTEL SITE (near intersection of Constitution and Pennsylvania avenues, approximately at the Canadian Embassy, NW). Chester Bailey, an American mail contractor then visiting the city, described the invading troops as they stopped opposite McKeown's Hotel as "the most hellish-looking fellows that ever trod God's earth."[19] On November 21, 1814, "The Star-Spangled Banner" was sung in Washington for the first time at this hotel at the retirement party of Secretary of Navy William Jones. It was sung publicly for the first time a week earlier on November 14, 1814, at Holliday Theater,* Baltimore.

> In the course of the toasts, the very beautiful and touching lines composed by a gentleman (F.S. Key, Esq.) of this District, whom circumstances had thrown on board the British fleet during its tremendous attack on Fort McHenry, and published in this paper on the 26th of September, were sung with great effect by several of the guests. (Washington *Daily National Intelligencer,* December 14, 1814)

NATIONAL INTELLIGENCER OFFICE SITE, also called the *Daily National Intelligencer* (6th Street and Pennsylvania Avenue, NW; postwar location at northeast corner of 7th Street where the Federal Trade Commission is now located). On July 23, 1814, at the urging of Brig. Gen. William H. Winder, the *National Intelligencer* adopted a policy of discontinuing the publication of military information. Traitors such as a Mr. Hopewell of Drum Point, Maryland, gathered the newspapers and presented them to British officers. On the morning of August 25, 1814, Rear Adm. George Cockburn ordered the burning of the *National Intelligencer* office (then located on 6th Street), but residents in the neighborhood successfully pleaded that private homes might also suffer. He therefore ordered the building torn down. Some accounts claim that when Cockburn was informed that the office did not belong to Joseph Gales, Jr., the newspaper's publisher, he ordered the presses, papers, books, and records to be destroyed, mostly in a bonfire outside the ransacked office. But most accounts claim a stout rope was passed through windows on the front side and by a strong pull the building front was tumbled down in ruins.

Ever since Rear Adm. George Cockburn's arrival in the Chesapeake in the spring of 1813, vicious articles had been written about him by the English-born publisher Joseph Gales, Jr., of the *Daily National Intelligencer.* Thus when Cockburn reached Washington, he was especially eager to destroy this newspaper. To ensure that the paper would not be able to abuse him by name again, Cockburn reportedly ordered Col. Timothy Jones to destroy every letter *c.*

Patrick Crowley, an apprentice at the *Daily National Intelligencer,* recorded the sacking and destruction of the city. Francis Scott Key sent Crowley a manuscript copy of his poem that eventually became "The Star-Spangled Banner" with permission to publish it. Crowley printed it on hand bills that he sold on the streets of Washington, earning a tidy profit of nearly $200.

Joseph Gales, Jr., was on a trip to Raleigh, North Carolina, at the time of the British occupation. His city house at 9th and E streets reportedly was saved from being burned by the British when a housekeeper closed up the home and placed a "For Rent" sign on the front door.

> Greater respect was certainly paid to private property than has usually been exhibited by the enemy in his marauding parties. No houses were half as much plundered by the enemy as by the knavish wretches of the town who profited by the general distress. (Joseph Gales, Jr., Washington *Daily National Intelligencer,* August 31, 1814)

★ NATIONAL MUSEUM OF AMERICAN HISTORY, Smithsonian Institution (National Mall at Constitution Avenue and 14th Street, NW). The Star-Spangled Banner garrison flag, which flew over Fort McHenry on September 14, 1814, is exhibited in a special gallery at the National Museum of American History. The flag, originally 32 by 40 feet, is significantly shorter because Lt. Col. George Armistead's family gave fabric squares from the flag to visitors as mementoes. A star from the flag is also missing, but no one knows who received it. A white *V*-shaped piece of material stitched over the stripes is thought to be part of an *A* for Armistead. Also in this gallery is a British bombshell of the type used during the bombardment of Fort McHenry; a punch bowl in the shape of a thirteen-inch British mortar presented to Lieutenant Colonel Armistead in 1816 by the citizens of Baltimore; and a charred Timber from the White House* believed to be a result of the August 24, 1814 British burning.

On exhibit is also a Congreve rocket, named after its inventor, Sir William Congreve (1772–1828). The rockets were a new and frightening but generally inaccurate weapon of war. At least one of the rockets was presented to the Smithsonian Institution by a delegation of British military officers on March 31, 1967. At the time, Maj. Gen. P. G. Glover, director of Great Britain's Royal Artillery Institution, said: "Now that a century and a half have elapsed, I am sure that the rockets' red glare of your National Anthem refers to Congreve rockets used in the bombardment viewed by Francis Scott Key."[20] A Congreve rocket is also on display at Fort McHenry.* Other War of 1812 exhibits can be found in the military gallery.

NATIONAL SOCIETY UNITED STATES DAUGHTERS OF 1812 HEADQUARTERS (1461 Rhode Island Ave., NW). NRHP. The National Society United States Daughters of 1812 was founded by Flora Adams Darling* on January 8, 1892, the seventy-seventh anniversary of the Battle of New Orleans. The 1884 home of Rear Adm. John Upshear (1823–1917) serves as the Society's headquarters and houses a War of 1812 museum and library. Artifacts include a sword presented to John Adams Webster,* a hero of the Battle for Baltimore. (A second presentation sword is in the collections of the Maryland Historical Society,* Baltimore.) From the flag pole, made from a mast of the U.S. frigate *Constellation* and located in front of the headquarters, flies an 1812-era replica flag.

★ **OCTAGON HOUSE** (1799 New York Avenue, NW). NRHP. Col. John Tayloe III of Mt. Airy Plantation, Richmond County, Virginia, said to be the wealthiest plantation owner in Virginia at the time, built Octagon House in 1801 as his winter house. During the British occupation of Washington, Tayloe asked the French Minister Louis Serurier and his wife to occupy the house to spare it from possible looting and burning. A makeshift Bourbon flag flew over the house, signifying that Octagon House was under the French king's protection. Serurier sent a letter to Maj. Gen. Robert Ross, who was then overseeing the burning of the President's House, asking a guard be placed at his residence for protection. Ross wrote back that the French king's house would be as respected as if His Majesty were there in person. White House doorkeeper or steward Jean Pierre Sioussat, known

as French John, took the mansion's pet macaw to Octagon House for safekeeping. A month later Serurier offered his house to President James Madison, who occupied it for six months after the President's House had burned. Here the president's cabinet members met on several occasions.

During the San Francisco, California earthquake of 1906, a woman who had bought the drum table on which was signed the Treaty of Ghent, concerned that it might be consumed in the fire started by the quake, reportedly chopped off the table legs, wrapped it in a blanket, and rolled it to safety although the flames ironically never reached her home. When the American Institute of Architects acquired the Octagon House in 1902, she reportedly returned the table to the house. However, no documentation of this story has been uncovered and until such proof emerges it must be considered a folktale.

Tayloe's son, John Tayloe IV, died of wounds he received while serving as a midshipman onboard U.S. frigate *Constitution* on August 19, 1812, during battle against H.M. frigate *Guerriere*. (*See also* Fort Covington, Baltimore and Bancroft Hall, U.S. Naval Academy, Annapolis.)

Following the signing of the Treaty of Ghent, one of the biggest of many social events at the Octagon House took place. Drinks were ordered for all the servants. French John, the White House doorkeeper, was said to be drunk for two days.

> Soon after nightfall, Members of Congress and others . . . presented themselves at the President's [Octagon] house, the doors of which stood open. When the writer entered the drawing room . . . it was crowded to its full capacity, Mrs. [Dolley] Madison (the President being with the Cabinet) doing the honours of the occasion . . . Among the members present were gentlemen of opposite politics, but lately arrayed against one another in continual conflict and fierce debate, now with elated sprits thanking God, and with softened hearts cordially felicitating with one another upon the joyful intelligence . . . But the most conspicuous object in the room was Mrs. Madison herself, then in the meridian of life and queenly beauty. (Joseph Gales, Jr.)[21]

The insignia of The National Society United States Daughters of 1812 is a star resting on an anchor encircled by a golden band. The star represents hope; the anchor faith; and the circle friendship. When the insignia is placed by the society on War of 1812 veterans' graves, the individual's name is usually included below the circle. (Ralph Eshelman 2006 photograph)

PATENT OFFICE SITE, also called Blodgett's Hotel (northeast corner of 8th and E streets, NW, now occupied by Hotel Monaco, the former Post Office Department and later the Tariff Commission Building). Although sometimes referred to as Blodgett's Hotel, this building was never used for pubic lodging. Designed by James Hoban, architect of the White House, and constructed in 1793, it served as the Patent Office and the Post Office Department beginning in 1810.

The Treaty of Ghent officially ending the war was ratified by President Madison here on February 16, 1815, when he signed it on the drum table located in the second-story Round Room also known as the Treaty Room. The table and a dispatch-box in which the treaty arrived are exhibited here. (Jack Boucher 1971 photograph; HABS, Library of Congress)

When the British threatened Washington in 1814, Dr. William Thornton, superintendent of patents, his clerk George Lyon, his messenger and model maker Thomas Nicholson, and two hired men used 402 feet of ¾ inch wooden lathe and 100 feet of sheet iron to make boxes for the packing of the Patent Office documents. They commandeered privately owned wagons and hired teamsters to haul the documents to the safety of Thornton's farm, located about eight miles away in what today is downtown Bethesda. They obtained wagons or teamster services or both from Burgess Willett, Charles Lemon, and Richard Fenwick. Similar efforts were made at the State Department* and in the Senate Wing of the Capitol* to save documents.

While the documents were carried to safety, the patent models, numbering in the hundreds, were too bulky to be moved to safety. When Thorton and Nicholson learned that the War Department and Blodgett's Hotel were about to be burned, they rushed to the Patent Office to save a musical playing instrument patent model that Thorton had invented and Nicholson was making. They approached a Major Waters, who told them the British had no intention of burning private property and they could remove anything they wished. Thorton and Nicholson explained that because the building contained hundreds of models it would be impossible to remove them all. Major Waters agreed to take Thorton to talk with his commander, Maj. Timothy Jones, who agreed to spare the building. Thus, Thornton saved not just his musical playing machine model but also the entire building and its contents.

The Patent Office operated from 1810 to 1836 in the Blodgett's Hotel, shown at right. The President's Mansion is visible above the cart. (Circa 1803 watercolor by Nicholas King, *View from Blodgett's Hotel to White House*; courtesy of the Huntington Library, San Marino, California)

I [Thornton] told [the British major in charge of the burning detail] that there was nothing but private property of any consequence, and that I was willing to have any other burnt in the street provided the Building might be preserved which contained hundreds of models of the Arts and that it would be impossible to remove them; and to burn what would be useful to all mankind would be as barbarous as formerly to burn the Alexandrian Library for which the Turks have been ever since condemned by all enlightened nations. The major [Waters] desired me to call again to Col. [Maj.] [Timothy] Jones . . . I went and was kindly received. They took their men away, and promised to spare the building. (Dr. William Thornton)[22]

Dr. [William] T [hornton]. went to the City [Washington], and by his exertions saved the patent office from destruction. They [British] were on the point of setting it on fire. And he represented to the officer [Maj. Timothy Jones] that it was the Museum of the Arts, and that it would be a loss to all the world. (Mrs. Anna Marie Brodeau Thornton, August 25, 1814)[23]

As one of the few public buildings to survive the burning of Washington, the Patent Office served as the temporary home for Congress from September 19, 1814, until December 8, 1815, when it moved to the Old Brick Capitol (where the U.S. Supreme Court* now stands). Tingey House,* the U.S. Marine Barracks,* and the Commandant House* also escaped destruction. A severe storm on the afternoon of August 25, 1814, toppled three chimneys and blew off part of the roof on the Patent Building. Ironically, many of the patent models saved in 1814 burned in a 1836 fire.

PENNSYLVANIA AVENUE. NHD. On August 24, 1814, the British marched down Pennsylvania Avenue from the U.S. Capitol to the President's House. At the intersection with 15th Street, where Pennsylvania Avenue turns, the British marched west to burn the President's House and the State Department and Treasury buildings. Like all the diagonal streets in the city, Pennsylvania Avenue was 160 feet wide.

The Admiral and General Ross then descended the Capitol hill, with about one hundred and fifty men, and entered the heart of the city, by the Pennsylvanian avenue. This was a fine and spacious causeway with a road on each side, for equestrians, outside of which were two broad pathways for the accommodation of the more humble pedestrian; the whole was beautifully planted with a row of trees separating them from each other. (Capt. James Scott, 1834)[24]

William Gardner watched from his home on Pennsylvania Avenue as the British marched down the road in twin columns, followed by four officers on horseback, each of whom doffed his hat to bid Gardner good evening. Gardner struck up a conversation with Rear Adm. George Cockburn, who assured him that private property would be respected.

QUALITY HILL, also called Worthington House (3425 Prospect Street, NW). NRHP. Dr. Charles Worthington, an opponent of the war with England, lived at Quality Hill. He took in some of the wounded British soldiers from the Battle of Bladensburg. In gratitude, one British officer reportedly later gave Dr. Worthington a gold snuffbox engraved with the words, "extreme kindness and attention."[25] The whereabouts of the snuffbox today is unknown.

RHODES TAVERN. *See* Bank of the Metropolis listing, Washington, D.C.

ST. ALBANS SCHOOL OF PUBLIC SERVICE. *See* Washington National Cathedral under Washington

SCOTT, WINFIELD, MONUMENT (Scott Circle, intersection of Rhode Island and Massachusetts avenues, NW). Although best remembered for his contributions during the Mexican War and Civil War, Gen. Winfield Scott* (1786–1866) attained the rank of major general in 1815 as a result of his leadership and heroism during the War of 1812. (*See* chapter 2 for details of Scott's War of 1812 accomplishments.) The bronze sculpture by Henry Kirke Brown, dedicated 1874, depicts Scott upon a stallion with a mare's body. Scott preferred to ride mares, but his family objected to an image of the general on a mare, so the artist modified the appearance of the horse. The sculpture was cast in bronze from Mexican War cannon captured by Scott.

★ **SEWALL-BELMONT HOUSE,** also called Alva Belmont House (144 Constitution Ave, NE). NRHP. Robert Sewall built this house in 1800 on three city lots. Incorporating part of an earlier house, the current structure dates from 1820 and is one of the oldest buildings in Washington. As the British marched down Maryland Avenue, someone (possibly U.S. Chesapeake flotillamen) fired shots from the house. One

View of Pennsylvania Avenue from the west terrace of the Capitol. The poplar trees that line the avenue were planted at the suggestion of Thomas Jefferson in 1803. Some sources claim this view dates from circa 1800, 1810, or 1813, but the image was actually executed circa 1828.

(John Rubens Smith, "Washington Looking up Pennsylvania Avenue from the Terrace of the Capitol," in *A System of Universal Geography,* vol. 2, 1834)

British soldier was killed and three others were wounded. Maj. Gen. Robert Ross's horse was also killed. The British retaliated by setting the house on fire. This was the only private residence deliberately burned by the British during the occupation. Three privately owned rope walks were burned, but these produced war materiel for the government. A rental house that was once owned by George Washington also burned, probably set afire by sparks from the nearby burning U.S. Capitol. A hotel belonging to Daniel Carroll was also destroyed. Robert Sewall's son William was living in the Sewall-Belmont House at the time, but he had been called into service with the militia. The shots fired from the house are the only resistance offered to the British during their occupation of Washington.

American account of the sniper attack: Master left a colored man and me sleve with a olde lady by the name of Mrs. Ried on Capitol Hill and as sone as got sight of the British army raising that hill they looked like flames of fier all red coats and the staks of their guns painted with red vermelion and iron work shimered like a Spanish dollar . . . The British army still continued ther march on toward the Capitol ontill they got against a large brick house on Capitol Hill fronting Maryland [Avenue] . . . This house now sets to the Northe east of the United States Senate and as the British army approach that house under the command of General [Robert] Ross and his aides, his horse wher shot from under him and in a twinkle of the eye the house wer sorounded by the British army and search all through upstairs an down-stairs . . . but no man whar found . . . They put a globe match to the house and then stood oft a sertin distance . . . and those rockets burst until they came to the explosion part they made the rafters fly East and West. (Michael Shiner)[26]

Second American account of sniper attack: That, on the retreat of the American forces from Bladensburg, on the 24th August, 1814, a party of Commodore [Joshua] Barney's men [U.S. Chesapeake flotillamen], then a portion of that force, threw themselves into the house of the petitioner, and made an attack from said house upon the advance party of the British army under the command of General [Robert] Ross; by which attack General Ross's horse was killed, one or two of his men also were killed, and several were wounded. This adventurous and heroic party were immediately overpowered by the British force; three of them were taken prisoners in the house, whilst the remainder made their escape by flight. The house of the petitioner [Robert Sewall], thus made a block-house of by this gallant little band, was instantly set on fire by order of General Ross, and destroyed with all its costly furniture. The house had been deserted by its inhabitants, the proprietor having several months before

removed to his farm [His Lordship's Kindness] in Prince George's county for the summer; and his son, Mr. William Sewall, in whose care the house had been left by his father, was then employed in the militia, who had been called into service some time before, when the enemy threatened the adjacent country. (Sonia Ressman Fuenties, 1819)[27]

American account of sniper attack: The house in which Mr. [Albert] Gallatin lived had been destroyed, in consequence of a barber and three or four men having got into it and firing from the windows! They shot general Ross's horse under him. (Philadelphia *American Weekly Messenger,* August 13, 1814)

British account of sniper attack: Advancing a short way past the first Houses of the Town without being accompanied by the Troops, the Enemy opened upon us a heavy fire of Musquetry from the Capitol and two other houses [one the Sewall-Belmont House], these were therefore almost immediately Stormed by our People, taken possession of, and set on fire, after which the Town submitted without further resistance. (Rear Adm. George Cockburn to Vice Adm. Alexander F. I. Cochrane, August 27, 1814)[28]

A plaque on the house claims "Commodore Joshua Barney and his men, from this house offered the only resistance." This text is misleading as Barney was wounded and left behind at Bladensburg; he was not present during the British advance into Washington. However, it is believed that some if not all the resistance came from his flotillamen.

Albert Gallatin,* the fourth secretary of the treasury, serving under Thomas Jefferson and James Madison from 1801 to 1814, leased the house, and from here financed the Louisiana Purchase in 1803. Ironically, at the time of the attack, Gallatin was in Ghent, present-day Belgium, serving as one of five American peace commissioners negotiating the end to the war. Some believe the kitchen wing of the Sewall-Belmont House may have survived the fire. Blackened bricks around the front door were discovered during a renovation in 2002, suggesting parts of the original walls also survive. Robert Sewall was justified in filing a claim for reimbursement for damages to his house and its contents because the British burned the building after it was used for military purposes. After years of legal maneuvering, the Senate Committee of Claims finally awarded compensation in 1847, some twenty-seven years after Sewall's death. The house now serves as the headquarters for the National Woman's Party.

THE SOCIETY OF THE CINCINNATI MUSEUM AT ANDERSON HOUSE (2118 Massachusetts Avenue, NW). The Society of the Cincinnati, organized by officers of the American Revolution in 1783, is headquartered in this palatial 1905 Beaux-Arts mansion known as Anderson House. At the end of the Revolutionary War, Maj. Henry Knox of the Continental Army proposed the establishment of a hereditary society of officers who had served in the war. It was named for Lucius Quinctius Cincinnatus, a citizen-soldier of early Rome who sacrificed his private pursuits for the sake of defending his country. The Society possesses a presentation sword given to Com. Joshua Barney on September 28, 1814, by the common council and aldermen of the City of Washington. A number of the War of 1812 officers who fought in the Chesapeake Campaign, including Com. Joshua Barney and generals Samuel Smith and John Stricker, were also Revolutionary War officers who belonged to the Society of the Cincinnati.

SUTER'S BOARDINGHOUSE SITE (southeast corner of 15th Street and Pennsylvania Avenue, NW). Maj. Gen. Robert Ross, Rear Adm. George Cockburn, and nine other British officers as well as a British spy (whose name is unknown) dined at Barbara Suter's Boardinghouse about midnight, August 24, 1814, after burning the President's House and adjacent U.S. Treasury and U.S. State Department buildings. The boardinghouse operated from 1807 until 1814. Rear Adm. George Cockburn reportedly rode into the boardinghouse on the back of a mule because his horse had been shot near Sewall-Belmont House* and blew out the candles, saying he preferred to eat by the light of the blazing buildings. Ms. Barbara Suter is said to have recognized the spy who visited her establishment only three weeks before. If Major General Ross and Rear Admiral Cockburn had already eaten at the President's House (White House*) as many sources claim, this would have been their second meal the same evening. More probably, other officers and men dined at the President's House and Ross and Cockburn only lightly refreshed themselves there, if at all. While it is probably true that Ross and Cockburn ate at Suter's, it is surely untrue that Cockburn rode a mule into the boarding house and doubtful that he blew out the candles to eat by the light of the burning city.

TENCH RINGGOLD, JOHN CHALMERS, AND RENNER & HEATH [Daniel Renner and Nathaniel K. Heath] **Ropewalk Sites** (near 7th Street and Mall, approximately where National Air & Space Museum and Hirshhorn Sculpture Garden located, SW). On August 24–25, 1814, the British burned three rope walks, one of which had been in operation for only ten days. The Ringgold rope walk served on August 19, 1814, as a militia mustering point.

> Two [actually three] Rope Walks of a very extensive Nature, full of Tar, Rope, &c. Situated at a considerable distance from the [Washington Navy] Yard were likewise set Fire to and consumed. (Rear Adm. George Cockburn to Vice Adm. Sir Alexander F. I. Cochrane, August 27, 1814)[29]

> Having spread quantities of the unwrought material along the centre of the roofed walk, and knocking out the heads of some dozens of tar-barrels, their contents were spread over the train. The whole was speedily in a state of ignition; black dense volumes of smoke rolled over the captured city, obscuring the heavens from the view of its inhabitants. (Capt. James Scott, 1834)[30]

TENLEYTOWN (area around the intersection of Nebraska and Wisconsin avenues, three miles north-northwest of Georgetown, NW). Brig. Gen. William H. Winder and parts of his exhausted and scattered army rendezvoused about midnight, August 24/25, 1814, at Tenleytown. Seeing the red glare of burning Washington, Winder pressed his men on to Montgomery Court House (Rockville*).

> On arriving at the capital, I understood that the city had been abandoned . . . encamped that night at Teny Town, about three miles back of Georgetown (Sgt. John Law, November 10, 1814)[31]

> A powerful army of Americans already began to show themselves upon some heights, at the distance of two or three miles from the city; and as they sent out detachments of horse even to the very suburbs, for the purpose of watching our motions. (Lt. George Robert Gleig, 1821)[32]

THEODORE ROOSEVELT ISLAND, then called Mason's Island (Potomac River, north of National Cemetery, access via George Washington Memorial Parkway, NW). National Memorial National Park Service designation. Capt. Samuel T. Dyson, in command of Fort Washington,* retreated with his troops to Mason's Island after blowing up the fort to keep it out of British hands. Dyson was dismissed from the army for not defending the fort. Units of the Northern Neck Virginia militia were also encamped here.

TUDOR PLACE (1644 31st Street, NW). NRHP. Tudor Place was constructed between 1794 and 1816 on the crest of Georgetown heights by Thomas Peter and his wife Martha Custis Peter, granddaughter of Martha Washington. Dr.

William Thornton, first architect of the U.S. Capitol and Octagon House,* designed the house in the neoclassical style. (*See* Latrobe Gate, Washington Navy Yard, Washington, for an account of a lawsuit between Thornton and Latrobe.) From here during the evening of August 24, 1814, Mrs. Peter, Dr. William Thornton, and his wife, Anna Marie Brodeau Thornton, watched the capital burn.

> We are all on the alert here to give the British a warm reception. An express arrived on Thursday last, saying they were in the river; and, as the wind was fair, we expected every moment to see their white sheets shivering in the breeze. The drums began to beat, the military to parade; and in a moment all was bustle and alarm. Before night, scarcely a man was to be seen in the streets: they were all posted at Fort Warburton [Washington] . . . The Secretaries of War and of the Navy joined the van; and each new-made officer vied with the other who should put on most finery; expecting, no doubt, by their dazzling appearance, to strike the enemy with dismay. (Martha Custis Peter to Mrs. Josiah Quincy, July 13, 1813)[33]

> We stayed all night at Mrs. [Martha Custis] Peter's and there witnessed the conflagration of our poor undefended and devoted city. (Anna Marie Brodeau Thornton, August 24, 1814)[34]

> For some weeks the citizens have expected a visit from the British, and repeatedly called upon the Secretary of the War Department and the President for protection. The first laughed at what he called their idle fears. The President said he was called on from all quarters for protection; that he could not protect everyone; and the District must take care of itself . . . About three days before the British came, Armstrong acknowledged that he now believed they would be here. The Cabinet then began to make great exertions, and assured the citizens that they would have so large a force, that it would be impossible for the British to penetrate through them. Knowing our Treasury to be much in want of money, the several banks in the District loaned the Cabinet two hundred thousand dollars for their defense. On Friday last, the troops were all ordered to march, as the enemy were landing, in considerable numbers, forty-five miles from Washington. Unfortunately, we never shut the stable-door till the steed is stolen . . . Two cannon were placed opposite the Capitol, two at the offices, and two at the President's house . . . On Wednesday, our troops received information that the enemy were at Bladensburg; and formed themselves in battle array on the ground between the city and that place. From what I can learn, nothing was ever worse ordered. For an hour before the engagement took place, the General was not to be found. The President was on the ground, who, no doubt, had some little curiosity to see what

sort of beings those were who dared to approach his Capitol, but I believe he was soon satisfied, as he fled so swiftly, that he has never been heard of since. The whole Cabinet are off, no one knows where. The citizens vow they will hang Armstrong on the walls of the Capitol when he returns. (Martha Custis Peter to Mrs. Josiah Quincy, August 26, 1814, two days after the burning of Washington)[35]

★ **U.S. CAPITOL** (intersection between Maryland and Pennsylvanian avenues and Constitution and Independence avenues) NHD. The U.S. Capitol was not complete in 1814. There was no central core with dome, only a north wing containing the Senate chamber, the Supreme Court chamber, and various other offices, and the south wing containing the larger House chamber and accompanying offices. The wings were connected by a wooden causeway some hundred yards long. Dr. William Thornton, an aide to Gen. George Washington, was the first architect of the Capitol. Thornton also designed Tudor Place and Octagon House.* The Capitol housed the three thousand-volume Library of Congress and the Supreme Court library. The Capitol building was burned by the British around 9:00 p.m., August 24, 1814. Separate fires were started in the House of Representatives Chamber, now known as Statuary Hall, South Wing, and the Old Senate Chamber or North Wing.

> Like other infant towns, it [Washington] is but little ornamented with fine buildings; for, except the Senate house [U.S. Capitol], I really know of none worthy to be noticed. This, however, is, or rather was, an edifice of great beauty. It stood, where its ruins now stand, upon a mound called the Capitol hill . . . from which circumstances, these modern republicans are led to flatter themselves, that the days are coming when it will rival in power and grandeur the senate-house of ancient Rome herself. It was built entirely of free-stone, tastefully worked and highly polished. (Lt. George Robert Gleig, 1821)[36]

> 50 men, sailors, and marines, were marched by an officer, silently thro' the avenue, each carrying long pole to which was fixed a ball about the circumference of a large plate,—when arrived at the building [capitol], each man was station'd at a window, with his pole and machine of wild-fire against it, at the word of command, at the same instant the windows were broken and this wild-fire thrown in, so that an instantaneous conflagration took place and the whole building was wrapt in flames and smoke. The spectators stood in awful silence, the city was light and the heavens redden'd with the blaze! (Margaret Bayard Smith)[37]

West elevation of U.S. Capitol as it appeared 1811–14. (Glenn Brown, *History of the United States Capitol*: vol. 1, *The Old Capitol—1792–1850*, 1900)

Congreve rockets were fired into the ceiling of the House of Representatives, but they had little effect because the ceiling was covered in sheet iron. Hence, mahogany tables, chairs, desks, and curtains were piled in the middle of the room, rocket powder was heaped on the mound, and rockets fired into it, which set off the blaze. The same method was used to burn the Senate wing of the U.S. Capitol as well as the Treasury building and the President's House.

American account of destruction: There was no want of materials for the conflagration, for when the number of members of Congress was increased the old platform was left in its place and another raised over it, giving an additional quantity of dry and loose timber. All the stages and seats of the galleries were of timber and yellow pine. The mahogany desks, table, and chairs were in their places . . . At last they made a great pile in the center of the room of the furniture and, retiring, set fire to a quantity of rocket stuff in the middle. The whole was soon in a blaze, and so intense was the flame that the glass of the lights was melted. (Benjamin Henry Latrobe)[38]

Second American account of destruction: The Vandals destroyed without remorse this collection of valuable and scarce books [Library of Congress], the loss of which is irreparable. If his incendiary hand were not to be arrested by the monument of art exhibited in the South Wing of the Capitol, it could not be expected the enemy would respect what none but Heathens or barbarians ever before wantonly

destroyed, a Public Repository of History, Science, and Law. (Boston *Weekly Messenger,* September 16, 1814)

British account of destruction: Unfortunately . . . a noble library, several printing-offices, and all the national archives were likewise committed to the flames, which, though no doubt the property of Government, might better have been spared. (Lt. George Robert Gleig, 1847)[39]

The vestibule at the entrance to the old Supreme Court chamber in the Senate wing survived the burning.

the ruin of the Capitol, which, I assure you, is a melancholy spectacle . . . However, many important parts are wholly uninjured, and what particularly is gratifying to me, the picturesque entrance of the house of Representatives with its handsome columns, the Corn Capitals of the Senate Vestibule, the Great staircase, and all the Vaults of the Senate chambre, are entirely free from any injury which cannot be easily repaired. (Benjamin Henry Latrobe to his wife Mary Elizabeth Hazlehust, soon after the burning of Washington, late 1814)[40]

The only exterior visible wall from 1814 is the sandstone wall on the west side of the Senate wing. An exact replica of the original wall was built in 1959–60 when the Senate wing was enlarged on the east side. A plaque, designated to commemorate the original Library of Congress, is located near the entrance to suite S-230-236.

The U.S. Capitol as it appeared after the British torching in August 1814. (1814 drawing by George Munger; Library of Congress)

It is well known that Dolley Madison saved a portrait of George Washington at the White House. Not so well known is Stephen Pleasonton's effort at the State Department to save the U.S. Constitution and other valuable documents and Dr. William Thornton's efforts to save the Patent Office documents. Also largely unknown is how Elias Boudinot Caldwell, clerk of the Supreme Court, moved the court's library into his house, saving the books from the fate visited on the Library of Congress.

British troops bivouacked on Capitol Hill, just to the east of the U.S. Capitol, during the night of August 24–25, 1814. The British raised the flag of Great Britain on Capitol Hill. In a room on the ground floor of the House Wing where President Madison maintained a work space, Rear Adm. George Cockburn took a bound volume of James Madison's personal copy of U.S. government receipts and expenses

(Right) The "corncob capitals" designed by Benjamin Henry Latrobe and carved by Giuseppe Franzoni in 1809 survived the fire and still stand in the east entry to the Senate Vestibule. (Library of Congress, Prints and Photographs Division)

for 1810. Stamped on the cover "President of the U. States," Cockburn wrote on the inside cover, "Taken in President's room in the Capitol of Washington 24th. August 1814." The memento was returned by a rare book dealer in 1940. The Library of Congress was reestablished using Thomas Jefferson's personal library as its nucleus. In 1815, Congress paid $23,950, which was considered about half the auction value. Portraits of Louis XVI and Marie Antoinette were also reportedly taken, but the culprit is unknown. A temporary hospital for treating British wounded was established on the U.S. Capitol grounds on September 2, 1814.

In the U.S. Capitol visitor center on the east side of the U.S. Capitol is an exhibition hall that contains numerous items related to the War of 1812. Among them is a model of Capitol Hill from 1789 to 1815 showing the appearance of the capitol building; a letter from Thomas Jefferson to Samuel Harrison Smith dated September 21, 1814, offering his library to replace the congressional library lost in the burning of the capitol; four original books belonging to Jefferson that he sold to the government to replace the library; a facsimile of the "Report of Destroyed House Records" dated September 1, 1814; a reproduction of Benjamin Henry Latrobe's corn cob column; and Latrobe's plan for the rebuilding of the capitol.

War of 1812–related sites in the U.S. Capitol include statues of Maj. Gen. Andrew Jackson in the rotunda and congressional War Hawk Henry Clay in Statuary Hall. The Old Supreme Court Chamber is a good location from which to view the original walls of the U.S. Capitol. However, the ceiling in this chamber was replaced after the burning. In the hall just before the entrance is the Senate Vestibule with six original columns depicting bundles of cornstalks and ears of corn at the top. On the ceiling of the ground floor east corridor of the House wing is a 1974 fresco by Allyn Cox entitled *British Burn the Capitol 1814,* which depicts British soldiers torching the U.S. Capitol.

In the stairwell between the second and third floors of the Senate wing is a huge and impressive oil painting by William H. Powell, executed in 1865, entitled *Battle of Lake Erie,* depicting Com. Oliver Hazard Perry on September 10, 1813, transferring from the U.S. brig *Lawrence* to the U.S. brig *Niagara.* After his victory, Perry wrote a message to Maj. Gen. William Henry Harrison: "We have met the enemy and they are ours." Powell took some artistic license in his composition of the painting. Eyewitnesses claimed there were only four men who rowed the craft, not six as depicted by Powell. There would not have been any waves due to light winds on the day of the battle. It is also doubtful Perry would have

been standing or waving his sword. Perry did not take the "colors" as depicted flying on the bow of his craft, but he did take his battle flag, which Powell does not show. The young boy pulling at Perry, urging him to sit down, is Perry's thirteen-year-old brother Alexander. Alexander did not accompany Perry in the boat during this transfer. Local lore claims that the painting frame was made from the wood of the *Lawrence,* but this is not supported by any contemporary evidence.

Reportedly, the following graffiti was found on the ruined U.S. Capitol walls after the fire: "George Washington founded this city after a seven years' war with England—James Madison lost it after a two years' war." "James Madison is a rascal, a coward and a fool." "Armstrong sold the city for 5,000 dollars." "The capital of the Union lost by cowardice." The Tripoli Monument, erected at the Washington Navy Yard in 1808 and reportedly damaged by the British during their attack, was moved to the terrace in front of the western portico of the U.S. Capitol in 1831 and then to its present site at the U.S. Naval Academy in 1860. (*See* Washington Navy Yard, Washington, D.C., and Tripoli Monument, U.S. Naval Academy, Annapolis.)

When the U.S. Capitol was rebuilt, the copper for the new roof (which survived from the 1820s until about 1861) came from Levi Hollingsworth's* Gunpowder Copper Works,* located on the Great Gunpowder River near the Baltimore County–Harford County border. Hollingsworth was wounded in the Battle of North Point.

U.S. MARINE BARRACKS AND COMMANDANT HOUSE, not to be confused with Tingey House, which is the Commandant's House of the Washington Navy Yard (north side of the U.S. Marine Barracks Quadrangle, G Street between 8th and 9th streets, SE). NRHP. The U.S. Marine Corps Commandant House, built in 1806, is probably the oldest public building in continuous use in the nation's capital. It has served as the Commandant's House or official residence of eighteen of the twenty commandants who have headed the U.S. Marine Corps. The house was considerably enlarged in 1836 from its original two-story hipped roof design. No one knows why the British did not burn the house during their occupation of Washington. One theory holds that the British used it for their headquarters. Another suggests that Maj. Gen. Robert Ross was so impressed by the stand the U.S. Marines made at Bladensburg that he ordered the house and barracks untouched as a gesture of soldierly respect. The most logical explanation is that either the British just missed it or the residents of the neighborhood pleaded with the British, pointing out that burning the barracks and house would almost certainly cause damage to adjoining private property. This same argument apparently saved the offices of the *Daily National Intelligencer** and the Patent Office.* Several houses were accidentally set ablaze by sparks from the British burning of the U.S. Capitol or the American and later British burning of the Washington Navy Yard.

> The British Army were momentarily expected—and as I mounted my horse, was told that the whistling of the balls, had been distinctly heard at the [U.S.] Marine Barracks; Which you heard, as well as myself. (Captain's Clerk Mordecai Booth to Capt. Thomas Tingey, August 24, 1814)[41]

U.S. NAVAL BUREAU OF MEDICINE AND SURGERY, also called Camp Hill or Peter Hill (E and 23rd streets, NW). NRHP. The U.S. Naval Bureau of Medicine and Surgery occupies a hill where the militia established a watch station during the War of 1812 to observe any British activity on the Potomac River. This hill became known as Camp Hill when Maj. Charles Pierre L'Enfant placed a military encampment here during the Revolutionary War.

U.S. STATE DEPARTMENT. *See* Executive Office Building, Original Site

U.S. SUPREME COURT/OLD BRICK CAPITOL SITE (One First Street, NE). In an attempt to keep Congress from moving the nation's capital elsewhere (most likely Philadelphia) after the burning of most of the public buildings, influential citizens of Washington erected a brick building as a temporary home for Congress. From December 8, 1815, to December 1819, it served this purpose. Known as the Old Brick Capitol, it was built on the site of Tunnicliffe's Tavern. Outside this temporary capitol, President James Monroe was inaugurated on March 4, 1817, marking the first time the oath of office was taken outdoors, a custom that has been maintained ever since.

U.S. TREASURY BUILDING SITE, also called the Southeast Executive Building (east side of White House and approximately parallel with its south facade; west side 15th Street between Pennsylvania Avenue and East Executive Avenue [closed to traffic]; a nearly identical building housing the Executive Office and War Department sat on the west side, NW). Built in 1798, the original brick treasury building burned in 1800. During the evening of August 24, 1814, the British burned the temporary treasury building as well as the Executive Office Building* where the War Department*

was located. A statue of Albert Gallatin, the fourth secretary of treasury, who served from 1801 to 1814, is located in front of the U.S. Treasury Building (north side). Ironically, at the time of the attack, Gallatin was in Ghent (in modern-day Belgium) working to restore peace.

> The Treasury was next visited, but the specie had been safely conveyed away. The building was fired before the discovery of a strong iron door, that resisted all the efforts made to break it open. It was presumed to be the stronghold and deposit of all the valuables. The window was forced in, and the first officer who descended into the apartment, gave information that it contained several weighty boxes . . . Great was the bustle attendant on handling through the window the supposed chests of treasure; our anxiety to extricate them from the flames ceased on finding that the contents would by no means compensate us for our exertions and possible suffocation, and they were left to their fate. (Capt. James Scott, 1834)[42]

WAR DEPARTMENT SITE. *See* Executive Office Building

WASHINGTON MONUMENT (National Mall between Lincoln Monument and National Capitol). Among the 192 commemorative stones located along the interior stairway of the Washington Monument (no longer open to the public) is one presented by the City of Baltimore in 1851. The granite stone depicts a monument that most people believe is the Washington Monument in Baltimore, considered the nation's first architectural monument to George Washington, begun in 1815 but not completed until 1829. While this conclusion is logical, it is inaccurate. The commemorative stone depicts Battle Monument,* erected by Baltimore as a tribute to those who defended the city in 1814. Battle Monument is the official emblem of Baltimore. Thus, a symbol of the War of 1812 graces the Washington Monument.

WASHINGTON NATIONAL CATHEDRAL (intersection of Massachusetts and Wisconsin avenues, NW). On the west wall of the crypt corridor, near the bookstore and beneath the south aisle of the nave, is a brass tablet honoring Francis Scott Key placed here by the District of Columbia chapter of the National Society United States Daughters of 1812 on April 26, 1931. Designed by Philip E. Frohman of Frohman, Robb and Little, Washington Cathedral architects, it depicts Fort McHenry against a rising sun. Above it are two flags: one with fifteen stars and the other with forty-eight stars. These were the flags in 1814 and 1931. Between the flags is the American eagle. The tablet mistakenly gives

The Treasury Building as it appeared in 1804 before being burned by the British. (*Harper's New Monthly Magazine,* March 1872)

Key's birth date as August 9, 1790. It should be August 1, 1779. Maj. Francis Scott Key-Smith, great-grandson of Francis Scott Key, gave a presentation on the life of Key during the dedication service. "The Star-Spangled Banner" and the hymn "Lord, with glowing heart I'd praise Thee," the words to both written by Key, were sung.

> MEMORIAL HONORS FRANCIS SCOTT KEY; Tablet Unveiled in Washington Cathedral to Author of National Anthem. GIFT OF WOMEN'S GROUP United Daughters of 1812 Hold Ceremony—Inscription Quotes the Lines of "Star-Spangled Banner." (New York *Times,* April 27, 1931)

Samuel Chester Reid (1783–1861), commander of the New York privateer brig *General Armstrong,* captured twenty-four British prizes during the war. In 1818, Reid collaborated with New York Congressman Peter H. Wendover to steer a bill through Congress that established uniformity in the design of the U.S. flag. Although the number of stripes was congressionally set at thirteen in 1777, a second Flag Act in 1794 authorized fifteen stars and stripes after the entry of Vermont and Kentucky to the Union. Afterward, the American flag varied widely. Reid suggested that stars be added as new states were admitted into the Union but that the stripes

remain at thirteen in honor of the original states. The desk of Samuel Chester Reid is said to reside in a guest house not open to the public on the grounds of Washington National Cathedral. This could not be confirmed.

★ **WASHINGTON NAVY YARD** (Anacostia River, 8th and M streets, SE). NRHP. Benjamin Stoddert, the first secretary of the navy, authorized the Washington Navy Yard in 1799, the U.S. Navy's oldest shore establishment. The U.S. sloop-of-war *Wasp,* built at the navy yard, participated in one of the earliest naval engagements of the war when under the command of Capt. Jacob Jones* it captured H.M. brig *Frolic* on October 18, 1812, but on the same day it was captured by H.M. ship-of-the-line *Poictiers.* The U.S. sloop *Scorpion* was rebuilt here and became the flagship of the U.S. Chesapeake Flotilla. The U.S. schooner *Lynx,* under construction, survived the 1814 burning and later served in the Mediterranean. The U.S. frigate *Constellation** sat in ordinary here prior to the war before being outfitted in early 1813 and then blockaded on June 22, 1813, in the Elizabeth River, Virginia. Sailors from *Constellation* helped to protect Craney Island* at the mouth of the Elizabeth River and thus helped save Norfolk,* Portsmouth,* and the *Constellation* from British capture.

The Washington Navy Yard served as the base for the defense of the Potomac River and the Potomac Flotilla. Brig. Gen. William H. Winder and his troops withdrew from Long Old Fields* to the Eastern Branch bridge* near the Washington Navy Yard on August 23, 1814, in the face of the British advance. Brigadier General Winder was conferring with President James Madison, Secretary of War John Armstrong, and other cabinet members at the nearby Griffith Coombe house about 10:00 a.m., when a scout reported the British were marching for Bladensburg. President Madison, his cabinet, and Winder's troops rode from the navy yard to Bladensburg. The nearby Eastern Branch bridge and much of the navy yard were set on fire by orders of Capt. Thomas Tingey at 8:20 p.m. on August 24, 1814, to keep them out of British hands.

The British showed up at the navy yard the next morning and burned almost everything remaining except the main gate and Quarters "A" and "B." The Tripoli Monument* was "slightly injured," reportedly by British officers. The schooner Lynx was only slightly damaged. The machinery of the steam engine and boiler survived the fire. Gun powder and part of the yard's provisions were recovered when a gunboat was retrieved from near Little Falls on the Potomac River. A second gunboat laden with provisions and gunpowder ran aground and was plundered by the inhabitants near the navy yard.

> It appear'd that they [British] had left the Yard, about ½ an hour when we arrived. I found my dwelling house [Quarters A] and that of Lieutenant [Nathaniel] Haraden [Quarters B] untouched by fire—but some of the people of the neighborhood had commenc'd plundering them . . . Could I have stayed another hour, I had probably saved all my furniture and stores—but being advised by some friends that I was not safe . . . I therefore again embark'd in the gig . . . I had no sooner gone, than such a scene of devastation and plunder took place in the houses (by the people of the neighbourhood) as is disgraceful to relate—not a movable article from the cellars to the garrets has been left us—and even some of the fixtures, and locks of the doors, have been shamefully pillaged. (Capt. Thomas Tingey to Secretary of Navy William Jones, August 27, 1814)[43]

> The buildings destroyed, by the fire . . . were, the Mast-shed, and timber-shed, the joiners & boat-builders shops, and mould loft—all the Offices—the medical store—the plumbers and smiths shops, and block-makers shop—the saw-mill & block mill, with their whole apparatus, tools and machinery—the building for the steam engine, and all the combustible parts of it's machinery and materials; the rigging loft—the apartments for the master, and the boatswain of the yard, with all their furniture—the gun carriage makers and painters shops, with all the materials and tools there in at the time: also the hulls of the old frigates Boston, New York and General Greene. (Com. Thomas Tingey to Secretary of Navy William Jones, October 18, 1814)[44]

On September 4 and 5, 1814, a few days after the British land forces withdrew, fire-vessels were readied and launched from the navy yard against the British naval squadron that was descending the Potomac River with plunder from Alexandria. The fire-vessels, however, did no damage. (See also Mount Welby, Fort Washington, and White House Gun Battery Site.)

During construction work at the Washington Navy Yard in 1905, the graves of fourteen soldiers and sailors of the War of 1812 were uncovered. The bodies were interred in Arlington National Cemetery.* A memorial was dedicated to them by the National Society United States Daughters War of 1812 in April 1976.

★ Latrobe Gate (8th and M streets). NRHP. The 1806 main gate and flanking guard houses, designed by Benjamin Henry Latrobe,* represent one of the earliest examples of Greek Revival architecture in the United States. The gate is one of the few structures to have survived the 1814 fire. The second story and Victorian style guard houses were added in 1880-81, greatly altering and largely hiding the original structure. The Latrobe Gate is the oldest continuously manned U.S. Marine sentry post in the nation. A great eagle and anchor, carved by Giuseppe Franzoni, once stood atop the arch of the gate, but they were removed when the additions were built. The eagle and anchor that were designed by Benjamin Henry Latrobe were ridiculed by Dr. William Thornton,* first architect of the U.S. Capitol, who wrote:

> such an arch as the interior one was never made to a Gateway before, and till the extinction of taste will never be made again . . . The eagle, which crowns it, is so disproportionate to the Anchor, that we are reminded of the Rook in the Arabian Nights Entertainments; but on reviewing it the Eagle looks only like a good fat Goose, and the Anchor fitter for a cock-boat than even a gunboat.—If the American hope rested on such an anchor she would soon breathe her exit in a sight of despair! (Washington Federalist, April 26, 1808)

Latrobe was so outraged by Thornton's comments that he sued him for libel and retained Francis Scott Key* as counsel. After many delays, the case was adjudicated in June 1813, awarding Latrobe one cent in damages and court costs.

Quarters "B" (northeast side of Leutze Park). NRHP. No public access. Quarters "B," built in 1801, served as the Washington Navy Yard's second officer's residence. It was occupied by Lt. Nathaniel Haradan during the British attack. Like Quarters "A" (the Tingey House), it escaped burning by the British. Subsequent additions and alterations, which have doubled the size of the building, have enclosed the original structure so that little of that structure is visible today.

Tingey House (Quarters "A"). NRHP. No public access. This 1804 house was occupied by and named for Capt. Thomas Tingey,* the first commandant of the Washington Navy Yard, who ordered the yard burned to keep it out of the hands of the British. Tingey House survived the fire. Tingey's 1808 rules for the operation of the Washington Navy Yard were adopted for all American naval stations on the Atlantic Coast. Tingey is buried at Congressional Cemetery,* Washington, D.C.

Tripoli Monument Site, originally called the Naval Monument (Leutze Park). Officers of the U.S. Navy erected the Tripoli Monument in 1808 at the Washington Navy Yard to eulogize six American naval officers who fell during the War with Tripoli in 1804. It was moved to the west front terrace of the U.S. Capitol in 1831. The monument, Washington's first outdoor monument, was reportedly vandalized during the morning of August 25, 1814, by British officers. In 1960, the monument was moved for a third time to the grounds of the Naval Academy* in Annapolis. (*See* illustration on page 41 and Tripoli Monument, U.S. Naval Academy, Annapolis, for a description of this monument.)

★ **National Museum of the U.S. Navy** (Building No. 76). The Navy Museum, housed in a six hundred-foot-long structure that accommodated the Breech Mechanism Shop of the old Naval Gun Factory, contains paintings, artifacts, and interpretive exhibits on the War of 1812. Artifacts include the sword that Midshipman David Glasgow Farragut* had onboard the U.S. frigate *Essex* in 1813; a powder horn inscribed "Ship Constellation—44" (number of guns) and dated 1813; a 12 pounder howitzer cannonball recovered from the Battle of Bladensburg*; and a presentation dirk given to Lt. William H. Allen of U.S. frigate *Chesapeake* after he was captured by H.M. frigate *Leopard.* It is inscribed "Given to Lt. William H. Allan as a token of esteem for his courage & endurance in the action on June 22nd 1807 by the officers of U.S. frigate Chesapeake."

WASHINGTON, GEORGE, RENTAL HOUSE SITE (Union Station Plaza near southeast intersection of Louisiana and New Jersey avenues, NW). George Washington had William Thornton design a double townhouse. Built in 1799, it was a three-story brick structure capable of accommodating between twenty and thirty boarders. When the city was threatened by attack, John Frost, a clerk in the House of Representatives, moved committee records, claims and pensions records, and revolutionary claims records here for safekeeping. Unfortunately, the house caught fire during the British occupation and the documents burned. It is probable that the house accidentally caught fire from sparks emanating from the burning of the nearby U.S. Capitol* or Sewall-Belmont House.* This area was then covered with oak trees, which may have helped spread the fire. Others suggest the British deliberately burned the house after learning records had been stored here. However no documentation supports this claim. A house that was built on the site in 1818 incorporating walls from the original house was demolished in 1913.

★ **WHITE HOUSE,** also known in 1814 as the President's Mansion, President's House, and Executive Mansion (1600 Pennsylvania Avenue, NW). The President's House, begun in 1792 and completed in 1802, was first occupied by President John Adams in November 1800. The British burned it about 11:00 p.m., August 24, 1814, leaving a roofless shell. The structure was rebuilt in 1815–17. Some scorch marks are still visible on the sandstone blocks forming the entrance arch of the original kitchen immediately below the north portico added in 1829-30, facing Pennsylvania Avenue. Scorch marks on the south wall are also exposed behind the South Portico added in 1824 at the level of the Truman Balcony on the private second floor. In the National Museum of American History* is a timber taken from the White House during a renovation phase that exhibits char marks believed to date from the British burning of the structure in 1814.

> Will you believe it my sister, we have a battle or skirmish near the city. I am still within sounds of the cannons, Mr. [James] Madison comes not. May God protect us. Two messengers came in and asked me to leave the capitol, I must stay here and wait for my husband. (An after-the-fact re-creation by Dolley Payne Madison to her sister Lucy Payne Todd of an event that took place after 3:00 p.m., August 24, 1814)[45]

> The President's house, . . . though likewise a public building, was remarkable for nothing, except the want of taste exhibited in its structure. It was small, incommodious, and

The White House as it appeared after being burned by the British.
(1814 engraving by William Strickland after drawing by George Munger;
Library of Congress)

plain; in no respect likely to excite the jealousy of a people peculiarly averse to all pomp or parade, even in their chief magistrate. (Lt. George Robert Gleig, 1821)[46]

While passing the President's House during the retreat from the Battle of Bladensburg, U.S. Chesapeake Flotillaman John Adams Webster* noticed a brass 6 pounder cannon on the grounds and took it and other cannon he had taken from the Bladensburg battlefield to the rendezvous site of Montgomery Court House (Rockville*).

The White House is made of tan-colored sandstone and, according to some accounts, "white washed" to hide scorch marks. However, white washing was a standard method of providing a protective coating, and the President's House was white washed as early as the fall of 1798, sixteen years before the British burning. As early as 1810 the term "White House" was in general use. Some accounts claim George Washington named the mansion after the white house where his wife, Martha Dandridge Custis, was living when he proposed. By the mid-nineteenth century it became known as the Executive Mansion. In 1901, President

Theodore Roosevelt signed an order officially naming the building the "White House." During exterior renovations, 1978–94, some thirty layers of paint and white wash were removed. The carved sill under one first-floor window on the north front, immediately west of the North Portico, has been left unpainted to show the original stone color. Thus while the house was no doubt painted white after being rebuilt in 1817, it was sometimes called the "White House" prior to the war.

According to British accounts, advance units that included Maj. Gen. Robert Ross and Rear Adm. George Cockburn found a "victory dinner" for forty persons at the president's mansion during the night of August 24, 1814, and ate some of the food and drank wine that had been laid out. Other accounts claim there was no prepared dinner, only such refreshment as was kept in readiness for messengers and officers returning from errands and the like. However, Paul Jennings, an African American who was a slave to President James Madison, said he set the table himself. More likely a table was set as James and Dolley often entertained, but this was not a victory dinner. Ross, Cockburn, and nine other officers ate that night at Suter's Boardinghouse,* only a few hundred yards from the President's House, making two meals that same evening. It seems more likely that Ross and Cockburn may have eaten some food at the White House but they ate their main evening meal at Suter's. Other officers and possibly troops also may have helped themselves to the food from Madison's table.

> Never was nectar more grateful to the palates of the gods than the crystal goblets of Madeira and water I quaffed off at Mr. [James] Madison's expense. (Capt. James Scott, 1834)[47]

Dolley Payne Madison is credited with saving the portrait of George Washington attributed to Gilbert Stuart, but she had plenty of help. Paul Jennings claims that while Dolley carried off some silver, Jean Pierre Sioussat (doorkeeper) and Tom Magraw (gardener), took the painting down and sent it off by wagon with some large silver urns, red curtains, papers, and other valuables. Two New Yorkers, Jacob Barker and Robert G. L. De Peyster, either oversaw or helped cut open the frame from the Washington portrait and personally removed the painting still on its stretcher. Barker returned it a few weeks later. The White House has a three-piece silver tea set reportedly given by the Madisons to Jacob Barker for his assistance.

> It is done . . . the precious portrait placed in the hands of the gentlemen [Jacob Barker and Robert G. L. de Peyster] for safe keeping. And now, dear sister, I must leave this house or the retreating army will make me a prisoner in it by filling up the road I am directed to take. When I shall again write to you, or where I shall be tomorrow, I cannot tell. (An after-the-fact re-creation by Dolley Payne Madison to her sister Lucy Payne Todd of an event that took place after 3:00 p.m., August 24, 1814)[48]

The Washington portrait that hangs in the East Room and a small wooden medicine chest in the Map Room are the only objects that remain in the mansion that were there before the conflagration. The medicine chest was returned by a Canadian named Archibald Kains, who claims his grandfather, a paymaster on H.M. bomb-vessel *Devastation,* took it. The *Devastation* was not present during the capture of Washington, arriving at Alexandria several days after the British land forces had withdrawn from Washington. How Kains acquired the object and whether it is authentic are unknown.

Another account claims Lt. Beau Colclough Urquhart of the 85th took President Madison's "fine dress sword." In the White House collection is a Windsor writing armchair referred to as the "Madison Chair" that he used between Au-

gust 26 and 27, 1814, at the Caleb Bentley House in Brookeville,* Maryland. The executive branch operated briefly from this house immediately after the evacuation of Washington. Also in the collection is a miniature painting of Capt. Richard Shaw of the 4th King's Own Regiment of Foot as well as his regimental belt plate. Engraved on the painting frame are the words "Capt. R. Shaw Honored by Fireing the American Capital 1814." None of these objects are on view to the public. However, the following portraits may be seen during public tours: James Madison (Blue Room), Dolley Madison (Red Room), James Monroe (Blue Room), William Henry Harrison (Green Room), Andrew Jackson (Green Room), and two sculptures of Henry Clay (statue on ground floor corridor and bust in Red Room).

The President's House doorkeeper (some accounts say Dolley Madison's steward) Jean Pierre Sioussat, known as French John, took the mansion's pet macaw to the Octagon House* for safekeeping. A slave, Paul Jennings, later reported that "a rabble, taking advantage of the confusion, ran all over the White House, and stole lots of silver and whatever they could lay their hands on."[49] A receipt in the National Archives made out to an African American named Nace Rhodes thanks him for the return of some of the house silver.

Related Delaware, North Carolina, and Pennsylvania Sites

The following selected sites from the neighboring states of the Chesapeake Bay are included because of their direct relationship to the Chesapeake Campaign. This is not meant to be a comprehensive listing of War of 1812 sites for these states as such a list is beyond the scope of this guide.

DU PONT GUNPOWDER COMPANY (Brandywine River, Hagley Museum and Library, off New Bridge Road [Route 141], northwest of Wilmington, Delaware). Éleuthère Irénée du Pont de Nemours (1771–1834), better known as Irénée du Pont, or E. I. du Pont, was a French-born American chemist and industrialist who worked at a French gunpowder mill near Paris and emigrated to the United States in 1799. In 1801, he founded the gunpowder company, E. I. du Pont de Nemours and Company. The company produced its first gunpowder in 1804 and by 1811 was the largest producer in the United States. In 1813, the U.S. government ordered 500,000 pounds of powder from the firm. In order to fill this order du Pont purchased the adjacent Hagley Estate downriver.

Fort McHenry* purchased gunpowder from du Pont during the War of 1812. So, too, probably did Fort Severn, Fort Norfolk, and other military installations. (*See also* Aetna Powder Mill and Bellona Powder Mill.) Organ Cave,* Virginia (now West Virginia), produced saltpetre, a necessary ingredient for the making of gunpowder. Some of the Organ Cave saltpetre is believed to have been processed into gun powder by du Pont. E. I. du Pont is buried in the family cemetery near the du Pont family home at Eleutherian Mills.

> I this morning rec⁴ a letter from Governor [Joseph] Haslet stating that considerable depredations, in Burning of Vessels &c. are committed by British Vessels of War about Lewes Town [Delaware Bay] in Sussex & requests of me to forward him six kegs of your best rifle Powder or such as is used for musketry, perhaps one of the kegs had best be of Cannon powder. (John Warner to E. I. du Pont, March 19, 1813)[50]

The Brandywine powder mills offered a prime target for the British during the war.

> I am uninformed of the plans of Government but . . . Suppose that they must be pointed against Philadelphia, Baltimore & Washington, if to the first the landing should be made at or near New Castle & Chester upon the Delaware or at the head of Elk [Elkton, Maryland]; at Brandywine the principal Mills for [gun] Powder & Flour are Situated which may be destroyed in passing. (Vice Adm. Sir Alexander F. I. Cochrane to Rear Adm. George Cockburn, July 1, 1814)[51]

> with the Expectation that the British will come up this [Chesapeake] Bay as they are now reinforced to the amount of 2500 and in all probability will go against Baltimore and then proceed on to Wilmington & Brandywine to destroy the public Property & Powder Mills if so there will come a part of them up this [Delaware] Bay to meet the others and there let them Embark onboard the Fleet. (William Frazer, Rich Neck Farm, Talbot County, Maryland, to his son William C. Frazer, Lancaster, Pennsylvania, September 1, 1814)[52]

During the War of 1812, E. I. du Pont and his older brother Victor both served as officers in the South Brandywine Rangers. Extraordinary measures were taken to protect the Brandywine mills from a British attack.

> All those men who did belong last year to the volunteer Corps of the Brandywine Rangers are hereby informed that the Captain is authorised by order of [Brig.] General [Joseph] Bloomfield to reorganize the Company under the immediate orders of the President of the United States—for the purpose of protecting the works on the Brandywine. They will be exempt from militia service and are not to be sent out further than the vicinity of Wilmington. (Victor du Pont, August 19, 1814)[53]

An inventory for June 30, 1814, lists over $52,000 worth of "Powder, in magazine or with agents" and puts the total worth of the mill at $351,704.11.[54]

Several structures from the War of 1812 era can be seen here, including a restored mill (number 3 distinguished by the double abutments on the land side), a glazing mill, a graining mill, and the walls of the packing mill. Although the external appearance of these restored buildings is the same or similar to what it was in 1812, the mill was transformed from a stamping mill into a rolling mill in the 1820s, and the glazing and graining equipment is of a later era. The ruins of a magazine from 1813 are located at the sharp turn in the road between the Composition House and the Steam Engine House. The original Eleutherian Mills, farther upstream, produced gunpowder used during the War of 1812. The saltpetre works and the first magazine were also located here. A model in the museum shows the site as it would have appeared in 1806. The du Pont office during the war was a three-story "lean-to" attached to the south side of the house. It was removed when du Pont's son built the current office near the house.

OCRACOKE (southern outer banks, Pamilco Sound on west and Atlantic Ocean on east, North Carolina). Because of the British blockade, some Chesapeake merchants were forced to use the inland waterways along the coast of Virginia and the outer banks of North Carolina.

> The waters of North Carolina, from Wilmington to Ocracoke, though not favorable to commerce in time of peace, by reason of their shallowness and danger of the coast, became important and useful in time of war, and a very considerable trade was prosecuted from and into those waters . . . and a coasting trade as far as Charleston, attended with the less risk than many would imagine. A vessel may prosecute a voyage from Elizabeth City to Charleston without being at sea more than a few hours at any one time.[55]

In late May the British sent a schooner, the former privateer *Highflyer,* to reconnoiter the area. This so alarmed the coastal inhabitants of North Carolina that they petitioned Governor William Hawkins to return two gunboats laid up in ordinary earlier that year by Secretary of Navy William Jones. The British extended their blockade southward to Ocracoke Island. On July 12, 1813, after they attacked Craney Island* and Hampton,* the British raided the North Carolina coast, including Ocracoke.

The whole [boats and barges] moved from the Ships toward the Shore . . . but owning to the great Distance . . . and the heavy swell . . . it was considerably after Daylight before the advanced Division turned a projecting Shoal Point . . . a heavy fire was opened on them from a Brig and Schooner which hoisted American Colours . . . the fire of the Brig began to slacken, and on . . . approaching her Bow . . . cut her cable and abandoned her, and the Schooner immediately struck her Colours . . . both almost instantly boarded and taken Possession of. The rest of the Vessels in the Harbor proving to be Neutral Merchant Vessels the advanced Division was immediately dispatched in chace of the some small Vessels which had brought down Goods to load the Vessels laying here, but which had made off up the River on our being first discovered, these however our Boats unfortunately failed in their Endeavours to overtake . . . The Troops . . . effected a landing on and without further Opposition took Possession of the Portsmouth and Ocracock Island, where all immediately submitted to our Mercy . . . They are now driving in Cattle &c. for the Refreshment of our Troops and Ships, and as we learn that there neither is at Washington [North Carolina] nor Newbern [New Bern, North Carolina] any Vessel of any size nor other object worthy our attention, this Harbor being the only Anchorage for Vessels drawing more than Eight feet Water loading from or trading to any Place within these Extensive Inlets, the passage of Roanoke and Carrituck being now filled up and impassable. (Rear Adm. George Cockburn to Adm. Sir John B. Warren, July 12, 1813)[56]

Your South Sea Ship came in here [Bermuda] very well & the Officers & men will be conveyed to you by Lieut. [Wentworth P.] Croke who is ordered to continue the Blockade of Ocracocke. (Adm. Sir John Borlase Warren to Capt. Robert Barrie, January 19, 1814)[57]

An estimated six hundred slaves were liberated and most sent to Bermuda. Among the vessels that the British captured was the Philadelphia letter-of-marque schooner *Atlas,* which was renamed *St. Lawrence.* The *St. Lawrence* played a significant role during the British campaign in the Chesapeake in 1814, especially during the battles of St. Leonard Creek.*

SCHUYLKILL ARSENAL SITE, later called the U.S. Arsenal (South 26th Street and 2620 Grays Ferry Avenue, Philadelphia, Pennsylvania). Originally built as a U.S. Navy powder magazine in 1799, this arsenal became an ordnance depot during the War of 1812, the third federal arsenal in the United States after Springfield, Massachusetts, and Harpers Ferry,* Virginia (now West Virginia). From here guns, ammunition, clothing, and textile materials (such as tents and canteens) were supplied to Fort McHenry* and probably other military installations, such as Fort Washington* and Fort Norfolk* in the Chesapeake Bay region.

On March 15, 1813, Schuylkill Arsenal provided 10,000 musket flints that were charged to the "Defense of Baltimore Accounts." On April 13, it provided 472 12-pound strapped shot, 128 12-pound canister, 50 portfires (used for setting fire to powder), 450 priming tubes and slow matches, and 36,900 musket cartridges. On March 1, 1814, it provided 20,000 pounds of cannon powder and 5,000 pounds of musket powder.[58]

All of the arsenal buildings were razed in 1963. The stone wall along Grays Ferry Avenue at the intersection with Washington Avenue may be part of the original stone and brick wall of the arsenal.

ACKNOWLEDGMENTS

Preparing this guide was possible only because we received a great deal of help from numerous individuals and organizations. The National Park Service provided support in several ways, most notably through its American Battlefield Protection Program. The Maryland Office of Tourism Development and the Maryland Tourism Development Board provided matching funds and logistical support. The Maryland Historical Trust also provided logistical support. In addition, we profited from the knowledge that many archivists, curators, librarians, and local experts freely shared with us. Property owners helped as well. We were never refused access to private property once we explained our project and requested information. A great many individuals stopped what they were doing and cheerfully helped us find a site we were searching for or put us in touch with someone they knew who could help us. To all these wonderful people, we extend our heartfelt thanks. They not only made it possible for us to complete this project, but they also renewed our faith in human nature.

More particularly, we would like to thank Douglas Rawlinson, who freely shared his extensive inventory of War of 1812 veterans buried in Maryland. His work is included in appendix B. Christopher George assisted this project during an early phase of the American Battlefield Protection Program work. Dr. Susan Langley and Ben Ford assisted this project during a later phase. Both Christopher George and Robert Reyes freely shared their knowledge of War of 1812 sites at North Point, Maryland. Stuart Butler, an authority on Virginia militia, reviewed the Virginia sites. William Allman, curator of the White House, reviewed the District of Columbia sites. Both provided important suggestions that improved this study. Donald Shomette reviewed the Maryland, Virginia, and District of Columbia chapters and he shared his knowledge of the war during numerous conversations.

In addition, the following individuals deserve thanks for their assistance: Gloria Allen, William G. Allman, Stewart Barroll, Mary Baumann, Paul Berry, Steve Bilicke, Jeff Bossart, Betty Bowen, the late Ronald Bozarth, Nancy Bramucci, Richard Brunkhorst, Robert Campbell, Ginger Carter, Ed Chaney, Bill Clark, Wayne Clark, Ann and Gary Collins, Kathy Concannon, Alice W. Cook, Jane Cox, Don Creveling, R. Thomas Crew, Jr., Ed Day, the late Jon Dean, Maria E. denBoer, Mike Dixon, William Dudley, Jim Dunbar, Van Dyke, Jeff Enright, Erich Eshelman, Evelyne Eshelman, Betsy Feiler, John Feiler, William Foote, Tom Fowler, Laura Galke, Tanya Gossett, Fred Grady, Chris Grazzini, Linda Green, Mary Kay Harper, William Hazel, Keith Heinrich, Fred Hopkins, Dave Howell, Mike Hughes, Maureen Kavanagh, Ross Kimmel, Julia King, Jeffery Korman, Greg R. Krueger, Frank Kubalis, Nancy Kurtz, Peter Kurtz, Susan Langley, Gareth McNair-Lewis, Kathy Lee Erlandson Liston, Rodney J. Little, James W. Loewen, David Lowe, Darrin Lowery, Rufus S. Lusk III, Tom Marsh, Phil Michel, H. Bryan Mitchell, Barbara Stewart Mogle, Russell Mogel, Vanessa Moineauz, Janie Morgan, Terry Nicholson, Rynell Novak, Apryl Parcher, Ken Parcher, Susan Pearl, William J. Pencek, Dwayne Pickett, Anthony S. Pitch, Jennifer Pollack, John Pousson, the late Stanley Quick, Jessica Reed, Susan Reidy, Linda Reno, Orlando Ridout, Franklin Robinson, Joanne Roland, Robin Roland, Ron Roller, Marci W. Ross, Warren Rowley, Mary Louise de Sarran, Wayne Schaumburg, Gary Scott, Betty Seifert, Edward Seufert, Debora Silvertson, Michael Smolek, Hugh Smith, James Stein, the late Stephen Strach, Edwin Swann, Peter T. Tattle, Richard Thomas, Bruce Thompson, Frank Thorton, Mrs. Carmichael Tilghman, Chris Van de Velde, Richard Van Stolk, Anna von Lunz, Elaine Ward, Donna Ware, Jenna Watts, John Weiss, Joseph A. Whitehorne, Glenn Williams, George Williams, James Wood, and Francis Zumbrum.

We encourage anyone who has information on any 1812 sites that we missed, or has any corrections or comments, to contact the lead scholar on this project, Ralph Eshelman. He can be reached by regular mail at 12178 Preston Dr., Lusby, Maryland 20657, and via e-mail at ree47@comcast.net.

MARYLAND

ARNOLD, PVT. JOHN, GRAVE (Broad Neck, intersection of Shore Acres Road and College Parkway, off Governor Ritchie Highway [Route 2], Arnold, Anne Arundel County). Pvt. John Arnold, who probably served in Capt. John Boone's Company, 22nd Maryland Regiment, is reportedly buried here, but no gravestone has been found. It may have been moved because of development

BARNET FARM CEMETERY (1.0 mile east of Gum Swamp, off Golden Hill Road [Route 335], Dorchester County). William W. Jones, who died September 14, 1863, in his eighty-second year, served as a lieutenant in Capt. Benjamin Leitch's Company, 31st Regiment. He is reportedly buried here, but the caretaker of Blackwater Sportsman Club, who has extensive knowledge about the area, knows of no such grave. Most of this area is now part of the Blackwater Wildlife Refuge and many roads, driveways, and homesteads have been abandoned. While many cemeteries were found in the Gum Swamp area, none contains a Jones grave marker.

BLIZZARD FAMILY CEMETERY (Woodenburg, Baltimore County). Ensign John Blizzard of the 15th Regiment is reported to be buried in the Blizzard Family Cemetery located near Woodenburg. This graveyard could not be found. The postmaster at Woodenburg knew of no such family, farm, or cemetery.

DALLMAN, WILLIAM, GRAVE (Aberdeen Proving Ground, possibly cemetery on east side of Emmorton Road [Route 24] 0.3 mile south of military boundary, Edgewood area, Harford County). Dr. William Dallam, a surgeon's mate with the 42nd Regiment, is buried within the Aberdeen Proving Ground, but the exact location is unknown.

ELLICOTT MILLS BURYING GROUNDS (Ellicott City, Howard County). The obituary of Capt. Edward Aisquith (1779–1815), of Fells Point 1st Baltimore Sharp Shooters, 3rd Brigade, claims he is buried at the Ellicott Mills Burying Ground. No such individual has been found in any of the cemeteries near Ellicott City. He may be buried at Oella Cemetery, located on the south side of Rest Avenue, 0.15 mile west of the intersection with Westchester Road, north off Frederick Road (Route 144), east of Ellicott City. This cemetery is abandoned and overgrown, and many gravestones are overturned. Another possibility is the Western Cemetery, which was located off St. John's Lane, just south of Frederick Road, before it was destroyed by developers in 1984–85.

FOWBLE FAMILY CEMETERY (off Black Rock Court, off Falls Road [Route 25], north of Butler, Baltimore County). 2nd Cpl. Peter Fowble, of Capt. Elias Stocksdale's Company, 15th Regiment, is buried in the Fowble family cemetery. There is no gravestone for any such individual in the Black Rock Church Cemetery, nor has any road called Black Rock Court been found.

GAYLEARD CEMETERY (6583 Cedar Lane, north off Exit 17, Savage Road [Route 32], at intersection with Pindell School/Cedar Lane, Columbia, Howard County). PRIVATE Richard Owens (1749–1819), a veteran of the Revolutionary War and War of 1812, unit unknown, is said to be buried here, but the address could not be found. A DAR marker is said to be located at the gravesite.

HAYWARD FAMILY CEMETERY (location unknown, Talbot County). William. Hayward, Jr., a veteran of the War of 1812 is said to be buried here, but the family cemetery could not be found.

HILLSBORO CEMETERY (Hillsboro, Caroline County). Dr. Marcellus Keene, who served as a surgeon in the 19th Regiment, is reported to be buried at "Hillsboro Cemetery." No grave marker for him was found at either Green Mount Cemetery off Cemetery Road or St. Paul's Episcopal Church Cemetery off Maple Avenue.

ISLINGTON (nearly opposite intersection of Bowie Shop and Solomons Island [Route 4] roads, 0.4 mile south of intersection of Arminger Road, north of Huntingtown, Calvert County). Islington, built circa 1790, was the home of Lt. Col. William Lawrence who commanded Fort Bowyer in Mobile Bay in 1814. Its exact location is unclear. Some sources suggest that it was located near Ponds Woods Road; others that it is the same structure known as the Armiger House, a mid-eighteenth-century house moved two hundred yards southeast from its original site in 1968 to make way for a widening of Route 4. Lawrence is buried in Congressional Cemetery* in Washington, D.C.

LONG GREEN CEMETERY (Putty Hill Farm, northeast of Loch Raven Reservoir, Baltimore County). James Chamberlain Morford, who at age nineteen served at North Point as quartermaster in the 46th Regiment, is interred in a family burying ground called Long Green. Morford was among the last survivors of the "Old Defenders," but not the last survivor, as is often claimed. William Welsh* is regarded as the last survivor. Moreford was originally buried at Green Mount Cemetery, Baltimore, but removed and interred at Putty Hill Farm in June 1899.

> He [James Morford] was the sole survivor at the last dinner given [December 17, 1888] to the Old Defenders, and after retiring from the dinner took the street cars by himself and went to Patterson Park, where a celebration was in progress, was introduced to the audience and made a few remarks. (O. F. Gregory, obituary, Baltimore *Sun,* September 12, 1913)

MCCREADY FAMILY CEMETERY (Somerset County). Pvt. Benjamin F. McCready, Sr. served in Wilson's Company, 23rd Regiment. He is buried in the McCready Family Cemetery but the location of this cemetery is unknown.

MOORE, NICHOLAS RUXTON, GRAVE (east side of Bellona Avenue [Route 134], 100 feet north of Malvern Avenue, Malvern, Baltimore County). Nicholas Ruxton Moore (1756–1816) served in the Revolutionary War and was appointed a lieutenant colonel of the 6th Maryland Cavalry Regimental during the War of 1812. He is probably buried in an unmarked grave in a cemetery located two hundred feet west of L'Hirondelle Club Road where it crosses Roland Run.

SHOWER, JACOB, GRAVE (near intersection of Hanover Pike [Route 30] and Manchester Road [Route 27], Manchester, northeastern Carroll County). Jacob Shower, a drummer boy of an unknown unit during the War of 1812, was born February 22, 1803, and died May 25, 1879. He would have been between nine and eleven during the war. He later became a physician

and politician in Carroll County. He is buried at Manchester, but the exact location is unknown.

SNOWDEN'S ENCAMPMENT SITE (presumed encampment at Snowden's Mill, along Paint Branch Creek in area east of Colesville, south of Fairland Road, west off Old Columbia Pike, east of New Hampshire Avenue [Route 650], and north of Randolph Road East, Montgomery County). PRIVATE Because they were short of men and unsure where the British would attack, American troops camped midway between Baltimore and Washington both before and after the attack on Baltimore. Secretary of State James Monroe sent the 36th and 38th Regiments of Infantry and Lt. Col. Jacint Lavall's U.S. Light Dragoons to Snowden's shortly after the Battle for Baltimore. Two brigades of militia from Richmond arrived on October 27, 1814, at Camp Snowden. By November 9, 1814, they were reassigned to Camp Crossroads at Ellicott Mills (now Ellicott City*). It is difficult to ascertain exactly where this encampment was located. The Snowden family home, called Montpelier, is located on the west side of the Patuxent River, at 9401 Montpelier Drive, west off Muirkirk Road, west off Laurel-Bowie Road (Route 197), in Laurel, Prince George's County.

> The enemy having taken possession of Kent Island are in a situation to make a rapid movement on Baltimore and I therefore wrote you this morning directing the movement of the force under your command at Snowdens and with you, toward Baltimore without delay. (Secretary of Navy William Jones to Com. John Rodgers, September 3, 1814)[1]

SPURRIER FAMILY CEMETERY (Joseph Spurrier Farm, north of Boteler Road between Ridge and Runkles roads, Hampton Knolls, east of Mount Airy, Carroll County). Pvt. Green (Greensbury) Spurrier, who served under Capt. John Fonsten's Company, 29th Regiment, and died in 1866, is reportedly buried on the Joseph Spurrier Farm. The location, however, is unknown.

STAG TAVERN SITE (location unknown, somewhere between Baltimore and Bladensburg). Stag Tavern is the site where Brig. Gen. Tobias Stansbury with his 1,353 men halted for the night of August 21–22, 1814, during their march from Baltimore to Bladensburg to engage the British. The site of the tavern is unknown.

WASHINGTON GUN POWDER MILLS SITE, also called Washington Mills (exact location unknown but probably near or upstream from the Carleton Mill Site,* Bladensburg, Prince George's County). Dr. Thomas Ewell (1785–1826), brother of Dr. James Ewell,* established in 1811 at Bladensburg the Washington Gun Powder Mills, which is said to have employed the first rolling mill in the making of gunpowder in the United States, although the technique had been in use in Europe for some forty years. When Ewell received sizable government contracts, he pleaded with E. I. du Pont, owner of the du Pont Gunpowder Company,* Wilmington, Delaware, to form a partnership or loan him an experienced superintendent. But Ewell's attempts to hire away laborers from du Pont's mills, coupled with Com. Stephen Decatur's lack of endorsement of Ewell, induced du Pont to withhold his financial support from Ewell. In December 1812, a powder drying house with two thousand pounds of powder exploded. Nevertheless, on December 7, 1813, Ewell received a patent for manufacturing gunpowder by boiling the ingredients and using rolling mills to reduce production hazards. Du Pont continued to use the less safe stamping mill process until he converted to rolling mills in the 1820s.

It is unclear how successful Ewell's mills were. In January 1813, Ewell completed trial firings of his powder both at his mill and at Greenleaf Point Federal Arsenal,* Washington, D.C. Lt. Samuel Perkins reported "Dr. Th[omas]. Ewell has deposited at this place [Greenleaf Point] two hundred and fifty barrels of Gun Powder (cannon and musket) one ounce of each barrel of which has thrown a 24 pound ball from two hundred to two hundred and seventy-five yards" (Washington *Daily National Intelligencer*, January 22, 1813).

> This is to certify that agreeably to the order of Captain [Charles?] Stewart, I attended at the powder yard of Dr. [Thomas] Ewell for selecting the powder for the frigate Constellation, where all the facilities for the trial were readily furnished, that on a trial of two hundred and one barrels there was but one found deficient, which fell short of the required proof (that is one hundred yards) [by] six yards, and that so good was the powder, that in one instance an ounce of it threw a twenty-four pound ball three hundred yards. (Washington *Daily National Intelligence*r, January 22, 1813)

Ewell sold the powder mills in 1817. The facility may have became the Stull & Williams Powder Works. Unaccountably, the British did not destroy the powder works during the Battle of Bladensburg. David Bussard operated a second powder mill near Bladensburg in 1817 or perhaps sooner.

VIRGINIA

DEEP CREEK (north of Onancock, off Pocomoke Sound, east end of Deep Creek Road [Route 657], Accomack County). The British supposedly raided Deep Creek on June 29, 1814, but were repulsed by the local militia. This poorly documented action is probably a skirmish that took place at Chesconessex* on June 25, 1814.

POTOMAC CHURCH SITE (Potomac Creek, southeast of Stafford Court House, Stafford County). Potomac Church was probably located near Daffan, end of Leeland Road between Potomac Run Road (Route 626) and Brooke Road (Route 608). Tradition claims that marauding British soldiers damaged Potomac Church during the War of 1812. The church, built in the 1660s and abandoned about 1804, would have been unoccupied for several years prior to the war, possibly making it a convenient place for soldiers to stay. However, there is no known British activity at nearby Stafford Courthouse or other places on Potomac Creek. This tradition is doubtful.

WILEY'S TAVERN SITE (east of 9800 area of Leesburg Pike [Route 7], south of Difficult Run, Fairfax County). Colvin Run Road (north of Difficult Run) and Locust Hill Drive (south of Difficult Run) are remnants of an eighteenth-century road from the Shenandoah Valley to Alexandria. Wiley's Tavern was located along a now abandoned portion of this road. The exact location is unknown.

Dolley Madison reached Wiley's Tavern on the night of August 25, 1814, just before a great storm passed through. Tradition claims that the wife of the tavern owner was infuriated to learn that the wife of the president was in her home while her own husband was out fighting the enemy. She reportedly shrieked at the First Lady, demanding she leave. It was only through the efforts of a friend that Dolley was permitted to remain. While en route to the tavern, President Madison sought sanctuary from the storm at the Crossroads, about five miles from the Little Falls bridge. After the storm passed, President Madison made his way to the tavern and was united with his wife. With rumors of the British approaching, President Madison left his wife and fled with his entourage to Conn's Ferry* in order to cross the Potomac River into Maryland.

This list was compiled principally by A. Douglas Rawlinson, with contributions from Ralph Eshelman, Scott Sheads, and Nancy Bramucci.[1] Many others assisted in numerous ways. Rawlinson has identified over 700 veterans buried in Maryland. Of these, 263 are buried at Green Mount Cemetery, Baltimore; 66 in Mount Olivet Cemetery, Frederick; and 436 elsewhere in Maryland. Rawlinson has found another 260 names on gravestones that match names on unit rosters, but it is unclear if these are the same men. Only the confirmed individuals in Rawlinson's list are included below. All units mentioned are militia from the state under which they are listed unless otherwise noted. Cenotaphs (an empty tomb built to honor a deceased person or monument erected to honor someone buried elsewhere) are included. Other burial sites for which the precise location could not be established are included in appendix A.

The Society of the War of 1812 in Virginia has an ongoing project to find and record the gravesites of Virginia's War of 1812 veterans. As of January 2007, over 2,300 sites had been recorded. This inventory is available on the world wide web.[2] There is no such Maryland inventory available on the web. The inventory found in this appendix is the most comprehensive inventory of Maryland and District of Columbia War of 1812 gravesites known. The appendix also includes the more significant or previously undocumented gravesites for Virginia.

MARYLAND

AARON FARM CEMETERY (east side of unimproved private road [chained] 0.5 mile west off Robinson Neck Road, 1.5 miles south of intersection with St. John Creek Road, and 2.5 miles south of intersection with Hooper Neck Road–Taylors Island Road [Route 16]). PRIVATE

Tall, Pvt. Elijah, Sr. 48th Regiment.

ADAMS FAMILY CEMETERY (near Finchville, Dorchester County).

Adams, Capt. Minos. 11th Regiment.

ALL HALLOWS PARISH CHURCH CEMETERY, also called the Brick Church (intersection of 3604 Solomons Island Road [Route 2] with Brick Church Road, near Davidsonville, Anne Arundel County).

Davidson, Pvt. Samuel. Baltimore Union Artillery.

ALMONY-AYERS FAMILY CEMETERY (Garrett Road, Baltimore County).

Almony, Capt. James. 41st Regiment.

ANGEL HILL CEMETERY (600 Ohio Street near intersection with Erie Street, Havre de Grace, Harford County).

O'Neill, John (1768–1838). Hero of the unsuccessful defense of Havre de Grace. Gravestone reads in part: "DEFENDER/JOHN O'NEILL."

ANTIOCH UNITED METHODIST CHURCH CEMETERY (11650 Somerset Avenue, Princess Anne, Somerset County).

Phoebus, James. Ballard's Company, 25th Regiment. Gravestone reads in part: "He was a soldier of the war of 1812."

APPLE'S REFORMED CHURCH CEMETERY, also called Apple's Lutheran Church and Jacob's Church (intersection of Graceham and Apples Church roads, immediately northeast of Thurmont, Frederick County).

Cover, 4th Cpl. Jacob. Galt's Company, 3rd Regiment.
Troxell, 2nd Lt. George. Reid's Company, 1st Cavalry District.
Troxell, Pvt. Jacob Samuel. Ogle's Company, 47th Regiment.

ASHBY FAMILY CEMETERY (end of Ashby Drive, off Goldsborough Neck Road, Ashby, west-northwest of Easton, Talbot County). PRIVATE

Goldsborough, Maj. Robert Henry. Captain, 9th Cavalry District, May 8, 1812. Promoted to major on February 13, 1813.

AUD FAMILY CEMETERY (west of Willard Road, near Poolesville, Montgomery County). Overgrown, no markers survive.

Aud, Orderly Sgt. Asa. Turbett's Company, 3rd Regiment.

BALDWIN MEMORIAL UNITED METHODIST CHURCH CEMETERY (southeast corner of intersection of Millersville Road [Route 175] and General's Highway [Route 178], Millersville, Anne Arundel County).

Baldwin, Ensign William H. Veitch's Company, 34th Regiment.

BALTIMORE CEMETERY (bordered by Edison Highway on east, Sinclair Lane on north, Federal Street on south, and Rose Street on west, Baltimore City).

Bandell, Pvt. William. Sheppard's Company, 6th Regiment. Buried in area S.

Barrett, 2nd Lt. John M. 38th U.S. Infantry. "A Defender of Fort McHenry in the 8th Regiment Infantry of the Line During the War of 1812."

Brewer, Lt. Nicholas. Galt's Company, 6th Regiment. Buried in area Q.

Cooper, Pvt. Samuel. Capt. Thomas Watson's Company, 39th Regiment. Served at the Battle of North Point.

Dalrymple, Pvt. William M. Nicholson's Company, Mechanical Volunteers. Buried in area Q. Wounded at Battle of North Point.

Downey, Pvt. Edmund. Smith's Company 51st Regiment. Buried in area BB.

Edes, Capt. Benjamin. 27th Regiment. Buried in area I.

Gehring, Pvt. John G. Sadtler's Company, Baltimore Yagers. Buried in area I.

Johnson, Pvt. Aquila. Smith's Company, 42nd Regiment. Buried in area N.

Knorr, Pvt. William. Pinney's Company, 27th Regiment. Buried in area G.

Lambdin, Capt. Thomas H. Extra Battalion, Dorchester County.

Leakin, Capt. Sheppard. 38th U.S. Infantry. Buried in area AA. Mayor of Baltimore, 1838–42.

Lightner, Henry (1798–1883). Twelve-year-old drummer boy, Berry's Washington Volunteer Artillerist, 1st Regiment, Maryland Artillery. Served during the bombardment of Fort McHenry. *See*

also Flag House and Star-Spangled Banner Museum, Baltimore, where Lightner's drum and drum sticks are exhibited.

McKenzie, Pvt. James. Pinney's Company, 27th Regiment. Buried in area JJ.

Meeks, William. No service record found. Buried in area I. "One of the Defenders of this Town at North Point 1814."

Morris, Cpl. Morris. Wilson's Company, 6th Regiment. Buried in area Q.

Mumma, Pvt. John. Bouldin's Company, Independent Light Dragoons. Buried in area N.

Peregoy, Ensign Joseph. James's Company, 7th Regiment. Buried in section N, lot 353.

Phelps, Pvt. Gardner. Faster's Company, 51st Regiment. Buried in area R, lot 94.

Scott, 1st Sgt. Abraham. 27th Regiment. Buried in area I. "Brave Defender of Baltimore in 1814."

Shrim, Capt. John. Baltimore Light Infantry. Buried in the Ancient and Honorable Mechanical Company of Baltimore plot.

Slott, Abraham. Served during the defense of Baltimore.

Spear, William. Captain of the privateer *Daedalus* (1813). Later sergeant in Stiles's Company, Marine Artillery. Buried in area BC.

Stansbury, Pvt. Elijah. Montgomery's Baltimore Union Artillery. Buried in Center 1. Served during the Battle of North Point.

Stephens, Pvt. Alexander. Long's Company, 27th Regiment. Buried in area R.

Wood, Pvt. Henry H. Biay's Company, 5th Cavalry Regiment. Buried in area J.

BARNESVILLE METHODIST EPISCOPAL CEMETERY (Barnesville, Montgomery County).

Nichols, 1st Lt. Jacob. Dawson's Company, 28th Regiment.

BAUST'S CEMETERY, also called Emanuel Lutheran and Reformed and Emanuel Baust Church (Old Taneytown Road [Route 832] near its intersection with Baust Church Road [Route 84], Tyrone, Carroll County).

Fleagle, Pvt. John. Fonsten's Company, 3rd Regiment.

BEAVER DAM BRETHREN CHURCH CEMETERY (Johnsville, Frederick County).

Haines, Pvt. Daniel. Crawford's Company.

BEAVER FAMILY CEMETERY (Westminster, Carroll County).

Robertson, Pvt. John. Durbin's Company, Randall's Battalion Riflemen. Buried in area Bv-10.

BENTON-SHIPLEY CEMETERY (south side of Benton Avenue between Oak Park and Golden Oak Drive, Linthicum, Anne Arundel County).

Linthicum, Capt. Abner. 22nd Regiment.

BETHEL EVANGELICAL LUTHERAN CHURCH CEMETERY (southwest corner of intersection of Opossumtown Pike and Bethel Road, Bethel, north of Frederick, Frederick County).

Ramsburg, Pvt. Frederick. Turnbull's Company, 1st Regiment.

BETHEL METHODIST CHURCH CEMETERY (Sams Creek Road, south of New Windsor, Carroll County, just east of Frederick County line).

Bennett, Pvt. Robert. Crawford's Company.

BETHEL PRESBYTERIAN CEMETERY (north side of Morrisville Road [Route 23], just west of Madonna, Harford County).

Amos (Amoss), Lt. William. Amos's Company, 40th Regiment.
Bay, Pvt. Thomas. Turner's Company, 42nd Regiment; John Smithson's Company, 49th Regiment.
Rampley, Capt. James.; 40th Regiment.
Wiley, Pvt. John. Thomas's Company, 49th Regiment.

BETHESDA UNITED METHODIST CHURCH CEMETERY (Bethesda Church Road, Browningsville, Montgomery County).

Watkins, Pvt. John. Thomas's Company, 2nd U.S. Infantry.

BOONE-MERRIKEN CEMETERY (Hidden Point Road, southwest of intersection with Pleasant Plains Road, Beechwood on the Burley, Anne Arundel County). This cemetery was located in the center of a field but apparently no longer exists.

Duvall, Lt. Col. Zachariah, Jr. 22nd Regiment.

BOONSBORO CEMETERY (Boonsboro, Washington County).

Huopt, Pvt. Jacob. Murray's Company.

BOSLEY UNITED METHODIST CHURCH CEMETERY (Thornton Road, 0.2 mile southeast of intersection with Princeville Road and 1.1 miles northwest of underpass of I-83, northwest of Hunt Valley, Baltimore County). This church was established in 1784 and the current structure built in1877.

Ensor, George. Probably private, Fizzell's Company, 15th Regiment.
Hall, Edward. Probably private, Moale's Company, Columbian Artillery.
Wheeler, Benjamin. Probably private, Deem's Company, 51st Regiment.

BRIDGETOWN METHODIST EPISCOPAL CHURCH CEMETERY (northeast intersection of Ruthsburg Road [Route 304] with Bridgetown Road, west of Bridgetown, Queen Anne's County).

Fountain, Pvt. Marcey. Potter's Company, 19th Regiment.

BRINKMAN-RINE CEMETERY (100 yards west on dirt lane off Oldtown Road [unpaved], 0.3 mile north of intersection with Mertens Avenue [unpaved], just north of power line crossing, opposite cleared grassy area campground number G4, approximately 5.0 miles north of intersection of Oldtown Road and Uhl Highway [Route 51], Green Ridge State Forest, Allegany County).

Rine (or Ryan), Pvt. Daniel. 1st Regiment, Virginia Militia. Buried with wife, Ann Hester, who received a widow's pension from 1878 until her death at age ninety-eight in 1915.

BROOK HILL METHODIST CHURCH CEMETERY (Yellow Springs, Frederick County).

Fox, Pvt. John. Murray's Company.

BROWN FAMILY CEMETERY (1795 Woodstock Road, Woodstock, Howard County).

Brown, 2nd Lt. John. Riggs 3rd Cavalry Regiment.

CAMPBELL FAMILY CEMETERY (Unionville, Frederick County).

Campbell, Pvt. John. Smith's Company, Watkin's Command.

CEDAR HILL CEMETERY (1.5 miles south of Baltimore City line, 5829 Ritchie Highway [Route 2], Anne Arundel County).

Johnson, Pvt. Samuel. Drummer, Piper's Company, United Maryland Artillery. Cemetery records identify two people named Samuel Johnson in the same lot; one died January 21, 1871, and the other January 8, 1885. Only one gravestone is present.

CEDAR PARK, also called Mercer Family Cemetery, and West River Farm (private drive east off intersection of Cumberstone and Bayfield roads, east off Muddy Creek Road [Route 468], just north of Galesville, Anne Arundel County). PRIVATE Overgrown cemetery.

Mercer, Lt. Col. John Francis (1759–1821). Wounded during the American Revolution at Brandywine, September 11, 1777. Tenth governor of Maryland from 1801 to 1803. Apparently at age fifty-five took an active role during the Battle of Kirbys Wind Mill on October 31, 1814. No gravestone found.

CENTRAL CHAPEL METHODIST CHURCH CEMETERY (New London, Frederick County).

Harding, Pvt. Philip. Darby's Company.
Lowe, 2nd Lt. John. Fonsten's Company, 3rd Regiment.

CHAPEL LUTHERAN CHURCH CEMETERY (Libertytown, Frederick County).

Filler, Pvt. Solomon. Wood's Company, 1st Regiment.

CHESTERFIELD CEMETERY (abandoned cemetery is located in woods just north of Centerville Elementary School, near intersection of Draper Lane and Homewood Avenue, Centreville, Queen Anne's County).

Chambers, Pvt. Perdue. Wright's 1st Queen Anne's Artillery Company, 38th Regiment. No gravestone found.
Vickers, Pvt. Samuel. Hand's Company, 21st Regiment. No gravestone found.

CHESTERTOWN CEMETERY (east side of High Street [Route 20], Chestertown, Kent County).

Chambers, Brig. Gen. Benjamin. 6th Brigade.
Chambers, Capt. Ezekiel Forman. 21st Regiment. Fought at Caulks Field.
Chambers, Capt. William Forman. 21st Regiment. Probably Ezekiel Forman Chambers. No gravestone for William Forman Chambers found.
Hand, Capt. Bedingfield. 21st Regiment. Too ill to serve during battle at Caulks Field.

CHESTNUT GROVE PRESBYTERIAN CHURCH CEMETERY (south side of Sweet Air Road [Route 145] 0.6 mile west of intersection with Manor Road, Chestnut Grove, Baltimore County).

Sterett, Capt. James. 1st Baltimore Hussars, 5th Cavalry District. Became colonel after the war.

CHRIST EPISCOPAL CHURCH CEMETERY (northwest corner of Church and High streets, Cambridge, Dorchester County). NRHP.

Brohawn, Capt. John. 48th Regiment.
LeCompte, Midshipman Samuel Woodward. Served aboard U.S. schooner *Nonsuch,* Charleston, South Carolina, 1812. Aboard U.S. gunboat *No. 164,* St. Mary's River, Georgia, September 1813. One of only six crew members who survived a storm with gale-force winds; twenty-five drowned. Aboard U.S. frigate *Java,* Baltimore, March 29, 1815.

CHRIST EPISCOPAL CHURCH I.U. CEMETERY (named for crossroads; north side of Fairlee–Still Pond Road [Route 298], 0.4 mile east of intersection with Worton Road [Route 297], near Worton, Kent County). NRHP.

Reed, Lt. Col. Philip. 21st Regiment. Commander of the American forces at the Battle of Caulks Field. Later promoted to general. Grave unmarked until 1902, when a granite marker was placed on his gravesite. Inscription on gravestone reads in part: "A Soldier of the Revolution and of the War of 1812."

CHRIST REFORMED CHURCH CEMETERY (12 South Church Street, Middletown, Frederick County).

Beckenbaugh, Pvt. John. Murray's Company.
Kinna, Pvt. James. Hall's Troop of Horse, 2nd Regiment.
Shafer, Pvt. George. Ent's Company, 3rd Regiment.
Titlow, Sgt. Maj. George. Dawson's Company, 28th Regiment.

CHURCH OF THE BRETHREN CEMETERY (Brownsville, Washington County).

Castle, Pvt. Eli. Marker's Company, 28th Regiment.

CHURCH OF GOD CEMETERY (Uniontown, Carroll County).

Christ, Cpl. Jacob. Duvall's Company, 29th Regiment.
Hollingberger, Pvt. Peter. Knox's Company, Randall's Battalion Riflemen.
Metcalfe, Sgt. Thomas. Cumming's Company, 15th Regiment.

CHURCHVILLE PRESBYTERIAN CHURCH CEMETERY (northwest corner of the intersection of Churchville Road [Route 22] and Priest Ford Road [Route 136]), Churchville, Harford County).

Archer, Stevenson. Paymaster, 40th Regiment.

DEER PARK UNITED METHODIST CHURCH CEMETERY, also called Deer Park Chapel (east side of Deer Park Road opposite Sulane Count, 1.0 mile north of intersection with Gamber Road [Route 91], Charolais Cares area, Carroll County). The two Ogg burials were originally located in the Ogg Family Cemetery on Bird View Road, near Holliday Lane, but at some unknown time were moved here.

Frizzell, Sgt. John. Gorsuch's Company. Buried in lot 30.
Ogg, George IV. No service record found.
Ogg, Pvt. James. Jameson's Company, 1st Regiment.
Wagers, Pvt. Luke, Jr. Gorsuch's Company, 1st Battalion of Riflemen.

DENTON CEMETERY (southeast corner of Easton–Denton Road [Route 328] and Hillsboro–Denton Road [Route 404 Business], Denton, Caroline County).

Potter, Lt. Col. William. 19th Regiment.

DETOUR METHODIST PROTESTANT CEMETERY (Detour, Frederick County).

Carmack, Pvt. Woods. Wood's Company, 1st Regiment.
Wilhide, Pvt. Jacob. Duvall's Company, 29th Regiment.

DODON FAMILY CEMETERY (presumably Dodon area, Dodon Road off Birdsville Road, south of Davidsonville, Anne Arundel County).

Steuart, Dr. Richards. Volunteer surgeon at Battle of North Point.

DONOHO FAMILY CEMETERY (north side of Wetipquin Road, 0.8 mile southeast of intersection with Royal Oak Road behind and northwest of black cemetery, Wetipquin, Wicomico County).

Donoho, Pvt. William. Humphrey's Company, 25th Regiment.

DRURY FAMILY CEMETERY (Bristol, Anne Arundel County).

Drury, Pvt. Henry. Child's Company, 2nd Regiment.

DUVAL FAMILY CEMETERY (former C. C. Beall Farm, State Highway Administration right-of-way, beyond southeast dead end of Bell Station Road at Annapolis Road [Route 450], Glenn Dale, Prince George's County).

Duval, Capt. Edmund B. 42nd U.S. Infantry.

EBENEZER UNITED METHODIST CHURCH CEMETERY (south side of Ebenezer Road, east of intersection with Earls Road and west of intersection with Bird River Beach Road, near White Marsh, Baltimore County).

Evans, Pvt. James. Ragan's Company, 1st Regiment.

ELKTON CEMETERY, also called Elkton Methodist Cemetery (south side of intersection of South and Howard streets; one block east off Main Street, Elkton, Cecil County).

Ford, Pvt. John Hyland. 8th Cavalry District.

ELKTON PRESBYTERIAN CHURCH CEMETERY (200 block of East Main Street, Elkton, Cecil County).

Mitchell, Col. George Edward (1781–1832). Major, 3rd U.S. Artillery in May 1812. Brevetted colonel in May 1814 for role in defense of Fort Oswego, New York. Cenotaph here; burial at Congressional Cemetery, Washington, D.C.
Whann, Maj. Adam. 8th Cavalry Regiment.

EMMITSBURG PRESBYTERIAN CEMETERY (also called Welty Cemetery, Emmitsburg, Frederick County).

Paxton, Pvt. John. Knox's Company, Randall's Battalion Riflemen.

ETTING FAMILY CEMETERY (northeast corner of North Avenue at Pennsylvania Avenue, Baltimore City). The cemetery is locked and surrounded by a brick wall, but the gravestones can be seen through the cemetery gate.

Etting, Solomon (1764–1837). Served in defense of Baltimore.

EVANGELICAL LUTHERAN CHURCH CEMETERY (Frederick, Frederick County).

Ebbert, Pvt. John. Ent's Company, 3rd Regiment.

FAIRMOUNT CEMETERY (south side of intersection of South Street and Liberty Road [Route 26], Libertytown, Frederick County).

Cummings, Maj. Gen. Robert. 2nd Division.

FAITH FAMILY BAPTIST CHURCH CEMETERY (formally Emmanuel Baptist Church and Mt. Pleasant Methodist Church, west side of Sykesville Road [Route 32], 0.4 mile south of intersection with Gamber Road [Route 91], near Gamber, Carroll County).

Gorsuch, Cpl. George W. Frizell's Company, 15th Regiment.

FIRST PRESBYTERIAN CHURCH BURYING GROUND, also called Western Burying Ground, Westminster Burying Ground or Old Westminster Cemetery (West Fayette and Greene streets, Baltimore City). Among those who are buried here are the following people connected to the War of 1812:

Buchanan, Col. James A. (Not to be confused with President James Buchanan.) Served in the Revolutionary War and the War of 1812.

Cunningham (Cunyngham), Pvt. John. Stiles's Company, Marine Artillery. Buried in plot 62.

Donaldson, Lt. James Lowry (Lowrie). 27th Regiment. Killed at the Battle of North Point. His obituary states: "While in the active performance of his duty, he received a musket or rifle ball through his head, which put an immediate period to his life" (Baltimore *Federal Gazette,* September 24, 1814).

Gold, Samuel. Buried in plot 59.

Gordon, Pvt. John. Buried in plot 116.

Harris, Lt. Col. David. 1st Artillery Regiment. Buried in plot 65.

Harris, Samuel. Buried in plot 178.

Hollins, Pvt. John. Addison's Company, Sea Fencibles. Buried in plot 88.

King, William. Buried in plot 108.

MacIntosh, Duncan. Buried in plot 60.

McClellan, 4th Sgt. Samuel. Sterett's Company, 5th Cavalry Regiment. Buried in plot 49.

McClellan, Pvt. Samuel. Warfield's Company, 5th Regiment. Buried in plot 4.

McDowell, Pvt. Maxwell. Thompson's Company, 1st Battalion Horse Artillery. Buried in plot 163.

McHenry, James. Fort McHenry named for him.

Mosher, James. In charge of construction of Spring Gardens Gun Battery, Baltimore. Buried in plot 26.

Schley, Pvt. Jacob. Harris's Company, 1st Artillery Regiment. Buried in plot 171.

Skinner, John Stuart. Purser of U.S. Chesapeake Flotilla and U.S. agent for prisoner exchange. Assisted Francis Scott Key in securing the release of Dr. William Beanes.

Smith, Maj. Gen. Samuel. Commander in chief during the defense of Baltimore. Buried in plot 85.

Sterett, Maj. Samuel. 5th Regiment. Buried in plot 74.

Stodder, David. Built U.S. frigate *Constellation.*

Stricker, Brig. Gen. John. 3rd Division, 3rd Brigade. Commander of American forces at the Battle of North Point. Buried in plot 19.

Watson, Capt. Thomas. 39th Regiment. Buried in plot 76.

FALLS ROAD UNITED METHODIST CHURCH CEMETERY, also Falls Road Chapel (east side of Falls Road, 0.3 mile south of intersection with Black Rock Road, north of Butler, Baltimore County).

Skipper, John. No service record found.

FOREST MEMORIAL UNITED METHODIST CHURCH CEMETERY, originally named Old Fields (3111 Forestville Road, near Forestville Plaza, Forestville, Prince George's County).

Darcey, Sgt. Francis. No gravestone found.

FOWLER-RINE FAMILY CEMETERY (Kemptown, Frederick County).

Simmons, Pvt. George. Dorsey's Company, 32nd Regiment.

FREDERICK REFORMED CEMETERY (Frederick, Frederick County). Abandoned.

Albaugh, Pvt. Solomon. Getzendanner's Company, 16th Regiment.

Albaugh Pvt. Solomon. Turbutt's Company, 3rd Regiment.

Dertzbaugh, 3rd Sgt. George. Steiner's Company, 1st Regiment.

Ely, Pvt. Daniel. Ent's Company, 3rd Regiment.

Hickson, Ensign Henry. Knox's Company, Randall's Battalion Riflemen.

Morgan, 3rd Cpl. Thomas W. Worthington's Company.

Ogle, Capt. Samuel V. 2nd Regiment.

Ott, Pvt. Peter. Turbott's Company.

Pyfer, Pvt. Philip, Jr. Steiner's Company, 1st Regiment.

Schissler, Pvt. John. Steiner's Company, 1st Regiment.

Staley, Pvt. Abraham. Turbott's Company.

Staley, Pvt. Peter. Turbott's Company.

GETZENDANNER FAMILY CEMETERY (Braddock, Frederick County).

Getzendanner, Capt. Jacob. Detachment of riflemen.

GLADE REFORMED CEMETERY (Walkersville, Frederick County).

Barrick, Capt. George. 29th Regiment.

Riner, Pvt. George. Smith's Company, Watkin's Command.

GLENDY GRAVEYARD, originally called Second Presbyterian Church Cemetery and Eastern Burial Ground (southwest intersection of Broadway and Biddle Street, bounded on south by Gay Street, four blocks north of Johns Hopkins Hospital). Over twenty veterans who fought at North Point and Fort McHenry

as well as others who served aboard many of Baltimore's privateers during the war are buried here. When the city extended
Broadway in 1874–75, many graves were removed. Most of the
remaining gravestones are located in the crawlspace below
the church. Among the former graves are the following people
connected to the War of 1812:

Beatty, James. Owner of the Aetna Powder Mill, U.S. Navy agent, and
   War of 1812 veteran.
Burke, Pvt. David, Jr. Lawrence's Company, 6th Regiment.
Chase, Thorndick. Sea captain, investor in Baltimore privateers,
   and owner of Chase's Wharf.
Cole, Pvt. Thomas. 6th Regiment.
Coulter Pvt. John P. Washington Blues, 5th Maryland Regiment.
Crawford, Pvt. William. 1st Rifle Battalion.
Dinsmore, Pvt. John. Ringgold's Company, 6th Regiment.
Dinsmore, Pvt. Patrick. Dobbin's Company, 39th Regiment.
Dinsmore, Pvt. Samuel. Pennington's Company, Baltimore Indepen-
   dence Artillery.
Duddy, Pvt. Henry. Phinney's Company, 27th Regiment.
Fulton, Sgt. James. Cozier's Company, 39th Regiment.
Fulton, Pvt. James. Levering's Company, Independent Blues. Prob-
   ably same as Sergeant Fulton above.
Gardner, 2nd Lt. Timothy. Marine Artillery of the Union.
Gibson, Pvt. James. Sterett's Company, Baltimore United
   Volunteers.
Gregg, Pvt. Alexander. Pennington's Company, Baltimore Indepen-
   dent Artillery.
Gregg, Pvt. James. Lawson's Company, Baltimore Patriots.
Hays, Pvt. William. U.S. Sea Fencibles.
Hollins, 1st Lt. John. Smith's 1st Baltimore Hussars.
Jephenson (Jephson), Pvt. John (1767–1814). Dillon's Company, 27th
   Regiment. Prisoner at North Point.
Kanes, Capt. Joseph M. 27th Regiment.
Kennedy, Capt. John. 2nd Company, 17th Regiment. Present during
   the Battle of North Point.
de Laroche, George F. Served aboard U.S. sloop-of-war *Erie*.
Mackenzie, Collin. No service record found.
McDonald, Capt. Samuel. 6th Regiment.
McDonald, Lt. Col. William (1758–1845). 6th Regiment.
McElderry, Pvt. John. Faster's Company, 51st Regiment.
McNeal, Pvt. James. Brown's Company, 1st Artillery Regiment.
McNeil, Pvt. James, Jr. Pennington's Company, Baltimore Indepen-
   dent Artillery. Probably the same as McNeal above.
Mezick, 2nd Lt. Baptist. Stiles's Company, Marine Artillery.
Miller, Pvt. George W. (1777–1836). Served at Fort McHenry. Father
   of Alfred Jacob Miller (1810–74), who painted the famous scenes
   depicting the bombardment of Fort McHenry.

Moore, 3rd Lt. Robert Scott. Pennington's Company. Located in
   the crawlspace under the church, gravestone reads in part:
   "Robert Scott Moore youngest Son of Robert, 3rd lieutenant of
   the Independent Artillerist, stationed at Fort McHenry, during
   the bombardment of the Fortress, by the British Fleet, on the 13
   September 1814, the fatigue and exposure he underwent on that
   memorable occasion brought on a disease of the Breast, under
   which he labored until the 2d January 1817, when he departed
   this life in the hope . . ." (rest of stone buried in ground).
Nelson [Neilson], Pvt. Oliver Hugh (d. 1821). Warfield's Company,
   Baltimore United Volunteers; quartermaster 51st Regiment.
Perry, Herman. Privateer officer.
Ramsey, Pvt. James. 1st Marine Artillery of the Union.
Roney, Capt. William (1782–1844). 29th Regiment.
Shaw, Archibald. Contributed ships to defend Baltimore.
Stiles, Capt. George (1760–1819). 1st Marine Artillery of the Union,
   3rd Brigade.
Trippe, A. C. No service record found.
Vickers, 1st Lt. Joel. 1st Marine Artillery of the Union.
Wynn, Cpl. Christopher. McKane's Company, 27th Regiment.

GOVANSTOWN CEMETERY, also called Govans Presbyterian
Churchyard (5828 York Road, near intersection with Bellona
Avenue and Orkney Road, near the northern boundary Balti-
more City).

Hall, Christopher. No service record found.
Tredway, Pvt. Thomas. 12th Regiment. Buried in lot 149.

GRACE EVANGELICAL AND REFORMED CHURCH CEMETERY
(Taneytown, Carroll County).

Clabaugh, Pvt. Jacob. Knox's Company, Randall's Battalion Riflemen.
Crouse, Capt. Joseph. Ogle's Company, 2nd Regiment.
Hiteshew, Pvt. Abraham. Knox's Company, Randall's Battalion
   Riflemen.
Hiteshew, Pvt. Gideon. Knox's Company, Randall's Battalion
   Riflemen.
Ott, Pvt. Michael. Knox's Company, Randall's Battalion Riflemen.
   Buried in area D, lot 10–16.
Ridinger, Pvt. Peter. Ogle's Company, 2nd Regiment.
Slick, Pvt. Francis. Magee's Company, 1st Regiment. Buried in area
   D, lot 7–8.
Snider, 1st Lt. Nicholas. Galt's Company, 3rd Regiment. Buried in
   area D, lot 5-3.
Thomson, 2nd Lt. Hugh Henry. Lowrye's Company, 1st Regiment.
   Wounded at Battle of Bladensburg. Buried in area D, lot 5-2.

GRASON, GOVERNOR WILLIAM, GRAVE, Wye River Farm (near 204 Governors Way North, north off Governors Lane, 0.2 mile east off Bennett Point Road, 1.0 mile south off Main Street [Route 18], south of Queenstown). PRIVATE

Grason, Gov. William (1788–1868). Twenty-eighth governor of Maryland, enlisted as a private in the 38th Regiment, Artillery Company, May 11, 1813; 3rd sergeant, August 6, 1813; 2nd lieutenant, September 12, 1813. During the Battle of Slippery Hill, Grason served in Wright's 1st Queen Anne's Artillery Company, attached to the 38th Regiment, 6th Brigade.

GREEN MOUNT CEMETERY (bounded by Greenmount Avenue on west, where entrance is located, North Avenue on north, Ensor Street on east, and Hoffman Street on south, Baltimore City). Green Mount Cemetery holds the remains of over 260 War of 1812 veterans. It is the largest known repository in the Chesapeake region. Killed in the early stages of the Battle of North Point, Pvts. Daniel Wells and Henry Gough McComas, originally buried together in Second Baptist (New Jerusalem) Cemetery near Broadway where Johns Hopkins Hospital now stands, were reburied in an unknown vault at Green Mount Cemetery before being moved on September 12, 1858, to their current resting place at the Wells and McComas Monument, Ashland Square.

Adgate, Pvt. Andrew. Warfield's Company, Baltimore United Volunteers. Buried in area Linden.

Albers, 2nd Maj. Solomon G. 1st Artillery Regiment. Buried in area K.

Alder, Pvt. Michael. Moore's Company, 6th Cavalry Regiment. Buried at entrance.

Allender, Surg. Joseph. 5th Regiment. Buried in area D, lot 18.

Andre, 1st Lt. Gregorius. Bader's Company, Union Yager. Buried in area T, lot 24. His epitaph reads in part: "fell at the Battle of North Point."

Appold, Pvt. George. Chalmer's Company, 51st Regiment. Buried in area I, lot 94.

Baltzell, Lt. Thomas. Sadtler's Company, 39th Regiment. Buried in area VV, lot 38.

Bandel (Bandle), Pvt. Frederick. McDonald's Company, 6th Regiment. Buried in area VV, lot 57.

Bangs, Pvt. John. Myer's Company, Franklin Artillery. Buried in area TT, lot 99.

Bankhead, Capt. James. U.S. Army. Buried in area Y, lot 7.

Banks, Pvt. Daniel Bower. Stapleton's Company, 39th Regiment. Buried in area U, lot 74–76.

Barger, Pvt. Deeter (?). Harris's Company, 1st Artillery Regiment. Buried in area K, lot 16.

Barney, Capt. John. Assistant district quartermaster general for the U.S. Army, August 1814 to June 1815. Buried in area F, lot 60.

Baughman, Pvt. Frederick. Howard's Company, 5th Regiment. Buried in area Q.

Baxley, Pvt. George. Berry's Company, 1st Artillery Regiment. Buried in area L, lot 93.

Baynard, Pvt. John. Warfield's Company, Baltimore United Volunteers. Buried in area TT.

Beard, Sgt. John. Schwarzaner's Company, 27th Regiment. Buried in area V.

Berry, Pvt. Benjamin F. Berry's Company, Washington Artillery. Buried in area TT.

Berry, Capt. John. Washington Artillerist, 1st Artillery Regiment. Buried in area A, lot 32.

Biays, Lt. Col. James. 5th Cavalry Regiment. Buried in area D, lot 18.

Biays, Pvt. Joseph, Jr. Shepard's Company, 6th Regiment. Buried in area D, lot 18.

Bixler, Pvt. David. 1st Baltimore Artillery. Buried in area Z.

Boehme, Pvt. Charles L. Sterett's Company, 1st Baltimore Hussars. Buried in area C.

Boggs, Pvt. Alexander L. Sterett's Company, 5th Cavalry Regiment. Buried in area Y, lot 35.

Boss, Pvt. George. Brown's Company, Eagle Artillery. Buried in area Poplar.

Bowen, Pvt. Richard. Dyer's Company, Fells Point Riflemen. Buried in area Poplar.

Boyer, Pvt. Jacob. Levering's Company, Independent Blues. Buried in area G.

Brundige, Dr. Henry. Surgeon's Mate. Buried in area B, lot 18.

Buckler, Pvt. John. Nicholson's Company. Buried in area J, lot 15–16.

Butler, Pvt. Absalom. Ede's Company, 27th Regiment. Buried in area V, lot 150.

Caldwell, John. No service record found. Buried in area C.

Cassard, Pvt. Gilbert. Berry's Company, 1st Artillery Regiment. Buried in area VV.

Chapman, Pvt. George. 27th Regiment. Buried in area V, lot 94.

Chaytor, Capt. Daniel. Privateer. Buried in area I.

Cherbonnier, Pvt. Pierre. Simpson's Company, Louisiana Militia. Buried in area VV.

Child, Pvt. William. Nicholson's Artillery Company. Buried in area N, lot 5.

Childs, Pvt. Samuel. Union Artillery. Buried in area TT, lot 111.

Clagett, Pvt. Elie. Warfield's Company, 5th Regiment. Buried in area V, lot 122.

Claxton, Lt. Alexander. U.S.N. Buried in area I.

Cobb, Pvt. Josiah. Marten's Company, Massachusetts Militia. Buried in area Cedar, lot 3.

Cole, Frederick. No service record found. Buried in area Z, lot 6.

Collmus, Pvt. Levi. Piper's Company, 1st Regiment. Buried in area U.

Conrad, Ensign David. 20th U.S. Infantry. Buried in area Y.

Corner, Pvt. James. Brown's Company, Eagle Artillerist. Buried in area I, lot 19.

Craggs, Pvt. Robert. Sheppard's Company, 6th Regiment. Buried in area Linden, lot 28.

Dalrymple, John H. No service record found. Buried in area U, lot 94.

Darling, Cpl. John. Chalmer's Company, 51st Regiment. Buried in area Ash.

Dashiell, Pvt. Henry. Stiles's Company, Marine Artillery. Buried in area E, lot 60.

Davis, Dr. Charles S. Surgeon's Mate, 15th Regiment. Buried in area TT.

Davis, George A. No service record found. Buried in area TT, lot 16.

Deems, Capt. Jacob F. 51st Regiment. Buried in area I, lot 7.

Dempsey, Sgt. Robert. McDonald's Company, 6th Regiment. Buried in area R, lot 79.

Diffenderfer, Dr. Michael. Surgeon's Mate, 1st Artillery Regiment. Buried in area V, lot 136.

Dryden, 1st Cpl. Joshua. Adreon's Company, 5th Regiment, and later major of the Old Defender's Association, 1883–97. Buried in area C, lot 37.

Duckhart (Dukehart), Pvt. Henri (Henry) V. A. Aisquith's Company, 1st Rifle Battalion. Buried in area Y, lot 60.

Duhamel, Pvt. James. 35th Regiment. Buried in area J, lot 8.

Durst, Pvt. John. Bader's Company, 1st Rifle Battalion. Buried in area VV.

Dushane, Sgt. Valentine. Deem's Company, 51st Regiment. Buried in area H, lot 48.

Edmondson, Maj. John. 10th Cavalry District. Buried in area WW, lot 13.

Egerton, Ensign Charles C. 39th U.S. Infantry. Buried in area Cypress, lot 12.

Ellender, Pvt. Frederick. Burke's Company, 6th Regiment. Buried in area Spruce, lot 44.

Elmore, Pvt. James. Peter's Company, 51st Regiment. Buried in area G.

Ensey, Pvt. Lot. Fowler's Company, 39th Regiment. Buried in area A, lot 14.

Ensey, Pvt. William. Jessop's Company, 36th Regiment. Buried in area A, lot 14.

Ensor, Pvt. James. Randall's Rifle Battalion. Buried in area WW, lot 7, Duhurst Vault.

Evans, John. No service record found. Buried in area Violet.

Fahnestock, Pvt. Derrick. Berry's Company, Washington Artillery. Wounded during bombardment of Fort McHenry. Buried in area A, lot 14.

Fahnestock, Pvt. Peter. Berry's Company, 1st Artillery Regiment. Buried in area H, lot 64.

Fahs, Pvt. Casper. Sadtler's Company, Baltimore Yagers. Buried in area TT, lot 77.

Farnandis, Pvt. Walter. Nicholson's Company. Buried in area G, lot 100.

Fisher, Abraham. Buried in area K.

Ford, Pvt. George W. Pennington's Company, Independent Artillerists. Buried in area D, lots 32–34.

Fossett, 4th Sgt. John. Wilson's Company, 6th Regiment. Buried in area W, lot 8.

Frailey, Maj. Leonard. 3rd Brigade. Buried in area V, lot 77.

Furlong, Pvt. William. Stiles's Company, Marine Artillery. Buried in area Springvale, lot 48.

Gatchaire, Lt. Francis. Privateer *Burrows*. Buried in area H, lot 78.

George, Pvt. James B. Addison's Company, Sea Fencibles. Buried in entrance area.

Gill, Capt. Stephen. 41st Regiment. Buried in area Lilac.

Gill, Midshipman William L. U.S.N. Buried in area Elm, lot 13.

Gist, 2nd Lt. William. 10th Regiment Cavalry. Buried in area K, lot 23.

Gold, Peter. Appointed to the Committee on Defense of Baltimore. Buried in area K.

Golder, Pvt. Archibald. Moale's Company, 1st Artillery Regiment. Buried in area S, lot 23.

Green, Pvt. Charles. Guiton's Company, 2nd Regiment. Buried in area Linden.

Griffith, Benjamin. Buried in area Tulip, lot 8.

Griffith, Pvt. Howard. Levering's Company, Independent Blues. Buried in area Cypress, lot 12.

Griffith, Pvt. Stephen. Roney's Company, 39th Regiment. Buried in area TT, lot 21.

Hall, Capt. Thomas W. Rifle Company, 5th Virginia Militia. Burial site unknown.

Harper, Maj. Gen. Robert Goodloe. 3rd Division. Buried in area U, lot 121.

Harris, Samuel. No service record found. Buried in area N.

Hayden, Pvt. Dr. Horace H. Watt's Company, 39th Regiment. Burial site unknown.

Herbert, Capt. John Carlyle. Bladensburg Troop of Horse, 2nd Cavalry District. Buried in area R, lot 83.

Hewitt, Pvt. Elmer. Ringgold's Company, 6th Regiment. Buried in area WW, lot 76.

?Higdon, Sgt. Benjamin D. Sterett's Company, 5th Calvary Regiment. Buried in area G, lot 98.

Hill, 1st Sgt. Thomas G. McKane's Company, 27th Regiment. Buried in area Maple, lot 48.

Hiss, Pvt. Philip. Steever's Company, 27th Regiment. Buried in area D, lot 17.

Hooper, Pvt. James. Lawrence's Company, 6th Regiment. Buried in area R, lot 23.

Hough, John E. No service record found. Buried in area VV, lot 117.

Howard, Brig. Gen. Benjamin Chew. 1st lieutenant, 2nd Regiment, 1813. Promoted to adjutant, 11th Brigade, 1813. Promoted to captain, 5th Regiment, 1814. Buried in area A, lot 5.,

Howard, Jacob. No service record found. Buried in area M.

Huball, Pvt. Ebenezer. Magruder's Company Artillery. Buried in area R.

Hugh, Pvt. Davey. Stiles's Company, Marine Artillery. Buried in area Juniper.

Hughes, Christopher, Jr. (1788–1846). Brother-in-law of Lt. Col. George Armistead. As secretary to the American delegation at Ghent, brought the first news of peace to the United States. Buried in area S, lot 16.

Hunt, Pvt. Jesse. Steuart's Company, 5th Regiment. Buried in area VV, lot 115.

Hutson, Pvt. John. Stiles's Company, Marine Artillery. Buried in area U.

Hyde, Lt. Samuel G. Ede's Company, 27th Regiment. Buried in area Y, lot 28.

Inloes, 1st Lt. William. 6th Regiment. Buried in area TT, lot 59.

Israel, 3rd Sgt. Fielder. Moale's Company, Columbian Artillery. Buried in area M, lot 19.

Jamart, Pvt. Jean Michel (Michael) Armand. Sterett's Company, 5th Regiment. Buried in area U, lot 69.

Jamison, Pvt. Caelilius C. Sterett's Company, 5th Cavalry Regiment. Buried in area Spruce.

Janvier, Pvt. Peregrin (?). Steuart's Company, Washington Blues. Buried in area M.

Jarret, Pvt. Asbury. Streett's Company, 7th Regiment. Buried in area TT, lot 51.

Johnson, Pvt. Reverdy. 22nd Regiment. Buried in area AAA.

Jones, Pvt. Talbot. Sterett's Company, Independent Company. Buried in area V, lot 76.

Jones, William Pace. Officer of unknown unit. Buried in area F, lot 75.

Jones, William R. Stewart, U.S.N. Buried in area M, lot 8.

Kalbfus, Sgt. Daniel. Stewart's Company, 51st Regiment. Buried in area D.

Kaufman, Pvt. Daniel. Miller's Company, 39th Regiment. Buried in area V, lot 123.

Kaylor, George. Sadtler's Company, Baltimore Yagers. Buried in area P, lot 37.

Keener, Pvt. Christian. Warfield's Company, 5th Regiment. Buried in area U, lot 108.

Keerl, Pvt. John C. Warfield's Company, 5th Regiment. Buried in area F, lot 64.

Keerl, Pvt. Samuel. Baltimore United Volunteers. Buried in area F, lot 117.

Keilholtz, Cpl. William. Pike's Company, Baltimore Volunteer Artillery. Buried in area U, lot 112.

Keirle, P. Henry. U.S.N. Buried in area F, lot 64.

Kell, 1st Lt. Thomas. Bouldin's Company, 5th Cavalry. Buried in area TT, lot 47.

Kelso, Cpl. John Russell. Steuart's Company, Washington Blues. Buried in area I, lot 58.

Kenly, Pvt. Edward. 27th Regiment. Buried in area R.

Kepplinger, Col. P. Buried in area A, lot 39.

Keys, Sgt. John. Pike's Company, Volunteer Artillery. Buried in area V.

Kimberly, Pvt. Nathaniel. Steuart's Company, 5th Regiment. Buried in area WW, lot 79.

Kiplinger, Pvt. Michael. Chalmer's Company, 51st Regiment. Buried in area A.

Kirkland, Cpl. Alexander. Harris's Company, 1st Artillery Regiment. Buried in area I, lot 47.

Kitts, John. Teamster. Buried in area F, lot 37.

Knup, Pvt. Abraham. Fowler's Company, 33rd Regiment. Buried in area H, lot 11.

Landstreet, Pvt. John. Sadler's Company, Baltimore Yagers. Buried in area TT.

Leary, 1st Lt. Peter. Warner's Company, 39th Regiment. Buried in area Poplar, lot 61.

Lemmon, William P. Moale's Company, 1st Artillery Regiment. Buried in area O.

Levering, Capt. Aaron R. Independent Blues, 5th Regiment. Buried in area WW, lot 66.

Levering, Pvt. Jesse. Sterett's Company, 5th Cavalry Regiment.

Lord, Walter. Buried in area Yew, lot 191/2. Author of *Dawn's Early Light* about the Battle for Baltimore. Buried in area V.

Lucas, James. U.S.N. Buried in area R, lot 118.

Ludden, Pvt. Lemuel. Sterett's Company, 1st Baltimore Hussars. Buried in area S.

March, Morris G. U.S.N. Buried in area ZZ.

Marean, Pvt. Thomas. Sterett's Company, 5th Cavalry Regiment. Buried in area Z, lot 81.

Marriott, Maj. William Hammond. 8th Maryland Brigade, later general of Maryland State Militia. Buried in area R, lot 39.

Martin, Capt. Samuel. Surgeon. Buried in area VV, lot 67.

McClain, Pvt. John. Harris's Company, 1st Regiment. Buried in area Hickory, lot 1.

McConkey, William. No service record found. Buried in area G, lot 44.

McCurley, Pvt. Felix. Garrett's Company, 51st Regiment. Buried in area V, lot 108.

McLane, Louis. Wilmington, Delaware Artillery Company. Buried in area VV, plot 36.

McLean, Cornelius. 2nd Regiment, Brent's District of Columbia Militia. Buried in area O or R.

McMurray, 1st Sgt. Samuel. Murray's Company, 36th Regiment. Buried in area I.

McPherson, William. U.S.N. Buried in area R, lot 7.

Mears, Jacob. No service record found. Buried in area Spruce, lot 37.

Medtart, Gen. Joshua. 1st lieutenant, 38th U.S. Infantry. Buried in area F, lot 117.

Meyer, Pvt. Godfrey. Sadlter's Company, 5th Regiment. Buried in area U.

Middleton, Pvt. Richard. Levering's Company, 5th Regiment. Buried in area TT, lot 58.

Miltenberger, Pvt. Anthony. Levering's Company, 5th Regiment. Buried in area M, lot 63.

Moore, John H. No service record found. Buried in area O, lot 2.

Mosher, Pvt. William. Shrim's Company, Baltimore Light Infantry. Buried in area U.

Mowton, Capt. John. 38th U.S. Infantry. Buried in area B, lot 26.

Munroe, Pvt. Isaac. U.S. Volunteers. Present at Fort McHenry. Buried in area N.

Myers, 1st. Lt. Jacob. Allen's Company, Maryland Chasseurs. Buried in area T.

Needham, Ensign Asa. Clare's Company, 31st Regiment. Buried in area R, lot 72.

Neilson, Pvt. Robert. Crook's Company, 27th Regiment. Buried in area B.

Neilson, Sgt. Thomas. Steuart's Company, Washington Blues. Buried in area B, lot 81.

Nicholson, Sgt. Christopher. Stewart's Company, 51st Regiment. Buried in area K.

Palmer, Pvt. Edward. Sterett's Company, 5th Cavalry Regiment. Buried in area V.

Parr, Pvt. David. Peter's Company, 51st Regiment. Buried in area N.

Peirce, Pvt. Israel. Watkin's Command. Buried in area R, lot 116.

Pennington, Pvt. Josias. Sterett's Company, 5th Regiment. Buried in area M.

Pentz, Pvt. Daniel. Piper's Company, 1st Artillery Regiment. Buried in area VV, lot 44.

Pentz, John J. Baltimore Independent Blues. Buried in area L.

Perine, Pvt. David M. Magruder's Company, 1st Artillery Regiment. Burial site unknown.

Perrigo, Cpl. Daniel. Ship joiner and grocer, Sheppard's Company, 6th Regiment. Buried in area Hickory, lot 1.

Peters, Pvt. Christian G. Sheppard's Company, 6th Regiment. Buried in area R, lot 92.

Peters, William. No service record found. Buried in area K.

Phelps, Pvt. John. Snowden's Company, 39th Regiment. Buried in area H, lot 44.

Pindell, Pvt. Lewis. Taylor's Company, 41st Regiment. Buried in area WW.

Pinkney, Maj. Ninian. U.S. Army. Buried in area Beech, lot 2.

Pinkney, Adj. William, Jr. (1789–1853). 1st Rifle Battalion, 3rd Brigade.

His father was a major in 1st Rifle Battalion and U.S. attorney general, 1812. Buried in area D, lot 42.

Price, Pvt. Walter. Peter's Company, 6th Regiment. Buried in area A, lot 53.

Proebsting, 2nd Lt. Theodore C. (?), Sadtler's Company, Baltimore Yagers. Buried in area Oak.

Rains, Pvt. Lewis. Lawrence's Company, 6th Regiment. Buried in area VV, lot 69.

Randall, Pvt. Aquilla. Howard's Company, Mechanical Volunteers, 5th Regiment. Killed at the Battle of North Point. Buried in outline area 2.

Randall, Pvt. William. Chalmer's Company, 51st Regiment. Buried in area Chestnut, lot 2.

Rau, Cpl. John C. Sadler's Company, Baltimore Yagers. Buried in area TT.

Ready, Cpl. Samuel. Conway's Company, 6th Regiment. Buried in area A, lot 3.

Redgrave, Pvt. Samuel. Conway's Company, 6th Regiment. Buried in area R, lot 55.

Reeder, Pvt. Charles. Howard's Company, 5th Regiment. Buried in area F.

Reigart, Pvt. Philip. Nicholson's Artillery Company. Buried in area V, lot 137.

Richstein, Pvt. George. Magruder's Company, 1st Artillery Regiment. Buried in area T, lot 31.

Ricketts, Pvt. David. Jessop's Company, 36th Regiment. Buried in area G, lot 49.

Rieman, Pvt. Henry. Hook's Company, 2nd Regiment. Buried in area L.

Rowe, Capt. John Kitchen. 6th Regiment. Buried in area V, lot 180.

Rusk, Pvt. George. Hanna's Company, 5th Cavalry Regiment. Buried in area Springvale, lot 74.

Rust, Pvt. Samuel. Baltimore Independent Artillery, 1st Regiment. Buried in area Lilac.

Rutter, Pvt. Thomas G. Hughes's Company, 1st Artillery Regiment. Buried in area E, lot 47, vault.

Sadtler, Capt. Philip B. 39th Regiment. Buried in area F, lot 5.

?Salzwedel, Pvt. John. Sadtler's Company, Baltimore Yagers. Buried in area F., lot 37.

Sands, Pvt. John. Levering's Company, 5th Regiment. Buried in area O, lot 11.

Sauerwein, Pvt. Peter. Sadtler's Company, Baltimore Yagers. Buried in area B, lot 23.

Schely, William. Buried in area EE.

Schuchts, Lt. Col. John Henry. 2nd Regiment; served in both Revolutionary War and War of 1812; participated at battles of Bladensburg and North Point. Buried in area Holly.

Shaffner, Jacob. Buried in area R, lot 103.

Shane, Pvt. Daniel. Shrim's Company, 5th Regiment. Buried in area U.

Shaw, Pvt. Samuel H. Sheppard's Company, 60th Regiment. Buried in area X.

Sheppard, Capt. Thomas. 6th Regiment. Buried in area U.

Sherwood, Pvt. Philip. Galt's Company, 6th Regiment. Buried in area Crescent.

Slemmer, Pvt. Christian. Peter's Company, 51st Regiment. Buried in area V, lot 137.

Slingluff, Cpl. Jesse. Thompson's Company, 1st Horse Artillery. Buried in area A.

Smith, Pvt. Job, Jr. Warfield's Company, Baltimore United Volunteers. Buried in area P.

Snow, Pvt. Freeman (?). Stiles's Company, Marine Artillery. Buried in area F, lot 113.

Snyder, John. Served in both Revolutionary War and War of 1812. Buried in area L, lot 75.

Sprigg, 1st. Lt. Daniel. Quantrill's Company, 24th Regiment. Buried in area G, lot 51.

Sprotson, Dr. George S. Assistant Surgeon, U.S.N. Buried in area Z, lot 32.

Stansbury, Pvt. Darius. Howard's Company, Mechanical Volunteers. present at battles of Bladensburg and North Point. Buried in area Chestnut, lot 1.

Stapleton, Capt. Joseph K. 39th Regiment. Buried in area WW.

Steever, Capt. George. 6th Regiment. Buried in area U, lot 94.

Steuart Capt. George H., Sr. 5th Regiment. Wounded in Battle of North Point. Later general of Maryland State Militia. Father of Confederate Gen. George H. Steuart, Jr. Buried in area F, lot 80.

Steuart, Capt. Robert S. J. 51st Regiment. Buried in area WW, lot 65.

Steuart, Lt. Col. William. 38th U.S. Infantry. Buried in area U, lot 59.

Stidger, Capt. George. 2nd Ohio Militia. Promoted to general in Ohio Militia. Buried in area V.

Strobel, 2nd Cpl. John Peter. McLaughlin's Company, 1st Artillery Regiment. Buried in area P, lot 19.

Strong, James. No service record found. Buried in area V, lot 121.

Sumwalt, Pvt. John Thornburg. Berry's Company, 1st Artillery Regiment. Wounded during bombardment of Fort McHenry. Buried in area VV, lot 117.

Sutter, Pvt. Henry. Shrim's Company, Baltimore Light Infantry. Buried in area Chestnut, lot 2.

Sykes, 3rd Sgt. James. Moale's Company, 1st Artillery Regiment. Buried in area I, lot 26.

Taylor, 2nd Maj. Lemuel G. Adjutant, 5th Cavalry. Buried in area R, lot 37.

Taylor, Pvt. Robert. Pennington's Company, Baltimore Independent Artillery, 1st Regiment. Buried in area L, lot 1.

Teal, Pvt. Archibald. McDonald's Company, 6th Regiment. Buried in area Walnut, lot 5.

Tennant, Col. Thomas. 6th Regiment. Buried in area N.

Thomas, Cpl. James H. McDonald's Company, 6th Regiment. Buried in area H, lot 78.

Thomas, Joseph. No service record found. Buried in area L, lot 80.

Thomas, Cpl. Sterling. Stuart's Company, 51st Regiment. Buried in area outline 4, lot 48.

Thompson, Capt. Henry. 1st Baltimore Dragoons. Buried in area V, lot 37.

Tittle, Pvt. Jeremiah. Pinney's Company, 27th Regiment. Buried in area F, lot 11.

Toy, Pvt. John D. Stewart's Company, 51st Regiment. Buried in area AA.

Tumblinson, Pvt. William. Brown's Company, 5th Regiment. Buried in area A, lot 3.

Turner, Capt. Daniel. Hero of the Battle of Lake Erie. Buried in area F.

Vickers, 2nd Lt. Joel. Stiles's Company, Marine Artillery. Buried in area V, lot 131.

Walker, Pvt. Sater T. Biays's Company, 5th Cavalry Regiment. Buried in area C.

Warner, Capt. Andrew E. 39th Regiment. Buried in area O, lot 5.

Warner, John. U.S.N. Buried in area I, lot 131.

Warner, Lewis M. No service record found. Buried in area VV, lot 150.

Warner, Capt. Thomas W. 39th Regiment. Wounded in action with loss of left leg. Buried in area O, lot 20.

Waters, Pvt. Joseph G. Magruder's Company, American Artillery. Buried in area R, lot 77.

Webb, Pvt. Abner. Rogers's Company, 51st Regiment. Buried in area B.

Welsh, Pvt. William H. Levering's Company, 5th Regiment. Last survivor of the "Old Defenders" of Baltimore (1800–1852). Buried in area outline 5, lot 10.

Werdebaugh, Pvt. John. Warfield's Company, Baltimore United Volunteers. Buried in area Z.

Wilkens, Dr. Henry. Surgeon, 39th Regiment. Buried in area G.

Willard, 2nd Lt. Julius. Meyer's Company, 1st Artillery Regiment. His stone includes image of cannon. Willard served in the defense of Baltimore. Buried in area G, lot 84.

Williams, Pvt. Amos A. Sterett's Company, 5th Regiment. Wounded September 12, 1814. Buried in area N, lot 5.

Williams, Pvt. George. Buried in area L, lot 26.

Williams, Pvt. Nathaniel. Sterett's Company, 5th Regiment. Wounded September 12, 1814. Buried in area M, lot 25.

Wilson, Greenbury. Buried in area V, lot 26.

Wilson, Pvt. John. Thompson's Company, 1st Baltimore Horse Artillery. Buried in area I.

Wilson, Pvt. Robert. Buried in area K, lot 78.

Wilson, Thomas. Independent Blues, 5th Regiment. Buried in area F.

Wilson, Pvt. Thomas. Buried in area G, lot 25.

Winder, Brig. Gen. William Henry. Commander of the American forces at the Battle of Bladensburg. Buried in area G, lot 54.

Wood, Pvt. John. Baltimore City 1st Artillery Regiment. Buried in area T, lot 20.

Wood, Matilda O'Neill. Daughter of John O'Neill, who helped seek her father's release from British after attack on Havre de Grace. Buried in outline 5.

Wood, Pvt. Nicholas Fowler's Company, 39th Regiment. Buried in area V.

Wood, Pvt. Samuel. Baltimore City 1st Artillery Regiment. Buried in area T, lot 20.

Wright, Cpl. John. No service record found. Buried in area Cedar, lot 4.

GREENWOOD CEMETERY (east side of Georgia Avenue, Brookeville, Montgomery County).

Bowie, Dr. John. Surgeon, 18th Regiment.

GROSSNICKLE'S BRETHREN CHURCH CEMETERY (Ellerton, Frederick County).

Eccard, Pvt. Peter. Marker's Company, 28th Regiment.

GUNPOWDER BAPTIST CHURCH CEMETERY, also called Old Middletown Cemetery (northeast corner of intersection of Middletown Road and Freeland Road, Middletown, northwestern Baltimore County). Gunpowder Baptist Church was established in 1808.

Hoffman, William D. Joseph. Green's Company, 1st Regiment.
Hoshall, 1st Lt. Jesse. Raven's Company, 2nd Regiment.

HAMMOND FAMILY CEMETERY (Gambrills, Anne Arundel County).

Hammond, Pvt. Resin. Linthicum's Company, 22nd Regiment.
Hammond, Silas W. No service record found.

HARLAN FAMILY CEMETERY (Woodsboro, Frederick County).

Harlan, Pvt. James. W. Wood's Company, 1st Regiment.

HARMONY CEMETERY (southeast side of McKendree Road, 0.5 mile south of Frederick Road [Route 144], southeast of Cookville, Howard County).

Hobbs, Pvt. Peregrine. Hood's Company, 32nd Regiment.

HARPER, COL. WILLIAM S., GRAVE (near flag pole at Eastern Shore Police Association of Maryland Camp ESPA, 0.4 mile down unimproved road southwest off Sharptown Road [Route 313], 1.1 miles southeast of intersection with Eldorado Road [Route 14], south of Eldorado, Dorchester County). PRIVATE

Harper, Capt. William S. 11th Regiment, Dorchester County. Promoted to the rank of colonel after the war.

HAUGH'S MT. ZION LUTHERAN CHURCH CEMETERY (Ladiesburg, Frederick County).

Hersh, Pvt. Philip. 1st Cavalry District.

HAWKINS FAMILY CEMETERY (also Hawkins Gate Cemetery, west side of Hawkins Gate Road, 1.7 miles south of intersection with LaPlata Road [Route 488], approximately 2.0 miles east of La Plata, Charles County). PRIVATE

Hawkins, Lt. Col. Samuel. 1st Regiment. Gravestone missing and reportedly stolen.

HEREFORD UNITED METHODIST CHURCH (Hereford, Baltimore County).

Gorsuch, Pvt. Thomas. Steever's Company, 27th Regiment.

HISS UNITED METHODIST CHURCH CEMETERY (west side of Harford Road [Route 147], just south of intersection of Putty Hill Road and north of Baltimore City line, Baltimore County).

Canoles, Pvt. William. Stansbury Miller's Company, 1st Regiment.

HOLY CROSS EPISCOPAL CHURCH CEMETERY (intersection of Rock Springs Road [Route 24] and Holy Cross Road, Bushs Corner, north of Bel Air, Harford County).

Streett, Lt. Col. John. 7th Cavalry District.

HOLY TRINITY EPISCOPAL CHURCH CEMETERY (Bowie, Prince George's County).

Isaac, Capt. Joseph. 34th Regiment.

HOYES UNITED METHODIST CHURCH CEMETERY (Hoyes–Sang Run Road and Friendsville–Hoyes Road [Route 42], Hoyes, Garrett County).

Dewitt, John. No service record found.

HYATTSTOWN METHODIST CHURCH CEMETERY (Hyattstown, Frederick County).

Hyatt, Pvt. Asa. Hall's Troop of Horse, 2nd Regiment.

JEFFERSON UNITED METHODIST CHURCH CEMETERY (Jefferson, Frederick County).

Culler, Lt. Henry. Shawen's Company.

JERUSALEM CEMETERY (Jerusalem, Frederick County).

Jacobs, Pvt. Ignatius. Ent's Company, 3rd Regiment.

JESSOPS METHODIST CHURCH CEMETERY (end of paved driveway south off York Road [Route 45] , 1.1 miles north of intersection with Shawan–Paper Mill Road [Route 145], Hunt Valley, Baltimore County). This church was founded in 1809. The Jessop Meeting House was built in 1811, enlarged in 1854, and remodeled in 1887 to present appearance.

Cole, Ensign Abraham. Taylor's Company, 46th Regiment.

JOHNSVILLE METHODIST PROTESTANT CHURCH CEMETERY (Johnsville, Frederick County).

Wolfe, Pvt. John. Duvall's Company.

JORDAN FAMILY CEMETERY (Gamber, Carroll County).

Jordan, Pvt. William. Gorsuch's Company.

KEMP FAMILY CEMETERY (Wades Point area, near McDaniel, Talbot County).

Kemp, Pvt. Thomas. Kierstead's Company, 6th Regiment.

KRAUSS FAMILY CEMETERY (north of Wyatt Lane, east off Jacob Tome Memorial Highway [Route 276], Harrisville, southwest of Rising Sun, Cecil County).

Krauss, Capt. Leonard. 30th Regiment.

KRIDER'S LUTHERAN & REFORMED CEMETERY (also called Old Krider's and St. Benjamin's Lutheran Church Cemetery, Krider's Church Road, west off Baltimore Boulevard [Route 97, north side of Westminster, Carroll County).

Byers, Pvt. Michael. Fonsten's Company, 29th Regiment.
Everly, Pvt. David. Blizzard's Company, 15th Regiment.
Grammar, Pvt. Jacob. Zacharias's Company, 2nd Regiment.
Hoppe, Trumpeter Frederick. Zacharias's Company, 2nd Regiment.

Marker, Pvt. David. Durbin's Company, Randall's Battalion Riflemen.
Sullivan, 3rd Sgt. David. Frederick County Militia.
Sullivan, Pvt. Jacob. Frederick County Militia.
Sullivan, 4th Sgt. William. Frederick County Militia.

LAKIN FAMILY CEMETERY (Catoctin Creek, Frederick County).

Lakin, Pvt. William. Turbutt's Company, 3rd Regiment.

LAMAR FAMILY CEMETERY (Jefferson, Frederick County).

Lamar, Sgt. Richard. Alexander's Company, 32nd Regiment.

LEEDS CEMETERY (Leeds Road, 0.2 mile northeast of intersection with Blue Ball Road [Route 545], Leeds, Cecil County). Leeds Cemetery occupies both sides of Leeds Road. Granite marker on south side of road just inside entrance to cemetery on west side (front side lists Civil War veterans; back side lists War of 1812 veterans): "WAR OF 1812–14/JOHN GALLAHER/ JOSEPH HALL SR/LT. ANDREW HARVEY."

Gallaher (Galleher), John. Damsell's Artillery Company, 1st Brigade.
Harvey, 1st Lt. Andrew. Damsell's Artillery Company, 1st Brigade.
Hall, Joseph, Sr. Probably buried in the north, older section of the cemetery either in an unmarked grave or under a stone now indecipherable. His son, Joseph Hall, a Civil War veteran, is buried under the tree in the northwest corner of the north side of the cemetery.

LEITERSBURG CEMETERY (Leitersburg, Washington County).

Lowman, Pvt. Daniel. Heath's Company, 2nd Regiment.

LLOYD FAMILY CEMETERY (Wye House, off Bruffs Island Road, Talbot County).

Lloyd, Lt. Col. Edward. 9th Cavalry District.

LORRAINE PARK CEMETERY (south side of Windsor Road, just northwest of Baltimore City limit and east of I-695, Woodlawn, Baltimore County).

Griffin, Pvt. George. Amey's Company, 51st Regiment. Buried in section 2, lot 172.

LOUDON PARK CEMETERY (main gate off Wilkens Avenue [U.S. Route 1], original gate at Frederick Avenue [Route 144] near intersection for both with Canton Avenue [Alternate U.S. Route 1], Baltimore City).

Bond, Thomas. No service record found. Buried in area Y.

Buck, Cornet Benjamin. Berry's Company, Washington Artillery.

Davis, Richard Thomas. Burgess's Company, 43rd Regiment. Buried in area AA.

Dolphin, Pvt. Francis. Miller's Company, 39th Regiment. Buried in area J.

Emmert, Cpl. Henry. Jessop's Company, 36th Regiment. Buried in area A.

Hugh, Pvt. Arthur. Jessop's Company, 36th Regiment. Buried in area VV.

Ijames, John. Baltimore City 51st Regiment. Buried in area J.

Kenner, Pvt. William C. Shrim's Company, Baltimore Light Infantry. Buried in area Q.

Luberson, John. Eight-year-old drummer boy.

Marine, William M. Author of *The British Invasion of Maryland 1812–1815*. Buried in area Y.

Marshall, Pvt. Thomas. Smith's Company, 51st Regiment. Buried in area C.

Matthews, Ensign William. Parnham's Company, 1st Regiment. Buried in area XXX.

Owens, Pvt. Joseph. Sterett's Company, 5th Regiment. Wounded at Battle of North Point.

Petticord, Pvt. John George. Steever's Company, 27th Regiment. Gravestone reads in part: "Old Defender." Buried in area VV.

Raborg, 1st Sgt. Christopher. Sterett's Company, 5th Regiment. Buried in area C.

Raborg, Pvt. Samuel. Sterett's Company, 1st Baltimore Hussars. Buried in area J.

Spies, John P. Andre's Company, Union Yagers. Buried in area KK, lot 14.

Watts, Pvt. Nathaniel. 6th Cavalry. Buried in area P.

LOWE FAMILY CEMETERY (Owings Mills, Baltimore County).

Lowe, Pvt. Amos. Randall's Battalion Riflemen.

Lowe, 2nd Lt. John.

LUTHERAN COMMUNITY CEMETERY, also called High German Lutheran Cemetery (one lot west of intersection of Cockeys Mill Road and Main Street, Reisterstown, Baltimore County). NRHP.

Aler (Ayler), Pvt. Thomas. Ducker's Company, 7th Regiment.

Beckley, Sgt. John. Ducker's Company, 7th Regiment.

Bennett, Pvt. Jesse. Snowden's Company, 6th Cavalry Regiment.

Choate, Pvt. Solomon. Ducker's Company, 7th Regiment. No gravestone found.

Clark, Cpl. Henry. Ducker's Company, 7th Regiment.

Cook, Pvt. Jeremiah. Ducker's Company, 7th Regiment.

Dickson, Maj. Isaac. 11th Brigade.

Ducker, Maj. Henry Howard. 11th Brigade.

Ducker, Capt. Jeremiah. 7th Regiment.

Dwyer, Pvt. William. Montgomery's Company, Baltimore Union Artillery.

Forney, Pvt. Michael. Ducker's Company, 7th Regiment.

Gore, Pvt. William. Carnan's Company, 6th Regiment Cavalry.

Gosnell, Pvt. Thomas. Ducker's Company, 7th Regiment.

Harryman, Pvt. Samuel. Dillon's Company, 27th Regiment.

Jessop, Pvt. Dominick B. Timanus's Company, 36th Regiment.

Larsh, Pvt. Charles. Levering's Company, Baltimore Independent Blues, 5th Regiment.

Norwood, 2nd Cpl. Nicholas. Ducker's Company, 7th Regiment.

Reister, Sgt. Peter. Ducker's Company, 7th Regiment.

Snyder, John C. Surgeon's Mate, 7th Regiment.

Stocksdale, Pvt. Solomon. Ducker's Company, 7th Regiment.

Stocksdale, Pvt. Thomas E. Ducker's Company, 7th Regiment.

Uhler, Pvt. Andrew. Hook's Company, 2nd Regiment.

MAGRUDER FAMILY CEMETERY ("The Forest Estate" located near intersection of Enterprise Road [Route 193] and John Hanson Highway [U.S. Route 50], Prince George's County).

Magruder, QM, Thomas. 14th Regiment.

MANCHESTER CEMETERY (Manchester, Carroll County).

Fair [Fehr], Pvt. John. Kerlinger's Company 15th or 36th [?] Regiment. Buried in area A, lot 19-25.

Sellers, Pvt. John. Shower's Company, 15th Regiment. Buried in area A, lot 7-5.

Shower, Jacob. Drummer boy. Buried in area D, lot 6-7d.

Shower, Capt. John Adam. 15th Regiment. Buried in area A, lot 2-9.

MANOKIN PRESBYTERIAN CHURCH, also called Old Manokin (11892 Somerset Avenue).

Handy, Capt. George, Jr. Commissioned lieutenant December 7, 1813, in Walter's Company, 23rd Regiment. Promoted to captain, September 10, 1814. Promoted to rank of general after the war.

MARTINGHAM SITE, then called Hambleton Farm (end of Old Martingham Road, just northeast of Martingham Drive, northeast of St. Michaels, Talbot County). PRIVATE

Freeland, Ensign William. Hewitt's Company, 4th Regiment.

Hambleton, Samuel. Purser in U.S. Navy and aide-de-camp to Com. Oliver Hazard Perry.

MCLAUGHLIN FAMILY CEMETERY (east side of Town Creek, near top of knoll near Hunters Paradise, approximately 1.1 miles southeast off Jacobs Road, 3.1 miles south from intersection with Mertens Avenue, Pumpkin Center area, Green Ridge State Forest, Allegany County). This cemetery is extremely difficult to find without a guide and requires either a four-wheel drive vehicle or a long hike. The McLaughlin home site can be recognized by a stone house chimney and dilapidated barn along the east side of an unimproved road on the east side of Town Creek just south of two hunting cabins at Hunters Paradise. McLaughlin is buried in the family cemetery located near the top of a knoll between and east of the cabins and home site.

McLaughlin, Capt. William. Commanded a company of 104 militia-
    men, 50th Regiment during the Battle of Bladensburg. Mustered
    out on October 13, 1814.

MCROBIE FAMILY CEMETERY (Green Glade Road, Garrett County).

McRobie, Elisha. No service record found.
McRobie, John. No service record found.

MERRYMAN FAMILY CEMETERY (dirt road on east side of Pot Spring Road, just north of intersection with Dulaney Gate Circle on east and just south of Colonade Road on west, opposite stone spring house on east; trail begins behind white wooden fence, proceeds around iron gate with sign "No Dumping/No Littering/Private Property/Baltimore Gas & Electric Co."; road winds down past pond on east, over bridge toward Lock Raven Reservoir, past side trail to east near bottom of hill, where stream enters reservoir, to a steep slope on east side down to reservoir at old quarry on west; just before quarry take trail on west; cemetery is surrounded by stone wall; near Cockeysville, Baltimore County). Micajah and Moses Merryman are buried under the same obelisk gravestone, which has been vandalized and knocked down.

Merryman, 2nd Lt. Micajah. Jarratt's Company, 7th Cavalry Regi-
    ment, cornet 1812 and 2nd lieutenant 1814.
Merryman, Moses. Surgeon's Mate, 7th Regiment.

MIDDLETOWN METHODIST CHURCH (Middletown, Carroll County).

Koons, Pvt. William. Reid's Company, 1st Cavalry District.

MIDDLETOWN (CHRIST) REFORMED CHURCH CEMETERY (Middletown, Frederick County).

Hyatt, Pvt. William. Hall's Troop of Horse, 2nd Regiment.

MONOCACY CEMETERY (Darnestown Road [Route 28], 0.2 mile west from intersection with Beallsville Road [Route 109], Beallsville, Montgomery County). This cemetery was established in 1747 and surrounded the Old St. Peters's Church, also known as Old Monocacy Chapel.

Allnut, James N. No service record found. Buried in row A, lot 3.
Dade, Capt. Robert T. 3rd Regiment. Buried in Old Ground.
Dawson, Pvt. Joseph N. Hood's Company, 32nd Regiment. Buried in
    row D, lot 12.
Dyson, Pvt. William. Watkin's Company.
Howard, 5th Sgt. Elisha. Hackney's Company, 3rd Regiment.
Poole, Capt. William. 2nd Regiment, 1st Cavalry District. Buried in
    row C, lot 15.

MORAVIAN CEMETERY (Graceham, Frederick County).

Eyler, Ensign John. Flautt's Rifle Company.

MOUNT BETHEL METHODIST CHURCH (Garfield, Frederick County).

Forrest, Pvt. Solomon. Marker's Company, 28th Regiment.

MOUNT CARMEL CEMETERY (Odonnell Street, Odonnell Heights, just west of Dundalk Avenue, Baltimore City).

Batchelor, Pvt. William. Chalmer's Company, 51st Regiment. Buried
    in section S, lot 174.
Bond, William. No service record found. Buried in section T, lot 81.
Cathcart (Kithcart), Pvt. John. Ringgold's Company, 6th Regiment,
    3rd Brigade. Fought at the Battle of North Point.
Randolph, Pvt. Thomson. Myers's Company, 39th Regiment.

MOUNT CARMEL CHAPEL, BEL AIR UNITED METHODIST CHURCH CEMETERY, also called Mount Carmel Methodist Presbyterian Church (northwest corner of intersection of Old Emmorton Road and Wheel Road, just east of Emmorton Road [Route 924], Emmorton, Harford County).

Montgomery, Capt. John. Baltimore Union Artillery Company. (Not
    to be confused with Pvt. John Montgomery, who is buried at St.
    Mary's Catholic Church, Bryantown, Charles County.)

MOUNT CARMEL UNITED METHODIST CHURCH CEMETERY (southeast corner of intersection of Mount Carmel Road [Route 137] and Prettyboy Dam Road, near Mount Carmel, Baltimore County).

Murray, Capt. William. 15th Regiment.

MOUNT OLIVET CEMETERY (northeast side of 2500 block of Frederick Avenue and Olivet Lane, Baltimore City).

Armstrong, Pvt. Peter. 36th U.S. Infantry. Buried in area B, lot 56 .

Baer, Dr. Jacob. Surgeon's Mate, 16th Regiment. Burial site unknown.

Barrow, 2nd Lt. Denwood. Hooper's Company, 10th Regiment of Cavalry. Buried in area I, lot 187 .

Beastson (also Beeston and Beison), Pvt. Thomas. Berry's Company, 1st Artillery Regiment,. Killed in action at Fort McHenry. Buried in area A, lot 147.

Bodensick, Pvt. Henry. Marsh's Company, 39th Regiment. Buried in area H, lot 136.

Brown, John. No service record found. Buried in area A, lot 258.

Buckingham, Pvt. Levi. Shrim's Company, 5th Regiment. Buried in area A, lot 31.

Christhilf, Pvt. Heinrich (Henry). Roney's Company, 39th Regiment. Buried in area B, lot 78.

Clayton, Samuel. Buried in area A, lot 24.

Davidson, Pvt. Nelson. Kennedy's Company, 27th Regiment. Buried in area I, lot 260.

Edwards, Pvt. Joseph. 4th Cavalry Regiment. Buried in area H, lot 17.

Gettier, Pvt. Jacob. Jessop's Company, 36th Regiment. Buried in area B, lot 110.

Gurney, Drummer Gridley. Ward's Rifle Battalion, Massachusetts Militia. Buried in area A, lot 199.

Jones, Pvt. Uriah. Deems's Company, 51st Regiment. Buried in area B, lot 187.

Knight, Pvt. John. Dobbin's Company, 39th Regiment. Buried in area H, lot 42.

Medairy (Medairy, Medary), Pvt. John. Adreon's Company, Union Volunteers. Buried in area A, lot 196.

Ogden, Pvt. Joseph Ireland. Maynard's Company, 22nd Regiment.

Rawlings, Lt. Benjamin. Long's Company, 27th Regiment. Buried in area I, lot 18.

Ringrose, Pvt. John W. 1st Regiment Artillery (Harris's). Buried in area D, lot 5.

Ruckle, Pvt. Thomas. Streett's Company, 7th Regiment. Buried in area A, lot 485.

Sanders, Joseph. Probably 39th Regiment. Buried in area H, lot 70.

Simonson, 1st Sgt. John. Shrim's Company, Baltimore Light Infantry.

MOUNT OLIVET CEMETERY (515 South Market Street, Frederick, Frederick County). There are over 32,000 individuals buried at Mount Olivet Cemetery. At least 83 have a connection to the War of 1812.

Baer, Pvt. William. Steiner's Company, 1st Regiment.

Balderson, Pvt. John. Brengle's Company. Buried in area B, lot 98.

Baltzell, Dr. John. Surgeon's Mate, 16th Regiment.

Bantz, Cpl. Henry. Brengle's Company. Buried in area G, lot 188.

Bartgis, Lt. Mathias Echternacht. Brengle's Company. Buried in area NN, lot 126.

Birely, Sgt. Valentine. Warner's Company, 39th Regiment.

Boteler, Pvt. Edward Simms. Sloan's Troop, Light Dragoons, Ohio Volunteers.

Boyd, Pvt. David. Steiner's Company, 1st Regiment.

Brengle, 2nd Lt. (John) Nicholas. Hauer's Company, 1st Cavalry District.

Brengle, Capt. John. Maryland Militia.

Brunner, Sgt. John. Brengle's Company. Buried in area E, lot 98.

Buckey, Daniel. A defender of Baltimore.

Butler, Pvt. Tobias, Sr. Brengle's Company. Buried in area E, lot 171.

Carmack, Pvt. Samuel. Duvall's Company, 29th Regiment.

Cline, Pvt. Casper. Ent's Company, 3rd Regiment.

DeGrange, John. Drummer, Turbott's Company.

Devitt, Pvt. David B. Brengle's Company, 1st Regiment. Buried in area E, lot 84.

Dill, 1st Sgt. Joshua. Ent's Company, 3rd Regiment.

Doyle, Pvt. Laurence. Ent's Company, 3rd Regiment.

Eader, Pvt. Thomas. Zacharias's Company, 2nd Regiment.

Eader, Pvt. William M. Smith's Company.

Ebberts, Pvt. Joseph. Ent's Company, 3rd Regiment.

Eichelberger, 2nd Maj. George. 3rd Regiment.

Englebrecht, Michael. Musician, Huston's Company, 1st Regiment.

Englebrecht, Pvt. William. Turbott's Company, Maryland Infantry.

Ent, Capt. George Washington. Reburied from old Lutheran Cemetery, East Church Street in area B, lot 1.

Faubel, Jacob. Musician, Steiner's Company, 1st Regiment.

Fauble, Cpl. John. Stembel's Company, 8th Regiment.

Frazier, Pvt. Jeremiah. Murray's Company.

Gladhill, Pvt. John. Marker's Company, 28th Regiment.

Goldsborough, Pvt. Nicholas. Duvall's Company, 28th Regiment.

Gomber, Pvt. Ezra. Ent's Company, 3rd Regiment.

Gonso, Pvt. Jacob. Brengle's Company, 1st Regiment.

Grahame, Pvt. Thomas J. Steiner's Company, 1st Regiment.

Green, Pvt. Benedict. Heeter's Company.

Grove, Pvt. Leonard. Shawen's Company, 1st Regiment.

Grove, Pvt. Reuben. Brengle's Company, 1st Regiment.

Hallar, Pvt. Philip. Brengle's Company. Buried in area NN, lot 130.

Haller, Pvt. Jacob. Huston's Company, 16th Regiment.

Hanshew, Pvt. Henry. Steiner's Company, 1st Regiment.

Harman, Pvt. Jacob. Steiner's Company, 1st Regiment.

Harrison, Pvt. Zephariah. Brengle's Company. Buried in area A, lot 72.

Hauer, Pvt. George. Worthington's Company.

Hawman, Pvt. Frederick. Stembel's Company 3rd Regiment.

Howard, Pvt. Thomas. Worthington's Company.

Hughes, Maj. Daniel. 2nd U.S. Infantry. Buried in area C, lot 59.

Johnson, Pvt. William. Steiner's Company, 1st Regiment.

Knauff, 6th Cpl. Jacob. Ent's Company, 3rd Regiment.

Kolb, Lt. John William. Brengle's Company. Buried in area B, lot 91.

Koontz, Pvt. John. Steiner's Company, 1st Regiment.

Lambright, Pvt. George. Ent's Company, 3rd Regiment.

Lambright, Pvt. Michael. Ent's Company, 3rd Regiment.

Lugenbeel, 2nd Lt. Moses. 1st Regiment.

Mantz, Capt. George. 16th Regiment.

Mantz, Pvt. Peter. Ent's Company, 3rd Regiment.

Markell, Ensign Peter. Worthington's Company.

Markell, QM John. Ragan's 1st Regiment.

Markey, Pvt. David. Brengle's Company, 1st Regiment.

Marquert, Pvt. George. Davidson's Company, Union Artillery, 1st Regiment, District of Columbia.

McLean, Pvt. Charles. McDonald's Company, 6th Regiment.

McPherson, Pvt. Robert G. Steiner's Company, 1st Regiment.

Medtart, Pvt. Lewis. Ent's Company 3rd Regiment.

Montgomery, Capt. John. 1st Artillery Regiment.

Musseter, 1st Lt. Christopher. Duvall's Company, 29th Regiment.

Nixdorff, Pvt. Henry. Steiner's Company, 1st Regiment.

Ramsburgh, Pvt. Lewis. Worthington's Company.

Riehel, Pvt. Jacob. Brengle's Company, 1st Regiment.

Robertson, 1st Sgt. Alexander. Brengle's Company. Buried in area C, lot 165.

Salmon, Pvt. George. Brengle's Company, 1st Regiment.

Schley, Lt. Henry. Cramer's Detachment.

Scholl, Pvt. Christian. Getzendanner's Company, 16th Regiment. Buried in area R, lot 165.

Scholl, Pvt. Henry. Brengle's Company, 1st Regiment.

Shawbaker, Pvt. George. Ent's Company, 3rd Regiment.

Shope (Shoup), Pvt. George B. Brengle's Company, 1st Regiment.

Shultz, 1st Sgt. George. Marker's Company, 16th Regiment.

Sponseller, Pvt. Jacob. Ent's Company, 28th Regiment.

Stephens, George Mull. Virginia Militia. Buried in area D, lot 62.

Steiner, Capt. Henry. Commander of artillery company, 1st Regiment.

Storm, Pvt. Peter. Ent's Company, 28th Regiment.

Swearingen, Brig. Gen. Joseph. 9th Brigade.

Vernon, Nathaniel. Served in Pittsburgh Blues, at Battle of Mississineway and siege of Fort Meigs.

Widerick, Pvt. John. Getzendanner's Detachment Riflemen.

Worthington, Thomas Contee. Captain in Frederick Company 1812. Later promoted to rank of brigadier general, 9th Brigade.

Yager, Pvt. Charles. Ent's Company, 3rd Regiment.

Young, Pvt. Conrad. Dawson's Company, 28th Regiment.

MOUNT PLEASANT METHODIST CHURCH CEMETERY. *See* Faith Family Baptist Church Cemetery

MOUNT VIEW CEMETERY (Sharpsburg, Washington County).

Miller, Capt. John. 10th Regiment.

Rohrback, Lt. Jacob. Miller's Company, 10th Regiment.

MOUNT ZION LUTHERAN CHURCH CEMETERY (formerly Evangelical Lutheran Church, northeast corner of intersection of Locust Grove and Rohrersville [Route 67] roads, Locust Grove, Washington County). Church established in 1844.

Young, Pvt. Davault. Dawson's Company, 28th Regiment. Present at Battle of Bladensburg.

MOUNT ZION UNITED METHODIST CHURCH CEMETERY (2901 Mount Zion Road, 0.2 mile south of Freeland Road, Freeland, Baltimore County). The present church structure dates from 1886.

Morris, Samuel III. No service record found.

MYERSVILLE LUTHERAN CHURCH CEMETERY (Myersville, Frederick County).

Smith, Pvt. Jacob. Shawen's Company.

NEW CATHEDRAL CEMETERY (4300 Old Frederick Road, Baltimore City). Over the plot of the Francis Scott Key family stands a bronze angel. However, Francis Scott Key is buried in Mount Olivet Cemetery, Frederick.

Jenkins, Pvt. Edward. Independent Company, 5th Regiment.

Laroque, Dr. John M. Hospital Service. Originally buried at Cathedral Cemetery that closed in the 1870s and probably re-interred here.

Lee, Col. John. Son of Mary Digges and Thomas Sim Lee, owners of Melwood, where British officers dined on their way to Washington.

Logan, Thomas White. Gravestone reads in part: "assisted his soldier father at the Battle of Ft. McHenry, 1814."

Lucas, Pvt. Fielding. McKane's Company, 27th Regiment.

Monmonier, Sgt. Frances. Dyer's Company, Fells Point Riflemen. Buried in section V.

NEW MARKET METHODIST EPISCOPAL CHURCH CEMETERY (New Market, Frederick County).

Wright, Pvt. Benjamin. Dorsey's Company, 32nd Regiment.

NEW WINDSOR PRESBYTERIAN CHURCH CEMETERY (east side of High Street [Route 75], New Windsor, Carroll County).

Baile, Pvt. Ludwick. Crawford's Company, Maryland Militia.

NICODEMUS FAMILY CEMETERY (northwest side of Bowersox Road, 0.1 mile south of intersection with Nicodemus Road, 1.3 miles northwest of Ridge Road [Route 27], near Camp Chal-Mar, southwest of Westminster, Carroll County).

Nicodemus, Pvt. Andrew. Crawford's Company.

NORTH EAST METHODIST CHURCH CEMETERY (Main Street, North East, Cecil County).

Brown, John H. No service record found.

OELLA CEMETERY (south side of Rest Avenue, 0.15 mile west of intersection with Westchester Road, north off Frederick Road [Route 144], Oella, east of Ellicott City, Baltimore County).

Armitage, Pvt. John. Stewart's Company, 51st Regiment.

OGG FAMILY CEMETERY. *See* Deer Park United Methodist Church Cemetery

OLD BOHEMIA CHURCH CEMETERY, St. Frances Xavier Church (north end of Church Road, north off Bohemia Church Road, 3.2 miles east of Augustine Herman Highway [Route 213], southeastern Cecil County).

Knight, Catharine "Kitty." War of 1812 heroine who saved the William Henry and Archibald Wright houses from burning during a British raid at Georgetown on May 6, 1813.

OLD CEMETERY (Baptist Road, near intersection with Taney-town Pike, near Taneytown, Carroll County). Name of this cemetery unknown.

Hays, Pvt. Abraham. Knox's Company, Randall's Battalion Riflemen.

OLDFIELDS CHAPEL CEMETERY, now called Oldfields Episcopal Church (near Hughesville, 0.7 mile west of intersection of Prince Frederick–Hughesville Road [Route 231] and Brandy-wine Road [Route 381], opposite Goode Road, Charles County). Two British soldiers are reportedly buried here, but no markers have been found.

Wise, Francis. Alexandria Troops. Killed in a skirmish at Benedict, Maryland, on June 21, 1814. No grave marker found.

OLD HOOPERS ISLAND GRAVEYARD (S. Hubert Applegarth home, Applegarth Road, west off Hoopers Island Road, just south of Fishing Creek Bridge, on Upper Hooper Island, Honga, Dorchester County).

Ruark, Pvt. Henry (1796–1842). The True Blues of America, 48th Regiment. No gravestone found.
Simmons, Pvt. Edward. Brohawn's Company, 48th Regiment. Participated in the Battle of the Ice Mound.
Travers, John. 48th Regiment.

OLD MOUNT ST. MARY'S ROMAN CATHOLIC CEMETERY (St. Anthony, Frederick County).

Orotin, Pvt. James. Galt's Company, 3rd Regiment.
Harris, Pvt. John. Duvall's Company, 29th Regiment.
Nussear, Pvt. Jesse W. Myer's Company, 39th Regiment.
Shorb, Pvt. John. 1st Cavalry District.
Taney, 3rd Cpl. Felix B. Galt's Company, 3rd Regiment.

OLD ST. ANDREWS EPISCOPAL CHURCH CEMETERY (2.6 miles southwest of Three Notch Road [Route 235] on St. Andrews Church Road [Route 4], St. Mary's County). NRHP.

Dent, Col. George. Gravestone reads in part: "Capt. Rev. War/Col. War of 1812."
Forrest, Capt. James. 4th Cavalry Regiment. Promoted to brigadier general. No gravestone found.

OLD ST. JOSEPH'S CEMETERY (north side of intersection of Waldorf–Leonardtown Road [Route 5] and Busy Corner Road, entrance off Busy Corner Road, Morganza, St. Mary's County). Not to be confused with the later St. Joseph's Cemetery located directly across the road from St. Joseph's Church.

Heard, Ensign Benedict I. (d. 1864). 14th U.S. Infantry. No gravestone found.
Mattingly, Pvt. Sylvester (d. 1872). Ashton's Company, 45th Regiment. No gravestone found although a stone was reported during a 1958 survey. Heard's farm suffered a loss estimated at $4,000 during a British raid in the summer of 1814.

On last Wednesday week a detachment from the enemy's shipping in the Patuxent, in pursuit of stock, landed at Mr. Benedict
Heard's in St. Mary's . . . they burnt every house on the land,
all of which had been recently repaired. (Baltimore *Federal
Republican*, July 29, 1814)

OLD ST. PAUL'S CEMETERY (between West Redwood and 700
West Lombard streets; immediately east of Martin Luther
King Junior Boulevard, Baltimore City).

Armistead, Lt. Col. George (1780–1818). Major 3rd Artillery 1813,
    Corps of Artillery 1814. Brevetted lieutenant colonel 1814.
    His gravestone reads in part: "the gallant Defender of Fort
    McHenry."
Brice, Nicholas. Served as special judge advocate, staff of Maj. Gen.
    Samuel Smith. Buried in plot 406.
Callender, Pvt. J. A. (1784–1832). Pennington's Company, Baltimore
    Independent Artillerists. Served at Fort McHenry during the
    war.
Cole, Pvt. Samuel. Levering's Company, Independent Blues, 5th
    Regiment.
Heath, Maj. Richard Key (1770–1822). 5th Regiment. Commander of
    the American advance guard that skirmished with the British
    forces before the Battle of North Point.
Hindman, Col. Jacob H. Captain in the 2nd U.S. Artillery 1812. Pro-
    moted to major 1813. Promoted to brevet lieutenant colonel for
    distinguished service in the defense of Fort Erie.
Hollingsworth, Pvt. Samuel (1756–1830). Sterett's Company, 1st
    Baltimore Hussars, 5th Cavalry District.
Howard, Gen. John Eager (1752–1827). Helped organize the defenses
    of Baltimore.
Hughes, Capt. Christopher, Sr. (1744–1824). Baltimore Independent
    Artillery.
Hush, Pvt. Samuel. Magee's Company, 1st Regiment. Wounded at
    Bladensburg. Died at home while on leave.
McCreery, William (1750–1814). Baltimore Independent Cadets.
McKim, Isaac (1775–1838). Aide to Gen. Samuel Smith during the
    Battle for Baltimore. President John Quincy Adams and Daniel
    Webster attended his funeral. (There is a cenotaph for McKim at
    Congressional Cemetery, Washington, D.C.)
Rodgers, Col. Nicholas. Unit unknown.
Small, Lt. Col. Jacob, Jr. (1772–1851). 39th Regiment. Quartermaster
    3rd Brigade.
Stevenson, Pvt. Alexander (1788–1824). Chalmer's Company, 51st
    Regiment. Present at Battle of North Point.

OLD TRINITY CHURCH CEMETERY, also called Trinity Episcopal
Church (1716 Taylors Island Road [Route 16], 8.5 miles west of
Ocean Gateway [Route 50], Church Creek, Dorchester County).

Dixon, Noah. Williams's Company, 48th Regiment.
Stewart, Lt. Levin. Linthicum's Company, 48th Regiment.
Woolford, Sgt. William. Woolford's Company, 48th Regiment.

OLIVET CEMETERY, St. Luke's Methodist Church (304 Talbot Street, across from the post office, St. Michaels, Talbot
County).

Dodson, Capt. William. Adjutant, 26th Regiment. Commanded the
    gun battery at Parrott Point.
Kemp, Col. Joseph. Captain 26th Regiment. Commander of the St.
    Michaels Patriotic Blues.
    In front of the Capt. William Dodson gravestone is a granite
    monument: "TO THE MEMORY OF/WILLIAM DODSON/A SAILING
    MASTER IN U.S. NAVY/BORN 1786–DIED 1833/HE COMMANDED
    A PRIVATE ARMED VESSEL/FURNISHED BY HIS FATHER IN THE
    EARLY/PART OF THE WAR OF 1812. GUARDING THE/WATERS OF THE
    EASTERN BAY/AND ITS TRIBUTARIES. HE WAS IN CHARGE OF PAR-
    ROT'S POINT/BATTERY AUG. 10, 1813, WHERE THE BRITISH/WERE
    DEFEATED IN THE ATTACK UPON THE/TOWN OF ST. MICHAELS./HE
    FOUGHT AT BLADENSBURG UNDER/COMMODORE BARNEY AND
    PARTICIPATED IN/THE DEFENCE OF BALTIMORE AND/FORT MCHEN-
    RY SEPT. 1814." (While the First Battle of St. Michaels is regarded
    as an American victory the British captured and destroyed the
    cannon at Parrott Point Gun Battery before being driven off.)

OWENS FAMILY CEMETERY (Bristol, Anne Arundel County).

Owens, Pvt. James. Burke's Company, 6th Regiment.

OWINGS FAMILY CEMETERY (Rose Haven, Anne Arundel
County).

Owings, Pvt. Samuel. Richard Amey's Company, 51st Regiment.

PERCY CEMETERY (1st Street, near intersection with Chestnut, one block north of West Mechanic Street [Alt. U.S. 40],
Frostburg, Allegany County). In response to President James
Madison's proclamation of July 4, 1814, calling upon the
governors of states to raise a militia for the nation's defense,
Capt. Thomas Blair formed one of two companies from Allegany County. Blair's company marched to Baltimore and
was stationed at Camp Diehl (location of Camp Diehl is unknown although there is a Diehl Avenue located immediately
northeast of Baltimore at Perring Village) from September 2
to November 6, 1814. The Cumberland Continentals, a local
military organization, buried Captain Blair with full military
honors in Percy Cemetery.

Blair, Capt. Thomas. 50th Regiment. Despite the use of colonel on his gravestone, there is no record of him ever attaining that rank.

PINEY CREEK CEMETERY, also called Piney Creek Presbyterian Cemetery (1.25 miles southeast of Harney, northwest of Taneytown).

Correll, Pvt. Christian. 24th Regiment.
Galt, Capt. John. 47th Regiment. Buried in area A, lot 6-16.
Knox, Capt. William. Randall's Battalion Riflemen.

PIPE CREEK CEMETERY (Uniontown, Carroll County).

Bond, Pvt. Benjamin. Fonsten's Company, 3rd Regiment. Buried in area A06-47.
Harman, Pvt. Jacob. Durbin's Company, Randall's Battalion Riflemen.
Roop, Pvt. Jacob. Crawford's Company. Buried in area A06-44.

PLEASANT GROVE METHODIST CHURCH CEMETERY, also called Sandymount United Methodist Church Cemetery (Old Westminster Pike, west of Baltimore Boulevard [Route 140] between Sandymount Road and Greens Mill Road, southeast of Westminster, Carroll County).

Hugh, Cpl. Bosley. Moore's Company, 6th Regiment of Cavalry. Buried in area 06-16.

PLEASANT VIEW BRETHREN CHURCH CEMETERY (Burkittsville, Frederick County).

Arnold, Pvt. John. Marker's Company, 28th Regiment.
Bear, Pvt. George. Marker's Company, 28th Regiment.

POPLAR GROVE CEMETERY (Emory Creek, in front of Poplar Grove Manor, Poplar Grove Farm Lane, southwest off Spaniard Neck Road, just northwest of intersection with Lands End Road, Indian Town area, northwest of Centreville, Queen Anne's County). PRIVATE

Emory, Maj. Thomas. 9th Cavalry District.

PORTER CEMETERY, also called Rose Meadow Cemetery (southeast side near end of Porter Cemetery Road, northeast of Frostburg, Allegany County).

Porter, Sgt. John M. "Squire Jack." McLaughlin's Company, 50th Regiment.

Frank Blackwell Mayer, a celebrated Baltimore artist, painted a portrait of "Squire Jack" in the early 1850s entitled *American Independence (Squire Jack Porter)*, depicting him at Rose Meadow on the porch of his stone cottage farm house in his shirt sleeves, smoking a corn-cob pipe, looking out over his farm. The painting won awards in Paris and London expositions in 1858–59 and now hangs in the National Gallery of Art in Washington, D.C.

PROSPECT HILL CEMETERY (east side of York Road [Route 40], 0.2 mile north of intersection with Dulaney Valley Road [Route 45], Towson, Baltimore County).

Hillen, Pvt. Solomon. Magruder's Company, American Artillerists.
Hillen, Lt. John. Sterett's Independent Company.
Stevenson, Pvt. Joshua. Hanna's Company, Fells Point Light Dragoons.

REISTERSTOWN UNITED METHODIST CHURCH CEMETERY (just south of Lutheran Cemetery at 246 Main Street, Reisterstown, Baltimore County). NRHP.

Core, Pvt. George. Carnan's Company, 6th Regiment Cavalry.
Stocksdale, Jesse. Surgeon's Mate, 7th Regiment.
Yingling, Cpl. David. McGee's Company, 20th or 24th Regiment.

RIVER VIEW CEMETERY (entrance at end of West Church Street at intersection of Commerce Street, Williamsport, Washington County).

Ardinger, Lt. Peter, Sr. Wolfe's Company, 10th Regiment. No gravestone found.
Downs, Cpl. Charles G. 3rd Regiment.
Hetzler, Pvt. John. Bader's Company, Union Yagers.
Hollman, Joseph. No service record found. An 1812 marker placed next to his grave may be misplaced.
Long, Pvt. Jesse. Washington Blues.
Patrick, Ensign Matthew A. 29th U.S. Infantry.
Williams, Capt. Edward Greene. 1st Cavalry District.
Williams, Maj. Otho Holland. 1st Cavalry District.

ROBERT BRIDGE ESTATE CEMETERY (Sharpsburg, Washington County).

Tilghman, Lt. Col. Frisby. 1st Cavalry District.

ROCKY SPRINGS CEMETERY (Rocky Springs, Frederick County).

Aubert, Pvt. Jacob. Getzendanner's Company.

Hinkle, Pvt. George. Ent's Company, 3rd Regiment.
Main, Pvt. John J. Getzendanner's Company.

ROSE HILL CEMETERY (Fayette Street, Cumberland, Allegany County).

Deems, Sgt. Frederick. Ragan's Company, 1st Regiment.
Thruston, Charles Mynn. U.S. Army Engineers. Buried in section 1, lot 6/7.

ROSE HILL CEMETERY (600 South Potomac Street, at intersection with Memorial Boulevard, Hagerstown, Washington County).

Biays, Lt. James. McDonald's Company, 6th Regiment.
Biershing, Pvt. Henry. Worthington's Company, 3rd Regiment. Buried in section D.
Mobley, Pvt. Elie. Worthington's Company, 3rd Regiment. Buried in section D.
McComas, Pvt. Zaccheus O. Lowry's Company, 1st Regiment.
Ragen, Lt. Col. John. 24th Regiment. Injured and captured at Battle of Bladensburg. Ragen commanded a company at the Battle of New Orleans.

ST. ANNE'S CEMETERY (Northwest Street, off Calvert Street, Annapolis, Anne Arundel County).

Brice, Pvt. John. Artillery Regiment.
Claude, Dr. Dennis. Surgeon, 23rd Regiment.
Hohne, 2nd Lt. Christopher I. Pinkney's Company, 8th Brigade.
MacKubin, Pvt. George. Artillery Company, 22nd Regiment.
Randall, Col. Daniel. Assistant district paymaster in U.S. Army.
Randall, 2nd Lt. Thomas. 14th U.S. Infantry. At Fort McHenry during bombardment.

ST. AUGUSTINE'S CHURCH CEMETERY, also called Cecil Church (southeast intersection of St. Augustine Road [Route 342] and Cayots Corner Road [Route 310], St. Augustine, Cecil County).

Wirt, Capt. John Thompson. Adjutant quartermaster in the Delaware 2nd Infantry.
Wirt, Pvt. John T. Veazey's Company, 49th Regiment.

ST. BARNABUS EPISCOPAL CHURCH CEMETERY (west side of West Friendship Road, at intersection with Forsythe Road, just south of Sykesville, Howard County).

Warfield, Pvt. Warner. Tilghman's Regiment of Cavalry.

ST. ELIAS LUTHERAN CHURCH CEMETERY (Emmitsburg, Frederick County).

Troxell, Pvt. Peter. Reid's Troop of Horse, 1st Cavalry District.

ST. GEORGE'S PARISH CEMETERY, also called Spesutie Church and Old Spesutie Church (intersection of Spesutie Road and Perryman Road [Route 159], Perryman, Harford County).

Michael, Capt. Jacob. 42nd Regiment.
Sewell, Cpl. Charles S. 42nd Regiment.

ST. IGNATIUS ROMAN CATHOLIC CHURCH CEMETERY (corner of Conowingo Road [U.S. Route 1] and Jarrettsville Road, Hickory, Harford County).

Cain, Cornet Matthew. Macatee's Company, 7th Cavalry District.
Macatee, Capt. Henry. 7th Cavalry District.

ST. JAMES BRETHREN (north side of Pappans Road, St. James, southeast of Williamsport, Washington County).

Ringgold, Brig. Gen. Samuel. 2nd Brigade.

ST. JAMES EPISCOPAL CHURCH CEMETERY, My Lady's Manor (3100 Monkton Road, just west off Old York Road, east-southeast of Monkton, Baltimore County).

Anderson, Pvt. Ira G. Moore's Company, 6th Cavalry District.
Hutchins, Capt. James. 41st Regiment.
Hutchins, William. No service record found. Buried in section 2, row 1.
Miller, James. No service record found. Buried in section 2, row 1.
Pearce, Pvt. Thomas. Edes's Company, 27th Regiment. Buried in section 3, row 1.
Stansbury, 1st Lt. Dixon. 13th U.S. Infantry, captured at Detroit. Buried in section 3, row 3.
Street, Dr. St. Clair. Surgeon, Hutchin's Company, 41st Regiment.

ST. JOHN'S CEMETERY (west side of Saint Johns Lane, north off Frederick Road, west of Elliott City, just west of exit 24 Columbia Pike [U.S. Route 29], Howard County).

Cline, Pvt. Philip. Marker's Company, 28th Regiment.
Dorsey, Capt. Charles W. 32nd Regiment. Later promoted to a major.
Hammond, Thomas Lloyd. Paymaster 32nd Regiment. Buried in section A-1, row 4.
Thomas, Capt. Allen. 3rd Cavalry District.

ST. JOHN'S EPISCOPAL CHAPEL CEMETERY (north side of Hudson Road [Route 343], 0.7 mile west of intersection with Bar Neck Road, Cornersville, west of Cambridge, Dorchester County). Hicks North and Richard North were originally buried on the nearby T. Ellsworth Marshall Farm off Ross Neck Road.

North, Pvt. Hicks. Brohawn's Company, 48th Regiment.
North, Pvt. Richard. Brohawn's Company, 48th Regiment.
North, Pvt. William. Brohawn's Company, 48th Regiment.

ST. JOHN'S EVANGELICAL LUTHERAN CHURCH CEMETERY (east side of Leisters Church Road, just south of intersection with Hampstead Mexico Road [Route 482], northeast of Westminster, Carroll County).

Late, Pvt. George. Wood's Company, 1st Regiment.
Mathias, Pvt. Griffith. Smith's Company, Watkins's Command.
Miller, Pvt. George. Smith's Company, Watkins's Command.
Six, Pvt. George. 1st Cavalry.
Trump, Pvt. Casper. Fonsten's Company, 3rd Regiment.

ST. JOHN'S LUTHERAN CHURCH CEMETERY (northwest side of intersection of Ward Kline Road and Church Hill Road, 0.6 mile west of Wolfsville Road [Route 17], Church Hill, near Ellerton, northeast of Myersville, Frederick County).

Bittle, Lt. John. Marker's Company, 28th Regiment.

ST. JOHN'S REFORMED CHURCH CEMETERY (Sabillasville, Frederick County).

Miller, John. No service record found.

ST. JOHN'S ROMAN CATHOLIC CEMETERY (Frederick, Frederick County).

Boone, Pvt. Robert. Steiner's Company, 1st Regiment.
Ways, Pvt. Basil. Kelb's Company.
Young, Pvt. Andrew. Brengle's Company, 1st Regiment.

ST. JOHN'S ROMAN CATHOLIC CEMETERY (Westminster, Carroll County).

Hayden, Pvt. Basil. Zacharias's Company, 2nd Regiment.
Lockard, Pvt. John. Blizzard's Company, 15th Regiment.
Yingling, Pvt. John. Fonsten's Company, 3rd Regiment.

ST. JOSEPH'S CARROLLTON MANOR ROMAN CATHOLIC CHURCH CEMETERY (Buckeystown, Frederick County).

Copelin, Pvt. Samuel. Marker's Company, 28th Regiment.

ST. JOSEPH'S CHURCH CEMETERY, also called Old St. Joseph's Church (1.5 miles south on Church Lane from intersection with Queen Anne Highway, also called Shore Highway [Route 404], southwest of Queen Anne Queen Anne's County. Talbot County).

Pascault, Louis C. One of the Old Defenders.

ST. JOSEPH'S ROMAN CATHOLIC CHURCH CEMETERY (east side of Seton Avenue, one block north of intersection with Main Street [Route 140], Emmitsburg, Frederick County).

Hann, Pvt. Henry. Knox's Company, Randall's Battalion Riflemen.
Storm, Pvt. James. Stebel's Company of Artillery.

ST. LUKE'S LUTHERAN CHURCH CEMETERY, also called Winter's Lutheran and Reformed Cemetery (New Windsor, Carroll County).

Crawmer, Pvt. Helpner. Fonsten's Company, 3rd Regiment.
Winter, John. Drummer, McGee's Company, 9th Regiment.

ST. LUKE'S METHODIST CHURCH OLD CEMETERY (northeast corner of Franklin and Fourth streets, Denton, Caroline County).

Young, 1st Maj. John. 15th Regiment.

ST. MARK'S EPISCOPAL CHURCH CEMETERY (Petersville, Frederick County).

Blessing, 2nd Lt. Abraham. Hackney's Company, 20th Regiment.
Marlow, Pvt. Hanson. Turbutt's Company, 3rd Regiment.
Staub, Pvt. Jacob. Wood's Company, 1st Regiment.

ST. MARY'S CATHOLIC CEMETERY (1200 Homeland Avenue, between Charles Street and York Road, Baltimore City).

Barrenger, John F. No service record found. Buried in row 5b, lot 7.

ST. MARY'S CATHOLIC CHURCH CEMETERY (St. Mary's Church Road, 0.2 mile east of Newport Church Road, 0.5 mile south of Penns Hill Road, Bowlingss Alley, southeast of La Plata, Charles County).

Merrick, 1st Lt. William Duhurst. 3rd lieutenant 36th U.S. Infantry. Promoted to 2nd lieutenant, August 15, 1813. Promoted to 1st lieutenant, September 30, 1814. Served as regiment adjutant April 14 to June 15, 1814.

ST. MARY'S CEMETERY (southeast corner of West Street and Brewer Avenue, opposite Brewer Hill Cemetery, Annapolis, Anne Arundel County).

Boyle, Col. James. Aide-de-camp to Brig. Gen. Osborne Williams.
Karney, 1st Lt. Thomas. 14th U.S. Infantry.

ST. MARY'S LUTHERAN CEMETERY (Silver Run, Carroll County).

Crawford, Pvt. Robert. Zacharias's Company, 2nd Regiment. Buried in old section 253.
Frock, Pvt. William. Fonsten's Company, 3rd Regiment. Buried in old section 052.
Humbert, Pvt. George. Fonsten's Company, 3rd Regiment. Buried in old section 558.
Myerly, Pvt. David. Fonsten's Company, 3rd Regiment.
Yeiser, Pvt. Daniel. Ogle's Company, 2nd Regiment. Buried in old section 843.

ST. MARY'S LUTHERAN AND REFORMED CEMETERY (across from St. Mary's United Church of Christ, Mayberry Road, east off Littlestown Pike [Route 97], Silver Run, Carroll County).

Myerly, Pvt. David. Stembel's Company, 3rd Regiment.

ST. MARY'S ROMAN CATHOLIC CHURCH CEMETERY (Barnesville, Montgomery County).

Beall, Pvt. John. Vinson's Company, 32nd Regiment.

ST. MATHEW'S LUTHERAN CHURCH CEMETERY (Ballender Creek Pike, Frederick County).

Hilderbrand, Ensign John. Getzendaner's Company.

ST. NICHOLAS CHAPEL CEMETERY (north side of Cedar Point Road, Patuxent Naval Air Station, off Three Notch Road [Route 235], Lexington Park, St. Mary's County). Military base, limited access. Carroll Michael Brown, who served at the Battle of New Orleans, may be buried here but no marker for him has been found.

Cissell, Pvt. George Enoch J. Millard's Detachment, 12th Regiment.
Combs, Capt. Cornelius. 12th Regiment. Later promoted to rank of colonel.
Flower, Pvt. Gustavus. 43rd Regiment.

Jarboe, Capt. James. 5th Brigade, 12th Regiment. Stationed at Cedar Point and Point Lookout in command of 68 men. Later promoted to the rank of colonel.
Peak, Pvt. John. Served in Joseph William's, Richard Clark's, James Jarboe's and Cornelius Comb's detachments, 12th Regiment.
Tarlton, Pvt. Elijah. Served in Joseph William's, Joseph Milburn's, Cornelius Comb's, and Richard Evan's detachments, 12th Regiment.

ST. PATRICK'S CEMETERY (Little Orleans, Allegany County).

Bevans, Capt. Walter. 1st Regiment.

ST. PAUL'S EPISCOPAL CHURCH, PINEY PARISH, CEMETERY, also Chapel of Ease Port Tobacco Parish (at St. Paul's Drive intersection with Piney Church Road, west off Renner Road, west off Waldorf–Leonardtown Road [Route 5], south of Waldorf, Charles County).

Berry, Pvt. John Nally. Dents Company, 43rd Regiment.

ST. PAUL'S EVANGELICAL LUTHERAN CHURCH CEMETERY (15801 Trenton Road, just east of intersection with Hanover Pike [Route 30], Upperco, western Baltimore County).

Algire, Pvt. George. Stockdale's Company, 36th Regiment.
Hauck, Capt. William. 6th Cavalry District. His cavalry saber is exhibited at Flag House, Baltimore.
Houck, John. His gravestone has the image of a standing militiaman wearing a derby hat and holding a gun. Houck died in 1873. The image appears more like a Civil War soldier than a war of 1812 militiaman. Gravestone reads in part: "A soldier in the war of 1812–14."

ST. PAUL'S EVANGELICAL LUTHERAN CHURCH CEMETERY (Utica, Frederick County).

Barrick, Pvt. Cornelius. Wood's Company, 1st Regiment.
Cramer, Lt. Col. Jacob. 29th Regiment.
Shryock, Cpl. Henry. Ragan's Company, 1st Regiment.

ST. PAUL'S LUTHERAN CHURCH CEMETERY (Uniontown, Carroll County).

Williams, Pvt. John B. Smith Company, 3rd Regiment.

ST. PAUL'S UNITED CHURCH OF CHRIST (north side of National Pike [U.S. Route 40], on east side of intersection with Saint Paul Road, 2.5 miles east of Clear Spring, Washington County).

Cushwa, Capt. David. 8th Regiment

ST. PETER'S EVANGELICAL LUTHERAN CHURCH CEMETERY
(Clearspring, Washington County).

Sponseller, Pvt. Frederick. Ent's Company, 3rd Regiment.

ST. PETER'S LUTHERAN CEMETERY (east side of Big Spring Road, at intersection with South Martine Street, 0.1 mile south of National Pike [U.S. Route 40], Clear Spring, Washington County).

Brewer, Lt. Daniel. Served in his father's unit, Capt. John Brewer's Company, 8th Regiment.

ST. PETER'S ROMAN CATHOLIC CHURCH CEMETERY (Hancock, Washington County).

Taney, Pvt. Ethelbert. Knox's Company, Randall's Battalion Riflemen.

ST. STEPHEN'S EPISCOPAL CHURCH CEMETERY (1110 Saint Stephen's Church Road opposite intersection of Martin Grant Court, 0.1 mile north at intersection with John Hopkins Road, near Crofton Village, northeast of Crofton, Ann Arundel County).

Williams, Brig. Gen. Osburn (1757–1819). 8th Brigade.

ST. STEPHEN'S EPISCOPAL CHURCH CEMETERY, also called North Sassafras Parish (northwest corner of intersection of Crystal Beach Road [Route 282] and Glebe Road, Earlville, west of Cecilton, Cecil County).

Veazey, Dr. Pvt. John Thompson. Morgan's Company, 49th Regiment. Participated in the defense of Fort Duffy at Fredericktown and Georgetown on May 5, 1813.
Veazey, Pvt. Thomas B. Morgan's Company, 49th Regiment.

ST. THOMAS' CHURCH CEMETERY, Episcopal Garrison Forest (232 St. Thomas Lane, east corner of intersection of Garrison Forest Road and St. Thomas Lane, 0.8 mile from intersection with Reistertown Road [Route 140], Owings Mills, Baltimore County).

Carroll, Pvt. Nicholas. Long's Company, 27th Regiment.
Cockey, Thomas. Probably 41st Regiment.
Latimer, 2nd Lt. James. Harris's Company, 1st Regiment.
Lyon, 1st Lt. Charles G. Carnan's Company, 6th Cavalry District.
Moale, Capt. Samuel. Columbian Artillery, 1st Maryland Regiment,

3rd Brigade. His epitaph reads in part: "Commander of the Columbian Artillery at the Defence of Baltimore in 1814."
Moale, QM Randall H. Columbia Artillery, 1st Maryland Regiment of Artillery.
Owings, Cornet Edward. Gist's Company, 2nd Regiment, 1st Cavalry.
Owings, Samuel. Paymaster, 6th Cavalry District.
Renell, Pvt. John N. Warfield's Baltimore United Volunteers, 1st Maryland Artillery.
Russell, 1st Lt. Thomas. Baltimore Independent Artillery; served at Fort McHenry.

ST. THOMAS EPISCOPAL CHURCH CEMETERY (also called Page's Chapel, intersection of St. Thomas Church Road and Croom Road [Maryland Route 381], Croom, Prince George's County). NRHP. The colonial cruciform chapel was completed in 1745, modified in 1859 by the addition of a east chancel; the bell tower was added in 1888 and a small northeasterly sacristy was added in 1905.

Bowie, Capt. Eversfield. Nottingham Cavalry Company.
Bowie, Pvt. Fiedler II. 17th Regiment.

ST. VINCENT DE PAUL CEMETERY (off Rose Street, west of intersection of Erdman Avenue and Belair Road, Clifton Park, near the old polo-pony barn that now serves as a Clifton Park utility building, Baltimore City). All that remains of this cemetery after years of neglect and vandalism are about thirty gravestones, piled or laid flat in four clusters, all overgrown with weeds.

Storm, Peter. Served in the defense of Baltimore. No gravestone found.

SAMS CREEK METHODIST PROTESTANT CEMETERY (south of Pearre Road, McKinstrys Mill, east of Johnsville, Frederick County).

Coppersmith, Pvt. Jacob. Zacharias's Company, 2nd Regiment.
Naill, Pvt. Peter. Zacharias's Company, 2nd Regiment.

SATER'S BAPTIST CHURCH CEMETERY (west end of Saters Lane off Falls Road [Route 25], just south of Chestnut Ridge County Club golf course, 1.0 mile north of Seminary Avenue [Route 131], Baltimore County).

Cole, Pvt. John. Levering's Company, Independent Blues. Participated in Battle of Bladensburg and a defense of Baltimore. No gravestone found.

Death of a Veteran of 1812–14.—Mr. John Cole, one of the defenders of Baltimore in 1812–14 . . . He took special pride in his agility, and would not permit a street car to stop for him, always preferring to board it while in motion . . . at the breaking out of hostilities in 1812 joined Captain [John] Bon's [Bond] company, which was transferred at Bladensburg to the command of Captain [Joseph] Hook of Hookstown, Baltimore County. After the defeat at Bladensburg the company was transferred to Chincapin [Chinquapin = Hampstead] Hill near the present site of Patterson Park, where the deceased served until the close of the war. He . . . helped to build the first steamboats made in Baltimore . . . The remains will be interred at Sater's Church, Baltimore County. (Baltimore *Sun,* November 27, 1882)

SHERWOOD EPISCOPAL CHURCH CEMETERY (south side of Sherwood Road, at intersection with Cedar Knoll Road, 0.1 mile east of York Road [Route 45], Cockeysville, Baltimore County).

Bosley, Amon. Moore's Company, 6th Regiment of Cavalry.
Gent, Pvt. William C. Moore's Company, 6th Regiment of Cavalry

SHOOK FAMILY CEMETERY (east side of Kemp Road, 0.25 mile north of intersection with Shookstown Road, Shookstown, just west of Fort Detrick, Frederick, Frederick County).

Bopst, Pvt. Daniel. Turnbull's Company, 1st Regiment. No gravestone found.
Bopst, Pvt. John. Markey's Company, Kolb's Command, 16th Regiment.

SHREWSBURY PARISH CEMETERY, also called Shrewsbury Episcopal Church or South Sassafras Parish (located at end of Shrewsbury Church Road, off Augustine Herman Highway [Route 213], 5.1 miles west of Galena, Kennedyville, Kent County). NRHP.

Blackiston, Pvt. James, Jr. Whittington's Company, 33rd Regiment.
Ferguson, Pvt. Colin. Hand's Company, 21st Regiment.
Maxwell, Lt. William. Blakistone's Company, 33rd Regiment
Merritt, Pvt. Benjamin. Boyer's Company, 8th Cavalry District.
Spencer, Cpl. Isaac. Paymaster, 8th Regimental Cavalry District.
Spencer, Lt. Col. William. 33rd Regiment.
Sutton, Pvt. John C. Mackey, Jr.'s Company, 49th Regiment.
Wethered, Samuel. Paymaster of the 33rd Regiment. Paymaster of the 6th Brigade.
Wilson, Pvt. James. Mackey, Jr.'s Company, 49th Regiment.

SIMMONS FAMILY CEMETERY (Park Mills, Frederick County).

Simmons, 1st Lt. James. Stembell's Company, 3rd Regiment.

SPRING HILL CEMETERY (west side of Aurora Street and north of intersection with Cherry Street, Easton, Talbot County).

Hollyday, Henry. Paymaster, 9th Cavalry District.
Martin, Maj. Daniel (1780–1831). Captain and then major November 3, 1812, 9th Cavalry District. Served as governor of Maryland, 1829–31. No gravestone found.
Martin, Dr. Ennalls. Surgeon's Mate. Buried in section PEC.
Stevens, Capt. Samuel, Jr. (1778–1860). 9th Regiment. Governor of Maryland from 1822 to 1826.

SUMMERS FAMILY CEMETERY (Ellerton, Frederick County).

Summers, Pvt. Jacob. Shawen's Company.

THOMAS FAMILY CEMETERY (Point of Rocks, Frederick County).

Thomas, 1st Lt. Otho. Stembell's Company, 3rd Regiment.

TOMLINSON FAMILY CEMETERY (Ellerslie, Allegany County).

Tomlinson, Pvt. Jesse. Blair's Company, 50th Regiment.

TOMS CREEK CEMETERY (Toms Creek, Frederick County)

Sluss, Capt. Michael. 47th U.S. Infantry.

TRINITY CHURCH CEMETERY, St. Mary's Parish (Church Point, west off Leonardtown-Point Lookout Road [Route 5], St. Mary's City, St. Mary's County).

Bennett, John White. No service record found.

TRINITY LUTHERAN CHURCH (Taneytown, Carroll County).

Harman, Pvt. John. Durbin's Company, Randall's Battalion Riflemen.
Naill, Pvt. Samuel. Knox's Company, Randall's Battalion Riflemen.
Sheets, Pvt. Jacob. Reid's Company, 1st Cavalry District.
Zumbrun, Pvt. Jacob. Knox's Company, Randall's Battalion Riflemen.

UNITED BRETHREN & BLUE RIDGE CEMETERIES (Thurmont, Frederick County).

Arthur, Pvt. John. Durbin's Company, Randall's Battalion Riflemen.
Barton, Pvt. Samuel. Galt's Company, 3rd Regiment.
Bussard, Pvt. Peter. Duvall's Company, 29th Regiment.
Foreman, Pvt. Valentine. Shrim's Company, 5th Regiment.
Moser, Pvt. Henry. Duvall's Company, 29th Regiment.
Moser, Pvt. Leonard. Creager's Company.

Shaffer, Pvt. Daniel. Creager's Company.

Stokes, 1st Sgt. George. Marker's Company, 28th Regiment.

UNITED BRETHREN CEMETERY (Wolfsville, Frederick County).

Stottlemyer, Pvt. George. Flaut's Company of Riflemen.

U.S. NAVAL ACADEMY CEMETERY (west side of Ramsey Road, southeast side of confluence of College Creek and Severn River; a foot bridge from McNair Road at the north end of the academy campus leads toward the cemetery, Annapolis, Anne Arundel County).

Ballard, Lt. Henry E. U.S.N. Served onboard U.S. frigate *Constitution*.

Mayo, Com. Isaac. Lieutenant in U.S. Navy.

VEAZEY FAMILY CEMETERY (Cherry Grove Road, west of intersection with Fingerboard Road, north of Earlesville, Cecil County).

Veazey, Lt. Col. Thomas W. 49th Regiment.

WALLIS AND COMEGY CEMETERY (Perkins Hill Road, near Chestertown, Kent County).

Comegys, Cornelius. There are two individuals with this name who are veterans of the War of 1812, one a private in Ringgold's Company, 6th Regiment, and one a 2nd lieutenant in the 14th U.S. Infantry.

WALNUT GROVE FARM CEMETERY, also called W. S. Hebb's Farm (5192 Sheppard Lane 0.9 mile north off Clarksville Pike [Route 108], northeast of Clarksville, Howard County). PRIVATE

Watkins, Lt. Col. Gassaway. 32nd Regiment. Veteran of both the American Revolution and War of 1812.

WAUGH UNITED METHODIST CHURCH CEMETERY (east side of intersection of Hannibal Road with Green Pike, west off Harford Road [Route 147], Greenwood north of Baltimore, Baltimore County).

Coe, Cpl. James. Street's Company, 7th Cavalry Regiment.

Coe, Joshua. No service record found.

WESLEY FREEDOM METHODIST EPISCOPAL CEMETERY (961 Johnsville Road, Eldersburg, Carroll County).

Little, Col. Peter (1775–1830). Lieutenant colonel in the 51st Regiment, 1808. Colonel in the 38th Regiment, May 19, 1813, to June 15, 1815. No gravestone found.

WESLEY UNITED METHODIST CHURCH CEMETERY (north side of Carollton Road, just east in intersection with Houcksville Road and just west of intersection with Wesley Road, Richards Mills, southwest of Hampstead, Carroll County).

Algier, Pvt. Nicholas. Lt. Col. John Henry Schuchts's 2nd Regiment.

Leppo, Pvt. Jacob. Blizzard's Company, 15th Regiment.

WESLEYAN CHAPEL UNITED METHODIST CEMETERY (east side of Paradise Road [Maryland Route 462], just south of West Chapel Road and north of Chaple Road intersections, Chapel, north of Aberdeen, Harford County). Wesleyan Chapel was founded in 1826.

Carroll, Pvt. Aquila. Ringgold's Company, 7th Regiment.

WEST HATTON, also called Wicomico House (West Hatton Point, Wicomico River, West Hatton Place, east off West Hatton Road, east off Mount Victoria Road, east off Rock Point [Route 257], Mount Victoria, Charles County). PRIVATE

Stoddert, John Truman. Aide-de-camp, 5th Brigade 1814.

WEST LIBERTY METHODIST CHURCH CEMETERY (20400 West Liberty Road, 0.3 mile east of intersection with Old York Road [Route 439], West Liberty, Baltimore County).

Meredith, Micajah. Gravestone states: "A soldier of the war of 1812." Possibly served in Pennsylvania unit.

WESTMINSTER CEMETERY, also called Westminster City Cemetery and Westminster Old City Cemetery; do not confuse with First Presbyterian Church Burying Ground in Baltimore, which is called Old Westminster (0.1 mile north on North Church Street off East Main Street [Route 97], Westminster, Carroll County).

Arbaugh, Pvt. John. 15th Regiment. Buried in area F, lot 13-16.

Beaver, Pvt. John. Stembel's Company, 8th Regiment. Buried in area K, lot 06-02.

Blizzard, Capt. William W. 15th Regiment. Buried in area J, lot 06-07a.

Colegate, Dr. George. Surgeon, 20th Regiment. Buried in area F, lot 07-17.

Crouse, Pvt. William. Fonsten's Company, 3rd Regiment. Buried in area C, lot 12-04.

Knight, Peter. Crawford's Company. Gravestone reads in part: "SOLDIER OF 1812."

Powder, 2nd Cpl. Jacob. Durbin's Company, 20th Regiment, Randall's Battalion. Buried in area G, lot 01-14.

WEST NOTTINGHAM PRESBYTERIAN CEMETERY (intersection of Harrisville Road and Firetower Road, off Jacob Tome Memorial Highway [Route 276], Colora, Cecil County). Patrick Ewing, Jr. Served as a private and was brevetted to ensign while serving in the 30th Regiment. Ewing is believed to have been buried at Polk Cemetery before being reburied here, but no stone has been found.

Atkins, Lt. Henry Byard. 2nd U.S. Light Dragoons.

Black, Brig. Maj. John N. 1st Brigade. Saw action at Elkton April 1813 and July 1814, and Hampstead Hill, Baltimore, in September 1814.

WESTERN CEMETERY (south side of Edmondson Avenue, east of intersection with Hilton Parkway, Rosemont area, Baltimore).

Carnes, Pvt. William. Dillon's Company, 27th Regiment. Buried in area L.

Carson, Pvt. David. Peter's Company, 51st Regiment. Buried in area S.

Milleman (Milliman), Sgt. George. Haubert's Company, 51st Regiment. Buried in area S.

Pastorious, Pvt. Samuel. Stewart's Company, 51st Regiment.

WOLFSVILLE REFORMED CHURCH CEMETERY (Wolfsville, Frederick County).

Hiltabidel, Pvt. George. Crawford's Company.

Marken, Pvt. Samuel. Marker's Company, 28th Regiment.

Wolfe, Pvt. Jacob, Sr. Shawen's Company, 28th Regiment.

WORTHINGTON FAMILY CEMETERY (Kahler Property, Dogwood Road, west of Baltimore City, Baltimore County).

Worthington, Rezin H. No service record found.

ZION EPISCOPAL CHURCH CEMETERY (Urbana, Frederick County).

Moling, Pvt. Edward. Getzendanner's Company.

ZION LUTHERAN CHURCH CEMETERY (Feagaville, Frederick County).

Greenwald, Sgt. Christian. Getzendanner's Company.

Holter, Pvt. William. Turbutt's Company, 3rd Regiment.

ZION LUTHERAN CHURCH CEMETERY (107 West Main Street, Middletown, Frederick County).

Ridgely, Pvt. Joshua. Alexander's Company, 32nd Regiment.

Swearingen, Pvt. Van. Alexander's Company, 32nd Regiment.

ZION REFORMED CHURCH CEMETERY, once called the German Reformed Church, now the Zion United Church of Christ (North Potomac and West Church streets, Hagerstown, Washington County). The following veterans of the War of 1812 may be buried here in unmarked graves: Pvt. Frederick Betz, Pvt. Jacob Binkley, Pvt. John Goll, Sgt. Jacob Huyett, Pvt. George Kershner, Pvt. Jacob Leider, Capt. Thomas Quantrill, Pvt. William Scleigh, Pvt. John Troxell, and Cpl. John Wolgamot.

Humrickhouse, Pvt. Frederick. Quantrill's Company, 24th Regiment.

Rench, Pvt. Daniel. Quantrill's Company, 24th Regiment.

Schnebley, Lt. Col. David. 8th Regiment, Maryland Volunteers.

Sheetz, Capt. Henry. Led a company of Pennsylvania volunteers at the Battle of Bladensburg.

Tice, Pvt. John. Shryock's Company, 24th Regiment.

VIRGINIA

ARLINGTON NATIONAL CEMETERY (off George Washington Parkway, Arlington, just across the Potomac River from Georgetown, Arlington County).

Auld, Lt. Col. Hugh, Jr. (1767–1820). Served in the 26th Regiment. Participated in the Battle of St. Michaels. Buried in section 2.

Cassin, Lt. Stephen. Commanded U.S. schooner *Ticonderoga,* during the Battle of Lake Champlain, September 11, 1814. Cassin received a gold medal from the U.S. Congress. Buried in section 1.

Custis, George Washington Parke. Grandson of Martha Washington. Volunteered in the defense of Washington, D.C. Buried in section 13.

Graham, Capt. George. Served in the Fairfax County Company of Horse. Buried in section 3.

Lingan, Brig. Gen. James McCubbin. Federalist stabbed to death during the Baltimore Riots of 1814. Buried in section 1.

Williams, Capt. John. Native of Stafford County, Virginia. Commanded twenty marines who were attacked by a large number of Indians. Died of wounds in a skirmish with East Florida Indians on September 29, 1812. Buried in section 1.

BAILEY CEMETERY (adjacent to the Great House site, northeast side of unpaved drive southeast off Great House Road [Route 1003] near intersection with Sigourney Drive [Route 1005], Kinsale, Westmoreland County).

Bailey, Maj. Robert. No service record found.

Signourney, Midshipman James B. Commanded U.S. schooner *Asp* during an engagement on the Yeocomico River on July 14, 1813, where he was killed. His grave is marked by a cast iron cannon on wooden carriage. His epitaph reads in part: "Midshipman James B. Sigourney/Of the United States Navy/ . . . Age 23 years;/ Who fell gallantly defending his Country's Flag/On board of the United States Schooner ASP,/Under his command in an action with five/British barges of very superior force/On the 14th day of July, 1813/ . . ."

BRUTON PARISH EPISCOPAL CHURCH CEMETERY (210 West Duke of Gloucester Street, Williamsburg City).

Cabaniss, James. Served under Gen. William Henry Harrison at Fort Meigs in 1813. His name is inscribed on the Capt. Richard McRae Monument at Blandford Church,* Petersburg (spelled Cabiness) as a member of the Petersburg U.S. Volunteers.

CEDAR GROVE CEMETERY (238 East Princess Anne Road, Norfolk).

Warrington, Com. Lewis. Commanded U.S. sloop-of-war *Peacock,* which captured H.M. brig *Epervier* off the coast of Florida in 1814. Fought last engagement of war in 1815 against armed East India cruiser *Nautilus* in Indian Ocean. Awarded the congressional Gold Medal for his service.

Immediately north and adjacent to Cedar Grove is Elmwood Cemetery. In the cemetery office is a National Society U.S. Daughters War of 1812 grave marker for Robert Barron Hunter (unit unknown). There are no records for such an individual buried here; he probably is buried in an unknown grave in one of the Hunter family plots.

CHRIST CHURCH (southwest side of intersection of Christ Church Road [Route 646] and Gaskins Road, north of Irvington, Lancaster County).

Kelley, Pvt. Charles. Yerby's Company, 92nd Regiment.
Kelley, James. Probably Fisher's Company, 66th Regiment.
Kelley, John. No service record found.

CHOLSON FAMILY CEMETERY (Brunswick, Brunswick County). The exact location of this cemetery is unknown.

Cholson, Thomas, Jr. (1768–1816). Served in U.S. Army. Died in 1816 from wounds received during the War of 1812.

HOLLYWOOD CEMETERY (412 South Cherry Street, Richmond City).

Archer, Dr. Robert. Physician at Fort Nelson.

Monroe, James. Secretary of state and secretary of war during the War of 1812. Took an active role in scouting the British position during the invasion of Maryland. Present at the Battle of Bladensburg.

LEE CHAPEL AND MUSEUM (on grounds of Washington and Lee University, Jefferson Street and Letcher Avenue, Lexington, Rockbridge County).

Lee, Gen. Henry (better known as "Light Horse Harry"). Re-interred in the Lee family vault located in the lower level of the Lee Chapel, which was completed in 1868 and renovated in 1999. General Lee was an ardent Federalist and supported Alexander Contee Hanson, editor of the Baltimore *Federal Republican,* which editorialized against the war. Lee was severely injured during the Baltimore Riots of 1812.*

MASONIC CEMETERY (900 Charles Street at George Street, Fredericksburg, Spotsylvania County).

Chew, John. No service record found.
Ellis, Robert. No service record found.
Grinnan, Daniel. Probably private in Quarles Company, 16th Regiment.
Minor, Brig. Gen. John. No service record found.

MOUNT HEBRON CEMETERY (305 East Boscawen Street, Winchester, Frederick County).

Tucker, Capt. Henry St. George. Commanded a troop of cavalry from Frederick County. Later served as a rifleman attached to the 57th Regiment. Still later served as brigade major of the 6th Brigade. He lived at Stone House Mansion.*

OLD CITY CEMETERY, also called Old Methodist Cemetery (401 Taylor Street, Lynchburg, Bedford County). Of the estimated 20,000 people interred here, 75 percent of whom are of African decent, only about 2,500 have markers.

Cobbs, Pvt. Charles Gwatkins (circa 1790–1827). Dunnington's Artillery. No gravestone found.

Gray, Pvt. French S. (1790–1820). Dunnington's Artillery.

Gray, Pvt. Robert Hening (1792–1865). Dunnington's Artillery.

Holmes, Col. Joshua Rathborne. No service record found.

Perry, Jesse L. (?–1839). No gravestone found.

Rohr, Philip. Wiatt's Company, Lynchburg Rifles, U.S. 4th Regiment.

Vawter, Pvt. John (1795?–1834). Dunnington's Artillery. Probably buried in an unmarked grave inside the stone wall of the Bransford Vawter plot.

Wiatt, William. Served during the War of 1812 and later promoted to rank captain of the Lynchburg Rifles.

PHILLIPS CEMETERY (intersection of Yeager, Fairhope, and Findley roads, Jimtown [Fairhope], Randolph, West Virginia). This abandoned cemetery served the poor and indigent.

Gibson, Pvt. Dudley A. Jackson's Company, 7th Regiment.

PRESBYTERIAN CEMETERY (907 Bailey Street, Lynchburg, Bedford County).

Hancock, Pvt. Ammon. Wiatt's Company, Lynchburg Rifles, U.S. 4th Regiment.

ST. JAMES EPISCOPAL CHURCH CEMETERY (east side of Church Street near intersection with Edwards Ferry Road [Route 7] near courthouse, Leesburg, Loudoun County, northern Virginia).

Dawson, Pvt. Samuel. Hopkins's Troop, 2nd Light Dragoons. Private Dawson's discharge certificate states:

> Camp Near Sackets Harbor 7th December 1813. The Bearer here of Samuel Dawson a private in Captain Samuel G. Hopkins Troop 2nd Regiment United States Light Dragoons has served for and during 18 months; his term of service having expired on the 7th day of December 1813, he is entitled to an honorable discharge. He has been paid up to the 31st day of May 1813, has returned his arms & accoutrements in good order and has received his full allowance of clothing. He is entitled to pay from the 31st day of May 1813, together with three months pay as his allowance upon being honorably discharged and pay and rations from this place to Frankfort in the State of Kentucky being his place of residence. To prevent imposition here follows a description of the said Samuel Dawson he is five feet five inches and half blue eyes fair complexion dark hair born in Amherst County in the State of Virginia and by Profession a Farmer. [signed] Samuel Goode Hopkins Capt. 2nd Reg. U.S. Light Dragoons.

Mason, Lt. Col. Armistead Thomson (1787–1819). Commanded the 57th Regiment. Killed by his brother-in-law, John M.

McCarty, on February 6, 1819, in a duel at Bladensburg Dueling Ground.* No gravestone found.

SHOCKOE HILL CEMETERY (4th and Hospital streets, north side of James River, Richmond City).

Francisco, Peter. Rank and unit unknown but served in War of 1812. Best remembered for his service during the Revolutionary War, when he was wounded at least four times during three battles and was present at the siege of Yorktown.

Leigh, Benjamin Watkins. Aide-de-camp to James Barbour, governor of Virginia.

SMITHFIELD PLANTATION (1000 Smithfield Plantation Road, off Duck Pond Drive, off Southgate Drive [Route 364], Virginia Tech University, Blacksburg, Montgomery County).

Preston, Lt. Col. James Patton (1774–1843). 75th Regiment of Virginia Militia. Wounded and crippled for the remainder of his life during the Battle of Crysler's Farm, November 11, 1813. Served as governor of Virginia from 1816 to 1819. Buried in unmarked grave in the Preston Cemetery located on the plantation.

SPRING HILL CEMETERY (3000 Fort Avenue, Lynchburg, Bedford County).

Garland, James (1791–1885). Probably Lt. James P. Garland, Coleman's Company, 80th Regiment.

SWEET SPRINGS CEMETERY (Kanawha Trail [Route 311], Sweet Springs, Monroe County, West Virginia).

Floyd, Governor John. Surgeon during the War of 1812. Floyd is buried in an unmarked grave, presumably in the small cemetery behind St. John the Evangelist Church at the intersection of Kanawha Trail and Route 3; there are three cemeteries in Sweet Springs.

TRINITY EPISCOPAL CHURCH CEMETERY (southwest corner of intersection of High and Court streets at 500 Court Street, Portsmouth).

Barron, Com. James. Commanded the U.S. frigate *Chesapeake* when it was attacked by H.M. frigate *Leopard* in 1807. Convicted in 1808 of "neglecting to clear his ship for action," he was suspended from command for five years and denied an active command during the War of 1812. Killed Com. Stephen Decatur in duel in 1820.

UNION CEMETERY (323 North King Street, Leesburg, Loudoun County, northern Virginia).

Mercer, Charles Fenton (1778–1858). Lieutenant and captain of cavalry (1798–1800) U.S. Army. Aide-de-camp to the Governor James Barbour in 1813. Major in Light Corps of 6th Regiment in 1814. Inspector general Virginia Militia in 1814. Lived at Aldie.*

VARMER, JOSEPH, GRAVESITE (in locust grove near intersection Hagans Lane [Route 696] and Abram Penn Highway [Route 626], north of Critz, west of Martinsburg, Patrick County).

Varmer, Joseph (1758–1848). Unit unknown. No gravestone found.

WASHINGTON, D.C.

CONGRESSIONAL CEMETERY (originally called Washington Parish Burial Ground [1807–46] and then Washington Cemetery [1846]) (1801 E Street, SE near the intersection of Potomac Avenue and 18th Street, near Barney Circle). NRHP. The thirty-two-acre Congressional Cemetery, established in 1807, is neither owned nor operated by the U.S. Congress, but because it has so many historical figures buried or memorialized here, Congress has occasionally made contributions toward its upkeep. Early congressional bills entitled "The Congressional Burying Ground" gave the cemetery its name. It was America's first de facto national cemetery before the establishment of a national cemeterial system begun in 1862 during the Civil War. Nearby Arlington Cemetery was established in 1864. Congressional Cemetery has been called "America's Westminster Abbey."

Congressional Cemetery has over 60,000 graves but only about 14,000 grave markers. Among those buried here are at least 100 veterans of the War of 1812 and at least 37 federal officials, employees, and civilians who played a role in the war. There are also 13 cenotaphs, including ones that honor War Hawks Henry Clay and John C. Calhoun. The cemetery offers several self-guiding walking tours, including "Walking Tour: the Burning of Washington" and "Walking Tour: The War of 1812."

There is a War of 1812 marker next to a Gerard Wood of Charles County, Maryland, who died at age fifteen, June 12, 1811. Is it possible this was a ships boy who died in some pre-war naval engagement? Is the 1812 marker misplaced? We will probably never know. The remains of Dolley Payne Madison, John Quincy Adams, and Louisa Adams were taken to the Public Vault until buried elsewhere. Dolley Madison's remains were here from 1849 to 1852, when she was moved to the James H. Causten Vault. She remained there until 1857, when she was buried with her husband at their family estate in Montpelier,* Virginia. Flora Adams Darling, founder of the Daughters of the War of 1812, is also buried here at R55/96-97.

Military Personnel[3]

Note: * = present at the Bladensburg and/or the burning of Washington; ** = present at Battle for Baltimore; ® = removed

Adams, John Quincy. Served as one of five commissioners to negotiate the end of the war. Cenotaph in R54/101.

Andrews, Col. Christopher. Served as an adjutant and rendered support during the American attempt to harass the British squadron during its descent of the Potomac River after occupying Alexandria. Buried in R69/152.

Ashton, Lt. Col./Dr. Henry. Served in the 49th Maryland Militia Regiment. Buried in R34/48.

Ball, William L. Served in the 92nd Virginia Regiment. Buried in R29/37-38.

Barry, Com. Thomas. Served as a gunner on U.S. frigate *United States*. He later oversaw the fitting out of most of the American frigates during the war. Buried in R42/19.

Baxter, James. Served in Stewart's Company, 31st Maryland Regiment. Buried in R87/281.

Beale, George. Fought under Commodore McDonough on Lake Champlain. Buried in R32/59.

Bestor, Chauncey. Served in the District of Columbia militia. Buried in R47/152.

Bestor, Harvey. Commanded a company in the 2nd District of Columbia militia. Buried in R47/143.

Black, James Augustus. Served in the 8th Infantry. Promoted to 1st lieutenant in 1813. Cenotaph in R55/104.

Booth, Mordecai. Served as captain's clerk to the commandant's office, Washington Navy Yard. Buried in R53/2.

Brady, John. Unit and rank unknown. Buried in R18/140.

Brown, Maj. Gen. Jacob. Wounded at the Battle of Lundy's Lane, July 25, 1814. Buried in R57/150-152.

Buck, Daniel A. Served as captain in the 31st U.S. Infantry. Buried in R41/78.

Bulley, Michael E. Served in the 4th Regiment. Promoted to 1st lieutenant in 1813. Buried in R51/50.

Burdine, William H. Worked at the Washington Navy Yard. Served in the local militia. Served as a guard and present during the burning of the Anacostia Bridge. Buried in R137/252.

Caldwell, Capt. Elias Boudinot. Served in the Washington Light Horse Cavalry during the Battle of Bladensburg. Buried in R51/13.

Carrico, William Bartholomew. Served as a private in the District of Columbian militia. Buried in R64/124.

Chauncey, Com. Isaac. Appointed commander of naval forces on Lakes Ontario and Erie. Buried in R30/34.

Clarke, Satterlee. Served in the U.S. Army pay department. Buried in R40/130.

Crane, Comm. William. Buried in R37/94-95.

Cross, Col. Truman. Served as Ensign in 12th Regiment of Infantry. Buried in R39/141.

Dawson, John Bennett. Served as aide to Gen. Jacob Brown and Gen. Andrew Jackson. Buried in R30/11-12.

Dorsett, Fielder R., Sr. Rank and unit unknown. Member of the Association of the Survivors of the War of 1812. Buried in R33/117.

Dove, Marmaduke. Sailing master, U.S. Navy. Served at the Norfolk Station during the war. Buried in R57/33.

Dumas, 1st Lt. Hippolete. Served as U.S. Army engineer. Buried in R52/86.

Duvall, William Pope. Commanded a company of Kentucky mounted militia during the Indian hostilities of 1812. Was the original "Ralph Ringwood" of Washington Irving and "Nimrod Wildfire" of James K. Paulding. Buried in R46/5.

Dyer, Capt. William D. Served in the 1st Rifle Battalion (Pinkney's) Maryland Militia. Buried in R34/55-56.

Easby, Capt. William. Militia unit unknown. Buried in R50/94.

Eaton, David. Served on U.S. sloop-of-war *Hornet* during its capture of H.M. brigs *Peacock* and *Penguin*. Buried in R37/48.

Edwards, 2nd Lt. James L. U.S.M.C. Buried in R54/198.

Elliot, Jonathan. Served in the U.S. Army. Rank and unit unknown. Buried in R31/15.

Elzey, Dr. Arnold. Garrison surgeon's mate and post-hospital surgeon, U.S. Army, 1814–18. Served as physician to President Madison. Buried in R33/7.

Farrelly, Maj. Patrick. Buried in R57/101-103 .

Forrest, Com. French. Served onboard U.S. sloop-of-war *Hornet* during battle with H.M. brig *Peacock* on February 24, 1813. Served during the Battle of Lake Erie on September 10, 1813. Buried in R45/42.

Frick, Henry. Unit and rank unknown. Cenotaph in R54/116-117.

Gardner, Lt. Col. Charles Kitchel. Present at the battles of Crysler's Farm, Chippawa, Niagara, and defense of Fort Erie. Buried in R55/190.

Gardner, Com. William Henry. Midshipman, U.S. Navy. Buried in R37/234.

Glynn, Lt. Anthony Greenville. Served as a paymaster during the war. Buried in R33/49.

Gibson, Maj. Gen. George C. Served as lieutenant colonel in the 5th U.S. Infantry during the War of 1812. President Abraham Lincoln attended his funeral. Buried in R56/140.

Grider, Hon. Henry. Rank and unit unknown. Buried in R59/125.

Hamilton, Dr. Charles. Service and unit unknown. Buried in Beale Vault.

Hamilton, Samuel. Served in an artillery company at the Battle of Bladensburg. Buried in R29/135.

Henderson, Archibald. Commanded the U.S. Marines at the Charleston Navy Yard, Boston. Served on U.S. frigate *Constitution* when it captured H.M. frigate *Cyane* and H.M. sloop-of-war *Levant*. Buried in R55/171.*

Henry, Robert Pryor. Rank and unit unknown. Cenotaph in R57/122-124.

Hook, James Harvey. Ensign 5th U.S. Infantry, 1812. Promoted to captain 38th U.S. Infantry, 1813. Buried in R37/51.

Huntt, Dr. Henry. Served as surgeon of the U.S. Hospital at Burlington, Vermont. Served as physician to five presidents of the United States. Buried in R46/55.

Jesup, Maj. Gen. Thomas. Captain U.S. Army in 1813. Promoted to major in 1813. Served on staff of Brig. Gen. William Hull. In 1814, commanded the 25th U.S. Infantry at Chippawa. Brevetted to lieutenant colonel. Fought at Lundy's Lane. Brevetted colonel. Buried in Vault.®

Jewell, David. Rank and unit unknown. Buried in R84/121.

Johnson, Hon. James. Served as a lieutenant colonel and commanded the American left wing in the Battle of the Thames. Cenotaph in R57/128-130.

Johnson, Dr. Richmond. Served as surgeon's mate, U.S. Navy, during the war. Buried in R31/154.

Johnston, Col. Josiah Stoddard. Organized a regiment of militia for the defense of New Orleans but arrived at the city after the battle. Cenotaph in R57/160.

Jones, Maj. Gen. Roger. Served in artillery at Battle of Chippawa, July 4–5, 1814. Brevetted major for distinguished service at battle. Buried in R57/253.

Jones, Gen. Walter. Present at the Battle of Bladensburg. Buried in R33/67.* ®

Kearney, Surgeon John A. Served as surgeon aboard U.S. frigate *Constitution* during its engagement with H.M. sloop-of-war *Levant* and H.M. frigate *Cyane*. Served as gunboat flotilla surgeon at Newport Rhode Island. Buried in R53/18.

Kleiber, Jacob. Rank and unit unknown. Buried in R26/202.

Lauck, Isaac S. Served in the Virginia militia. Rank and unit unknown. Buried in R39/200.

Lawrence, Lt. Col. William. Commanded Fort Bowyer at Mobile Bay, Louisiana, where he successfully defended the fort twice from superior British forces where he was wounded. Buried in R54/78.

Lenox, Capt. Peter. Unit unknown. Buried in R32/91.*

Lovell, Dr. Joseph. Served as surgeon of the 9th U.S. Infantry. Buried in R54/149-152.

Macomb, Gen. Alexander. Defended Plattsburg. Voted a gold medal by Congress for his service. Buried in R55/147-149.

Manning, Capt. Richard Irvine. Unit unknown. Cenotaph in R31/65.

McCalla, Gen. John M. Buried in R52/164N.

McKenney, Benson. Rank and unit unknown. Buried in R54/255.

McKim, Hon. Isaac. Served as aide-de-camp to Gen. Samuel Smith. Cenotaph in R30/57-59.

McNeill, Lt. Col. John. Fought at battle of Chippawa. At Niagara he was severely wounded in both legs by cannister shot. Buried in R53/248.

Meade, James. Rank and unit unknown. Buried in R44/185.

Mitchell, Col. George Edward. Served as a major in the 3rd U.S. Artillery. Promoted to lieutenant colonel in 1813. Brevetted to colonel in 1814 for his gallant conduct in repelling a British attack at Fort Oswego, New York. Buried in R29/53-55.

Morgan, Com. Charles W. Commanded U.S. frigate *Constitution* in 1812 during its engagement with H.M. frigates *Guerriere* and *Java*. Buried in R81/105.

Newton, Com. John T. U.S. Navy. Buried in Vault.®

Nye, Capt. John. 2nd Regiment Massachusetts militia. Buried in R16/67.

Paine, Capt. Thomas. U.S. Navy. Severely wounded in attack against American gunboats near Savannah. Buried in R86/86.

Palmer, Sgt. Morris. U.S. Marine Corps. Served at the Marine Barracks* in Washington. Buried in R55/79.

Parker, Gen. Daniel L. Paymaster general during the War of 1812. Cenotaph in R45/45.

Patterson, Com. Daniel Todd. Served as commander of the Naval Station at New Orleans. Buried in R55/150-152.

Pickett, James C. Midshipman U.S. Navy. Promoted to 2nd lieutenant by end of war. Buried in R31/45.

Pinkney, Maj. William.* Served with the Rifle Battalion, 5th Baltimore Regiment of Volunteers. Buried at Green Mount Cemetery, Baltimore. Cenotaph in R29/35-37.*

Pushmataha. Choctaw American Indian chief. Along with five hundred of his warriors, he joined the U.S. southern army, fought in twenty-four battles, and served directly under Andrew Jackson in the Pensacola Campaign, including the Battle of New Orleans. Buried in R31/41-42.

Robertson, Henry B. 1st Regiment, District of Columbia militia. Buried in R138/237.

Robinson, Sgt. John G. Served in Dade's Company at the Battle of Bladensburg. Buried in R69/179.*

Rodgers, Com. John. Commander of the U.S. frigate *President* against H.M. sloop-of-war *Little Belt* off Cape Henry. Buried in R56/152.**

Schwartz, Maj. John. Unit unknown. Cenotaph in R60/72.

Seaton, Col. William. Served in the Battle of Bladensburg. Co-owner of the Washington *National Intelligencer*. Mayor of Washington for five terms from 1840 to 1850. Buried in R57/165.*

Simonton, Col. John W. Served as a private in John B. Moorhead's Company, 1st Regiment Pennsylvania militia. Buried in R46/43.

Smoot, Joseph. Served as Midshipman aboard U.S. sloop *Hornet* throughout the war. Buried in R52/103.

Smyth, Brig. Gen. Alexander. Served as inspector general U.S. Army. Buried in R29/43-44.

Stettinius, Samuel. Rank and unit unknown. Buried in R64/106.

Stevens, Com. Thomas. U.S. Navy. Commanded one of the vessels in Battle of Lake Erie. Cenotaph in R55/240.

Stuart, Brig. Gen. Philip. 5th Brigade. Present at the Benedict and Lower Cedar Point skirmishes. Buried in R52/24.

Thomas, Col. James. Unit unknown. Buried in R57/82.

Thompson, Col. Samuel. Served as aide to Gen. Andrew Jackson at Battle of New Orleans. Buried in R29/136.

Tingey, Capt. Thomas. Commandant of the Washington Navy Yard during the War of 1812. Buried in R57/1.*

Totten, Maj. Gen. Joseph G. U.S. Army. Brevetted lieutenant colonel for gallant conduct at Battle of Plattsburg. Buried in R44/36.

Trimble, Col. William A. Major of Ohio Volunteers 1812. Captured at Detroit. Major of 26th U.S. Infantry 1813. Brevetted to lieutenant colonel in 1814 for gallantry at Fort Erie where he was severely wounded. Commanded 1st U.S. Infantry in 1814. Buried in R29/34-35.

Wadsworth, Com. Alexander S. Unit unknown. Buried in R45/244?

Walker, Maj. David. Served on staff of Governor Shelby of Kentucky in Battle of the Thames. Buried in R29/22-23.

Walker, Zachariah. Rank and unit unknown. Buried in R55/26.

Ward, Capt. Charles. Served as lieutenant of ordnance, U.S. Army during war. Buried in R25/149.

Warrington, Com. Lewis. Rank and unit during war unknown. Buried in Public Vault.®

Washington, Dr. Bailey. Served as surgeon on U.S. schooner *Enterprise* when it captured H.M. brig *Boxer*. Served as fleet surgeon on Lake Ontario. Buried in R27/166.

Watterston, George. Served in Benjamin Burch's Company at Battle of Bladensburg. Buried in Hamilton and Watterston Vault.*

Weightman, Gen. Roger Chew. Served as an officer in a District of Columbia cavalry company. Took a commission in the District of Columbia militia. Buried in R53/134.*

Woodward, Amon. Served as ensign in Carberry's Company, 36th U.S. Infantry. Fought at the Battle of Bladensburg. Received a pension of $8.00 per month commencing in 1871 and received a bounty of 160 acres for 361 days of service during the war. Buried in R35/176.*

Selected Federal Employees and Other Civilians

Note: * = present at the Bladensburg and/or the burning of Washington; ** = present at Battle for Baltimore; ® = removed

Bassett, Simeon. Stone mason who worked on capitol reconstruction following the British burning. Buried in R77/D-4.*

Berry, Brook M.. A civilian who was taken from his federal office to man an artillery company during the Battle of Bladensburg. No gravestone found. Buried in R52/23.

Booth, Mordecai. Principal clerk of the Navy Yard, ordered to burn the yard in 1814. Buried in R53/2.*

Calhoun, John Caldwell. War Hawk. Cenotaph in R60/146.

Campbell, Mary J. Ingle. Then an eleven-year-old who wrote of her remembrances of the British burning of Washington. Buried in R37/213.*

Clay, Henry. War Hawk. Cenotaph in R60/149-151.

Coombe, Griffith. A prominent citizen of Washington who wrote of his remembrances of the British occupation. Buried in R50/20.*

Crowley, Patrick. Apprentice at the *National Intelligencer* during the war. He printed copies of "The Star Spangled Banner" and made more than $100. He wrote of his remembrances of the British occupation. Buried in R84/231.*

Frost, John T. Served as a clerk in the House of Representatives. Buried in R48/5.*

Gales, Joseph, Jr. Editor of the Washington *National Intelligencer.* Buried in R55/165.*

Gerry, Elbridge. Served as vice president under President Madison. Buried in R29/9-11.

Graham, George. Recruited and commanded the Fairfax light-horse. He served as chief clerk in the War Department under Secretary James Monroe. Buried in R30/42.*

Hadfield, George. Designed the treasury and executive offices that were burned by the British. Buried in R33/30.*

Madison, Dolley. Buried temporarily in 1849 in the Causten Vault R49.®

Moore, Capt. William Walker. Enrolled at age eleven in a company of youths to prepare ammunition against a possible second attack on Baltimore. Buried in R80/D3.**

Otis, Samuel Allyne. Served as the secretary of the U.S. Senate until his death in 1814. Buried in R30/14.

Pleasonton, Stephen. Clerk of the State Department. Saved many national documents, including the Declaration of Independence, Articles of Confederation, the correspondence of Gen. George Washington, and the Secret Journals of Congress. Buried in R43/244.*

Ringgold, Tench. Owned one of the three rope walks burned by the British. Buried in R45/55.*

Thornton, Dr. William. First architect of the U.S. Capitol, Octagon House, and Tudor Place. Superintendent of the Patent Office where because of his personal appeals saved the patent models from burning. Buried in R33/39.*

Todd, John Payne. Son of Dolley Todd Madison, served as one of Albert Gallatin's attachés for the peace mission to Ghent. Buried in R41/230.

Tucker, Thomas Tudor. Served as U.S. treasurer. Buried in R30/37-38.*

OAK HILL CEMETERY (north off R Street, at intersection with 30th Street, NW, Georgetown)

Adlum, Maj. John. Served as a captain during the War of 1812.

Heath, James P. Aide-de-camp to Brig. Gen. William H. Winder.

Peter, Maj. George. Organized a battery of flying artillery.

Sprigg, Cornet Samuel. 2nd Cavalry District, 4th Brigade June 18, 1814. Offered but declined a commission as 2nd lieutenant in July 1814.

Towson, Maj. Gen. Nathan (1784–1854). Commissioned a captain in the 2nd U.S. Artillery in March 1812. Brevetted a major on October 8, 1812. Brevetted a lieutenant colonel on July 5, 1814.

DELAWARE

WILMINGTON AND BRANDYWINE CEMETERY (701 Delaware Avenue, Wilmington).

Davis, Col. Samuel B. (1765–1854). Served in the U.S. Army during the War of 1812.

Jones, Com. Jacob* (1768–1850). Master commandant and hero of the U.S. sloop *Wasp,* which captured H.M. sloop *Frolic* October 18, 1812.

Tilton, Gen. James (1745–1822). Surgeon General of the United States from 1813 to 1815. Gravestone not found.

PENNSYLVANIA

CHRIST CHURCH BURIAL GROUND (Arch and 5th streets, Philadelphia).

Bainbridge, Capt. William. Commanded U.S. frigate *Constitution,* which captured H.M. frigate *Java* December 29, 1812. Plaque on gravestone alludes to fact that the U.S. Naval Training Center at Bainbridge,* Maryland, is named after him.

ST. PETER'S EPISCOPAL CEMETERY (313 Pine Street, Philadelphia).

Decatur, Com. Stephen. Commanded U.S. frigate *United States,* which captured H.M. frigate *Macedonian* October 25, 1812. Gravestone reads in part: " . . . SUSTAINED BY HIS/INTREPID ACTIONS/THE INSPIRING SENTIMENT/'OUR COUNTRY: RIGHT OR WRONG,'/GAVE HIM IN RETURN/ITS APPLAUSE AND GRATITUDE."

All the engagements, events, localities, and vessels mentioned in this appendix are discussed in more detail within the text of this guide.[1] Please consult the index for more details on these entries.

1807

March 3	United States rejects Monroe–Pinkney Treaty with Great Britain
June 22	H.M. frigate *Leopard* attacks U.S. frigate *Chesapeake* off the Virginia Capes
Dec. 22	United States adopts embargo prohibiting U.S. ships and goods from leaving port

1808

	As a consequence of the *Chesapeake–Leopard* affair, forts such as Powhatan, Norfolk, and Boykin are strengthened (VA)
Sept. 30	The "Gin Riot" against tax takes place on Hampstead Hill, Baltimore (MD)

1812

May 16	Fifty leading citizens from Baltimore meet to petition Congress to declare war on Great Britain (MD)
June 18	United States declares war on Great Britain
June 22	Baltimore mob destroys office of *Federal Republican* newspaper (MD)
July 12	The first Baltimore privateers depart to prey upon British shipping (MD)
July 24	Three companies of the 14th U.S. Infantry recruited in Maryland leave for Canada
July 27–29	Baltimore mob destroys office of *Federal Republican* newspaper and attacks Federalists defending office (MD)

August 4	Baltimore mob threatens to tear down post office to get copies of *Federal Republican*
Sept. 9	1st Baltimore Volunteers leave for Canada (MD)
Oct. 13	Great Britain authorizes reprisals against United States
Oct. 21	Petersburg U.S. Volunteers leave for Canada (VA)
Mid-Nov.	Brawl erupts when Federalist Meshack Browning tries to muster his militia unit (MD)
Dec. 26	British government orders blockade of Chesapeake Bay

1813

	British burn three vessels and damage Poplar Hall on Broad Creek near Norfolk (VA)
Feb. 4	British squadron arrives in Chesapeake Bay to begin blockade; U.S. frigate *Constellation* blockaded in Elizabeth River at Norfolk (VA)
Feb. 6	British declare blockade of Chesapeake Bay
Feb. 8	British establish anchorage in Lynnhaven Bay (VA)
Feb. 8	British capture privateer *Lottery* in Lynnhaven Bay (VA)
Feb. 14	British raid Cape Henry lighthouse (VA)
March 3	Rear Adm. Sir George Cockburn arrives in Chesapeake Bay
March 6	380 additional 14th U.S. Infantry recruits leave Baltimore for Canada (MD)
March 9	British raid Cherrystone Inlet (VA)
March 10	First runaway slaves in Chesapeake Bay seek refuge on H.M. ship-of-the-line *Victorious*
March 10	British raid Cape Charles (VA)
March 10	Naval skirmish at Gwynn Island (VA)
March 11	U.S. engineers begin improvements on Fort McHenry near Baltimore (MD)
March 14	British ships move into Choptank River near Cambridge (MD)

March 20	British cancel attack planned on U.S. frigate *Constellation* at Norfolk (VA)	May 26	Adm. Sir John B. Warren issues proclamation blockading U.S. coasts from New York to New Orleans
March 26	British raid Sharps Island (MD)	spring	British raid mouth of Patuxent River (MD)
March 28	Construction begun on Fort Stokes on Tred Avon River to protect Easton (MD)	June 12	H.M. frigate *Narcissus* captures U.S. revenue cutter *Surveyor* in York River (VA)
April 3	British capture *Arab, Lynx, Racer,* and *Dolphin* in Rappahannock River (VA)	June 15	British destroy corn mills near Cape Henry (VA)
April 4	British raid Chewnings Point, Carter Creek (VA)	June 18	British reinforcements enter Chesapeake Bay
April 6	British threaten Urbana (VA)	June 20	British reconnoiter Norfolk (VA)
April 6	British destroy six American vessels in Rappahannock River (VA)	June 20	U.S. gunboats unsuccessfully attack H.M. frigate *Junon* (VA)
April 6–7	British probe Potomac River	June 22	British attack on Craney Island repulsed (VA)
April 7	Militia establish base below mouth of Nomini Creek (VA)	June 25	British sack Hampton (VA)
April 11	British establish temporary base on Tangier Island (VA)	June 26	Skirmish at Pagan Creek (VA)
		June 29	British raid Mount Pleasant (VA)
April 12	British raid Sharps Island (MD)	July 2	British raid at Burwell Bay repulsed (VA)
April 16	British threaten Baltimore (MD)	July 4	British raid St. Jerome Creek (MD)
April 16	British raid Sharps Island (MD)	July 1–10	British raid James River (VA)
April 17	American Jacob Gibson frightens residents of St. Michaels by approaching in vessel disguised to appear British (MD)	July 6	British raid Lawnes Creek (VA)
		July 6–23	British occupy Kent Island (MD)
		July 7–27	British raid Potomac River (MD/VA)
April 18–19	British raid Poplar Island (MD)	July 12	British attack Ocracoke Island (NC)
		July 14	British watering party attacked at Cape Henry (VA)
April 19	Maryland public records removed from Annapolis to Upper Marlboro (MD)	July 14	British capture U.S. schooner *Asp* in Yeocomico River (VA)
April 20	British capture of Queenstown packet curtails cross-bay travel (MD)	July 14	British sound Potomac River (MD)
		July 16	Skirmish at Woodland Point (MD)
April 20	British raid Deal Island (MD)	July 18	British raid at Rosier Creek repulsed (VA)
April 23	British seize Spesutie Island (MD)	July 19–21	British occupy Blackistone (St. Clements) Island (MD)
April 24	British occupy and establish battery on Pooles Island (MD)	July 19	British raid on Mattox Creek repulsed (VA)
April 24?	Americans repulse British at Still Pond (MD)	July 19	British occupy St. George Island (MD)
April 26– May 3	British survey mouth of Severn River (MD)	July 19	Courier warning system established at Point Lookout (MD)
April 27	British raid Worton Creek (MD)	July 21	British occupy St. Catherine's Islands (MD)
April 29	British burn Frenchtown after skirmish (MD)	July 21	British raid Hollis's Marsh, Currioman Bay (VA)
April 29	British land at White Hall (MD)	July 24	Torpedo (water mine) prematurely explodes near H.M. ship-of-the-line *Plantagenet* at mouth of Chesapeake Bay (VA)
April 29	British attack at Elk Landing repulsed (MD)		
late April	British bombard Howell Point (MD)	July 26	British raid Lower Machodoc Creek (VA)
late spring	Militia attacks British party attempting to scuttle grounded ship off Point Lookout (MD)	August 6–23	British occupy Kent Island (MD)
May 3	British loot and burn Havre de Grace after skirmish (MD)	August 8	British fleet threatens Baltimore (MD)
		August 10	British attack on St. Michaels repulsed (MD)
May 3	British destroy Principio Iron Works (MD)	August 12–13	British sound the mouth of Severn River (MD)
May 3	British raid Bell's Ferry (MD)		
May 6	Charlestown capitulates to British (MD)	August 13	British attack on Queenstown leads to Battle of Slippery Hill (MD)
May 6	British loot and burn Fredericktown and Georgetown after skirmish (MD)	August 19	False reports circulate of British landing at Sandy Point (MD)
May 6	British raid Turners Creek (MD)		

August 19	Mary Young Pickersgill finishes making garrison and storm flags for Fort McHenry (MD)	June 1	British burn American schooner near Cove Point (MD)
August 26	British land at Wades Point (MD)	June 3	British raid Cedar Point (MD)
August 26	British capture fourteen Americans at Harris Creek (MD)	June 6–8	British fleet arrives at mouth of Patuxent River (MD)
August 26	British attack on St. Michaels repulsed (MD)	June 8–9	British probe St. Leonard Creek and skirmish with U.S. Chesapeake Flotilla (MD)
Sept. 21	Skirmish at Cherrystone Inlet (VA)	June 9	British raid Rousby Hall (MD)
Sept. 22	British raid Pleasure House, Lynnhaven Bay (MD)	June 10	First Battle of St. Leonard Creek (MD)
Sept. 22	Virginia militia deployed to Hague, Kinsale, Lynchs Point, Pickatone, Ragged Point, and Sandy Point (VA)	June 10	British attempt to cut off American reinforcements at Sotterley (MD)
Nov. 1–9	British occupy St. George Island (MD)	June 11	British raid St. Leonard Creek (MD)
Nov. 2	British raid St. Clements (Blackistone) Island (MD)	June 12	British raid Broomes Island (MD)
Nov. 5	Skirmish at St. Inigoes Creek (MD)	June 14	British raid Sotterley Plantation (MD)
Nov. 7	Bulk of British fleet in Chesapeake leaves for Bermuda (VA)	June 15	British raid Benedict (MD)
Dec. 20	British barges attack American privateer *Tartar* near Cape Henry (VA)	June 15–16	British raid Lower Marlboro (MD)
		June 16	Skirmish at Hall Creek (MD)

1814

Jan. 25	Vice Adm. Sir Alexander F. I. Cochrane assumes command of the North American Naval Station	June 17	British raid Magruders Landing (MD)
		June 17	Skirmish at Hollands Cliffs (MD)
March	British raid Wicomico River (MD)	June 17	British raid Cedar Point (MD)
March 17	British raid New Point Comfort (VA)	June 18	British raid Coles Landing (MD)
April 4	British raid Corotoman Plantation and Carter Creek (VA)	June 21	British raid of Benedict repulsed (MD)
April 7	British raid Little Annemessex River (MD)	June 25	Skirmish at Chesconessex (MD)
April 8	British raid Zachariah Crockett's house on Tangier Island (VA)	June 25–late Sept.	Mount Lubentia becomes temporary repository of Prince George's County records (MD)
April 9	British raid on Wicomico River repulsed (MD)	June 26	British raid Point Patience (MD)
April 14	British reoccupy Tangier Island (VA)	June 26	Second Battle of St. Leonard Creek (MD)
April 18	British raid Carter Creek (VA)	July	British raid Trent Hall (MD)
April 22	British raid Carter Creek (VA)	July	British raid on Lower Cedar Point repulsed (MD)
April 23	British raid near Windmill Point repulsed (VA)	July 1	President James Madison convenes emergency meeting of cabinet to discuss defenses and appoints Brig. Gen. William Winder as commander of the newly formed 10th Military District (DC)
April 25	Vice Adm. Sir Alexander F. I. Cochrane issues proclamation to blockade U.S. coast from Maine to Louisiana		
spring	British raid Smith Island (VA)	July 2	British raid St. Leonard Town (MD)
April–May	British raid Potomac River (MD/VA)	July 4	British raid St. Jerome Creek (MD)
May 19	British attack vessel on Big Annemessex River repulsed	July 11	British raid at Worton Creek repulsed (MD)
		July 12	British raid at Elk Landing repulsed (MD)
May 30	Skirmish at mouth of Onancock Creek (VA)	July 14	British burn lighthouse at Smith Point (MD)
May 30	Battle of Pungoteague Creek (VA)	July 16	British raid Calverton (MD)
summer	British raid Smith Island (MD)	July 16–17	British raid Sheridan Point (MD)
summer	British occupy St. Clement's (Blackistone) Island (MD)	July 17	British raid Cedar Point (MD)
		July 17	British raid Gods Grace (MD)
summer	British raid Bryantown (MD)	July 17	British raid Huntingtown (MD)
June 1	British raid St. Jerome Creek (MD)	July 19	British land at Newtown and raid Leonardtown (MD)
June 1	Naval skirmish off Cedar Point (MD)	July 19	British raid Prince Frederick (MD)
		July 20	British damage Taney Place at Battle Creek (MD)
		July 20	Fearing British attack, residents of Port Tobacco flee (MD)

July 20–21	British raid Nomini Creek (VA)
July 21	British raid Hallowing Point (MD)
July 23	British raid St. Clement Bay (MD)
July 26	British raid Lower Machodoc Creek (VA)
July 29	British land at Hamburg (MD)
July 30	British raid Chapitco (MD)
August 1	British raid at Dares Landing repulsed (MD)
August 2	British raid Slaughter Creek (MD)
August 2	British reinforcements enter Chesapeake Bay
August 3	Skirmish at Mundy Point and Kinsale (VA)
August 3	British raid at Cherry Point repulsed (VA)
August 7	British raid Coan River (MD)
August 11–12	British raid St. Marys River and burn Great Mills cloth factory (MD)
August 13	British raid Carroll Plantation (MD)
August 16	British reinforcements under Rear Adm. P. Malcolm rendezvous with Rear Adm. George Cockburn's ships off mouth of Potomac River
August 18	British raid Eastern Bay (MD)
August 19	British raid St. Leonard Town (MD)
August 19–20	British troops occupy Benedict and march to Washington (MD)
August 20	British raid Rock Hall and Swan Creek (MD)
August 21	Secretary of State James Monroe joins the American troops at their encampment at Woodyard (MD)
August 21	Skirmish at Nottingham (MD)
August 21	British raid Hollowing Point (MD)
August 22	Skirmish near Bellefields (MD)
August 22	British raid Woodlawn on Lyons Creek (MD)
August 22	Skirmish at Pig Point (MD)
August 22	U.S. Chesapeake Flotilla scuttled in Patuxent River (MD)
August 22–23	British occupy Upper Marlboro (MD)
August 24	British occupy Mount Calvert (MD)
August 24	Battle of Bladensburg (MD)
August 24	British burn schooner *Lion* on Bodkin Creek (MD)
August 24	U.S. forces burn Washington Navy Yard and two U.S. ships (DC)
August 24–25	British occupy Washington after brief skirmish at Sewall-Belmont House and burn public buildings (DC)
August 26	Brig. Gen. William H. Winder tries unsuccessfully to regroup forces at Montgomery Court House (MD)
August 26–27	Brookeville becomes temporary seat of national government from about 6:00 p.m., August 26, to about noon, August 27 (MD)
August 26–27	British occupy Upper Marlboro (MD)

August 27	Baltimore Capt. Thomas Boyle of U.S. privateer *Chasseur* proclaims mock blockade of Great Britain and Ireland
August 27	U.S. forces destroy Fort Washington (MD)
August 27	British raid St. Clements Bay (MD)
August 27	Skirmish at Porto Bello (MD)
August 28	British raid Fairlee Creek (MD)
August 28?	British fire rockets at Mount Welby (MD)
August 28	Alexandria capitulates to British (VA)
August 29–30	British forces re-embark ships at Benedict (MD)
August 30	British raid Fairlee Creek (MD)
August 31	Battle of Caulks Field (MD)
August 31	American troops at Montgomery Court House (Rockville) ordered to Baltimore (MD)
fall	British sink several fishing boats in Breton Bay (MD)
Sept. 2–18	British loot Drum Point (MD)
Sept. 3	British raid Maj. Joseph Mitchell's house at Tolchester Beach (MD)
Sept. 2–5	Battle at White House (VA)
Sept. 5	Skirmish at Indian Head (MD)
Sept. 12	British land at North Point and march on Baltimore (MD)
Sept. 12	British burn Todd House at North Point (MD)
Sept. 12	Maj. Gen. Robert Ross killed during skirmish at North Point (MD)
Sept. 12	Battle of North Point (MD)
Sept. 12	British bombard Sollers' house at Sollers Point (MD)
Sept. 13	British raid Sollers' house at Sollers Point (MD)
Sept. 13–14	British bombard Fort McHenry (MD)
Sept. 14	British launch flanking attack on Fort McHenry (MD)
Sept. 14	British army withdraws from Baltimore (MD)
Sept. 14	Francis Scott Key writes "Defence of Fort M'Henry" later known as "The Star-Spangled Banner" (MD)
Sept. 15–16	British army re-embarks at North Point (MD)
Sept. 16	American flag-of-truce vessel *President* arrives at Hughes Wharf, Fells Point, with Francis Scott Key and his poem "Defence of M'Henry" (MD)
Sept. 16–17	British fleet withdraws down the Patapsco River to Chesapeake Bay (MD)
Sept. 17	Francis Scott Key's poem "Defense of Fort M'Henry" is printed as a handbill by Baltimore *American* (MD)
Sept. 18–19	British fleet anchors under protection of Drum Point (MD)

Sept. 20	Francis Scott Key's poem "Defense of Fort M'Henry" is printed for first time in a newspaper (Baltimore *Patriot & Evening Advertiser*)
Sept. 27	British raid St. Marys River area (MD)
October	British occupy Tilghman Island (MD)
Oct.–Nov.	British fleet patrols between Patuxent and Choptank rivers
Oct. 4–5	British land simultaneously at Nomini Bay, Ragged Point, Mundy Point (Yeocomico River), and Black Point (Coan River) and attack Northumberland Court House near Rowes Landing (VA)
Oct. 7	British raid Dividing Creek (VA)
Oct. 19	British raid Castle Haven (MD)
Oct. 19	Bulk of British fleet departs Chesapeake Bay for Gulf of Mexico
Oct. 25	British occupy Tilghman Island (MD)
Oct. 27	Skirmish at Tracys Landing (MD)
Oct. 31	British raid St. Inigoes (MD)
Oct. 31	British raid at Kirbys Wind Mill repulsed (MD)
Nov. 2	British naval force enters the Rappahannock River (VA)
Nov. 6	British barges capture American schooner *Franklin* near Hampton (VA)
Nov. 11	British capture American sloop *Messenger* near Pooles Island (MD)
Dec. 2	British raid Tappahannock (VA)
Dec. 6	Skirmish at Farnham Church (VA)
Dec. 7	Skirmish at Jones Point on Rappahannock River (VA)

Dec. 13	British abandon base on Tangier Island (VA)
Dec. 24	United States and Great Britain sign Treaty of Ghent in what today is Belgium
Dec. 27	Great Britain ratifies Treaty of Ghent

1815

January	British evacuate St. George Island (MD)
Jan. 12	British raid Lakes Cove (MD)
Feb. 6	British raid Madison (Tobacco Stick) (MD)
Feb. 7	Battle of the Ice Mound off James Island (MD)
Feb. 13	News of Treaty of Ghent reaches Annapolis (MD) and Washington (DC)
Feb. 14	Official copy of Treaty of Ghent reaches Washington (DC)
Feb. 15	Baltimore celebrates peace with a "general illumination" (lighting of the city) (MD)
Feb. 16	U.S. Senate unanimously approves Treaty of Ghent (DC)
Feb. 16	President James Madison ratifies Treaty of Ghent (DC)
Feb. 17	United States and Great Britain exchange ratifications of Treaty of Ghent (treaty becomes binding)
March 10	Last British warship, H.M. frigate *Orlando,* leaves the Chesapeake
March 28	News of Peace reaches London (GB)

This appendix is a compendium of all military actions, war-related incidents, and defense preparations in the Chesapeake region during the War of 1812. We have included battles, skirmishes, raids, and capitulations; the construction or improvement of forts and earthworks; the use of booms, chains, and sunken vessels for defense; and the launching of fire-vessels and torpedoes.

There is no universally accepted definition of a battle, skirmish, or raid. A battle is generally understood to be a large-scale engagement. A skirmish is a brief and usually disorderly kind of combat waged by small parties that are detached from the main body of troops. A raid is an offensive operation into enemy territory in which the attacker does not intend to hold the objective once it is taken. Raids can be on a small (tactical) scale for the purpose of capturing prisoners, knocking out enemy gun positions, or securing food or other supplies. A raid might also be designed to disrupt an enemy attack before it starts, in which case it is known as a "spoiling attack." Raids are typically unexpected and often meet with little or no resistance.

All of these distinctions, however, are arbitrary, and are not universally accepted. Local tradition may well pin any of these labels on a particular action without regard to logic or consistency. For the purposes of this study, we have defined a battle as any military engagement that involved at least a hundred men on each side and a skirmish as any engagement that involved fewer than a hundred men on either side. We have labeled any sudden military descent into enemy territory that meets with no resistance a raid. If there is resistance, then we have classified it as a battle or skirmish.

By our definition, there were 162 military actions in the Chesapeake region: 11 battles (7 in Maryland and 4 in Virginia), 64 skirmishes (31 in Maryland, 32 in Virginia, and 1 in the District of Columbia), and 87 raids (66 in Maryland and 21 in Virginia). Of the 162 actions, 104 took place in Maryland, 57 in Virginia, and 1 in the District of Columbia. There were also at least 39 military encampments (20 in Maryland, 15 in Virginia, and 4 in the District of Columbia).

We have also identified a number of other war-related incidents that we have included here. Two towns capitulated to the British rather than risk looting or destruction. To defend the region, 64 fortifications were established: 9 masonry forts and 59 earthworks. The earthworks ranged in size from small batteries mounting a single gun to elaborate trenches and redoubts over a mile long. Of the masonry forts, 5 were in Maryland and 4 in Virginia; and of the 59 earthworks, 42 were in Maryland, 14 in Virginia, and 3 in the District of Columbia. Some forts, such as Fort Powhatan, were brick lined inside and earthen covered outside.

To prevent the Royal Navy from sailing into navigable waterways, booms (floating devices) and chains were deployed in six places (five in Maryland and one in Virginia); and merchant ships were sunk in three (two in Maryland and one in Virginia). Fire-vessels were launched against British squadrons twice (both times in Maryland), and on two other occasions torpedoes (water mines) were launched against British ships (once in Maryland and once in Virginia).

While we might have missed some minor war-related actions or incidents, we believe that our list is more comprehensive than any ever assembled.

BATTLES

Maryland (7)

Battle for Baltimore
    Battle of North Point, September 12, 1814
    Bombardment of Fort McHenry, September 13–14, 1814
Battle of Bladensburg, August 24, 1814
Battle of Caulks Field, August 31, 1814
First Battle of St. Leonard Creek, June 10, 1814
Second Battle of St. Leonard Creek, June 26, 1814
Battle of St. Michaels, August 26, 1813[1]

Virginia (4)

Battle of Craney Island, June 22, 1813
Battle of Hampton, June 25, 1813
Battle of Pungoteague, May 30, 1814
Battle of White House, September 3–6, 1814

Skirmishes

Maryland (31)

Bellefields, August 22, 1814
Benedict, June 21, 1814
Big Annemessex River, May 19, 1814
Cedar Point, June 1, 1814
Dares Beach, August 1, 1814
Elk Landing, April 29, 1813
Elk Landing, July 11, 1814
Fort Washington, August 27, 1814[2]
Fredericktown/Georgetown, May 6, 1813
Frenchtown, April 29, 1813
Hall Creek, June 16, 1814
Hollands Cliffs, June 17, 1814
Havre de Grace, May 3, 1813
Indian Head, September 5–6, 1814
James Island (Battle of the Ice Mound), February 7, 1815
Kirbys Wind Mill, October 31, 1814[3]
Lakes Cove, January 12, 1815
Lower Cedar Point, July 1814
Nottingham, August 21, 1814
Pig Point, August 22, 1814
Point Lookout, late spring, 1813
Porto Bello, August 27, 1814
Queenstown (Battle of Slippery Hill), August 13, 1813[4]
St. Inigoes Creek, November 5, 1813
St. Leonard Creek, June 8–9, 1814[5]
St. Michaels, August 10, 1813
Still Pond, April 24?, 1813
Tracys Landing, October 27, 1814
Wicomico River, April 9, 1814
Woodland Point, July 16, 1813[6]
Worton Creek, July 11, 1814

Virginia (32)

Burwell Bay, James River, July 2, 1813
Cape Henry, July 14, 1813
Cape Henry, December 20, 1813[7]
Carter Creek, April 22, 1814
Cherrystone Inlet, March 9, 1813
Cherrystone Inlet, September 21, 1813
Chesconessex, June 25, 1814

Chowning Point, Carter Creek, April 4, 1813
Coan River, August 7, 1814
Coan River, October 4, 1814
Farnham Church, December 6, 1814
Gwynn Island, March 10, 1813
Hampton, November 6, 1814[8]
Jones Point, December 7, 1814
Kinsale, August 3, 1814
Lawnes Creek, July 6, 1813
Lynnhaven Bay, February 8, 1813[9]
Lynnhaven Bay area, October 1813[10]
Mattox Creek, July 19, 1813
Munday Point, August 3, 1814
Nomini, July 21, 1814
Norfolk, March 20, 1813[11]
Norfolk, June 20, 1813[12]
Northumberland Court House, October 4–5, 1814
Onancock, May 30, 1814
Pagan Creek, June 26, 1813
Rappahannock River, April 3, 1813[13]
Rosier Creek, July 18, 1813
Tappahannock, December 2, 1814[14]
Windmill Point, April 23, 1814
Yeocomico River, July 14, 1813[15]
York River, June 12, 1813[16]

District of Columbia (1)

Sewall-Belmont House, August 24, 1814

Raids

Maryland (66)

Bell's Ferry, May 3, 1813
Benedict, June 15, 1814
Bodkin Creek, August 24, 1814
Brenton Bay, fall 1814
Broomes Island, June 12, 1814
Bryantown, summer 1814
Calverton, July 19, 1814
Carroll Plantation, August 13, 1814
Castle Haven, October 19, 1814
Cedar Point, June 3, 1814
Cedar Point, July 17, 1814
Chaptico, July 30, 1814
Coles Landing, June 18, 1814
Cove Point, June 1, 1814
Drum Point, September 2–18, 1814[17]
Eastern Bay, August 18, 1814
Fairlee Creek, Skidmore, and Waller Farm, August 28, 1814

Fairlee Creek, Great Oak Manor, August 30, 1814
Gods Grace Plantation, July 17, 1814
Great Mills, August 12, 1814
Hallowing Point, July 21, 1814
Harris Creek, Talbot County, August 26, 1813[18]
Howell Point, late April 1813[19]
Huntingtown, July 17, 1814
Leonardtown, July 19, 1814[20]
Little Annemessex River, April 7, 1814
Lower Marlboro, June 16–17, 1814
Madison (Tobacco Stick), February 6, 1815
Magruders Landing, June 17, 1814
Mitchell house, Kent County, September 3, 1814
Mount Welby, August 28?, 1814[21]
Patuxent River, spring 1813[22]
Point Patience, June 26, 1814
Pooles Island, April 24, 1813
Poplar Island, April 18–19, 1813
Prince Frederick, July 19, 1814
Principio Iron Works, May 3, 1813
Rock Hall, August 20, 1814
Rousby Hall, June 9, 1814
St. Clement Bay, July 23, 1814
St. Clement Bay, August 27, 1814
St. Clement Island, November 2, 1813
St. George Island, November 1–9, 1813
St. Inigoes Manor, October 30, 1814
St. Jerome Creek, July 4, 1813
St. Jerome Creek, June 1, 1814
St. Leonard Creek, June 11, 1814
St. Leonard Town, July 2, 1814
St. Leonard Town, August 19, 1814
St. Marys River, August 11–12, 1814
St. Marys River, September 27, 1814
Sharps Island, April 12, 1813
Sharps Island, April 16, 1813
Sheridan Point, July 22, 1814
Slaughter Creek, August 2, 1814
Smith Island, summer 1814
Sollers Point, September 12 or 13, 1814
Sotterley, June 14, 1814
Spesutie Island, April 23, 1813
Taney Place, July 20, 1814
Todd House, September 12, 1814
Trent Hall, July 1814
Turners Creek, May 5, 1813
Wicomico River, March 1814
Woodlawn, August 22, 1814
Worton Creek, April 27, 1813

Virginia (21)

Cape Charles, March 10, 1813
Cape Henry lighthouse, February 14, 1813
Cape Henry area, June 15, 1813
Carter Creek, April 18, 1814
Cherrystone Inlet, March 9, 1813
Corotoman Plantation, April 4, 1814
Dividing Creek, October 7, 1814
Hollis's Marsh, July 21, 1813
James River, July 1813[23]
Lower Machodoc Creek, July 26, 1814
Lynnhaven Bay, February 8, 1813[24]
Mount Pleasant, June 29, 1813
New Point Comfort, March 17, 1814
Nomini, July 20–21, 1814
Nomini Bay, October 4, 1814
Pleasure House, September 21, 1813
Poplar Hall, Broad Creek, 1813
Smith Island, spring 1814
Smith Point, July 14, 1814
Tangier Island, April 8, 1814
Yeocomico Creek, July 14, 1813[25]

ENCAMPMENTS

Maryland (20)

Belle Chance (Andrews Air Force Base)
Benedict
Camp Eagleston
Camp Lookout
Caulks Field
Ellicott City
Fairfield (Baltimore)
Gaithersburg
Kent Island (Belle Vue)
Largo
Long Old Fields
Lowdnes Hill
Montgomery Court House (Rockville)
Nottingham
Piscataway
St. Leonard Town (plus Fort Hill)
Snell's Bridge
Snowden's
Upper Marlboro
Woodyard

Virginia (15)

Camp Bottom's Bridge

Camp Carter
Camp Chesconessex
Camp Holly Springs
Camp Fairfield
Camp Malvern Hill
Camp Mims
Camp Mitchell
Little England Farm
Macclesfield
Onancock
Pungoteague
Rosier Creek
Shooters' Hill
Tangier Island

District of Columbia (4)

British Reserve Camp (Old Circus Grounds)
Lafayette Square
Mason's Island
Tenelytown

CAPITULATIONS

Maryland (1)

Charlestown, May 6, 1813

Virginia (1)

Alexandria, August 28, 1814

FORTS (MASONRY)

Maryland (5)

Fort Covington, Baltimore
Fort McHenry, Baltimore
Fort Madison, Annapolis
Fort Severn, Annapolis
Fort Washington, Potomac River[26]

Virginia (4)

Blockhouse, Craney Island, Elizabeth River
Fort Norfolk, Norfolk
Fort Nelson, Portsmouth
Fort Powhatan, James River

ENTRENCHMENTS AND BATTERIES

Maryland (42)

Blakeford, Queenstown
Charlestown, North East River

Chestertown, Chester River
Creswell, Port Deposit, Susquehanna River
Federal Hill, Baltimore
Ferry Point Redoubt, Baltimore
Fort Babcock, Baltimore
Fort Defiance, Elk River
Fort Duffy, Fredericktown, Sassafras River
Fort Frederick, Elk River
Fort Hill, St. Leonard Creek
Fort Hollingsworth, Elk River
Fort Horn, Annapolis, Severn River
Fort McHenry water batter, Patapsco River
Fort Nonsense, Annapolis, Severn River
Fort Point, Centreville, Corsica River
Fort Stokes, Easton, Tred Avon River
Fort Washington water battery, Potomac River
Fort Wood, Baltimore
Frenchtown, Elk River[27]
Gamble's Redoubt (Bastion No. 4), Baltimore
Havre de Grace
    Concord Point, mouth of Susquehanna River
    Potato Battery, near mouth of Susquehanna River
Kent Narrows[28]
Lazaretto Gun Battery, Baltimore
Lowndes Hill, Bladensburg
North Point
Unfinished lower earthworks, narrows between Humphry
    Creek and Back River
Upper earthworks, narrows between Bear Creek and
    Back River
Parrott Point, St. Michaels[29]
Pearce Point Fort, Georgetown, Sassafras River
Pooles Island, Chesapeake Bay
Principio Iron Works, Furnace Bay
Ramage's Redoubt, Baltimore
Rodgers's Bastion (Bastion No. 5 or de la Roche's
    Redoubt), Baltimore
St. Leonard Lower Battery, St. Leonard Creek
St. Leonard Upper Battery, St. Leonard Creek
Salter's Redoubt, Baltimore
Spring Gardens Battery, Baltimore
Stiles's Redoubt, Baltimore
Tracys Landing, Herring Bay[30]
Unnamed redoubts at north end of defensive line,
    Baltimore[31]
Vienna, Nanticoke River

Virginia (14)

Chesconessex, Pocomoke Sound
Coan River

Craney Island, mouth of Elizabeth River
Fort Albion, Tangier
Fort Barbour, Norfolk
Fort Boykin, James River
Fort Tar, Norfolk
Gosport Navy Yard, Portsmouth
    Battery inside yard
    Breastwork outside yard
Hampton
    Large Battery, mouth of Salters Creek, Hampton Creek
    Small Battery, mouth of Sunset Creek, Hampton Creek
Unnamed battery, Rappahannock River below
    Fredericksburg[32]
Yeocomico River
    Mundy Point
    Thicket Point

District of Columbia (3)

Barney Battery, Anacostia River[33]
Greenleaf Point, Anacostia River
Windmill Point, Anacostia River

BOOMS AND CHAINS

Maryland (5)

From Fort McHenry to Lazaretto Point, Baltimore
From Ferry Point to Moale's Point, Baltimore[34]
Across Elk River, Fort Frederick[35]
Across St. Leonard Creek, Fort Hill
Across entrance to St. Michaels harbor

Virginia (1)

At Gosport Navy Yard, Portsmouth[36]

SUNKEN VESSEL DEFENSES

Maryland (3)

Between Fort McHenry and Lazaretto Point, Baltimore
Between Fort McHenry and Cromwells Marsh, Baltimore[37]
Elk River channel at Fort Frederick

Virginia (1)

In Elizabeth River, Norfolk

FIRE-VESSELS

Maryland (2)

White House, Potomac River, September 4, 1814
White House, Potomac River, September 5, 1814

TORPEDOES (WATER MINES)

Maryland (1)

White House, Potomac River, September 5, 1814

Virginia (1)

Torpedo attack, Cape Henry, July 24, 1813

Introduction

1. To our knowledge, no other region of the United States or Canada has been so extensively examined as has the Chesapeake. Additional survey work, especially in the Great Lakes states such as New York, will doubtless reveal previously unknown sites. However, we still believe the Chesapeake in general and Maryland in particular sustained more raids, skirmishes, and battles than any other comparable region in the nation. This was because the British targeted the region for almost two full years (including the winter months) and explicitly wanted to bring the war home to people living in the Chesapeake. In the 1990s, the American Battlefield Protection Program employed local experts to conduct a state-by-state inventory of War of 1812 battle sites. This survey found a total of 78 significant engagements: 15 in Alabama, 13 in New York, 11 in Maryland, 7 in Louisiana, 6 in Michigan, 5 in Maine and Ohio, 4 in Virginia and Indiana, 2 in Florida and Illinois, and one each in the District of Columbia, Georgia, Iowa, and Wisconsin. In our more detailed study of the Chesapeake, we found 162 military actions: 11 battles, 64 skirmishes, and 87 raids. Of the 162 actions, 104 took place in Maryland, 57 in Virginia, and one in Washington, D.C. We know of no other theater that comes close to this magnitude of action. Until such time that the other War of 1812 theaters of war are as extensively studied and their numbers prove otherwise, we stand by our claim that the Chesapeake, and Maryland in particular, suffered more military activity during the War of 1812 than any other region or state in the Union.

2. Figures based on conversion tables in Samuel H. Williamson, "Five Ways to Compute the Relative Value of a U.S. Dollar Amount, 1790–2005, at www. measuringworth.com.

Chapter 2. Warfare in the Chesapeake

1. *Niles' Weekly Register* 4 (May 15, 1813), 182; 7 (October 27, 1814), 110; (Supplement), 158.

2. Journal of Charles Napier, August 12, 1813, in William F. P. Napier, *The Life and Opinions of General Sir Charles James Napier*, 4 vols. (London, 1857), 1:221.

3. James Scott, *Recollections of a Naval Life,* 3 vols. (London, 1934), 3:314–15.

4. Niles to [U.S. Claims Commission?], January 28, 1827, in Collections of Fort McHenry National Monument, microfilm edition, reel 62.

5. *Niles' Weekly Register* 6 (June 25, 1814), 279.

Chapter 3. Maryland Sites

1. There was an earlier gunpowder mill established in 1791 on Gwynns Falls that received government orders for gunpowder in 1812. This mill suffered a major fire on September 17, 1812. William Lorman, head operator of the mill, in a letter dated September 26, 1812, to E. I. du Pont, wrote, "I believe it did not originate from design." Du Pont, fearing the fire might have been set by a British sympathizer, was relieved. He feared his own works near Wilmington, Delaware, might be targeted by arsonists. See Arlan K. Gilbert, "Gunpowder Products in Post-Revolutionary Maryland," *Maryland Historical Magazine* 52 (1957): 192.

2. Walter Lowrie and Matthew St. Clair Clarke, eds., *American State Papers, Documents, Legislative and Executive, of the Congress of The United States, From The First Session Of The First To The Second Session Of The Fifteenth Congress, Inclusive: Commencing March 3, 1789, and Ending March 3, 1819* (Washington: Gales and Seaton, 1832), 543.

3. Indiana University, Lilly Library, Bloomington, Indiana, War of 1812 manuscripts.

4. National Library of Scotland (NLS), Edinburgh, Alexander F. I. Cochrane Papers, MS 2333, fols. 173–78.

5. Robert J. Barrett, "Naval Recollections of the Late American War, No. 1," *United Service Journal* (April 1841): 461.

6. NLS, Alexander F. I. Cochrane Papers, MS 2329, fol. 17.

7. Maryland Historical Society (MHS), Baltimore, Winder Family Letters, MS 919.

8. Lowrie and Clark, *American State Papers,* 544.

9. Lowrie and Clark, *American State Papers,* 544.

10. Probably Capt. Thomas W. Warner, 1st Baltimore Volunteers, 39th Regiment, who lost his leg during the war. This letter was from Sacket's Harbor, New York, to his wife. Five Thomas H. Warner (1780–1828) letters, including this one, are available at www.haemo-sol.com/thomas/thomas.html.

11. Fort McHenry National Monument Site and Historic

Shrine, Baltimore, research library (FMRL). This letter is also copied in Sallie A. Mallick and F. Edward Wright, *Frederick County Militia in the War of 1812* (Westminster, MD: Family Line Publications, 1992), 25. Crumbaker served in the 16th Regiment, Maryland Volunteer Infantry, Frederick County militia.

12. MHS, Hollingworth Papers, MS 1849; transcript only, location of original unknown.

13. Brown University, Providence, Rhode Island, John Hay Library (JHL), Henry Wheaton Papers, 1786–1899.

14. Library of Congress (LC), Manuscript Division, James Madison Papers, series 1, reel 17; reprinted in J. Thomas Scharf, *History of Baltimore City and County, Maryland* (Philadelphia: Louis H. Everts, 1881), 98.

15. Baltimore *Federal Republican,* June 20, 1812.

16. National Archives and Records Administration (NARA), RG45, MC, 1814, vol. 2, no. (M147, roll no. 5).

17. Boyle apparently was aware of an earlier proclamation by Paul Jones, Bunker Hill, Massachusetts, published in Baltimore *Niles' Weekly Register,* June 4, 1814, as his wording is nearly identical.

18. Massachusetts Historical Society, Boston Appleton Family Papers.

19. "Reminiscences of Captain John A. Webster to Mayor Brantz Mayer, July 22, 1853," MHS, Vertical Files, printed in William M. Marine, *The British Invasion of Maryland, 1812–1815* (Baltimore, 1914), 179.

20. William D. Hoyt, Jr., "Civilian Defense in Baltimore, 1814–1815: Minutes of the Committee of Vigilance and Safety," *Maryland Historical Magazine* 41 (1944): 295.

21. Scharf, 1881, 89.

22. JHL, Henry Wheaton (1790–1870) Papers; copies of correspondence at Fort McHenry Research Library (SC 75).

23. NARA, RG107, Letters Received by the Secretary of War, Registered Series, S-141 (8) (M221, roll no. 66), and Samuel Smith Papers, MSS 18974, Library of Congress.

24. NLS, Alexander F. I. Cochrane Papers, MS 2334, fols. 20–27.

25. FMRL, letter.

26. "Autobiography by John L. Dagg." Dagg served in the Virginia militia. His autobiography is available at www.founders. org/library/dagg-bio.html.

27. John Harris was a drummer in the U.S. Marines. He is describing the view of Fort McHenry and the British army about a mile away from his position on Hampstead Hill. MHS, MS 1846, War of 1812 Papers.

28. National Archives of the United Kingdom (NAUK), London, WO 1/141, 75–89.

29. John Thomas Scharf, *The Chronicles of Baltimore; Being A Complete History of 'Baltimore Town' and Baltimore City From The Earliest Period To The Present Time* (Baltimore: Turnbull Brothers, 1874), 781–82.

30. LOC, Rodgers Family Papers, series III-B, container 51, fols. 5562–63.

31. NARA RG217, Claims of State of Maryland Relating to War of 1812, Defense of Baltimore, Vessels Sunk in Harbor, deposition August 9, 1832.

32. NARA, RG107, Letters Received by the Secretary of War, Registered Series, S-141 (8) (M221, roll no. 66).

33. NLS, Alexander F. I. Cochrane Papers, MS 2329, fols. 41–42.

34. Scharf, 1881, 89.

35. MHS, MS 1846, War of 1812 Papers.

36. Samuel Tyler, *Memoir of Roger Brooke Taney, Chief Justice of the Supreme Court of the United States* (Baltimore: John Murphy & Co., 1872), 116.

37. John Brannan, *Official Letters of the Military and Naval Officers of the United States, during the War with Great Britain in the Years 1812, 13,14, & 15* (Washington, DC: Way & Gideon, 1823), 65.

38. NARA, RG45, Letters Received by the Secretary of Navy: Miscellaneous Letters, 1814, vol. 6, no. 57 (M124, roll no. 65).

39. Lowrie and Clarke, *American State Papers,* 555.

40. John Armstrong, *Notices of the War of 1812* (New York: Wiley & Putnam, 1840), vol. II, appendix no. 29, 234.

41. Gleig quote in C. R. B. Barrett, ed., *The 85th King's Light Infantry (Now 2nd Battn, The King's Shropshire Light Infantry) by "One of Them"* (London: Spottiswoode & Co. Ltd, 1913), 137.

42. *American State Papers,* Public Lands, December 8, 1835, to February 28, 1837, vol. 8, no. 1463, 532–33.

43. Washington *Daily National Intelligencer,* June 30, 1814, also carried an ad by Benjamin Oden but the reward was only for $20; the date on the ad (not the newspaper) is April 25, suggesting Oden later upped the reward.

44. NLS, Alexander F. I. Cochrane Papers, MS 2333, fols. 106–10.

45. LC, Papers of George Cockburn, container 14, vol. 38, Letters Received 1812–1815, fols. 341–43.

46. Quote in Edward S. Delaplaine, *Francis Scott Key: Life and Times* (New York: Biography Press, 1937), 130. Delaplaine does not give source.

47. NAUK, Adm. 1/4260, fols. 133–34.

48. Historical Society of Pennsylvania, Philadelphia, Papers of Joshua Barney. Letter book copy at NARA, RG45, CLS, 1814, 182.

49. LC, Manuscript Division; copy at Calvert Marine Museum library, Solomons, Maryland.

50. [George Robert Gleig], *Subaltern In America; Comprising His Narrative of the Campaigns of the British Army, at Baltimore, Washington, &c., &c., During the Late War* (Philadelphia: E. L. Carey & A. Hart, 1833), 7–8.

51. Gleig, 1833, 10–11.

52. [George Robert Gleig], *A Narrative Of The Campaigns of the British Army At Washington And New Orleans, Under Generals Ross, Pakenham, And Lambert, In The Years 1814 and 1815; With Some Account Of The Countries Visited. By An Officer Who Served In The Expedition* (London: John Murray, 1821), 93–94.

53. NAUK, Adm. 51.

54. National Maritime Museum, London, Papers of Sir Edward Codrington, COD/6/4.

55. NAUK, Adm. 51.

56. LC, Manuscript Division, James Madison Papers.

57. George Robert Gleig, *The Campaigns of the British Army at Washington and New Orleans* (E. Ardsley, Eng.: E. P. Publ. Ltd., 1972, reprint of 1847 ed.), 115. This view can be best seen at Bladensburg Waterfront Park.

58. Gleig, 1821, 153.

59. *A Narrative of the Life and Adventures of Charles Ball, A Black Man* (Lewistown, PA: John W. Shugert, 1836), reprinted in Yuval Taylor, ed., *I Was Born a Slave: An Anthology of Classic Slave Narrative*, vol. I, *1770–1849* (Chicago: Lawrence Hill Books, 1999). Ball, apparently an alias, was a former slave who joined the U.S. Chesapeake Flotilla and helped man one of the cannons in Barney's battery. Ball, who had lived at the Washington Navy Yard with a previous owner, later worked at a fishing camp at the mouth of the Patuxent River that was raided by the British in 1813. Still later, he served against the British in the Baltimore campaign.

60. MHS, MS 919, William H. Winder Papers.

61. NAUK, Adm. 1/506, fols. 606–13.

62. Letter reprinted in Barrett, 1913, 153.

63. Historical Society of Pennsylvania, Philadelphia, William Jones Papers, Clarke Smith Collection, 1378A.

64. J. Woods to unknown correspondent in England, February 4, 1836. Copy of letter in archives of Prince George's County Historical Society, Glenn Dale, Maryland.

65. Lt. Col. Harry Smith, of the 20th Foot, wrote an autobiography, circa 1824, reprinted as G. C. Moore-Smith, ed., *The Autobiography of Lieut. General Sir Harry Smith,* 2 vols. (London: John Murray, 1902).

66. Gleig, 1847, 78.

67. Letter written by officer in Lt. Col. Frisby Tilghman's 1st District Cavalry, written from Montgomery Court House to his friend in Hagerstown. Quote in John Thomas Scharf, *History of Western Maryland. Being A History of Frederick, Montgomery, Carroll, Washington, Allegany, and Garrett Counties From the Earliest Period to the Present Day; Including Biographical Sketches of Their Representative Men,* vol. 1 (Baltimore: Regional Publishing Company, 1968), 189–90.

68. James Scott, *Recollections of a Naval Life,* 3 vols. (London: Richard Bentley, 1834), 3:314.

69. NAUK, WO 1/141, 31–38.

70. "General Stansbury's Report" Documents Accompanying the Report of the Committee Appointed on the Twenty-Third of September Last, to Inquire into the Causes and Particulars of the Invasion of The City of Washington, by the British Forces in the Month of August, 1814 (Washington, DC: A. and G. Way, Printers, 1814), 24.

71. Gleig diary quote in Barrett, 1913, 138.

72. NARA, RG45, Letters Received by the Secretary of Navy: Miscellaneous Letter, 1814, vol. 6, no. 57 (M124, roll no. 65).

73. Henry T. Tuckerman,, *The Life of John Pendleton Kennedy* (New York: G. P. Putman's Sons, 1871), 77–78. Kennedy marched, fought, and during the retreat carried his wounded friend James McCulloch on his back to safety, all while wearing his pumps.

74. Lowrie and Clark, *American State Papers,* 572.

75. Quote in "The Battle of Bladensburg," *Maryland Historical Magazine* 5 (1910): 344.

76. Gleig, 1847, 79.

77. Elkton *Cecil Whig,* September 11, 1991.

78. NARA, RG107, Letters Received by the Secretary of War, Unregistered Series, S-1814 (M222, roll no. 14).

79. Quote from Gaillard Hunt, ed., *The First Forty Years of Washington Society* (New York: Charles Scribner's Sons, 1906), 105.

80. Hunt, *The First Forty Years,* 100.

81. Hunt, *The First Forty Years,* 104.

82. Hunt, *The First Forty Years,* 107.

83. Norman Harrington, *Easton Album* (Easton, MD: Historical Society of Talbot County, 1986), 57–59.

84. NLS, Alexander F. I. Cochrane Papers, MS 2329, fols. 30–31.

85. Baltimore *Niles' Weekly Register,* Supplement to vol. 7, 151–52.

86. Frederick Chamier, *The Life of A Sailor* (London: Richard Bentley, 1850), 185.

87. NLS, Alexander F. I. Cochrane Papers, MS 2333, fols. 98–99.

88. NARA, RG45, Letters Received by the Secretary of Navy: Miscellaneous Letter, 1814, vol. 4, no. 86 (M124, roll no. 63).

89. NARA, RG45, Letters Received by the Secretary of Navy: Miscellaneous Letter, 1814, vol. 4, no. 86 (M124, roll no. 64).

90. NAUK, Adm. 1/507, fols. 110–11.

91. Peter Rowley, "Captain Robert Rowley Helps to Burn Washington, DC," *Maryland Historical Magazine* 82 (1987): 245–46.

92. Brannan, *Official Letters,* 449–50.

93. Baltimore *Niles' Weekly Register,* April 28, 1814.

94. NAUK, Adm. 1/503, fols. 679–85.

95. The British prisoners are almost certainly those captured during a skirmish at Benedict, June 20, 1814.

96. Pennsylvania Historical Society, Welma Clarke Smith Collection, William Jones Papers.

97. Gleig, 1847, 63.

98. NLS, Cochrane Papers, MS 2333, fols. 98–99; also copy in NAUK, Adm. 1/507, fols. 74–75.

99. LC, Papers of George Cockburn, MSS 17575, containers 14–15, reel 9.

100. LC, Papers of George Cockburn, container 14, vol. 38, fols. 372–74, reel 9.

101. NARA, RG45, MLR, 1814, vol. 3, no. 40 (M124, roll no. 62).

102. NARA, RG45, Letters Sent by the Secretary of Navy to Officers, vol. 11, p. 394 (M149, roll no. 11).

103. *A Narrative of the Life and Adventures of Charles Ball, A Black Man.*

104. NAUK, Adm. 51.

105. University of Michigan, William L. Clements Library, Ann Arbor, Michigan, Robert Barrie Papers.

106. Gleig, 1847, 109.

107. National Maritime Museum, London, Papers of Sir Edward Codrington, COD/6/4.

108. NLS, Alexander F. I. Cochrane Papers, MS 2329, fols. 15–16.

109. Quote in Norman Harrington, *Easton Album* (Easton, MD: Historical Society of Talbot County, 1986), 43.

110. LC, Samuel Smith Papers, MSS 18974.

111. MHS, Forman Papers, MSS 403, 1732–1908.

112. NLS, Alexander F. I. Cochrane Papers, MS 2333, fols. 173–78.

113. The poem placed on the ox has been attributed to George Ricketts of Elkton.

114. Lowrie and Clark, *American State Papers,* 571.

115. Columbia University, Samuel Smith Papers. Lt. Col. Minor commanded the 60th Virginia Regiment, Fairfax County.

116. Western Reserve Historical Society (WRHS), Cleveland, Ohio, MS 1236 Microfilm Cabinet 40, Drawer 8. Journal kept during the years 1813–14 aboard H.M. frigate *Menelaus* by Lt. Benjamin G. Benyon, RM.

117. Fort McHenry National Monument, NPS—Historical and Archeological Research Project (HARP), Research Library, Special Collections No. 87, original letter.

118. WRHS, MS 1236 Microfilm Cabinet 40, Drawer 8. Journal Kept During the Years 1813–14 aboard H.M. frigate *Menelaus* by Lt. Benjamin G. Benyon, RM.

119. Walter Lord, *The Dawn's Early Light* (New York: W. W. Norton & Co., 1972), 274. This quote has not been found within the Samuel Smith Papers at Library of Congress, University of Virginia or Columbia University.

120. Gleig, 1833, 157.

121. James Wilkinson, *Memoirs of My Own Times,* 4 vols. (Philadelphia: Abraham Small, 1816).

122. LC, Joseph H. Nicholson Papers.

123. James Stevens (1776–1859) to Mrs. Julian Pernell, Huntington County, Pennsylvania, September 29, 1814. "A Letter Describing the Attack on Fort McHenry," *Maryland Historical Magazine* 51 (1956): 356. Maryland Historical Society, MS 1846, War of 1812 Papers; copy at FMRL, Special Collection 75-014.

124. Elkton *Cecil Whig,* "Recollections" and "Reminiscences," 1872 to 1881. Judge Sample was only fourteen years old at the time of bombardment.

125. The letter was sent to the editor on September 17 and it was published on September 30. See also Scott S. Sheads, "'Yankee Doodle Played,' A Letter from Baltimore, 1814," *Maryland Historical Magazine* 76 (1981): 381–82.

126. Barrett, 1841, 464.

127. James E. Hancock, *Fort McHenry,* Baltimore, Maryland Trust Company, n.d. [1928?].

128. LC, George Washington Papers, 1741–1799: Series 4, General Correspondence 1697–1700, image 73.

129. James Wilkinson, quoted in John S. Williams, *History of the Invasion and Capture of Washington . . .* (New York: Harper & Brothers, 1857), 285.

130. NLS, Alexander F. I. Cochrane Papers, MS 2333, fols. 173–78.

131. Major General Elers Napier, *The Life and Correspondence of Admiral Sir Charles Napier, K.C.B., From Personal Recollections, Letters, and Official Documents* (London: Hurst and Blackett, Publishers, 1862), 80. This is a reprint from Napier's own account published earlier in the "Narrative of the Operations in the Potomac by the Squadron under the orders of Capt. Sir. James A. Gordon in 1814," *United Service Journal* 11 (1833): 469–80.

132. Diary entry from her home in Washington, quoted in S. A. Wallace, "Georgetown is Saved from the British," *The Social Studies* 63 (1952): 235.

133. NARA, RG45, Letters Received by the Secretary of Navy: Captain's Letters, 1814, vol. 5, no. 138 (M125, roll no. 38).

134. Quote in [James P. Wilmer], *Narrative Respecting the Conduct of the British from Their First Landing on Sepecutia Island Till Their Progress to Havre de Grace . . . By a citizen of Havre de Grace* (Baltimore: P. Mauro, 1813), 28. Quote also in Donald G. Shomette, *Lost Towns of Tidewater Maryland* (Centreville, MD: Tidewater Publishers, 2000), 281.

135. LC, Papers of George Cockburn, container 9, Letters Sent, 3 Feb. 1812–6 Feb. 1814, 171–79.

136. Lowrie and Clark, *American State Papers,* 571.

137. LC, Papers of George Cockburn, container 9, Letters Sent, 3 Feb. 1812–6 Feb. 1814, 171–79. See Fredericktown for the rest of this quotation.

138. LC, Papers of George Cockburn, container 14, vol. 38, 368–70.

139. LC, Papers of George Cockburn, container 14, vol. 38, 405–8.

140. LC, Papers of George Cockburn, container 14, vol. 38, 405–8.

141. NARA, RG45, Letters Received by the Secretary of Navy: Miscellaneous Letter, 1814, vol. 5, no. 111 (M124, roll no. 64).

142. NAUK, Adm. 1/507, fols. 119–20.

143. Chamier, 1850, 176.

144. George Huntington Williams, professor of geology, Johns Hopkins University, 1880s. Quote from John W. McGrain, *From Pig Iron to Cotton Duck: A History of Manufacturing Villages in Baltimore County* (Towson, MD: Baltimore County Heritage Publication, 1985), 328.

145. NAUK, Adm. 1/507, fols. 110–11.

146. NLS, Alexander F. I. Cochrane Papers, MS 2329, fol. 17.

147. LC, Papers of George Cockburn, container 9, Letters Sent, 3 Feb. 1812–6 Feb. 1814, 162–70.

148. *Sea Soldier. An Officer of Marines with Duncan, Nelson, Collingwood and Cockburn: The Letters and Journal of Major T. Marmaduke Wybourn, RM, 1797–1813,* ed. Anne Petrides and Jonathan Downs (Tunbridge Wells: Parapress, 2000), 183.

149. Daniel Mallory, *Short Stories and Reminiscences of the Last Fifty Years by An Old Traveller,* 2 vols. (New York: R. P. Bixby & Co., 1842), 150–52.

150. Benson J. Lossing, *The Pictorial Field-Book of the War of 1812* (New York: Harper Bros., 1868), 674.

151. Benjamin Henry Latrobe, *The Correspondence and Miscellaneous Papers of Benjamin Henry Latrobe,* ed. John C. Van Horne and Lee W. Formwalt. vol. 3, 1811–1820 (New Haven: Yale University Press, 1988).

152. [Rev. James Jones Wilmer] *Narrative Respecting the Conduct of the British from their First Landing on Spesutia Island, Till their Progress to Havre de Grace* (Baltimore: P. Mauro, 1813).

153. [Wilmer], *Narrative.*

154. Latrobe, *The Correspondence and Miscellaneous Papers of Benjamin Henry Latrobe.*

155. Latrobe, *Correspondence.*

156. LC, Papers of George Cockburn, container 14, vol. 38, Letters Received 1812–1815, fols. 368–70.

157. "Report (No. 1) concerning the Military defence of the river Potomack, the City of Washington and adjacent country: founded on a survey and investigation of prominent features of the premises, by William Tatham." Typed transcript on file, Fort Belvoir, Virginia; original NARA.

158. NARA, RG45, Letters Received by the Secretary of the Navy: Captain's Letters, 1814, vol. 6, no. 34 (M135, roll no. 39).

159. NAUK, Adm. 1/507, fols. 153–57.

160. Scott, *Recollections,* 3:160–61.

161. Chart insert, in French, on "Carte De La Baie De Chesapeake et de la Partie navigable de Riveres, James, York, Patowmack, Patuxen, Patapsco, North-East, Choptank et Pokomack . . . " This is a second edition engraved in Paris by Le Rouge, 1778, based on the 1776 chart, "A New and Accurate Chart of the Bay of Chesapeake . . . " Chart is figured in Russell Morrison, Edward C. Papenfuse, Nancy M. Bramucci, and Robert J. H. Janson-La Palme, *On the Map* (Chestertown, MD: Washington College, 1983), figure 40.

162. NARA, RG107, Letters Received by the Secretary of War, Registered Series, S-191 (8) (M221, roll no. 66).

163. NAUK, Adm. 1/507, fols. 153–57.

164. NAUK, Adm. 1/509, fol. 195.

165. St. Clements Island Potomac River Museum, Colton Point, Maryland, letter in collections. Captain Forrest served with the St. Mary's Cavalry.

166. NAUK, Adm. 1/507, fols. 101–2.

167. This newspaper account claims to be *St. Mary's Beacon,* but the earliest newspaper in Leonardtown was the *Leonard Town Herald* published in 1839 that became the *St. Mary's Beacon* in 1852. Therefore, this is apparently from a different unknown newspaper.

168. St. Clement's Island and Potomac River Museum, Colton Point, St. Mary's County, Maryland, archival collections, original document.

169. Lowrie and Clark, *American State Papers,* 536.

170. James Wilkinson, *Memoirs of My Own Times,* 4 vols. (Philadelphia: Abraham Small, 1816).

171. LC, Rodgers Family Papers, Series III-B, container 51, fols. 5534–35.

172. NARA, RG233, Report of the Navy Department in Records of the Select Committee, HR13a-D15.3. Johnson served as a colonel of a regiment of mounted Kentucky riflemen and was wounded at the Battle of the Thames on October 5, 1812.

173. NARA, RG45, Letters Received by the Secretary of Navy: Miscellaneous Letter, 1814, vol. 6, no. 47 (M124, roll no. 65).

174. Lowrie and Clark, *American State Papers,* 556.

175. Gleig, 1821, 112.

176. NARA, RG107, Letters Received by the Secretary of War, MC, S-191 (8) (M221, roll no. 66).

177. NLS, Alexander F. I. Cochrane Papers, MS 2333, fols. 106–10.

178. LC, Manuscript Division; copy at Calvert Marine Museum library, Solomons, Maryland.

179. NAUK, Adm. 1/506, fols. 602–5.

180. *A Narrative of the Life and Adventures of Charles Ball, A Black Man,* 21 and 404.

181. Scott, *Recollections,* 3:282.

182. [Obituary] " Funeral of a Distinguished Veteran," Baltimore *American,* July 9, 1877; and "Death of Capt. John A. Webster," Baltimore *American,* July 13, 1877.

183. Katherine M. Brevill, "Captain John A. Webster, Died July 4, 1877," *The Patriotic Marylander* 2 (1914): 37–40.

184. NAUK, Adm. 1/506, fols. 602–5.

185. NAUK, Adm. 1/506, fols. 606–13; enclosed in Cochrane to Croker, September 2, 1814, 226–28.

186. Prince George's County Court Records, June 25, 1814.

187. Mary Welby DuButts to her sister Millicent Welby Ridgehill of Welbourne, Lincolnshire, England, written from Mount Welby, March 18, 1815. Copies in the collections of National Colonial Farm, Mount Welby, National Park Service, Oxen Hill, Maryland; originals in Richmond Historical Society, Virginia.

188. NAUK, Adm. 1/507, fols. 153–57.

189. NAUK, WO 1/141, 75–89.

190. NARA, RG107, Letters Received by the Secretary of War, Registered Series, S-141 (8) (M221, roll no. 66).

191. NLS, Alexander F. I. Cochrane Papers, MS 2332, fols. 20–27.

192. NLS, Alexander F. I. Cochrane Papers, MS 2332, fols. 20–27.

193. Gleig, 1833, 132–33.

194. LC, Samuel Smith Papers.

195. Quote in Byron A. Lee, *The Mercers and Parkhurt* (Harwood, MD: Byron A. Lee, 1999), 56.

196. NLS, Alexander F. I. Cochrane Papers, MS 2332, fols. 20–27.

197. Scott, *Recollections,* 3:342.

198. Gleig, 1847, 102.

199. "Report on the Road to North Point" LC, Samuel Smith Papers, MSS 18974, reel 4, container 5-6.

200. "Report on the Road to North Point" LC, Samuel Smith Papers, MSS 18974, reel 4, container 5-6.

201. "Report on the Road to North Point" LC, Samuel Smith Papers, MSS 18974, reel 4, container 5-6.

202. Gleig, 1847, 57.

203. LC, Manuscript Division; copy at Calvert Marine Museum library, Solomons, Maryland.

204. Lowrie and Clark, *American State Papers,* 537.

205. "Calendar of the General Otho Holland William Papers," Maryland Historical Society, prepared by the Maryland Historical Records Survey Project Division of Professional and Service Projects, Works Projects Administration, November 1940, 353.

206. Gleig, 1847, 56,

207. NAUK, Adm. 1/506, fols. 602–5.

208. Gleig, 1821, 103–4.

209. Gleig, 1821, 144.

210. Gleig diary quote in Barrett, 1913, 154.

211. Quote in Caleb Clarke Magruder, Jr., "Dr. William Beanes, the Incidental Cause of the Authorship of the Star-Spangled Banner," *The Columbia Historical Society* 22 (1919): 219. No source given.

212. Jack D. Brown et al., *Charles County, Maryland: A History, Bicentennial Edition* (South Hackensack, NJ: Custombook, Inc., 1976), 97.

213. Gleig, 1847, 53–55.

214. NAUK, Adm. 1/506, fols. 602–5.

215. NAUK, Adm. 1/506, fols. 602–5.

216. NAUK, Adm. 1/506, fols. 602–5.

217. NAUK, Adm. 1/506, fols. 602–5.

218. Lowrie and Clark, *American State Papers,* 566.

219. Scott, *Recollections,* 3:158.

220. [Robert J. Barrett], "Recollections of the Expedition to the Chesapeake and Against New Orleans in the Years 1814–15, by an 'Ols Sub,'" *United Service Journal* (Part 1, April 1840, and Part 2, May, June, July 1840), 457.

221. NARA, RG45, MLR, 1814, vol. 5, no. 12 (M124, roll no. 64).

222. NARA, RG45, MLR, 1814, vol. 5, no. 12 (M124, roll no. 64).

223. LC, Papers of George Cockburn, container 14, vol. 38, 405–9 (reel 9).

224. For further information, see Frank J. Schwartz and James Green, "Found: One Anchor from H.M.S. Dictator," *Maryland Historical Magazine* 57 (1962): 367–70.

225. Scott, *Recollections,* 3:96.

226. Quote in Arthur Hecht, "The Post Office Department in St. Mary's County in the War of 1812," *Maryland Historical Magazine* 52 (1957): 144.

227. LC, Papers of George Cockburn, container 14, vol. 38, 368–70 (reel 9).

228. Part of this letter is reproduced in Hulbert Footner, *Sailor Of Fortune: The Life and Adventures of Commodore Barney, U.S.N.* (New York: Harper & Brothers Publishers, 1940), 276–77. Copy of the letter can be found in the Calvert Marine Museum archives, Solomons, Maryland. A copy of the letter was sent to the Maryland Academy of Sciences, Baltimore, on August 12, 1954, by Howard J. Cassidy, grandson of Thomas King. This suggests the original letter belonged to the family at that time. The location of original today is unknown.

229. LC, Papers of George Cockburn, container 9, Letters Sent, 3 Feb. 1812–6 Feb. 1814, 162–70.

230. NARA, RG45, Confidential Letters Sent by the Secretary of the Navy, 1814, 150–51.

231. NARA, RG45, MLR, 1814, vol. 8, no. 1 (M124, roll no. 67).

232. Capt. Frederick Robertson, Royal Artillery, account in H. William Nod, *The Life and Letters of Admiral Sir Charles Napier* (K.C.B. London: Hutchinson, 1917).

233. Quote in Henry C. Rhodes, *Queenstown: The Social History of a Small American Town* (Queenstown, MD: Queen Anne Press, 1985), 72–73.

234. See Frederick Emory, *Queen Anne's County, Maryland Its Early History and Development* (Queenstown, MD: Queen Ann Press, 1981), 433.

235. Hecht, "The Post Office, Department," 150.

236. Hecht, "The Post Office Department," 151.

237. Margaret L Callcott, *Mistress of Riversdale: The Plantation Letters of Rosalie Stier Calvert, 1795–1821* (Baltimore: Johns Hopkins University Press, 1991), 253.

238. Callcott, *Mistress of Riversdale,* 253.

239. Callcott, *Mistress of Riversdale,* 275. Mrs. Calvert is referring to two English officers who were wounded in the Battle of Bladensburg and stayed behind to recuperate.

240. Callcott, *Mistress of Riversdale,* 279.

241. Callcott, *Mistress of Riversdale,* 282.

242. Historical Society of Pennsylvania, Philadelphia, Clarke Smith Collection, 1378A, William Jones Papers.

243. W. Emerson Wilson, ed., *Plantation Life of Rose Hill: The Diaries of Martha Ogle Forman, 1814–1815* (Wilmington: The Historical Society of Delaware, 1976).

244. NAUK, Adm. 1/507, fols. 108–9.

245. NARA, RG107, Letters Received by the Secretary of War, Registered Series, S-191 (8) (M221, roll no. 66).

246. University of Georgetown Library, Archives of the Maryland Province of the Society of Jesus at Georgetown, Box: 58 Fold: 18 Correspondence [204 S1-9] Nov 1813; quote in Edwin W. Beitzell, *Life on the Potomac River* (Abell, MD; privately printed 1979 edition), 28.

247. NLS, Alexander F. I. Cochrane Papers, MS 2574, fols. 91–99.

248. "Journal Kept During the Years 1813–1814 aboard H.M. Frigate *Menelaus* by Lt. Benjamin G. Benyon, R.M." (Western Reserve Historical Society, Cleveland, Ohio, MS.1236 microfilm cabinet 40, drawer 8).

249. NLS, Alexander F. I. Cochrane Papers, MS 2336, fols. 25–26.

250. LC, Papers of George Cockburn, container 14, vol. 38, 502–4 (reel 9).

251. Edwin W. Beitzell, *The Jesuit Missions of St. Mary's County, Maryland* (Leonardtown, MD: St. Mary's County Historical Society, 1998), 107–10. Michael Crawford and Christine Hughes, *The Naval War of 1812: A Documentary History,* vol. 3 (Washington, DC: Naval Historical Center, 2002), 338, footnote 3, give the date of the raid as November 1, 1814, but a careful reading of the mission records, particularly correspondence by Brother Joseph P. Mobberly, from the Georgetown University Maryland Jesuit archives, confirms that the raid took place on October 31, 1814.

252. NARA, RG107, Letters Received by the Secretary of War, Unregistered Series, S-1814 (M222, roll no. 14).

253. "The Robbery of St. Inigo's House," *The American Historical Record* 2, no. 24 (1873): 557 reports that Hancock was demoted of rank and placed onboard a vessel of inferior grade. This account also states the value of damage was at least $1,800 and the amount left by Hancock for repayment was $113.

254. NARA, RG45, Letters Received by the Secretary of Navy: Miscellaneous Letter, 1814, vol. 4, no. 105 (M124, roll no. 63).

255. *A Biographical Memoir of the Late Commodore Joshua Barney: From Autographical Notes and Journals in possession of his family, and other authentic sources* (Boston: Gray and Bowen, 1832), 257–58.

256. Brannan, *Official Letters,* 340.

257. NARA, RG45, Letters Received by the Secretary of Navy: Miscellaneous Letter, 1814, vol. 4, no. 111 (M124, roll no. 63).

258. *Public Documents printed by order of The Senate of the United States, during the First Session of the Twenty-Sixth Congress begun and held At the City of Washington, December 2, 1839,* vol. V (Washington, DC: Blair and Rives, 1840), 213.

259. Copy of copy in Calvert Marine Museum archives, location of original unknown. Source of first copy is Vanirdk E. Fehr, Spout Farm, St. Leonard Creek, Calvert County.

260. NARA, RG45, Letters Received by the Secretary of Navy: Miscellaneous Letter, 1814, vol. 5, no. 12 (M124, roll no. 64).

261. NLS, Alexander F. I. Cochrane Papers, MS 2333, fols. 146–47.

262. NARA, RG45, Letters Received by the Secretary of Navy: Miscellaneous Letter, 1814, vol. 4, no. 111 (M124, roll no. 63).

263. LC, George Cockburn Papers.

264. NARA, RG45, Letters Received by the Secretary of Navy: Miscellaneous Letter, 1814, vol. 5, no. 4 (M124, roll no. 64).

265. NLS, Alexander F. I. Cochrane Papers, MS 2333, fols. 104–5.

266. NARA, RG45, Letters Received by the Secretary of Navy: Miscellaneous Letter, 1814, vol. 4, no. 111 (M124, roll no. 63).

267. NAUK, Adm. 1/507, fols. 119–20.

268. See also "Extract of a letter from Col. Fenwick, of the Maryland Militia, to the Secretary of War, Leonardtown, September 17, 1814," Baltimore *Federal Gazette,* October 5, 1814. Lt. Col. Athanasius Fenwick, 12th Regiment, Maryland militia, and a detachment of Virginia militia captured the British barge.

269. NAUK, Adm. 1/503.

270. NARA, RG45, Letters Sent by the Secretary of Navy to Officers, vol. 11, 219–20 (M149, roll no. 111).

271. NARA, RG45, Letters Received by the Secretary of the Navy: Miscellaneous Letters, 1814, vol. 3, no. 40 (M124, roll no. 62). "Col. Spencer" may be Richard Spencer, a shipbuilder in St. Michaels at this time and member of the Kent County militia.

272. MSA, vol. 3159, 564.

273. Scott, *Recollections,* 3:163.

274. Lowrie and Clark, *American State Papers,* 555.

275. Quote in William Gribbin, "American Episcopacy and the War of 1812," *Maryland Historical Magazine* 38 (1943): 33.

276. Meshach Browning, *Forty-Four Years of the Life of a Hunter, Being Reminiscences of Meshach Browning, a Maryland Hunter, Roughly Written Down by Himself* (Winston-Salem, NC: Winston Printing Company, 1942), 166–67.

277. Quote in Norman Harrington, *Easton Album* (Easton, MD: Historical Society of Talbot County, 1986), 57–58.

278. Testimony of John Smith who served in Capt. Jacob Franklin's Company. House of Representatives, 29th Congress, 1st Session, Committee of Claims, Report No. 131, 5.

279. Testimony of William G. Jones. House of Representatives, 29th Congress, 1st Session, Committee of Claims, Report No. 131, 10–11.

280. LC, Washington, DC, Papers of George Cockburn, container 14, vol. 38, 372–74.

281. NLS, Alexander F. I. Cochrane Papers, MS 2333, fols. 18–23.

282. Lowrie and Clark, *American State Papers,* 559.

283. Lowrie and Clark, *American State Papers,* 585.

284. NARA, RG45, Letters Received by the Secretary of the Navy: Miscellaneous Letters, 1814, vol. 5, no. l11 (M124, roll no. 64).

285. Scott, *Recollections,* 3:229.

286. Scott, *Recollections,* 3:227.

287. NLS, Alexander F. I. Cochrane Papers, MS 2333, fols. 106–10.

288. LC, Papers of George Cockburn, container 14, vol. 38, 368–70.

289. "Calendar of the General Otho Holland William Papers," 354.

290. Com. Joshua Barney to Secretary of Navy William Jones, July 8, 1814, NARA, RG45, Letters Received by the Secretary of the Navy: Miscellaneous Letters, 1814, vol. 5, no. 43 (M124, roll no. 64).

291. Com. Joshua Barney to Secretary of Navy William Jones, July 8, 1814, NARA, RG45, Letters Received by the Secretary of the Navy: Miscellaneous Letters, 1814, vol. 5, no. 43 (M124, roll no. 64).

292. "The Claim of James Tongue, John Scrivener, and William Hodson's Representatives," in *American State Papers: Documents, Legislative and Executive, of the Congress of the United States* (Washington: U.S. House of Representatives, 1842), 2. A copy of this pamphlet is at the Library of Congress.

293. Letter reprinted in *A Sketch Of The Events Which Preceded The Capture Of Washington By The British On The Twenty-Fourth Of August,1814* (Philadelphia: Carey & Hart, 1849), 49.

294. Gleig, 1821, 107.

295. Gleig diary quote in Barrett, 1913, 137.

296. Gleig, 1847, 58–59.

297. NAUK, Adm. 1/506, fols. 606–13.

298. Gleig diary quote in Barrett, 1913, 137.

299. Quote in Edward S. Delplaine, *Francis Scott Key: Life and Times* (Brooklyn: Biography Press, 1937), 154, original letter at Independence Hall, Philadelphia.

300. Magruder, "Dr. William Beanes," 212.

301. Sister Mary Xavier Queen, Grandma's Stories and Anecdotes of "Ye Olden Times," in *Incidents of the War of Independence, Etc.* (Boston: Angel Guardian Press, 1899), 96–97.

302. Letter reprinted in *American State Papers, Documents, Legislative and Executive, of the Congress of The United States, From The First Session Of The First To The Second Session Of The Fifteenth Congress, Inclusive: Commencing March 3, 1789, and Ending March 3, 1819* (Washington: Gales and Seaton, 1832), 538.

303. John Armstrong, *Notices of the War of 1812* (New York: Wiley & Putnam, 1840), vol. II, appendix No. 29, 233; *see also* Long Old Fields under Forestville.

304. Pennsylvania Historical Society, Welma Clarke Smith Collection, William Jones Papers.

Chapter 4. Virginia Sites

1. Captain Gordon (1782–1869) lost his leg on March 13, 1811, during an Anglo-French engagement in the Adriatic when a 36 pounder French shot passed through a portal of his frigate, graz-

ing a gun carriage and taking off a sailor's leg before hitting him in the knee. Although his leg hung only by tendons, he continued to give orders before being taken below deck to have the leg amputated. Gordon later lost an arm in combat.

2. Walter Lowrie and Matthew St. Clair Clarke, *American State Papers: Documents, Legislative and Executive, of the Congress of the United States . . . Military Affairs* (Washington, DC: Gales and Seaton, 1832), 590.

3. Lowrie and Clarke, *American State Papers,* 591; John Armstrong, *Notices of the War of 1812* (New York: Wiley & Putnam, 1840), vol. II, appendix no. 25, 227–28; and in several newspapers such as Annapolis *Maryland Republican,* September 3, 1814.

4. Library of Congress (LC), Charles Simms Papers, vol. 6, Peter Force Collection, Series 8D, fols. 35428–29 (reel 66).

5. Charles G. Muller, "Fabulous Potomac Passage," *U.S. Naval Institute Proceedings* (1964): 89.

6. LC, Charles Simms Papers, vol. 6, Peter Force Collection, Series 8D, fols. 35428–29 (reel 66).

7. Lady Jane Barbara Bourchier, ed., *Memoir of the Life of Admiral Sir Edward Codrington,* vol. 1 (London: Longmans, Green, and Co., 1873), 317–18.

8. James Scott, *Recollections of a Naval Life,* 3 vols. (London: Richard Bentley, 1834), 3:65.

9. Scott, *Recollections,* 3:63.

10. National Archives United Kingdom (NAUK), London, Adm. 1/505, 139–41.

11. National Library of Scotland (NLS), Edinburgh, Alexander F. I. Cochrane Papers, MS 2333, fols. 123–32.

12. National Archives and Record Administration (NARA), RG45, Letters Received by the Secretary of the Navy: Miscellaneous Letters, 1814, vol. 6, no. 20 (M124, roll no. 65).

13. NARA, RG45, Letters Received by the Secretary of the Navy: Miscellaneous Letters, 1814, vol. 7, no. 34 (M124, roll no. 66). Lambert's letter is based on a letter from John Hall, postmaster at Kilmarnock.

14. NLS, Alexander F. I. Cochrane Papers, MS 2336, fols. 25–26.

15. NARA, RG45, Captain's Letters to the Secretary of Navy, 1813, vol. 2, no. 78 (M125, roll no. 27).

16. NARA, RG45, Captain's Letters to the Secretary of Navy, 1813, vol. 4, no. 107 (M125, roll no. 29).

17. NAUK, London, Adm. 1/503, 743–46.

18. These Independent Companies of Foreigners behaved so poorly at Hampton that they were banned from any further participation in the war.

19. NARA, RG45, Letters Received by the Secretary of the Navy: Miscellaneous Letters, 1814, vol. 7, no. 34 (M124, roll no. 66). Lambert's letter based on a letter from John Hall, postmaster at Kilmarnock.

20. Shenandoah County, Virginia, Court Records for 1813.

21. NAUK, Adm. 1/509, fols. 188–92.

22. NAUK, Adm. 1/509, fols. 188–92.

23. Virginia State Records (VSR), Governor's Office (RG3), Executive Papers, Governor James Barbour, 1812–1814. Major Wilson forwarded the letter to Governor Barbour.

24. NARA, RG45, Masters Commandant Letters Received by the Secretary of the Navy, 1813, no. 34 (M147, roll no. 5).

25. NARA, RG45, Captain's Letters to the Secretary of Navy, 1813, vol. 4, no. 119 (M125, roll no. 29).

26. NAUK, Adm. 1/503, 779–82. Beckwith apparently was unaware that Williams had been killed during the engagement.

27. Quote from Hampton History Museum exhibit, source given as Dorothy Rouse-Bottom.

28. National Archives of Canada, Ottawa, Ontario, British Military and Naval Records, RG8, I, "C" Ser., vol. 679, 189–91; and Public Record Office, Adm. 2/504.

29. Benson J. Lossing, *The Pictorial Field-Book of the War of 1812* (New York: Harper Bros., 1868), 687, footnote 2.

30. NARA, RG45, Letters Received by the Secretary of the Navy: Captain's Letters, 1814, vol. 7, no. 117, enclosure (M125, roll no. 40).

31. Richmond *Virginia Argus,* July 8, 1813.

32. Scott, *Recollections,* 3:76–77.

33. George Robert Gleig, *The Campaigns of the British Army at Washington and New Orleans* (E. Ardsley, England: E. P. Publ. Ltd., 1972, reprint of 1847 edition), 112.

34. "Autobiography by John L. Dagg." Dagg served in the Virginia militia. His autobiography is available at www.founders. org/library/dagg-bio.html.

35. Edward Duncan Ingraham, *A Sketch of the Events which Preceded the Capture of Washington by the British on the Twenty-Fourth of August, 1814* (Philadelphia: Carey and Hart, 1849), 47–49.

36. NAUK, Adm. 1/507, fols. 110–11.

37. Richmond *Enquirer,* October 8, 1813.

38. LC, Papers of George Cockburn, container 16, vol. 44, 327–33.

39. NAUK, Adm. 1/505, fols. 131–33.

40. Scott, *Recollections,* 3:65–66. Some of the smaller privateers used Cape Charles Passage to escape the British blockade.

41. Executive Papers, Archives Division, Virginia Library.

42. Alfred M. Lorrain, *The Helm, The Sword and the Cross: A Life Narrative* (Cincinnati, 1862), 103.

43. Marc Leepson, *Saving Monticello: The Levy Family's Epic Quest to Rescue the House that Jefferson Built* (New York: Free Press, 2001).

44. This seemingly unlikely event is made without citation by Charles G. Muller, "Fabulous Potomac Passage," *U.S. Naval Institute Proceedings* (May 1964): 88.

45. Maj. Gen. Elers Napier, *The Life and Correspondence of Admiral Sir Charles Napier, K.C.B., From Personal Recollections, Letters, and Official Documents* (London: Hurst and Blackett, 1862), 80.

46. NLS, Alexander F. I. Cochrane Papers, MS 2574, fols. 91–99.

47. Scott, *Recollections,* 3:181.

48. This copy of a letter to the editor dated March 18, 1814, is signed as "A friend to Brave Patriot."

49. NAUK, Adm. 1/507, fols. 103–6.

50. NAUK, Adm. 1/507, fols. 103–6.

51. Scott, *Recollections,* 3:243–44.

52. Baltimore *Niles' Weekly Register,* August 6, 1814.

53. Howard J. Strott, "A Seaman's Notebook: The Travels of

Captain George De La Roche," *Maryland Historical Magazine* 62 (1947): 265.

54. NARA, RG45, Captain's Letters to the Secretary of the Navy, 1813, vol. 1, no. 53 (M125, roll no. 26).

55. NARA, RG107, T-55 (7).

56. NARA, RG45, Captain's Letters to the Secretary of Navy, 1813, vol. 4, no. 97 (M125, roll no. 29).

57. NAUK, Adm. 1/504, 313–14.

58. NARA, RG107, T-1814 (Unregistered Series).

59. Duane De Paepe, *Gunpowder From Mammoth Cave: The Saga of Saltpetre Mining Before and During the War of 1812* (Hays, KS: Cave Pearl Press, 1985), 7, 31.

60. Thomas Jefferson, *Notes on the State of Virginia* (Philadelphia: Prichard and Hall, 1788), 31–32.

61. NARA, RG45, Letters Sent by the Secretary of the Navy to Officers, vol. 11, fol. 278 (M149, roll no. 11).

62. NARA, RG45, Letters Received by the Secretary of the Navy: Captain's Letters, 1814, vol. 6, no. 77 (M125, roll no. 39).

63. NARA, RG45, Letters Received by the Secretary of the Navy: Captain's Letters, 1814, vol. 6, no. 57 (M125, roll no. 39).

64. VSR, Governor's Office (RG3), Executive Papers, Governor James Barbour, 1812–1814; reprinted in Ralph T. Whitelaw, *Virginia's Eastern Shore: A History of Northampton and Accomack Counties* (Gloucester, MA: Peter Smith, 1968), 816.

65. NLS, Alexander F. I. Cochrane Papers, MS 2333, fols. 123–32.

66. Scott, *Recollections,* 3:78–83.

67. VSR, Governor's Office (RG3), Executive Papers, Governor James Barbour, 1812–1814. Quote reprinted in Alton Brooks Parker Barnes, *Pungoteague to Petersburg:* vol. I, *Eastern Shore Militiamen Before the Civil War 1776–1858* (Lee Howard Book, 1988), 71.

68. Scott, *Recollections,* 3:117.

69. NLS, Alexander F. I. Cochrane Papers, MS 2333, fols. 53–59.

70. NAUK.

71. Adam Wallace, *The Parson of the Islands; A Biography of the Rev. Joshua Thomas . . .* (Cambridge, MD: Tidewater Publishers, 1961), 151.

72. NLS, Alexander F. I. Cochrane Papers, MS 2334, fols. 81–82.

73. NAUK, Adm. 1/509, fols. 188–92.

74. NAUK, Adm. 1/509, fols. 188–92.

75. VSR, Governor's Office (RG3), Executive Papers, Governor James Barbour, 1812–1814. It is unknown where the Ritchie family vault was located but presumably near the Ritchie house located on the northeast corner of the intersection of Prince and Cross streets; no evidence of such a vault survives; the original interior wood paneling from this house is now displayed at Winterthur Museum, Wilmington, Delaware.

76. NAUK, Adm. 1/509, fols. 188–92.

77. William Stanhope Lovell, *From Trafalgar to the Chesapeake: Adventures of an Officer in Nelson's Navy* by Vice Adm., R.N., K.H. (Annapolis, MD: Naval Institute Press, 2003), 166–67.

78. Frederick Chamier, *The Life of A Sailor* (London: Richard Bentley, 1839), 195.

79. This quote refers to the action of April 2, 1813, involving *Dolphin, Racer, Lynx,* and *Arab.*

80. "Report (No. 1) concerning the Military defence of the river Potomack, the City of Washington and adjacent country: founded on a survey and investigation of prominent features of the premises, by William Tatham." Typed transcript on file, Fort Belvoir, Virginia, original NARA.

81. University of Michigan, William L. Clements Library, Ann Arbor, Michigan, David Porter Papers.

82. Diary entry from her home in Washington, quoted in S. A. Wallace, "Georgetown is Saved from the British," *The Social Studies* 63 (1952): 237.

83. Napier, "Life and Correspondence," 85.

84. John Brannan, *Official Letters of the Military and Naval Officers of the United States, during the War with Great Britain in the Years 1812, 13,14, & 15 . . .* (Washington, DC: Way & Gideon, 1823), 409–10.

85. NAUK, Adm. 1/507, fols. 153–57.

86. William James, *The Naval History of Great Britain, from the Declaration of War by France in February 1793, to the Accession of George IV, in January 1812* (London: Harding, Lepard, and Co., 1826), 458.

87. NARA, RG45, Letters Received by the Secretary of the Navy: Captains' Letters, 1814, vol. 6, no. 27 (M125, roll no. 39).

88. William Tatham to Secretary of War, John Armstrong, May 27, 1813, "Report (No. 1) concerning the Military defence of the river Potomac . . . by William Tatham."

89. NARA, RG45, Letters from Officers of Rank Below that of Commanders Received by the Secretary of the Navy, 1813, vol. 3, no. 33 (M148, roll no. 12).

90. This account incorrectly names the commander of the *Asp* as Liggany; it is apparently a corruption of Sigourney.

91. NAUK, Adm. 1/504, fols. 69–71.

92. Scott, *Recollections,* 3:254.

93. NARA, RG45, Letters Received by the Secretary of the Navy: Miscellaneous Letters, 1814, vol. 6, no. 20 (M124, roll no. 65).

94. NAUK, Adm. 1/507, fols. 112–15.

95. John Thomas Scharf, *History of Maryland from the Earliest Period to the Present Day,* 3 vols. (Hatboro, PA: Tradition Press, 1967, reprint of 1879), 3:48. Quote source not given.

Chapter 5. The District of Columbia and Other Sites Related to the Chesapeake

1. By an Act of Congress and in accordance with the local residents, the Virginia portion of the district was returned to the Old Dominion in 1847. Although Alexandria was part of the district during the War of 1812, we have included it in Virginia in this guide.

2. Gaillard Hunt, ed., *The First Forty Years of Washington Society* (New York: Charles Scribner's Sons, 1906), 99. Margaret Bayard Smith was the wife of Samuel Harrison Smith, president of the Bank of Washington and commissioner of revenue in the Treasury Department.

3. National Archives of the United Kingdom (NAUK), London, War Office, 1/141, 31–38.

4. NAUK, Adm. 1/506, fols. 606–13.

5. [George Robert Gleig], *A Narrative Of The Campaigns of the British Army At Washington And New Orleans, Under Generals Ross, Pakenham, And Lambert, In The Years 1814 and 1815; With Some Account Of The Countries Visited. By An Officer Who Served In The Expedition* (London: John Murray, 1821), 128.

6. Alexandria *Gazette,* September 8, 1814. Madison's claim that the American forces were outnumbered is incorrect.

7. James Scott, *Recollections of a Naval Life,* 3 vols. (London: Richard Bentley, 1834), 3:322.

8. [George Robert Gleig], *Subaltern In America; Comprising His Narrative of the Campaigns of the British Army, at Baltimore, Washington, &c., &c., During the Late War* (Philadelphia: E. L. Carey & A. Hart, 1833), 86–87.

9. Dolley Madison Aide-de-Memoire, Dolley Madison Papers, Library of Congress (LC), Manuscript Division. Reprinted in *Memoirs and Letters of Dolly Madison: Wife of James Madison, President of the United States,* ed. Lucia B. Cutts (Boston: Houghton, Mifflin and Co., 1886), 110. Cutts was the grand-niece of Dolley Madison; she used the spelling Dolly.

10. Walter Lowrie and Matthew St. Clair Clarke, eds., *American State Papers, Documents, Legislative and Executive, of the Congress of The United States, From The First Session Of The First To The Second Session Of The Fifteenth Congress, Inclusive: Commencing March 3, 1789, and Ending March 3, 1819* (Washington: Gales and Seaton, 1832), 585.

11. National Archives and Records Administration (NARA), RG45, Naval Shore Establishments, 1814–1911.

12. Historical Society of Pennsylvania, Philadelphia, Uselma Clark Smith Collection, William Jones Papers.

13. NARA, RG233, Report of the Navy Department in Records of the Selected Committee, HR13A-D15.3.; also Lowrie and Clarke, *American State Papers,* 576.

14. Gleig, 1821, 125, 128, 141.

15. Dolley Madison Aide-de-Memoire, Dolley Madison Papers, LC, Manuscript Division.

16. Lowrie and Clarke, *American State Papers,* 538.

17. Stephen Pleasonton to William Winder, August 7, 1848. Letter reprinted in John C. Hildt, "Letters Relating to Capture of Washington," *South Atlantic Quarterly* 6 (1907): 65.

18. Quote in John S. Williams, *History of Invasion and Capture of Washington and All the Events Which Preceded and Followed* (New York: Harper & Bros., 1857), 275.

19. Baltimore *Patriot,* August 26, 1814.

20. Washington *Evening Star,* April 1, 1967.

21. Written after the event, quote in Harold Donaldson Eberlein and Cortlandt Van Dyke Hubbard, *Historic Houses of George-Town & Washington City* (Richmond, VA: Dietz Press, Inc., 1958), 312.

22. LC, Manuscript Collection.

23. Diary entry from her home in Washington, quoted in S. A. Wallace, "Georgetown is Saved from the British," *The Social Studies* 63 (1952): 235.

24. Scott, *Recollections,* 3:303.

25. *Transactions and Proceedings of the 75th Anniversary of the Medical Society of the District of Columbia,* February 16, 1894, 30–31.

26. Washington slave, recorded in his diary, LC, Manuscripts Division.

27. Senate Report, 15th Congress, 2nd Session, #480 (1819).

28. NAUK, Adm. 1/506, fols. 606–13.

29. NAUK, Adm. 1/506, fols. 606–13.

30. Scott, *Recollections,* 3:311–12.

31. Lowrie and Clarke, *American State Papers,* 586.

32. Gleig, 1821, 136.

33. Eberlein and Hubbard, *Historic Houses,* 128. Source of quote not given.

34. Wallace, "Georgetown," 235.

35. Eberlein and Hubbard, *Historic Houses,* 129–30.

36. Gleig, 1821, 233–34.

37. Hunt, *The First Forty Years,* 112.

38. Quote reprinted in Glenn Brown, *History of the United States Capitol*: vol. 1, *The Old Capitol—1792–1850* (Washington, DC: Government Printing Office, 1900).

39. George Robert Gleig, *The Campaigns of the British Army at Washington and New Orleans* (E. Ardsley, Eng.: E. P. Publ. Ltd., 1972, reprint of 1847 edition), 70. Although Gleig claims all the papers in the archives were burned, many important documents, including the Declaration of Independence, were actually removed prior to the British occupation of the city. Twenty-four-year-old clerk Lewis H. Machen and the office messenger, Tobias, transported the executive proceedings of the U.S. Senate to Brookeville Academy, Brookeville, Maryland. *See also* Rokeby Mansion, Virginia, to which other documents were taken.

40. Benjamin Henry Latrobe, *The Correspondence and Miscellaneous Papers of Benjamin Henry Latrobe,* ed. John C. Van Horne, vol. 2 (New Haven, CT: Yale University Press, 1986), 32.

41. NARA, RG45, Naval Shore Establishments, 1814–1911.

42. Scott, *Recollections,* 3:305.

43. NARA, RG45, Letters Received by the Secretary of the Navy, Captain's Letters, 1814, vol. 5, no. 18 (M125, roll no. 38).

44. NARA, RG45, Letters Received by the Secretary of the Navy, Captain's Letters, 1814, vol. 7, no. 50 (M125, roll no. 40).

45. Dolley Madison Aide-de-Memoire, Dolley Madison Papers, LC, Manuscript Division.

46. Gleig, 1821, 135.

47. Scott, *Recollections,* 3:303.

48. Dolley Madison Aide-de-Memoire, Dolley Madison Papers, LC, Manuscript Division.

49. Paul Jennings, *A Colored Man's Reminiscences of James Madison,* Baldensburg Series, Number Two (Brooklyn: George C. Beadle, 1865), Special Collections Library of James Madison University, reprinted in *White House History,* White House Historical Association, 1 (1981): 46–51.

50. Quote in *Life of Eleuthère Irénée de Pont from Contemporary Correspondence 1811–1814,* vol. 9 (Newark: University of Delaware Press, 1925), 91.

51. National Library of Scotland, Edinburgh, Alexander F. I. Cochrane Papers, MS 2346, fols. 8–9.

52. Hagley Museum & Eleutherian Mills Historical Library (HEHL), Longwood Manuscripts, Box 9, Group 8 Acquisitions, Series A—Dealers & Donors, Me to Z, Unknown Sources (Part 1), unknown Source V # 184.

53. HEHL, Letters of Victor du Pont, Accession 146, box 6 of 15, file 67.

54. Quote in *Life of Eleuthère Irénéé de Pont from Contemporary Correspondence 1811–1814*, vol. 9, 222–23.

55. Quote from unnamed Norfolk newspaper, no date given, in Sarah McCulloh Lemmon, *North Carolina and the War of 1812* (Raleigh: Division of Archives and History, North Carolina Department of Cultural Resources, 1984), 37.

56. George Cockburn Papers, LC, container 9, Letters sent 3 Feb. 1812–6 Feb. 1814, 217–21. Jon Latimer, *1812: War with America* (Cambridge, MA: Harvard University Press, 2007), 172, states the British made two raids on Ocracoke, July 2 and July 12, but Cockburn's letter of July 12 clearly states the *Anaconda* and *Atlas* were captured July 12, 1813; July 2 is apparently a misread of July 12.

57. Duke University, Rare Book, Manuscript, and Special Collections Library, Durham, North Carolina, Sir Robert Barrie Papers.

58. NARA, RG 217, extracts of contracts for ordnance stores, "General Accounting Office, Third Auditors Report, Defense of Baltimore Accounts."

Appendix A. Sites Whose Locations Could Not Be Established

1. LC, Rodgers Family Papers, Series IH-B, Container 51, fols. 5551–52.

Appendix B. Gravesites Connected to the War of 1812

1. Sources used in compiling this appendix include Charles Lawrence Bishop, *Frederick's Other City: Mt. Olivet Cemetery* (Frederick, MD: Mt. Olivet Cemetery, Inc., 2002); Dennis F. Blizzard and Thomas L. Hollowak, "A Chronicle of 1812 Soldiers, Seamen and Marines" (Maryland Society of the War of 1812, 2001); Stuart Lee Butler, *A Guide to Virginia Militia Units in the War of 1812* (Athens, GA: Iberian Publishing Company, 1988); Stuart Lee Butler, *Virginia Soldiers in the United States Army 1800–1815* (Athens, GA: Iberian Publishing Company, 1986); *Directory of Maryland Burial Grounds* (Westminster, MD: Family Line Publications, for Genealogical Council of Maryland, 1996) (Anne Arundel, Carroll, Montgomery, and Prince George's counties); Jacob Mehrling Holdcraft, *Names in Stone: 75,000 Cemetery Inscriptions from Frederick County, Maryland,* vols. 1 and 2 (Ann Arbor, MI, 1966; reprinted Baltimore: Genealogical Publishing Company, 1985); John E. Jacob, *Graveyards and Gravestones of Wicomico* (Westminster, MD: Family Line Publications, 1998); Sallie A. Mallick and Wright, *Frederick County Militia in the War of 1812* (Westminster, MD: Family Line Publications, 1992); William M. Marine, *The British Invasion of Maryland 1812–1815* (Hathboro, PA: Tradition Press, 1965); Mt. Olivet Cemetery, Caretaker Records; Lillian Bayly Marks, "War of 1812 Soldiers buried in Baltimore County, Maryland," *The Maryland and Delaware Genealogist* 112 (1987): 136–38; Lillian Bayly Marks, "Grave Locations of Maryland War of 1812 Soldiers with Miscellaneous War of 1812 Material" (copies of grave files from Maryland State Society United States Daughters of 1812, Maryland State Law Library); Nellie M. Marshall, *Tombstone Records of Dorchester County, Maryland 1678–1964, 1678–1964,* vol. 1 (Dorchester County Historical Society, Inc., 1993); Henry C. Peden, Jr., *St. John's and St. George's Parish Register Baltimore and Harford County, 1696–1851: transcribed from Microfilm in the Maryland Historical Society Library in Baltimore, Maryland* (Westminster, MD: Family Line Publications, 1987); Clarence Stewart Peterson, *Known Military Dead During the War of 1812* (Baltimore: C. S. Peterson, 1955); Jean A. Sargent, *STONES and BONES: Cemetery Records of Prince George's County, Maryland* (Bowie, MD: Prince George's County Genealogical Society, Inc., 1984); Jane B. Wilson, *The Very Quiet Baltimoreans: A Guide to the Historic Cemeteries and Burial Sites of Baltimore* (Shippensburg, PA: White Mane Publishing, Inc., 1991); and F. Edward Wright, *Maryland Militia: War of 1812,* 11 vols. (Lewis, DE: Colonial Roots Collection, 2006).

Reports from many churches and organizations were also used. These include the Maryland Society of the War of 1812; Westminster Cemetery & Presbyterian Church (Baltimore); Maryland Historical Society; DAR "Cemetery Records of Anne Arundel County, Maryland"; DAR "Tombstone Records of Cecil County"; Genealogical Society of Allegany County, "Allegany County, Maryland Rural Cemeteries"; Dale W. Morrow, "Washington County, Maryland Cemetery Records"; and Mt. Olivet Cemetery (Frederick) Caretaker Records. Obituaries such as from the Baltimore *Sun,* the World Wide Web, and physical tombstone inscriptions were also most helpful.

2. See www.1812va.org/index.php.

3. Taken from Congressional Cemetery web page, last updated September 15, 1999, at www.congressionalcemetery.org. Go to genealogy, click on lists/rosters, click on veterans, click on War of 1812.

Appendix C. Chronology of the War in the Chesapeake

1. This chronology is based on the research conducted for this guide, Ralph E. Eshelman and Christopher T. George, "Maryland War of 1812: Battlefields, Selected Skirmishes, Encampments, Earthworks and Related Sites" (American Battlefield Protection Program, National Park Service, December 2000); Ralph E. Eshelman, Susan Langley, and Ben Ford, "Maryland Revolutionary War and War of 1812 Battlefields/Skirmishes and Associated Historical Properties Survey" (American Battlefield Protection Program, National Park Service, March 2002); Joseph A. Whitehorne, *The Battle for Baltimore 1814* (Baltimore: Nautical & Aviation Publishing Company of America, 1997; appendix A, several dates in error); Donald R. Hickey, *Don't Give Up the Ship! Myths of the War of 1812* (Champaign: Illinois University Press, 2006, chronology chapter); and an unpublished chronology by Edward A. Seufert. When dates are unclear, only the month, season, or year is given.

Appendix D. Military Actions and Other War-Related Incidents in the Chesapeake

1. Only a few shots were actually fired in this battle.
2. Artillery bombardment.
3. It is possible enough men participated for this engagement to qualify as a battle, but the evidence is inconclusive.
4. Although more than a hundred men were on each side, only about twenty Americans engaged in the fire fight.
5. These skirmishes were part of the First Battle of St. Leonard Creek.
6. More than a hundred American militia skirmished with an unknown number of British soldiers. This could qualify as a battle, but the evidence is inconclusive.
7. Naval engagement.
8. Naval engagement.
9. Naval engagement.
10. Engagement between volunteer association and escaped slaves.
11. Naval engagement.
12. Naval engagement.
13. Naval engagement.
14. American militia apparently did not return fire, so this could be classified as a raid.
15. Naval engagement.
16. Naval engagement.
17. The British burned and looted while anchored here.
18. The British captured fourteen Americans, apparently without any resistance.
19. Artillery bombardment.
20. There were more than a hundred men on each side, but the Americans offered no resistance.
21. Artillery bombardment.
22. The British destroyed a fishery and plundered a home at the mouth of the river.
23. The British destroyed vessels and plundered homes near Hampton.
24. The British captured the privateer *Lottery*.
25. The British captured the U.S. schooner *Asp*.
26. This was a star fort and blockhouse.
27. This fortification was made of logs.
28. This site was occupied by both sides at different times in the war.
29. The other two batteries at St. Michaels were apparently not protected by earthworks.
30. An earthwork was reputed to be established here but only a temporary fortification made of tobacco hogsheads was used during the skirmish.
31. There were three such redoubts here.
32. It is unclear whether earthworks were established here.
33. It is unclear whether earthworks were established here.
34. This was put in place after the British attack.
35. This was a double chain; a sunken vessel also impeded movement on the river.
36. There were at least two booms here.
37. These vessels were sunk after the Battle for Baltimore was over.

The literature on the War of 1812 is vast. In the essay that follows, we have focused on those studies that we found most useful for our project. They fall into three broad categories: (1) those works that are especially strong on the Chesapeake; (2) those that contain information that we needed but could not find elsewhere; and (3) those that in some other way contributed to our understanding of the war in the region. Although this essay does not list all works bearing on the war in the Chesapeake, it should provide a good starting point for anyone interested in doing research on this theater of operations.

General Histories of the War

There are many broad studies of the War of 1812. One of the most detailed and still the most useful is the classic written by Henry Adams, *History of the United States of America [during the Administrations of Jefferson and Madison]*, 9 vols. (New York: C. Scribner's Sons, 1889–91). Although Adams's judgments must be treated with caution, vols. 6–7 provide a good overview of the political, diplomatic, and military history of the war. Also indispensable is Benson J. Lossing's remarkable work, *The Pictorial Field-Book of the War of 1812* (New York: Harper & Brothers, 1868), which is based on the author's extensive travels in the 1850s and includes hundreds of sketches of 1812 sites as they appeared some forty years after the war. For a contemporary history of the war from the British perspective, see William James, *A Full and Correct Account of the Military Occurrences of the Late War between Great Britain and the United States of America*, 2 vols. (London: privately printed, 1818). The best American counterpart are two works by Charles J. Ingersoll, *Historical Sketch of the Second War between the United States of America, and Great Britain*, 2 vols. (Philadelphia: Lea and Blanchard, 1845–49), and *History of the Second War between the United States of America and Great Britain*, 2 vols. (Philadelphia: Lippincott, Grambo & Co., 1853). Both James and Ingersoll were witnesses to the war, James as an enemy alien in the United States and then a refu-

gee in Halifax, and Ingersoll as a member of Congress from Pennsylvania.

Among the modern accounts that are most valuable are John K. Mahon, *The War of 1812* (Gainesville: University of Florida Press, 1972), and Robert S. Quimby, *The U.S. Army in the War of 1812: An Operational and Command Study*, 2 vols. (East Lansing: Michigan State University Press, 1997). Both works present a detailed account of the military history of the conflict. While these works focus on the American side of the contest, there is no comparable work written from the British perspective, although Reginald Horsman, *The War of 1812* (New York: Knopf, 1969), does a good job of presenting both sides of the story. Two works that present the war from the Canadian perspective (although their treatment of the Chesapeake theater is cursory) are J. Mackay Hitsman, *The Incredible War of 1812: A Military History* (1965; updated by Donald E. Graves, Toronto: Robin Brass Studio, 1999), and George F. G. Stanley, *The War of 1812: Land Operations* ([Toronto]: Canadian War Museum and Macmillan of Canada, 1983).

Another overview of the war, one that focuses on the American side and includes political, diplomatic, and financial as well as military history, is Donald R. Hickey, *The War of 1812: A Forgotten Conflict* (Urbana: University of Illinois Press, 1989). Hickey's companion volume, *Don't Give Up the Ship! Myths of the War of 1812* (Toronto: Robin Brass Studio, and Urbana: University of Illinois Press, 2006) challenges many widely held misconceptions about the war, including a fair number bearing on the Chesapeake. Two other works that are worth consulting are David S. Heidler and Jeanne T. Heidler, eds., *Encyclopedia of the War of 1812* (Santa Barbara: ABC-CLIO, Inc., 1997), which has considerable information on the war in the Chesapeake, and Robert Malcomson, *Historical Dictionary of the War of 1812* (Lanham, MD: Scarecrow Press, 2006), which is especially strong on naval aspects of the war.

Naval and amphibious operations loomed large in the Chesapeake. For this dimension of the conflict, a good place to start is the pioneering pro-British work of William James:

A Full and Correct Account of the Chief Naval Occurrences of the Late War between Great Britain and the United States of America (London: Egerton, 1817), and *The Naval History of Great Britain, from . . . 1793, to . . . 1820,* rev. ed., 6 vols. (London: Harding, Lepard, and Co., 1826), especially vol. 6. Future president Theodore Roosevelt delivered a compelling American rejoinder to James in *The Naval War of 1812,* 3rd ed. (New York: G. P. Putnam's Sons, 1882).

Documentary Collections and Documents

One of the most useful documentary collections bearing on the war is the wide-ranging U.S. Congress, *American State Papers: Documents, Legislative and Executive, of the Congress of the United States,* 38 vols. (Washington: Gales and Seaton, 1832–61), which is available online through the Library of Congress's American Memory project at: http://memory.loc.gov/ammem/amlaw/lwsplink.html. For understanding the military and naval history of the war, the most useful series are *Military Affairs,* 7 vols. (1832–61), especially vol. 1, and *Naval Affairs,* 4 vols. (1834–61), vols. 1–2. There is information on pensions, military land warrants, and claims for compensation for property destruction in the volume on *Claims* (1834) and scattered through the series on *Public Lands,* 8 vols. (1834–61) and *Finance,* 5 vols. (1832–n.d.). Congress considered some claims as late as the 1850s. Although there is no comparable collection for Great Britain, the best substitute is William Wood, ed., *Select British Documents of the Canadian War of 1812,* 3 vols. (Toronto: Champlain Society, 1920–28), which has been put online by the Champlain Society at www.champlainsociety.ca/cs_publications-digital.htm.

Two other documentary collections that are useful are John Brannan, ed., *Official Letters of the Military and Naval Officers of the United States, during the War with Great Britain in the Years 1812, 13, 14, & 15* (Washington: Way & Gideon, 1823); and Herman A. Fay, ed., *A Collection of the Official Accounts, in Detail, of All the Battles Fought by Sea and Land Between the Navy and Army of the United States and the Navy and Army of Great Britain* (New York: E. Conrad, 1817). Fay was a U.S. Army officer who was in command of forts Madison and Severn in Annapolis during the war.

For a compilation of known War of 1812 sites in the United States, see *Report to Congress on the Historic Preservation of Revolutionary War and War of 1812 Sites in the United States* (prepared for the Committee on Energy and Natural Resources United States Senate and The Committee on Resources United States House of Representatives by the American Battlefield Protection Program, National Park Service, U.S. Department of Interior, 2007).

For documents bearing exclusively on the naval war, William S. Dudley, Michael J. Crawford, et al., eds., *The Naval War of 1812: A Documentary History,* 4 vols. (Washington, DC: Naval Historical Center, 1985–), is of incomparable value. There is no British counterpart, but many significant British naval documents were printed in the *Naval Chronicle,* a periodical published by J. Gold in London from 1799 to 1818. The modern reprint of this work should be avoided because it leaves out too many important documents. Also valuable for understanding British operations in the Chesapeake are the official reports, letters, and ship logs in the Public Record Office at the National Archives of the United Kingdom in London, England. These documents are filled with information on ship locations, weather conditions, and victualing and water-gathering details. They are also essential for establishing time lines for amphibious raids. Similarly, the George Cockburn Papers, available on microfilm at the Library of Congress, Washington, D.C., include orders, reports, and other documents dealing with the British campaigns in the Chesapeake Bay.

Two essential collections of documents published by Congress that have considerable material on the war in the Chesapeake are "Committee Report on Spirit and Manner in Which the War Is Waged by the Enemy, July 31, 1813," and "Committee Report on Capture of Washington," November 29, 1814. These reports were widely reprinted under different titles and can be found most conveniently in *American State Papers: Military Affairs,* 1:339–82 and 524–99. For a particularly interesting claim made by the master of a runaway slave for the latter's military service, see "Committee Report on a Claim to a Bounty Land Warrant for the Military Services of a Slave," March 3, 1836, in *American State Papers: Public Lands,* 8:532–33.

Other printed sources include Margaret L. Calcott, ed., *Mistress of Riversdale: The Plantation Letters of Rosalie Stier Calvert, 1795–1821* (Baltimore: Johns Hopkins University Press, 1991) (Calvert was an antiwar woman); Christopher George, ed., "The Family Papers of Maj. Gen. Robert Ross, the Diary of Col. Arthur Brooke, and the British Attack on Washington and Baltimore of 1814," *Maryland Historical Magazine* 88 (1993): 300–316; David Brown, ed., *Diary of A Soldier, 1805–1827 [of the] 21st Royal North British Fusiliers* (Ardrossan, Scotland: Guthrie & Sons, n.d.); "Admiral Cockburn's Plan," *Maryland Historical Magazine* 6 (1911): 16–19; Franklin R. Mullaly, ed., "A Forgotten Letter of Francis Scott Key," *Maryland Historical Magazine* 55 (1960): 359–60; and Howard J., Strolt, ed., "A Seaman's Notebook: The Travels of Captain George De La Roche," *Maryland Historical Magazine* 42 (1942): 261–69 (De La Roche was a U.S. Navy midshipman during the war).

Newspapers and Magazines

The newspapers of the day published many public documents and sometimes carried eyewitness accounts of events that include information found nowhere else. Even newspapers far removed from the Chesapeake might have a knowledgeable correspondent visiting the region who wanted to share what he had seen or heard with friends and family back home. The Chesapeake newspapers that we found most useful were the Alexandria *Gazette,* Annapolis *Maryland Gazette and Political Intelligencer,* Annapolis *Maryland Republican,* Baltimore *Federal Gazette,* Baltimore *Federal Republican,* Baltimore *Patriot,* Cecil County *Whig,* Easton *Republican Star,* Richmond *Enquirer,* Washington *National Intelligencer,* and Wilmington *American Watchman & Delaware Republican.* Those newspapers outside of the Chesapeake that we found useful were the Salem (Massachusetts) *Essex Register,* Hartford *Connecticut Mirror,* Salem (Massachusetts) *Gazette,* Worcester (Massachusetts) *Spy,* and the London (England) *Evening Star.*

In a class by itself is *Niles' Weekly Register,* a magazine published in Baltimore that carried eyewitness accounts, government documents, and statistical tables that shed light on military operations in the Chesapeake.

Autobiographies and Memoirs

There are several autobiographical accounts of men who fought in the Chesapeake region that provide fascinating and sometimes surprisingly detailed information about the war, but some caution must be exercised in using these sources because most were compiled years later when memories had begun to fade.

Among the most descriptive of these works are those produced by 2nd Lt. George Robert Gleig, who served in the British 85th Regiment. We drew heavily on [George Robert Gleig], *A Narrative of the Campaigns of the British Army at Washington, Baltimore and New Orleans under General Ross, Pakenham and Lambert in the Years 1814 and 1815* (London: John Murray, 1821), and George Robert Gleig, *The Campaigns of the British Army at Washington and New Orleans* (London: William Clowers and Sons, 1847). We also used Charles R. B. Barrett, ed., *The 85th King's Light Infantry* (London: Spottiswoode, 1913), which reproduces Gleig's diary (as distinct from his memoirs), and "Letter of Mr. George R. Gleig," *Magazine of American History* 15 (1886): 508–9.

Gleig wrote another work, *A Subaltern in America; Comprising His Narrative of the Campaigns of The British Army, at Baltimore, Washington, &c. &c. during the Late War* (Philadelphia and Baltimore: Carey, Hart & Co., 1833). But he exercised some

literary license to enliven his text, and we have therefore used this work sparingly.

Other British memoirs and autobiographies of merit are James Scott, *Recollections of a Naval Life,* 3 vols. (London: Richard Bentley, 1834) (Scott was an aide to Rear Adm. George Cockburn); Lady Jane Barbara Bourchier, ed., *Memoir of the Life of Admiral Sir Edward Codrington,* 2 vols. (London: Longmans, Green, 1873) (Codrington was a British naval captain whose daughter deleted all critical references to Rear Admiral Cochrane prior to publishing his memoir); Frederick Chamier, *The Life of A Sailor* (London: Richard Bentley, 1839) (Chamier was a British naval lieutenant who served with Sir Peter Parker aboard H.M. frigate *Menelaus*); George Laval Chesterton, *Peace, War and Adventure: An Autobiography of George Laval Chesterton,* 2 vols. (London: Longman, Brown, Green, 1853) (Chesterton was a captain in the Royal Artillery); Vice Admiral William Stanhope Lovell, *Personal Narrative of Events From 1799–1815* (London: W. Allen, 1879), which was reprinted as *From Trafalgar to the Chesapeake* (Annapolis, MD: Naval Institute Press, 2003) (Lovell was the captain of a British troop transport); G. C. Moore-Smith, ed., *The Autobiography of Lieut. General Sir Harry Smith,* 2 vols. (London: John Murray, 1902) (Smith was an aide to Maj. Gen. Robert Ross); William Jarvis Neptune, *The Life and Adventures of W.J. Neptune, Commonly Called General Jarvis* (Hull, England: Peck, Smith, 1832) (Neptune was a British sailor who witnessed the sacking of Washington and the capitulation of Alexandria); "Historical Memoirs of Admiral Sir George Cockburn, G.C.B.," in James Ralfe, *The Naval Biography of Great Britain: Consisting of Historical Memoirs of Those Officers of the British Navy Who Distinguished Themselves During the Reign of His Majesty George III,* 4 vols. (London: Whitmore and Fenn, 1828), 3:257–307; Anne Petrides and Jonathan Downs, eds., *Sea Soldier, An Officer of Marines with Duncan, Nelson, Collingwood and Cockburn: The Letters and Journal of Major T. Marmaduke Wybourn, RM, 1797–1813* (Tunbridge Wells: Parapress, 2000); and [Robert J. Barrett], "Recollections of the Expedition to the Chesapeake and Against New Orleans in the Years 1814–15, by an 'Ols Sub,'" *United Service Journal and Naval Military Magazine,* Part 2, May, June, July, 1840, 25–36.

American memoirs and autobiographies worth noting are Mary Barney, ed., *A Biographical Memoir of the Late Joshua Barney from Autobiographical Notes and Journals in Possession of His Family and Other Authentic Sources* (Boston: Gray and Bowen, 1832); John Leadley Dagg, *Autobiography of Rev. John L. Dagg* (Rome, GA: J. H. Shanklin, 1878) (Dagg was a private in the Virginia militia); Daniel Mallory, *Short Stories and Reminiscences of the Last Fifty Years by An Old Traveller,* 2 vols. (New York: R. P. Bixby & Co., 1842); Samuel Tyler, *Memoir of Roger*

Brooke Taney, L.L.D. (Baltimore: John Murphy & Co., 1872) (Taney talked with Francis Scott Key about his poem after the bombardment of Fort McHenry); James Wilkinson, *Memoirs of My Own Times,* 4 vols. (Philadelphia: Abraham Small, 1816) (Wilkinson was an American general during the war); Sister Mary Xavier Queen, *Grandma's Stories and Anecdotes of "Ye Olden Times"* (Boston: Angel Guardian Press, 1899); Narrative of Richard Rush, July 10, 1835, in John S. Williams, *History of the Invasion and Capture of Washington and the Events that Followed* (New York: Harper and Bros., 1857), 274–81; Joseph S. Van Why, ed., "Martin Gillette's Letters About the War of 1812," *Connecticut Historical Society Bulletin* 23 (1958): 81–84 (Gillette was a private in the Maryland militia); Statement of John Stuart Skinner, in Baltimore *Patriot,* May 23, 1849, reprinted as "Incidents of the War of 1812," *Maryland Historical Magazine* 32 (1937): 340–47; William Henry Winder, "General Winder and the Capture of Washington," *Historical Magazine* 5 (1861): 227–29; and the many narratives written by participants in the war that appear in William M. Marine, *The British Invasion of Maryland, 1812–1815* (Baltimore: Society of the War of 1812 in Maryland, 1913, reprinted by Hatboro, PA: Tradition Press, 1965).

Biographies

There is considerable biographical information readily available on the characters, major and minor, who played a role in the war in the Chesapeake. Of special note are Gerson G. Eisenberg, *Marylanders Who Served the Nation: A Biographical Dictionary of Federal Officials from Maryland* (Annapolis: MD State Archives, 1992), and Charles, J. Peterson, *The Military Heroes of The War of 1812 with a Narrative of the War,* 10th ed. (Philadelphia: Leary & Getz, 1858).

Also valuable are Frank A. Cassell, *Merchant Congressman in the Young Republic: Samuel Smith of Maryland, 1752–1839* (Madison: University of Wisconsin Press, 1971); Roger Morris, *Cockburn and the British Navy in Transition: Admiral Sir George Cockburn, 1772–1853* (Columbia: University of South Carolina Press, 1997); James Pack, *The Man Who Burned the White House: Admiral Sir George Cockburn, 1772–1853* (Annapolis, MD: Naval Institute Press, 1987); Elers Napier, *The Life and Correspondence of Admiral Sir Charles Napier, K.C.B.* (London: Hurst and Blackett, 1862), which was reprinted as *The Life and Letters of Admiral Sir Charles Napier, K.C.B* (London: Hutchinson, 1917) (Napier was a British Royal Navy captain who in 1814 served under Capt. James A. Gordon); Scott Sumpter Sheads, *Guardian of the Star-Spangled Banner: Lt. Colonel George Armistead and The Fort McHenry Flag* (Baltimore: Toomey Press, 1986); and Henry T. Tuckerman, *The Life of John Pendleton Kennedy* (New York: G. P. Putman's Sons, 1871).

Still other works that are worth consulting are Charles Oscar Paulin, *Commodore John Rodgers: Captain, Commodore, and Senior Officer of the American Navy 1773–1838* (Cleveland, OH: Arthur H. Clarke, 1910); John H. Schroeder, *Commodore John Rodgers: Paragon of the Early American Navy* (Gainesville: University Press of Florida, 2006); David D. Porter, *Memoir of Commodore David Porter of the United States Navy* (Albany, NY: J. Munsell, 1875); Hulbert Footner, *Sailor of Fortune: The Life and Adventures of Commodore Barney, U.S.N.* (New York: Harper & Brothers, 1940); Ralph D. Paine, *Joshua Barney: A Forgotten Hero of Blue Water* (New York: Century Co., 1924); Louis Arthur Norton, *Joshua Barney: Hero of the Revolution and 1812* (Annapolis: Naval Institute Press, 2000); James T. de Kay, *A Rage for Glory: The Life of Commodore Stephen Decatur, USN* (New York: Free Press, 2004); Robert J. Allison, *Stephen Decatur: American Naval Hero, 1779–1820* (Amherst: University of Massachusetts Press, 2005); Spencer Tucker, *Stephen Decatur: A Life Most Bold and Daring* (Annapolis: Naval Institute Press, 2005); and Leonard F. Guttridge, *Our Country, Right or Wrong: The Life of Stephen Decatur, the U.S. Navy's Most Illustrious Commander* (New York: Forge, 2006).

Still other biographical studies worth noting are William L. Calderhead, "A Strange Career in a Young Navy: Captain Charles Gordon, 1778–1816," *Maryland Historical Magazine* 72 (1997): 373–86; Ruth Kimball Kent, "The Convivial Dr. Beanes," *Maryland Historical Magazine* 73 (1978): 389–93; and Caleb Clarke Magruder, Jr., "Dr. William Beanes, The Incidental Cause of the Authorship of the Star-Spangled Banner," *Records of the Columbia Historical Society* 22 (1919): 207–25.

General Works on the Chesapeake Region

There are several good works devoted exclusively to the War of 1812 in the Chesapeake. Walter Lord, *The Dawn's Early Light* (New York: W. W. Norton, 1972), is a popular account focusing on the war in Maryland and Washington that is both engaging and generally reliable. Christopher T. George, *Terror on the Chesapeake: The War of 1812 on the Bay* (Shippensburg, PA: White Mane Publishing Company, 2000), is a more recent account. Like Lord, George focuses on the war in the Upper Chesapeake, although he does include a chapter on the Virginia engagements at Craney Island and Hampton. Joseph A. Whitehorne, *The Battle for Baltimore 1814* (Baltimore: Nautical & Aviation Publishing Company, 1997), and Anthony Pitch, *The Burning of Washington: The British Invasion of 1814* (Annapolis: Naval Institute Press, 2000) both cover the Chesapeake Campaign during 1813 and 1814. Whitehorne has an appendix listing British and American troops present during major operations in Maryland and Virginia and includes a chronology, but some of the dates and locations are wrong. Pitch's work is heavily laced with anecdotes and thus engaging. Gilbert Byron, *The War of 1812 on the Chesapeake Bay* (Baltimore: Maryland Historical Society, 1964), is a brief history. Finally, Robert E. Reyes, Ray Stolle, Amber Sessler, and Mike Wieczorek, *Star Spangled Banner Trail: A Guide to the Chesapeake Campaign of 1814* (Riviera Beach, MD: privately printed, 2000), is a useful illustrated guide with maps. Although few copies of this work were printed, one is available at the Research Library, Fort McHenry National Monument & Historical Shrine.

Works on the Militia

For information on the Maryland militia, one should consult Sallie A. Mallick and F. Edward Wright, *Frederick County Militia in the War of 1812* (Westminster, MD: Family Line Publications, 1992); and F. Edward Wright, *Maryland Militia: War of 1812,* 11 vols. (Silver Spring, MD: Family Line Publications, 1979–86). These volumes are also available on compact disk in *Maryland Militia in the War of 1812* (Lewis, DE: Colonial Roots Collection, 2006). Over half of William M. Marine's work, *The British Invasion of Maryland, 1812–1815* (Baltimore: Society of the War of 1812 in Maryland, 1913), consists of a list (compiled by Louis H. Dielman) of more than 11,000 Maryland militiamen who served in the war.

For the Virginia militia, see Stuart Lee Butler, *Virginia Soldiers in the United States Army 1800–1815* (Athens, GA: Iberian Publishing Company, 1986), and *A Guide to Virginia Militia Units in the War of 1812* (Athens, GA: Iberian Publishing Company, 1988); and *Pay Rolls of Militia Entitled to Land Bounty Under the Act of Congress of Sept. 28, 1850* (Richmond, VA, 1851), which was reprinted as *Virginia Militia in the War of 1812,* 2 vols. (Baltimore: Genealogical Publishing Company, 2001).

Works on African Americans

For the role of African Americans in the Chesapeake, see Stuart L. Butler, "Slave Flight in the Northern Neck During the War of 1812," *Northern Neck of Virginia Historical Magazine* 62 (2007): 6821–43; Christopher T. George, "Mirage of Freedom: African Americans in the War of 1812," *Maryland Historical Magazine* 91 (1996): 426–50; the account of escaped slave Charles Ball, *A Narrative of the Life and Adventures of Charles Ball, A Black Man* (Lewistown, PA: John W. Shugert, 1836); Paul Jennings, *A Colored Man's Reminiscences of James Madison,* Bladensburg Series, Number Two (Brooklyn: George C. Beadle, 1865), John G. Sharp, "The Diary of Michael Shiner Relating to the History of the Washington Navy Yard 1813–1869," www.ibiblio.org/hyperwar/NHC/shiner/shiner_diary.htm; and Scott Sumpter Sheads, "A Black Soldier Defends Fort McHenry, 1814," *Military Collector and Historian* 41 (1989): 20–21.

General Works on Maryland

The general works cited above on the Chesapeake all provide good material on the war in Maryland. In addition, one should consult the oldest, and in some ways still most useful, work on the conflict in this state, which is William M. Marine, *British Invasion of Maryland,* cited above. Marine was the first to go beyond the engagements at Bladensburg and Baltimore, and he presents some important source material as well. Other useful works on the war in Maryland are "Maryland in the War of 1812," in Matthew P. Andrews, *Tercentenary History of Maryland,* 4 vols. (Chicago: S. J. Clarke, 1925), 1:686–739; David Healey, *1812: Rediscovering Chesapeake Bay's Forgotten War* (Rock Hill, SC: Bella Rosa Books, 2005); Edward Duncan Ingraham, *A Sketch of the Events Which Preceded the Capture of Washington by the British on the 24th of August, 1814* (Philadelphia: Carey & Hart, 1849); and Charles G. Muller, *The Darkest Day: 1814: The Washington-Baltimore Campaign* (New York: J. B. Lippincott Company, 1963).

Of special importance for understanding the war in Maryland are two American Battlefield Protection Program reports that unfortunately are not widely available although both can be found in the Research Library at Fort McHenry National Monument & Historic Shrine. These are Ralph E. Eshelman and Christopher T. George, "Maryland War of 1812: Battlefields, Selected Skirmishes, Encampments, Earthworks, and Related Sites," American Battlefield Protection Program Report (National Park Service, December 2000); and Ralph Eshelman, Susan Langley, and Ben Ford, "Maryland Revolutionary War and War of 1812 Battlefields/Skirmishes and Associated Historical Properties Survey," American Battlefield Protection Program Report (National Park Service, March 2002). These reports laid the foundation for the Maryland inventory in our work.

During the centennial commemoration of the British invasion of Maryland, Wilfred M. Barton retraced the British route in *The Road to Washington* (Boston: Richard G. Badger, 1919). Barton provides some photographs of sites along that route that have since been greatly altered or destroyed.

Three scholarly works in progress should shed further light on the war in Maryland. The late Stanley Quick worked on a general account of the war in the Chesapeake Bay that hopefully will be published; Donald G. Shomette has a revised and expanded edition of his work, *Flotilla: Battle for the Patuxent* (Solomons, MD: Calvert Marine Museum Press, 1981), retitled *Flotilla: The Patuxent Campaign in the War of 1812,* published by Johns Hopkins University Press in May 2009; and Scott Sheads and Ralph Eshelman are working on an account of the war in Maryland that focuses on the role of the citizen-soldier and -sailor.

Maryland County Histories

The most useful county histories are Frederick Emory, *Queen Anne's County: Maryland Its Early History and Development* (Baltimore: Maryland Historical Society, 1950); George Johnson, *History of Cecil County, Maryland, and the Early Settlements around the Head of the Chesapeake Bay* (Baltimore: Genealogical Publishing Co., 1989); and Fred G. Usilton, *History of Kent County, Maryland, 1630–1916* (n.p., 1916?). Histories of individual towns and cities are also often useful as is Harry C. Rhodes, *Queenstown: The Social History of a Small American Town* (Queenstown: Queen Anne Press, 1985).

Maryland County Libraries and Historical Societies

Vertical files in local libraries, museums, and historical societies can be a good source of information on the war. A good example is a brochure entitled *A Cecil County Historic Tour Guide* (Elkton?, MD: Cecil County Bicentennial Committee, 1976?). While concentrating on sites associated with the American Revolution, it also has information on sites related to the War of 1812, most notably Rodgers Tavern, Principio Furnace, and Rose Hill (home of Gen. Thomas Marsh Foreman). Similarly, the vertical file in the Maryland Room of the Talbot County Free Library in Easton has considerable information on Fort Stokes, and the Maryland Room of the Enoch Pratt Library in Baltimore has many newspaper clippings and pamphlets bearing on the war.

Other Works on Maryland

A host of other works shed light on the battles, campaigns, and other topics related to Maryland.

Battle of Havre de Grace

For details on this battle, see Jared Sparks, "Conflagration of Havre de Grace," *North American Review* 14 (July 1817): 157–63; Blaine Taylor, "May 3, 1813, Cockburn vs. O'Neill at Havre de Grace: Britain's Sea-Going Commando Burns the 'Harbor of Mercy,'" *Harford Historical Bulletin* 43 (1990): 1–20; Herbert G. Adams, *The Life and Writings of Jared Sparks,* 2 vols. (Boston: Houghton Mifflin and Co., 1893), 1:66–67; George W. Archer, "Our Local History: Details of the Capture of Havre de Grace by the British, May 3rd, 1813, and of the Barbarities Committed by them on that Occasion" (paper read before the Harford Historical Society on December 15, 1885, Havre de Grace *Republican,* July 18, 1886); Christopher T. George, "Harford County in the War of 1812," *Harford Historical Bulletin* 76 (1998): 3–61; John S. Hanna, *History of the Life and Services of Samuel Dewees. A Native of Pennsylvania and Soldier of the Revolutionary and Last War* (Baltimore: R. Neilson, 1844) (Dewees

served as a musician in the Maryland militia); and [Rev. James Jones Wilmer], *Narrative Respecting the Conduct of the British from their First Landing on Spesutia Island, Till their Progress to Havre de Grace* (Baltimore: P. Mauro, 1813).

Battles of St. Michaels

For the British attacks on this town, see Gilbert Byron, *St. Michaels, The Town that Fooled the British: A Complete Account of the British Attacks on St. Michaels during the War of 1812,* 3rd ed. (Easton, MD: Loskamp Printing Co., 1986); Norman H. Plummer, "Another Look at the Battle of St. Michaels," *The Weather Gauge* 31 (1995): 10–17; and Thomas H. Sewell, "The Battle of Saint Michaels 1812–1913" (facsimile copy in Howard I. Chapelle Library, Chesapeake Bay Maritime Museum, St. Michaels, MD).

Battles of St. Leonard Creek

For this series of engagements, see Ralph E. Eshelman, *Maryland's Largest Naval Engagement: The Battles of St. Leonard Creek, 1814, Calvert County, Maryland,* Studies in Archaeology No. 3 (St. Leonard, MD: Jefferson Patterson Park & Museum, 2005); *Flotilla: Battle for the Patuxent* (cited above) and Donald G. Shomette, *Tidewater Time Capsule: History Beneath the Patuxent* (Centreville, MD: Tidewater Publishers, 1995).

Battle of Bladensburg

For details on the American defeat in this critical battle, see Albert K. Hadel, "The Battle of Bladensburg," *Maryland Historical Magazine* 1 (1906): 197–210; Glenn F. Williams, "The Bladensburg Races," *The Quarterly Journal of Military History* 12 (1999): 58–65; Horatio King, "The Battle of Bladensburg," *Magazine of American History* 14 (1885): 438–57; Horatio King, "The Bladensburg Races," *Magazine of American History* 15 (1886): 85–88; Thomas Lorraine McKenny, *A Narrative of the Battle of Bladensburg in A Letter to Henry Banning, Esq., By an Officer of General Smith's Brigade* (Washington, DC: n.p., 1814) (McKenny was an aide to Brig. Gen. Walter Smith in the 1st Brigade of the District of Columbia militia); Thomas Parker, "A Narrative of the Battle of Bladensburg in a letter to Henry Banning, Esq." (typescript at the Military History Institute, Carlisle, PA); and Samuel Williams, "Leaves From An Autobiography," *Ladies Repository* 14 (1854): 156–60 (Williams was a clerk in the general land office).

Battle of North Point

Works on this battle include Frederick M. Coleston, "The Battle of North Point," *Maryland Historical Magazine* 2 (1907): 111–25; John L. Sanford, "The Battle of North Point," *Maryland Historical Magazine* 24 (1929): 356–64; Thomas M. Spaulding, "The Battle of North Point," *Sewanee Review* 1 (1914): 319–29;

and B. Wheeler Jenkins, "The Shots That Saved Baltimore," *Maryland Historical Magazine* 77 (1982): 362–64. See also the three works by Kathy Lee Erlandson: "Archival and Archaeological Investigations at the Patapsco Neck Methodist Meeting House Site, 18BA443, Baltimore County, Maryland," report submitted to the Maryland Historical Trust, 1998; "Archival and Archeological Investigations at the North Point Battlefield/North Point Road at Trappe Road Site, 18BA456, Baltimore County, Maryland," report submitted to the Maryland Historical Trust, 1999; and "Where Are the British Soldiers Killed in the Battle of North Point Buried?" *Baltimore County History Trails* 33 (1998): 1–8.

Battle for Baltimore

For details on the Baltimore campaign, see Scott Sumpter Sheads, *The Rockets' Red Glare: The Maritime Defense of Baltimore in 1814* (Centreville, MD: Tidewater Publishers, 1986); Charles C. Saffell, *The Citizen Soldiers at North Point and Fort McHenry, September 12 and 13* (Baltimore: Privately printed, 1889); Frank A. Cassell, "Baltimore in 1813: A Study of Urban Defense in the War of 1812," *Military Affairs* 33 (1969): 349–61, and "Response to Crisis: Baltimore in 1814," *Maryland Historical Magazine* 66 (1971): 261–87; Franklin R. Mullaly, "The Battle for Baltimore," *Maryland Historical Magazine* 54 (1959): 61–103; Barbara K. Weeks, "'This Present Time Of Alarm': Baltimoreans Prepare For Invasion," *Maryland Historical Magazine* 84 (1989): 259–66; William D. Hoyt, Jr., "Civilian Defense in Baltimore 1814–1815: Minutes of the Committee of Vigilance and Safety," *Maryland Historical Magazine* 39 (1944): 199–225, 293–309 and 40 (1945): 7–23; Melinda K. Friend, "Defense of Baltimore Correspondence," *Maryland Historical Magazine* 86 (1991): 443–49; Robert Henry Goldsborough, "Report of the Battle of Baltimore," *Maryland Historical Magazine* 40 (1945): 230–32; William G. Hawkins, *The Life of John H. W. Hawkins* (Boston: Briggs, Richards, 1863) (Hawkins was a clergyman); "Charles Carroll of Carrollton's Letter Describing the Battle of Baltimore," *Maryland Historical Magazine* 34 (1939): 244–35; and James Piper, "Defense of Baltimore, 1814," *Maryland Historical Magazine* 7 (1912): 375–84 (Piper was a captain in the United Maryland Artillery).

Bombardment of Fort McHenry

For the assault on Fort McHenry, see Scott Sumpter Sheads, *Fort McHenry* (Baltimore: Nautical and Aviation Publishing Company, 1995); Scott Sumpter Sheads, "H.M. Bomb Ship *Terror* and the Bombardment of Fort McHenry," *Maryland Historical Magazine* 103 (2008): 257–67; John Baxley, "Description of the Bombardment of Fort McHenry," *DAR Magazine* 49 (1916): 254–55; S. Sydney Bradford, "Fort McHenry: The Out Works in 1814," *Maryland Historical Magazine* 54 (1959): 188–209; "Of-

ficial Report of the Bombardment of Fort McHenry," reprinted in *Patriotic Marylander* 1 (1914): 20–23; and Richard Walsh, "The Star Fort," *Maryland Historical Magazine* 54 (1959): 296–304.

Fort McHenry Flag and "The Star Spangled Banner" Song

Works on the famous flag and song include P. W. Filby and Edward G. Howard, comps., *Star-Spangled Banner: Books, Sheet Music, Newspapers, Manuscripts, and Persons Associated with "The Star-Spangled Banner"* (Baltimore: Maryland Historical Society, 1972); *Poems of the Late Francis Scott Key* (New York: R. Carter & Bros., 1857) (includes introductory letter by Roger Brooke Taney narrating what Key said about the origins of the song); and Sally Johnson, Beth Miller, and Pat Pilling, *The Star-Spangled Banner Flag House: Home of America's Flag* (Lawrenceburg, IN: Creative Company, 1999).

Baltimore Riots

For information on the pro-war riots that rocked Baltimore in 1812, see Frank A. Cassell, "The Great Baltimore Riot of 1812," *Maryland Historical Magazine* 70 (1975): 241–59; Paul A. Gilje, "The Baltimore Riots of 1812 and the Breakdown of the Anglo-American Mob Tradition," *Journal of Social History* 13 (1980): 547–64; and two works by Donald R. Hickey: "The Darker Side of Democracy: The Baltimore Riots of 1812," *Maryland Historian* 71 (1976): 1–19, and *The War of 1812: A Forgotten Conflict* (Urbana: University of Illinois Press, 1989), ch. 3 .

Todd House

Works on this site are Margaret Burke, "Significance of Todd's Inheritance," in *The Todd House: Friends of Todd's Inheritance* (Patuxent Publishing Company, 2000); Kathy Lee Erlandson, "After the British Fire, Baltimore County War of 1812 Damage Claims: The Todd and Sollers Families and the U.S. Congress," *Journal of the War of 1812* 2 (1997): 14–18, and "The House the Todds Built: Preliminary Investigations into Todd's Inheritance on the Patapsco Neck," [Baltimore County] *History Trails* 32 (1997): 1–8.

Miscellaneous Sites

For information on other sites in Maryland, see Edwin Warfield Beitzell, *The Jesuit Missions of St. Mary's County, Maryland* (Leonardtown, MD: St. Mary's County Historical Society, 1998); Stuart Lee Butler, "Thomas Swann and the British in St. Mary's County," *Maryland Historical Magazine* 73 (1978): 71–78; Amy Cheney Clinton, "Historic Fort Washington," *Maryland Historical Magazine,* 32 (1937): 228–47; M. Keith Ellingsworth, "Tracey's or Tracys Landing?" *Anne Arundel County History Notes* 26 (1995): 1–2, 8–9; Janet A. Headley, "The Monument Without a Public: The Case of the Tripoli Monument," *Winter-*

thur Portfolio 29 (1994): 247–64; Peter Himmelheber, "Sotterley Plantation During the War of 1812," *Chronicles of St. Mary's* 51 (2003): 90–93; Clayland Mullikin, "When A British Fleet Attacked Easton" (typescript in Fort Stokes file, Maryland Room, Talbot Free Library, Easton, MD); Ralph Robinson, "New Light on Three Episodes of the British Invasion of Maryland in 1814," *Maryland Historical Magazine* 37 (1942): 273–90; Mary Runde, "Fort Stokes: Easton's Guardian in War of 1812," Easton *Star-Democrat,* March 21, 1973; Donald G. Shomette, *Lost Towns of Tidewater Maryland* (Centreville, MD: Tidewater Publishers, 2000); and Robert G. Stewart, "The Battle of the Ice Mound, February 7, 1815," *Maryland Historical Magazine* 70 (1975): 372–78.

General Works on Virginia

The general works on the war in the Chesapeake cited above provide some information on the conflict in Virginia (although not nearly as much as they provide on Maryland). Moreover, there is no comprehensive study of Virginia during the War of 1812, but several works deal with specific events or actions in Virginia. Norma Lois Peterson, ed., *The Defense of Norfolk in 1807 as told by William Tatham to Thomas Jefferson* (Chesapeake, VA: Norfolk County Historical Society, 1970), provides primary source material about Norfolk at the time of the *Chesapeake–Leopard* affair in 1807. W. P. Palmer et al., eds., *Calendar of Virginia State Papers and Other Manuscripts . . . Preserved in the Capitol at Richmond,* 11 vols. (Richmond: State of Virginia, 1875–93), provides a wealth of detailed information on state problems, such as the difficulty in supplying arms and food to the militia. Stuart Lee Butler, *Real Patriots and Heroic Soldiers: Gen. Joel Leftwich and the Virginia Brigade in the War of 1812* (Westminster, MD: Heritage Books, Inc., 2008), provides a history of the Virginia Brigade that marched to Ohio and helped establish Fort Meigs. Butler is also working on a book about the Virginia militia during the war that should significantly add to our understanding of the conflict in this state.

Other Works on Virginia

Battle of Craney Island

For details on the largest battle to take place in Virginia during the war, see John M. Hallahan, *The Battle of Craney Island: A Matter of Credit* (Portsmouth, VA: Saint Michael's Press, 1986), which also has a chapter on the Battle of Hampton; William H. Gaines, Jr., "Craney Island, or Norfolk Delivered," *Virginia Cavalcade* 1 (1951): 32–35; James Jarvis, "A Narrative of the Attack on Craney Island on the 22nd June, 1813," *Virginia*

Historical Register 1 (July 1848): 137–41; John D. Richardson, *Defense of Craney Island on the 22nd of June, 1813* (Richmond, VA, 1849); and William Maxwell, ed., "The Defence of Craney Island," *Virginia Historical Register and Literary Advertiser* 1 (1848): 132–41.

Battle of Pungoteague

For the largest battle on Virginia's Eastern Shore, see Alton Brooks Parker Barnes, *Pungoteague To Petersburg,* 2 vols. (Bowling Green, VA: privately printed, 1988), 1:1–107.

Battle of White House

For information on this battle, see Bertram H. Groene, "A Trap for the British: Thomas Brown and the Battle of the 'White House,'" *Virginia Cavalcade* 18 (1968): 13–19, and Charles G. Muller, "Fabulous Potomac Passage," *U.S. Naval Institute Proceedings* 90 (1964): 85–91.

Other Sites

For information on other sites in Virginia, see "War's Wild Alarm, Richmond 1813, Baltimore 1814," *Virginia Magazine of History and Biography* 49 (1941): 217–33; Lewis P. Balch, "Reminiscences of the War of 1812," *Historical Magazine* 7 (1863): 383–84 (Balch was a private in Virginia); Stuart Lee Butler, "Captain Barrie's Last Raid," *Northern Neck of Virginia Historical Magazine* 54 (2004): 6441–52; Marshall W. Butt, *Portsmouth Under Four Flags* (Portsmouth, VA: Messenger Printing Co., 1973); J. Mackay Hitsman and Alice Sorby, "Independent Foreigners or Canadian Chasseurs," *Military Affairs* 25 (1961): 11–17; Floyd Painter, ed., *The Legend, History, and Archaeology of Fort Boykin in Virginia* (Norfolk, VA: Chesopeian Library of Archaeology, 1982); Parke Rouse, Jr., "The British Invasion of Hampton in 1813: The Reminiscences of James Jarvis," *The Virginia Magazine* 76 (1968): 318–36; James H. Ryan and Lee A. Wallace, Jr., "Duty and Honor: Petersburg's Contributions to the War of 1812," *Proceedings of the Historic Petersburg Foundation* 11 (2004): 1–41; Joseph F. Skivora, "The Surrender of Alexandria in the War of 1812 and the Powers of the Press," *Northern Virginia Heritage* 10 (1988): 9–13; George Holbert Tucker, *Norfolk Highlights: 1584–1881* (Portsmouth, VA, 1972); Ralph T. Whitelaw, *Virginia's Eastern Shore: A History of Northampton and Accomack Counties,* 2 vols. (Richmond: Virginia Historical Society, 1952); William Tatham, *Report Concerning the Military Defence of the River Potomack, the City of Washington and Adjacent Country . . . Submitted to the Secretary of War, May 27, 1813* (original document in National Archives; typed copy on file at Fort Belvoir, VA); and Lee A. Wallace, Jr., "The Petersburg Volunteers, 1812–1813," *Virginia Magazine of History and Biography* 82 (1974): 458–85 (also available at www.newrivernotes.com/va/pete1812.htm).

Works on the District of Columbia

The best place to start for the war in the District of Columbia are the general works on the war in the Chesapeake cited above but especially Anthony Pitch, *The Burning of Washington: The British Invasion of 1814*. Other pertinent works are Carole L. Herrick, *August 24, 1814: Washington in Flames* (Falls Church, VA: Higher Education Publications, Inc., 2005) (also covers the flights of the President and First Lady); George Delacy Evans, *Facts Relative to the Capture of Washington, in Reply to Some Statements Contained in the Memoirs of Admiral George Cockburn* (London: Henry Colburn, 1829) (Evans was a British army lieutenant who took part in the campaign); John C. Hildt, "Letters Relating to Capture of Washington," *South Atlantic Quarterly* 6 (1907): 58–66; "Col. McLane's Visit to Washington in 1814," *Bulletin of the Historical Society of Pennsylvania* 1 (1845): 16–22; Peter Rowley, "Captain Robert Rowley Helps to Burn Washington, DC," *Maryland Historical Magazine* 82 (1987): 240–50; Milton S. Davis, "The Capture of Washington," *U.S. Naval Institute Proceedings* 63 (1937): 839–51; Mary Hunter, "The Burning of Washington," *New-York Historical Society Bulletin* 8 (1925): 80–83 (which reproduces a contemporary account); Willis Thornton, "The Day They Burned the Capitol," *American Heritage* 6 (1954): 48–53; and Frederick P. Todd, "The Militia and Volunteers of the District of Columbia, 1783–1820," *Records of the Columbia Historical Society* 50 (1952): 379–439.

Other works include Thomas B. Brumbaugh, "A Letter of Dr. William Thornton to Colonel William Thornton," *Maryland Historical Magazine* 73 (1978): 64–70; Rene Chartrand, ed., "An Account of the Capture of Washington, 1814," *Military Collector and Historian* 37 (1985): 182 (reproduces British account written by Lt. David Dennear of the Royal Artillery Drivers); Allen C. Clark, *Life and Letters of Dolley Madison* (Washington, DC: W. F. Roberts, 1914); John C. Hildt, ed., "Letters Relating to the Burning of Washington," *South Atlantic Quarterly* 6 (1907): 56–66 (prints letters of Stephen Pleasonton, chief clerk of the State Department); Gaillard Hunt, ed., *The First Forty Years of Washington Society* (New York: Charles Scribner's Sons, 1906) (narrative of Margaret Smith, wife of editor of *Daily National Intelligencer*); Ray W. Irwin, ed., "The Capture of Washington in 1814 as Described by Mordecai Booth," *Americana* 28 (1934): 7–27; Dorothy T. Madison, ed. "At a Perilous Moment Dolley Madison Writes to Her Sister," *Madison Quarterly* 4 (1944): 27–28; James Monroe, "Letters of James Monroe," *Tyler's Quarterly Historical and Genealogical Magazine* 4 (1923): 405–11; and Norman S. Pringle, ed., *Letters by Major Norman Pringle, Late of the 21st Royal Scots Fusiliers, Vindicating the Character of the British Army Employed in North America in the Years 1814–1815* (Edinburgh, Scotland: Blackwood, 1814).

Armistead, Walker K., 238

Armstrong, John (gunsmith), 114

Armstrong, John (Sec. of War): at Bladensburg, 83, 86, 270, 288, 291; at Frederick, 124; at Griffith Combe House, 294; office of, 276; and Pleasonton, 278; on possible British attack on Washington, 288; on Washington's military value 270. Correspondence: from Dyson, 123; from Granger, 183; from Stuart, 144, 148, 186; from Tatham, 141, 265; from Taylor, 251; with Winder, L., 108; from Winder, W. H., 28, 36, 205

Arnold, John (Pvt., Md. Militia), 303

Arnold, Maryland, *27*

Ashby Family Cemetery (Md.), 308

Asp (U.S. schooner), 154, 234, 266, 267, 268, 335

Asquith, George (Acting-Midshipman), 190

Atkinson, Isaac, 147

Atlanta (privateer), 112

Atlas (privateer), 299, 363n6

Auld, Hugh, Jr. (Lt. Col., Md. Militia), 193, 208–9, 334

Auld's Point (Md.), 208, 209

Aveilhe-Goldsborough House (Md.), *133, 135*

Babcock, Samuel (Capt., USA), 51, 60

Babcock Battery. *See* Fort Babcock

Baden, Nehemiah (Lt., Md. Militia), 173

Bailey, Chester, 280

Bailey Cemetery (Va.), 334

Bainbridge (Md.), *27*, 42

Bainbridge, William (Com., USN), 5, 42–43, *43*, 340

Baker, Henry L. (Capt., RN), 192

Baldwin Memorial United Methodist Church Cemetery (Md.), *27*, 307

Ball, Charles (USN): bio, 355n59; at Bladensburg, 84; as cook, 149; and fishery at Drum Point, 105; at Lower Marlboro, 149

Ballard, Charles (Maj.), 260

Ballard, Levin, 149

Ballards Landing (Md.), 148

Ball House (Portsmouth, Va.), 255

Baltimore, Battle for, 11, 17, 60, 63

Baltimore *American* (newspaper), 13, *45*, 48, 50, 54, 57, 77, 126, 149, 153, 160, 164, 165, 357n182

Baltimore Cemetery, *45*, 58, 308

Baltimore Clipper(s), 14, 43, 54

Baltimore Committee of Observation, 77

Baltimore Committee of Vigilance and Safety, 56, 69, 166

Baltimore *Daily Gazette,* 198

Baltimore *Evening Post,* 16

Baltimore *Federal Gazette and Baltimore Daily Advertiser,* 24, 46, 49, 53, 78, 98, 153, 176, 178, 211, 312, 359n268

Baltimore *Federal Republican* (newspaper), 34, 49, 50, 54, 78, 79, 122, 129, 141, 146, 175, 176, 186, 201, 203, 205, 207, 208, 219, 257, 262, 325, 335, 354n15

Baltimore *Federal Republican and Commercial Gazette,* 15

Baltimore Fencibles, 15, 47, 50, 63, 102, 115, 117, 118, 119, 120, 158, 212

Baltimore Flotilla, 55, 67

Baltimore Light Infantry, 308, 317, 318, 321, 323

Baltimore *Patriot & Evening Advertiser,* 13, *45*, 49–50, 54, 55, 84, 89, 108, 110, 112, 127, 178, 198, 222, 223, 237, 238, 240, 251, 261, 267, 269, 362n19

Baltimore Public Hospital, 70, 76

Baltimore Riot(s), 17, *31*, 34, 50, 201, 220, 334

Baltimore *Sun* (newspaper), 52, 59, 65, 161, 304, 332

Baltzell, Thomas (Lt./Adj., Md. Militia), 158, 313

Bancroft Hall (U.S. Naval Academy, Annapolis), *33, 34*, 37

Bank of the Metropolis (Washington, D.C.), 273–74

Bank of Washington, 93, *271*, 273, 361n2

Barbour, James (Va. Gov.), 232, 251; bio, 19; boyhood home, 244; call for volunteers, 258; county named for, 213. Correspondence: from Bayly, 257, 262; from Cocke, 263; from Cropper, 259; from Ritchie, 263; from Tatham, 244

Barclay, Thomas H. (Col., British Agent for Prisoners in America), 88

Barker, Jacob, 297

Barney, John (Capt., USA), 314

Barney, Joshua (Com., USN), 42, 58, 61, 68, 192, 274–75, 276; battle of Bladensburg, 10, 84, 89–90; battle of Cedar Point, 103; battles of St. Leonard Creek, 9, 168, 188–91; bio, 14; complaint of Calvert militia, 202; 1813 plan to Navy Department, 9; at Long Old Fields encampment, 147, 211; medical treatment of, 90–91; Md. Historical Roadside Marker, 75, *157;* as member of Society of the Cincinnati, 287; musket ball that took life of, *277;* portrait, 69; as privateer, 14, 53, 75, 195; proposed attack near Gods Grace, 129; rage against, 177, 190; sketch of Patuxent River, 100, *106;* and sniper attack on Capital Hill, 286; suggestion of gun battery at Point Patience, 175; testimony on damages to Prince Frederick courthouse, 177. Correspondence: from Jones, 89, 178, 195; from Stricker, 165, 168, 195; to Jones, 75, 90, 99, 100, 104, 130, 148, 175, 178, 188, 189, 190, 191, 192, 201, 359nn290, 291

Barney, William B. (Maj., USN), 136; Baltimore riots, 50, 74; at Battle of North Point, 158; at battles of St. Leonard Creek, 188; location of home, *45*, 49

Barney Gun Battery (near Barney Circle, Washington, D.C.), *32, 83, 85*, 147, *271*, 274

Barney House (Md.), *25*, 75

Barney Marker (Fort McHenry, Md.), 118

Barney Monument (Bladensburg, Md.), *83*, 90

Barossa (H.M. frigate), 251

Barr, Jacob (Capt., Md. Militia), 131

Barrett, Robert J. (Midshipman, USN), 29, 117, 174

Barrie, Robert (Capt., RN): attack on Tappahannock River, 262; at Benedict, 78; decision not to attack Fredericksburg, 234. Correspondence: from Alexander, 144; from Cockburn, 105; from Jackson, 224; from Warren, 299; to Cockburn, 77, 99, 103, 149, 192, 201, 231, 264; to Warren, 243

Barroll, James Edmondson, 102

Barron, James (Capt./Com., USN), commander of U.S. frigate *Chesapeake,* 89, 234, 248; duel with Decatur, 43, 89, 277; family home, 239; gunboat model, 252; place of burial, *336*

Barry, Standish (2nd Maj., Md. Militia), *158*

Barry, William F. (Gen., USA), 153

Bartholomew, David E. (Capt., RN), 266

Basilica of the Assumption (Baltimore), *45,* 50

Bastion No. 5 (Baltimore), 72

Bathurst, Henry (3rd Earl Bathurst, British Sec. of State For War and the Colonies): letters from Brooke, 64, 158; letters from Ross, 87, 272

Battery Decatur (Fort Washington, Potomac River), 124

Battery Jameson (Fort Lincoln, Md.), 90

Battery McFarland (Fort Armistead, Patapsco River), 58

Battery Many (Fort Washington, Potomac River), 124

Battery Park (Baltimore), *32, 44,* 55, 56, 60–61, *61,* 68, 71

Battery Towson (Fort Carroll, Patapsco River), *44,* 75

Battery Winchester (Fort Armistead, Patapsco River), 59

Battle Acre (North Point Battlefield, Md.), monument at, *157,* 158, 160

Battle Ground Methodist Episcopal Church (Md.), 161

Battle Monument (Baltimore), 23, 30, *45,* 50, *52,* 53, 57, 182, 292

Bayly, Thomas M. (Lt. Col., Va. Militia), 224, 253, 257, 262

Bayou Hotel (Havre de Grace, Md.), *133,* 135, 136

Beall, Upton, 184

Beall, William D. (Col., Md. Militia), *85,* 113, 128

Beall-Dawson House (Md.), 184

Beanes, William (Dr.), 12–13, 21–22, 151, 170, 177, 191, 197, 208, 211; grave, *206,* 208; house, *206,* 207

Beanes, William Bradley, 154, 197, 207

Bear Creek (Md.), 75, *157,* 158, *158,* 160, 200

Beatty, James, 24, 78

Beaver Creek Plantation (Va.), *215,* 221

Beckett, John (Capt. USA), 104, *105*

Beckwith, Sir Thomas Sidney (Col., British Army), 560n26; at Battle of Slippery Hill, 179–80, 182; letters to Warren, 237; near St. Michaels, 195

Beeston (Beaston), Thomas V., 117

Belair (Mansion) (Md.), *27,* 76

Belches, Alexander (Lt., USN), 254

Bellefields (Md.), *26, 31,* 76, *77,* 147–48, 197

Belleville Cemetery (Md.), 108

Bellevue (Md.), 259, 276

Bellona Arsenal (Richmond), 258, *259*

Bellona Gunpowder Mills (Md.), *27,* 77–78

Bell's Ferry (Susquehanna River, Md.), *31,* 78, 172

Belmont (Md.), 15, 49

Belvidera (H.M. frigate), 16, 139

Belvoir (Mansion) (Va.), 264, 267

Benedict (Md.), *8, 9,* 20, *26,* 78–82, *80,* 102, 105, 123, 124, 148, 149, 168, 170, 171, 176, 177, 202; British encampment, *81;* British invasion at, 78–80; D.C. militia encampment, 79

Bennett, Charles, 55; house (Fells Point), *45*

Bennett, Henry (Capt., Md. Militia), 112

Benson, Perry (Gen., Md. Militia), 82, 108, 195, 209; battle of St. Michaels, 193–95; grave, *28,* 82; letter from Bryan, 145

Bentley, Caleb, 94

Bentley, Caleb, House (Md.), 94, *95*

Bentley, Henrietta, 94–95

Benton-Shipley Cemetery (Md.), *27,* 309

Benvenue (McLean, Va.), 224, *271*

Berge, Edward, 37, 117

Bermuda, 80, 99, 106, 244, 262, 299

Berry, John (Capt., Washington Artillery), 61, 118, 314

Berry, John Nally (Pvt., Md. Militia), 95, 330

Betsey (merchant ship), 346

Beynon, Benjamin George (1st Lt., RM), 114, 186

Biays, James (Lt. Col., Md. Militia), *158,* 313

Bibb, Sally Wyatt, 236

Big Annemessex River (Md.), *28, 31,* 82, 147

Big Fairlee (Md.), 114

Binns II, Charles, 242

Blackbeard Point (Hampton, Va.), *235, 236,* 236, 238, *239*

Bladensburg (Md.), *8, 9,* 10–11, *25, 32,* 84–92, 270, *271*

Bladensburg, Battle of (Md.), *10,* 12, 14, 15, 16, 17, 20, 21, 56, 57, 75, *85, 87,* 154, *183,* 313, 317, 318, 322, 324, 326, 328, 331, 332, 334, 335, 337, 338, 339, 400

Bladensburg Waterfront Park (Md.), *83,* 87

Blackistone Island (Md.), *26, 31,* 186

Black Point (Coan River, Va.), 225

Blair, James (Sgt. Maj., Md. Militia), *158*

Blair, Thomas (Capt., Md. Militia), 326

Blake, James H. (Mayor), 279

Blake, Peregrine (Maj.), 180

Blake, T., 177

Blakeford (Md.), *179,* 181

Blakistone, Thomas (Lt. Col., Md. Militia), 146

Blandford Church (Va.), 254

Bleeker, Harmanus, 96, 199

Richmond *Enquirer* (newspaper), 214, 232, 234, 245, 246, 255, 263, 360n37

Richmond *Virginia Argus* (newspaper), 244, 254, 260, 360n31

Richmond *Virginia Patriot* (newspaper), 245, 246

Ridge (Md.), *26*, 182–83

Ridgely, Charles Carnan, 131, 156

Ridgely (Charles S.?) (at Brookeville, Maj., Md. Militia), 95

Ridgely House (North Point, Md.), *157, 165*, 165–66

Riley, Thomas (Cpl., British deserter), 203

Rinehart, William Henry, 35

Ringgold, Tench, 272, 287

Rising Sun (merchant ship), 75

Ritchie, Archibald (Lt. Col., Va. Militia), 263

Ritchie, Meriwether, House (Tappahannock, Va.), 262, *263*, 361n75

Rivardi, J. J. Ulrich (Maj., USA), 120

Riversdale Mansion (Md.), *26*, 183, *183*

River View Cemetery (Md.), *26*, 327

Robert, Joseph, 185

Robertson, Frederick (Capt., Royal Artillery), *125*, 180

Robyns, John (Capt., RM), 172–73

Rock Hall (Md.), *8, 27, 31*, 176, 184

Rocks Plantation (James River, Va.), 213

Rodgers, John (Capt./Com. USN), 26, 42, 72, *72, 73*, 120, 124, 135, 139–40, 196, 219, 276, 339; bio, 16; launch of fire ships against British, 156, 266–67. Correspondence: letters from Jones, W., 147, 304; letter from Monroe, 265; letter from Rutter, 67; letters to Jones, W., 156, 218

Rodgers' Bastion (Baltimore), *45*, 72, *72*

Rodgers House (Havre de Grace, Md.), 133, 138, *138*

Rodmon, Solomon (Sailing Master, USN), 120

Rokeby Farm (near Chain Bridge, Va.), 224, 230, 245, 259, *271*

Rokeby Mansion (near Leesburg, Va.), *215, 242*, 243, *243*, 276, 277

Rolla (privateer), 55

Roosevelt, Theodore (Pres.), 42, 298

rope walks, at Baltimore, 64, *65, 71*; at Washington, D.C., *10*, 11, 21, 270, 272, 286, 287, 340

Rose Hill (Cecil County, Md.), *27*, 184

Rosier Creek (Potomac River, Va.), *8, 215, 216*, 259

Ross, David, Jr. (Dr.), 91

Ross, Gen. Robert (Maj. Gen., British Army), 12, 14, 192, 207, 208; at Bladensburg, *10*, 83, 84, *86*, 91; invasion of Md., 9, 24, 76, 80, 147, 148, 149, 151, *152*, 169, 170, 207, 209, 211; letters to Bathurst, 88, 272; mortal wounding of, 12, 17, *47*, 51, 52, 58, 64, 75, 106, 119, 157, *158*, 160, *161*, 163, 165, 168; at North Point, 12, 46, 160, 167; and ruses, 76, 148; at Washington, D.C., 274, 275, *276*, 282, 284, 286, 287, 291, 296, 297

Ross, Gen. Robert, Roadside Marker (North Point), *157*, 160

Ross House (Annapolis, Md.), *83*, 91–2, *92*

Rossie (privateer), 14, 17, 55, 75, 195

Rousby Hall (Md.), *26, 31*, 185

Row, Jacob (Capt., Md. Militia), 114

Rowley, Robert (Capt., RN), 101

Royal Oak (H.M. ship-of-the-line), 174

Rush, Richard (Attorney General), 84, 86, 94, 192; letter to Williams, 279

Rutherford, Archibald, 239

Rutter, Solomon (Capt., USN), 67, 120; letter to Rodgers, 67

Sadtler, Philip Benjamin (Capt., Md. Militia), 158, *158*

Sailor's Battery (Baltimore), 59, 60. *See also* Fort Babcock

"Saint Michaels Patriotic Blues," 196, 326

Salem (Massachusetts) *Essex Register* (newspaper), 79

Salem (Massachusetts) *Gazette,* 54

Salona (Va.), 230, 245, *271*

Salter, William D. (Midshipman, USN), 72

Salters Creek (Hampton, Va.), *235*, 238

Salter's Redoubt (Baltimore), *45*, 72, *72*

saltpetre (saltpeter), 18, 253, 298

Sample, John (Capt., Md. Militia), 111

Sample, Thomas J. (Judge), 111, 112, 117, 128, 356n124

Samuel Chaplin's Hotel (Centreville, Md.), 100

Sanders, Edward, 231

Sanders, James (Capt., RN), letter to Cockburn, 251

San Domingo Creek (Md.), *194, 196*, 197

Sandy Point (Md.), *27, 36*, 198

Saracen (H.M. sloop-of-war), 187

Sarah Ann (privateer), 65–6

Saranac (privateer), *55*

Saratoga (U.S. sloop-of-war), 38

Sater's Baptist Church (Md.), *27*, 331, 332

Schrader, George, 247

Schuler, Hans, 72

Schuylkill Arsenal (Philadelphia), 299

Scorpion (U.S. sloop), 99, 172, 188, 190, 192, 267, 293

Scott, James (Lt./Capt., RN), 87, 143, 151, 163, 172, 173, 175, 196, 201, 222, 241, 244, 247, 248, 258, 260, 268, 272, 284, 287, 292, 297

Scott, James (Lt. Col., Va. Militia), 228

Scott, William (Lt. Col., USA), *86*, 173

Scott, Winfield (Brig. Gen., USA), 5, 18, 69, 228, 260; bio, 20

Scott, Winfield, Monument (Washington, D.C.), *272*, 285

Seahorse (H.M. frigate), 213, 214, 246

Sears, William, 176

Seatack (Va. Beach City, Va.), *215*, 249, 260

Seaton, William Winston, 21

Seavers, Richard, 207

Appendix B consists of 1,125 individuals involved in the War of 1812 who are buried or have cenotaphs to them in the Chesapeake region. Of these, 826 served in Maryland militia (MM) units.

Gales, Joseph, Jr. (editor, Washington *National Intelligencer*), 340

Gallaher (Galleher), John (MM), 320

Galt, John (Capt., MM), 327

Gardner, Charles Kitchel (Lt. Col.), 338

Gardner, Timothy (2nd Lt., MM), 313

Gardner, William Henry (Midshipman, USN), 338

Garland, James, 336

Gatchaire, Francis (Lt., Privateer *Burrows*), 315

Gehring, John G. (Pvt., MM), 308

Gent, William C. (Pvt., MM), 332

George, James B. (Pvt., US Sea Fencibles), 315

Gerry, Elbridge (Vice President under Madison), 340

Gettier, Jacob (Pvt., MM), 323

Getzendanner, Jacob (Capt., MM), 312

Gholson, Thomas, Jr. (USA), 335

Gibson, Dudley A. (Pvt., MM), 336

Gibson, George C. (Lt. Col., USA), 338

Gibson, James (Pvt., MM), 313

Gill, Stephen (Capt. MM), 315

Gill, William L. (Midshipman, USN), 315

Gist, William (2nd Lt., MM), 315

Gladhill, John (Pvt., MM), 323

Glynn, Anthony Greenville (Lt./paymaster), 338

Gold, Peter (Baltimore Committee on Defense), 315

Gold, Samuel, 312

Golder, Archibald (Pvt., MM), 315

Goldsborough, Nicholas (Pvt., MM), 323

Goldsborough, Robert Henry (Capt./Maj., MM), 308

Goll, John (Pvt.), 334

Gomber, Ezra (Pvt., MM), 323

Gonso, Jacob (Pvt., MM), 323

Gordon, John (Pvt., MM), 312

Gore, George (Pvt., MM), 327

Gore, William (Pvt., MM), 321

Gorsuch, George W. (Cpl., MM), 312

Gorsuch, Thomas (Pvt., MM), 319

Gosnell, Thomas (Pvt., MM), 321

Graham, George, 340

Graham, George (Capt., Va. Militia), 334

Grahame, Thomas J. (Pvt., MM), 323

Grammar, Jacob (Pvt., MM), 320

Grason, William (Md. Gov./Pvt./3rd Sgt./2nd Lt, MM), 314

Gray, French S. (Pvt., MM), 336

Gray, Robert Hening (Pvt., MM), 336

Green, Benedict (Pvt., MM), 323

Green, Charles (Pvt., MM), 315

Greenwald, Christian (Sgt., MM), 334

Gregg, Alexander (Pvt., MM), 313

Gregg, James (Pvt., MM), 313

Grider, Henry, 338

Griffin, George (Pvt., MM), 320

Griffith, Benjamin, 315

Griffith, Howard (Pvt., MM), 315

Griffith, Stephen (Pvt., MM), 315

Grinnan, Daniel (MM), 335

Grove, Leonard (Pvt., MM), 323

Grove, Reuben (Pvt., MM), 323

Gurney, Gridley (drummer, Massachusetts Militia), 323

Hadfield, George, 340

Haines, Daniel (Pvt., MM), 308

Hall, Christopher, 313

Hall, Edward (MM), 309

Hall, Joseph, Sr., 320

Hall, Thomas W. (Capt., Va. Militia.), 315

Hallar, Philip (Pvt., MM), 323

Haller, Jacob (Pvt., MM), 323

Hambleton, Samuel (purser/aide-de-camp to Com. Oliver Hazard Perry, USN), 321

Hamilton, Charles (Dr.), 338

Hamilton, Samuel, 338

Hammond, Resin (Pvt., MM), 319

Hammond, Silas W., 319

Hammond, Thomas Lloyd (paymaster, MM), 328

Hancock, Ammon (Pvt., USA), 336

Hand, Bedingfield (Capt., MM), 310

Handy, George, Jr. (Lt./Capt., MM), 321

Hann, Henry (Pvt., MM), 329

Hanshew, Henry (Pvt., MM), 323

Harding, Philip (Pvt., MM), 310

Harlan, James W. (Pvt., MM), 319

Harman, Jacob (Pvt., MM), 323, 327

Harman, John (Pvt., MM), 332

Harper, Robert Goodloe (Maj. Gen., MM), 315

Harper, William S. (Capt., MM), 319

Harris, David (Lt. Col., MM), 312

Harris, John (Pvt., MM), 325

Harris, Samuel, 312, 315

Harrison, Zephariah (Pvt., MM), 324

Harryman, Samuel (Pvt., MM), 321

Harvey, Andrew (1st Lt., MM), 320

Hauck, William (Capt., MM), 330

Hauer, George (Pvt., MM), 324

Hawkins, Samuel (Lt. Col., MM), 319

Hawman, Frederick (Pvt., MM), 324

Hayden, Basil (Pvt., MM), 329

Hayden, Horace H. (Pvt., MM), 315

Hays, Abraham (Pvt., MM), 325

Hays, William (Pvt., U.S. Sea Fencibles), 313

Karney, Thomas (1st Lt., USA), 330

Kaufman, Daniel (Pvt., MM), 316

Kaylor, George, 316

Kearney, John A. (Surgeon, USN), 338

Keener, Christian (Pvt., MM), 316

Keerl, John C. (Pvt., MM), 316

Keerl, Samuel (Pvt., MM), 316

Keilholtz, William (Cpl., MM), 316

Keirle, P. Henry (USN), 316

Kell, Thomas (1st Lt., MM), 316

Kelley, Charles (Pvt., Va. Militia), 335

Kelley, James (Va. Militia), 335

Kelley, John, 335

Kelso, John Russell (Cpl., MM), 316

Kemp, Joseph (Col., MM), 326

Kemp, Thomas (Pvt., MM), 320

Kenly, Edward (Pvt., MM), 316

Kennedy, John (Capt., MM), 313

Kenner, William C. (Pvt., MM), 321

Kepplinger, P. (Col.), 316

Kershner, Jacob (Pvt.), 334

Keys, John (Sgt., MM), 316

Kimberly, Nathaniel (Pvt., MM), 316

King, William, 312

Kinna, James (Pvt., MM), 310

Kiplinger, Michael (Pvt., MM), 316

Kirkland, Alexander (Cpl., MM), 316

Kitts, John (teamster), 316

Kleiber, Jacob, 338

Knauff, Jacob (6th Cpl., MM), 324

Knight, Catharine Kitty, 325

Knight, John (Pvt., MM), 323

Knight, Peter (MM), 334

Knorr, William (Pvt., MM), 308

Knox, William (Capt., MM), 327

Knup, Abraham (Pvt., MM), 316

Kolb, John William (Lt., MM), 324

Koons, William (Pvt., MM), 322

Koontz, John (Pvt., MM), 324

Krauss, Leonard (Capt., MM), 320

Lakin, William (Pvt., MM), 320

Lamar, Richard (Sgt., MM), 320

Lambdin, Thomas H. (Capt., MM), 308

Lambright, George (Pvt., MM), 324

Lambright, Michael (Pvt., MM), 324

Landstreet, John (Pvt., MM), 316

Laroque, John M. (Hospital Service), 324

Larsh, Charles (Pvt., MM), 321

Late, George (Pvt., MM), 329

Latimer, James (2nd Lt., MM), 331

Lauck, Isaac S. (Va. Militia), 338

Lawrence, William (Lt. Col., USA), 338

Leakin, Sheppard (Capt., USA), 308

Leary, Peter (1st Lt., MM), 316

LeCompte, Samuel Woodward (Midshipman, USN), 310

Lee, Henry (Federalist injured at Baltimore riots), 335

Lee, John (Col., MM), 324

Leider, Jacob (Pvt.), 334

Leigh, Benjamin Watkins (aide-de-camp to Gov. Barbour), 336

Lemmon, William P., 316

Lenox, Peter (Capt.), 338, 340

Leppo, Jacob (Pvt., MM), 333

Levering, Aaron R. (Capt., MM), 316

Levering, Jesse (Pvt., MM), 316

Lightner, Henry (drummer boy, MM), 308

Lingan, James McCubbin (Federalist killed at Baltimore riots), 334

Linthicum, Abner (Capt., MM), 309

Little, Peter (Col., USA), 333

Lloyd, Edward (Lt. Col., MM), 320

Lockard, John (Pvt., MM), 329

Logan, Thomas White, 324

Long, Jesse (Pvt., MM), 327

Lord, Walter (author), 316

Lovell, Joseph (Surgeon, USA), 338

Lowe, Amos (Pvt., MM), 321

Lowe, John (2nd Lt., MM), 310, 321

Lowman, Daniel (Pvt., MM), 320

Luberson, John (drummer boy), 321

Lucas, Fielding (Pvt., MM), 324

Lucas, James (USN), 316

Ludden, Lemuel (Pvt., MM), 316

Lugenbeel, Moses (2nd Lt., MM), 324

Lyon, Charles G. (1st Lt., MM), 331

Macatee, Henry (Capt., MM) 328

MacIntosh, Duncan, 312

Mackenzie, Collin, 313

MacKubin, George (Pvt., MM), 328

Macomb, Alexander (Gen., USA), 338

Madison, Dolley (temporary burial), 340

Magruder, Thomas (QM, MM), 321

Main, John J. (Pvt., MM), 328

Manning, Richard Irvine (Capt.), 338

Mantz, George (Capt., MM), 324

Mantz, Peter (Pvt., MM), 324

March, Morris G. (USN), 316

Marean, Thomas (Pvt., MM), 316

Marine, William M. (author), 321